9/53

KANSAS

KANSAS

THE HISTORY OF

THE SUNFLOWER

STATE, 1854–2000

CRAIG MINER

PUBLISHED IN ASSOCIATION WITH THE

KANSAS STATE HISTORICAL SOCIETY BY

THE **UNIVERSITY PRESS OF KANSAS**

Published by the University Press of Kansas (Lawrence, Kansas 66049), which was organized by the Kansas Board of Regents and is operated and funded by Emporia State University, Fort Hays State University, Kansas State University, Pittsburg State University, the University of Kansas, and Wichita State University

Library of Congress Cataloging-in-Publication Data

Miner, H. Craig.

Kansas : the history of the Sunflower State, 1854–2000 / Craig Miner.

p. cm.

Includes bibliographical references and index.

ISBN 0-7006-1215-7 (alk. paper)

1. Kansas—History. I. Title.

F681 .M54 2002

978.1—dc21

2002007025

British Library Cataloguing in Publication Data is available.

Printed in the United States of America

10   9   8   7   6   5   4   3   2   1

The paper used in this publication meets the minimum requirements of the American National Standard for Permanence of Paper for Printed Library Materials z39.48-1984.

TO MY PARENTS,

NATIVE KANSANS

STAN (Ness County)

AND

MARYBEL (Brown County)

CONTENTS

ILLUSTRATIONS

PREFACE

This project began on a mild winter day early in 1998 as I was driving southwest through the Kansas Flint Hills in my 1958 Mercedes 190SL. There had been a meeting of the Editorial Committee at the University Press of Kansas in Lawrence. I was finishing someone else's term, after having served on the same committee years before. At the meeting, the press's director Fred Woodward had spoken with me about my current research. He had been doing that since the early 1980s, when the project was a history of early western Kansas.

This time my response disappointed him. My study of Latin and Greek had led to an interest in the reasons for the decline of the classical curriculum. Fred politely asked whether with my academic background in American history and a lifetime of living in Kansas and writing regional history, I had much business writing about the status of classical languages. Fred was the acquisitions specialist in Kansas history, but he was also someone who had known me a long time and had an eminently practical sense about getting worthwhile projects done. He owned a classic Corvette, too, so he had to be a trustworthy person. Thus, with some of the most glorious prairie scenery in the world going by as I drove with the roadster's top down, I rethought my immediate future.

I had recently published a book, *Harvesting the High Plains,* with the University Press of Kansas. Woodward and I had talked about a sequel to my 1986 book *West of Wichita,* which might follow the history of that region into the twentieth century. I had some notes on that labeled "Dust to Dust," running from the 1890s to the 1930s. Now, however, I had the thought of a complete history of Kansas. No Kansas history extant had much coverage of the period since World War II, most were written specifically as textbooks for middle or high school use, and none since William Connelley's in 1918 had been based to any extent on primary sources. Might it be desirable, I asked, to write a chronologically balanced history for the twenty-first century that "could serve not only as a text for classes in the history of Kansas and as a good read for Kansans looking at themselves, but as a model study of a regional culture?"

Woodward's reply was positive. He had wanted to publish a history of the state since he had come to Kansas in 1981. We corresponded for some months. By June 1998, I had some chapter titles (not one survived to the final draft) and some ideas about documenting the "complex and deep nexus between particular people and their achievements, and the times and places that are their stage." Fred, in a gratifying letter, expressed the thought that I was "obviously . . . on the brink of writing the book that . . . [I] was meant to write." If so, I had him partly to thank for getting my nose pointed in the right direction.

There were six readers of an extensive proposal. The most important and regular comment from this group was a warning that no one could or should try to write a "definitive," in the sense of "encyclopedic," history of Kansas. That heavy tome would be likely to do duty as a paperweight. Each author who had written a Kansas history over the years had a unique take on it, and this try would be no different. The author should be certain to keep things grounded in events, lest the history "become a mishmash of local, national, and human 'experience,' or a vaporous set of cultural identities chasing each other in a fog." He should guard against "style fatigue" in writing the lengthy work and maintain a sense of humor. With these caveats, the readers agreed that it might be done and might be done well.

James Malin of the University of Kansas, one of the great historians ever to arise in the state, thought that there was "no field of historical study more intriguing than the history of Kansas."[1] He wrote a series of articles on previous histories of Kansas, and many people hoped, even expected, that he would write a one-volume study of the state's history. But he seemed incapable of writing briefly about anything and became so upset with "totalitarian" editors trying to trim his extensive research into more accessible form that he decided to have his books printed himself.[2] He had such strong methodological ideas and political views that historian Roy Nichols warned in 1957 that Malin should end any Kansas history he might write in 1918, so as not to fall into the same trap of emotion and conditioning about his own times that had plagued local historians before him.[3]

Indeed, the writing of histories of Kansas since the 1880s, when semi-academic works began to replace passionately personal ones, has been an industry both energetic and variable.[4] Kansans were among the most literate people in the nation. They believed they had been and still were participating in momentous events beyond mere local significance, and they were diligent in collecting archives, forming in 1875 the Kansas State Historical Society to house them. They were therefore critical of such histories as were published, not only in regard to emphasis and tone but also to style. An 1868 review from Topeka of John Holloway's *History of Kansas* concluded that in that volume "words have broken loose from their ordinary moorings, and seem to be drifting in every direction. The parts of speech seem to be on a general rampage."[5]

Any historian now working with the history of the state is daunted as well as gratified by the scope and depth of the historical record. The Kansas State Historical Society's archives and manuscript collection is enormous, and its newspaper collection is without parallel among state societies. By 1937 there had existed 4,368 newspapers in Kansas, more than in any other state.[6] There existed over five hundred state agencies before 1956, and over twenty thousand state publications appeared before 1958.[7] The number and diversity of events that could be called significant during 150 years over an area of 50 million acres was considerable. Daniel Wilder used 1,170 pages in his *Annals of Kansas* to document events to 1886. Kirke Mechem used another 962 pages to bring that compilation to 1925. Homer Socolofsky and Virgil Dean's 1992 bibliography of secondary literature on Kansas contains 4,565 entries.[8] The local historian wonders at the energy and temerity of Arnold Toynbee and Will and Ariel Durant in their sweeps over the history of civilization.

As a practical matter, space for the published discussion of Kansas history is not as extensive as it once was. William Connelley's *Standard History of Kansas and Kansans* (1918) was five folio volumes, and John Bright's *Kansas: The First Century* (1951) was four. Biographies filled some of the space, but there was plenty of room for history. Connelley complained even so that he had written nine hundred thousand words on the first sixty years of the state's history but that "the history of Kansas, to be complete, cannot be confined to the narrow bounds of two volumes." He hoped that "some future historian" would be allowed more scope.[9] That hardly seems likely.

There are numerous routes by which a state history may find both boundaries and a point of view. This one isolates historical moments that were pivotal in taking Kansas in a direction that could have been otherwise. It tries to isolate and treat those events that were key to forming state culture and to illustrate how they looked from the perspectives of different observers. And it tries to suggest the simultaneity of reality rather than dividing human affairs too neatly. The economic, social, political, and intellectual spheres are interdependent, and cross influences are important.

Hindsight is wonderful, but readers of a state history should be able to empathize with the conditions of uncertainty in which decisions were made. The Roman historian Tacitus observed that "achievements often are estimated best in the times in which they are brought forth most easily."[10] The goal of good local history, Isaiah Berlin wrote, is to understand what people "thought, imagined, felt, wanted, strove for in the face of physical nature at a particular stage of social development, expressed by institutions, monuments, symbols, ways of writing and speech, generated by their efforts to represent and explain their condition to themselves."[11] Kansas has suffered some for having been the center for movements that are seen in hindsight as "losers," in the march of the mainstream. Prohibition, the currency reform elements of Populism, and movie censorship are examples. Yet taken on their own terms and in the tenor of their times, their force and dignity in addressing universal human concerns becomes evident.

There is a "local logic" to state history, requiring that the historian not depend on applying national textbook categories to regional development. The cattle trade, the grasshopper invasion, and Indian removal, for example, were important in Kansas in the 1870s in a way that standard national Reconstruction issues were not. Certain dates—1887 for municipal suffrage for women; 1928 for the creation of a state highway system; 1951 for dams in the wake of floods; or 1986, when liquor by the drink and the state lottery upset a century of tradition—are uniquely important to the region.

Culture influences places just as places influence culture. There were "states" of Kansas over time, each the result of action by people with certain understandings of it, preconceptions about it, and visions for its future. Coronado, the conquistador, saw the resources and possibilities of the state in one way; Joseph G. McCoy, the cattleman, in another. Laura Johns, the feminist, focused on one state; Erasmus Haworth, the petroleum geologist, on another. George Washington Carver, experimenting with plant varieties in Ness County in the 1880s; Ray Garvey, building a power-farming wheat empire from a base in Thomas County in the 1940s; and Wes Jackson, working with prairie perennials to try to create a sustainable agriculture and rural community in Saline County in the 1980s, exemplified radically different points of view on farming. But they were all Kansans.

Sometimes these states arose successively in changing times, but sometimes the visions were contemporary and conflicting. It would be a mistake for the scholar to posit a single "spirit of the age" into which all those warring visions were conveniently absorbed. Complex value struggles between railroad people, Indian agents, trail promoters, farmers, and town speculators created a culture in their time to which conflict and paradox were endemic.

I confess that I started researching state and local history in the 1960s because of weariness with the cheap hotels where I had to stay in Washington while working at the National Archives. Also, I reasoned that should my interpretive or stylistic abilities be weaker than some writers, my work would still have the virtue of originality in the telling of things new to the academic world. Perhaps I could emulate Francis Parkman, who said that he created the taste by which his work was appreciated.

Later, I found that one could not altogether avoid Washington when writing about Kansas (though I learned to avoid certain hotels) and also that regional history had more possibilities than as a haven for those who did not care for travel and shied from drawing monumental conclusions. There was a "universe in a grain of sand" indeed, and there was the prospect of following those great regionalists in literature and art in the writing of a genre of regional history that was anything but trivial or amateur.

My predecessors in this kind of work inspired me. As a student, and ever since, I have been strongly influenced by the work and person of William E. Unrau. Unrau in turn had as teachers and mentors both James Malin and Robert Athearn. When I worked with Athearn on my Ph.D., he sometimes called me a "grandchild" for that reason. All these people had a strong regional focus to their work as well as a penchant for deep primary research. Athearn used to joke that his colleagues got to travel to Paris and London for their sabbatical leaves while he repaired to the railroad yards in East St. Louis. But he delighted in the steam, brick, and drama of nearby places. His chapter titles alone showed that. Unrau taught me to take Kansas history seriously and gave it a dignity and sweep for me as a student that was unforgettable and undeniable.

I had a less frequent but regular contact, too, with Nyle Miller, Robert Richmond, and Joseph Snell at the Kansas State Historical Society, and with all the magic of the catacombs of the 1910 Memorial Building in Topeka where it was once housed. When laptop computers came, it was hard to find a plug there, but the smell of wood and paper, and the marble bathrooms, convinced me that it was a special place. Being escorted through the stack levels, as we regulars sometimes were in the past, led the imagination toward many subjects otherwise not to be broached, so rich and rare were the contents of those metal shelves. One-of-a-kind items could be ordered out to the reading room, one after another.

I well remember standing in those stacks once, looking at historical clippings books that had been kept for each county and recognizing that those volumes were a base for examining the personal reminiscences of hundreds of ordinary people in sixty Kansas counties. I wrote a title on a card: "West of Wichita." As so often happens, the idea for the book came from a glimpse of the archive, the actual start from recognition of a practical possibility rather than from desultory reading or abstract thinking.

This book started too with the thought of all that old paper, now transferred to a modern building adjoining an early mission structure. I remember in the early 1980s the look of shock on the face of the person at the retrieval desk in Topeka when, asked "what county?" I came up with a list of sixty. The book was more demanding still for carrying boxes back and forth, yet the staff tracked down every request enthusiastically and swept up when, after a day with old clippings, my place at the table was a blizzard of tiny paper remains. My association there in recent years with the executive director, Ramon Powers, has been helpful and inspiring from the moment I first met him and we talked about his research on the Dull Knife raid. And there were productive times in the Kansas Collection of the University of Kansas and in the Special Collections rooms of Kansas State and Wichita State Universities.

I had a companion most of those days with the archive boxes, Julie Courtwright. Julie was a student in Wichita State University's master's program in history and was, thanks to funding from the College of Liberal Arts there, my research assistant for two years. She went on to the Ph.D. program at the University of Arkansas and to an impressive start on a publication program of her own in the history of Kansas—a "great grandchild" perhaps of Malin, Athearn, and Unrau. I thank her for her friendship as well as for her excellent work.

My thanks go also to Fred Woodward and the staff at the University Press of Kansas. The press has meant a great deal to me over the years, publishing as it does the kinds of books on Kansas that Kansans need to read. I appreciate the constructive criticism received from all the readers of the manuscript. Some were anonymous, but the two who made the final comments on the completed work were Virgil Dean and Thomas Isern. Both these men are at the very top of any list of scholars of high achievement in the study and interpretation of Kansas history, and I feel lucky to have had the benefit of their careful and high-quality analysis and suggestions. Nancy Sherbert, the photo archivist at the Historical Society, was a particular help with the photo and map selection in the final editing stages.

Finally, every scholar, every person, owes much to family, living and dead. As I write this in the wake of the terrorist attacks of September 2001, I can't help being especially aware how tenuous is the combination that allows civilization to thrive, and how important is the mix of education and love we find at different stages of our personal lives. Having become with a shock part of the elder generation, my wife Suzi and I work at being the patriarch and matriarch of our little clan, consisting of adult sons Hal and Wilson. This group has always been patient with me and respected what I was trying to do. Wilson even said recently that he might consider reading this book of mine. It makes me feel I might be getting somewhere after all.

INTRODUCTION: THE FAR LOOK

Analyzing the Kansas character and the state's prospects based on its history has been a national spectator sport and a regional compulsion. William Seward noted on the floor of Congress in 1856, "The circumstances of Kansas, and her relations toward the Union, are peculiar, anomalous, and deeply interesting."[1] What that history portends, however, is problematic. "Even historians don't understand Kansas," wrote a Kansas City reporter in the 1920s. "I wonder sometimes if anybody except God understands Kansas and sometimes I think Kansas even has him fooled."[2]

It has been said that Kansas was not only a place where people attempted to put ideals into practice, the "electric light of the Union" as one person called it, but one where in the process the moderate middle dropped out, and the extremes locked in struggles of pointless fury.[3] Always its people were energetic and pushed a long way without much hesitation in whatever direction they faced. The history of Kansas, wrote its longtime senator John Ingalls, "is written in capitals. It is punctuated with exclamation points. Its verbs are imperative. Its adjectives are superlative. . . . The aspiration of Kansas is to reach the unattainable."[4] A Salina reporter added in 1893, "There was never a middle ground in Kansas. It was either the heights of ecstasy or the black abyss."[5]

That determination could be seen as "cranky." Ingalls observed that "prohibitions, female suffrage, fiat money, free silver, every incoherent and fantastic dream of social improvement and reform, every economic delusion that has bewildered the foggy brains of fanatics, every political fallacy nurtured by misfortune, poverty, and failure, rejected elsewhere, has here found tolerance and advocacy."[6] But it could be uplifting. "Kansas wouldn't be much of a state," wrote one of its residents, "without her ingrates, her silly laws, her cultural veneer, her pride of being God's footstool to balance her agricultural activity."[7] William Simpson argued in 1889 that accomplishments of Kansans came precisely from "a prevailing condition of mental unrest and 'yeastiness,' " which sometimes caused them to be a laughingstock. "Their very impetuosity cleared the way for right thinking on the part of slower minds" and translated into economic growth. "There is something in our inheritance of John-Brownism and Jim-Laneism," Simpson thought, "that makes prosperous and progressive towns where in the ordinary course of events only a few sleepy hamlets would vex the morning breezes as they swept the broad plains."[8]

Like the Hebrews, who felt that their unique history made them a "light to lighten the Gentiles," Kansans doted on their past as more than a collection of facts. Edwin Manning, in his presidential address to the Kansas State Historical Society in 1911, commented, "If it were possible to obliterate the history of Kansas there would be little found within its boundaries to make it distinguished among the states of this Union."[9] The difference in Kansas resided heavily in the special culture that developed through a special history. "The Kansas idea in morals is above the age," wrote Simpson. "From the chilly peaks of righteousness we overlook the pleasing valleys of sin, and try to induce those below to come up higher."[10] Kansas senator Arthur Capper said that his state was "in many respects . . . the political and economic experiment station of the American people."[11] Not to be progressive in Kansas, he said once, "is almost to be convicted of intellectual and moral sluggishness."[12]

Even Capper, however, had to admit, "I was born there when it took some nerve to be born in that part of the country."[13] Robert Bader, in *Hayseeds, Moralizers, and Methodists: The Twentieth Century Image of Kansas,* argued that the state's inferiority complex originated with the Dust Bowl.[14] Dr. Karl Menninger, head of the Topeka Menninger Clinic for mental health, thought there were psychological roots for the "self-depreciation" of Kansans that were deeper, growing from an inability to live up to their own high ideals.[15] Perhaps it was partly the state's central geographical location in the United States, and the resultant ecological variety, weather range, flat accent, and uncertain regional cultural identification. And doubtless there was an element of plain difference from the majority norms, which might or might not be an element of local pride. Kansas, wrote Charles Edson, "exemplifies everything that a civilized metropolitan or cosmopolitan mind despises."[16]

There was no shortage of external critics to reinforce whatever doubts Kansans had about themselves. Heywood Broun in the early 1930s wrote that Kansas, at least from his Pullman car window, was "a place devoid of beauty, where existence is an endless and deadly monotony."[17] A 1950 article on

Kansas in *American Mercury* related the story of a Kansas farmer who, when asked where he was from, said, "Kansas. Now, gosh darn ye, laugh."[18] Fred Brinkerhoff, editor of the Pittsburg *Headlight,* wrote in 1964: "I am going to say Kansans have an inferiority complex. . . . They permit bad tales to be told about Kansas and, in fact, pass them along themselves. . . . They let easterners talk about Mary Lease, Carry Nation, Brinkley, cyclones, grasshoppers, dust and drought and never say a word about Eisenhower, a Kansas boy, Charley Curtis, an Indian kid, and Will White and Ed Howe."[19] In 1969 Richard Rhodes published "Death All Day in Kansas."[20] In 1978 Frank and Deborah Popper of Rutgers University suggested in *Planning* magazine that large portions of the Great Plains, including much of Kansas, be returned to bison range for the enjoyment of tourists. Farming the prairie, they said, was "the largest, longest-running agricultural and environmental miscalculation in American history."[21] These minor classics joined their lugubrious fellows over the years to form a familiar litany.

There were roots to the ambiguous image through Kansas history. Coronado had the guide who brought him to Kansas strangled. In the late nineteenth century a story circulated about the visit of Grand Duke Alexis of Russia to the state for a bison hunt in 1872. The lieutenant governor strode up to him during a legislative reception in Topeka, pointed to the Kansas seal on the wall with its motto, "Ad Astra Per Aspera" (To the Stars Through Difficulty), and said, "Duke, them words is Latin."[22] Charles Gleed, a Topeka attorney, wrote in 1894, "We are done up in satire, strung all over with barbed wit, and blistered with abuse. We are described as cranks, fad-chasers and political unaccountables."[23] In the *Oxford English Dictionary* one of the illustrative quotations for the word *derelict* comes from the *Voice* (New York), 1888: "The derelictness of many officials in Kansas."[24] William Allen White concluded in 1896, "Go east and you hear them laugh at Kansas; go west and they sneer at her; go south and they 'cuss' her; go north and they have forgotten her."[25]

There were early attempts to explain the state's mixed reputation. White blamed the Populists. Charles Gleed wrote, "We talk too much. We think out loud," and therefore "we ourselves are unnecessarily responsible for much of the feeling adverse to us."[26] But the most common explanation was exaggeration in the news reports of the national media. Noble Prentis commented in 1891 that the "hysterical historians" in the media had a "disposition to see something extraordinary, striking and unheard-of" in everything coming from Kansas: "So every high wind in Kansas is, in report, a terrific cyclone; every snow storm a fearful blizzard attended by great loss of life; . . . every county seat fight is marked by the crash of arms and the shedding of rivers of gore."[27] Ingalls thought the exaggerations began with the "Bleeding Kansas" territorial struggles. "No time," he wrote, "was ever so minutely and so indelibly photographed upon the public retina."[28] But whenever it started, it continued a feature. Speaking to a New York audience in 1898, J. W. Gleed of Kansas said, "When only the prodigious gets into print, false ideas are inevitable. The freak will fix the type."[29]

Kansas history was both a defense against this reputation and an inspiration. Kansas governor Lyman Humphrey said in his inaugural address in 1889 that Kansas history was "a living, energizing force in all our moral, social, and material progress." Kansas was "rich in retrospection and opulent in hope."[30] Charles Gleed thought Kansas history was the best argument that it was not "a state of cranks and fools and villains," but he blamed Kansans for not knowing that history well or using it effectively.[31] Charles Sheldon, the Topeka minister who wrote the best-seller *In His Steps,* noted in 1931 that he liked Kansas because of the "atmosphere." He did not mean, he said, "the mean temperature," but the history of the place. "Kansas boasts of raising the best wheat in the world. But I like the state because it has raised some questions about human behavior that are worth more than the grain that pours into the elevators."[32]

Because of the perceived importance of local history, certain historical events became iconographic in ongoing debates about current identity. But the problem with regional history as a palliative for stereotypes was that in Kansas the facts emphasized and the significance assigned to key events changed with the needs of the interpreters. And emotions clouded the view.

An example is John Brown. There was agreement on the basic facts: that he was a radical abolitionist, beloved of eastern reformers and African Americans for his uncompromising devotion to freedom, and that he was closely implicated in the 1856 massacre—with short swords, in the dead of night, before their families—of five helpless people along Pottawatomie Creek in southeast Kansas. The problem was what to make of the public identification of the state with this man and his actions.

In 1885, Leverett Spring, a minister and a professor of English at the University of Kansas, published *Kansas: The Prelude to the War for the Union.*[33] This account of struggles during the Kansas territorial period seemed straightforward enough. James Malin, one of the premier historians of Kansas in the twentieth century, concluded that Spring "wrote with moderation and perspective" and that his book "was undoubtedly the best Kansas history of its time."[34]

In 1885, however, there was strong criticism from Kansas. Daniel Wilder concluded of Spring: "Kansas does not know him and he does not know Kansas." He said Spring was a "sniveling idiot" who should be dismissed from his academic post.[35] Another local review concluded, "The book is hopelessly bad. . . . For him to attempt to teach the language is a grotesque absurdity."[36] Commented another, "This historian writes of Kansas as Morton of Merrymount writes of Massachusetts—with no more appreciation of the free state men who saved Kansas from slavery, than the English rascal had of John Winthrop and the Puritans."[37]

One problem was that Spring, though ultimately praising the results of Brown's action, was critical of his technique. He called the Pottawatomie massacre a "ghastly affair."[38] In doing so he put himself in the middle of a hornet's nest of debate on Brown, which had been going on in both the Kansas and the national press actively for at least seven years, and which had aroused enormous emotion on both sides.[39]

On one side were Brown's defenders, mostly old partisans who had been active in the territorial struggles, or modern politicians who had an interest in the uses of historical mythology. It was hard for them to deny, as some of the earliest writers had, that there had been a massacre, but they justified Brown's actions in various ways. They questioned the right of historians who were not there to interpret events.[40] They argued that the murdered men were themselves murderers and Brown was a savior.[41] "No Hebrew prophet," Ingalls wrote in 1884, "no Christian martyr ever spoke in loftier and more heroic strains than this 'Coward and Murderer.' "[42]

The detractors found Brown wanting. George Martin of the *Junction City Union* editorialized against the collecting by the state historical society of every relic connected with the life of Brown—an "endless litter of relics and curiosities," he thought, appropriate to a saint perhaps, but not to Brown. The society's "John Brown tendencies," Martin said, caused "wide-spread disgust," even in Kansas.[43] David Utter, a Unitarian minister in Chicago, pointed out that "to John Brown the fates had been unusually kind. His story fell upon a time when the world was eager for a hero, and when the people of the northern United States must make one of whatever material came to hand."[44] But that did not justify his "moral hallucination" and consequent actions in 1856. "A man who did not know the difference between midnight assassination and war deserves not the name of 'liberator of Kansas.' " And who was Utter to say so? Simple: "I am the voice of a new generation."[45]

That approach interfered with the myth that many people held dear. "Gods are made, I suppose of just such material as the *hero* John Brown," wrote one observer who was there and yet criticized Old Brown—George Brown, editor of the *Herald of Freedom.*[46] Local patriotism was strong. One Kansan wrote, "The deeds done in Kansas, may have been small things . . . but they cast great shadows on the blank wall of American history, and they should be treated with dignity and forbearance. . . . Kansas has been a brave field for adventure and romance, which its historian ought duly to recognize."[47] Spring, in calling John Brown "a parenthesis in the history of Kansas," had not presented it quite that way.[48]

Charles Gleed characterized the Kansas reviews of Spring's book as "a lynching" rather than literary opinion. He had to admit, however, that it was difficult in 1885 for a scholarly account of Kansas history to be accepted among the state's factions.[49] In 1888 Noble Prentis spoke of the impossibility of writing a decent biography of Kansas senator James H. Lane: "To go anywhere near the old Lane–[Charles] Robinson fight, is like smoking a cigar in a powder magazine. A mild-mannered professor in the State University tried it not long ago, and was blown clear through the state by the explosion."[50]

No wonder Wilder had not dared to write a "real history" but had just compiled facts without comment. Wilder's *Annals of Kansas,* Gleed wrote, "tells the day and date when Billy Patterson was struck but it does not tell who did the striking or why." Yet maybe that was all that could be done in the 1880s. "If Mr. Wilder were to write a history of Kansas of the other sort, his excellency the governor would have to call in all the militia of the state to keep his able and scholarly assistant from being murdered."[51]

In 1892 the publication of former governor Charles Robinson's memoir *The Kansas Conflict* heated up the Brown argument again. Wilder wrote Robinson, "I am decidedly on the other side on the main part of your version or perversion. Your wife's book is better than yours."[52] Robinson in an 1877 address had compared John Brown to Jesus of Nazareth. In his later memoir, however, he was critical both of Brown and of the role partisan feeling had in the writing of Kansas history.[53] In 1860 he had written a woman inquiring about some facts: "I am truly gratified at the interest you manifest in Kansas history & that you are disposed to examine for yourself the random thrusts of the press."[54] He felt he had only done the same in regard to Brown. In *Kansas Conflict* he noted that "the time for writing the true history of Kansas has not yet arrived. . . . Distance lends enchantment to a view, and clearness to the vision of the historian."[55]

Neither distance nor research, however, necessarily changed conclusions. In 1901 the Ft. Scott attorney and poet Eugene Ware tried to get the budding historian and oilfield promoter William Connelley a commission from the widow of Senator Ingalls to write a biography of Ingalls. In recommending Connelly, Ware emphasized that "anybody can take a lot of clippings and throw them together in a book" but that a good biography must "be a photograph of the times and occasions and the circumstances."[56] Yet Connelley's book on Brown, published in 1900, incorporated his prejudice against the Robinson family as much as it did new research and defended Brown against any and all detractors. Connelley shortly became secretary of the Kansas State Historical Society, that storehouse of Brownania.[57] Ware, however, did think that research was the key to honesty in history. "I'm glad the Alexandrine library was burned," he wrote. "What an enormous amount of lying biographies it must have contained." It was time to write straightforwardly about the "meatheriums and reptiles" he had seen in Kansas politics.[58]

John Brown continued to be an issue in 1910, when Theodore Roosevelt came to Kansas and gave his famous address in Osawatomie. That TR wanted to identify the Progressives with the history of Kansas and to appear before a friendly audience was clear. But by 1910, too strong an identification with John Brown, to whom the day Roosevelt appeared was dedicated, was dangerous, even in Kansas. Times had changed and so had the interpretation of the past. A reporter in 1928 noted that "however nostalgic Kansans might be for "familiar things which were a part of the panorama," they must realize these old pictures were sometimes stereotypes and had "no place in the living stream of events that is the Kansas of today."[59]

Modern interpreters of local history, TR warned in private, could see the "insurgents" in the Republican Party posing the same threat to sane politics that Brown once had. And if there was a lesson in that history, it was that

Brown's strategy led to blood and chaos without even the cover of law. Roosevelt wanted, he said, "to be radical as Lincoln was radical," not as Brown was.[60]

William Allen White agreed that Brown should be downplayed. "I am not sure how much good he really did," he wrote his friend the president. "I do not know exactly how much good the extremist does."[61] There were many, he said, "who unfold their ample jaws and yip and kyoodle about old John and the Cause of freedom," who, when faced with the modern struggle for reform, "pull down their blinds [and] fasten the doors."[62] In the speech TR gave in Kansas, Brown's name appeared only twice.[63]

Oswald Garrrison Villard noticed the continued sensitivity about Brown. Villard published a biography of Brown in 1910, claiming that "so complex a character as John Brown is not to be dismissed by merely likening him to the Hebrew prophets or to a Cromwellian Roundhead."[64] In 1914 he spoke in Kansas at a newspaper meeting on the subject of Brown. "The modern historian," he said, "is not merely a eulogist, nor is the eulogist of the past necessarily a historian." The "trouble with much Kansas writing," Villard said, was that "the idea has been to bang your neighbor over the head, metaphorically speaking, with the heaviest club in your possession and bolster up your hero by charging the other man with being a midnight assassin or a horse thief. . . . Take all possible adjectives, then add more adjectives in a ratio of one hundred to each statement of fact, mix well, and then heat to the temperature of the prairies in mid-July—this seems to have been the prescription for producing such so-called history of Kansas."[65]

The situation had not changed in the 1920s. Responding to a paper on Brown, the young University of Kansas history professor James Malin said it was too much of the old school. "From what I've done in Kansas history," he wrote, "only one conclusion is possible; that Kansas history is most remarkable for what has been omitted from the books. I have enough stuff to start a riot in Lawrence or in the historical society any day."[66]

Malin learned what kind of local pressure could be applied to would-be Kansas historians in 1929. That year KU Chancellor Ernest Lindley determined to push for collection from the federal government of compensation for the burning in 1856 of the old Free State Hotel, owned by the New England Emigrant Aid Company. The claims of the company had been assigned to the university.[67] Malin responded in print to an article in the *Daily Kansan,* pointing out that the sheriff who did the burning was not acting under orders from Washington and therefore there was no basis for the claim.[68]

It was then that scholarship intersected interest. The chancellor called Malin to his office, where he got a tongue-lashing, but not before Lindley had loudly berated him on Fourteenth Street in Lawrence. "Among other things," Malin remembered, "he prohibited me absolutely from publishing anything more on that period in Kansas history."[69] Something similar had happened years earlier to Frank Hodder, Malin's colleague and teacher. Hodder had stopped writing Kansas history because, according to the historian Roy Nichols, he "questioned the accepted canon and thereby gained the condemnation of certain of the local historians of influence dedicated to free state hagiography."[70]

One didn't have to write history to feel the heat. In 1941 a native son and nationally known artist, John Steuart Curry, painted a giant image of John Brown, eyes blazing, a rifle in one hand, a Bible in the other, blood on his hands, and a tornado behind him on the walls of the state capitol. Curry only wanted, he said, to show the contrast in Kansas between struggle and success and "to picture what I feel about my native state."[71] Although one student noted that in retrospect the controversy over the Brown image had "seriocomic overtones," people in Kansas felt strongly enough about it that the state legislature refused to remove any more of the Victorian marble on the walls to make room for modern murals. Curry came to have such mixed feelings about what he once called his best work that he did not sign the mural. *Time, Life,* and *Newsweek* magazines chided Kansas for its failure to appreciate Curry's art.[72] But art was not the real issue; history was. "Many Kansans," wrote a longtime political commentator at the state capital, "always edgy about hot weather, tornadoes, prohibition, and being the butt of so many jokes of radio comedians, were on the defensive."[73]

There were different sorts of objections to the Curry murals. The single African-American member of the Kansas legislature protested the depiction on the grounds that it was disrespectful to a defender of black people.[74] One Kansas woman, who had not seen the murals, wrote Governor Payne Ratner that she did not have to view them because "if they tend to besmear or under-value our beloved State instead of portraying its values, beauty, the high ideals and standards our fore-fathers had . . . please throw them out."[75]

The most articulate editorial response objected not so much to the art as to Brown's prominence in Kansas history. "From a tempestuous start," the editorial held, "Kansas has slowly been refining into a state of considerable culture and consequence. Kansas is NOT John Brown." How could "the picture of a bearded maniac" be considered an allegorical representation of the state except by the "sophisticated smart aleck crudeness of our time?" After all, the writer emphasized, "Kansas is healthy. Kansas is not berserk."[76] The image, of course, outlasted its critics. In 1957, William Zornow's widely adopted *Kansas: A History of the Jayhawk State* used as its dust jacket a photograph of Curry's version of John Brown.[77]

Charles Edson, who was employed with the Works Progress Administration's (WPA) Federal Writer's Guide in Topeka about the time Curry was painting his murals, felt strongly that Kansas as late as the 1930s and 1940s still was not ready to hear its true history. Edson was an eccentric, a Democrat and sometime socialist in a Republican state, and there were those who claimed he was mentally ill. But he was an experienced journalist and a tireless researcher with a strong interest in Kansas history. Edson claimed that the Kansas volume in the WPA's State Guide series was censored by chamber of commerce types defensive of the image of the state to the point that it became "illiterate, inaccurate and uninteresting."[78] The director of the *Guide,* A. Q. Miller, editor of the *Belleville Telescope,* was, according to Edson, so pressured by the establishment that he refused to allow the statement that Kansas was subject to dust storms or that counties had been often fraudulently organized in Kansas history. There was a kind of "state religion," Edson claimed, conducted "in the manner of camp meeting revivals" with which state history must jibe. "No true history of Kansas has ever been published," he wrote, "because the politicians and businessmen of the State are ashamed of their work and will not permit the record to be spread before a candid world."[79]

James Malin, who came to the conclusion that Brown was as much a legend as a historical figure, documented the history of Kansas's cultural relation with that fiery old man at nearly eight-hundred-page length in his *John Brown and the Legend of Fifty-six* (1942). But he had to admit, after having considerable difficulty publishing his big book and being frustrated that so few read it, that "the role of Legend in shaping the behavior of our society is more significant than historians have yet recognized adequately."[80] Roy Nichols, a Malin student, noted in 1957 that in the minds of Kansans their early history had been the field on which "the children of light had been beset by the children of darkness, but righteousness had triumphed. So a pantheon had been created in the emotions of future Kansans where were enshrined the heroes of the faith. This interpretation was not only written in books but more important it was inscribed in the minds and memories of the citizens of the blood-born commonwealth."[81]

The passage of time should create a perspective, however, which might serve as a filter. The thick books full "of a number of things," the heavy volumes stuffed with pages of long quotations in the interest of preservation, the atavistic rhetoric, marshaling ancestors behind our banners, are no longer appropriate. Rolla Clymer, editor of the *El Dorado Times,* in one of his meditations on the surrounding Flint Hills, commented that "there are many places within easy walking distance of our homes where we can ascend into a high place, and let our eyes, both mental and spiritual, take in the far look. The little, trifling things that have bothered us seem to shrink into insignificance." There was no worthy achievement, Clymer said, without the achiever's having first taken something like that look from a hilltop into the possibilities within, and those of the time and the place. That look, for Kansans, should be into the past as well as toward the physical horizons.[82]

Kansas extremes were not entirely a media invention. The state could contain both the national headquarters for the socialist newspaper *Appeal to Reason* and for the stridently entrepreneurial Pizza Hut fast-food franchise. It could be a center for antiabortion protest and also be in the 1990s one of the few places in the country where one could obtain a late-term abortion.[83] It was always a pioneer in women's rights, yet it produced some of the most quoted antifeminist newspaper rhetoric of the nineteenth century. It had in the late nineteenth century more miles of railroad per capita than any other state yet was accused of socialism in 1905 when it tried to build a government oil refinery operated by prisoners to compete with Standard Oil. Carrie Nation only advertised the flaws in practice of its prohibition law. A Philadelphia newspaper wrote acerbically of the Kansas moral range in 1877: "Its best people are Puritanic, and the rest Satanic—the one class being as disagreeable as the other is dangerous."[84]

But it is too easy and too distorting to quote the entertaining anecdotes endlessly and to let the "freak fix the type." The common serious thread running through the eccentricity was that Kansans were idealistic, progressive, and pragmatic—"practical idealists," as White put it. They tried to achieve what other people only discussed in the abstract. Many tributes at the death of General Frederick Funston in 1917 turned upon the special

Kansas qualities of this famous American. "His high ideals," one writer said, "never beclouded his practical, woodsawing common sense." He and others from his state had what Emerson called "a sort of far flung idealism combined with a clear sense of the world that must be lived in—a wagon hitched to a star that would, nevertheless run and run well."[85]

But it is well to note, local patriotism aside, that these "natural crusaders" could be narrow, prissy, intolerant, insufferable, even vicious.[86] An article in a national magazine in 1950 had it that since Kansans were "taught from infancy that God is a Republican and a Methodist, they consider it only fitting that he should provide abundant rain for Kansas while visiting the Democratic, Roman Catholic Babylons of the East with burning droughts to warn the inhabitants."[87] Ray Garvey was only half kidding when in the midst of the Dust Bowl he wrote that it was time to leave this age of "Dust and Democrats" for one of "Rain and Republicans."[88]

Sometimes the narrowness was not so innocent or funny. The anti-Semitic elements in the Populist tirades from 1890s Kansas against eastern bankers have been well studied by historians. Strong isolationism was followed in both world wars by what some observers would call mindless patriotism in the state. The Ku Klux Klan flourished at times, and the state universities always suffered from a constricted anti-intellectualism in the state, encouraged by smart but somewhat smart-aleck newspaper editors who took their good-old-boy pragmatism to an extreme. Film censorship in Kansas went too far for many people. And of course the major reform with which Kansas was long identified, prohibition of alcohol consumption, brought mixed reviews, with plenty of critics characterizing it as moral busybodyism or worse.

There was enormous nerve in Kansas in pushing its agenda. That was connected with a sales and growth mentality, perhaps compensation for self-doubt, and encouraged the critics. A Missouri paper in the 1880s commented, "A board of trade in an enterprising Kansas town recently bought 5,000 copies of the Bible, printed a map of the city on the fly leaf, ran a description of the county around the margin of the book of Genesis, 'inducements to capitalists' in green around the psalms, and cards of real estate dealers in blue at the beginning of each book in the New Testament, and sent the volumes back east as boom literature. And it is further said that when a poor deluded fool in Missouri read in the good book 'In the beginning God created the heavens and the earth' he exclaimed as natural as life, 'That's another Kansas lie!' "[89]

Kansans were great talkers, sterling editorial writers. But their literature was in newspaper and pamphlet screeds, ephemeral by definition and circumstance, and tied to issues and action rather than to the more Olympian musings of high art. Edith Coe, a Kansas writer, said in 1975, "I grew up believing the great names in writing were William Allen White, Rolla Clymer, Margaret Hill McCarter and Peggy of the Flint Hills."[90] Of course, that could only be believed in Kansas. William Allen White was surely right in saying that "a first rate poet in Ford county would do more to bring Western Kansas into the approval of mankind than a packing house," but the local talent ran to packing houses.[91] Jim Lane was a spellbinder on the stump, but his personal charisma was lost in the reading of his words. Ed Howe's *Story of a Country Town* (1883) was a touching, if melodramatic, piece of realism, but hardly in the class of Howells and James. John Ingalls was articulate for a U.S. senator, but his locally famous poem on bluegrass would no more ring down through the ages than the *Rhymes of Ironquill* by Eugene Ware, the poet of industry from Ft. Scott. Kansas never had a great literary regional interpreter in the mode of Willa Cather or Ole Rolvaag. White, for all the force of his editorials, was in a lower tier as a novelist, and his books, bestsellers for a time, now litter the shelves of tacky used book stores rather than gracing the rare-book catalogs dealing in American literature. Noble Prentis, Eugene Ware, and John Ingalls, an author once commented, might have been first-class writers, had they not been so busy working their jobs and trying to change the world.[92]

The Kansas flower is the sunflower, adopted as the first state symbol, outside the seal, in 1903. The familiar state song, "Home on the Range," is, by comparison, a newcomer, adopted in the 1950s, and the state reptile, the box turtle, is a creation of schoolchild exercises of the late twentieth century.[93] This "tough daisy" is no lacy columbine, but that may be just as well. It is appropriate to the acquired taste one may with time and a little study discover for the real Kansas. "The sunflower is not pretty," wrote Ed Howe. "All that can be said of it is that it is cheerful, and refuses to be downed, and shows a perseverance worthy of a prettier flower."[94]

The sunflower's popularity was hardly immediate. Though Thomas Say admired them on his trip through the area in 1820, and an observer admiring the dense growth of "rampant sunflowers" in the capitol square in Topeka in 1880 thought it should be an emblem for the state, it was declared a noxious weed by the residents of that same building in 1895.[95] Yet when *Harper's Weekly* ran a full-page photo of Frederick Funston on board the ship *Tartar,* returning in triumph from the Philippines in 1899, there was attached to his neat uniform a small felt sunflower to mark his origin.[96]

"The sunflower always was out in the open," wrote a nostalgic former Kansan in 1904. "It did not hide in dark places and it did not seek the shade. It made its own way. It was no parasite. It stood by the dusty roadside and out on the high prairie—and you always knew what it meant. . . . It turned its gold petals and black center always toward the sun. No matter how fiercely the heat beat down, it faced the music and never blinked. . . . It was the last bit of vegetation to surrender to the hot winds and it was blithe to the last. It loved life and it was genuine."[97] Any Kansan who has traveled through the state in late August or early September, before the break in the heat, has seen a landscape dominated by sunflowers, looking bright and vigorous and turning toward the fiery orb when everything else, including the residents, are brown and wilted. Noble Prentis wrote a poem about 1900 suggesting the sunflower as an appropriate state symbol:

> Child of the grassy plain
> Facing the Day
> Blooming in sun and rain
> Evermore gay,
> Coming the first to bless
> Wide-spreading wilderness,
> Flaunting and free,
> Coming in power,
> Kansas is like to thee,
> Sunflower—[98]

Legislators in 1903 designated the "wild sunflower" as the state flower, although there were twelve species in the state. Tradition has established an annual plant known as the common sunflower, or *Helianthus annuus,* as the true thing.[99] It was perhaps less attractive than the glorious *maximiliani* but was felt to be more appropriate than the hothouse-bred types "that rear monster heads in the back and front yards."[100] The statute stated that the sunflower was "of definite, unvarying and striking shape . . . ideally adapted

Sunflowers.
Gloria Hunter, photographer.

for artistic reproduction . . . a flower that a child can draw on a slate." It also bespoke regional history that was not flashy but deep, enduring, and, when familiar, inspiring.

As the sunflower needs appreciators, so does the state, and as symbols focus emotion, so does regional history focus the intellect upon the meaning of one's home. In the late 1990s I heard the story of a couple entering Kansas from the West. Impressed by the "glorious upland" of the High Plains they got out their small automatic camera to record it. The autofocus just buzzed, unable to fix on anything in particular amid the magnificence of things in general under that broad heaven.

The associations that outsiders and too often residents have concerning the history of Kansas are too simple and stereotyped, just as their images of its geography and climate are. William Allen White stands for its newspaper editors, but that class was a varied host. Other names (Marsh Murdock, Henry Allen, Clyde Reed, Sol Miller, Fred Brinkerhoff, Jess Denious for a sample) must be known and appreciated. Too many names, vital to the past of Kansas, seem to its younger residents as the names of the nineteenth-century politicians Thomas Wolfe's father spoke of and that seemed to the young novelist the names of "lost men . . . more far from me than the Tartarian coast, more haunting strange than Cipango, or the lost facts of the first dynastic kings that built the pyramids."[101]

That should not be. People from Kansas history in many fields should take a place in the regional consciousness alongside the accepted heroes in the general American history textbooks. Until the Kansans everybody knows—Amelia Earhart, John Brown, Wyatt Earp, Ike Eisenhower—or think they know—Matt Dillon or Dorothy Gale—are joined by many others, our sense of place and our understanding of the local legacy will be pallid. Adaptation is possible. Capper, running for governor in 1915, was moved when driving down a road in western Kansas to see a group of children, half of them foreign-born, waving American flags and wearing sunflower pins.[102] The difficulty of the "eclipsed civilization" is not so much a native strain that has died. There has not yet been time for that. Rather, it is an insufficient understanding of the past that must be present for residents of any place to move appropriately into their own special future. And, too, any careful student of the past recognizes that while the times and the place dictate much, it is the force and insight of particular people, and not just outsized attracters of publicity, that create of the materials at hand either a Bach fugue or a maddening and distracting counterpoint of mere noise.

Kansas always drew deep praise as well as lightning. Wrote Victor Murdock, the Kansas editor and congressman, "I suppose that what gets me is a combination of amplitude in sky and plain—the same thing that warms an Arab to the desert and a sailor to the sea. To the prairie-born, immensity and monotony are identical and both are vocal. To a prairie soul, a diffuse landscape has in it . . . identity—a great, glad aboriginal fellowship. But who in the dickens would know what that meant?"[103] The people spoke what Capper called the "Kansas language." To Capper, it was a beacon in a storm, a home light in "strange times," when the world was in a fog, and where Kansans "stay on their feet more firmly, keep their heads, think more sanely than any people I know."[104] Henry Allen, once governor, said, "I am an incurable Kansan. I couldn't leave here any more than I could give up the habit of drinking coffee, or of giving advice. . . . I want to stay on and see what is going to happen next."[105]

In multiple jeremiads over a forty-year political career, Capper reminded the state's citizens to study their history, to cherish the proper "precious memory" of the crises that gave their state birth.[106] He wrote in 1927, "All

Kansas is studying, thinking, doing; seeing, hoping, testing; believing, trying, accomplishing; learning, sometimes thru error, sometimes thru attempting the impossible and realizing it is impossible—in which case we admit our mistake and start over again."[107]

For nothing had ever been automatic in Kansas nor ever would be. No irresistible scenery or climate would draw wealth. Kansas, an early editor said, was "the hottest, coldest, driest, wettest, thickest, thinnest country in the world."[108] It was "one of the lean cuts. It furnishes more laborious chewing to get the best taste."[109] Success on the prairie was a continuing responsibility, and it was a region where things that did not move died. "The world's work," Capper said, "is done by men and women . . . schooled and trained in DOING. . . . I wish I could set all Kansas afire with this idea—so true that it is as inevitable as death—that every man and every woman in this state has the future progress and greatness of Kansas in his or her keeping. . . . We shall go ahead, or we shall go back."[110] Wrote a Kansan in 1936, "Kansas is simply Kansas. May she never be tempted to become anything else."[111]

Olin Templin of the University of Kansas, bracing an audience in the middle of the depression to hold to their ideals, told a story of St. Simon, the French reformer, who directed his valet to call him each morning with the exhortation, "Waken, Monsieur Le Compte! We have great things to do today." It was the same with Kansans, Templin said. Citizens there should ask their children to "waken," as had their fathers and mothers before them, and face the sun in its whole course, as "we have great things to do to-day."[112]

CHILD OF THE GRASSY PLAIN

There was no political unit called Kansas until 1854 and no state until 1861. The area was for a long time what Governor John Martin called "a fiction of the geographers."[1] The concept of surveyed boundaries, as contrasted to those enforced by ecology or warfare, was alien to the people who moved back and forth across the region for 10,000 years. The ram-nosed tylosaurs, which swam 80 million years ago in the Cretaceous sea and whose bones were locked in western Kansas rock formations, could not have cared less.

Kansas prehistory is extensive, but an understanding of it is necessarily limited. The first scientific archaeological dig in Kansas was at Twelve-Mile Creek in Logan County in 1895. But well into the 1930s some people argued that there had been no occupation of the Great Plains by paleo-Indians prior to the introduction of the horse by Spanish explorers in the sixteenth century.[2] The combinations of tribes and the "flamboyant" native horse cultures observed by explorers and travelers along trails in the Kansas region were recent and represented adaptations to a changing environment as well as political and economic realignments among tribes in response to events mostly unrecorded.[3] Even the landscape, supposedly fixed from time immemorial, had undergone recent change, part of it due to human intervention, such as purposeful burning. The weather had cycles deeper and longer than any early settler was able to research or observe.

Not that nothing had happened. Elliott West has emphasized that one delusion of Europeans encountering the Plains was that they were bringing history and change to an area and a people that had remained static for thousands of years, denizens of a "timeless past."[4] A second delusion was that it would be easy for nineteenth-century civilization to make more efficient—they might have used the word "better"—use of resources there than did its long-term residents. The Europeans plunged in, and the result, in West's phrase, was "energy loosed, connections broken and realigned, ideas ebullient, biota merged, death invigorated, imaginations freed, the world remade,"—in short, a "bewildering, calamitous, glorious mess."[5]

The invasion was of an ancient world, filled with human cultures. As West emphasized, "In terms of human history, Bob Dole's Kansas is far older than Thomas Jefferson's Virginia or John Winthrop's Massachusetts." James Mead, a founder of Wichita, made much the same point in the 1890s: "The present inhabitants of the [Arkansas] valley, fondly imagine that before their arrival there was nothing here but earth, sky and river. In this they are in error. It is fair to assume that while Joseph was laying up grain in Egypt against years of famine, there were people here laying up stores of provisions for winter use and for traffic with their neighbors."[6] To see Kansas as a "new country" simply because there had been no recording of the details of the far past would be a fundamental error.[7]

There was, surely, plenty of imagination applied to the possibilities of deep time. Charles Sternberg, who from the 1870s forward dug out fossils from the Niobrara chalk in western Kansas, could envision a strange and exotic setting. "How often in imagination," he wrote, "I have rolled back the years and pictured central Kansas, now raised two thousand feet above sea level, as a group of islands scattered about in a semi-tropical sea! There are no frosts and few insect pests to mar the foliage of the great forests that grow along its shores, and the ripe leaves fall gently into the sand, to be covered up by the incoming tide and to form impressions and counterparts of themselves as perfect as if a Divine hand had stamped them in yielding wax."[8]

The combination of science, exotica, and western camping represented by Sternberg's expeditions was irresistible to his age. So were the investigations of Victorian geologists, which shortly had a practical offshoot in the development of Kansas oil exploration beyond the "creekology" or medium-consultation stage. Lewis Lindsay Dyche was a good scientist and a master promoter. He gave magic lantern slide shows around the country, and his exhibit of stuffed animals in the Kansas Building at the 1893 Chicago World's Fair was popular.[9] His long, flowing hair and his sense of adventure were as much a part of the Museum of Natural History at the University of Kansas, where he taught and curated, as was the fierce-looking marine carnivore

Ram-nosed tylosaur.
Courtesy of the Kansas State Historical Society.

Xiphatinus molossus; the avian Pteranodon sternbergi, with its bizarre crest and twenty-foot wingspan; the Superbison latefrons, with ten-foot-wide horns; the dire wolf; the mammoths and mastodons; or the rhinolike Teleocaras fossiger.[10] The entomologists, too, had a field day with Kansas prehistory, though a cowboy, seeing them rushing around with their nets, once commented, "I don't believe it. They are grown men."[11]

For a historian, knowledge about ancient times in the Kansas region is short on the specific. On a hillside in Graham County still spreads the giant body of a man outlined on the grass in stone. It is called Penokee Man, after a nearby town. There used to be some stone shrines connected with the man, but the highway department hauled them away to put into roads in the 1930s. The figure looks over the country from the tallest hill around, and the complex must have had some important ritual significance. But no one knows what it was or who built the complex.[12] That is typical. At the end of the twentieth century, hardly more was known about the Osages of five hundred years earlier than about the habits of the three-toed horse.

Still, there are basics of landscape, soil, and sky that are givens to current

Charles Sternberg preserving a fossil in the field.
Courtesy of the Kansas State Historical Society.

Kansans and that derive from that far, unrecorded past. The succinct and commonsense conclusion is easy to state. The political unit that is the State of Kansas, four hundred by two hundred miles, fifty million acres, is a new invention. Human occupancy is much older. And what was thus circum-scribed was, like all places, almost unimaginably ancient.

John McPhee wrote that Kansas was a "sedimentary wedge" coming off the "rain shadow" of the Rockies. "Kansas and Nebraska," he wrote, "are like pieces cut from a wheel of cheese—lying on their sides, thick ends to the west."[13] The eastern valleys are at about seven hundred feet above sea level. Mount Sunflower in Wallace County, near the Colorado line, seems only a rise, but at the top one stands at over four thousand feet, most of the gain to the Rockies having passed behind on the increasingly arid and open High Plains. The Mississippian geologic strata, which outcrop in the east, are deeply buried in the west. The ten landforms of Kansas (Cherokee Lowland, Osage Plains, Glaciated Region, Flint Hills, Smoky Hills Upland, Great Bend Prairie, Blue Hills Upland, Red Hills, Sand Hills, and High Plains) may seem a subtle variety to a Californian, but they are distinct. And there is a special break between the east and the west ecosystems, which begins at the Wichita-Salina line, about one-third of the distance across the state.[14] This geography affects people, their organization, and their attitude. "It would be as untrue to classify together the Egyptian, the Indian and the Central American," William Allen White once wrote, "as to speak of the Kansas man without distinguish-ing between the Eastern Kansan, the Central Kansan and the Western Kansan."[15]

On the prairies, the intersection of land and sky is obvious, and from both come gifts and terrors. Although the *Encyclopedia Britannica* in 1911 described the Kansas climate as "exceptionally salubrious," it noted there were exceptions that made some years "memorable by particularly severe storms." There were two regular kinds of trouble, the writer noted, "freshets and droughts," which could "work havoc." In addition, there was the "not infrequent affliction" of the tornado.[16]

Located five hundred miles from the nearest large body of water, the Gulf of Mexico, the state has a continental climate and is influenced by cyclonic storms (not always of Oz intensity) when prevailing southwest winds cause warm moist air pushed up from the Gulf to meet dry, cold air from the north and west. These storms can be one thousand miles in diameter, and they revolve counterclockwise toward a low-pressure center, giving the region

Tornado in Anderson County, 1884. This is the earliest photographed tornado in Kansas.
Courtesy of the Kansas State Historical Society.

world-class weather.[17] "It is a place," wrote William Least Heat-Moon, "of such potential celestial violence that the meteorologists at the National Severe Storms Forecast Center in Kansas City, Missouri, are sometimes called the Keepers of the Gates of Hell."[18]

The tornado, an extreme of such storms, has become associated with Kansas. The state is certainly in the tornado belt and leads the country in incidence of the most powerful kind. It is true, also, that spring storms are characterized by dark rolling clouds, strong winds, spectacular lightning, and hail. Temperatures have serious range, from a 121-degree high in 1936 to a 40-degree-below-zero low in 1905.[19] Professor Francis Snow of the University of Kansas provided an "elaborate and conspicuous schedule" of the state's weather to newspapers nationally through the 1870s.[20] In the early twentieth century, the pioneer meteorologist S. D. Flora played the same role.[21] The "rain follows the plow" speculations about the possible redemption of the desert by civilization there focused attention also on the details.[22]

But like its politics, Kansas weather is notable as much for the way it has been publicized as for its actual behavior. The *Topeka Capital* reported in July 1911, when it was for a few days a record 106 degrees, that it must have been 200 degrees and women were fainting. At one dry-goods store the wax mannequins in the window melted, providing, the editor said, a "gruesome sight. . . . The eyes were protruding and the mouths were dry. The hands were drawn in painful positions seeming to picture intense suffering."[23]

The tornado was the most tempting phenomenon to elicit word pictures, often excessive. Kansans themselves were "enterprising enough to take advantage of this gratuitous billing and bulletining of their state," though most lifelong residents had never seen a tornado and had only a one-in-five-thousand chance of being killed by one.[24] The tornado frightened and attracted through the weirdness of its effects, the suddenness of its appearance, its random path, and its awesome power. It seemed, wrote an editor in 1881, "as if the demons of destruction were turned loose, and human life and property destroyed by the monsters of the air, in the twinkling of an eye. . . . The unbridled wantonness of the winds, the demonic fury of the electric current and the cruel touch of the cyclone, coming without warning; irresistible in power, carrying death and desolation in their wake, are more dreaded than war; more inexplicable than pestilence, as heartless as famine."[25] Probably the most famous tornado story ever to come from Kansas was in 1930 when Will Keller near Greensburg looked up into the core of one passing overhead and described it to the delight of newspapers everywhere.[26] And of course there was Dorothy and her flying Kansas house.[27]

Part of the fascination of describing tornadoes in Kansas, particularly in the pioneer period, was the counterdistinction between nascent civilization, as represented by the small town, and the elemental terror of the heartless wind. A regular descriptive theme was the suddenness of the change some spring afternoon from order to chaos. An example was the town of Irving, Kansas, where a tornado struck in May 1879. Fifteen people died, and many descriptions of the scene went to newspapers. Nude bodies of women "covered with mire" lying dead on the street before the gaze of passengers aboard the regular train that pulled into town just as the storm moved out provided a particularly appalling contrast to the travelers' orderly schedule and expectation of a hot bath and meal. "Every house was torn to atoms and everything movable hurled into space," a reporter wrote.[28] "All the sermons in the world on the ineffectiveness of man as opposed to nature," a writer for *Harper's Weekly* claimed in 1882 when describing a tornado in south central Kansas, "could never prove the text so thoroughly as a great tornado might do in the space of sixty seconds."[29]

The Irving experience was repeated with variations regularly enough to keep Kansas tornadoes in the news. There were 889 of them between 1916 and 1954.[30] Kansas town names like Andale, Udall, El Dorado, Hesston, Andover, and perhaps even the state capital, Topeka, are known in other places more for their association with killer tornadoes than for anything else. Nineteen fifty-five was a particularly bad year, with 144 tornadoes in the state, including the "town-erasing" one that struck the little south-central Kansas town of Udall on Memorial Day eve, killing eighty-two people.[31] That "maniacal" storm made a "low whistle like an old tin horn," stopped clocks at 10:30 P.M., and left the switchboard operator dead at her post. It ranked with Quantrill's raid on Lawrence in 1863 as among the worst disasters in Kansas.[32]

Even short of a cyclone, the wind in the state, the "Kansas zephyr," was a subject for comment. A legislator attending the first session of the state legislature, held in a Congregational Church in Topeka during the howling March winds of 1861, wrote, "Pipes were blown from our mouths; tobacco quids sent whirling from annoyed cheeks . . . hedges transplanted; bumble bees confused and gophers taken bodily from their holes."[33] Marshall Murdock, editor of the *Wichita Eagle,* commented in 1880 that his own "blowing pretensions" had been bested by the Kansas wind. The wind that week, he said, "has just sat on its hind legs and howled and screeched and snorted until you couldn't tell your grandfather from a jackass rabbit. . . . We saw a preacher standing on the corner the other day with his back up, his coattails over his head and his chapeau sailing heavenward, spitting mud out of his mouth and looking unutterable things."[34]

Kansas suffered adverse publicity when it was dry and when it was wet. The image of "droughty Kansas" was so much pushed in the east that Governor George Hodges in 1913 formally complained that "the suffering of men and beast by the drought and the total destruction of Kansas crops are confined entirely to the pages of Eastern newspapers."[35] Still, the impact of drought cannot be underestimated. When Kansas was new as a state in 1861, not only did it have to endure shaky finances and the disruptions of the Civil War but also a devastating drought, which created an embarrassing necessity for "begging" relief from eastern philanthropy.[36] John Ingalls wrote his father in Massachusetts in 1862 that a dry season early that year created fears of another famine. "Living as you do in a country where agriculture is a secondary interest, you can hardly realize the interest and anxiety excited by the weather in those whose only resource is the product of the soil."[37] The same dry pattern plagued Kansas in 1880, through much of the 1890s, in the 1930s Dust Bowl, and in the 1950s.

But the flood disasters drew attention also. The Kansas River in the eastern part of the state was the main offender, particularly its rampages of 1903 and 1951 during times of torrential rain. However, even the "desert" far western counties could be affected, as evidenced by the experience of Elizabeth Bacon Custer, who in spring 1867, as she was camped along Big Creek near Ft. Hays, discovered "what Kansas could do" in the way of rain. The creek, "which we had last seen, the night before, a little rill in the bottom of the gully," rose thirty-five feet in a short time, leaving the tops of good-sized trees on the bank barely visible and drowning seven men near the Custer tent. There was panic in the night amid lightning. It rained for three days, and Libby, alone while her husband George was on maneuvers, had to face the prospect of being tied to a Gatling gun to keep her from floating away. In the glare of lightning she saw "the men waving their arms imploringly as they were swept down with tree-trunks, masses of earth, and heaps of rubbish."[38]

The flood of 1844, documented by Indian agents, was the Kansas champion until 1903. But smaller events in the interim aggravated people. Alden Stevens, camped near Paola, Kansas, in May 1859, wrote, "But Lord, how it did thunder and lighten & rain all night! Lightning was so quick, rapid, and vivid that it shone all the time, and the thunder, it was rolling, clapping & growing all the time." The next morning the party found North Sugar Creek "running, roaring & foaming as loud as a Loch Isle."[39] His son Robert, who managed the Missouri, Kansas, and Texas (MK&T) Railroad, reported in June 1873 on damage to rail operations from flooding. The Kansas Pacific west of Junction City had no trains for four days and lost its bridge over the Solomon River. The MK&T suffered bridge and track damage along the length of the Neosho Valley.[40]

It had been happening forever. A reporter wrote, "Time after time in the

Missouri Pacific bridge in Kansas City, Kansas, after the 1903 flood.
Courtesy of the Kansas State Historical Society.

course of unrecorded centuries the Indians must have watched the flood eddying through the cottonwoods of the bottom wilderness and listened at night with awe to the crash of the great trees falling as the water loosened the soil about their roots."[41] However, the developed downtowns of Kansas City, Topeka, and Manhattan sustained a different level of damage in 1903 than had the mobile tribes or rude forts, or even the pioneer railroads and small towns of earlier days. The engine house and the city electric plant at Abilene were underwater that spring from the ravages of the Smoky Hill, and at Atchison "a seething, roiling mass of mud, water and floating debris" played havoc with the pace of ordinary life.[42] The city of Armordale, in the Kansas City packing district, which had a population of sixteen thousand, was nearly deserted, and property damage in Topeka was estimated at two hundred thousand dollars.[43] "Scourged by fire, the plaything and toy of an awful flood, and with starvation waiting around the corner," an eyewitness wrote on May 31, "the conditions of the cooped-in unfortunates in North Topeka this morning defies descriptive adjective."[44] More than forty people died in Topeka due to the flood and subsequent fire, and seven thousand to ten thousand were homeless.[45] In Kansas City "dead bodies by the scores were seen floating down the rapid side of the current, which was running like a mill race beneath the Seventh Street viaduct."[46] Terrible sights caused one man to comment, "I have lived two or three hundred years in the past two or three days."[47]

Major flooding recurred in Kansas in 1908, 1914, 1926, and 1935, but it was the disaster of 1951, spawned of a series of record rains, that shocked to the degree necessary to bring forth major expenditures for control.[48] The flooding was statewide. The Arkansas was out of control in Wichita, in Arkansas City, and in Garden City and Dodge City, adding to the misery already caused by the Kaw, the Smoky Hill, and the Blue.[49] Hays had eleven inches of rain in one night, and a flash flood inundated eighty blocks.[50] Two hundred blocks flooded in Manhattan, and most of the population of the city sought the high ground at Kansas State College.[51] While deaths (fourteen) were fewer than in 1903, property damage was greater—close to $1 billion.[52] "Mud, mud, mud," a Lawrence reporter observed, "soft, slimy mud all the way from ankle deep to knee deep along the streets, in the yards, and even in the homes. A vast sea of sticky slime."[53]

And it could be dangerous in Kansas when it was clear. The "heated term" in July and August was not an event to attract tourists to Kansas. And Kansans, like others, tended to focus on the extremes. Emory Lindquist, a history professor and the president of Wichita State University, told a story of people discussing the weather in Kansas. When there was a beautiful, cool day in the summer, they would say, "Isn't this just like Colorado?" On a warm, sunny day in winter it was "isn't this just like California?" Only on a stormy day with hail or in the most searing heat would they admit to its being real Kansas weather.[54]

What many people overlooked was that the weather could be lovely and very often was. The summer clouds over the prairie, sometimes triple the height of Pike's Peak, were a substitute for mountains and were much admired by Kansas aviators. Said one: "Probably in no other section of the earth do these billowy giants present themselves in such numbers and grandeur as above the prairies of Kansas."[55] There were three hundred days of sunshine a year in the western part of the state. The dry, mild Indian summer, sometimes lasting well into December, impressed all who experienced it. Ingalls called the late October Kansas weather in 1858 "inexpressibly fine: the days of a happy medium between hot and cold which combine the attractions of both, and the nights as bland and beautiful as June."[56] In early January 1863, he reported "a long succession of golden and luxurious days

1951 flood, Topeka.
Courtesy of the Kansas State Historical Society.

which are degenerating almost into a monotony of splendor." Such prairie brightness and shirtsleeves days, when people huddled around fires in Maine and Minnesota, gave the future senator, a person prone to melancholy and cynicism, "strength to the frame and satisfaction to the heart."[57] A Wellington editor wrote in 1880, "November, which elsewhere is regarded as fit only to die in, in Kansas is one of the most charming of the twelve . . . a season of glorious days, gorgeous sunsets and brilliant nights. Just warm enough in day time for comfort and cool enough at night to sleep." It was a time when "a flood of softened, mellow light covers the whole earth, when the physical seems to blend into the spiritual, and all unconscious of our bodies we live in the soft, ethereal glory that envelops us."[58]

Deep winter weather, as in others seasons, was, however, variable and could be severe. Numerous contemporary observers felt that the calm that prevailed for several months after the famous Wakarusa War in late 1855 in Kansas Territory was due as much to the bitter weather, with snow and the thermometer sometimes dropping to twenty below, as to any propensity of the battling parties to resolve their differences peaceably. Sara Robinson wrote in her diary in January 1856, "No security from the murderous midnight assassin can be more sure than the heavy drifting snows which cover the whole country."⁵⁹ In 1861, another cold winter, Ingalls wrote that "contrasted with the Cuban softness and beauty of the preceding winter here, this Arctic season comes with a peculiarly bad grace."⁶⁰ A farmer near Baldwin City reported in 1879 that much in contrast to the year before, that winter was early and severe, with more snow on the ground than at any time since the winter of 1855–1856. Eighteen to twenty inches fell in two days early in December "and made the best sleighing I ever saw in Kansas."⁶¹

During dry periods, rural Kansas could enjoy the starry heavens in an atmosphere of unusual transparency. Amateur astronomers are amazed that on the Plains one can often see extended objects, like globular clusters, rated at 6.5 magnitude with the unaided eye. The Milky Way appears bright and granulated, and the Andromeda Galaxy, at a distance of over 2 million light years, appears as obvious to the uninitiated gazer as the moon.⁶² The night sky was a sight former Kansans recalled with emotion. Remembered a man in 1961: "Nowhere else can one see the stars so near, so brilliantly clear and so countless as one can on a still, dry night in the Flint Hills. I recall one night when my wife, Eastern-born, and I stood looking up into the sky, so filled with stars that there seemed scarcely room for another and she remarked that never before had the words of the Psalm seemed so real to her: 'The heavens declare the glory of God; and the firmament showeth His handiwork.' "⁶³

Below the vast sky is the land. That Kansas is the heart of America geographically (Smith Center) and geodetically (near Osborne) is an artificial aspect of recent science. But that it has seemed to so many a heartland in other ways is knowledge with a deeper root.

It was rich land, much of it passed over at first by people estimating it according to its sparse look and their primitive technology. Certainly Kansas as a wheat state was slow to emerge. The insight was not immediate that soil that supported prairie might support crops and that the land, particularly with new farming methods, had the "long-lasting requirements for production of the tame-grass field crops with which the northern European migrant was familiar."⁶⁴ At first it was seen as a place where the "deer and antelope play" and where Indians and possibly herdsmen might be added. An article on western Kansas warned in 1879 against overestimating the region based on experience in the eastern part of the state. "Nature's lessons," the author wrote, were never "written so plainly on the fact of any country as that of the great plains of Western Kansas and Eastern Colorado."

It was fine for grazing, but "to attempt to make it corn country is like planting yams in Canada."[65]

It took Kansans some time to become truly nostalgic about the prairie. But whether the Kansas prairie will ever be a tourist attraction, it has been and remains what Walt Whitman called "North America's characteristic landscape," and its silent presence was the enduring background for the history of the state. Tall grasses grew to nine feet in the east of the state while a blanket of short buffalo grass extended all around in the west. It was, wrote the native Kansan and *Wall Street Journal* reporter Dennis Farney in 1975, "an utterly open landscape, a place of lonely windmills turning in a ceaseless wind, of red-tailed hawks circling in an empty sky." This openness, he noted, tended "either to invigorate people or to terrify them."[66] Willa Cather once noted that "those scorching dusty winds that blow up over the bluffs from Kansas seem to dry up the blood in men's veins as they do the sap in the corn leaves."[67]

As time passed, Farney thought, urbanized people came to feel both safe enough in being able to make a living there to appreciate the "harsh and sharp-edged beauty" of the Plains and fragmented enough to yearn for something enduring.[68] And they came to admire those closest to nature and the land. Least Heat-Moon said of Flint Hills residents he observed during a sojourn there that "they often seem to be people from another time, people who desire permanence over continuity, who just happen to find themselves surfaced in an era of X-rated movies, the Internal Revenue Service, Styrofoam burger boxes and nuclear medicine."[69]

Ironically, the more latter-day Kansans loved their native landscape, the less they could enjoy it. Late twentieth-century urban Kansas was isolated from dark skies and wide horizons. Cities tended to be in river valleys with minimal topographic relief and maximum light pollution. Railroads and interstate highways followed river valleys, giving travelers a view of Kansas distorted toward the monotonous. In these cities, and along these roads, with their national franchise eateries and syndicated car dealerships, the sense of place was lost, replaced by what the landscape historian John Stilgoe has called a "metropolitan corridor."[70] With it, doubtless, went some of the sense of community. Many analysts have found a shared sense of place and of its permanence in the face of human frailty an essential element in the building of community.[71] The kind of prairie the first settlers saw, dependent as it was on a bison-fire relationship on a vast scale, doubtless has disappeared forever in reality, but not to memory or suggestion. John Madson wrote in 1995 that he felt in his love for the prairie like "a modern man fallen in love with the face in a faded tintype." Only the frame—the sky and the winds, the setting and the mood—were any longer real.[72] But the need for it remained.

The tendency early was to plow, without much thought that the grassland was precious. In 1980 Kansas had 25 million acres of prime farmland, 48 percent of its surface, second only to Texas in the nation. Most of it was flat, with little erosion, and required minimal fuel and labor to cultivate.[73] In fact, lack of rainfall contributed to the richness of the soil. Like hell, the joke went, all Kansas needed was water and a few good people. With the introduction of numerous wheat varieties and farming methods adapted to Kansas, however, it did well at wheat culture. The first 1-million-bushel Kansas crop came in 1866; the first 10-million-bushel crop in 1875; the first 100-million-bushel crop in 1914; the first 200-million-bushel crop in 1931; the first 300-million-bushel crop in 1952; and the first 400-million-bushel crop in 1979. The trend has been upward in yield of high protein wheat (from under 20-bushel averages in the 1940s to around 40 in the mid-1980s), upward in farm size and mechanization, and, since the 1930s, downward in total acreage planted.[74] Farmers, consequently, have had a diminishing political influence, even in the Wheat State, and precisely because of their success in wheat culture.

What the eye could see did not limit the resources that abided. There was wealth underground. The Nemaha Mountains, one of the great ranges of the primeval world, lying northeast to southwest across eastern Kansas, were important to the oil-well drillers of the early twentieth century. They are granite, with a precipitous east face and a sloping western approach. The view, however, is hardly a modern tourist attraction, as the summits of what is properly called the Nemaha anticline are now six hundred to four thousand feet beneath the surface.[75] Likewise invisible, but economically significant, is the Ogallala formation, an extensive substrata containing substantial groundwater slowly recharged by percolating surface water.[76] There were over 3 million irrigated Kansas acres by the mid-1970s, dependent mostly on this resource. In 1967 there were over forty-six thousand miles of oil and gas pipelines under the surface of Kansas, well in excess of its rail mileage.[77] They carried natural gas from the Hugoton gas field in southwest Kansas to cities in the upper Midwest. Hugoton was one of the largest reserves in the nation and produced 70 percent of the natural gas, ranking Kansas for many years in the top half-dozen producers of that commodity in the nation.[78]

So abided the land and its potential under that variable sky for eons of unrecorded human activity. In 1541 Francisco Vasquez de Coronado visited with a small body of men. Journals of that journey survived.[79] For some time it was only an occasional explorer and some entries in a report, a campsite, or a flag-raising in some native village that informed the world of the area that was marked on early nineteenth-century maps as part of the "Great American Desert." The American presence began with the Louisiana Purchase in 1803 and the Lewis and Clark expedition, which crossed the region on its outward journey in 1804 and on the way back in 1806. There followed incursions by Zebulon Pike (1806), Stephen Long (1819–1820), and John Frémont (1842), among others. In 1822 the Santa Fe trade began, and the Santa Fe Trail, mostly following the course of the Arkansas River, became a feature of the region when surveyed and marked in 1825. Through a northeast corner of what became Kansas ran the Oregon Trail, which in the territorial period was called the California Road.

The Kansas area was then viewed by traders as a road to somewhere else, an image from which it has suffered since. But superimposed on that in the early nineteenth century was another "state"—that of a home for Indians, both those indigenous and those removed from the path of white civilization farther east. Had one asked in the 1830s what the Arkansas, Smoky Hill, and Kansas River country was called, the answer would have been "Indian Territory." The Reverend Isaac McCoy was only the most articulate in advancing the idea of a haven for native civilization among many missionaries who established early fixed outposts of U.S. occupation among the tribes. In the 1820s and 1830s such indigenous tribes as the Kansas and Osages were moved onto fixed reserves; others, like the Wyandots, Delawares, Potawatomies, and Shawnees, with whom territorial settlers would become so familiar, were removed by treaty from their homes in the East and upper Midwest to what became eastern Kansas.[80]

There was at first no question of statehood for such a region. The Trade and Intercourse Acts, designed to provide continued coexistence of the two cultures, specifically forbade white settlement on Indian lands, introduction of whiskey and firearms, or trading without obtaining a license and posting a bond with the Indian Office in Washington. Therefore, the primary classes of people seen in the region before 1854 were travelers on the trails and aboard steamboats, soldiers stationed at forts, missionaries at the church outposts, licensed traders, Indian agents, and members of the tribes. It is no accident that the admission date of the state of Missouri was 1820 and of Arkansas 1836, but of Kansas, 1861; Nebraska, 1867; and Oklahoma, 1907. The central region's westward movement was halted not only by debate over the extension of slavery but also by the establishment of reserves in Indian Territory guaranteed to the tribes removed there.

Still, small groups of structures appeared. Ft. Leavenworth (1827), Ft. Scott (1842), and Ft. Riley (1853) were the major forts, and there was hardly a tribe that by the late 1830s did not have a mission establishment operated by a religious denomination. The first printed work published in Kansas was an edition of three hundred copies of the missionary Jotham Meeker's "Delaware Primer and First Book," printed on his press in 1834. Shawnee Mission (1829) was to become in the early twentieth century one of the first preserved historic sites in Kansas, and the Potawatomie Baptist Manual Training School (1849), after a time as a farmstead barn, was at the turn of the twenty-first century part of the museum and archives complex of the Kansas State Historical Society.[81]

The removal policy as a solution to the "Indian question" depended on treaties negotiated under pressure and the existence of bodies of land thought unsuited for American agriculture located at the frontiers of the Louisiana Purchase next to Mexico. That changed for three reasons: the war with Mexico in 1848, which put the Kansas region in the middle of the expanded continental United States rather than on its southwestern edge; the development of railroad and telegraph technology sufficient to connect the eastern states with newly acquired and gold-laden California; and the realization that prairie lands, though barren of trees, could have soil rich enough to grow abundant crops.

Two obstacles, however, were in the way of a change: Indians and slaves. New removal treaties might be negotiated with the Indians by the same, sometimes crude, combinations of carrots and sticks, as the earlier ones had been. But where would the tribes go? The slavery question had by 1850 been heating up for some time between the sections of the United States. The Missouri Compromise of 1820 had seemed to settle matters by providing that in new states lying north of thirty-six degrees, thirty minutes north latitude, except for Missouri, slavery would be forever banned.

The south boundary of Kansas, as eventually organized, was thirty-seven degrees north.

The Kansas-Nebraska bill, which passed in May 1854, changed that situation. Based on the ideas advanced in the Compromise of 1850 that Congress should not interfere with the question of slavery, and on Stephen A. Douglas's idea of popular sovereignty, the Kansas-Nebraska Act repealed the Missouri Compromise. Douglas, a Democrat, championed the idea that a vote of actual settlers in a new territory should determine whether a state would come into the Union with or without slavery, wherever it was geographically positioned. It was widely assumed that under such a system Nebraska, which was clearly too far north to support agriculture based on slavery, would enter the Union as a free state, but that Kansas, contiguous as it was to slaveholding Missouri, might well be added to the slave South.

The bill organizing Kansas and Nebraska as territories did not sail through the Congress on a wave of good feeling. "It is a question of political morality," wrote the popular minister Theodore Parker. "Shall the Government be a commonwealth where all are citizens, or an aristocracy where man owns his brother man? Shall there be the schools of Ohio, or the ignorance of Tennessee?"[82] And what of the Indians? There were ten thousand on specific reserves in Kansas. Senator Sam Houston of Texas queried, "You may ask, what shall be done with them? You have given them a country, can they ever become civilized, if you keep forcing them from wilderness to wilderness?" The United States was forming territories, he noted, in advance of extinguishment of Indian title and in violation of pledges made to tribes. "Sir, these people are friendless. They have no political influence; they have no hopes; no expectations to present to the ambitious and aspiring. They have no wealth with which to recompense their advocates and friends."[83] Will you bring the Indians back across the Mississippi, William Seward asked. What was the Kansas-Nebraska bill to them but "the consummation of a long-apprehended doom?"[84] Some few might be assimilated, a New York newspaper reporter noted, "but the great mass can neither use nor be used by civilization."[85]

Proponents of the bill, however, emphasized that civilization, as it was defined by midcentury Americans, must progress. When the Indian commissioner George Manypenny visited the region that was to become Kansas in 1853, his threat to enforce the Trade and Intercourse laws by removing white intruders on Indian lands until satisfactory removal treaties could be negotiated was met with disdain from spokespersons on both sides of the slavery controversy. He was even criticized by members of Indian tribes, who had decided that the best route to prosperity was through investment in the new order. Abelard Guthrie, a mixed blood, thought that Indian title should not stop townsite promotion. Guthrie later was a partner with Charles Robinson in the ill-fated Missouri River town of Quindaro. Some tribal members were slaveholders, complicating the situation further. One member of Congress, looking at the native situation, predicted, "Their bones— their very ashes—will be converted into bread to pamper their destroyers." Manypenny, as he started negotiating new treaties in 1854 for the opening of Indian lands and their removal elsewhere, was shocked at the disregard for the old ones. "Are treaties merely made for fun," he wrote, "and hence to be looked on as maneuvers played off the benefit of a hungry crowd of land speculators?"[86]

Southerners imagined there was some "natural law" regulating these matters, with which human agency had nothing to do. Northerners did not see it that way. Said Henry Ward Beecher, "If the South inoculates the State with her leprosy, the plains of Kansas are fairer and richer to-day as a wilderness, than they ever will be again."[87]

The Kansas-Nebraska Act became the "Organic Law" for the original administration of Kansas Territory, which extended from Missouri to the Rocky Mountains. Territories were in effect colonies administered by the federal government. The president appointed the territorial governor and arranged for the election of a congressional delegate and the territorial legislature. He also issued or refused to issue certificates of election in any contests where there were charges of voting fraud. Because the president, Franklin Pierce, was a Democrat and a Southerner, and because those men closest to Kansas to travel to the polls on voting day were from the slaveholding state of Missouri, the system presented a discouraging prospect for slavery opponents.

Andrew Reeder of Easton, Pennsylvania, became governor in June and took up residence in Ft. Leavenworth in October. The election for congressional delegate occurred November 29, 1854, and, after a census, that for the legislature on March 30, 1855. Both elections were victories for the Pro-Slavery faction, amid charges of fraud on both sides. The mistake of the Missourians, Robinson later said, was to overreact, to bring in too many nonresidents to vote, and thus to create a scandal unifying the opposition.[88]

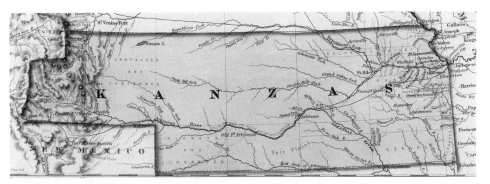

A cropped view of a map of Nebraska and Kansas, published by J. H. Colton, 1855.
Courtesy of the Kansas State Historical Society.

In June, at a convention in Lawrence, the Free State group, bolstered by New England emigrants and by the groups led in from the North through Iowa and Nebraska by James Lane, repudiated the legislature and its laws. On July 2 the legislature gathered at the designated capital of Pawnee, a town formed within the limits of the Ft. Riley reservation, partly because federal lands were about the only places to which secure title could be gained as Indian land-cession treaties were negotiated and sent to Washington.

As with everything in Kansas in its formative stages, however, that simple story is an outline imposed over a reality boiling with enmity and fraught with complications. James Malin, whose *Nebraska Question* remains a classic account, observed that "one thing that emerges clearly from a study of the 1850s is the power of fanatical propaganda—unending repetition of unscrupulous falsehoods—syllogizing in semantic confusion—intolerance masked under moral and religious symbolism—all leading the public to frustration and defeatism, which at long last found escape from stalemate in the Civil War. The United States has been conspicuously addicted to the delusion that the passing of a law, based upon some doctrinaire principle, can work miracles; as though a mere statute could solve anything."[89]

That the statute did not eventually result in adding Kansas to the slaveocracy as expected was not the responsibility entirely of New England. But New England's role was large, and the moral fervor and Puritan heritage of that region clearly fit the way crusading Kansas later wished to view itself. Charles Robinson went to Kansas as an agent of the New England Emigrant Aid Company, a successor to the Massachusetts Emigrant Aid Company, organized by Eli Thayer in April 1854. Robinson earned a salary of one thousand dollars a year, plus a 2.5 percent commission on all sales and receipts from the business of colonization. That business, in a way parallel to the aims of the original English Massachusetts Bay Company, which had planted the American Atlantic colony in the seventeenth century, was expected to turn a profit as well as to establish a "city on a hill" for the moral and religious edification of the benighted elsewhere. The company spent one hundred forty thousand dollars and sent thirteen hundred people to Kansas in 1854 and 1855. Its major Kansas town, Lawrence, a tent city that groups from Boston reached in summer 1854, took its name from Amos Lawrence, a principal of the company. The company subsidized its infrastructure and aided it with cash and expertise in negotiations with Indians for land. The company hired George W. Brown, a newspaperman from Pennsylvania, to establish the *Herald of Freedom*. It sent Sharp's rifles, known for their accuracy, fast firing, and killing power, in boxes marked "books." Thayer spoke of the necessity of bringing emigration "into a system." Robinson wrote a detailed plan of operations for the enterprise before anyone left Boston. Other states followed suit with their own Kansas organizations.

The New England connection can be overdrawn. John Holloway in his 1868 *History of Kansas* emphasized that benefits given to those who came under the New England Company's auspices were limited to reduction of rail fare and the pleasure of company. "The direct effects of these societies," he wrote, "were as a drop in the ocean in the settling of Kansas with freemen."[90] By 1865 those in Kansas born in New England were outnumbered over ten to one both by those hailing from the upper Midwest and those from the South. There were 1,177 Massachusetts-born people in Kansas that year, the largest representation from any New England state, but there were over 20,000 born in Missouri and over 11,000 from Ohio.[91]

Still, influence is not measured wholly in numbers. George Brown pointed out that a little yeast could leaven a large loaf.[92] Influential men, such as Samuel Pomeroy, later a Kansas senator; Isaac Goodnow, a prominent educator and founder of Manhattan; and Robinson had direct connections with the company. Massachusetts origins were respected for qualitative reasons beyond mere numbers. Robinson wrote the company that people from other states were claiming the Bay State as their own: "Everybody you meet is *from* Massachusetts."[93]

The New Englanders who did come had in their minds that they were the heirs of colonial pioneers. They sang to the tune of "Auld Lang Syne" a poem by John Greenleaf Whittier: "We cross the prairies as of old / the pilgrims crossed the sea, / To make the West, as they the East / The homestead of the free."[94] Thayer, speaking in the House of Representatives in spring 1858, claimed, "It was necessary that Plymouth Rock should repeat itself in Kansas. The Puritan character was needed there; but how could it be had except by such discipline as made the Puritans?"[95] Added a Washington paper, "The only famous emigrants . . . worthy to stand side by side with those of Kansas . . . are the Pilgrim fathers. . . . All is stern, majestic, colossal. . . . Everything about them smacks of winter."[96]

The existence of a system such as the Aid Company instituted confirms historians' insight that the image of the lone and self-sufficient western pioneer is misplaced. The system also enhanced the influence of a few. It is a prime example of the kind of practical idealism for which Kansans would come to be known.

An interesting example of systematic group colonization driven by ideology, though this time of a religious rather than of a political nature, is the Ebenezer group. This organization, consisting of two thousand recent German immigrants, ultimately rejected Kansas in favor of Iowa, where it founded seven towns at Amana as a communal enterprise into the 1930s. It did, however, send a pilot expedition of four men into Kansas Territory in September 1854 and made a serious attempt to buy land directly from the Delaware Indians.

The group departed from the society's lands in Ebenezer, New York, under the leadership of Christian Metz, who was an esteemed *Werkzeug*— that is a seer, wizard, or tool of God. They traveled by steamboat and train and eventually arrived on the Missouri River steamboat *Admiral* at the town of Parkville, Missouri, near today's Kansas City. There they hired a Delaware subchief, Charles Journeycake, a prominent "progressive" well known to travelers, who provided food and a covered wagon for the journey west. The prevailing drought made the journey uncomfortable for lack of water, but the group traveled over forty miles into Kansas before one of their horses ran away. Stuck at a stream called Mud Creek, Metz, so ill he feared death, looked to God for guidance. The message that came to him was, "The Lord is sun and shield, a helper who makes night to morning and grants the right to examine beyond on an orderly path. Do not rely only on your own quick decisions and be mindful of the will of the Lord." Pondering that, Metz decided the Lord was telling him to get out of this country while he could. When their stray horse returned, the party retraced its steps.

They had done some exploring during their four days and found the country promising, especially the wolf-infested area around what later became Topeka, Kansas. Therefore, they made several attempts over the next weeks to convince the Delawares to sell them land. The Indians said their agent had forbidden them to sell any more land to private individuals. The group returned to New York. Shortly, a second group departed for Iowa.[97]

The New England Emigrant Aid Company was just as well organized for colonization and just as focused for the moment on the importance of group mutual aid in going into the wilderness as any communal religious group. It was also ostensibly a no-nonsense business, with investors providing capital in expectation of financial return. The historian William Connelley went so far as to write of the company in 1918 that "benevolence had no place in its designs. It was a money-making enterprise."[98]

Evaluated financially, however, the company was a failure. The original objective was to raise $5 million to support emigration to Kansas; in fact, the concern raised less than $.2 million from stock sales, donations, and sales and rents in Kansas. Less than half of the 8,346 shares the corporation issued were held in lots of 25 or more, no individual holding over 150. This suggests "the stock was not generally regarded as either a good investment or an attractive speculation." Probably people who bought 1 to 5 shares regarded their contribution in the same way as did people who bought small-denomination war bonds during the two world wars of the twentieth century. The company's town lots did so poorly that their eventual sale after Kansas became a state barely paid the company's debt and kept it from bankruptcy.[99]

An early example of the gap between financial expectation and return was Edward Everett Hale's book *Kansas and Nebraska*, published in August 1854. Hale was a key official of the company, and early ads for the book claimed it was being published under company sanction.[100] Both Hale and the publisher, Phillips Sampson and Company of Boston, were sanguine at first about the sales possibilities, since the nation seemed to be talking about Kansas. The publisher proposed both a hardbound and paperbound edition and pushed both the stereotypers and Hale to produce the book in less than two weeks at a rate of twenty-five to thirty pages a day.[101] A year later, however, the publishers reported they had lost $108 on the book and that Hale's royalties amounted to only a little over $200. "To you," Phillips, Sampson wrote Hale, "it was a venture in precisely the same way it was to us, & I suppose the grand difficulty in both was in overestimating the public interest in that new world."[102]

It was too bad for Hale and the investors that the Emigrant Aid Company's activity could not have been evaluated instead by the return in "social overhead capital," as is often done with the pump-priming activities of governments in new ventures. The returns in the sense of eventual economic development in the new region from this initial planting were vast, and Hale's well-crafted little book provided the first useful guide to and compendium of reasons for the trip. Hale knew the rewards were not all financial. The company, he wrote, was the pioneer, and its stockholders received "that satisfaction, ranked by Lord Bacon among the very highest, of becoming founders of states, and, more than this, states which are prosperous and free." The enterprise was, he wrote, "an effort which the whole providence of God demands, and which is made easy by the wonderful arrangements of his wisdom."[103]

Just as there were people who criticized the company for being too fixed on profits and political influence, there were critics too of its disorganization, and particularly of the dreamy rhetoric of Thayer. Thomas Webb, the company's secretary, complained in May 1854 that the company's techniques were "perfectly Quixotic."[104] Horace Greeley, who endorsed the company editorially, privately wrote, "I am myself deeply dissatisfied with and distrustful of Mr. Thayer and his management."[105] As more parties went out early in 1855, an observer recommended to a company officer: "For Humanity's sake do something to prevent the fleecing of your emigrants through the inexperience of their leaders. You *must* listen to experience and Western men if you do not want to pay high prices. The agents of the E. A. Company have so far been as green as grass and the emigrants have suffered accordingly. Poetry is a very good thing in its place but I assure you by the time emigrants arrive here [Alton, Ill.] they have got over their singing enthusiasm."[106] Robinson remembered later that "many looked upon Eli Thayer as mad, and his project as madness. Who could be found to go to Kansas with the certainty of meeting a hostile greeting of revolvers, bowie knives, and all the desperadoes of the border. . . . These men were regarded with as much interest as would be a like number of gladiators about to enter into deadly conflict with wild beasts, or each other. Hundreds of people gathered to bid them farewell, and ovations greeted them at all principal points between Boston and Chicago."[107]

They did come, however, and the effect was cumulative. Senator David Atchison of Missouri was standing one day in 1855 on the wharf in Kansas City when a riverboat approached with one of the Aid Company's steam engines for powering a sawmill on its deck. Atchison turned to friends and asked, "What is that on the deck of the steamer?" They replied, "Senator, that is a steam engine and a steam boiler." Atchison exclaimed, "You are all a pack of —— fools; that is a Yankee city going to Kansas, and . . . in six months it will cast one hundred Abolition votes."[108]

A telling example of the powerful influence of the Aid Company in the field was the experience of the Reverend Isaac Goodnow of East Greenwich, Rhode Island. Goodnow, late in 1854, collected material from several aid companies.[109] But it was a Thayer lecture early in December 1854 and a conversation with Thayer at his hotel afterward that convinced Goodnow to organize a group of people "of the right stamp" to found a new town in Kansas Territory (KT). Thayer emphasized that Goodnow could double his money every year, but that was not what most excited the minister. He was impressed with the travel setup. "With their organization," he wrote a friend, "emigrating is a very different affair from going *alone* into the woods!" And he craved the moral and political challenge. "I well understand that Kansas must & will be Free! There is no necessity about it: indeed it is *doubtful!* There is only *one way* to have it, this is for every lover of Freedom with a strong will & the ability to start to make his arrangements with his best friends, or without them to go right on to the ground, and whatever he has of talent, money & influence, to use them *heartily* for Liberty!"[110] Kansas, he wrote in his diary, "is the *all engrossing subject!*"[111]

Goodnow resigned his teaching post in January 1855 and traveled up the Missouri River aboard the steamer *Kate Swinney* with 120 emigrants, 93 U.S. troops, 80 horses, and a military band. He wrote his first letters to his wife Ellen from Wild Cat Creek near Boston (later Manhattan), KT, in March.[112] Lawrence, he wrote after having seen that city in the snow, "looks new & rough, about as I expected."[113] But the countryside he described as "magnificent! Oh the *moonlight* scenery!"[114] His first home along the Big Blue was a tent with walls of turf around it, where he was cold but happy.[115] "Election Day," he wrote a few days after arriving, "Voted for Freedom."[116]

Isaac Goodnow.
Courtesy of the Kansas State Historical Society.

Ellen Goodnow.
Courtesy of the Kansas State Historical Society.

Goodnow's enthusiasm reminds one of Per Hansa's whistling optimism in Ole Rolvaag's classic novel of Dakota pioneering, *Giants in the Earth.* But the fears of his wife, who is so haunted by the wilderness that she crawls into her trunk, brought from the Old Country, to escape, are mirrored in the mixed attitude of Goodnow women toward flipping flapjacks and drinking limewater at the claim at the far limit of western navigation of the Kansas River. Isaac's wife's health was poor; Ellen Goodnow was willing to go to Kansas but asked many questions about the climate and the rigors of travel. She emphasized that these concerns "are no index of the heart. I would be with you as soon as steam would carry me, if it were best."[117] But it was a challenge. Eventually, with aid from railroad conductors and a hack driver in Kansas City with her two hundred pounds of luggage, she paid a fare of $38.75 to Kansas City and traveled alone, arriving at the Goodnow claim in June.[118] Isaac's brother William was also in Kansas, but his wife, Harriet, was far less amenable to joining her husband. "To think of you far away," she wrote, "destitute of the Comforts of Life and in poor health—is to me a sad and gloomy repletion." She was willing to leave him there with God, "to whom I daily commend you," and without her.[119] She would send him letters, she said, through Ft. Leavenworth, but that was all. "How can you wish me to leave my beautiful home that I have worked so hard for, and suffer the privation and hardship of one in a new country? I hope you will not let your mind rest one moment on such an idea. If you can do well there, I have no objection. *I* can do *well* here, and feel perfectly contented, why should I not?"[120]

It has been suggested that perhaps the contrast in the attitude of these two women had partly to do with different political sensibilities and partly with a degree of flexibility about living in primitive conditions or facing danger. It may also have involved differences with husbands about "wifely duty." Ellen's attempts at reassuring Harriet, after Ellen herself had arrived in Kansas, were to no avail.[121] At best, however, residence in Kansas did not then seem a heady prospect for a woman faced with keeping house and maintaining civilization.

Josiah Miller, who hailed from South Carolina but became the editor of the *Kansas Free State* in Lawrence early in 1855, was another emigrant on the Spartan model.[122] In summer 1855, established in his newspaper office in Kansas, Miller advised his parents, who were thinking of coming, that they should bring their beds and bedding: "Feather beds cannot be had in this country at all."[123] Guns, however, could be had. "Two revolvers & a knife is all I want," Miller wrote, "& the first man that touches me in a violent manner I blow him through. . . . *I am ready.*"[124]

So was the Emigrant Aid Company. It sent party after party, nearly weekly, until by the March 30, 1855, election over 800 had arrived. By fall the company had sent 1,312 people directly from Boston and Worcester, where it organized the trips. Thomas Webb, its secretary, thought that an equal number went "under our auspices" from other places in New England and that a still greater number went to Kansas from points in the West "in consequence of our movements and doings."[125]

Being a business as well as a crusade, the Aid Company's influence was for "prudence" and the "dictates of . . . good sense, and wise forecast." Webb was constantly talking Robinson out of resigning and at the same time restraining him and the radicals around him from scotching the whole enterprise by precipitate or intemperate action.[126] The company had enough of a problem raising money, as "patriotism and pockets do not harmonize," and any suggestion that the settlers were irresponsible would dry up the support.[127]

There was an ideal balance—firm in resolve but not overly aggressive, united in spirit while free to disagree, and committed but not uncooperative. "We regret," Webb wrote Samuel Pomeroy in March 1855, "to see by the Papers that there is a factious & turbulent spirit prevailing among some at Lawrence. Not looking for perfection in poor humanity, we did not suppose that harmony & unanimity would at all times bear sway, but it was reasonable to presume that those, who were permitted to become citizens, and were graciously granted lots, would for appearance, if not from a sense of honor, avoid manifesting their propensities. If however they will only prove true to Freedom & act harmoniously in the approaching election, we shall care but little about the venom spit out upon us, however poisonous it may be; knowing that our Cause is just."[128]

Violence was not in the planning. The Emigrant Aid organization in the earliest days would have had philosophical difficulty sending the weapons that it later shipped in quantity. "When the first hundred rifles were solicited [probably in spring 1855]," Webb remembered early in 1856, "people shrank with a kind of holy horror at the idea of sending such murderous weapons." He and another Aid Company principal had to finance the first shipments personally.[129] But subsidy for economic development of the territory and domination through that means of Free State principles was a purpose about which the company never had doubt. Ellen Goodnow remembered that the arrival in the new town of Manhattan of the Emigrant Aid Company mill, drawn by twenty oxen, "was a greater event to those early settlers than that of the Union Pacific Railroad . . . later."[130]

The Goodnows reported in mid-June 1855 that the legislature was to meet about ten miles from them.[131] And so it did. There are various evaluations of how much a part Andrew Reeder's interest in developing a town site played in the location of that capital of Pawnee. Witnesses differed on how poor the accommodations there were. But the stone capitol surrounded by the tents of the legislators on the open prairie did present a primitive picture. "We want [the capital city]," said one legislator, "at some point where there are no bullheads or horned frogs."[132] Pawnee, wrote a student of the times, was "a town of the smallest realized attainments."[133]

A six-year-old girl, whose father was the contractor for the building, watched the legislative proceedings, seeing "the fighting . . . the swearing and everything that transpired." On July 4, the second day of the meeting, her father saw her and said this was no place for a woman. To that, Governor Reeder responded, "Let the child remain. She is the only redeeming thing in the room. Come and have a seat near me." She was escorted to the front amid cheers, tugging at her pantalets, which were showing.[134]

It was an enormous domain they were trying to govern, and deep, complex divisions among a hard and loud people were unresolved. B. F. Stringfellow knocked Reeder down at Shawnee Mission late in June when Reeder called him a border ruffian.[135] "The Governor would have killed the dog," wrote a freighter to Mrs. Goodnow, "if he had not been prevented by some friends who were present."[136] Also, those people whom such "civilization" was to replace had not yet departed. In mid-June, as the legislature was about to meet just over a hill or two from his cabin, William Goodnow wrote his wife that "between 100 & 200 mounted Indians have just passed us by for Buffalo hunt in great style."[137]

As the debates proceeded at Pawnee, resolutions of repudiation for any measures the legislature might take came from Lawrence, a town where visitors slept on prairie-hay beds in a hotel made of poles and thatch with cloth on the cable ends and ate at a common dining hall feeding one hundred at a time.[138] "It is our purpose," Charles Robinson wrote, "to so conduct ourselves in this trying time as to meet the approval of the whole North & all good men, & it is very gratifying to know that leading men in the East appreciate our position & sympathize with us. . . . I am not in the habit of looking upon this struggle as a local one & confined to Kansas."[139] He told an audience of two thousand, including some Shawnee and Delaware Indians, gathered for the Independence Day celebration, that they were "in a new and strange country and surrounded by circumstances interesting and peculiar. . . . I seem to hear the millions of freemen and the millions of bondsmen in all countries, the spirits of the revolutionary heroes, and the voice of God—all saying, to the people of Kansas, 'Do your duty.'"[140]

Pro-Slavery statements were no less firm. "We would not like to see the Governor dangling in the air, by the neck," wrote one journalist. "He will soon be dead, dead, dead without that—merely because we consider him a fair specimen of Eastern chivalry, and a very fair sample of a Free Soiler; but if he is an Abolitionist at heart and in action, and would abet in running off darkies into Canada, it might be well enough to place a noose around his neck, by way of experiment, if it were only to hear him cough and see him make *pretty* faces."[141] The *Kansas Herald* in Leavenworth, only a little grown up from its first publication outdoors under an elm tree, called the Emigrant Aid Society people "conspirators" and "criminals."[142]

On June 27, 1855, settlers organized a Kansas Democratic Party in a meeting chaired by a firebrand and an electrifying speaker recently arrived from Indiana—James H. Lane.[143] Lane by August had joined the Free State cause, either from conviction or ambition, and had no connection with the restraining hand of the Aid Company. A handful of towns were established. The territory grew fast from its population of eighty-five hundred, revealed by the spring 1855 census, and its newspaper presses spewed out rhetoric. Leavenworth and Atchison were the main Pro-Slavery towns while Lawrence and Topeka were Free State centers. A gaggle of smaller towns—Kickapoo, Franklin, Tecumseh, Wyandotte, Quindaro, Delaware, Sumner, Emporia, Doniphan, Ft. Scott, Osawatomie, Palermo, Elwood, Lecompton, Grasshopper Falls, Manhattan, and Council Grove, among those of some pretension —rounded out the primitive panoply within the next several years.[144]

The seal of Kansas Territory, designed by Reeder and engraved in Philadelphia, juxtaposed the buffalo, agriculture, and the primitive pioneer with the goddess of the harvest, Ceres with her sheaf. The motto was *Populi voce* (by the voice of the people).[145] One observer wrote, "The whole earth seems to be reeling to and fro."[146] For the newest American political unit, it was not going to be a gentle beginning.

2

TRAMPLING OUT THE VINTAGE, 1855–1865

On Thursday evening, August 20, 1863, Robert Stevens, a speculator in lands and a lobbyist for Kansas interests around the Indian Department in Washington, checked into the Eldridge House in Lawrence, Kansas, probably to attend a railroad meeting.[1] A few blocks south, Charles and Sara Robinson went to bed in their house on Massachusetts Street on a still night under a full moon. They talked about Charles's rising early to attend to some horses at their barn on Mt. Oread. When he left in the predawn dark, Sara asked him what time it was. He said quarter to five. She turned over and napped until the housekeeper rushed in with a cry that the town was under attack. Miss E. P. Leonard was visiting, a tall woman (five feet, eight inches), who had just had a narrow escape from drowning on a return by steamship from Europe. "Wheel left," Sara heard a horseman say, "kill every man, woman and child."[2]

Stevens was awakened shortly after 5:00 A.M. by gunshots and shouting. Pulling on his pants and coat, he realized the raiders were about to burn him and his companions inside their hotel. Luckily, the leader of the band of Missouri bushwhackers was William Quantrill, a former client of Attorney Stevens. Stevens met with him and negotiated the evacuation of the Eldridge House guests but could not otherwise moderate the savagery.[3] When Robinson returned from his bird's-eye perch on the hill as the raiders departed, he had to pass bodies and burning homes. The Eldridge House was on fire, "truly a wall of fire," Sara wrote, that "never wavered."[4] "O God!" Stevens wrote to his family in New York. "No pen, no language, can fitly describe the awful scene. It was not a fight, not a murder, but the most terrible, cold-

Robert Stevens.
Courtesy of the Kansas State Historical Society.

"Dead Brother," an image of Kansas violence from a popular contemporary book.
Courtesy of the Kansas State Historical Society.

blooded, fiendish massacre ever heard of in this country, or any other where civilized people pretend to live."[5]

Horrid scenes were legion. There was the spectacle of Katherine Riggs being dragged through a lot and over a woodpile as she hung on the bridle of a man's horse to keep him from shooting her fleeing husband, to say nothing of the terrors to which children and old people were subjected.[6] H. M. Simpson, a banker who handled Massachusetts resident Hiram Hill's investments in Lawrence, wrote Hill that he, his wife, his father, and his children stood hiding in a cornfield for over three hours that hot day. The children, Simpson wrote, seemed to know not to cry, but the baby got hungry. He gave it an ear of raw green corn to eat. "Mrs. Simpson is quite well," the letter continued, "but has not yet entirely got over the effect of the terrible scenes she has passed through."[7]

The morning after the raid a wailing arose. A woman found among the ashes of a large building held the blackened skull of her husband, who had been shot and burned in his place of business.[8] The cemetery in the next days, was, in Stevens's words, a "most busy place; many men were at work; long trenches were dug, two sets working, one digging, the other following & covering coffins."[9]

On Monday John Ingalls came down from Atchison as part of a column of relief. Lawrence was smoking ruins, "and the charred and distorted corpses" of the victims still littered the streets. "Absolutely nothing remained. Not a yard of calico, a pound of flour or sugar, a nail or a pan or pair of shoes could be purchased in a town where stocks of not less value than a million and a half of dollars were exposed two days before."[10] Simpson estimated the business loss to Lawrence at $1.1 million. He himself lost everything and had to "commence life again at the bottom of the ladder."[11]

Governor Thomas Carney visited Lawrence and called it a "disaster."[12] He wrote the military authorities, "The track of the enemy from the Missouri border to Lawrence may be traced in blood. Ruins of villages, towns & cities, the sacrifice of millions of property & sadder yet the sacrifice of hundreds of the lives of our best citizens proclaim the success of the brutal marauders." He could admire the skill of the bushwhackers as horsemen but could hardly condone the federal government's lack of attention to the defense of Kansas.[13]

The next Sunday people feared the raiders might return. As Ingalls described the scene, "Women with a single night dress, the only garment left them from the destruction of their houses, naked infants, wrapped in old quilts and scraps of carpeting, men haggard and desperate, fled in one tumultuous flood to the ferry landing with shrieks & cries that were pitiable to hear." The wind suddenly blew with frightful coldness from the north and a thunderstorm "poured its torrents upon the hungry and half-clad multitude as they huddled upon the banks of the forbidding stream." Ingalls spent the evening until midnight standing in front of the Eldridge House with his revolver until word came that the rumor was just a rumor. "You can easily imagine," he wrote his father, "what a feeling of exasperation exists among the people of Kansas."[14]

Thus was the much-written-about Quantrill's raid, the most famous incident of the Civil War in the new state of Kansas. One hundred fifty were killed, and newspapers across the nation competed with one another to describe the details.[15] The contrast of civilization and sudden chaos was almost as striking and as tempting to describe as the Kansas tornado.

Yet Quantrill's raid was neither an official military engagement nor without provocation from the "innocents" of Kansas. And it had precedents dating to long before the nation was plunged into war. Lawrence had been burned before. "Bleeding Kansas" had long been in the news. The chaos of the territorial period and first years of statehood amid war, extending from 1854 to 1865—a time when *inter arma leges silent* (among arms, laws are

John Ingalls.
Courtesy of the Kansas State Historical Society.

silent)—represents not only the first definable era in the history of Kansas proper but also one saturated with the drama of vivid contrasts and enduring in its impact on regional culture. "We do not intend to abandon the place," Simpson wrote as he picked up the pieces of his life in 1863, "no matter what may happen."[16]

Wichita, later the state's largest and most industrialized city, did not exist in the 1850s, its geographic place occupied by Osage Indian traders; and western Kansas was yet the bison hunting grounds of the Cheyennes, Arapahoes, and Sioux, facts that are significant in understanding the relative short shrift that that city and that section seemed to get from the Kansas political and social establishment of the twentieth century. Not only did the Indian reserves situation in the territorial era concentrate the state institutions in its northeast corner, but also Wichita and Hays did not figure in the hallowed traditions of the Bleeding Kansas era, which mattered so deeply for so long to the cultural and political elite there.

The mythology developed even as the events unfolded. Robert Stevens wrote territorial governor James Denver in 1858: "People here [Washington] so dreadfully misunderstand the real situation in Kansas that it is the next thing to an impossibility to enlighten them. Having got certain ideas in their heads, they are determined not to be convinced."[17] John Martin, a Civil War hero with the Eighth Kansas at Chickamauga, spoke in 1886 during his gubernatorial term about the importance of the "armed camp" era of Kansas history. "That a State cradled amid such events, schooled during such a period, and inspired by such sentiments, should, in its growth and development, illustrate these mighty energies and impulses, was inevitable."[18] Eli Thayer, founder of the New England Emigrant Aid Company, wrote a few years later that the years after the passage of the Kansas-Nebraska bill were the "controlling and dominating epoch" that determined "the character and destiny of a nation."[19] Governor Lyman Humphrey in 1889 emphasized the same theme. He said that Kansas late in the nineteenth century "beautifully exemplifies in her present conditions, the philosophy of De Tocqueville that the growth of states bears some marks of their origin; that the circumstances of their birth and rise affect the whole term of their being." Kansas started on a high social and moral plane, he thought, and that had "dominated and propelled her with the gathering momentum of a falling body." Territorial history, he said, was "an influence that runs like a golden thread throughout our later experience, at once charming, fascinating, and yet powerful." That history had become "classic" and read like "an epic poem."[20]

The territorial period in Kansas was enormously complex—"wheels within wheels," as the prophet said. It contained a war of individuals and of factions. "I can scarcely dignify with the name of party," one observer said, "those who condescend to such a petty warfares as exist between Kansas agitators."[21] There were always two governors, competing congressional delegates, two capitals, and two legislatures, one called "revolutionary" and "treasonous" by the Pro-Slavery Law and Order Party and the other called "bogus" by the Free State faction. There were divisions within the factions. The Democratic governors regularly fell out with the Democratic legislature. The Free State group tried to contain people who, though all against slavery, had shades of view on race ranging from support of a state voting right for blacks to insistence on banning all African Americans from residence in Kansas. There were competing elections in which only one faction participated, and therefore with results that only one faction recognized. John Brown and Jim Lane moved in a swirl of violence and demagoguery while Charles Robinson, no less radical and physical in temper, was restrained by the economic goals of the New England Emigrant Aid Company from the wages of anarchy. There were arrests and counterarrests, killings and revenge killings, raids and counterraids, in which every good horse that a thief might steal was characterized as a part of enemy contraband and every town that might be burned and plundered as a stronghold of opposing ideology.

There were, in succession, four official capitals (Ft. Leavenworth, Pawnee, Shawnee Mission, Lecompton), while the Free State legislature gathered in Topeka, its capital. There were two more de facto capitals where the legislature met without legal sanction: Minneola and Lawrence. There were four Kansas constitutions written in addition to the Organic Law organizing the Territory initially (Topeka, 1855; Lecompton, 1857; Leavenworth, 1858; Wyandotte, 1859). Six Democratic territorial governors (A. H. Reeder, 1854–1855; Wilson Shannon, 1855–1856; John Geary, 1856–1857; Robert Walker, 1857; James Denver, 1857–1858; Samuel Medary, 1858–1859) left Washington to go to what came to be called the "graveyard of governors."[22] Four acting governors supplemented these in interim periods. Land titles were confused by the fact that when the territorial government was created, it was superimposed upon an area that had been envisioned twenty years earlier as a permanent Indian frontier. Consequently, no land was initially available for settlement by whites. The early concentrations of population clustered in its northeast corner, where alone, through direct negotiations with the tribes and the location of "floats" (land claims with no specific location given in treaties that could be purchased from the Indians), towns with tenuous title could be carved out of the wilderness. The Territory itself extended west to the Rocky Mountains, and, in the middle of the slavery battles, there was a gold rush to Cherry Creek, attracting thousands more people. On top of that, the Santa Fe Trail trade continued across the region where several dreams of the future had already established themselves.

Robert Richmond has called the Kansas territorial era "one of the most confused—and confusing—in American history."[23] Governor Denver's sister warned him about the impossibility of bringing any order out of it. She wrote to him in Kansas in 1858, reminding him of a time when as an adventurous boy he had climbed a tree in quest of a crow's nest, only to find that he could not make his way back down. His siblings watched, "lest their ambitious brother should become a prey to the crows, which he wished to destroy, rather than the destroyer." It might be thus in Kansas. "Why is it," she wrote, "that the people in Kansas will not be guided by reason, instead of allowing their wild passions to urge them to destruction?"[24]

Despite the complications, certain events are clear and simple. Everything dated from the March 1855 election, flawed as it was, that established what the Free State faction, history, and hindsight have called the bogus legislature. That legislature, however, was recognized by two Democratic administrations (Pierce, Buchanan) in Washington. It represented the way territories were technically supposed to be administered. The rest was revolution.

It is significant, also, that Kansas, which became one of the most consistently Republican states in the nation, harbored, in the time of its origin, a plethora of Democrats. Just as Kansas prohibition may be explained partially by the alcoholic excesses of the territorial and cattle-trade era, so also might its Republicanism have been influenced partly by these disastrous Democratic regimes.

But the Free Staters were not Republicans: that party was not officially organized nationally until 1856, or in Kansas until 1859. They were a moral interest group, and like people impassioned on both sides of the abortion issue in the late twentieth century, focused on "higher law" in a way that cut across party lines. However careful some of them were not to confront directly the federal authority, with the military behind it, there was a real question whether they were obeying the actual sublunary law. The heroes of Kansas history, as later written by the victors, were at the time regarded by the self-designated Law and Order (Pro-Slave) faction as criminals, and their treatment ranged from the indictment and arrest of Governor Charles Robinson to active military pursuit of John Brown. The election of 1855 was corrupt, no doubt, with voting fraud on both sides, but the result probably represented the views of the majority on the ground. That the balance soon changed was the result of organization and money as well as ideology and aggression. Robinson described the delicate problem of overturning an established government when he wrote, "It is easy to commence operations, but difficult to stop at the right time & in the right way."[25]

And at its simplest, the Kansas conflict was about the moral issue of slavery. There have been generations of revisionist historians to talk about the sectional conflict as economic division or disagreement over states' rights. Paul Gates has made a strong case for the importance of land speculation as a factor in the Kansas struggle.[26] And certainly opposition to slavery in 1850s Kansas did not imply a modern view of racial equality. But the overwhelming emphasis in contemporary statements by both sides on slavery, either as a biblical contradiction or as a fundamental property right, must lead one to the conclusion that those moral passions were more than window dressing for some economic core.

Another key feature, easily understood, was violence. Guerrilla action was constant. Locals called it war, but it was not really a war. Between 1854 and 1861, fifty-six people died in the confrontations in Kansas. There was much exaggeration. Sol Miller humorously noted in 1858 that the statistics of the "last civil war in Kansas were: Killed—0; Wounded, contusion of the nose—2; Missing—0; Captured—3; Frightened—5,718."[27] To catalog that violence in detail, however, would be a lengthy and repetitive process. William Phillips noted in 1856 that to detail all the "Kansas outrages" would fill "a book as big as 'Webster's Unabridged,' and more frightfully dreary."[28]

The violence, however, was brutal and domestic—more shocking in a way to bystanders, neighbors, and families than the numbing spectacle of lines mown like grass in formal battle. Just as accounts of men being beaten and shot at their homes before their wives by the Quantrill raiders were capable of deeply disturbing a nation inured to war, so did details of such a personal killing as that of Reese Brown early in 1856. Brown, a Free State man captured by the Kickapoo Rangers, was helpless and unarmed when his captors hacked him to death with hatchets. While his brains oozed from a deep gash, and while he pleaded with his captors as he struggled in the agonies of death, they jumped on him, kicked him, and cursed at him, one of them even leaning over and spitting tobacco juice in his eyes. Such incidents, multiplied by both sides, made vengeance the order of the day. There was a wearing constancy about the skirmishes (Black Jack, Hickory Point, Ft. Titus), the massacres (Pottawatomie, Marais des Cygnes), the raids on towns (Lawrence, Osawatomie, Franklin), and the just plain one-at-a-time killings that straddled the line between battle and murder in the way the raids did between war and plunder. As the historian Thomas Goodrich wrote, "The continual stress of the guerrilla war, the day-in, day-out uncertainty of life and property, quite simply exhausted the meager resources of the territory not only physically and financially, but emotionally as well."[29]

As outsized as the violent incidents became in the press and in the minds of the participants, so also loomed large the human characters in the piece. But oversimplification is a danger everywhere. The winning side got the best of it in the telling. David Atchison, John Stringfellow, Samuel LeCompte, and John Calhoun were men as riveting as Charles Robinson, Samuel Pomeroy, James Lane, and John Brown. There were doubtless Southern women as outstanding as Sara Robinson or Clarina Nichols. The Pro-Slavery bastions of Atchison and Leavenworth were places as vital as Lawrence and Topeka, and their communications in the *Squatter Sovereign* newspaper as full of bold rhetoric as was the *Herald of Freedom*. But the Pro-Slavery group seemed not to share the glory of the Lost Cause that attached over time to the secessionists of the 1860s. Their leaders and arguments were ultimately consigned mostly to the shadowy limbo reserved for the also-rans.

John Brown was no farmer, and he did not come to Kansas by accident. He came because Kansas was the "cockpit of the Nation" and because he wanted to be a warrior in the fight brewing there.[30] But so did many others. It was a self-selected slice of society, young and brash mostly, that dared to pull up roots for a frontier such as the highly publicized one that existed in Kansas in the 1850s. Cyrus Holliday in his report as adjutant general of Kansas in December 1864 explained the high success of Kansas in recruiting and the special bravery of Kansas's men in the Civil War with reference to territorial history. "The reputation required by our settlers in our early Kansas troubles," he wrote, "aroused the military spirit in sympathizing breasts all over the country, and from that consideration, and the additional fact that Kansas came to be regarded as a dangerous place for settlement, the result was, that the large proportion of the immigration to our State was composed of the most daring and hardy sons of the Republic."[31]

Of the Free State leaders themselves, there has been much stereotyping, as John Brown exemplifies. Sophisticated researchers, as well as popular writers, have portrayed the divisions within the Free State faction as a kind of

James Lane.
Courtesy of the Kansas State Historical Society.

split personality characteristic of Kansas itself, represented by the contrasting figures of Charles Robinson and James Lane. Lane, the "Grim Chieftain," has been portrayed as an amoral demagogue, changing sides at will, stooping to any stratagem to gain power, and yet possessed of an alluring charisma that moved all who met him. He demonstrated the characteristics of a manic-depressive personality, sailing sometimes to the heights in impossibly eloquent speeches, advancing clever ideas and stratagems, overwhelmed and overwhelming at times with frantic energy while at other times he was confined to bed in the entropy of melancholy. Few can resist characterizing him in the most colorful, extreme, and probably irresponsible terms. But Robinson, who gets the statesman's role, has been distorted, too, partly to serve as Lane's psychological foil, as he was surely his political opponent. Robinson also was a radical, tuned for those times. A Lawrence resident, writing to an eastern investor about the "old timers" in town in 1878, mentioned, "Gov. Robinson still is always on the 'opposite side' of whatever is up for discussion."[32] The bitter enmity between Lane and Robinson, as well as the success of both in the situation, was partly because they were alike—eloquent, courageous, hot tempered, cocksure, and confrontational. "In the history of the world," Isaac Goodnow wrote of those times, "Providence has raised up men qualified for particular work."[33]

It was supposedly Robinson who kept the fragile peace that maintained the respectability of his cause for another day of political action while Lane and Brown would have run amok. Robinson in later years said that Lane was "destitute of principles or convictions of any kind, and of moral or physical courage." He seemed almost feral to the doctor, "pawing the earth," he wrote, "beating the air and bellowing . . . like a bull of Bashan." Sol Miller, the editor of the *Kansas Chief*, said that Lane's characteristic action was "bulldozing and deceit."[34] Hannah Ropes, who was a witness to the negotiations that ended the Wakarusa War of late 1855, observed that Lane, with a "wonderful ingeniousness," tried to keep up a "wicked spirit of vengeance." Any reader of human faces, she wrote, "can never study his without a sensation very much like that with which one stands at the edge of a slimy, sedgy, uncertain morass." Robinson, on the other hand, she characterized as "honest in expression, simple and unaffected in manner, and brave as a lion."[35]

But Lane as well as Robinson was instrumental in the Wakarusa War negotiations with Governor Wilson Shannon and was criticized along with Robinson by observers who thought too many compromises had been made. Lane was a close friend and adviser of Abraham Lincoln during the Civil War, a man without whom most scholars think Lincoln could not have been renominated in 1864. The question of how the fatherlike Lincoln was linked with the libertine madman "with the eyes of a harlot" who took off his clothes and screamed on the stump is as fascinating as why Henry Thoreau, Ralph Emerson, and Theodore Parker met with and supported the "lunatic" John Brown.

Robinson explained the Lane-Lincoln connection by saying that Lincoln was a "weak" man, quoting with favor the opinion that Lincoln was "subject to like passions as the rest of us, subject to flattery and coercion."[36] Given what we know about Lincoln, that seems hardly credible. Robinson was Lincoln's personal and political enemy. Certainly, there is a great myth of Lincoln as sainted martyr, which clouds our view of the real man, who could appreciate a crude story, a political scheme, or a grandiose idea (the Emancipation Proclamation, the March to the Sea) that might come from Lane.

Lane was at times supposed to be a rapist, wife abuser, and murderer; Robinson a manipulator, speculator, and an embezzler.[37] The charges were plausible because contemporaries judged both men capable of such acts. Both, however, were at all times certified leaders and could mesmerize audiences with the "Kansas language" of the great crusade for freedom. Robinson was the savior of Kansas in his own mind, and he and his enthusiastic wife Sara lived a long time and wrote much, interpreting historical events from their perspective.[38] But in fact, it is certain that Lane was more of a statesman and Robinson more of a stinker than is generally communicated.

It is vital to keep in mind in analyzing this and other issues the extreme partisanship of virtually every primary source for the territorial era. Douglas Brewerton, whose *War in Kansas* is one of the few accounts contemporary with the events to try to balance the views, noted that, like all causes, this one was greatly afflicted with cant. He thought that the people in "politics-ridden" Lawrence would do best with less talk and more work.[39] And the media was as much an influence, on the actors as well as on the observers, as in any modern political crisis. When in 1858 there was a rump meeting called to try to arrange for the Free State group to vote for the "regular" legislature and thus resolve issues peacefully, that meeting was, according to a participant, so disrupted by newspaper correspondents who led a "wild, hooting, disorderly rabble" into the hall, "filling every aisle and vacant place, jumping upon seats, and cheering at the hight [*sic*] of their voices," that the organizers had to douse the lights and move to another building under cover of darkness. According to George Brown, the newspapers had an interest in prolonging the Kansas strife: it was selling papers.[40] James Christian, a Southerner with Union sympathies living in Kansas in the 1850s, wrote, "I have seen, as yet *nothing* in the public prints, which may be regarded as strictly true, on either side of this question, for editors and letter-writers are like lawyers, very apt to tell but one part of the story, and that in their own way."[41]

There was never agreement in the press or in books published at the time on the details of events. Did Franklin Coleman attack a helpless Charles Dow on the Santa Fe Road in November 1855 to touch off the Wakarusa War, or did Dow first curse Coleman and come at him with a wagon skein? Did the town of Lawrence threaten to resist the law and the military by force, or was there a difference of opinion on the wording of resolutions? Did John Brown and his friends really cut up helpless men with swords that May night in 1856, or did the Pro-Slavery people die in an equal fight, the mutilations being accounted for by people brought in from an Indian attack on the prairie? Was Brown a martyr or a fanatic? A devil or, as Henry Thoreau once called him, "an angel of light"? Was Douglas County sheriff Samuel Jones a tyrannical monster, who took fiendish delight in the torching of Lawrence, or a fine-looking twenty-eight-year-old trying to do his duty in enforcing the law? Did Governor Shannon after the Lawrence threats of 1855 give Lane and Robinson carte blanche authority to defend themselves, or was it only permission to take arms against an immediate threat the night the document was signed? Was the Eldridge House in Lawrence built as a fort? Were the Free Staters akin to the revolutionaries of 1776 in disobeying authority in defense of freedom, or were they a minority pursuing through direct action what they could not for the moment achieve through legal process? One finds versions, tinged with emotion, that support all these interpretations. The caveats of analysis, however, and the necessity to modify with some salient detail the sweeps of the broader brushes that have painted the scene do not diminish the story of earliest Kansas as a great one.

It appeared that mutability was the key to the political fortunes of Kansas, as it was to its weather. Mild days and hope of peace seemed to alternate with storms of hail and of passion. "The inclemency of the season," Ingalls wrote in 1862, "appears to be in unison with the rude fortunes of our youthful State."[42]

The initial pioneers of 1854 and 1855 were enthusiastic about the place. An emigrant writing in January 1855 said that the climate "is one of the best in the world" and was "in raptures with the magnificent, rich, rolling prairies."[43] Julia Lovejoy commented, "It seems to us impossible that any spot on earth, uncultivated by art, can be more inviting in appearance than this country."[44] Yet the weather and the mood changed radically within a year. Winter 1855–1856 was harsh, and the political situation deteriorated apace, climaxing in the horrible cluster of events in 1856. In the middle of that year one man wrote, "The existing state of things in Kanzas is a disgrace to our country and our civilization."[45] Governor Wilson Shannon, resigning his office late in the summer, exclaimed, "Govern Kansas! . . . You might as well attempt to govern the devil in hell."[46]

The factual sequence of escalation from the time of the meeting of the Pawnee legislature in summer 1855 may be traced in many histories.[47] After meeting for only two days, the legislature voted to move itself and the capital to Shawnee Mission, on the Missouri line, closer to those "fleshpots of Egypt" as well as to decent lodgings. That first legislature was in session fewer than fifty days but adopted laws filling more than one thousand pages by the simple device of adopting the Missouri code nearly wholesale, with a few "odious" additions that one author claimed were written "under the evil influence of bad whiskey."[48] The president removed Andrew Reeder as governor late in July at the behest of the legislature. The primitive town of Lecompton, nine miles west of the Free State stronghold of Lawrence, became the permanent capital. In October the Free State group, in convention in the new town of Topeka, drew up a constitution that prohibited slavery. It also organized a state government as an alternative to the elected territorial government. Late in the year 1855 began the dueling elections phenomenon. The Pro-Slavery group elected J. W. Whitfield as the delegate to Congress in an election the Free State people boycotted. The Free Staters, after working up their principles of responsible resistance at a two-day September convention in Big Springs (a camping ground on the California Road east of Topeka), elected former governor Reeder as their delegate, who, according to Robinson, "was completely cured of his Bogus Legislature and could talk repudiation with the loudest."[49] Both delegates journeyed to Washington and presented their credentials to a confused Congress.

There was violence from the start. Governor John W. Geary's secretary, John Gihon, noted that the Pro-Slavery Party would "have a terrible catalogue for which to account; but in the great day of retribution their political opponents will not entirely escape condemnation."[50] In November 1855, the killing of Charles Dow, a Free Stater murdered by a Pro-Slavery man over a land claim, created a series of responses known as the Wakarusa War (the Wakarusa was a stream running through Lawrence). Douglas County Sheriff Samuel Jones arrested a Free State man who was associated with Dow in the land dispute and was pursuing Dow's murderer by vigilante action. A body of riders headed by Samuel Wood freed the captive, and in turn a band of Missourians led by David Atchison marched on a fortified Lawrence. A treaty, in which the Free Staters pledged not to resist the law, resolved the issue. Governor Wilson Shannon promised not to call on the Missourians for aid, and the force backed off—all parties retaining their arms and ideologies. It was at that time that Shannon authorized self-defense by Lawrence, in a more or less limited way, depending on which account one accepts.

That cleared the way for the *annus diabolis* of 1856. President Franklin Pierce started it late in January with a firm denunciation of the Free State rebels, who had just elected state officers under their Topeka Constitution and asked for admission to the Union. Congress sent an investigating committee west, headed by William A. Howard, to take testimony. It held its first meetings in Lecompton in April 1856. On April 23, while this committee was in session, someone shot and wounded Sheriff Jones, who was in Lawrence trying to arrest some Free State leaders. The official Lawrence leadership denied responsibility, but there were two immediate upshots. One was the indictment of a number of Free State leaders for treason. Robinson was arrested and detained early in May, while his wife Sara went to Washington to plead the Free State case and to deliver Howard Committee testimony. Reeder, who was indicted, escaped Kansas in disguise. The second upshot was an attack on Lawrence on May 21, led by the wounded Jones. His men burned the Free State Hotel and destroyed the equipment of the *Herald of Freedom*.

None of these actions, however, prepared anyone for John Brown's night visits on Pottawatomie Creek on May 24. It seemed that those brutal killings—"ordained by God," as Brown said, or not—removed the last restraints to full civil conflict in Kansas. Captain Henry Pate, trying to capture Brown, was himself defeated at the Battle of Black Jack (June 2) near present-day Baldwin. On July 4, Federal troops broke up the meeting of the Free State legislature in Topeka. In August Free State militia groups attacked four Pro-Slavery forts, most prominently the so-called Ft. Titus. Governor Shannon,

Samuel Wood.
Courtesy of the Kansas State Historical Society.

who replaced Reeder, resigned at the end of that month. His secretary, Daniel Woodson, temporarily in control, declared Kansas to be in open rebellion. And so it was. Brown and an army of Missourians fought the Battle of Osawatomie; Lane led an army toward Lecompton, stopped only by intervention of Federal troops from Ft. Leavenworth; and there was a battle at Hickory Point on September 13, again with Mexican War veteran Lane in command of the Free State forces. Raiding was rampant. It was almost a footnote that another new governor, John Geary, arrived in Lecompton on September 11, or that the national elections in November returned again a Democrat, James Buchanan, to the White House. John Frémont, the presidential candidate of the new Republican Party, wrote his friend Charles Robinson in March 1856: "Your position will undoubtedly be difficult. . . . No man can give you counsel. . . . All history teaches us that great results are ruled by a wise providence & we are but units in a great plan."[51]

Robinson's wife Sara was not so sure. Informed that her husband was well treated during his long house arrest of 1856, she nevertheless felt the strain. She recalled that the May raiders of Lawrence burned the couple's first house on Mt. Oread, walnut woodwork, personal effects, and all. "My husband confides too much in the generosity of his enemies & it is this which fills me with fear."[52] Charles, however, needed to be active: "I expect to please myself as well as I can & hope to do some good in the world."[53]

Lane was a potential firebrand. He had successfully pushed a "black code" through the 1855 Topeka Constitutional Convention barring emigration of blacks to the proposed free state and exercised considerable influence otherwise in that meeting. But a scandal about him circulating in Lawrence caused Lane during those proceedings to challenge Governor Reeder's secretary G. P. Lowry to a duel. Robinson went to the Garvey House in Topeka to dissuade Lane and found him "in bed and greatly agitated." Lane withdrew from the duel at the last moment and returned to his leadership role at the convention.[54] But could he be trusted to remain steady in his leadership?

The Aid Company hoped so and hoped in general to maintain its conservative ground in the whirl. Amos Lawrence wrote Robinson that he should avoid direct confrontation and maintain a "deadly though smiling quiet" until legal processes had time to work.[55] "A battle is to be fought," said Henry Beecher in Congress. "If we are wise, it will be bloodless. If we listen to the pusillanimous counsels of men who have never shown a throb of sympathy for Liberty, we shall have blood on the horses' bridles."[56]

The Wakarusa War, however, advanced the mood in favor of vigorous, and, if necessary, armed, self-defense against unofficial militias or "creatures" of the "bogus" legislature and courts with their writs and indictments. E. J. Nute wrote, "The men of Lawrence are wrought up to the fighting pitch" and agreed with the maxim, "First Pure then Peaceable." Six months ago, he noted, he could not believe his trust would be "put in carnal weapons. But when men behave like wild beasts, what can we do but treat them as such & make men of them as quick as possible?"[57]

Strategists made detailed suggestions for more aggressive action. At a meeting in Boston in June 1856, former governor Reeder proposed that the North establish five thousand armed settlers in Kansas and provision them for one year, using a $2 million fund controlled by a National Central Committee for Kansas, with headquarters in Chicago. There should be a road opened through Iowa from the north. "Shun their steamers, river & places of business entirely. Proclaim to the world that the Missouri River is infested with pirates and wholly unsafe as a highway of travel."[58]

The northern route became the Lane Trail, when Lane, disguised as "Spanish Joe," with his "Army of the North," went down it that summer.[59] The new route was expensive. But it was effective. Thaddeus Hyatt from New York met Lane at Tabor, Iowa, and thought him perfect for the job. Lane had, Hyatt said, "dark twinkling eyes, deep set & restless, but penetrating subtle & determined in their expression."[60]

Clarina Nichols spoke on behalf of Kansas through summer and fall 1856 throughout the East. Her goals were, she said, were, first, to subsist her two sons in the Free State Army of Kansas through the pay she received for her lectures (an average of ten dollars over expenses) and, second, to aid in the election of Republican presidential candidate John Frémont "by showing how Kansas, alias Freedom, is being stabbed in the house of its pretended friends in the North." Third, she hoped "to open the hearts & purses of people to sustain the Free State sufferers."[61] The National Kansas Committee began regularly to receive letters from eastern women's committees, asking how they should pack supplies for Kansas and to whom they should address the cash they had raised.[62]

By summer 1856, after the destruction of Lawrence and the dispersion of the Topeka legislature, sentiments had gone still further in the direction of firmness to the brink of violence. Nute wrote in August that Boston doubt-less had rumors "of the first horrors of the renewed contest—so horrible that you will refuse to believe them. . . . But I can assure you the worst is true. Nothing more horrible, more devilish, than the truth can be told." The Free State forces hoped to have one thousand men armed with Sharp's rifles in Lawrence, and they had five hundred pounds of type from the *Herald of Freedom* office cast into balls for artillery.[63] Nute wrote again in November that it was major news in Kansas that he had managed to raise a flock of

Clarina Nichols.
Courtesy of the Kansas State Historical Society.

chickens, but he had done so only by posting a nightly armed guard.[64] When Thomas Barber was killed, one of the Manhattan colony wrote that the Free State men "could hardly be restrained from rushing out and taking vengeance upon their savage enemies." When Governor Shannon proposed during the Wakarusa War that the people of Lawrence give up to his army their Sharp's rifles and obey the laws of the territorial legislature, Robinson made a reply that was "worthy of one of the old Romans": "We will compromise, *keep the rifles & give them the contents.*" Sharp's rifles, with their rate of fire of ten shots a minute and deadly accuracy in the hands of trained men, one correspondent thought, "did more to cool the ardor of the mob than anything else."[65] In May, as the buildup for the Lawrence attack occurred, William Goodnow wrote his wife that there was "great excitement & preparations for War! War!! War!!!"[66]

Still, key people exercised a moderating influence. George W. Brown, in captivity with Robinson, was afraid that Lane would try to rescue them, as he had offered. But even Lane knew that a rescue would escalate tensions and suggested that the prisoners escape, so that he could meet them and appear only to be defending them in their effort, not directly attacking the authority of the court. Brown wrote in August 1856 that it would be necessary for the Free State people to form small detachments "on fleet horses" to cut off bodies of invaders as they came down the public highways, but he advised that "if Uncle Sam's troops fire upon us, companies B & D will aim too high to injure any one. You should do the same. . . . Don't meddle with Lecompton, nor any private property . . . maintain a steady hand, commit no violence on any one, labor to keep excitement down, but be prepared to put down any new rising of the demons who threaten our destruction."[67] That odd combination of visceral vindictiveness and cerebral conservatism was typical of the Free State leaders at the time.

There was a propaganda war in 1856 and 1857 as active as the physical struggle. And the Free State faction won it. In newspaper bombast, the Pro-Slavery group gave as good as it got. The *Kansas Herald* (Leavenworth), *Kansas Pioneer* (Kickapoo), and *Squatter Sovereign* (Atchison) were no shrinking violets compared to the *Herald of Freedom, Lawrence Tribune,* and *Kansas Freeman* (Topeka). The pamphlet exchange was balanced. But in books with a national circulation, there was no comparison. Probably it mattered that the centers of publishing were Boston and New York, not Atlanta and Charleston. The nature of the books was a far cry from Edward

Hale's gentle paean to Kansas agricultural possibilities of 1854. The books of 1856 and 1857 were personal eyewitness accounts, and they were mostly propaganda, more or less heavy, for the Free State perspective.

The most outstanding, and close to the most irresponsible, was Sara Robinson's *Kansas: Its Interior and Exterior Life.* She wrote it when she joined her husband under comfortable but confining house arrest during summer 1856 and based it on diaries she had kept earlier. She admitted to "bitterness," not only over the policy of the Kansas government but over the idea that "the clanking of chains" connected with slavery would blemish the beauty of the region. She was not alone in pointing out that Governor Shannon was a drinker. But to ask if his brain had "become so muddled in the bad whiskey in which it floats, as to dull all his perception of justice and right" was to go beyond most critics. She called the president of the United States an "imbecile" and the Pro-Slavery activists "demons of darkness."

But Robinson was a woman tempered in an atmosphere that hardly sheltered women. "The women . . . of Kansas," she wrote, "have shared in this quickening of the perceptive and reflective faculties. . . . Some, who would have floated gaily down life's smoother tides . . . and would have asked not the great questions of life, of its import, of its destiny, have learned that 'life is real, life is earnest.'" A few women made cartridges, two went through the lines and returned with ammunition hidden in their dresses, but for the most part, Robinson wrote, women simply acted directly as citizens on a frontier that could not afford to shuffle them aside. One woman walked thirty-five miles from Leavenworth to Lawrence in the snow at the height of the dangers to visit her brother and to keep family bonds strong. The Ladies' Sewing Circle and the Temperance Society never ceased meeting as Kansas bled, epitomizing the expectation that civilization would prevail.

Polemic was a Robinson specialty. "Let the booming cannon battering down hotels," Sara wrote, "and printing presses thrown into the Kansas River, tell afar the bloody despotism that rules our land." Ghosts crying "I am murdered" called to her, she wrote, on every breeze, and the threats to women by the bushwhackers echoed in her memory. "Men of the North," she asked at the end of her book, "shall the brave hearts in Kansas struggle alone?"[68]

Just as strongly Free State in sentiment was William Phillips's *Conquest of Kansas by Missouri and Her Allies,* a book that indulged in conspiracy theory. Phillips, who later served in Congress from Kansas, was at the time a correspondent for the *New York Tribune,* and he moved freely between the sides. He said of Governor Shannon that he had "acquirements not much above mediocrity and abilities rather below it." John Brown did not fare much better: "He is one of those Christians who have not quite vanished from the face of the earth ... a strange, resolute, repulsive, iron-willed, inexorable old man." Phillips said that Kansas was "politically prostrate" and that Free State and Pro-Slavery interests could never live together.[69]

Less strident were Douglas Brewerton's *War in Kansas,* Hannah Ropes's *Six Months in Kansas by a Lady,* Thomas Gladstone's *Kansas; or Squatter Life and Border Warfare in the Far West,* and John Gihon's *Geary and Kansas.*[70] Brewerton stayed at the governor's office in Shawnee Mission, in Lawrence, and in the developing town of Lecompton during the severe weather at the end of 1855 and beginning of 1856. He conducted extensive interviews with Governor Shannon and with Charles Robinson and published both their versions of events. Ropes was a woman from Boston, whose book reproduces letters to her mother written during the Wakarusa War. She makes few interpretive comments, unless her report that she used the *New York Journal of Commerce* to protect her bread from the dust broom is one.[71] Gladstone was from England, reporting the Kansas phenomenon to interested readers of the *London Times.* Lawrence, to him, was the "Western Sebastopol," and he was shocked that under the stern laws of the Kansas legislature, which punished by death the introduction of anything calculated to incite slave rebellion, "the man ... who possesses a copy of 'Uncle Tom's Cabin' is on a par with the murderer." Though Gladstone had considerable contact with Southerners early in his visit, he came to sympathize with the Northern and Free State cause.[72]

Though no doubt less read than the journalistic accounts (it is 1,206 close-spaced printed pages long), the Howard Report of 1856 was a part of the print war also. The conclusion, sympathetic to the Free State position that the 1855 legislative elections were fraudulent and should be set aside, was preordained, and the majority and minority reports split along strict party lines. But the report contained massive testimony and documents, not only on the elections but also on violent incidents, including the siege of Lawrence, and on secret societies and squatter associations.[73]

Yet surely the greatest of the propagandists of 1856 was a man who wrote no book: James Lane. Lane toured the East in 1856 speaking for Free State

Kansas. He raised money, and he was a sensation. "We all have our moments of nervous exaltation," one observer wrote. "It was this set of nerves which that cunning anatomist, Lane, knew how to play upon. He sent a shiver down the backs of his auditors like a charge of electricity down a lightning-rod, and raised the goose-flesh on their skins as though a regiment were marching over their collected graves. . . . Every sentence was a lighted transparency, uttered as if written in Roman capitals."[74] Thomas Wentworth Higginson heard Lane in Chicago at the end of March 1856: "Never did I hear such a speech; every sentence like a pistol bullet; such delicacy and lightness of touch; such natural art; such perfect adaptation; not a word, not a gesture could have been altered; he had every nerve in his audience at the end of his muscles; not a man in the United States could have done it; and the perfect ease of it all, not a glimpse of premeditation or effort; and yet he has slept in his boots every night but two for five weeks."[75] He may have been a "strip tease orator," as one Kansas critic charged, heavy on special effects; he may have been a former Democrat with no love for racial equality, but Lane drew people to the Free State cause as effectively as he drew them to himself.[76] "No one liked him," one man wrote, "but they couldn't resist him."[77]

After the battles of summer and fall 1856, there followed what might be called a "constitutional interlude," characterized more by debate over the Lecompton Constitution than by bloodshed. Governor Geary recommended moderating the laws but fell out with the territorial legislature, and Robert Walker replaced him in March 1857. Walker tried to conciliate the Free State faction by claiming that climatic conditions made Kansas unsuited for slavery, and he hoped to salvage it as a state dominated by the Democratic Party. He was unable, however, to convince Robinson to abandon the passive resistance policy or the Free State faction to participate in the regular elections. In October, a constitutional convention drafted what was called the Lecompton Constitution and decided to allow Kansas voters to vote, not on whether to accept or reject the constitution but whether to accept it with or without the slavery clause.

There was a key change, however, in the interim before the constitutional vote. The Free State faction, confident of its strength and of Walker's basic honesty, participated in the October 1857 elections for territorial delegate and members of the legislature. It won a legislative majority. In effect this represented the end of the "civil disobedience" phase of the Topeka movement. That change also made it clear to the Pro-Slavery Party that its last chance was in the ratification of the Lecompton Constitution.

The Free State Party boycotted the vote on the Lecompton Constitution, held in December 1857, as set up by the old territorial legislature, and therefore the side favoring the constitution with slavery won. But a few weeks later, in January 1858, there was a special referendum authorized by the new territorial legislature, allowing a vote on accepting or rejecting the Lecompton Constitution as a whole. This time the Free State group participated and the Pro-Slavery people abstained. There were over ten thousand votes against the constitution, and only twenty-three for it with slavery.

President James Buchanan, not wishing to accept the obvious, submitted the Lecompton Constitution to Congress, where William English proposed a compromise: Kansans would be given another chance to vote on the Lecompton Constitution. Acceptance would give them immediate admission as a state; rejection would force them to wait until they reached the required population. And there were offers of federal land to the state included in the package. The Free State faction, meeting in Leavenworth, drafted yet another alternative constitution.[78]

Isaac Goodnow, who was a delegate to the Leavenworth Constitutional Convention, wrote that the corner was turned. The Leavenworth Constitution, he thought, would be one "of the people! One that will be no discredit to their heads nor their hearts." In fact, it was the most liberal of the proposed constitutions, constructed by men of stern morality and a "fairness and integrity worthy of the old Puritans." It had no Black Law barring African Americans from emigrating or voting. It gave power to the legislature to prohibit the manufacture and sale of liquor. Foreigners of one-year's residence were enfranchised. Goodnow thought Lane's actions at the Leavenworth convention were wonderful: "He is the man for the hour & fills a place in our history that no other man can."[79]

Goodnow thought the worst of the bleeding was over and was planning for civilization in 1858. In June, his wife Ellen killed a rattlesnake in their log home near Manhattan and drew venom from the leg of a boarder. She "drew and spit" while he drank whiskey borrowed from a neighbor and so did she, as the taste in her mouth got bitter. She complained about wildcats killing their chickens.[80] But those primitive surroundings did not keep Goodnow from forming Bluemont College, hiring professors, and arranging for the construction of a building for it.[81] The Emigrant Aid Company helped by donating half the proceeds of twenty of its Manhattan town lots to the school.[82] In an 1888 address to the Kansas State Historical Society, Goodnow recalled that although supplies had to come 120 miles by river, he preferred his town site to any between there and the Missouri River.[83]

But Goodnow's optimism was premature. There was great excitement in Washington and in the national press over the possible ratification of a constitution that seemed the last chance to establish slavery or even the Democratic Party in Kansas Territory. And this was accompanied by a renewal of factional violence in Kansas. President Buchanan minced no words. The Lecompton Constitution was created in a "regular" way, he said. If the backers of the Free State faction had not wished to participate in the scheduled elections concerning it, they must bear the consequences. "The sacred principle of popular sovereignty has been invoked in favor of the enemies of law and order in Kansas. But in what manner is popular sovereignty to be exercised in this country, if not through the instrumentality of established law?" Why not accept the Lecompton Constitution, he asked, localize the conflict by admitting Kansas under it as a state, and then, if necessary, the constitution could be quietly changed later?[84] The majority on a congressional Committee of Fifteen agreed with this interpretation. The opposition to the Lecompton Constitution, the committee report stated, "consisted of persons engaged in insurrection, rebellion, and revolution. . . . It is alike impolitic and unjust to grant the turbulent demands of the disorderly, be they few or many."[85]

Ultimately, neither the threats, nor the appeals, nor the offers of land and privilege in the English bill could save the Lecompton Constitution or the style of territorial government once ensconced in the town by that name. In August 1858 Kansans voted down the Lecompton Constitution again, federal blandishments or no, by a huge majority. However, that result must have seemed inevitable to many observers for months. Therefore it was a surprise to moderates that 1858 was a year not only of political debate in Washington but also of renewed violence in Kansas.

Governor James Denver, who was in office for less than a year during 1858, was a strong administrator with considerable Washington experience and seemed to have an excellent chance of getting control of Kansas politics.[86] Instead, he had to deal with a series of guerrilla actions centered in southeast Kansas and typified by the Marais des Cygnes massacre of May 19, 1858. Missourians under the command of Charles Hamilton executed five

Free State men without trial along that stream, almost equaling Brown's toll at Pottawatomie Creek two years earlier. That action seemed to release any inhibitions. James Montgomery, a minister, and Charles Jennison, a dentist, led quasi-military groups known as Jayhawkers in attacks on and around Ft. Scott. These bands were regarded by some people as nothing more official than the personal raiders of James H. Lane. The Jayhawkers did not seem concerned about the ideology of those whom they plundered, nor did they share the earlier Free State scruple about killing U.S. soldiers who got in the way. John Brown, who had been absent from the territory for a time, returned to add his brand of inflammation. Bleeding Kansas again justified its name.[87]

Denver had heard that "the passions of many have been so thoroughly aroused, and long-standing difficulties have so embittered the feelings of one portion of the community against another, that it has been represented as almost impossible to find anyone willing to listen to the voice of reason." But like others before him, he hoped to find a rational core somewhere.[88] The secretary of the interior, Jacob Thompson, reassured Denver, upon his appointment as governor, that he had the full support of the Washington administration. The president would recommend admission of Kansas with the Lecompton Constitution, and he would send Kansas a powerful message to comply. "To turn aside now," Thompson wrote, "is downright weakness. . . . You know there is no want of cool courage & self reliance with the President." Denver should begin his western sojourn, Thompson thought, by vetoing any bill coming out of the new Free State–dominated territorial legislature outlawing slavery, on the grounds that such legislation was against the Supreme Court's *Dred Scott* decision and therefore unconstitutional. "Every step they [the legislature] take leads to additional confusion. . . . We are now like the man who held the wolf. To hold one is bad enough, to let go is inevitable death."[89]

Denver offended some people by vetoing a bill to move the capital to Minneola, and his promotion of the Lecompton Constitution offended others. President Buchanan wrote Denver in March, "The public is tired even *ad nauseam,* with the Kansas situation" and warned that continued unrest there would "reduce the value of property & injuriously interfere with our revenue trade."[90] But Buchanan could not impose the Lecompton Constitution unilaterally, and Denver could not stop armed confrontations. Kansas, as always, was "a bubbling sea of troubles."[91]

Lane was forever difficult, not only as an overt or covert military commander but also as a political strategist, stump speaker, and moral bellwether. In June 1858 he shot and killed Gaius Jenkins, another Free State leader, in an argument over a land claim. While Denver thought that most people condemned Lane for that, "quite a number of his 'boys,'" he wrote his wife, still adhered to him.[92] A friend suggested that Denver should "give [Lane] a thrashing" but confessed, "I think the governorship of that Territory the most difficult place to fill in America."[93] Another warned the governor to be careful dealing with "that dirty scoundrel Jim Lane," lest action backfire. "You remember the old fable of the Skunk challenging a Lion & the Lion's reply, 'that he could not accommodate him, for if he should whip the skunk he would get no credit for the act, while he would not be able to get rid of the odor in a long time.' So it is with this creature."[94]

The reinvigorated guerrilla war was a problem for government. J. W. Williams, a judge at Ft. Scott so notorious among the Free State people for his supposed partisanship that they set up their own squatter court, wrote the governor in May that "civil war in all its honors" was initiated. Montgomery "and his murderers & robbers" had commenced operations in broad daylight, and the Ft. Scott community had vowed retaliation. He was, Williams reported, "between two fierce fires," both sides having threatened his life for trying to enforce the law. He recommended that federal troops help officers of the law arrest Montgomery and break up his ranks around Osawatomie and Maneka. "There is the nest, where are gathered the operators who so kindly come down on Fort Scott & this neighborhood to execute the plans of the 'higher law' commanders."[95]

On May 30, 1858, there was a confrontation at Ft. Scott that was typical except for its special intensity. That Sunday in the early afternoon two companies of men with Sharp's rifles, one headed by Samuel Walker and the other by Montgomery, appeared in town, arrested a man, and surrounded the house of G. W. Clark, who was accused of murder. There were loud arguments about the authenticity of the writs for arrest. Townspeople threatened Walker for bringing "a band of robbers to town to arrest honest men." The groups had cocked weapons aimed at each other for a few tense moments.[96]

The protection of U.S. troops was no longer sufficient, as Montgomery was determined to "destroy the charm of invincibility which was supposed to reside in gilt buttons with an eagle stamped on them." On June 6 Montgomery set fire to several buildings in Ft. Scott. When Lane ordered him to disband his company, Montgomery replied that he was no longer a militia officer responsible even to Lane, but "I am identified with a popular movement in this section of the country, having for its object the redress of grievances."[97]

Denver went with Robinson to Ft. Scott in June and spoke to a crowd of several hundred about calming the conflicts. Six feet, two inches tall and weighing 250 pounds, Denver was an imposing figure but could not by physical presence or force of personality entirely quell the passions of the region.[98] He expressed to Secretary of the Interior Thompson his "anxiety to return" to Washington and resigned in October.[99] His successor as acting governor, his former secretary Hugh Walsh, published a reward of three hundred dollars for Montgomery and five hundred dollars for John Brown.[100] Walsh's successor, Samuel Medary, promised to "clean out" southeast Kansas, but the federal troops, with which he proposed to "whip Montgomery and Brown out," were withdrawn to other duty. Medary wrote, "It is impossible for these things to be understood at Washington as they really exist here."[101] It was several months before Montgomery came to trial for his extralegal raiding.[102]

By 1859, however, admission as a state seemed imminent. Attention focused again on constitution making, this time the creation of the Wyandotte Constitution, ratified in July 1859. Modeled largely on other state constitutions, the document had some unusual features. It did not give the vote to African Americans, as had the Leavenworth Constitution. Though Robinson said the earlier "whites only" provisions of Kansas constitutions were to conciliate Washington more than local opinion and that "no valid argument can be produced against the right of suffrage for the colored man," black franchise in Kansas waited for the Fifteenth Amendment to the U.S. Constitution. But by a narrow vote, the Wyandotte document allowed blacks and mulattos to reside in the state. Proposals to exclude blacks from the common schools failed. Women were not extended the vote, either, by this constitution, though there was strong sentiment for that. At least a petition from women was heard. "I think," said delegate William Hutchinson, "no evil consequences can result from giving our attention to a question so interesting to half the people of the Territory." There was a section in the new constitution guaranteeing the rights of married women to property "separate and apart from the husband"—a milestone at a time when most law regarded women as chattel. Equally progressive was the Homestead exemption in section nine, protecting a farmstead or home from attachment and sale for taxes or debt. Advanced by Samuel Kingman, it was designed to protect the family from disintegration and was widely adapted by other states thereafter. Other provisions of obvious significance were ones delineating the boundaries of the state (giving up the future ski slopes of Colorado, claims to southern Nebraska, and, in one debate, almost giving up everything west of Salina), a provision against the state's participation in the funding of internal improvements, a lid on allowable state debt, and a clause for "a uniform and equal rate of assessment and taxation." And there were a few curiosities, such as forbidding any person who had given or accepted a challenge to a duel from holding any office of "trust or profit" in the new state. Perhaps, given recent local history, that was not so curious after all.[103]

Clarina Nichols was at the Wyandotte convention as an unofficial delegate representing Kansas women. These women, according to one of them, had lived through scorching days in primitive houses "sometimes with a lean-to kitchen, roofed with tarred paper which on occasion of a company dinner was apt to ooze through and flavor whatever was on the cook stove." They deserved some legal rights. Nichols was "a pleasant-faced woman of middle age," wrote a friend later. "Often she sat knitting, but more often busy with pencil or pen and with bright eyes always on the alert for the 'business before the house.' She was there a self-appointed delegate, uninvited and uninstructed; there because she knew that legal rights when secured in a constitution were not so easily abrogated." In addition to the better-known clauses relating to women, Nichols achieved equal educational privileges for women in colleges in the state, equal rights for them in the formation and conduct of the common schools, equal rights for mothers with the fathers to the custody and control of their offspring, and the right of a wife to sue in defense of the community fund.[104]

The members of the convention, overall, were pleased with their product, having had by then considerable practice in constitutions. Some observers, however, felt less sanguine. Abelard Guthrie, who was married to a Wyandot Indian woman, claimed to be largely responsible for the movement in Congress leading to the Kansas-Nebraska Act.[105] He had since fallen on hard times, though he had high hopes that his speculation in the town site of Quindaro would one day make him rich. He was an intelligent and savvy political operative who attended the Wyandotte convention and recorded his impressions in his extensive diary. He was upset that there were no real declarations of principles. He signed a petition presented by Nichols for granting women the same political rights as men and even lent her a pony to attend the convention. But he attached a proviso that women in return should "renounce the privileges and immunities now exclusively enjoyed by them."[106] He was not impressed by the debates at Wyandotte. "They did not display much depth of thought or research, but a good deal of that prudent brevity which usually attends conscious ignorance." He voted against the constitution on the grounds that people already were taxed too much, that the franchise was withheld from Indians, and that the territory was not yet ready for statehood. He thought that "swindlers and demagogues" would be the only class with time to engage in electioneering in Kansas.[107] It turned out there was no such rush about ratification anyway. The Democrats in Washington delayed admission of Kansas as a state, and, constitution or no, that cause did not advance again until the election of Abraham Lincoln and the Republican Party in 1860.

Kansas was in 1859 solidly in the Republican fold, but in the presidential campaign it mostly ignored the rail-splitter from Illinois in favor of William Seward, who had defended the Free State cause eloquently. Mark Delahay of Leavenworth was a relative by marriage of Lincoln. He urged the candidate to come to Kansas and campaign. Lincoln wrote in May 1859 that he could not attend the Kansas Republican Convention to which Delahay invited him but that he would like to "see your fine new Country and to meet the good people who have cast their lot there."[108] In November Delahay invited him again.[109] This time Lincoln agreed.

Candidate Lincoln arrived in Kansas Territory on December 1, 1859, the day before John Brown was hanged in Virginia for his Harpers Ferry raid. He spoke that evening before forty people at the Great Western Hotel in Elwood, KT. He was too tired, he said, to deliver a full speech, but he did comment that John Brown, "though of great courage and unselfishness," was wrong in spilling blood. Lincoln would not say which faction was most to blame for violence in Kansas Territory but did say that the ballot box was a bloodless means of ending slavery.

Lincoln remained in the territory, traveling through the cold between towns (Troy, Atchison, Leavenworth) for five days.[110] Albert D. Richardson, a well-known writer, heard him at Troy, noting that "in the imaginative language of the frontier, Troy was a town . . . but . . . its urban glories were visible only to the eye of faith. . . . The sweeping prairie wind rocked the crazy buildings, and cut the faces of travelers like a knife." Lincoln's party arrived there wrapped in buffalo robes, and Lincoln spoke for an hour and a half.[111] Colonel D. R. Anthony of the *Leavenworth Conservative* remembered that Lincoln was as impressive informally as formally. After his speech to a crowd of nearly four hundred in Leavenworth, a small group went back to Anthony's room and talked into the night, warming themselves around a stove fueled by patent office reports from Washington.[112] Leavenworth was much larger than Troy, the biggest city in Kansas, but still a primitive place, where, according to John Ingalls, there was in the late 1850s no observation of the Sabbath ("no change of dress or manner indicates the advent of holy time and the most of the citizens employ the day in hunting prairie chickens"), and the whiskey shops were "full of cursing democrats & the click of billiard balls."[113] Anthony remembered in 1902, "Mr. Lincoln sat . . . for hours, his feet against the stove, his chair tilted back. His reputation as a storyteller is deserved, for he was leader in swapping tales that night. In appearance Lincoln was not the impressive man the next few years made him. He was made up of heads, hands, feet and length. The lines that gave his face and figure a majesty of sadness were yet to come."[114] Perhaps Kansans did not expect he would even be elected.

During the delay in admission for the state, there was a drought. From June 1859 until November 1860 hardly any measurable rain fell.[115] Nathan Starks, the tenant farmer for the eastern investor Hiram Hill, wrote in June 1860, "The drought is very severe. I never saw anything to compare. . . . Vegetation droops, the earth dusty & hot, the springs . . . dried up. The hot wind sweeps over the land blinding one with the dust or blistering the skin. The sun rising and setting daily only at long intervals obscured by a flying cloud, no rain no hope. The poor squatter looks to his withered crops and sits down in despair."[116] On July 1, Starks wrote that is was 105 degrees in the shade, "wind blowing strong & hot burning my body under my clothing— the grass as dry and dead as if in a Dry Kiln, not any favorable circumstances for writing a pleasant letter."[117] Ingalls noted in August 1860 that the weeks of heat "were only fit for a Hottentot, accustomed to the ardors of Sahara."[118] Charles Robinson told Sara in fall 1860, "We are left to eke out an existence where *starvation* is said to stare the whole people in the face."[119] Once more, Kansas became an object of publicity and charity. Thaddeus Hyatt, a New York businessman who had been active in the supply efforts during the crisis of 1856, associated himself with W. F. N. Arny and Samuel Pomeroy in organizing relief for the drought sufferers.

Pomeroy was later criticized for making political capital out of his relief efforts.[120] But there is every evidence that despite a tendency to dramatization (his letters are sprinkled with underlining and exclamation points), he was in 1859 sincere in his sympathy for a real crisis. Hyatt was frustrated in fall 1860 because people thought only of the presidential elections and not of the starving farmers of Kansas. "It is always difficult," he wrote, "to make people with full bellies feel for empty ones."[121] Pomeroy provided him with sad tales from the field. "My ear is pained," he wrote, "my heart is sick of every day's report."[122]

Hyatt directed a caravan of fleeing emigrants to call at the office of the *Leavenworth Herald* to inform the editors there of the real situation. The "terrible drouth," wrote Hyatt, "has baked every thing else to a crisp," but "the owners of 'corner lots' remain as green as ever." It seemed a shame that the territory, where farmers had so long been prevented from bringing in crops by political troubles, suffered now from the caprices of nature.[123]

The admission of Kansas as a state on January 29, 1861 (an unfortunate date for later chilly celebrations) was an anticlimax. It was a cold time, below zero day after day that year. There had recently been over twenty inches of drifting snow, and the mail was irregular.[124] The exchange at the Eldridge House in Lawrence, it was said, "was vocal with a strange combination of sounds . . . and the throng seemed festive and jubilant, save where some forlorn Democratic officials wander through the crowd like condemned ghosts on the banks of the Stygian stream gazing at the fields from which they are forever excluded."[125]

There was some hopefulness. Mary Holliday, writing from Topeka to her husband Cyrus, who was in Washington pushing for federal aid to Kansas railroads, observed, "It does me good to notice the difference in our citizens since our admission and the calling of the Legislature. They are as active as bees, and their countenances have lost that forsaken look."[126] Most people felt, too, that the approach of civil war was not all bad, as at least it would most likely eliminate slavery. Hyatt decided to settle in Atchison, despite the wind and all the troubles. "I want to live in Kansas to enjoy its *sun-sets*. You can have no idea of their rare beauty."[127] The new state seal displayed the motto contributed by John Ingalls: "Ad Astra per Aspera" (To the Stars Through Difficulties).[128]

For a time, emphasis was on the difficulties. The effects of the drought remained. Kansas was in debt with little in the treasury and a record of only about 30 percent of taxes due being paid.[129] The nation was on the brink of coming apart, and a distracted Congress was unlikely to worry either about the security or the financial problems of its newest state. People in Kansas drank some at the admission news, fired off "Old Sacramento," a cannon from the territorial struggles, and sighed with relief that it was finally done.[130]

"The legislature is not doing much," the never cheery Ingalls wrote on January 19, "except discussing Union resolutions . . . and divorcing everybody that applies for rupture of the bonds of matrimony."[131] A newspaper agreed that legislative activity was largely formal: "Everybody in Kansas has been incorporated, and nearly everybody has been divorced. Every other section of land has a city on it. Every village has its university, its college, its church, and seminary."[132]

The legislative hall was primitive, and so were its residents. A newspaper concluded, "Weak, inexperienced, or corrupt men have been thrust into places for which they were totally unfit, either because of their deficiency in positive traits of character, their skill in intriguing for a nomination, or their personal interest in the location of some county boundary or county seat."[133] A year later a reporter commented that the capital city of Topeka was still "a howling wilderness" with only eight hundred people and no sidewalks. But the legislators, meeting in rented buildings, were at least, he thought, no longer a "thick-headed assembly made up of 'undone minds,' " as before.[134]

Lincoln had said that no Kansas appointments would be made until the senators were elected.[135] That decision has traditionally been blamed on the manipulations of Lane, but there is evidence that Robinson partly brought it on himself by delaying the meeting of the legislature until late March in order to line up support to defeat Lane for the senatorship. Senator Lyman Trumbull wrote Mark Delahay that the delay was "utterly inexcusable." After all, secession was going on and there was a war coming.[136]

M. J. Parrott, Samuel Pomeroy, James Lane, and F. P. Stanton were the possibilities for senator. "If abdomen were the test," Ingalls commented, Pomeroy would be a sure winner. But Lane was an even stronger candidate. Ingalls thought Lane was "one of the most remarkable men I ever knew: a perfect demagogue, charlatan, knave," but with "energy, magnetism and nerve."[137] There were five thousand men under arms in the state by May and drilling constantly. Lane was head of the state militia and making the most of it.[138]

The general atmosphere in the state was bleak. The Hannibal and St. Joseph Railroad, the state's only connection with the "bread-giving East," might be shut down if Missouri seceded. The river route was again closed. Kansas had no banks of its own, and Ingalls declared conditions "miserable and wretched."[139] "Whether we shall revert into anarchy and fight out our destiny in fratricidal war, or relapse into the original solitude of the desert I do not know: but it seems even to the calmest and most dispassionate observer, as though the calamities of our history . . . never cease."[140]

Robinson, now indeed the official governor, was worried, too. "No State Executive," he wrote twenty years later, "was so unfortunately situated as the Executive of Kansas" during his term, "and none has been so misrepresented and misunderstood." There was not a dollar in the state treasury. There was a question whence the one-hundred-dollar rent for the Representatives' Hall or the governor's two-thousand-dollar salary were to come. There were no guns or ammunition in the armory. State bonds, which had been issued for war and general expenses, would not "bring a dollar in any stock market in the world." There were two hundred miles of border with Missouri, full of unfriendly elements, and twice that number of miles of Indian frontier to the West, with the tribes well aware of the opportunity the white man's war provided.[141]

Robinson's message to the first state legislature was, accordingly, grave. He said that the federal government should pay the bills for Bleeding Kansas damages done under its auspices, estimated at five hundred thousand dollars, but it probably would not. It should pay the one-hundred-thousand dollar debt of Kansas, but it probably would not. The state should help the drought sufferers, but it probably could not. And then there was the Civil War. "When Kansas applied for admission into the Union, it was supposed there was a Federal Government that would endure until the present generations, at least, should pass away. Recent developments, however, have given rise to serious doubts as to its existence." It might happen that no laws of the United States would be enforced anywhere in a few months. "Our government, once regarded as a power in the earth, will become a hissing and a byword among the nations—a stench in the nostrils of all men." Still, Kansas, "though last and least of the States in the Union, will ever be ready to answer the call of her country."[142]

Certainly that last observation was true. There were only minor battles on Kansas soil, almost all the official ones (prominently Mine Creek) connected with the Sterling Price raid into Missouri and his feint into Kansas in 1864.[143] But Kansans served with distinction in every theater. The state had a good enlistment record, and its eighty-five hundred casualties in the war was the highest ratio of any state relative to those engaged. It was a pioneer, too, in the use of African-American and Native-American troops.[144]

But not all was as it seemed. The sterling troop-raising record was partly related to false propaganda and to patronage and power ploys operated by Lane in his enmity toward Robinson. The military actions by Kansans in their own region included all too much Jayhawking of a type condemned by both the governor and the official military, and probably counterproductive to Union strategy. The old territorial Free State factions complicated elections from the first. The financial tribulations of the state led quickly to a bond scandal and an impeachment. And in the center of it all came Quantrill, down "like a wolf on the fold" on an undefended Lawrence.

The election of U.S. senators, one of the first items on the agenda, illustrated complications that were only to deepen. "Lane has undertaken a personal fight on me," Robinson wrote Sara.[145] Robinson himself was "in a perfect whirl of agitation talking from morning till morning not getting to bed till one & two o' clock often. We have defeated Lane in all his schemes for endorsement & he is terrible *mad*."[146] The senatorial contest, he predicted, would be "exceedingly bitter."[147]

So it was. Lane, himself poor and "ragged as Diogenes," stumped the state and met the people. He promised jobs, advocated stay and minimum interest laws that would appeal to debtors, and, with his appealing romanticism, outlined grandiose canal and railroad systems.[148]

Lane wrote Delahay a "strictly confidential" letter in December 1860, illustrating how closely he planned. He had arranged for his friend John Speer to buy the *Lawrence Republican,* provided Lane could raise five hundred dollars. "For days & weeks," Lane wrote in one of his few surviving letters, "I have been laboring night and day to accomplish this result and now there must be no failure in this. I scarcely know where to go but raise it I must & will. Think and keep thinking until I come over." He hoped to raise five thousand dollars for his campaign and begin distributing it the moment news came of the admission of Kansas. "I do not believe the whole batch of our opponents can raise as much. . . . The people are for me . . . & by god they shall not defraud me out of my election."[149] Lane promised offices right and left. Sol Miller wrote of this, "Lane has no more right to bargain off that nomination than his distinguished ancestor had to promise the world to Christ."[150] Levity aside, he did it, and did it effectively.

In the voting, fifty-eight of the ninety-eight members of the joint legislative session changed their votes from one to six times, and 297 different votes were cast in all. Lane and Pomeroy were elected. It is interesting that these two so vilified in hindsight—Lane, the supposed demagogue and womanizer, and Pomeroy, the fat, cigar-smoking model for Mark Twain and Charles Warner's corrupt senator in *The Gilded Age*—were the choice of people closest to events at the time.[151] As the legislators, having voted, filed out of the room, they found Lane sitting on a sofa teary-eyed and holding a pistol, which he said he would have used to blow his brains out had the result been different. Thus was the new senator from Kansas, who had to borrow money on his life insurance policy to buy new clothes and pay his fare to Washington.[152]

Arriving there, Lane found the city in tumult over the firing on Ft. Sumter and immediately formed the Kansas Frontier Guard, which camped for a time at the White House and acted as a personal bodyguard for Abraham Lincoln. That endeared Lane to the national press and further to the president. Robinson, on the other hand, as was his temperament and lifelong habit (he ran for governor of Kansas as a Democrat in 1890), bolted from the regular party candidates and came during the war actively to dislike Lincoln and to say so often.[153]

It has been a mystery to many observers since how "a man of Lincoln's perception" could have failed to see "the true inwardness of the whole business" and have allowed himself, as one man put it, to "become a dupe of Lane."[154] There was the matter of political loyalty and effectiveness, certainly. Lane was a great speaker and Lincoln needed one. However erratic Lane was, he was magnetic and confident, a westerner of bold and sometimes crude humor, a populist who took care of his friends, and a man with none of the churchy New England superiority to the masses about him. He seemed to many in the East and West a kind of bright beacon in a time of great uncertainty.

The "wild fanaticism" of those like Lane had its appeal in the great emergency when all the negotiations of the "practical reformers" and "safe counselors" seemed to have led only to disaster.[155] "No one who did not live in and through the stormy period that darkened our political horizon in the fifties can imagine," a Kansan wrote later, "much less realize, what it was—

Samuel Pomeroy.
Courtesy of the Kansas State Historical Society.

the strange unrest and the anxious foreboding, the alternation of hope and despair, the uncertainty that was more alarming than actual knowledge could be, however dark."[156]

An additional alarm for Kansans was provided by impeachment. The impeachment trials in 1862 of Governor Charles Robinson, Secretary of State John Robinson, and Auditor George Hillyer arose partly from irregularities in the sale to the Indian Office in Washington, through Robert Stevens, of otherwise almost unsalable Kansas bonds, and partly from the enmity between Robinson and Lane, which led the Lane faction to push every advantage.

That first Kansas legislature appropriated twenty thousand dollars to defray the expenses of raising troops and one hundred fifty thousand dollars to meet the general expenses of the new state. But having no cash, these appropriations were in bonds, and the bonds had no market. Their sale was finally negotiated by Robert Stevens to the Indian Office at a considerable profit to Stevens and a deep discount in the proceeds coming to the state treasury. Lane, who, along with Pomeroy, may well have been in on the deal, refused for a time to approve it, suspecting Stevens and knowing that he was close to Robinson and perhaps a candidate for senator against Lane. Lane eventually led the charge of those who saw corruption in it and an excuse to remove the state administration in favor of Lane's backers. That led to an impeachment in the Kansas House of Representatives and a trial in the Senate in 1862. At the impeachment proceedings, Lane testified that the bond sellers had asked him to go before Lincoln "and make one of *my appeals* in favor of the negotiation." He did that, he said, but then realized that the money was to be used against him and his friends instead of going into the state treasury.[157] Robinson escaped removal. The other two, the evidence revealed, were probably more ignorant than dishonest and perhaps made the best deal the state could have expected. But they were removed from office, and Robinson's reputation was forever after besmirched.[158]

Wilson Shannon, the former governor, wrote Stevens, "It is a mistaken notion that those men under the lead of Lane can be conciliated. It cannot be done. The more you yield to them the more insolent and violent they become."[159] So it increasingly seemed. Robinson wrote Sara in spring 1862: "I intend to make the fur fly here [Washington] unless I am permitted to get my business done without hindrance from Lane. He is endeavoring to levy black mail upon everybody."[160] However, just as Robinson was doing his utmost to fight the impeachment and respond to the bond charges, he contracted smallpox and had to spend weeks at the Sisters of Charity sanitarium in Buffalo, New York, feverish and incapable of his usual vigorous response.[161]

That moment and that scandal were not the only fronts on which Lane and Robinson were engaged and where the nature of the new state was forged. The creation of the Republican Party in Kansas in 1859 ended the Free State name, but not its factions.[162] Lane saw his political machine as dependent upon patronage, and the war situation was an opportunity, not only to benefit contractors who would then be loyal to him but also to control the appointment of military officers in state volunteer regiments, although that was usually the duty of state governors. That angered Robinson no end, not only personally but also as an insult to his office.

And all the while there was the Jayhawking, growing out of the activities of Montgomery and Jennison in the territorial period and climaxing in the raid on Osceola, Missouri, led by Lane personally, on September 23, 1861. His force robbed a bank and pillaged stores and homes, and when he withdrew, the wagons of the drunken men groaned with a load of plunder that included a piano and a pile of silk dresses as the Grim Chieftain's share.[163]

Robinson had warned his friend Frémont on September 1 that "an effort is being made to get up a panic in our State" by people who wanted a war on the border. He asked that Lane's Kansas brigade be removed from the border and that the government stores convenient to them at Ft. Scott be sent back to Ft. Leavenworth. Kansas, he said, had little to fear from the rebels in Missouri. "But what we have to fear, and do fear, is that Lane's brigade will get up a war by going over the line, committing depredations, and then returning into our State."[164]

Lane was writing Frémont, too, reporting on his efforts to organize seventeen hundred troops around Ft. Scott and to call on people to rally to him. "Kansas is destitute. I have a thousand horses now arriving and eager men to mount them, but without arms or equipment."[165] Late in the month Lane moved to Kansas City with seven hundred cavalry, five hundred infantry, one hundred artillery, and a battery of four howitzers. He reported rumors of a large force moving on Kansas in the wake of the Union defeat at Wilson's Creek and added, "I trust you will approve the march on Osceola and its destruction. It was the depot of the traitors for Southwestern Missouri."[166]

Kansas was his home, he said in a speech in Springfield, Missouri, in

November, the home "of my adoption, and toils and strife. . . . For Kansas have I wrestled as wrestles the mother when she brings forth her first-born into the world. . . . Kansas, as my home, as the living present, absorbs my thoughts and sways my destiny." Yes, he had been criticized for his language and his actions, "but whether excited or calm, whether my language be rough or smooth, principle and duty require that our policy [Jayhawking] be rigidly adhered to until condemned by the Government." Boldness, he said, was all. Let Kansas "inscribe 'freedom to all' upon our banners, and appear just what we are."[167]

Robinson was not impressed. An investigation in 1910 showed that Lane never formally accepted his brigadier generalship of volunteers, but having an acting senator in de facto command of troops was irregular.[168] And that was not to mention Lane's methods. Robinson compared the Osceola raid with Quantrill's attack on Lawrence. Sol Miller wrote, "A system of terrorism was practiced upon loyal and good citizens who were not in the army, by means of deputy marshals, so-called detectives, and desperate, irresponsible men under other guises to keep them in subjection to the wishes of Lane." A dispatch in 1861 read, "The conduct of the forces under Lane and Jennison has done more for the enemy in this state than could have been accomplished by twenty thousand of his own army." To make Lane a brigadier of volunteers was, one officer said, "offering a premium for rascality and robbing generally."

Was it any wonder, Robinson asked in 1893, that people from Osceola joined Quantrill's band? It was Lane that the Quantrill raiders primarily sought.[169] "The victims of Quantrell's [sic] massacre have been counted," Robinson noted, "but those whom Lane and Jennison left in the hands of their executioners, who shall chronicle them? They are unnumbered as the murders of Attila."[170]

Thomas Carney succeeded Robinson as governor of Kansas. The removal of the person of Robinson, however, did not stop the conflict between the office and the ambitions of Lane or reduce the place of Kansas as a kind of entertainment for the national press. Carney thought James G. Blunt, whom Lane maneuvered into a position of military authority in Kansas, was a toady and a drunk. "The disordered and anarchical condition to which the State of Kansas has been reduced by some of the military officials operating in that State, and acting under Federal authority," he wrote Lincoln in spring 1863, "reluctantly compels me as the Executive of that State to . . . address you."[171] Could a state governor be "the mere clerk of the military officer in command of a Department?"[172]

Lane, however, had charisma, and he had an unerring sense of the dramatic. Representative of his vision was his use of the issue of freeing and arming African Americans. He constantly recommended to Lincoln an emancipation proclamation and the early use in Kansas of African-American troops. He participated in slave-liberating expeditions. He introduced a resolution in the Senate in 1862 to authorize field commanders in Kansas to muster into service all persons who presented themselves. He hedged about arming blacks but was cheered when he said he would say to Negroes, "I have not arms for you, but if it is in your power to obtain arms from rebels, take them, and I will use you as soldiers against traitors." Later he said it would give him "no pain" to see a black man handling a gun. If Southerners objected to being killed by an African American, they should lay down their arms. Despite Lincoln's objections, Lane began signing up a black regiment in early August 1862, and the press reported the men of the First Kansas Colored Volunteers were eager to fight under his leadership.[173] Lane continued to say that blacks were inferior and proposed colonizing them in Africa or setting them aside on lands in Texas after the war. But his actions in recruiting them were bold for the times.[174]

Lane's style was well illustrated, too, by his proposed Great Jayhawker expedition into Indian Territory and Texas in 1862. The idea was for Lane to command ten thousand Kansas troops and four thousand Indians in an invasion of Texas. Major General David Hunter, commanding the Department of Kansas, was not informed of this plan, however, until it had received considerable newspaper publicity. He stated that he would have enough trouble defending Kansas with the resources he had, that there was no chance to invade Texas, and if that were done, he would certainly command the expedition, not Lane.[175]

Hunter reported that Lane's brigade was in "demoralized condition," that its regimental and company officers "knew nothing of their duties & apparently had never made returns or reports." Their camps, he wrote, were "little better than pig-pens," with officers and men sleeping and meeting together. Furloughs in great numbers were granted, and the units were "a ragged, half-armed, diseased, mutinous rabble taking votes as to whether troublous or distasteful orders should be obeyed." Hardly the material for a major expedition! "With Lane at the head of an army of 10,000 to 12,000 men, 4,000 of them Indians," wrote Samuel Smith some years later, "recruited, armed, clothed, organized & fed by his direction, a raid would have been made on the Treasury more direful in its results than any damage his forces would inflict on any enemy."[176]

Lane aimed for the presidency through these military devices, Abelard Guthrie wrote from Washington. He was "a great lion here and his room is always filled with visitors; at this moment there is not a man in Washington more sought after."[177] Later, however, Guthrie added, "There seems to me a species of insanity in some of this man's eccentricities."[178]

Lane's enemies grew apace. At one point in 1864, it seemed he was ruined. Carney even organized an election for senator a year early and was himself elected to Lane's post. He visited Washington and convinced Lincoln and Stanton to reduce Lane's appointment powers. But the Price raid confirmed the danger that Lane had always warned of and allowed him to charge Carney with negligence for not being well prepared. Lane's people dominated the fall 1864 legislative election, the new legislature set the earlier senatorial election aside (perhaps encouraged by thirty thousand dollars estimated to have been distributed by Lane's friends), and Lane was returned to the Senate with a one-hundred-gun salute fired in his honor. Yet even the patient Lincoln was growing tired of the Kansas way of doing politics. He wrote Pomeroy, "I wish you and Lane would make a sincere effort to get out of the mood you are in. It does neither of you any good—it gives you the means of tormenting my life out of me, and nothing else."[179]

But with Lincoln, as with Kansas's voters, Lane was a phoenix. The Great Emancipator was up for reelection in 1864, running on the Union Party ticket with former Democrat Andrew Johnson, and there was some question whether his Republican backers would nominate him. Lincoln and Lane appeared together on the same platform during the campaign, and Lane spoke often and eloquently for Lincoln's candidacy and for the cause with which the party was identified in the struggle. Was Lincoln not radical enough? Look at the Emancipation Proclamation, said Lane, "striking the shackles from the limbs of every human being in the rebellious states." Lincoln was a hero in Lane's eyes, and Lane worked to make him one in the vision of the voters.[180] "Uniting prudence and firmness," Lane said of Lincoln on the Senate floor, "wisdom and simplicity, integrity and sagacity, generosity and elasticity of spirit, in a singular degree, with that practical knowledge of men and things which places him, head and shoulders, above his peers for all the purposes of government," the president had piloted the ship through the greatest of storms.[181]

At a critical moment during the meeting of the Grand Council of the Union League, the day before the Republican convention in Baltimore, Lane rose to counter the "appalling charges" being made against the president.[182] "I am speaking individually to each man here," he said. "Do you, sir, know in this broad land, and can you name to me, one man whom you could or would trust, before God, that he would have done better in this matter than Abraham Lincoln has done, and to whom you would be now more willing to trust the unforeseen emergency or peril which is to come? That unforeseen peril, that perplexing emergency, that step in the dark, is right before us, and we are here to decide by whom it should be made for the Nation. Name your other man."[183]

Shortly after, Lincoln was dead, and the war was over. Neither was good for Lane. Without his high-placed friend, he became enmeshed in the scandal to which his daring was prone. In May 1866, he asked a fellow senator about "slanders . . . whispered in your Ears, prejudicial to my honor as a Senator."[184] He had always thrived on contracting through government offices, probably benefiting himself. In June 1866 the *New York Tribune* broke the story that Lane had received twenty thousand dollars as compensation for obtaining favors for contractors supplying Indian refugees.[185] His attempt to curry favor with the new president backfired as Lane backed Johnson's vetoes of civil rights bills that were popular in Kansas, and an all-powerful Congress moved to impeach Johnson. Lane collapsed in St. Louis in June and was taken back to his farm near Leavenworth to recuperate.[186]

The man had been challenged and charged before, and he had taken to his bed with melancholia induced by stress and overwork before, and always before he had emerged stronger than ever. "He would have defied the King of Terrors himself," wrote a Kansas associate, "and lived in spite of fate."[187] As late as May that seemed his stance. He wrote his friend John Speer that he would fight it out in the political trenches. "It seems to me I am entitled to be heard before condemnation. I think I can show that the civil rights bill is mischievous & injurious to the best interests of the black man but if I cannot the Legislature shall fill my place."[188]

This time, however, something was different. Speer visited Lane at his farm late in June, meeting him at the doorway. He joked that he heard Lane was ill but thought he was worth a dozen dead men yet. Lane responded,

"The pitcher is broken at the fountain. My life is ended." Two days later, July 1, 1866, he jumped out of a carriage in which he was riding, pulled out a pistol and fired a ball through the roof of his mouth and into his brain. He lingered eleven days, even recognizing his friends sometimes, but finally died.[189] "Lane had not the disposition to become 'a canker of a calm world and a long peace,'" wrote an associate.[190]

Lane's nemesis, Robinson, was out of the cockpit of Kansas too, reading Buckle's *History* at Oakridge, his thousand-acre farm near Lawrence. He reflected one spring day in 1865 that the state university was under way in Lawrence, a freedman's college was to be built at Quindaro, railroads were the subject on everyone's lips, the government was running smoothly, and there had been no guerrilla excitement in a long time: "They are almost forgotten in the hurry of business." He wrote Sara, "It seems as though we might be real happy."[191]

Thus ended the first and never-to-be forgotten era in Kansas history.

3 "HOW THE IRON MUST BURN"

In the first days of October 1865, midway between the time Governor Robinson wrote happily to Sara that the guerrillas were gone and the time Jim Lane put a pistol in his mouth, Black Kettle of the Cheyennes stood at a point a bit north of the juncture of the Big and Little Arkansas Rivers in south-central Kansas. He listened to the proceedings of one of the many treaty conferences with which the new state was necessarily laden, and he spoke about his feelings toward the changes. J. B. Sanborn, who headed the commission sent from Washington, apologized to the gathered Cheyennes, Arapahoes, Kiowas, Apaches, Wichitas, and others for the massacre of Cheyennes the year before at Sand Creek in Colorado Territory by militiamen under the command of the Reverend John Chivington. The government would pay compensation for the Cheyenne losses. But such incidents provided even more reason why the Indians "should be located on seperate [*sic*] lands and hunting grounds" where they could be protected from the whites by law. "War simply annoys and troubles the whites, while it destroys . . . [the Indians.] We have lost more men in the last four years, among the whites, than all the Indians put together. We have destroyed and vanquished our enemies, and our towns and country are still full of soldiers."

The message was clear. It took time and more treaty conferences, but in 1870 the city of Wichita was incorporated at the site where Black Kettle and Sanborn stood. By 1887 Wichita was the fastest-growing city in the nation and by the twentieth century the largest and most industrialized city in Kansas. Little Raven of the Arapahoes said at the Little Arkansas Treaty conference, "Our friends are buried here and we hate to leave these grounds." Black Kettle was not sure he trusted whites. "When I come in to receive presents, I take them up crying," he said. "My shame is as big as the earth."[1]

Some tribes were aggressive. The Cheyenne dog soldiers kept up a running battle with white troops in Kansas well into the 1870s. "The white chief is a fool," said Little Mountain of the Kiowas. "He is a coward; his heart is small—not larger than a pebble stone; his men are not strong—too few to contend against my warriors; they are women."[2] Satanta of the Kiowas said he had no desire to kill the white people but that these white men killed buffalo and let their carcasses rot on the prairie. They destroyed the grass and caused Indian ponies to die of starvation. They cut down timber and made large fires, while the Indian cooked with only a few dry limbs. "I picked up a little switch in the road," Satanta complained, "and it made my heart bleed to think that small limb so ruthlessly torn up and thoughtlessly destroyed by the white man would have in the course of time become a grand tree for the use and benefit of my children and grandchildren."[3]

Eloquence in defense did not stop the process. The ten thousand Indians residing in Kansas in 1854 were reduced by removal to Indian Territory to the south to fewer than one thousand in 1875.[4] A *Wichita Vidette* reporter observed in 1870 that as the Osages moved away, "the air was filled with the cries of the old people, especially the women, who lamented over the graves of their children, which they were about to leave forever."[5] They said goodbye to their way of life and to the sea of grass on which it was lived, while railroads, farmers, stockmen, drovers, and townsite speculators fought over their patrimony.

Paul Gates spent nearly twenty years researching his book, *Fifty Million Acres.* In it, he made the point that land hunger and inadequate provision for transfer of lands both from Indians to the United States and from the public domain to individual settlers were major factors in the turbulence of early Kansas history. The Kansas story, Gates wrote, was "a grotesque composite of all the errors involved in the growth of the American West."[6]

When the moral struggles waned, business, which had been just below the surface, got fuller attention. George Brown ceased publication of the *Herald of Freedom* in 1859, ostensibly because the freezing of the Missouri River blocked his supply of printing paper but actually because the cause that boomed his circulation was won and because he had become interested in the oil business.[7] Brown in 1860 became business manager for the firm of Brown,

Solomon and Company, which drilled three oil wells about one hundred feet in depth near Paola, Kansas.[8] The company had a thirty-year lease on land owned by Johnson Lykins, a partner in the oil company who was in charge of the Baptist Mission to the Shawnees. Their third well was, Brown said, "blasted . . . through solid rock" and produced a good deal of salt water and a little petroleum.[9] Brown loaded his wife, camping equipment, and geological library into a carriage and spent four months in summer and autumn 1860 studying possible signs of petroleum in eastern Kansas.[10]

The wells at Paola were pioneering ventures. Edwin Drake's oil well in Pennsylvania, the first in the United States, was dug in 1859, less than a year before Brown's well in Kansas Territory. Brown was from Pennsylvania and had not only read reports from there and observed the Drake well, but since 1855 he also had studied "mineral oil" samples from places in Kansas. Robert Stevens walked into the *Herald* office in 1857 with a bottle of oil from springs along Wea Creek at Paola, exactly where Brown later drilled.[11]

Yet there were problems. The start of the Civil War made oil-field labor difficult to find. Lykins was, according to Brown, an opium addict and therefore unreliable as a businessperson. He was also of the Pro-Slavery persuasion, had been a member of the bogus legislature, and was arrested by Jayhawkers in 1861. He escaped hanging but thought it best to sell out his mission and leave the territory. Another partner, Maltravis Solomon, was convinced that the explorers had found gold and copper as well as oil and therefore refused all offers to sell. Soon the offers ceased. There was no nearby refinery and therefore not much of a market outside perhaps a local one for lubricants. However, although the company's location method was not scientific (it involved following surface oil seeps and consulting a spiritual medium), there was at least production.[12] The activities of a man who discovered in 1857 that gypsum, a grayish rock found along the Blue River, could be used to plaster his cabin did not have great impact at the time, either. The commercial development of petroleum and gypsum, as well as the lead and zinc mineral resources known to abound in the southeast corner of the state, awaited different times, different markets, and different promoters.[13]

Not so with railroads. Railroad corporations, those artificial beings with "no body to kick or soul to damn," became powerful players in Kansas, baffling as they were sometimes to husbandmen and politicians as well as to Indians. Railroad building, with its attendant land buying, bond debt, and town development concomitants, involved all the boiling elements of the Kansas stew in a high-stakes game.

Although the territorial legislature chartered fifty-one rail companies, no track existed in Kansas until 1860 (the Elwood and Marysville). The Pacific of Missouri reached Kansas City in 1865, but there was no continuous rail connection with eastern systems until the Missouri River was bridged in 1869.[14] The first rail empires were modest. Charles Gleed wrote that the initial expedition of the Elwood and Marysville was a "merry mob," which rode behind a "scrap head" of a locomotive. A participant claimed that "the occasion was characterized by the most ardent, wide-spread and all-prevailing inebriety ever attained in the state."[15]

But steam and credit were the watchwords of the age, and Kansas especially was enmeshed from the start in every twist of those miracles of modernity. The possibility of a Pacific railroad and telegraph, ballyhooed as a "Seal of Union" and "Highway of Nations" from every street corner and press-room since the Mexican War, was in the wings during the Kansas-Nebraska Act debates.[16] The Pacific Railroad Surveys were by then published in their twelve folio volumes, recommending that a transcontinental rail route avoid the snows of the north and the heat of the southern desert. William Gilpin proclaimed the influence of "isothermal lines" and marked the geographical center of the nation in Kansas as a key point on the future rail route. "The holy question of our *Union*," Gilpin wrote in his *Central Gold Region* in 1860, "lies in the bosom of *nature;* its perpetuity in the hearts of a great democratic people, imbued with an understanding and austere reverence for her eternal promptings and ordinances; it lies not in the trivial temporalities of political taxation, African slavery, local power, or the nostrums of orators."[17] In Kansas, which "erupted during an age of romanticism," with its attendant hopes of human perfection, the alliance of science and morality in the railroad vision could not have fallen on more fertile ground.[18] By the late 1880s Kansas, with nearly nine thousand miles of railroad line, or five and one-half miles for every one thousand people, was better equipped per capita with railroads than any other state in the Union or any country in the world.[19]

Initially, there was much more paper than rail, and the planning was of a type where every prospect pleased. Johnston Lykins's project, the Kansas City, Galveston and Lake Superior, was too ambitious for 1850s realization. But he predicted that "cities at some day, greater than Babylon, Nineveh, or

Thebes will tower above [Kansas's] green hills and become the wonder and glory of the world;—when the passage from Galveston to Lake Superior will be as through an enchanted Eden."[20] A cynic wrote in 1857 that Governor Robert Walker "enlarges upon the varied resources of the Territory, and speaks as though air-line railroads would be immediately put into operation (under his auspices) in every quarter of Kansas. If I am not greatly mistaken the address will prove to be wishy-washy, verbose and meaningless—full of gas and buncombe. . . . Walker has come out here with a tremendous flourish, but I'll wager ten to one that he ends in smoke."[21] Still, an observer of the Kansas scene wrote in 1860, "Railroads are all the go. Everybody talks about railroads. Everybody builds railroads (in the air) and every body has the most practicable route."[22]

Every town expected a railroad, and people speculated in lots as though one were sure to come. Often it did not. Hiram Hill, like Charles Robinson and Abelard Guthrie, invested in the town of Quindaro, which they thought would rival Leavenworth as a Missouri River port and railroad hub. But Quindaro was a failure. "It is about the same," a friend wrote to Hill in 1860 concerning the state of the town, "I would feel in communicating the condition of a very sick friend, in whom the chances for life and death were about equally balanced, death seemingly having a little advantage."[23] In 1867 the situation was no better and the friend was trying to sell Hill's town lots in several Kansas spots, "if you don't ask fancy prices." Thaddeus Walker had been "stirring up the whole Neosho Valley with the prospect of a rail road from Junction City down the Valley of Neosho, and many of the people in the little villages in the Valley behold future great cities—and want prices for lots, now, that they will not command ten years hence, and what lots would only sell for if they had the cities they anticipate."[24] That, Hill's friend thought, was dreaming.

Still, there were practical goals amid the fluff. A major early one was to connect Kansas's river towns and those slightly inland with the Hannibal and St. Joseph Railroad, which had extended through Missouri close to the Kansas border. Whatever town got the best connection and bridge would have an advantage—the advantage Kansas City eventually gained in 1869 when the Hannibal and St. Joseph Bridge across the Missouri River opened at that point. Another was to connect eastern towns with their near western hinterlands. The historian Charles Glaab pointed out that the best promoters were those who were able to translate, largely through newspapers, local business interests into a compelling community ideology, which included a practical railroad strategy.[25]

The problem was money. Cyrus Holliday, a founder of Topeka, had a plan as early as 1856 to build a railroad from Leavenworth to Topeka and on to Ft. Riley to replace the unreliable steamboat transport on the Kansas River. By 1857 he had even conceived the idea of extending his project southwest toward Santa Fe, New Mexico. "I have thought of this matter much," he wrote, "but am too confounded poor to put it in execution."[26] The Elwood and Marysville, the Atchison & Pike's Peak, the Leavenworth, Pawnee and Western, and Holliday's Atchison and Topeka were all typical of the dreams of towns hoping that a regional feeder and even a Pacific connection were possible outgrowths of a bit of bond aid and some track running a few miles to a neighboring burg. That the latter two (renamed the Kansas Pacific and the Atchison, Topeka and Santa Fe) would form the nuclei of the first two railroads to cross the state was an outcome that was totally unpredictable when the outbreak of the Civil War made any significant actual construction for the time impossible.

Some rail strategists gained serious attention. One of them was Jim Lane. "General Lane made a Railroad speech at Elwood yesterday," wrote Jeff Thompson to Cyrus Holliday in 1858. "Several hundred of us went over to hear him . . . and he was listened to with the greatest attention and respect. The Genl. confined himself entirely to the Rail Road, speaking of the troubles in Kansas as having passed, and that now the time had arrived for tying us together by Bands of Rail Road Iron. I was laughed at a good deal by some of the folks on this side of the River for having anything to do with him, and really was placed in an awkward position as I conscientiously believe he has no principles at all—but our project must place us above personal dislikes."[27]

The other senator from Kansas, Samuel Pomeroy, was also railroad conscious early. At the same time in 1857 that he was arranging to purchase a steamboat called the *Lightfoot*, Pomeroy wrote to Thaddeus Hyatt that a railroad from Leavenworth and Doniphan to St. Joseph, Missouri, was sure, and he, Pomeroy, wanted to be certain to control any resultant town site, particularly land there for railroad machine shops and a foundry. He proposed to "lay off a Town, to harmonize the Streets with the R.R. Track and sell lots to mechanics and all sorts of laborers and others who want to use them." If the railroad could be put through that season, Pomeroy thought, "we can sell lots enough to make such sinners as we are rich as sinners ought to be."[28]

William Hutchinson, in a speech at a railroad meeting in Lawrence in December 1858, put the stakes clearly: "No higher or more important question of secular interest at the present time, can engage the attention of the people of Kansas. The building of railroads has become to our country like the building of churches & school houses, one of the fixed emblems of civilization and national progress, and even more than these latter, they exhibit a superlative regard for the promotion of American production and home labor." A channel of communication between producers and consumers, the speaker noted, "is a jugular vein to the commonwealth." Without it, "life becomes a gradual death—and the people aspire to nothing but a scanty subsistence—they live, die & are forgotten." It was not so much for the stockholders that the railroads were built—these often lost money in the pioneer ventures—but for the community and its property values. Kansas was ready and, despite the fact that "our hecatombs of resolutions . . . our unnumbered Conventions have all sung the old sing song of politics," Kansans were "inured to the shrill voice of the locomotive" and would adapt to its ways. Kansas was at the center of the continent, and it must be a link in the railroad chain. "Now before we can have 2,000 miles of RR we must begin somewhere and build *one* mile. And then another."[29]

There would be no direct state investment in Kansas railroads, as there had been in Missouri, largely because the disastrous results in that neighboring state had led Kansas to prohibit state aid to internal improvements in its Wyandotte Constitution.[30] Instead, the future taxing power of the towns and counties would be tapped through the issuance of railroad bonds. By 1860, there was talk also of federal aid, which might come to a Kansas railroad either through its being on a sponsored transcontinental route or through receiving a land grant on its independent promise. Pacific railroad bills passed the Congress in 1862 and 1864, with the recalcitrant Southern members absent. There was recognition that rivers could not be relied upon in Kansas for internal communication, that the Pony Express and the Butterfield Stage were hardly adequate to develop its western region, and that some connection with the great building fever that was sure to follow the war was therefore essential. "Of course, according as the resources of the country are developed," a newspaper noted early in 1860, "lines will be made in all directions, but without doubt those that run east and west will be the ones first undertaken, and are the only ones that will command attention in the east."[31]

One of the most important railroad conventions ever held in Kansas occurred in Topeka October 17, 1860. Significantly, it created a unified strategy among the warring towns of Kansas to send with lobbyists to Washington. It was no modest plan. The convention, in which some 150 delegates from nineteen counties were represented, proposed five railroads. One was to run from Atchison to the west boundary of Kansas; a second from Atchison to Topeka and southwest to Santa Fe; a third from Wyandotte up the Kansas River Valley to Junction City, and then west up the Smoky Hill River Valley to the western border of Kansas; the fourth from Lawrence down the Neosho Valley to the southern boundary of Kansas and then on to Ft. Gibson and Galveston; the fifth from the Osage Valley in Missouri to Emporia, Council Grove, and Ft. Riley. All but the fifth were eventually built, in part because of the convention's partial stilling of the wrangling that had preceded it.[32]

That economic wrangling, partly because it was an outgrowth of the political battles centering in the towns, had been fierce. "I have to fight the Lawrence battle entirely alone," Charles Robinson wrote to Sara in 1859. "Leavenworth men are unwilling to make Lawrence a point on the road south. We shall make it a point west. I shall try to fasten the Southern road also at Lawrence. Were it not that I have, with Stevens, the advantage of these fellows, Lawrence would not have a single road, if they could help it."[33] There was even a struggle within Lawrence between those who wanted a railroad on the north side of the Kaw River and those who pushed for the south side.[34] But it was railroad people, a Lawrence paper pointed out, who would make things happen, not "designing politicians or visionary enthusiasts." It was unwise, the reporter added, to push railroads "into sparsely settled sections of the country, with the expectation that they will produce business for themselves by bringing in emigration. . . . It is better to be slow and safe, than to gridiron the Territory with unfinished or bankrupt roads."[35]

The trunk-line railroad plan showed signs of viability in the next several years, while a myriad of local projects, most hoping to graft themselves to the main lines, rose and fell. There were several important reasons. First, the time between the beginning of the Civil War and the end of federal granting of lands to railroads in 1871 was the golden age of federal largesse to the western rail industry. Second, the same period, from the time the Civil War threatened the old settlement patterns and Indian agreements to the end of federal treaty making with the Indians in 1871, was the golden age, seen from the white developer's perspective, of the capitalization of Indian lands for the uses of industrial and agricultural civilization. Third, there was considerable bond aid from ambitious towns and counties.

A Kansas City editor in 1863 made sport of the pretensions of the "Great Pacific Railroad," as represented by the Union Pacific, Eastern Division (UPED). He wrote that the entire editorial force of Leavenworth had turned out "with pick and shovel and gone to work on the road, and expect to have it completed through to California in a couple of weeks. They are going to have it run three times around Leavenworth, so as to be sure it will stop there. But the great difficulty for them to determine is whether they will build most of it by telegraph, stage or newspaper puffs—probably the latter." Nine months later, however, track began to go down under the supervision of general superintendent Samuel Hallett. He had one hundred thousand dollars in bond aid from Wyandotte County, and a second locomotive, the *Delaware*.[36] "The Kansas Valley," wrote the *Kansas City Daily Journal of Commerce* in commenting on the completion of forty miles in November 1863, "is bound to be the great trunk line of the Pacific road. . . . The march of events is startlingly rapid. We must be up and doing, if we would secure those advantages which our position entitles us to, but which mere position will not suffice to secure."[37]

Events did march. Kansas in 1866 divided the five hundred thousand acres it received upon entering the Union from the federal government for the support of internal improvements. It went to four railroads: the Northern Kansas; the Kansas and Neosho Valley; the Leavenworth, Lawrence and Ft. Gibson; and the Union Pacific, South Branch (shortly Missouri, Kansas & Texas), all running along routes outlined by the 1860 Topeka convention. The Leavenworth, Pawnee and Western (to operate on the Wyandotte/ Smoky Hill Valley route west) changed its name in 1863 to the Union Pacific, Eastern Division, and in 1869 to Kansas Pacific. Thanks to the help of Senators Lane and Pomeroy in Washington, that company received the right to buy two hundred twenty-five thousand acres of former Delaware lands at $2.25 an acre. Also, as part of the four-pronged political monstrosity that the Union Pacific Railroad originally was, the UPED collected a federal land grant of ten sections and a loan of $16,000 in U.S. bonds for every mile of track laid. The Atchison and Pike's Peak Railroad (which became the Central Branch, Union Pacific in 1867) shared also in the federal Pacific railroad largesse but lost the race west to the 100th meridian and never became a major trunk line. The Kansas and Neosho Valley, chartered in 1865, reflected enlarged ambitions by changing the corporate name to the Missouri River, Ft. Scott and Gulf in 1868. That railroad's great Indian lands coup was the purchase of the Cherokee Neutral Tract of six hundred thirty-nine thousand acres in southeast Kansas. The Leavenworth, Lawrence and Ft. Gibson, with James H. Lane as its president, received bonds and state lands and changed its name to Leavenworth, Lawrence, and Galveston (LL&G) in 1869. The Union Pacific, South Branch, received a federal land grant also, thanks to the influence of Robert Stevens, who became its general manager, and a right-of-way through Indian Territory to the south, if it could beat the Kansas and Neosho Valley to the southern line of the state. Several of these southern companies had their eyes also on the Osage reserve, amounting to nearly 8 million acres and extending from the border tier of Kansas counties to the 100th meridian in the West. But they failed to recognize the mounting strength of the settlers' opposition to railroad grants and purchases. The last, and ultimately most important, of the Kansas chartered roads arising from the 1860 convention was the Atchison, Topeka and Santa Fe (ATSF), which began life, with typical early modesty, as the Atchison and Topeka in 1859. In 1863 it received a federal land grant of sixty-four hundred acres per mile, which eventually gave the road over 2 million acres of Kansas land. And this is the barest outline. Between 1864 and 1910, eleven hundred railroad charters were filed with the Kansas secretary of state. Kansas was a latter-day frontier, where "instant civilization" was thought possible.

Heavy construction was not immediate. There were only 71 miles of track in Kansas in 1865, and 1,234 in 1870. But that latter figure included one line, the Kansas Pacific, which had crossed the state and was heading for Denver (reached in August of that year), and another, the Santa Fe, which was pushing hard in the same direction. It reached the western border of Kansas in the Arkansas River Valley in 1872. In 1880 Kansas had 3,104 miles of railroad track.[38]

Many people in 1860s and 1870s Kansas were involved in some way in railroad promotion, more were involved in its ancillary town sites, and probably most were investing in real estate that would benefit from the prosperity brought by both. There was a rare excitement in founding a town

Railroad water tank in Manhattan, Kansas, 1867.
Courtesy of the Kansas State Historical Society.

with prospects that were limited only by the unknown parameters of the future. However unpromising a few buildings might seem in reality, their prospects glowed. Cyrus Holliday wrote eastern friends in 1858 about "extraordinary inducements to investments in Kansas," once there was no slavery question. The political troubles had temporarily reduced the prices of property far below their proper value, and now there would be opportunity to make large money. Plenty of common prairie land could be bought, said Holliday, for $1.50 to $3.00 an acre that would be worth $5.00 "the very instant you have them in your possession." Town-lot investments were more unsafe "but much more speedy in return," and loans in the territory earned from 2.5 to 5 percent a month. The insecurity of land title, with the Indian treaty situation still uncertain and the unknown pattern of the railroads, created risk but also great upside potential.[39] Holliday said in an 1886 address before the State Historical Society, "New towns or cities—everything was a city then—were being daily organized, surveyed, platted and sold." Most ended up returned to cornfields, but some made fortunes for their projectors. Holliday became a member of the legislature in 1858, mainly to push the incorporation of railroads and towns.[40]

George W. Brown was an original projector of Emporia, one of those towns that lasted and grew. He selected the town site on a ten-day horseback tour along the snow-covered Neosho Valley in 1857, became president of the Emporia Town Company, and named it and all its north-south streets. He and George Deitzler paid $1,800 in gold for a float from the Wyandot Indians and laid out the town on 320 acres of the section thus acquired. Preston Plumb, later a Kansas senator and the man who is often credited with founding Emporia, was a boy of nineteen at the time, working in Brown's *Herald of Freedom* office. Brown brought Plumb into the town company on credit and bought a printing press and fixtures for him to use in starting the *Emporia News*. The other four projectors of Emporia subscribed for twelve hundred copies of the new paper. Plumb later paid for his loan with appreciated Emporia town lots—just the way things were supposed to work.[41]

The best towns were associated with the best people—those who were clever and tough. Nor were they rubes. In 1882 a young man came into Brown's office claiming that Brown had made a mistake in the naming of Emporia. The singular ending should be Emporium and the plural Emporiae. Emporia, the man said, was a "barbaric" name. Brown let him talk a time and then noted on a map that the Greeks had a colony named Emporia. "Those old Greeks," Brown then told the man "must have been simpletons, who located colonies and gave them 'barbaric' names. It is to be regretted that they had not the services of some modern college sophomore to have instructed them in a proper use of their language."[42]

The towns would not thrive, however, and land values would not go up without railroad connections, nor would good title be passed without the removal of the Indian tribes and some solid arrangement for the transfer of Indian title. Thus a major policy question was to whom would Indian lands be transferred. Would they go to actual settlers, 160 acres at a time; to railroad companies in large blocks for resale; to town sites in the form of floats to be located at places and times of the buyers' choosing; to out-of-state speculators hoping for a fast profit; or to some combination of all these? On that question there was no consensus, and pragmatic pressures ruled.

Another post–Civil War complication of the aboriginal history of the Kansas region was that nomadic tribes who roamed through the western two-thirds of the state, sustained by the dwindling bison herds, had to be corralled, it was thought, to more limited ranges—preferably by treaty but by force if necessary. Eighteen sixty-five marked the practical opening to white settlement of western Kansas, a distinctly different ecological zone of arid high plains far from Topeka, where railroads and modern agricultural techniques were vital for sustaining life and economic viability.

Some of the more ambitious individuals moved west early. William Phillips in 1860 wrote Samuel Wood from Salina, on the frontier. Wood edited a paper in Council Grove then and soon moved on to cattle ranching in the Flint Hills at Cottonwood Falls. Phillips was concerned that any railroad chartered to come in his direction should recognize the town he was developing. He offered to take ten thousand dollars in stock in any company that could be formed to continue the Pacific railroad on a central route and asked Wood to oppose any Kansas road up the Republican River Valley or any other route northward into Nebraska, "as all such roads will merely tend to make us a tributary to a Pacific railroad up the Platte." Salina could use a post office and mail service, too.[43]

Wood agreed about the transportation. The stage fare from Council Grove to Leavenworth in 1864 was eleven dollars a passenger. Four ranch men from the Flint Hills "swore like troopers when they came to pay their fare that it would be the last time ever this stage company would get any of their money."[44] But short of starting private stage companies, there was little the westerners could do except lobby the legislature, attend railroad conventions, and encourage the military to make the West safe for settlers. They pushed hard. Wood by 1872 was promoting the town of Great Bend near the 99th meridian, and by the time of his murder in 1891 the former territorial-wars activist was in the middle of a county seat fight in Stevens County in the far southwest corner of the state.[45]

On the matter of the transfer of the eastern land once assigned to emigrant tribes, the controversy was deep. Horace Greeley, on a tour of Kansas in 1859, complained that "the infernal spirit of Land Speculation and Monopoly" had seized everyone there. "There are too many idle, shiftless people in Kansas," he wrote. "To see a man squatted on a quarter section in a cabin which would make a fair hogpen, but is unfit for human habitation . . . with hardly an acre of prairie broken . . . waiting for some one to come along and buy out his 'claim' . . . this is enough to give a cheerful man the horrors."[46]

At first, some elements of the Indian tribes saw advantages, given the inevitability of the change to white civilization, of ceding some of their lands, retaining some, and encouraging railroad development in order to boost the value of the remaining tribal property in Kansas. Railroad sales yielded immediate cash to the tribes, whereas sales to individual settlers would be slow in coming. The survey and transfer costs were paid by the railroad. Thieves were taking timber from Indian lands and reducing their value every year sale was delayed. Money sometimes stuck to the fingers of clerks in Washington in the case of a sale to the United States. The Delaware treaty of 1860, therefore, gave the Leavenworth, Pawnee & Western Railroad the right to purchase lands ceded by the tribe near those allotted to individual Indians, provided the company build a railroad and begin disposing of its land to white settlers within seven years. Other Kansas treaties in the early Civil War period contained similar provisions. "We would like to accommodate the Rail Road Company," wrote Delaware officials John Conner and Charles Journeycake in 1862. "We want to help them all we can and will do provided we can and do justice to our people."[47]

More often, however, it was a question of the Indians or their representatives resisting a sale or transfer method that seemed unfair. It was difficult to know where justice lay in the rapidly changing circumstances and among all the constituencies. "I have never known such a bungling business as this subdivision and assignment of Wyandot lands," wrote Abelard Guthrie, who was frustrated at unsuccessfully pursuing claims through his wife's connection with both the Wyandots and the Shawnees. "The partiality of the commissioners, the dishonesty of the chiefs and the rapacity of the Indians have given rise to much difficulty and many glaring acts of injustice."[48] Just as Robert Stevens and numerous railroad attorneys did, Guthrie drafted language for treaties, which they tried to persuade tribal delegations and the Indian Office in Washington to adopt. Guthrie thought that the Delaware treaty, which he wrote in 1858, would "secure the Delawares from being defrauded by the harpies that are flocking to Washington in the hopes of securing slices of their land."[49] In 1862 Guthrie canvassed squatters on these same Delaware lands, who were "very restive" about the claims of the Leavenworth, Pawnee & Western Railroad to this property. He gave a speech at a blacksmith shop that year to the farmers in hopes that they would elect him to Congress to advance their claims.[50] Senators Lane and Pomeroy, both of whom had been given substantial stock interests in the UPED Railroad for helping it to get federal aid, were giving speeches urging removal of about two thousand settlers already there "to make room for an imaginary railroad company." Timber was being cut at "a dreadful rate."[51] To a close observer in 1863, the Indian bills in Congress, including one advanced by Lane for the wholesale removal of all the Indians from Kansas, displayed "a most reckless disregard of the commonest principles of justice and humanity, and of course a folly and ignorance in proportion."[52] Another commentator, watching Stevens supervise sales of Indian lands, characterized the Kansas squatter as a man "of varied cast, just emerged from the ordinary walks of a fixed state of society into an untried experience, where 'Chaos is come again,' and order is yet to be brought forth."[53]

During the Civil War, treaties recognized the possibility of some Kansas land being retained by the tribe or allotted to individual Indians. However, treaties negotiated at the end of the war in an atmosphere of threat, such as Black Kettle and his friends experienced in Wichita in 1865, provided for complete removal except for a few of the most intransigent bands (Kickapoos, Sac and Fox, and Prairie Pottawatomies prominently, who retained small reserves in the state). Stevens in 1868 published a flyer for the sale of sixty thousand acres of Sac and Fox lands, with the UPED on the north and the LL&G on the west soon to be in operation, and the ATSF running straight through it. "TITLE PERFECT," claimed the flyer, "by patent direct from Government. One quarter cash, and balance in three equal payments with annual interest. Situate as these lands are, in the centre of the State, contiguous to all its large cities, and surrounded by railways, probably such facilities for securing choice selections of land for actual settlement and homes were never afforded at any sale heretofore held in Kansas."[54] That kind of language illustrated how quickly the transition away from Indian Kansas was made.

Some of the schemes for profit and position that accompanied the treaty making are a mystery yet; others required specialist study years later to unravel them fully. This was true, for example, of the ongoing speculations in Kansa Indian lands around the town site of Council Grove and of the complex maneuvering for the Kansa half-blood lands that formed part of the town site of the Kansas capital of Topeka. The fact that the mother of Charles Curtis was a Kansa Indian who owned one of these tracts had much to do with his becoming a wealthy Topekan, a senator from Kansas, and later vice president of the United States.[55] More newsworthy at the time, but scarcely clear in all its implications, was the combination townsite/university design created through removal treaty terms with the Ottawa tribe. What seemed a way to use funds generated by the transfer to educate Ottawas wishing to send their children back to Kansas to school became in practice a means of town booming, constructing a Baptist College well beyond the requirements of natives, and lining the pockets of enterprising and colorful characters. These included Ottawa agent C. C. Hutchinson (for whom Hutchinson, Kansas, was later named), the Reverend Isaac Kalloch (known because of his alleged active hormones as "the roan stallion of the Marais des Cygnes"), and the Ottawa mixed-blood John Tauy Jones (who attempted to turn whatever leverage the Ottawas had to the financial advantage of at least some of them).[56]

But of all the complex struggles between settlers and railroads for Indian land in Kansas, with the government and courts in the middle, those conflicts over the Cherokee Neutral Lands and later, the Osage lands, achieved the greatest publicity and aroused the greatest public passion at the time. The Cherokee Neutral Lands comprised a tract of eight hundred thousand acres in the southeast corner of Kansas purchased in 1868 by the Missouri River, Ft. Scott and Gulf Railroad through its backer, James F. Joy of Detroit. The Cherokees had never occupied this Kansas land, but many settlers had, albeit illegally—an estimated two thousand by 1860.[57] The railroad land prices did not appeal to settlers, who organized the Cherokee Neutral Land League and threatened railway surveyors and construction workers with physical violence. Kansas representative Sidney Clarke became the league's champion, coming close in some of his speeches to encouraging violence. There was a newspaper in Columbus at the time, the *Workingman's Journal*, which advocated the abolition of private property. Settler action, ranging from boycott of stores to whippings, and the tone of its rhetoric were precursors not only of the region's Balkans reputation but also of the later Populist anticorporate focus in Kansas. A lawsuit eventually resolved the challenge to title in favor of the railroad. Joy thought that was right. "Why should we," he wrote, "who shall have opened the country, given it the advantages of railway accommodations, and given it this value, and have had the title sustained . . .

sell these lands to the men who have been our enemies, and given us all this trouble for a quarter of the price which others will be glad to pay us?"[58]

The Osage imbroglio, coming later, had a different result—the denial, for the most part, of railroad purchase of the Osage reserve. Though moves by railroads to buy the Osage lands seemed not unlike the controversial Pottawatomie lands purchase by the ATSF, those of the Kickapoos by the Atchison and Pikes Peak, or the railroad offers for the Kansa lands, this issue hung fire longer, got more publicity, and gave the settlers' interests a chance to organize more effectively. There was also the fact that the "land monopoly," complained about by many critics, meant that between Indian treaties and land grants, over 40 percent of the area of Kansas was taken out of the public domain and was therefore unavailable to farmers, either free under the Homestead Act of 1862 or for $1.25 an acre under the various preemption acts.[59]

The first cession treaty for the fifty-by-thirty-mile Osage tract was negotiated in September 1865. It ceded over 4 million acres under provisions that barred preemption and homestead claims and did not allow for the donation of school lands. In 1868, William Sturges, president of the Leavenworth, Lawrence and Galveston Railroad, proposed, with the help of James Joy, to purchase the whole Osage reserve, not just the portions ceded by the 1865 treaty, for $.20 an acre. Railroad representatives brought generous presents and bribes to the Osage Council and got their treaty signed by some of the principal chiefs.[60]

That action created a furor both in Kansas and in Washington. "It was a wholesale deal," wrote a Neosho County man later, "a monstrous proposition," and it had upon the settlers "the same effect that a red flag is said to have upon a bull. It made them fighting mad."[61] The announcement of the 1865 treaty led, even before its ratification, to extensive settlement on the Osage tract, largely by Union army veterans who expected not only to be able to purchase the lands at $1.25 an acre under the terms of the treaty but also that the Homestead Law might apply to make their selections nearly free. "*All* . . . went vigorously to work," Governor Thomas Osborn commented, "built their houses; put up their orchards, and improved their farms in the confident assurance and belief that they could purchase the lands at the government price; or at the most at but slight advance over it."

This hope was complicated not only by the so-called Sturges treaty of 1868 and by the push of towns, like Wichita, that had established themselves in the Osage lands on the promise of a resolution of the title, but also by the claims of the LL&G and the Missouri, Kansas & Texas (MK&T) Railroads that their federal land grants (1863 and 1866) should include part of these former Indian lands. The settlers, who said they would fight rather than be bested and who looked to Clarke as their Moses, applied to Washington for relief. They achieved a joint resolution in 1869 that allowed any bona fide settler to enter the lands under the preemption laws for a period of two years. But many settlers were prevented by want of means and other impediments from making the entries within the time period, and in 1872 the secretary of the interior, at the behest of the railroad companies, vacated a number of them and suggested that all of them might be void. This, wrote Osborn, caused "great apprehension and consternation among these people. . . . It is difficult to understand on what ground the General Government can justify itself, in inviting its citizens to settle upon its domain; receive their money; encourage them to make improvements that shall largely appreciate the value of the lands, and then quietly abandon them to the tender mercies of grasping corporations."[62] Peter McVicar, working for the settlers in Washington, wrote to Isaac Goodnow in Manhattan in 1868 that the Sturges treaty was "an outrageous swindle on Kansas" and that in opposing it the settlers "ventilated" a number of other treaty scams. "We are fighting all swindles as opposed to the interests of our people & schools," he wrote.[63] Cyrus Holliday, whose ATSF Railroad was for a time cut in on the possible Osage railroad sale, wrote, also from Washington in 1869, that "attending these meetings and writing and printing papers concerning our Osage Treaty keeps me very busy, so that I scarcely have time to smoke my cigar."[64]

By a complicated process, the Congress finally did open the Osage lands largely to settlers at $1.25 an acre. The Sturges treaty was dropped, but it took three pieces of legislation and a U.S. Supreme Court decision to make the settlers' rights version of the issue stick.[65] These decisions weakened the LL&G and the MK&T as potential trunk lines to the Gulf for Kansas. It weakened them also in comparison to the Kansas Pacific (KP) and the ATSF, moving with federal land aid to the west. And this was not to mention the land problems the southern lines had in trying to push through the Indian Territory (later Oklahoma) south of the state line. The 1870 joint resolution provided for the Osages to remove entirely from the state. In September a conference was held with them, explaining the will of Congress, and they prepared to go. The *Wichita Vidette*, already angling to make its town a center for the cattle trade from Texas, reported that "the air was filled with the cries of the old people," among the Osages, whose way of life was about to change forever.[66]

Change came also to Native Americans in the western sections of Kansas but in a different way, and with a much larger mix of military action. A line of forts populated the river valleys of the high plains of Kansas with soldiers and denied to Indians, their ponies, and the bison they hunted several major timber and watering areas in a place where such havens were scarce in winter's cold. The wood and tie camps of the railroads increased the pressure on the environment so critical to Indian survival.[67] When settlers began to follow soldiers past the sacred Waconda Springs (a place now at the bottom of one of the federally funded reservoirs of Kansas), the Indians established a "dead line" on the latitude of Salina, almost exactly where nature divided the more eastern ecosystems from the western ones, the tall grass from the short grass prairies in Kansas. Beyond that, they swore, whites would not go unopposed.[68]

Ft. Riley (1853), Ft. Larned (1859), Ft. Harker (1864), Ft. Hays (1865), and Ft. Wallace (1865) guarded the northern emigration and overland express routes, and Ft. Zarah (1864) and Ft. Dodge (1865) protected the Santa Fe Trail. With them came a network of military roads and the nuclei of what would become western towns.[69] At Larned there was a flagpole one hundred feet high mounting a thirty-six by twenty-foot flag, as though to advertise to all concerned the new dispensation.[70]

A soldier wrote Samuel Wood from "out here in the 'wilderness'" (Ft. Larned) in 1864. Things were quiet with the Indians, he said, "although old residents here and traders along the route predict that it is only the calm that precedes the storm." Apaches were camped near the fort and "profess the greatest friendship for the whites." But Kicking Bird of the Kiowas had visited, exchanged "high words" with the commander of the post, and left in a "bad state of mind." Thereafter, the Kiowas and Comanches moved their villages south for making medicine, "leaving the whites to conjecture what kind of medicine they are preparing."[71]

At first the classic era of Indian warfare was not impressive in Kansas. During the so-called Indian War of 1864, centered mostly in Nebraska, General Samuel Curtis wrote from a camp on the Solomon River, "Indians scarce & signs show only scattered bands."[72] But as settlers moved into the western part of the state and railroad crews became active there, confronta-

Ft. Hays, June 8, 1867.
Courtesy of the Kansas State Historical Society.

tions increased. There were thirty-one engagements between Indians and U.S. troops in Kansas in 1867 and fifty-eight in 1868—the height of the Indian-military activity there.[73] The Indian "depredations" were isolated, and the military response resulted in no pitched battles of massed forces, but the horror was often domestic, the chase frustrating, and the embarrassment nettling. Well into the 1870s there was violence visited on the Kansas frontier by Indians.[74] As former governor Samuel Crawford wrote in 1867, "If those who believe that the Indian embodies in his nature everything that is noble and great could see their friends butchered and mangled as we of the West have seen ours the probability is that they would change their opinions."[75]

Typical of interactions between the military and Indians in Kansas was the April 1867 expedition into western Kansas led by General Winfield Scott Hancock, hero of Gettysburg. William Sherman had given him the order that he was "to go among the Cheyennes, Arapahoes, Kiowas, or similar bands of Indians, and notify them that if they want war they can have it now; but if they decline the offer, then impress on them that they must stop their insolence and threats."[76] The tribes did not do direct battle with Hancock's force of fourteen hundred. Tall Bull of the Cheyennes said in a visit with

Hancock at Ft. Larned while smoking a peace pipe, "We never did the white man any harm. We don't intend to. The buffalo are diminishing fast. The antelope, that were plenty a few years ago, are now few. When they shall all die away, we shall be hungry; we shall want something to eat, and will be compelled to come in the fort. Your young men must not fire on us."[77]

The Hancock march was therefore mostly shadow chasing, climaxed by the burning of a Cheyenne-Sioux encampment on the Pawnee Fork in present-day Ness County. There were some meetings at forts between Hancock and tribal leaders and exchanges of gifts and promises. There was also one tense confrontation on a hill near the camp Hancock was to burn. A line of soldiers and scouts, including Hancock, Custer, and James "Wild Bill" Hickok was on the one side, with artillery and cocked rifles.[78] In the facing line were Pawnee Killer, Roman Nose, and other leaders of the Sioux and Cheyenne, all in the various regalia and paint that had marked their success on the Plains as hunters and fighters for centuries. The war chiefs showed their bravery by facing the blue coats in the afternoon sun, but then withdrew not only from the fight but also from the camp, where the soldiers found only a few women and old people. Guerrilla tactics were their only chance, and even those created only a temporary respite.

Opinions about the western tribes and the proper policy to be pursued toward them varied a great deal in Kansas. On the one hand, there were those like Samuel Crawford, governor of Kansas from 1865 to 1868. Crawford referred to Indian males as "bucks" and averred that "a wild Indian in those days had no respect for anything but force. . . . They roamed the plains in search of something to kill or somebody to rob." Crawford made the official request for the Hancock expedition in response to petitions from settlers and railroads that were under sporadic attack by Cheyenne, Arapahoe, Sioux, and Kiowa Indians. These Indians followed, in Crawford's words, "a bloody trail," subsidized by annuities from the federal government and its avowed "peace" policy. Crawford wrote to General William Sherman in June 1867 that any withdrawal of force "leaves our frontier settlers, railroad men and all others in western Kansas, exposed and liable to be murdered and scalped at any moment." He believed that the organization of counties in the western part of the state helped bring law to Indians as well as to bandit whites there and that had Hancock been given more leeway by federal officials, the deaths in Kansas from Indian raids in 1868 might have been prevented. To Crawford, the Medicine Lodge treaty negotiations were a "farce," by means of which

Old Sioux Indian captured by the Hancock expedition, April 1867.
Courtesy of the Kansas State Historical Society.

Bull Bear of the Cheyennes, Satanta and Tall Bull of the Kiowas, and to a
lesser extent Little Raven of the Arapahoes, Ten Bears of the Comanches, and
Kicking Eagle of the Kiowas, pretended to agree to removal south and cessa-
tion of raids on Kansas in order to ensure winter rations while seriously
contemplating an attack on the peace commissioners themselves.[79]

Indian lodges at Medicine Creek, site of the peace conference, 1867.
Courtesy of the Kansas State Historical Society.

A contrasting view was held by James Mead, who had come at age twenty-three from Iowa to Kansas to establish a hunting and trading business, first near Salina and then near the future site of Wichita. Mead's business, carried out sometimes in conjunction with Jesse Chisholm, a part Cherokee with considerable knowledge of Indian languages, not only required but depended upon coexistence between whites and the Indian tribes. Mead and the Indian agent Jesse Leavenworth thought Crawford and others exaggerated the Indian danger in order to push economic development with troop presence.[80] Mead personally never felt insecure, even when riding alone on the prairie with thousands in cash from hide sales in Leavenworth. In 1867, when the Indians were said to be on the warpath, he recorded that he traveled over the Plains as usual, unmolested. "The writer is not one of those who believe that only dead Indians are good Indians," Mead wrote in 1910. "During the five years' residence of the Wichita Indians on the Little Arkansas [during the Civil War], I knew of but one crime committed in the country. . . . In the first five or six years after the Indians had left, and the country was open for settlement, I have a record of some twenty men who came to a sudden and violent death. Most of these were no special loss to the country."[81]

Mead was an amateur ethnologist, who studied Indian culture, collected examples of tribal dress and ornament, and filled notebooks with representations of pictographs from ancient natives he found on limestone faces during his hunts. In 1894, going down the trail he and Chisholm had established in 1865 and visiting the remnants of the tribes with which he was once familiar, now confined to reservations, he found the Cheyennes and Arapahoes "to be but the dejected, miserable remnants of a former proud and haughty race. . . . They seemed to be about as spiritless and worthless as a lot of wild animals brought from the wilderness of Africa and confined in cages for the purposes of exhibition." That was not the purpose for which God made the Indian, Mead mused, and in retrospect he wondered whether the blessings of civilization were really not something of a "myth," compared to the freedom that he and the Indian had enjoyed in those happier times.[82]

Certainly, too, there were stereotypes in operation concerning Indians, their nature, and their historical role. The extremes always seem to get the attention, and perhaps unfortunately, it is the extremes that often dictate policy. The Southern Cheyennes, for example, were deeply divided about policy toward whites. The Black Kettle faction worked with the army out of Ft. Riley but in doing so endangered themselves with the more radical dog soldier part of the tribe. And the whole group suffered when Custer attacked their village in November 1868. As James Sherow and William Reeder have written, "Just as some Dog Soldiers wished to eliminate all whites, some whites wished Indians gone from the earth forever. Neither of these extreme groups would ever achieve its goals, but others who desired little more than simple lives died in the crossfire."[83]

Although in the 1870s, with the railroads finishing track across the state, the Indian question seemed increasingly historical, Kansas governors were still touchy about it. This was particularly true when it seemed that eastern officials distributed philanthropy to the possible peril of Kansas. Governor James Harvey complained in May 1870 that there was "consternation prevailing" in western Kansas due to reports of hostile Indians in the vicinity. "I feel apprehensive," he wrote, "that terrible massacres, such as have been perpetrated there for years past, may be again impending."[84] Shortly after, he thanked Major General John Pope for assigning George Custer to the protection of Kansas settlements along the Republican Fork and the upper Saline and Solomon Rivers.[85] Still, in July, Indians were "lurking on the plains."[86] The next spring Harvey complained that the Office of Indian Affairs gave permission to Red Cloud and bands of Sioux to cross the Platte and hunt bison along the Kansas Pacific Railroad and south as far as Ft. Zarah and the Arkansas River. Harvey asked the president to have these Indians removed. "It can hardly be deemed necessary to remind you that for years every incursion of Indians into this State upon pretense of hunting has resulted in attacks made by them upon the citizens accompanied by atrocities of the most horrible nature." The governor blamed it on the "Indian Bureau" and threatened to take state action against any trouble caused by the "hordes of savages" if the policy were not changed.[87]

For a short time, there was a mix of cultures in the towns receiving or awaiting railroads, just as there had long been at forts. People speculated in town lots while at the same time hunting game and associating with Indians. Robert Wright, who shipped two hundred thousand buffalo hides and two cars of tongues from Dodge City the first winter after the ATSF reached there, emphasized that some of the "wild and wooley" tales of Dodge and Hays were overblown but did confess that the "hell of wheels" towns of Kansas attracted their share of aggressive persons. "Getting drunk and riding up and down the sidewalks as fast as a horse could go, firing a six shooter . . . were favorite pastimes, exciting, innocent, and amusing."[88] A correspondent for the *Lawrence Kansas Weekly Tribune* observed in spring 1868 that Hays, a city then of 150 houses, had few places of business that did not serve liquor, "and a drunken man does not excite any surprise."[89] Hunter George Anderson, visiting Wichita in 1871, observed all the businesses open on the Sabbath and frequented by "Texans, Mexicans and Greasers, and the hardest set of men we had yet encountered; every one carrying a huge bowie knife; a brace of Navy revolvers; large spurs with bells tingling from their heavy cavalry boots; rawhide breeches with the hair on. They were swearing, drinking and doing much as they pleased."[90]

W. E. Webb published in 1872 a minor classic of western Americana, *Buffalo Land*, illustrating the same mix of frontier and urban civilization in the earliest days of railroad towns. Webb, observing the great herds of bison as he hunted them around Hays, had a typical Gilded Age response. "What an immense aggregate of animal power was running to waste before us," he wrote, wondering why the bison were not harnessed to the plow. He also seemed to think the life of the Indians was a sort of waste and made lame attempts at humor about their efforts to adjust to relations with the residents of Hays City. He described the roofs of Hays as "glistening across the plains, as they say those of Damascus do to the East," but White Wolf, a Cheyenne chief whom Webb's hunting party met, hardly fit in, with his ragged military coat and limited English. Webb commented: "His stock of gastric juices seemed to have been well-nigh bankrupted by a fifty years . . . of jerked buffalo." It was not what the novels of James Fenimore Cooper had led him to expect in the way of native color, and he was certain that the sooner that part of the scene disappeared, the better.[91]

Governor Thomas Osborn, Harvey's successor, still had problems with the transition from Indian Kansas. The best arms he had to send to a group in Decatur County, worried about attack by Cheyennes in 1873, were U.S. .58-caliber rifle muskets—no breech-loading modern rifles were on hand in the state.[92]

That year, probably because the militia was armed against perceived threats from Kiowas and Comanches, there was a controversial incident relating to the generally peaceable Osages. Captain C. M. Ricker, commanding a party of Kansas militia on August 7, intercepted what he said was a war party of Osage Indians. These Indians were near Medicine Lodge in Barber County, Kansas, on a bison-hunting trip from their new reserve in Indian Territory. Ricker ordered his men to load their guns as they advanced. When he encountered three Indians, he ordered the tribesmen to give up their arms, which they did. Two more came up and were similarly treated. Others then approached, understood that they were being ordered to go back, and did. The order came for the militia to fire. At that point the disarmed Osages tried to escape and four of them were killed. According to an eyewitness, "The Indians did not fire a single shot or make any attempt toward self-defense," except one struck a militiaman with his whip as he was trying to hold the Indian's horse.[93] The hunt itself was with the permission of the Osage agent and was for the purpose of acquiring meat for the subsistence of the tribe.

The response in Kansas illustrated that even at such an early date, the Indians had local defenders and the military its local detractors. There was a careful investigation by the state, and a commission headed by former territorial governor Wilson Shannon took testimony from militiamen and Osage Indians. The conclusion was that the militia had "no facts upon which to base their suspicion that this particular band had been engaged in marauding." It was not the custom of the Osages, the commission concluded, to set out on hostile expeditions with women and children along, as this group had. The Indians interviewed denied in detail the claim of the militia that it had been fired upon. The commission agreed that it was unlikely that eight or nine Indians would make war on a company of fifty militia in full view, or that they would give up their arms to a single man if the rest of the militia were hidden. These were the only two versions of events available.[94]

Recent scholarship has asked whether the so-called Border War, of which this incident was a part, was real or pure exaggeration. The governor's office did receive reports of killings by Indians, including Osages, in the west; and the Wichita Eagle, representing the young cattle town that had grown up on the former Osage reserve, strongly supported keeping the Osages at a distance. But the threat quickly diminished, and no doubt the towns were overreacting.[95]

What is surprising, however, is not the fear of Indians but the severity of criticism from Kansans of the militia's action toward the Osages. However much Kansans wanted Indians removed from the path of commerce and supported defense from raids, they did not countenance unwarranted abuse. "Osborn's Minions Declared Guilty of Cowardly Murder of Inoffensive Osages," read the headline in the *Kansas City Star*, February 19, 1875. The "war," the paper said, was a pretext to keep the militia in service to protect certain bond swindlers in the area who were supporters of Governor Osborn.[96] Osborn denied this. He claimed that the official report was in error and that the Osages were hostile. He called the attention of the secretary of the interior to the general statistics of numbers of people killed in Kansas by Indians, as though this justified any attack.[97] He was nearly the only one, however, including the militiamen present, to push this version of events. The commissioner of Indian Affairs wrote to the secretary of the interior in January 1875 in response to a telegram from Osborn expressing alarm at a new party of Osages going on a bison hunt. Why had Kansas not punished the offenders from last summer and returned the property taken from the Indians then, the commissioner asked. "Until this is done, it will be difficult . . . to prevent the Osages from giving occasional causes of alarm to a people who must be conscious of having deeply wronged them."[98]

Osborn had a difficult year in 1874. He had to deal with the grasshopper invasion, which decimated the corn crop in the western sections, and the investigation of the gruesome murders of unwary travelers committed by Kate Bender and her kin at their grim little hostel in southeast Kansas. But he continued to act against Indian incursions into Kansas from Indian Territory. He claimed, "Frequent outrages are depleting the country contiguous to the Indian Territory," and he reported that he was organizing state militia companies to counter the threat. The state, Osborn said, had spent over three hundred fifty thousand dollars since 1861 defending its citizens against Indians.[99]

The most caustic and public critic in Kansas of Osborn's Indian policy was former governor Charles Robinson, now deeply involved in the reform movement. Robinson opposed a bill in the state legislature introduced in 1875 to appropriate money for an Indian war. It was a fraud, he said, to transfer money "from the pockets of the destitute taxpayers to the hay and quartermaster's departments of the state militia" and to create a casus belli by being overprepared. The militia money, Robinson said, was used for electioneering, and the "alleged hostility of the Osages was a ruse."[100]

The initial support of Kansas for Northern Cheyennes trying to escape from Indian Territory and across Kansas back to their homes in 1879 re-affirmed the basic sympathy of the people in the state for the plight of the tribes. But it showed also the limits of that tolerance. When those Cheyennes killed forty-one settlers and raped twenty-five females, one eight years old, the tone changed. If there were a peaceful and relatively humane way to remove Indians from the path of Kansas railroads and towns, fine, but Kan-sans would brook no violent interference with that process for any reason. An editor wrote in the late 1870s, "It is about time that the border states and territories took a contract for missionary work, in which a few companies of frontiersmen should civilize or exterminate these Government pets."[101]

The 1860s and early 1870s, as the old and the new coexisted, were espe-cially a study in contrasts in Kansas. A young man's letter from Ft. Harker in July 1869 described the scene there. He was, he wrote, "nearly burned up by excessive heat, eaten up by mosquitoes, and having the blues, thinking . . . all [his] friends had forgotten & forsaken [him]." There had been a fight with Indians who had been raiding on the Saline and Republican Rivers, which this correspondent felt "will put an end to the Indian War I think." But in addition to his news, he commented that he was glad to hear of Goodnow's work at Bluemont College in Manhattan. He would not be able to attend that fall, but hoped to shortly. That young man was Charles Sternberg, who later became one of the country's leading field paleontologists.[102]

The development of cultural institutions could hardly wait for rain to follow the plow, for the local railroads to develop their networks, or for the Indians entirely to remove. The New Englanders in the Kansas mix, espe-cially, were fixed on the common school and institutions of higher learning from the start.

That did not mean that there was deep understanding of the mission of schools and universities or that enthusiasm was necessarily accompanied by wisdom. Clifford Griffin, the historian of the University of Kansas, has written, "When the University of Kansas opened on September 12, 1866, the only things it had in common with the genuine universities of the time were a name, a charter, and a quarrelsome faculty." The Wyandotte Constitution required Kansas to create a state university that was nonsectarian and open to both sexes. Griffin concluded, however, that the political movement of the early 1860s, which resulted in Kansas's having three institutions of higher learning—in Lawrence, Manhattan, and Emporia—was a tissue of corruption, with the result that the state was suddenly as oversupplied with colleges as it soon would be with railroads. The towns quarreled over the locations of the university, the state capital, and the penitentiary. There were powerful figures (most prominently Robinson in the case of Lawrence and Goodnow in the case of Manhattan) backing the ambitions of specific towns. The Morrill Land Grant Act of 1862 allowed the boon of the agricultural college to go to Manhattan, instead of being a part of KU, and then a normal school at Emporia was thrown in for good measure as a way of holding together the legislative coalition. Three colleges were chartered as state institutions in 1863; none thrived much for some time. In fact, only at Manhattan, where Goodnow was operating Bluemont College in a limestone structure built in 1859, was there any momentum at all.[103]

Robinson had worked with Amos Lawrence of Boston almost from the founding of Lawrence to establish a college on the hill called Mount Oread, where the governor built his first home. Amos Lawrence proposed a "model" common school in 1857 and gave ten thousand dollars for the Free State College. He emphasized that the hill was the place for it. "Trade will not go up to the hills except to get prospect of a good bargain & there is no risk in locating a college or a church on a hill even in a large city. . . . It ensures a good view & seclusion."[104]

On the same day early in 1864 that Charles reported to Sara Robinson that their piano had arrived in Lawrence from the East with its legs wrapped in newspapers, he wrote also that he thought the legislature would provide a female department for the university.[105] The piano had to be placed far from the stone walls of their house, and the new university had to be protected from the machinations of politics.[106]

Robinson recruited Francis Snow, twenty-six years old, of Fitchburg, Massachusetts, as chancellor in 1866. He advertised that the university had an endowment of seventy-six sections of land, a fifty-acre site on a nice hill, and ten thousand dollars in interest-bearing bonds. He thought the legislature would appropriate four thousand dollars to pay teachers. "Of course we are weak & small compared with Eastern institutions," he admitted, "but we intend to have none but first class teachers & hope to soon have an institution that no young man need be ashamed of."[107] Snow accepted, agreeing to chair the department of mathematics and natural sciences in addition to handling the entire administration. He wrote that the university was likely to "be the most important institution of the kind in Kansas."[108]

That did not happen quickly. Robinson received a letter from KU in 1876, commenting on the actions of a stingy legislature toward higher education. "The faculty of this University are no *literary paupers* dependent on state aid. Nor are we a set of *tramps* foisting ourselves into comfortable quarters. We are here for honest hard work. . . . Does the state expect us to prepare for charity burials, or should she force us into business operations outside of our profession to save old age from relentless poverty?" How could the legislature continue to "freeze [the faculty] in unprotected rooms—and apply repeated scourgings because he does not draw to his cold embrace more ardent youths in the pursuit of knowledge?"[109] It was 1887 before Chancellor Joshua Lippincott could assure Robinson that "the University of Kansas is fully and fairly established not more securely on beautiful Mount Oread than in the hearts of the people of the state."[110]

Some of the complaints of the compromises involved in being a state institution continued into the twenty-first century. But in Kansas, democratic tendencies and the desire for universal education overcame questions of ultimate academic quality. There were individuals at the outset who were against public universities, but the decision was to take that path, to admit women, to move as quickly as possible to make tuition free for all Kansans, and eventually (1915) to create an open admissions policy for all Kansas high school graduates.[111] It was part of the style of the place.

Isaac Goodnow was the champion of the agricultural college, later Kansas State University. And it came very close to being the single state university. Goodnow started Bluemont Central College with financial help from the New England Emigrant Aid Company as part of its program of profitable community development. The company's Thomas Webb authorized Goodnow in 1858 to dispose of twenty of its town lots in Manhattan for cash and to give half the proceeds to the college project.[112] He told Goodnow that education at all levels "will aid materially in promoting the mental, moral, and physical well-being of those who may be trained under its auspices, and thus impart a healthy and vigorous tone to the community in which their lot may hereafter be cast, and over which some portion of them will be destined to exercise a guiding and controlling influence."[113] Goodnow was just then dealing with a plague of wildcats eating hens at his farm, little knowing that that animal would become the mascot of his institution of higher learning.[114]

Goodnow worked personally on painting and door hanging at the college and lived with his wife in the new building for a time in 1859.[115] "We must not be weary in *well doing*," he wrote a friend. "With a good press, good churches, & a College we shall have a chance to take breath. . . . The Lord knows what is best for us. We should die with the 'harness' on!"[116] He introduced a bill into the state legislature in 1861 to make Bluemont the state university, but it failed that year, despite the efforts of two lobbyists financed by the Manhattan City Council.[117] The next year Goodnow was in the legislature and pushing full time on the issue in the midst of the impeachment of the governor.[118] A bill for the benefit of the Manhattan school passed the house—"a triumph of the right, over local selfishness, & the advocates of allowing ignorance to stalk abroad a few years longer."[119] But the bill was killed in the senate, "crucified between two thieves," Goodnow said.[120] In 1863, with the Morrill Act in place, Goodnow accepted status as the agricultural college; and as such his bill passed both houses unanimously, with deals for Lawrence and Emporia thrown in. "This is one of the wonders of Kansas legislation. It has come to be considered a truthful maxim that no important legislation can be done on its own merits!"[121]

The state budget for the new institution was twenty-seven hundred dollars for two fiscal years, nine hundred of it to pay debts.[122] So primitive were conditions that Goodnow believed for a time in 1866 a report that two of his professors had frozen to death in going from the town up to the college.[123] By 1871, however, the Kansas State Agricultural College letterhead read that there was no tuition and no contingent fees and that the curriculum included "Agriculture, Military Science, Mechanic Arts, Literature and Science, Veterinary Science, Horticulture, Pomology, Entomology, Sylvaculture, Ornithology, Nursery Practice."[124]

The idea of a normal school in Emporia arose in that same 1863 session. The friends of Manhattan and Emporia had united to put the agricultural college in Manhattan and the state university in Emporia, as opposed to Lawrence. Emporia had a good chance at the main prize, Goodnow recalled later, but Lawrence won it "by means of bribery as it was thought." C. V. Eskridge, the champion of Emporia, introduced a bill calling for an investigation of the means by which the Lawrence victory was secured, and in response the Lawrence backers, "feeling well over their success & generous

Building the Kansas statehouse, 1867.
Courtesy of the Kansas State Historical Society.

towards their rival & to stop the investigation," put forward a bill to place the
state normal college in Emporia and endow it with thirty-eight thousand
acres of state lands. Eskridge agreed, and there was no investigation. The first
term of the Kansas State Normal School was in February 1865.[125]

There were plenty of other signs in the earliest statehood days of interest
in matters beyond economics. The state capitol was an elegant Victorian
structure designed by John Haskell of Lawrence.[126] A sign that social experiment had not been forgotten was the continued debate over the political
place of women in the new state. "It is not at all impossible," wrote the *New
York Times* in 1859, "that Kansas may set a brilliant example to the rest of the
world. . . . Apparently, nothing is needed but a determined prosecution of
the campaign, so brilliantly inaugurated, to insure the success of the cause of
woman's rights, after the manifold snubbings to which it has been subjected

in this older and less gallant portion of our slightly disunited States." The *Herald of Freedom*, which employed a female typesetter and office manager, encouraged women to demand their equal rights and emphasized that petitions would force the legislature to obey the voice of the populace.[127]

Clarina Nichols was an effective activist. She had proposed striking the word "male" from the suffrage clause of the Kansas Constitution when it was being debated in 1859, and she secured liberal property rights for women, equal guardianship of children, and the right to vote in school-district elections.[128] In 1860 Nichols persuaded the territorial legislature to pass a law that gave women the right to sue or to be sued, independently of their husbands. She argued in 1861 that women should be given the right to vote or be exempted from taxation. That session the legislature passed two laws providing for the relief and protection of widows.[129]

In 1867 the state legislature, choosing "opportunism over racism," according to the historian Michael Goldberg, proposed constitutional amendments granting the vote to African Americans. Samuel Wood, to the dismay of some Republicans, amended that bill to include women. There was then a compromise that the legislature would pass both measures, provided they were submitted to the electorate separately.[130]

Some African-American leaders in Kansas opposed the compromise. Charles Henry Langston, who had met John Brown just before the Harpers Ferry raid and had subsequently moved to Leavenworth to open a grocery store and to crusade for education and rights for blacks, was one of these. The editor of the *Leavenworth Daily Conservative* responded to a Langston petition in 1866 by stating, "We do not think the Negroes do, or should, lay any claim to social equality, nor do we believe that the masses of them are fitted at this time to be invested with all the political privileges accorded to the white people of this country. We do claim, however, that they should be protected in all their natural and civil rights, and should be allowed to enjoy them as fully and freely as we of a fairer complexion." Langston wanted black suffrage to be presented to the electorate without the association with the vote for women. He thought that black suffrage had a better chance than woman suffrage at that time and that the proposition should be merely to strike the word "white" from the voting clause of the Kansas Constitution.[131]

Both suffrage measures were defeated in a general election, but many prominent Kansans supported them. The campaign was an education for the state in women's as well as race issues. Lucy Stone, a leader in the national women's movement, came to Kansas for the initial meeting of the Impartial Suffrage Association, organized by Sam Wood, and stayed for a lecture tour lasting several weeks. "With the help of God and Lucy Stone," Wood said, "we shall carry Kansas. The world moves!" He wrote in the *Emporia News,* "I advocate 'Negro suffrage' not because they are black—not because they are of the male sex, but because they are human beings and entitled to all the rights of other human beings. If women are not human beings, then they are not entitled to the rights of human beings; but if you once raise them above the brute creation and admit them to be human beings, that ends the argument."[132] Nichols was proud that Kansas had the first legislature to propose constitutional female suffrage and noted, "Kansas has already taken a long stride in advance of 'the Fathers' in securing *civil* rights to women." But she also emphasized that "the present government of Kansas is 'bogus' to the women and the blacks of the state" as much as the territorial legislature had been seen as bogus by the Free Staters earlier.[133]

Prominent male politicians and editors in Kansas supported the women's initiative. Charles Robinson, who had been a neighbor of the feminist Lucy Stone in his youth and who was married to the inimitable and well-connected Sara, was, according to a woman who accompanied Stone to Kansas in 1867, "always true as steel upon the woman suffrage question." He once made a tour of the state with Elizabeth Cady Stanton, holding daily meetings on women's rights and throwing all his influence behind the issue.[134] In 1869 Robinson, at the behest of Stone, delivered an address to a national convention on woman suffrage.[135]

Wood was likewise committed. "You have my entire good will on in the matter," Nichols wrote him. "I only felt you could not be a *woman* to feel all I have."[136] Wood persuaded Congressman Sidney Clarke to come out in favor of the suffrage amendment.[137] In 1871 and 1872 he worked hard to establish the eligibility of women for appointments as notaries public and for county superintendents of public instruction, on the grounds that the Constitution did not specifically prohibit it.[138]

Also active among men in the women's cause was Sol Miller, editor of the *Kansas Chief.* Thanking him for his support of the Kansas municipal suffrage bill in 1887, Lucy Stone recalled her visit to Miller and Kansas in 1867. "It is . . . powerlessness," she wrote, "which drives people wild. . . . It will be all the better for Kansas when it gives its women full suffrage."[139]

There was no question that even short of their goal of full enfranchisement, Kansas women used political power and moral suasion well. Their influence was key in advancing the "Kansas Idea" of prohibition of alcohol, which resulted in the Kansas constitutional amendment of 1880. And it should therefore come as no surprise that women influenced the champion of that reform, Governor John St. John. Susan B. Anthony wrote him in 1881 after a visit with St. John and his wife in Kansas: "The trouble is *you've got 'the cart before the horse,'* in Kansas. It should be *women suffrage first,* and after that, Prohibition. . . . *Woman's instinct of self-interest makes her the sworn enemy to the Grog shop, the gambling House and the Brothel*—the great overshadowing trinity that now *legally* rob her of house and home—of Father, Husband and son, yes, and sometimes of Mother, daughter and sister."[140] Charles Eskridge once said, "Next to the grasshopper humbug, in point of damage to the State, is this question of Female Suffrage. It is the most impudent, frivolous, uncalled for proposition ever crammed into the throats of the people by a *shystering* legislature."[141] But folks of that opinion, as political movers in the Sunflower State, were on the way to becoming extinct, with legislative and social results of the utmost significance.

Women traditionally played a large role in churches, and churches thrived in Kansas in the 1870s when establishment replaced mission as the typical mode. The Roman Catholics had a college, St. Benedict's, an abbey, and an impressive accompanying church in Atchison in those years.[142] The Episcopal Church was so well entrenched that Charles Edson charged that there had long been an unholy alliance between that denomination (which he called the "British machine") and the Kansas Republican Party.[143] The Presbyterian Synod of Kansas formed in 1869, and the development of Presbyteries parallels the growth of counties. The Baptists, premier missionaries that they were, increased from 146 to 334 churches during the 1870s and by 1880 had over thirteen thousand members. The Methodists, which became the largest Protestant denomination in Kansas, had fifteen thousand members and 115 churches by 1880, up from 22 churches and four thousand members at the end of the Civil War. The Kansas Conference of the African Methodist Episcopal Church was organized in Ft. Scott in 1876. About two thousand Quakers came to Kansas between 1860 and 1871, and there were four thousand in the Society of Friends in 1880. The Congregationalists founded over 300 churches in the state in the late nineteenth century and developed Washburn College in Topeka and Fairmount College in Wichita.

The Lutheran Church, early plagued by "serious wedges of separation," due to its German connections, thrived particularly in the Smoky Valley area around Lindsborg, led by Olaf Olsson, from Sweden. These Swedes became famous for their yearly performances of the *Messiah* at Bethany College in Lindsborg, but the community itself was really their great creation. Olsson wrote home in 1869, "The view of the prairies is at first lonely. Many who come, despair over this lonely plain, and do not give themselves enough time to dig a hole to observe the rich soil which produces the luxuriant grass." To the practical, however, progress was quick. "It has been wonderful," wrote Olsson, "to see this summer the large planted fields, which a few years ago belonged to buffalo and Indians." These people debated the atonement one hour and fought grasshoppers or subscribed to railroad bonds the next. The Mennonites also had strong ethnic connections and a substantial presence in central Kansas as they were forced out of Russia and recruited by the Santa Fe railroad to buy and farm its lands there in the mid-1870s. Kansas made accommodations for them regarding militia service in order to attract a prosperous and experienced farming population. Like many other denominations, they founded schools, notably Bethel College in Newton. A Jewish congregation appeared in 1857 in Leavenworth, and there were seven Jewish agricultural colonies attempted in Kansas, though there were only about three thousand Jews in the state in 1904.[144] Wichita had a Jewish mayor, Sol Kohn, in 1879, who was also one of its most successful businesspeople.[145]

The ethnic influx of the 1870s, from Volga Germans from Russia building Catholic cathedrals on the plains near Hays to black Exodusters coming from the South and worshipping in dugouts in Graham County, broke the relative social homogeneity of territorial Kansas, even as the emergence of women modified its political monolith.[146] Moreover, it added sturdiness, flexibility, and more alternatives for the future. Noble Prentis noted that these expert farmers, with their unwavering faith in God and wheat, had brought the area around Newton out of the disastrous downturn of the 1873 panic combined with the 1874 Kansas grasshopper invasion and had created a strong community. He saw a Russian farm wagon with a flaring bed painted green, and he had a black man for a German interpreter. Alexanderwohl, Hoffnungsthal, and Gnadenau were towns such as Kansas had never seen, but the crops grew well and the architecture was interesting.[147] The myth of the Turkey Red hard winter wheat that allegedly came in the bag-gage of a small Mennonite girl and by itself saved Kansas agriculture is overdrawn.[148] But the contributions of these industrious people and others like them are not.

Still, above and beyond the political debate, the agricultural explosion, the church building, and the school founding rang the whistle of the locomotive and the hammering of the track crews as the "Steel Nile" flung its branches over the land, planting towns where farmers could shop as it went. It touched all as it flew, it was on every tongue, and it became a kind of mania that would have been tiring had it not presented such continuing thrills.

The true object of the railroad, said Congressman Sidney Clarke in 1865, was not to build a few towns or enrich a few people but to develop an entire region. "Let us make no mistakes in laying the foundations of our new State. We must build upon the immutable laws of industry and production." The initiative and the management should be private, Clarke thought, but bond aid should be forthcoming from towns to support their part of the "connecting links, the web-work, the outlets and inlets of vast national through fares, crowded with the mighty traffic of the continent." The plans for an east–west and north–south grid must be carried out. "We must be equal to our advancing destiny. We must act and act now. . . . Our geographical location is directly in the track of empire."[149]

Company by company, route by route, the isolated track pieces of the 1860s became the rail system of the 1870s. The UPED was the first to bridge the state east to west (1868) along the Smoky Hill River route, with an eventual (1870) extension to Denver. Standing at Ft. Harker (present-day Ellsworth) in 1867, General Hancock told members of the senatorial excursion to the end-of-track on this land-grant railroad that such expeditions as his that year against the western Kansas Indians would shortly be unnecessary, as "this great railroad brings civilization with it, so that when the Rocky Mountains are reached, the wild Indian and the buffalo will have passed away." The Kansas Pacific, as the railroad was called between 1869 and 1880, was never a financial or an operational success, cut off as it was by the front range of the Rockies from the true transcontinental routes, saddled with shoddy construction, and stuck with its role as pioneer in developing a seeming desert country on the high plains of western Kansas. Fewer than 10,000 acres of its 4-million-acre 1866 land grant were occupied when it pushed construction west of Salina in 1867. But as one supporter put it, it

Fifth Street, Leavenworth, Kansas, 1867.
Courtesy of the Kansas State Historical Society.

meant that people in the region "are now in the world and belong to the 'rest of mankind.'" The trim wooden rail station in Wallace, Kansas, at the far western border of the state, dispatching through trains to Denver in the early 1870s, provided a veneer of urban civilization.[150]

The Atchison, Topeka & Santa Fe started construction southwest from Topeka toward New Mexico along the Arkansas River Valley. By the time the Kansas Pacific moved into Colorado in 1870 the Santa Fe system extended only twenty-seven miles.[151] But it made up for lost time spectacularly.

The Santa Fe was the vision and life's work of Cyrus Holliday. It was more important to him even than to Topeka, to which he linked the corporate headquarters in perpetuity in return for a vital early bond issue. It was long a laughingstock, locally and nationally, and, wrote a *Topeka Record* correspondent in 1860, "a prolific theme for prosy disquisitions by the score, upon the drouth, benevolence, railroads."[152] Most people thought it was a mistake when the St. Joseph and Topeka and the Atchison and Topeka merged to form the ATSF and believed that at most in the lifetime of the projectors the road would reach from Topeka, by way of Cottonwood Falls, to the valley of the Arkansas River.[153] But it received a land grant in 1863 and managed, by completing its line across the state late in 1872, to fulfill the construction conditions to develop that vast property.[154]

None promoted Kansas better. C. B. Schmidt went sub rosa into Czarist Russia on behalf of the company to recruit Mennonites and other farmers. Other Santa Fe agents took its literature and land flyers elsewhere. Through the efforts of the company, one reporter recalled, "the name of Kansas soon became as familiar to the household of the German peasant as that of Canaan was to the Israelites in bondage." The company wanted permanent settlers of good morals "and reliable in affairs in business." So important was immigration to Kansas that Schmidt suggested in 1881 that the Kansas prohibition amendment be repealed, as the Germans thought it an act of tyranny against their beloved beer.[155]

In 1881 the Santa Fe road reached California; in 1882 it started building entire engines, the first ever constructed west of the Mississippi, in its two-hundred-thousand-dollar Topeka shops. These shops employed five thousand workers. In 1883 the company built a new office building in Topeka, sprawling on nine lots and designed by architects Burnham and Root of Chicago.[156] Of all the changes since Kansas statehood, none was any more striking than the apotheosis of the ATSF. Charles Gleed thought the history of the company was a "romance" and that "there can never be again in this country such a life as was led by President [William B.] Strong. Strictly within the bounds of civil life, he was yet as free as Columbus to discover new commercial worlds, declare war and wage it, organize and build communities, overturn political powers of long standing, replace old civilizations with new—and do all this asking no men's leave, save those whose money was to be risked."[157]

The road grew beyond Kansas, but its roots there were vital. The purchase and reselling of the Pottawatomie Indian tract was a good boost, as was local bond aid.[158] A "plain and convincing statement" made to the voters of Shawnee, Atchison, Jefferson, Osage, Morris, Lyon, Wabaunsee, and Chase Counties in 1865 for bond aid illustrated the Santa Fe's vision perfectly. The election, the rail promoters said, was "more important to the material interests of these counties than *all* the elections that have hitherto engrossed our attention from the organization of our territory in 1854 down to the present time." The aid was not a donation but an investment. If the counties gave, they would "become rich and populous by the very act of giving: while by refusing to give they remain poor and weak." The company in which the counties would receive stock for their bonds "will stand as first among the great paying enterprises of the day." Interest would need to be paid only by the present generation. By the time principal was due, "a new people able and willing to pay the principal will be occupying the cities originated and built by this great Rail Road or farming the rich lands along its track, made a hundred fold more valuable by the proximity of the Rail Road: or else Kansas will be proven to be unfit for the presence of white men, and will have reverted back to the Indian and the Buffalo." The railroad machine would bring markets "to our very doors" and cause "intelligence to quicken and the whole country to be invested with keen life and energy and money to abound. . . . This is an opportunity that occurs but *once* to a community in its existence."[159]

The Union Pacific, South Branch (which became the Missouri, Kansas & Texas, or "Katy," in 1870) was a less impressive part of the 1860 Kansas plan but key in that it represented the connection of Junction City, Kansas, where the MK&T crossed the KP, with the trade of Texas and the Gulf Coast. After winning a three-way race for the Indian Territory border with the Missouri River, Ft. Scott & Gulf (MRFtS&G) and the Leavenworth, Lawrence & Galveston, the Katy reached Denison, Texas, in 1872.[160] The LL&G and the MRFtSG became substantial local feeders in the eastern tiers of Kansas counties and tempting bases for system builders of the future.[161]

Robert Stevens became general manager of the MK&T in the 1870s. Isaac Goodnow became its land agent. Stevens, supervising from his private car *Prairie Queen,* kept up a correspondence, much of which has survived.

Levi Parsons, the Katy president, depended on Stevens to organize and push. "Things seem to be in much confusion at Parsons," he wrote late in 1870. "Goodnow does not seem to know how to handle the matter. . . . I think you had better go over there and take charge."[162] Stevens could assure squatters at Parsons, the president wrote, "that we will take up track & lay it ten miles from there & not stop any trains for them before we will submit to their actions."[163] In July, with the heat ranging up to 108 degrees ("think how the iron must burn"), Stevens pushed the crews to lay one mile of track a day.[164] On reaching the Indian Territory border and winning the race to get the single north–south right-of-way allowed by treaty through the Indian Territory and for the grant of state lands, Stevens wrote his wife, "You ought to read the comments of Kansas Press on me now, and compare them with those of *1862* [when Stevens was criticized in connection with the Robinson bond/impeachment scandal]. (Such is life.) I only wish you were here with me. Life is stirring, but very lonely." To his son Freddie he described his railroad car, with beds, writing desk, kitchen, and water closets. "Tell mother her boy will be home soon, but is very black and tanned up."[165]

Stevens clearly recognized that what was a miracle one day would be a commonplace the next and that he would soon be struggling with land leagues and political attacks on railroad rates from the people who had been crying for the lines at any cost a few years earlier. Kansas politicians, led by Congressman John Anderson, conducted a crusade in the 1870s and early 1880s, first in agitating for the patenting and taxation of railroad land grants in the state and then in trying to create a state agency to regulate railroad rates and practices. A regional railroad speech in 1873 noted that "we want the train to go thundering through every county . . . but wish its shrieking whistle may sound to the citizen as a note of rejoicing and not as a beast of prey."[166]

Stevens struggled with "land grangers," who, he thought, "are soon to control several of these western states" and whose "chief antagonism is against railroad companies."[167] Even M. W. Reynolds, the hand-picked editor of the *Parsons Sun,* whose costs were paid by the Katy railroad, "adopted the 'Grangers' theory'" in 1873. Consequently, Reynolds began paying his own rent and railroad fare.[168] Meanwhile, Stevens was irritated by the people applying for free passes on the excuse that they were viewing lands to buy. "If we were to give gentlemen who proposed to ship freight over our line, free passage, we could keep two or three coach loads on every train, and if it was understood that every man who wanted to examine or look for land, could ride free, we would have a million land hunters between Hannibal & Denison in less than 30 days."[169]

The panic of 1873 did not help. Stevens met with T. J. Peter of the ATSF about the low earnings of their two roads and difficulties with customers and shippers. The Katy spent one hundred thousand dollars in cash for land ads in Kansas in 1873, and, Stevens wrote early in 1874, "it remains to be seen whether it was a good investment or not." Sales of land were only about two hundred thousand dollars that year. A few smaller roads might go bankrupt. "It seems to me that our prospects are not quite so dark, although it may be like the boy who kept whistling through the grave yard to keep up his courage."[170]

Stevens summed up the changes to Levi Parsons late in 1872: "You say very truly 'the American people are too apt to take great results as mere necessities and that those who labor the hardest and most continuously, frequently receive the least commendation and are soon forgotten.' Yet why should we complain?"[171] Why indeed? There were ups and downs, but by 1880 Kansas had over three thousand miles of railroad track constructed by forty companies, forming a system as coordinated as open competition allowed.[172]

Sometimes musical pieces are said to be idiomatic to a certain instrument —Chopin's nocturnes, for example, to the nineteenth-century piano, or Bach's polyphony to the harpsichord. In that sense the cattle trade in Kansas was idiomatic to the railroad. Joseph McCoy's idea of creating traffic for the new Kansas railroads on their return haul by concentrating Texas longhorns at a created town with services for cowboys was not an idea that everyone grasped immediately as promising.[173] He was thrown out of the offices of the Pacific Railroad of Missouri, partly because of his rough looks and partly because the complacent denizens of the city of St. Louis felt no need for his entrepreneurial scheme. The UPED, with its Chicago connections, was friendlier, and in 1868 McCoy was able to establish the tiny town of Abilene as a terminus for the cattle drives. These drives had been taking advantage of free Indian Territory grass, semiwild but tough longhorn cattle, ethnically mixed drovers, and eastern demand for beef since the end of the Civil War in drives to such points as Sedalia, Missouri, or Baxter Springs, Kansas. The MK&T reached northern Texas in the early 1870s, but being the sole line out of Texas to the north, its rates were high. Beeves worth three dollars a head on the Texas range brought fifteen dollars in Kansas and could bring twenty-five dollars a head after fattening and shipping on the railroad to the packinghouses.

The problem in the successive Kansas cattle centers of Abilene, Wichita, Ellsworth, Caldwell, and Dodge City was controlling vice and violence and reconciling a large transient, young, and male population with a permanent family and agricultural frontier. The farmers and ranchers of the state were understandably distraught at the prospect of roving herds trampling their crops, not to mention infecting their blooded cattle with "Spanish fever," a type of pneumonia carried by ticks and not affecting the longhorns. They were also disturbed at the increases in prices and interest rates in the cattle towns, the perceived discrimination against them by merchants, and the temptation for the towns to finance their limited governmental needs through the promotion of and taxation of vice.

There was a yearly struggle in Kansas over the quarantine line, behind

The end of the track for the Union Pacific, Eastern Division, in western Kansas, 1867.
Courtesy of the Kansas State Historical Society.

which Texas cattle could not be driven during the disease season. Its course regularly eliminated aspiring cattle towns due to the lobbying of their growing farm and ranch population. Natural growth in and around the towns also destroyed the open prairie that was necessary to hold the Texas cattle until the early autumn heat broke and rail shipment could begin. There were moral issues, too. People in Abilene objected to the lifelike genitalia shown on the sign at the Bull's Head Saloon on Texas Street, and they objected to the atmosphere of drunken violence, however well it might be controlled by the likes of Wild Bill Hickok as peace officers. The Dickinson County Farmers' Protective Association protested many aspects of the trade, despite the dollar gain to the community. Wichita, where the trade moved in 1872, had its Wyatt Earp, its policy of compensating farmers for damages without question, and its isolation of the leavings of sin in the township of Delano across the Arkansas River by toll bridge from the city proper. But the trade there also engendered an active Patrons of Husbandry (Grange) boycott movement against local merchants and bankers and a banking scandal, due to too many cattle deals, which ruined one of the town's leading lights.

Despite modest actual gunplay statistics and strict gun control laws, the cattle towns could not avoid the fascination dime novelists had with the whole genre and the consequent exaggerated and not-so-desirable reputations these Kansas towns enjoyed in the East as "wild, woolly, and wicked" places. W. E. Webb described the herders that frequented these places as "a distinctive and peculiar class . . . in appearance a species of centaur, half horse, half man, with immense rattling spurs, tanned skin, and dare-devil almost ferocious faces. . . . A majority of these herders would think no more of snuffing out a life than of snuffing out a candle."[174] Reporters were much more interested in the mud wrestling and the "Race of the Amazons," involving betting on prostitutes running in the nude, than they were in the low tax rate and booming grocery and boot business. "Wichita especially," wrote one paper, "is a most abandoned place—a sort of pandemonium where the offscourings of humanity have congregated as harpies to feed upon the moral and physical being of Texas shippers." Wilson Purdy, who was trying to get a start in agriculture in the region, wrote of Wichita in the early 1870s, "I would not live there for a good-sized farm."[175]

The cattle era was brief in Kansas. The progress of the ATSF westward and the tribes in eastern Indian Territory beginning to tax cattle herds pushed the trade westward in the 1880s and eventually killed it, though not without a famous last blooming at Dodge City. But it was profitable, showing what railroads and towns coordinating a business could do; it had a romantic appeal in generating more of that kind of publicity that Kansas probably did not need; and it influenced Kansans in their thinking about morality and economics. That prohibition found such fertile ground in Kansas may be due as much to a decade of experience with the effects of unregulated liquor consumption in the cattle towns as to the lobbying of women and churches.

The Long Drive and the Chisholm Trail were not all the Iron Horse wrought for Kansas. Perhaps most important were the towns along their rights-of-way and the agricultural hinterland their wheat- and corn-hauling capacity engendered. Kansas with railroads was a place tied to markets. It was a region where agriculture could become specialized and commercial, focusing on plants, like wheat, that thrived best in its climate, and using the new agricultural machinery, shipped in by the railroads, to farm larger acreages faster. Land sales and development became a business and a science.

The firm of Alexander Case and Levi Billings in Marion, Kansas, sold thousands of acres, not only to people immigrating to Kansas to farm but to the agents of William Scully, a wealthy Irishman, who by 1900 owned over two hundred thousand acres, much of it in Kansas, the largest farm acreage in one person's hands in the United States. Scully made his first Kansas purchase in 1870 and invested heavily thereafter, so heavily that he was a factor in the state's 1890s legislation against alien land ownership.[176]

Not every owner studied the prospects for agriculture as carefully as Scully, but the surviving records of Case and Billings for the 1870s reveal that real estate firms communicated the stakes of farming as a business to potential owners very carefully. Alexander Case at first sold sewing machines on the side but found land sales at an average of about $5.50 an acre in the relatively moist central part of the state a full-time affair.[177] Marion Centre, he wrote one client in 1876, had two banks, five general stores, one grocery and crockery store, two drugstores, one millinery, one furniture, one hardware, one harness shop, a wagon shop, two blacksmiths, a livery stable, and two meat markets, among other attractions. "There is a great body of first rate land [that] can be had very cheap. A splendid chance for a fellow and there are good openings for business."[178]

For the small Kansas farmer and merchant in the 1870s, however, it was a struggle. Abram Backus, who farmed with a mortgage from Hiram Hill in Clay County, and James Sands, who ran a business in Lawrence with loans from Hill, kept up a running correspondence through the 1870s with their boss and benefactor in Williamsburg, Massachusetts. These letters reveal the quotidian pattern of tentative development, rural and urban.

Backus, farming near Clay Center, reported in 1870 sowing twenty acres of wheat and the same in corn and potatoes, all fenced. "We have plenty of everything to live on but fruit, but we have got used to that and don't miss it so much."[179] Later, things looked considerably worse. During the panic of 1873, he wrote that farm prices were poor. Corn was worth twenty-five cents a bushel, wheat seventy-five cents, and potatoes one dollar, "but it is most impossible to get money for anything."[180] The next year the grasshoppers came, and Backus wrote, "I have struggled hard to gain an honest living but have never succeeded in laying up anything for a dark day." The grasshoppers ate his crop, and he had no corn or potatoes or garden, only a little pork. He asked Hill too for an extension of his loan—"hope you can bear with me another season."[181]

It was the same for many other ordinary farmers. Daniel Warden in Osborne County wrote in summer 1874: "Sometimes I almost give up but you know my fortitude is Elastic even if my Patience is mostly exhausted."[182] But by winter he was more desperate, writing that he was "actually afraid myself and Children will parish [*sic*]. . . . It may seem absurd to make sutch [*sic*] a Statement, but it is absolutely the truth, and there is scarcely a cow or any four fotted [*sic*] Beast that is fit to Eat but has been killed, and them that had no stock has killed the first animal they come to, the buffalo are too far out to get any, and we have not got a team in the Co. that could haul a load of meat two miles."[183] Howard Ruede, whose journal of life in a dugout in late 1870s Osborne County was published as *Sod House Days,* benefited from increased wheat prices brought about by the Russo-Turkish War. But he still had to get by in a dugout constructed for $10.05 and found bacon so beyond his means "that we are often vegetarians perforce."[184]

That struggle was not reflected in the official agricultural propaganda for Kansas. An 1874 broadside for Chase County, in the center of the tall-grass cattle-grazing country of the Flint Hills, was sanguine about the agricultural future. The southwest slopes of the region could be farmed and the "finest of grass, indigenous to this country" would support ranching royally. "The fallacy that Kansas suffers from drouth is now so completely exploded that a denial of it is unnecessary. . . . Stagnant water is not to be found, and a stiff breeze is always in motion during the summer months, invigorating the system and rendering outdoor labor during the warmest season of the year pleasant and agreeable." For "young men with small means and willing hands," Chase County was said to be a paradise. "Here you can have the great unsettled commons for stock to range upon that costs you nothing except a little looking after. . . . Why not come to it, own a few stock and help graze it down, and thus make wealth out of that which is now, every fall, committed to the destructive element known as prairie fire."[185]

James Sands illustrates urban struggles. Sands started a saddle and harness making shop in Lawrence, with "Indian goods" as a sideline. He felt the pinch of 1873 also. "In common with all business men," he wrote in October, "I am *prospectively* hard up. Like many others my fall stock remains unsold." He asked for an extension on his loan.[186] Santa Claus, he wrote December 26, "seems to feel the panic, judging by his conduct here yesterday, but having established with us a good reputation we will accord to him the same latitude we claim for ourselves."[187] Things were still tight in 1875. "I cover my face with shame and mortification at not being able to remit today." But he was working on a large government contract for Indian supplies.[188]

It was not until 1877 that Sands reported making profits.[189] Even then there were reverses. In 1878 he could not pay his debt to Hill because of tremendous rains. "We have *stood still*, in a business point, now *three* months, with an uninterrupted run of mud to such an extent that communication with the country is principally by horseback. In many cases corn is still ungathered [in February] & where in shock almost impossible to reach it. So with an enormous crop of Hogs, corn & c, in the hands of our farmers yet unable to reach the market suspends trade more completely than I ever saw." Three of Lawrence's five banks had closed.[190] Sands could not stabilize his business until the early 1880s, when he added hardware and numerous patent devices of his own invention to his saddlery business.[191]

There were a few glimmers, to be sure, of something more. The Kansas wheat crop in 1870 was less than 2.5 million bushels. In 1880, it was 25 million and was to be 35 million by 1890. Kansas hard winter wheat was particularly adapted to the new roller mill technology of the 1880s.[192] Petroleum remained a possible winner, and so did lead and zinc. Natural gas was largely flamed in "fire fountains" in the 1870s—a "freak of nature, or . . . an interesting sort of plaything," an editor called it—but it would not be long before it would power towns and industries.[193] Salt discoveries, combined with the technology of mining, separation, and distribution, made that industry a possibility for future growth—a growth that was realized in the next decade. However, the great salt discovery at Hutchinson did not come until 1887.[194] Strip coal mining had been a Kansas business for some time, but the first coal shaft was not sunk until 1874, and the business peaked in the 1880s with the development of machinery for mining.[195] Lead and zinc in southeast Kansas were found at shallow depths. In 1877 the mines started using horsepower and a more sophisticated system called a "whim," which allowed a horse, attached to a sweep, to gain leverage by powering a drum around which a rope was passed. The next year a geared horse hoister appeared, as well as a windlass. And new technology came into the separating of ore from waste. In 1881 came a sophisticated mill at Empire City for the crushing and cleaning of the ore. It was powered by steam and had a capacity of fifty tons in twelve hours. In 1879 the Galena Lead and Zinc Company built the first modern refinery in the state for the reduction of lead ore into pig lead. These developments, too, reached critical mass only in the 1880s.[196]

The hard times brought intimations of reform, which seemed for a time simply to mean changing the currency to help debtors and excoriating the railroads and their rates. "You ought to hear the *grangers* squeal," a correspondent wrote to Eugene Ware in 1874. "They like to go for *reform* when it does not touch their own pockets."[197] The railroads that depression year provided seed wheat to help settlers, but the legislature in a special session decided that constitutional scruples prevented it from doing anything other than authorizing a few counties without railroad debt to issue relief bonds.[198] In 1875 George Martin took the risk of publishing D. W. Wilder's *Annals of Kansas*, which gave reformers not only a compendium of history on which to build but also a load of political information and statistics on which to base proposals for change.[199]

The reform movement gained strength, not just from the hard times that seemed to provide a cause for complaint but from the better times, which created a revolution of rising expectations and the leisure to contemplate the alternatives the new tax wealth created for a legislature. One correspondent, sitting in the office of the chief attorney of the Santa Fe railroad, wrote state legislator Ware in 1880 expressing concern over the lack of appreciation from Kansans for the benefits such relatively untrammeled capitalism had brought them. He celebrated what he considered "the subjugation through you of the sporadic partisan, communism, socialism & c that were comprehended in the opposition & which have always seemed to flourish in the air of this District."[200]

But it was not only in the southeast that the radical tune was sung at the turn of the new decade. A tenant farmer wrote in 1879, "Still the old flame of reform is blazing in my boosum as it did when we used to get togather to reform meetings and labord so earnestly for that caus [*sic*]."[201] "Two things hurt us," wrote the tenant farmer William Roe near Vinland to his landlord W. C. Howard in 1879, "our heavy bonded debt and high R.R. rates with the power to put up or down at their pleasure." The local Grange, he added, was prosperous and had completed a new hall costing nine hundred dollars.[202]

Towns were not immune from the hurt and the reform impulse. Lawrence, despite its railroad planning and some early success under the aegis of Lane, entered in the 1870s a period that the historian I. E. Quastler called "years of bonds and sorrow." Lawrence was no Quindaro, but it was no Kansas City, either. The community was disappointed with its rail connections and oppressed by railroad bond debt. Towns like Lawence, wrote an editor there in 1873, were "now paying in sorrow the onerous tax for what they supposed was to be an immense benefit, but which turned out to be no benefit at all." By the late 1870s the tone was harsher still. "The monopolists of money and of freight cars gobble the products and leave to the producers of all this wealth only a meager subsistence. We have taxed ourselves to the verge of ruin to build railroads and *given* them into the hands of *private corporations* whose only aim seems to be to extort from the people the utmost penny they can for every service they perform."[203] Efforts were made in court to renege on the debt, and then came a series of meetings with the railroads to create a compromise. The hard truth was that Lawrence simply could not pay. The bonded debt of Douglas County that year for railroads was $854,250, for school district bonds $10,100, for all purposes of the City of Lawrence $464,000. There were township bonds in addition, bringing the debt total to over $1 million on a property evaluation of less than $5 million.[204]

As Kansas boomed in the 1880s, its residents reflected on the hard times they had passed through and that would return. They thought ever more seriously about the nature of the good life and found there was more to it than railroads.

TOWARD A BRIGHTER DAY

H. M. Hoxie, vice president of the Missouri Pacific Railroad, tele-graphed Kansas governor John Martin on March 9, 1885: "A mob has control of our Engines, Trains, Shops and Round House at Atchison and Parsons, and our men are powerless to move our passenger and freight trains and do the business of the Company." He asked the intervention of the state in a strike caused by a sudden 10 percent reduction in wages and the cutting of work hours for shopmen.[1]

That much was standard procedure. What was surprising was that Martin hesitated, saying that the strikers seemed peaceful and that the state militia should be used only as a last resort.[2] His response may have been based in part on political savvy. Governor George Anthony had intervened quickly with the militia in a Santa Fe shopmen's walkout in Topeka and Emporia in 1878 and garnered so much enmity from the friends of the strikers that some observers thought it cost him the next election.[3] But Martin's response grew also from his temperament and his view of the state's changing priorities. "I have seen enough of war and its horrors, and would prefer to spend the remainder of my life in a land at peace with itself and the world."[4]

Martin thought there should be alternatives. Kansas had operated a Board of Railroad Commissioners since 1883 to adjudicate rates and railway practices through moral suasion. And at the behest of the Knights of Labor, it created a Bureau of Labor in the same month that the strike broke out, March 1885. That bureau was to collect industrial and labor statistics, with a view toward applying public pressure on injustices.[5] Martin asked the Board of Railroad Commissioners to arbitrate the Missouri Pacific strike.[6] In a second strike the next spring he personally met with the strikers and company representatives and, in conjunction with the governor of Missouri, brought about a resolution. That time there was more violence and taking of property, and Martin had to call in the militia when local authorities lost control of the situation.[7] In both incidents, however, he praised the strikers for their restraint and good sense and was critical of the railroad for its arbitrary action and reluctance to negotiate. "They are employees," Martin wrote Hoxie in 1885, "as any private citizen would be glad to have. Their character and intelligence deserves respect and consideration. . . . I appeal to you to abandon any purpose of provoking a collision, if you entertain it."[8]

It was not a radical stance, but it was comparatively liberal, and it fit the times. In 1885 Kansas had just experienced a Democratic governor, George Glick, and had passed a good deal of mildly interventionist legislation. Martin's implementation, therefore, fitted a trend. "Is it true," wrote one worker, "that a people incur God's displeasure when they permit Labor to be oppressed and defrauded; and his vengeance when they permit it to be robbed, degraded and enslaved? . . . Is it putting it too strong to say that Labor is now the mud-sill which supports the entire superstructure of our immense modern civilization?" If so, the union man said, it was time for state government to help unions lift it out of the mud.[9] Out of their correspondence and Martin's thinking came an articulated theory of the role of the state in the economy that represented substantial change.

Martin wrote to the history and political science professor James Canfield at the University of Kansas, who had caused a ruckus among conservatives in the state with his advocacy of free trade, that the strike experience convinced him "that it is vitally important to provide some legal measures or authority through which differences of this character may be settled. The railroad companies and their employees are not the only parties to be considered. The public, whose business is interrupted, whose commerce and travel are impeded, has rights which must be protected." The time was "near at hand," Martin claimed, when state authority must be invoked to protect working people, just as the new State Board of Railroad Commissioners adjudicated damage claims and arguments over freight charges. "How much more important is it that honest, industrious and intelligent mechanics and working men should have a right to appeal to the State for protection against the greed or rapacity of these great and arbitrary corporate powers?"[10]

There was a mood of intervention in the interest of society. Shortly after the settlement of the 1885 strike, Martin announced the establishment of a

State Board of Health and a policy to outlaw racial segregation in the state orphans' home.[11] On the labor front, he signed a law creating a means for arbitration through petitioning the district court in each county, which would then set up a tribunal with labor and management representatives to hear labor cases. This legislation lasted only one year, but Kansas was not through with such experiments.[12]

Former governor Charles Robinson filled the regional press in the late 1870s with his ideas about the proper relationship between the state and the people, with great emphasis on the power of the people. During the national railroad strikes of 1877, Robinson wrote that any discussion that failed to see that the railroads were the aggressors was misguided. "The largest and most lawless money interest in this country is the railroad interest. It has walked over the people like a remorseless and tyrannical giant defying the general government, the State governments and the people; it has bribed, bullied, brow beaten, and bombarded every popular interest until men despaired of any remedy or relief. At last the worm, tired of being trodden upon, has turned."[13]

Many people agreed. "Kansas has taken the lead on many questions," the *Topeka Commonwealth* editorialized, "but on few more important than this, an impartial Executive coming in between the contending forces and arbitrating a peace in favor of the laboring class."[14] The *Kansas Farmer*, the official organ of the State Agricultural Society, wrote during the 1886 strike, "A bayonet has no satisfying power. Away down at the bottom of this movement the men are right and the railroad company is wrong." It expressed strong sympathy with the workers: "They stand with sweated face and bare arms while the millionaires rush by with the speed of wind . . . and they see no hope for the poor man except in counter organizations. . . . The people might as well make up their minds to face a revolution, for one is coming."[15]

There were incidents during the strikes that frightened the public. This was partly because the Missouri Pacific strike was the type that would later be called a sit-down strike, where strikers tried to control the equipment belonging to the railroad in order to prevent the response of simply firing them all. That was strictly and legally a confiscation of property. To railroad officials, Martin's actions were weak and wrong. "It is a matter of wonder to us," one of them wrote him in 1886, "that for a space of nearly three weeks a mob should defy the authority of the peace officers in several important towns in this State. It is all right for these men to stop work whenever they please and by all peaceful means induce others to do so, but the moment they lay their hands on property that does not belong to them or by force prevent other men from working . . . they are in a condition of anarchy."[16] Even when Terence Powderly of the Knights and Jay Gould of the Missouri Pacific called off the national strike, local people experienced problems. On March 30, 1886, a railroad attorney reported that the strike was "more formidable and vicious than ever" and that there was a one-thousand-strong "mob" at Atchison. "The people are afraid to appear as witnesses or to identify the wrong-doers, and we are powerless to prosecute."[17] The next day men attacked shops in Atchison, and in Parsons they slapped the sheriff in the face and spit on him.[18] A Law and Order League formed in Parsons to protect the town after the militia was withdrawn.[19]

Still, the tendency at the statehouse remained toward tolerance and arbitration and against automatic intervention on behalf of property interests. The Kansas Board of Railroad Commissioners noted that "strikes are exceedingly wasteful methods of obtaining redress of grievances" but that there were legitimate labor grievances that should be redressed somehow.[20] Senator Preston Plumb believed that "Mr. Hoxie was an irritable person anyhow" and that Martin had done well.[21] Martin's statements and strike actions in 1885 were only the beginning of a decade-and-a-half-long swing to the left in Kansas, in social as well as in economic affairs, played out in the best and the worst of times.

The 1880s in Kansas were boom times of far more than ordinary import. The 1,268,530 people recorded by the 1885 state census in Kansas were nine times as many as were there in 1865, and up from less than 1 million in 1880 and about .5 million in 1875.[22] Population peaked in 1888 with 1,518,552, an increase of 20 percent in three years.[23] That population was not reached again until 1904.[24] Wichita was for a time during the 1880s the fastest growing city in the United States. It was third in the nation in volume of real estate transactions, regardless of population. Topeka was tenth, ahead of San Francisco, Detroit, and Cleveland.[25]

The editor of the *Oberlin Eye* wrote in 1888 that Kansas was indebted to real estate agents for what it became in those days. "Large-brained, clear-eyed, strong to plan and to do, a well-stored mind, the Kansas land agent is surely one of the beloved. The Missouri land man paints fences, barns and outhouses on the roads leading to his village; the Kansas man takes out a full-page advertisement in his local paper, a column or two of reading

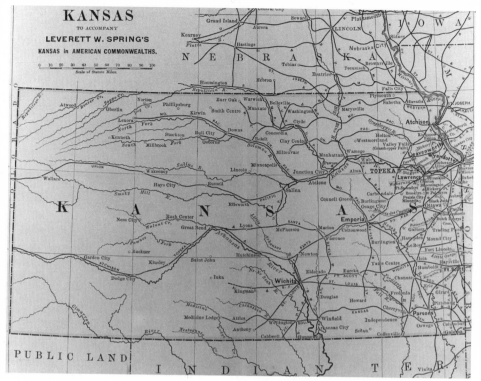

Map of Kansas, 1885. Taken from Leverett Wilson Spring's Kansas: The Prelude to the War for the Union. *Wichita State University Libraries, Department of Special Collections.*

notices, and orders a thousand extra copies of them broadcast through the East. . . . He lies? Perhaps. But the noblest liar of them all hangs his head in shame, in a few short years—mayhap months—the lies he told are so far below the truth Kansas progress makes possible."[26]

The railroad system blossomed into a world-beating plethora of convenient lines. To the core trunk lines of the 1870s were added in the 1880s the prominent systems of the Missouri Pacific and the Chicago, Rock Island and Pacific. The Missouri Pacific reached the west line of Kansas late in 1887 and soon provided an alternative route to Colorado, terminating at Pueblo. The Rock Island built over 1,000 miles in Kansas between 1886 and 1889, crisscrossing its southwest section.[27] In 1886 there were 950 miles of railroad built in Kansas, and the next year 1,680. Eight hundred miles more were added in 1888, bringing the total mileage near 9,000. The Board of Railroad Commissioners was amazed: "We doubt whether in the whole history of railroad building in this county, a parallel in rapidity of extension of her system of railroads can be found in any other state to the example now furnished by Kansas." Railroad building kept employment and real estate values up, leading to "unwonted prosperity." The only concern was the level of local bond aid and the possible fragility of the bubble.[28]

The idea that rain follows the plow seemed proved in the wet cycle of the mid-1880s. Land offices in western Kansas were packed with people. An 1887 railroad report claimed, "The universal belief, which until within a very recent period prevailed, that the whole west half of the State could never be utilized for any purposes of production, except the growth of wild or native grasses upon which to graze domestic herds . . . has gradually given way to the conviction . . . that climatic conditions favorable to agriculture are surely being established throughout the region."[29] Ditch irrigation from the Arkansas River helped, as did experimental farms established by railroads and the federal agricultural establishment to demonstrate grains and trees that might thrive in the high plains environment. Towns and railroads kept printing presses busy with purple descriptions. In 1887 the Garden City land office had over 16,000 homestead entries involving over 1.5 million acres of land. In western counties a doubling of population year to year during the mid- and late 1880s was common, and many reached their peak population of all time during that era.

So significant was the growth of western Kansas that there was a movement in the 1880s in favor of its secession from the rest of the state, or at least to recognize industrial reality over territorial history by moving the capital of Kansas to Wichita. T. B. Murdock of the *El Dorado Times* wrote, "Not all the virtue of the party is centered in a half-dozen pot-bellied politicians nor can all the brains of the party be found in a half-dozen counties bordering on the Missouri river."[30] A sorghum sugar industry for the west emerged for a time, and towns the size of Dodge City and smaller promoted colleges and streetcar lines. "Enthusiasm," wrote a chagrined Wichita booster from the perspective of later years, "is the temporary idiocy of a man who, on ordinary occasions, has common horse sense."[31]

The bust was as painful as the boom had been stimulating. Drought and depression in the 1890s severely inhibited the growth of Kansas and in the west rolled it back with a vengeance. The weather turned consistently dry, railroad debt became as much a biblical burden as the grasshoppers, and bitterness led to political backlash. Over one-third of the Kansas railroad

The family of Mennonite Abraham Bekker, Marion County, 1883.
Courtesy of the Kansas State Historical Society.

system was by 1888 operating at a net loss.[32] In 1890 only eighty-five miles of railroad were built in Kansas. "The prevalence of drought and hot winds . . . and the general financial depression," a state official wrote, "have produced a condition decidedly unfavorable to the profitable operation of railroads."[33] In 1892 Kansas was still third in the nation in rail mileage, and railroad corporations there employed over twenty-seven thousand Kansans.[34] But expectations had exceeded reality by a painful margin.

The boom and bust, said one analyst, was "only one of the many instances of overmomentum in western ambition and energy. . . . Every city, county and hamlet in Kansas has had one or two railroad projects in hand continuously, to which they offered all that the law would allow them to give, and often more. . . . Not content, those with one road wanted two, and those with two were clamorous for more."[35] Most people saw that but wondered what could have been different. Marshall Murdock of the *Wichita Eagle* noted that "the lurch to ruin" was "violent and maddening" but that the town that never got a second or third railroad often disappeared altogether.[36]

As in the boom, in the bust statistics told a story, this time a sadder one. Kansas in 1891 had 1,338,811 people, down by over 179,000, or about 11 percent. It was worse in some of the cities. Leavenworth dropped from 35,227 in 1888 to 20,802 in 1892.[37] Wichita by 1892 lost one-third of its peak boom population of over 33,000 (up from 5,000 in 1880), and about 50 percent of its assessed valuation. Like many towns, it had invested in street paving, railroad bonds, and public buildings. The fixed debt upped the mill levy in the 1890s, worsening the downward spiral and leaving many residential palaces to renters or weeds.[38]

Kos Harris, the Wichita attorney and historian, wrote in the 1890s that if on the festive evening of July 4, 1887, "an absolutely true and correct horoscope of Wichita ten years hence could have been shown us, the drug stores would have run short of arsenic, prussic acid, antimony, strychnine, hemlock, hellebore, nightshade, belladonna, aconite, laudanum and all kindred poisons."[39] But the optimists had no such foresight, and the decade of the 1880s had begun with unmixed hope and a strong feeling that the workings of the economy could bring to Kansas the means for realizing the better world its practical idealists imagined. Perhaps they could implement an Earthly Kingdom without waiting for the Second Coming.

It was appropriate that the eighth state governor of Kansas was named St. John: the two administrations of John St. John (1879–1883) were every bit as much a religious crusade as a political program. St. John made no secret that his interest was in improved morality, beginning with passage and enforcement of a prohibition amendment.[40] "Our covenant touching this matter is with the Lord," he said, "and we propose to complete the good work."[41] He would rather be right, St. John emphasized, "though it cost a defeat, than to gain victory at the expense of being wrong. . . . I am not now, nor have I ever been, a politician in the sense of pulling wires and packing primaries."[42] When asked for printed copies of his temperance speeches, St. John could not send them, for he never used even notes on his Sunday tours of the state. He spoke extemporaneously and from the heart, depending upon sincerity to carry him.[43]

The initial opportunity for St. John to put the stamp of his personality and priorities on the reputation of the State of Kansas, however, did not have to do with temperance but with the Exoduster movement. Blacks were escaping the South at the end of Reconstruction with hope of finding independence and respect on homesteads in Kansas. To Kansas, the mass movement presented a considerable refugee problem.

The outline of events is as simple as it was dramatic.[44] In 1876 there was a close election for president and some political dealing. The Republicans put Rutherford Hayes in the White House. In turn, the Democrats gained an agreement that Republicans would back off from the military occupation of the South and the radical advancement of Reconstruction legislation promoting African-American voting rights and equality in accommodations. Consequently, it was no surprise that after 1876 there was a migration away from the South by blacks. Although there was much debate about the extent to which these people were migrating west to escape actual persecution as contrasted to seeking economic opportunity, it was always the view of Kansas leaders that the situation for them in the South was genuinely oppressive and that to welcome them to Kansas was a humanitarian act. It was also the view of the St. John faction in Kansas that accepting the black exodus was in the tradition of Kansas and would eventually prove beneficial.

There were two phases to the migration. The first was associated with two black leaders: Henry Adams, a "faith doctor" from Louisiana, and Benjamin "Pap" Singleton, a carpenter and coffin maker from Tennessee. Singleton visited Kansas in 1873, and in fall 1876 the black town of Nicodemus in Graham County was established with the cooperation of W. R. Hill, a white minister and speculator. There were also two black colonies in Hodgeman County. Though these colonists were poor (one man who later became a prosperous farmer started by breaking an acre of prairie for wheat with a spade), they had more resources than the next wave, which came in larger numbers on riverboats and congregated in Topeka dormitories in 1879 and 1880.

F. W. Giles, an early resident and historian of Topeka, estimated that seven thousand blacks reached that city by August 1, 1879, and that one hundred to three hundred a week arrived steadily thereafter. At one time, Giles estimated, the population of Topeka was close to 30 percent African American, congregated in a section called Tenneseetown. Many had had "a vague knowledge" since the mid-1850s "that somewhere on the broad earth was a place known as Kansas, and they fancied that in some way the question of their emancipation was connected with it."[45]

But what was Kansas to do with them? "Persons of limited intelligence are often not unlike unreasoning animals," one person exclaimed, "in the way of following blindly on a given direction in which they have been started, like a flock of sheep jumping over a fence. The migration of the blacks having begun, it is not easy to tell where it will end. Something much like a panic

Exodusters at Floral Hall, Topeka, July 5, 1879.
Courtesy of the Kansas State Historical Society.

seems to have set in."[46] The *Kansas Pioneer* in Wyandotte called the exodus a "Dusty Stream," a "stampede . . . like a flock of frightened sheep, or a drove of insane swine."[47] Giles, sympathetic enough, was, however, awestruck and frightened by the situation of people "without quarters, without subsistence," who stood along the banks of the Mississippi by the hundreds to be shipped West by steamboat as "fourth-class freight."[48] Wrote a Leavenworth reporter, "Is Kansas a grand asylum for decrepit and destitute blacks?"[49]

Kansans generally rejected the suggestion of turning these people away. The dual solution was, first, to turn over the administration of relief to a private charity. This was done through the Kansas Freedman's Relief Association, supported by well-wishers nationwide and run by a Quaker woman from Chicago, Elizabeth Comstock. The second part of the plan was to distribute the new emigrants around the state so that no community would be required to absorb more than a portion. Governor St. John, speaking from the stage of the Topeka Opera House to a great crowd on Sunday, April 20, 1879, was hopeful that an emigration of "many years" could be handled in this way.

There were hitches in that program, the main one being prejudice. There was a proclamation by the Wyandotte mayor threatening legal action against individuals bringing black migrants into the town.[50] Atchison and Leavenworth did everything possible to divest themselves of the blacks as soon as they unloaded from the steamboats.[51] When the relief association assigned a group of blacks to Wichita in 1879, the city council sent them back to Topeka on the official grounds that they might be diseased. *Eagle* editor Murdock wrote, "If the women understood house work and the men ordinary labor several hundred could find employment in this section, but they seem entirely ignorant of any work, except that of cotton raising and picking and sugar planting." When criticized by the *Topeka Commonwealth*, Murdock suggested that his interlocutor's brains were "the product of a cross between a Zulu wench and a striped hyena."[52] When Newton, thirty miles to the north, criticized Wichita, Murdock responded, "Had we known sooner that Newton was losing sleep for the want of a whiff of the exodusters we would have acted more promptly, but as soon as we found it out, application was made to the large tender-hearted Topeka committee on her behalf."[53] Despite their mean welcome in some quarters, Giles remembered that "few could be induced to go anywhere but to Kansas, and on they came."[54]

Robert Athearn has concluded that St. John was "more concerned over ideological than practical matters." But it was definitely St. John who tipped the balance on the issue with his eloquent sincerity.[55] His outgoing correspondence, preserved intact in letterpress books, is filled with the shape of the daily administration of a moral initiative. Kansas, he wrote to a minister in Illinois in January 1880, had received and cared for at least fifteen thousand black refugees in the past few months, and it was a new state without the resources of Illinois to do so. The point, he said, was "not so much to give bread to these poor people as to secure for them an opportunity to earn it."[56] Yes, he wrote a black man from Indiana, you may run your business here (he enclosed a report from the State Board of Agriculture), and, no, the motivation of Kansas was not political. "We are not specially inviting *Black* Republicans to this State, as Kansas can to-day give a Republican majority of 70,000. . . . Kansas has no sentinel at her portals to make birthplace, race, condition, color, politics or religion a condition precedent to the right of any one to enter her borders. All that is required of those who come here is to obey our laws and to join us in an earnest, honest effort to make this a great state. I feel sure that you would like Kansas, and I know that you would be cordially welcomed by our people."[57]

The numbers made it difficult, and St. John realized that early. He wrote in January 1880 that enough had already arrived. But that did not change the ideal. "Do not understand me by this as saying that Kansas is complaining, or that she proposes to ever close her doors against any of God's people who are willing to put forth an effort to make an honest living. I only speak with reference to what is best for the poor and unfortunate class for whom we are laboring." He had the greatest confidence in Mrs. Comstock, who at sixty "labored incessantly, almost day and night, without a murmur, and is now at her post with a crowd of the destitute around her, distributing such articles as are necessary for their comfort and help." Feeding three hundred to five hundred people and securing homes and paying rail fare cost money, and the contributions were short. St. John, however, thought that God would find a way, and he was convinced something had to be done to allow the freedmen to escape the South. "All the refugees . . . tell substantially the same story of cruelty, outrage and wrong heaped upon them by the whites of the South, until they could no longer bear their burdens, and so were compelled to leave everything and come northward, as best they could."[58] What did they need? Just think, he told people, "what white people would require who are destitute of food, thinly clad, in a cold climate and without money."[59] Poor people had built Kansas, he noted, and corn yielded just as well for a black man as for a white one.[60] St. John regularly ended his letters on several subjects with the phrase "trusting that there may be a brighter day," or "trusting that a brighter day may soon dawn."

The *Colored Citizen*, published in Topeka by and for the Exodusters, followed much the same line. What would be the result of this movement? "We answer, first it will for the present, save the lives and liberty of those who leave; and in the future when the present generations of heartless planters are entirely broken up and utterly ruined . . . will make it possible for people to live there without being afraid to sleep at night lest they be killed before morning."[61] It was better to leave, however risky the economic circumstance, than to submit quietly. "Remember," said the paper, "that in Kansas every-body must work or starve. This is a great state for the energetic and indus-trious, but a fearful one for the idle or lazy man."[62]

The women running the relief association never underestimated the diffi-culty, sociological as well as economic. Laura Haviland noted that there were hundreds of applications from Kansas for black workers, but the real need was to place whole families. "In the cursed bondage of the past the breaking up of families was the most bitter trial of their hard lot. . . . Put ourselves in their place. Remember that they cannot read or write. That communication by mail is practically denied them. That they have been robbed all their lives of all those things wherein you are different from them . . . that family attachments constitute their *worldly all*." With "just treatment and kind usage," Haviland thought these people would be happy and add to the wealth of the state, never amounting to more than 10 percent of its population.[63]

That proved to be the case, as the white population of Kansas rapidly grew. In 1870, blacks composed 4.7 percent of the state's population; in 1880, 4.3 percent; and in 1890, 3.5 percent.[64] F. W. Giles admitted that "the ingenuity of the ablest was taxed to devise ways for them to become self-supporting," but writing in 1886, he thought this had been achieved. The black population of Kansas, he wrote, "show a degree of advancement in all conditions of civil life very surprising. . . . Some have become property holders in sums of thousands of dollars, and their children vie with the white children for prizes in the city high schools."[65] But ultimately that was not what mattered most to the St. John Republicans. Wrote the *Topeka Commonwealth*, which was St. John's organ, "The question of the exodus is not one of business merely, as shallow thinkers and flippant writers would have us believe. . . . A large portion of the American people will ignore the humanitarian side. Kansas cannot afford to do so."[66]

St. John's style, and consequently partly the emerging Kansas style, may be illustrated in several other issues of the early 1880s. His dealings with the drought in western Kansas, in 1880, for example, or the claims arising from the Dull Knife raid, when Northern Cheyennes tried to escape across Kansas from Indian Territory in 1879, show a remarkable combination of the pragmatic and the moral/religious. He was not afraid to appeal to the railroad tycoon Jay Gould for money for the relief of suffering farmers in western Kansas, though there were plenty in the state who criticized the substantial gift St. John received from Gould as tainted.[67] When regional newspapers, motivated by the damage that news of the drought was doing to prospects of immigration and town growth, began to talk about "the Destitution Fraud," St. John responded that though the problem might be exaggerated, it was certainly real. The government could do little directly, but the political leadership could and should do all it could to encourage private charity. "I have lived in the West all my life," he wrote one critic. "I know what it is to be poor; I know what it is to be hungry and without bread; I know what it is to live on the frontier. . . . If you were here [Topeka] just a few weeks, and could see daily, men in their poverty and rags and destitution from frontier counties, who have been forced to leave there to prevent starvation, I would think you would not wonder at the fact of some of us, at least, being impressed with the idea that many who remain there are in need of food." He told a businessman at Wakeeney on the KP line in Trego County that if locals could take care of needs in their county, he, St. John, would have the relief train bypass their station. He would then expect no cases of suffering in that region.[68] As for himself: "I would rather feed a dozen men who are unworthy than to turn away one man who is really worthy and without bread."[69]

But on no issue did St. John and Kansas come into greater prominence than on that of the constitutional prohibition of liquor.[70] From the Bismarck Grove rallies to bring people to take the Murphy Pledge in 1879, through the singing of hymns by women in saloons, to the publishing of temperance newspapers, Kansas promoted governmental control of liquor. The prohibition amendment to the Kansas Constitution was the first such provision in the country, though Maine had had a state law since 1851. Following the amendment, Kansas dealt with enforcement problems. It plugged loopholes, ranging from the "original package" court decisions allowing liquor to be shipped into the state to the problem of compliant druggists filling prescriptions with bourbon. It passed a Metropolitan Police Law in 1887 to try to control the Wichita Police Department directly from the statehouse and thus to enforce the liquor laws. Carrie Nation's smashing of Kansas bars and her visit to Governor W. E. Stanley in Topeka at the turn of the century highlighted hyposcrisy and led to the "bone dry" Kansas enforcement law of 1917. Until 1948, when Kansas repealed constitutional prohibition, a constituency was always there for enforcement. And even then, Kansas continued to outlaw the shot-glass drink and the open saloon into the mid-1980s. In the twenty-first century, it was still regulating sale of liquor in groceries and requiring any employee opening a wine bottle in a restaurant to be over twenty-one. Prohibition, the "Kansas idea," has been identified with the state, fairly and unfairly, as has almost nothing else. "Kansans," said one wag, "will vote dry as long as they can stagger to the polls."[71]

Charles Driscoll, a Wichita journalist, caught the flavor of the Kansas temperance establishment well, as seen at least by its detractors. Driscoll recalled that in his childhood Wichita was not going along with the program. His father, an Irish Catholic, made two or three barrels of wine from his own grapes every fall. When he offered it to visitors, they would sniff and say that it was evil. Steve Balch, who lived next door, made wine, too, and he told the preachers to go to hell. "He explained . . . that he didn't mean anything, since there really wasn't any hell. He just wanted to frighten the prohibitionists." In his early boyhood, Driscoll wrote, prohibition had been "merely a blunt instrument, used to extort blackmail from saloon keepers. It had no more force and effect than the Ten Commandments." If one wanted a drink, there were many "sample rooms" in Wichita.

Driscoll remembered that at school there was a large chart about the evil effects of liquor on the human body. "Some of the more nervous girls were unable to look at this chart without becoming very ill, but most of us became so accustomed to the revolting sketches, in five colors, of an ulcerated stomach and a disintegrating liver, life size, that we much preferred them to the dull pink map of the British Isles which clamored weakly for attention on the opposite wall. . . . Since it was much easier to tell about the depravity of habitual drunkards and the horrible deaths they invariably met than it was to teach the fundamentals of the Arabic system of notation and numeration, we spent much of our time taking notes upon prohibition discourses." Kansans crusaded throughout the country. "They went into far fields," Driscoll wrote, "stumping the East and the West for silly-looking Prohibition Party candidates for every imaginable office, and taking defeat with the same angelic smile with which an idiot takes castor oil."[72]

Marshall Murdock, the Wichita editor, took a similarly jaundiced view. One could not stop the publication of newspapers by breaking their presses to pieces, nor drinking by closing saloons. It was the demand of the public that must be changed through education. Mrs. Nation, he wrote in 1901, "might with persistence and her little hatchet render the bed of the Arkansas River dry by diverting its waters, but she can never stay their flow or force them to run back up to their mountain source."[73]

Charles Robinson took an antiprohibition stand, though a teetotaler, for much the same reason. No law would stop intemperance, he argued, and people who were not allowed to make choices never learned anything.[74] Every known vice or virtue could be practiced in Lawrence, Kansas, Robinson noted in 1890, "and individual character is the only protection."[75] Sam Wood was against prohibition, though he remembered that his Quaker father would not sell grain to be made into liquor.[76] But that was intellect and hindsight. Despite the Driscolls, the Murdocks, the Woods, and the Robinsons (and later in a more quiet way William Allen White and Rolla Clymer), the Kansas press was not only full of the issue for years and years but also heavily in favor of regulation.

In 1880 John St. John had his finger on the pulse of the masses and was hand-picked for the task of making prohibition a practical proposition in his state.[77] Former governor Robinson might think that a teenage boy or an alcoholic man had better sink or swim morally by facing temptations openly offered in the stream of commerce, but a great number of Kansas mothers and wives felt otherwise. St. John, himself the son of an alcoholic father, was a powerful advocate. He proposed to blot out what he called the "curse of the age." No, he did not believe that the amendment would stop drinking. Anyone who wanted to get to hell would find a way. But it would slow it for the morally uncertain.[78] It was ironic to him that people expended at least $3 million a year for liquor while settlers starved.[79] Would a prohibition amendment drive away business and population? If so, Kansas did not need that business or those people. "It seems to me, if drunkenness and crime are necessary to the growth of any city, that the quicker the city can stop growing the better, if it depends on such influences for its prosperity."[80] Would the amendment reduce crime? Inevitably. Most of the inmates in Kansas prisons, St. John claimed, blamed drink for their crimes.[81] St. John said, "The whole civilized world is looking to Kansas to-day."[82] And these matters were serious. "Our people have not entered into this contest for fun merely, but they are in *earnest,* and do not intend to take any backward steps in the matter."[83]

At first it seemed that the Kansas experiment might be doomed to failure. St. John went down to defeat in 1882, mostly because he was running for an unprecedented third term as governor, but partly because of the backlash over prohibition and some sympathy for "resubmission." When he ran as a Prohibition Party candidate for president of the United States in 1884, thus splitting the Republican vote and electing Grover Cleveland, he so alienated the Kansas Republican establishment that he became a pariah in his home state. In 1887 a bitter legislature changed the name of St. John County, Kansas, to Logan County.[84] In 1881 a Kansas antiprohibition newspaper wrote, "The future that St. John has before him is easily predicted. He will become the saint of strong-minded but superannuated old women: he will become a fanatic and orator at Sunday School conventions; and his portrait, for awhile, will figure at temperance meetings, and then be consigned to some cobwebbed garret or barn loft, or be used to replace a broken sash in some wash house."[85]

Although that was a sound prediction about the fortunes of the man,

St. John, like his state, was more complex and more interesting than the pale picture of him offered by the latter-day unsympathetic. His pioneering in women's and African-Americans' rights was as determined and as prescient of a future trend as his advocacy of prohibition was determined and unprophetic. And the course for the state was set.

St. John was a reformer but a Republican. His replacement, George Glick, was a Democrat. And Glick was not the most radical candidate in that election. Charles Robinson, running for the Greenback Party, advocated peoples' colleges, taxing of mortgages of nonresidents, lowering the legal rate of interest, and instituting woman suffrage. Robinson polled over twenty thousand votes in that election.[86] Rock-ribbed Kansas conservatives were distraught, but they were in for some tough years.

Among the specific actions of the Glick administration, none was more prominently debated or more significant than the legislation creating the Board of Railroad Commissioners in 1883. Although its specific enforcement powers were at first minimal, its investigations, arbitration, and the publicity of results had an impact. It operated until 1898, was replaced for two years by a Board of Visitation, was declared unconstitutional in 1900, was reconstituted the same year, and lasted in that form until 1911, when it merged into the new Public Utilities Commission. The political genealogy from there goes straight to the Public Service Commission, 1925–1933, and the Kansas Corporation Commission, created in 1933.[87]

Many people in positions of responsibility were making reform noises about railroad abuses. Eugene Ware of Ft. Scott, a member of the law firm of Gleed, Ware and Gleed of Topeka, which had the Santa Fe Railroad Company as a major client, dared to write in 1883: "The [railroad] rates are made in the back room by a professional rate-maker who is not a philosopher or a humanitarian. He does not make the rates at what 'the traffic will bear,' . . . he makes the rates the highest that he thinks the RR Co. can get. The Manager bears about the same relation to the Rate-maker that the Preacher does to the Deacon, one soars into office while the other passes the corn-popper around."

A. E. Toulazin, vice president and general manager of the ATSF, understandably had a sharply contrasting view. He wrote shortly after the Board of Railroad Commissioners legislation passed that the people of Kansas would eventually "tear the railroads out root and branch. . . . How far removed are principles and sentiments like these [used in creating the board] from Communism? Where in the world has Communism done anything but paralyze and destroy?"[88]

Communism itself did not seem so impossible in the state at the time. In 1883 there were press and letter exchanges about nihilism at the University of Kansas. "Almost every paper read by students and by some of the professors, for the last two or three years," wrote the *Topeka Commonwealth* in fall 1883, "has been imbued with the spirit of Communism—worse Nihilism."[89] Sol Miller of the *Troy Chief* picked up the theme with a passion. KU, he wrote, was like a "house with bed bugs," and he suggested burning it down. The state should withhold appropriations, Miller thought, for five years until "the present outfit get scattered to the four winds, then start her again, under new auspices, and on the American plan."[90] Charles Gleed, who was a regent of the university, told Miller that "your facts are all fancies, and your fancies are all follies."[91] But the charges and changes were in the air.

The reply from the Board of Railroad Commissioners to Toulazin emphasized that their mission was hardly communistic. "These roads are in fact an absolute gift to the stockholders from the toiling masses from which you are gleaning vast revenues, and still are clamoring for millions more. . . . Any State that permits the exercise of an unrestricted power by a railroad corporation to tax the people is derelict in its paramount duty of protection to its citizens. You may call this Communism, but the alternative is the subjection of the rights and property of one class to the irresponsible despotism of the other."[92]

That attitude had evolved. A. C. Greene, a member of the board, wrote that in the early building stages of Kansas railroads there had been "no more thought of attempting to enforce the principle of state control than there was of tearing up the tracks. . . . The man who would have raised a question of regulation . . . would have been regarded as a public enemy." But the roads "presumed somewhat upon this cordial expression of popular approval, and entrenched themselves in a position which they fondly hoped to make impregnable." That led to a switch in public opinion, and as early as 1877 Governor George Anthony suggested a law defining the powers of the corporations and the rights of the people. St. John pushed it also, and bills were introduced in his administration.[93] By 1883 it was a certainty that it would be done. "I have no fears as to the temper of our people on the importance and necessity of effective legislation on the RR question by the Legislature," a friend wrote Glick in February 1883.[94]

The railroads lobbied strongly against the change. Three Union Pacific attorneys in a pamphlet published in Topeka in 1883, *The Railroad Problem*, went into the question from the corporate perspective. People who complained about railroads, the attorneys claimed, misunderstood the true situation, and it was the job of government to protect property held by a minority against the whims of a majority. "We know [state politicians] have no sympathy with communism, no desire that those who, by superior industry or care, have been able to save some portion of their earnings, should be deprived of their property or its just use." Corporations were just people combined to do bigger things, the attorneys argued. "The State has not in any sense created the Railroads; it has merely furnished means by which its citizens and those of other States could unite for the accomplishment of a common object in which the State is largely interested." The Kansas Pacific was not paying dividends on its 479 miles of main lines and 516 miles of branch lines in Kansas. These had been built in advance of the requirements of the county "as a means of building up and developing the fertile lands of Kansas," and to cut rates through regulation would be "an act of wanton and unjustifiable oppression." If the railroad commission bill passed, the next thing would be that the state legislature might try to figure out the cost of raising wheat per bushel and then fix the maximum price that could be charged for it by farmers.[95]

The Santa Fe had its pamphlets also. "Public policy," declared one, "requires that enterprises should be encouraged in proportion to the benefits which they confer on the people." The interest of the state was "to allow the owners to make the railroad as largely profitable as the energy, intelligence, and enterprise of those owners may enable them to accomplish."[96]

But this was swimming upstream in Kansas. Ware advised Glick in 1882 on a whole series of legislative initiatives, including a law to collect state tax from corporations by a tax on their gross receipts, an employer's liability act, a road-building law, and a system of railroad, telegraph, express, and transportation tariff laws.[97] He collected data from other states that had railroad regulation, including Iowa and Massachusetts.[98] He emphasized that eleven states had railroad commissioner laws, that the public liked them, and that the courts upheld them. "It may be safely said that the Commissioner System forms no barrier to railroad enterprise and prosperity. . . . The 'Railroad Problem' is a problem that no one can solve. The railroads cannot solve it themselves. There is no use waiting for a solution, all that can be done is to *regulate, partially after a fashion, the best we can,* and that all such regulation must be flexible, because in that sphere all is progress, invention and activity."[99]

Charles Gleed looked back on the recent economic and regulatory trends in 1886 in a speech at Valley Falls. "General education," he said, of which Kansas was so proud, "is our chief communist and our chief conservative." Brainpower was ultimately the only defense against "brute force and the arrogance of Godless wealth"—that and a diversity of internal conditions and checks and balances. The freedom of Kansas was not the kind of freedom advocated by the Chicago anarchists, who had just been arrested after the Haymarket Labor riot—"we are all enthusiastic socialists but we are not crazy socialists. . . . We discover a moral inequity, the effect of which is to make one class poor in purse and in mental and moral condition, to the benefit of another class, and so we pass a prohibitory law." There had to be communication and cooperation with private companies. "Were we to do otherwise we should be like the buffalo that bucked the locomotive— admired for our pluck but damned for our discretion." Gleed quoted Epictetus, the Greek philosopher, that "in every act consider what precedes and what follows, and then proceed to act." Anything "thoughtless, incoherent, sporadic, spasmodic," or "red-flag" emotional action, would only result in an embarrassing retreat in the end for being inappropriate to the real circumstances and to human nature.[100]

The ATSF, especially, remained a force in Topeka, hardly reduced from Olympian proportions by the scratchings of the 1883 legislature. Still, the Board of Railroad Commissioners bill was critical to what James Malin has called the "emergence of the administrative state" in Kansas.[101] There was a feeling that the government had to be reformed structurally and then used effectively.

Structural changes were many. The legislature met yearly until 1877, when the long Kansas tradition of biennial legislative meetings with minimal pay for legislators began.[102] With fewer meetings, there were calls for more seriousness. Many private bills were being considered, leading reformers to charge that "every winter time has been frittered away upon local measures and pointless and vapid discussion." Some complained, too, that the bureaucracy was bloated with a "multitude of officials drawing large salaries or reaping fortunes from litigation in the way of fees." Yet they realized that more state action would doubtless require more state employees and more tax revenues.[103]

Bessie Wilder's account of the creation of Kansas agencies illustrates their proliferation in the late nineteenth century and a change in their type. Early there were standard offices, most related to fundamental taxation, educational, correctional, or eleemosynary work: Adjutant General's Office (1861); Board of School Fund Commissioners (1861); Quarter-Master General (1861); State Library (1861); Board of Equalization (1861); State Penitentiary, Lansing (1863); Asylum for the Insane, Osawatomie (1863); Bureau of Immigration (1864); Surgeon General (1865); Asylum for the Deaf and Dumb (1866); Horticultural Society (1867); Asylum for the Blind (1867); Geological Survey (1867); State Printer (1868); Insurance Department (1871); Board of Agriculture (1872); Board of Education (1873); Historical Society (1875)); Land Office (1876); Commissioner of Fisheries (1877); Asylum for Idiotic and Imbecile Youth (1881). But after 1880 there is a definite specialization, suggesting a belief in the scientific management of society by government. There was the Mine Inspector (1883); Board of Railroad Commissioners (1883); Livestock Sanitary Commission (1884); Military Board (1885); Board of Pardons (1885); Bureau of Labor and Industrial Statistics (1885); Board of Pharmacy (1885); Labor Commissioner (1885); Kansas State Industrial Reformatory, Hutchinson (1885); Board of Health (1885); Children's Receiving Home (1885); Agricultural Experiment Stations (1887–1917); Board of Police Commissioners (1887); Beloit Industrial School for Girls (1889); Bank Commissioner (1891); Board of Public Works (1891); State Accountant (1895).[104]

In 1890, when a legislative commission was appointed to codify and revise the state laws and define the duties of state officers, it was a considerable task. The committee concluded that not only were the rules about state agencies and their administration inconsistent but also that even the fundamental laws about administering educational institutions were vague and conflicting, with a "total lack of any fixed principles or knowledge about how these institutions ought to be governed." There should be one state library, which should include the state historical society. The state should investigate free textbooks, or at least the printing of textbooks by the state printer. Government control of charities should be "systematic and uniform," and specific law should provide for the organization and powers of the trustees. The state should not maintain a dining room at the penitentiary or supply guards with clothes. The overflow from insane asylums should not be sent to county jails. The Board of Railroad Commissioners should be elected, not appointed. The fish commissioner needed more power to balance sport with the environment. A number of agencies should be eliminated all together. The list was long but in its tedious detail was a specific passion for reform.[105]

Strangely, given this seeming liberal agenda and the great pride in Kansas literacy, in 1879 the state's school finances suffered a reverse. Although the U.S. Supreme Court ruled in 1874 that state tax money could be used for secondary education, the Kansas legislature and the Kansas Supreme Court questioned the practice. Therefore the legislature in 1879 eliminated the one-mill state tax levy, which had been in place for eighteen years, and reduced the school fund suddenly by 50 percent. Meanwhile, school enrollment for the grades went from 142,606 in 1875 to 405,450 in 1889—the latter figure higher than the elementary school enrollment for the state in 1962.

This action, wrote the historian of the Kansas State Teachers' Association, C. O. Wright, was untypical of state action elsewhere at the time and "spelled the death knell for any concept of shared state responsibility. It started Kansas on the way to a provincial, narrow, local approach to schools that retarded education." Perhaps the enormous expenditure on building the capitol with its imported Italian marble and planned artistic adornments left little for schools. Perhaps it was lack of organization among teachers. Only 497 of 11,888 teachers attended the Kansas State Teacher's Association meeting in 1892. But whatever the cause, the cuts were surprising.[106]

Another state hope and pride that could be threatened was its relatively progressive record on women. That was tested in 1887 with the passage of the Municipal Suffrage bill, allowing women to vote in municipal elections and to hold municipal offices. As had the Exodusters, this issue brought out unkindness in the temperamentally unyielding. Marshall Murdock, editor of the *Wichita Eagle,* was outspoken against activist women. His 1887 contribution was an editorial, "Bulldozing Females." The woman who "pants for public life," he characterized as hardly a "lady" and suggested that "in nine cases out of ten that class of hens do their crowing and rule the roost." He recommended that "home-living wives" should "snub the pernicious noses of these intermeddlers" and ignore "imported screechers and peripatetic old maids" who had persuaded the state legislature to pass "the so-called political abortion, known as the Female Municipal Suffrage Bill."[107]

John Ingalls put it as harshly, referring to all reformers, male and female, as "sexually unemployed." "I have heard a great many women," Ingalls said, "regret that they were not men, but I have never heard a man wish that he was a woman, or regret that he had not been born a woman."[108] That kind of talk and Ingalls's suffrage views roused Mary Elizabeth Lease of Wichita, founder of the local Hypatia Club, which was even then discussing birth control. Ingalls's 1887 suffrage lectures, Lease said, were "reared upon the crumbling ruins of the feudal ages." There were many examples, she said, of the "helplessness of men and absolute dependence upon tradition among men," but she was surprised to see it in one as intelligent as Ingalls. "The fact that the accident of birth made you a male perhaps renders you (in your own estimation at least) a superior being, but there are differences of opinion."[109]

For the nascent national women's rights movement the Kansas campaign of 1867 had been a major activity, using most of the resources of the Equal Rights Association to import workers to help local women in the first popular test in the nation of woman suffrage. The historian Ellen DuBois notes that it was precisely the defeat of slavery that created the political atmosphere for "a general flowering of radical ambitions for social change," including votes for women. Failure of black and woman suffrage in Kansas in 1867 then created a woman suffrage movement independent of the campaign for equal rights for blacks, with Kansas still a central opportunity. "These Kansas women are ready for the new doctrine of woman suffrage," Elizabeth Stanton wrote in 1867. "You need not wonder said one of them to me the other day if after all the difficulties and dangers we have encountered . . . that we should think that 'our divinely constituted heads' are on our shoulders. We should have been in a poor fix if they had not been."[110]

So it was that in the 1880s Kansas was again at the forefront in women's rights. In 1880 Sarah Brown was a Democratic candidate for state superintendent of schools. "It is fitting," noted a flyer from the National Woman Suffrage Association to the Voters of Kansas published that year, "that Kansas, whose soil is already classic through many well fought battles for freedom, should be the first place to place a noble representative of a disfranchised class in a position so honorable, dignified and elated."[111] Susan Anthony wrote Governor St. John in 1881, enclosing a copy of *History of Woman Suffrage* and expressing a wish that St. John and his wife, whom Anthony had met on the train on her last Kansas visit, would read and reflect upon it. Both Kansas senators were against votes for women, but there was

Dressed in black, Mary Lease in the 1890s.
Courtesy of the Kansas State Historical Society.

still the house and the committees. "Why may not *women*, as well as *Indians*, &c, &c have a standing com?" She thought that St. John should recommend at least municipal suffrage, which could be secured by legislation without a general vote of the people. "We cannot hope to reach the masses of men who neither read nor attend lectures, & they are the great balance of power always against woman's enfranchisement—But we can reach our representatives in Legislatures & Congress."[112]

The municipal suffrage debate brought the eighteenth annual American Woman Suffrage Association meeting to Kansas. Julia Ward Howe, author of the "Battle Hymn of the Republic," spoke: "I do not think a man can be considered a fair and just man unless he is willing to allow every other human being on the face of the earth the same rights which he claims for himself. . . . I want every avenue in life to be open just as wide to my little girls as to my little boys. . . . They say woman has her influence and does not need to vote; what would you say if your vote was taken and your influence left?"[113] Said another woman toward the end of the convention: "When your good friend with a kind and prosperous husband, a pleasant home, and nothing lacking that better laws could secure her, says that she thinks women are already pretty well treated and she don't know that she would care for the ballot, ask her how she would feel if she were a teacher and expected to work beside a man equal work and equal time, he to get $60, she $40 a month? Ask her whether she would not want to vote then."[114]

But there was disagreement among women. The Lyons County Anti Female Suffrage Organization, for example, consisted largely of women.[115] Some of the variety of views is reflected in the files of Governor John Martin, who was a known opponent of the municipal suffrage bill. Eliza Homans, an eastern woman, wrote Martin in 1886 thanking him for slowing the move toward municipal suffrage in Kansas and sending him antisuffrage literature. "Though the suffragists have the persistency of fanatics and 'cranks,' " she wrote, "we hope to as continuously . . . ward it off in the future as we have in the past."[116] Most letters from Kansas women to the governor's office, however, supported the bill. Dr. Nannie Stephens, the first female physician in Wichita, wrote, "My husband laughingly said to-day it would be a joke on us women if you would veto the bill." Stephens asked that the governor please not do so, as the statute would "benefit our State more than all the bills that have ever been passed."[117] Eva Stevens of Anthony, Kansas, wrote the governor in a different vein: "God will work & man may only *retard* His work but never thwart it. My dear Governor do not imagine that the women of our 1/2 free land want to enter the political field—far from it, but very many of us are in earnest on this matter & crave a voice in any measure that touches The Home & believe that we—Man & Woman—are to be coworkers together that the highest goal of all may the more speedily be accomplished."[118] Two other Anthony women wrote, "Every sincere, honest man must admit that woman is man's equal both intellectually and morally. Then why not give her the right to have a voice as to who shall make the laws that govern her?"[119] The Dickinson County Equal Suffrage Society felt the same way. If some women did not want to vote, the members wrote, they did not have to, but the right should be there. "We who are engaged in business, are property holders, taxpayers holding positions in public offices, newspaper offices, and participants in the world's work, feel the necessity of the ballot. . . . Hundreds of the most intelligent, thoughtful, earnest and consecrated women in Kansas have asked for this privilege by petition."[120] Sarah Hall was more personal: "I don't suppose you can fully comprehend what you have never felt, the *degradation* of being *disenfranchised*. Are we the mothers of the land to be always classed with the felons, lunatics, Indians and idiots? . . . For one hour, if possible, place yourself in thought where *we* are in fact."[121] The municipal suffrage movement, wrote an Ottawa man, "is not simply the work of 'cranky women'. . . . I believe it is one of the progressive movements of the day & bound to come."[122]

Turnout among women in the first municipal election in which they were qualified to vote was modest. So were the immediate results. Kansas elected a woman, Mrs. Susanna Salter, as mayor of Argonia, the first woman mayor in the United States. Five women served on the city council in Syracuse, in western Kansas. Two women were elected to the school board in Parsons, and in Abilene the women's vote defeated all councilmen opposed to woman suffrage.[123] Women held the mayor's office and all five council seats in Oskaloosa in 1888, and several other towns had women mayors within the next two years.[124]

It was only a start. Mary Lease called it "a pitiful crumb."[125] But the Municipal Suffrage Law of 1887 was a key turning point, a significant date in the local logic of Kansas history, which speeded an already strong turn toward reform along its irreversible way. Wrote Laura Johns of Salina, who had worked hard for the municipal suffrage law, "Women sometimes voted against husbands and against the election of the husbands of their dearest lady friends, and there were no rows about it. . . . In Kansas, the women are better educated than the men. . . . With the advent of municipal suffrage, and with their advancement in experience comes a new day."[126]

Indeed Kansas grabbed headlines in the 1880s for events incalculably less important than this, and the more bizarre the bigger the headline. As usual,

Laura Johns.
Courtesy of the Kansas State Historical Society.

this tended to dilute the real reform accomplishments in the public mind. While Governor Martin was reading letters on municipal suffrage, he was corresponding with Dr. S. S. N. Foote of Lebo, Kansas, about aerial navigation. Foote claimed in 1885 that he had invented an airplane and that "the world rests in the hollow of my hand. With a dozen machines and thirty operators, I could destroy the whole military and naval power of the globe without the loss of a man." He could also provide a transcontinental transportation system, which, if the state government would just help him financially, could and should center in Kansas.[127] Foote also had learned "by actual experimentation that copulation is not essential to fecundity" and thought the state might want to back his artificial insemination experiments.[128] He was still pushing his schemes in 1887, claiming he was no "harebrained enthusiast," and that Kansas could get in on the ground floor of navigating the air "with speed and certainty."[129]

Also of the epoch was Moses Harmon's Kansas-based free love movement. He changed the name of his newspaper from the *Kansas Liberal* to *Lucifer, the Light Bearer* in 1883 and embarked on a career from his home in the tiny town of Valley Falls, Kansas, that landed him often in courtrooms and in the tabloids. Harmon supported universal woman suffrage in Kansas, but, like the idiosyncratic male feminist George Francis Train, his identification with the movement was no particular blessing. The marshal arrived one day in February to arrest the staff of the *Lucifer,* and Harmon promulgated his doctrines (among which was a campaign against traditional marriage and one for "anarchistic eugenics") for a time from a jail cell in Oskaloosa, Kansas.[130]

There was, too, the Dodge City "war" of 1883, when a "shotgun brigade" of local vigilantes boarded trains to try to keep Luke Short, charged with assault in a saloon brawl about a woman, from returning to town. "The men driven out," wrote the *Kansas City Journal,* "may be men who are classed with the sporting fraternity, but as far as known they are no worse than the men who have been chiefly instrumental in driving them out." The arrival in Dodge of Bat Masterson, Wyatt Earp, and Rowdy Joe Lowe was thought not to be helpful for the reputation of civilization in Kansas.[131]

Intervention by the state militia was not only a part of that Dodge incident but also of several county seat Cowboy Wars, taking place all over western Kansas in the mid-to-late 1880s. Sometimes even the *New York Times* found lurid accounts of these battles, and the hauling of county records from one town to another in a rain of fire, part of "all the news that is fit to print." These battles were, a western Kansas editor agreed, "a disgrace to any county, and especially to the fair name of Kansas." Jokes could be cruel. There was the one about a man reaching the gates of heaven and being told that his life had been sinful and he would have to go to hell. "Oh, Lord," he said, "will I have to go back to Dodge?"[132]

Always there was something dramatic from Kansas and sometimes there was a bit of the heroic in it. In October 1892 it was the Dalton gang's raid on Coffeyville and the killing of four and the wounding of a fifth by the armed citizens of that town. That was the stuff of legend in the cattle town vein, and it did not inure entirely to the detriment of a state that was seen through that lens as rough-edged but courageous and independent. Thomas Beer, in his impressionistic 1926 history *The Mauve Decade,* gave the incident top billing. "Citizens grabbed their rifles with which the antecinemic West did its serious shooting and the fight began. Bright spires of glass toppled from frames of windows; smoke went in surges along the street as men fired busily from porches or through doorways. . . . Gratton Dalton ran down the sidewalk with blood on his face and paused to rip the green handkerchief from his throat in full range of the batteries before he turned at the corner of a stable and fired back, killing the city's marshal with a superb shot from the hip. . . . Men hurried up and a thick group formed around Bob Dalton in his carmine puddle on the clay. The body heaved in its blood but he kept yelling 'Ride!' "[133]

Late in the decade of the 1880s, however, bad economic news began to pile up to add to the prevailing negative image of the state, engendered partly, as was usual, by one of those large turns in the weather cycle that regularly frustrated farmers there. The blizzard of 1886 rang in the bad times, with its high sustained winds, bitter cold, and heavy snow taking a severe toll not only on cattle but also on the spirits of sod house pioneers. Then came diminished rainfalls, a dry cycle that lasted through much of the 1890s, and accompanying hot winds, which made crops impossible and mortgages a special burden.[134] The panaceas of county seat towns, street railways, new industries, and booming population disappeared, it seemed, in a flicker. Some of the most serious hopes of a better world suddenly appeared a laughingstock, even to some Kansans.

Out of bad times, most observers said, came the People's Party, the Kansas phenomenon perhaps most written about by academic historians. Many

A sod house family, western Kansas.
Courtesy of the Kansas State Historical Society.

have concluded that the movement that party engendered, Populism, was the heir of the "crazy" legacy of Kansas "freak" movements. But it could as well be argued that it was the legitimate though extreme offspring of the liberal direction that had developed during the St. John, Glick, and Martin administrations and perhaps had its far roots in the moral idealism and stubborn persistence of Kansas in the territorial era.

Recently, Gene Clanton has called the People's Party, which originated in Kansas in 1890 and became one of the most important third-party movements in American history, "the humane preference." Clanton emphasizes that it was hardly the "irrational or at best idiosyncratic" movement that emerges in discussions of it in many textbooks. He highlights the "soft" rather than the "hard" issues of Populism, that is, the concerns about the humanization of the economic system rather than the too easy focus on the debtor's cry of "free and unlimited coinage of silver at a ratio of 16 to 1." The Populist issues had roots in the Enlightenment. And they had a native genealogy in Kansas, going at least back to the Greenback, Independent Reform, and Union-Labor movements, the Alliances, and Farmer's Cooperatives.[135]

If one had to locate a "pivotal moment" when the turn was made regionally in the direction that became Populism, it would have to be the two administrations of Governor John St. John. His was a partly middle-class, partly urban reform of good economic times and belies the interpretation of the Richard Hofstadter school that Populist principles were largely a case of sour grapes by farmers failing as business people.[136] A study of the 1880s reform impulse in Kansas should also place in question the idea that Populism was a discontinuity. Elizabeth Barr, writing in 1918, noted, "It was not Populism that distinguished Kansas, but Kansas that distinguished Populism. Neither the conditions nor the proposed remedy was new, but the Kansas method of handling them was novel."[137]

The interpretations of Populism have run a considerable gamut. John Hicks's *Populist Revolt* (1931) saw it as interest-group politics using popular control of the government and government action to regulate corporations and political conspiracy. Chester Destler in his 1946 account de-emphasized the regional aspects and saw the People's Party as part and parcel of long-held radical ideas on natural rights. Richard Hofstadter thought Populists were provincial, backward-looking, failed business people—Nativists, anti-Semites, and anti-intellectuals to boot. Victor Ferkiss in 1957 went so far as to trace a relationship between Populism and fascism.

Recent studies have been more kind. Walter Nugent's *Tolerant Populists* (1963) argued that they were not irrational bigots but parts of a pragmatic farmers' movement. They were not against capitalism or cities but only protested the abuses the economy could inflict on people. Norman Pollack, representing the New Left view of the 1960s, stated in *The Populist Response to Industrial America* that the Populists had mounted a coherent, radical critique of the industrial system, which was still valid. Peter Argersinger's and Gene Clanton's careful studies of the Kansas movement, written during the 1970s, made a strong case that although the Populists were not as radical in legislative practice as perhaps they were in speeches, there was a great deal to choose on the reform front between them and the Republicans. Clanton's later work, especially *Populism: The Humane Preference* (1991), echoed Destler's emphasis on the radical tradition harking back to Jeffersonian democracy. Robert McMath, in *American Populism: A Social History* (1993), emphasized that Populism was especially strong in Kansas because the mainstream party response to farm problems was ridicule and intransigence. Had there been some bend in the Republican establishment, perhaps there need not have been such a fracture.

Worth Robert Miller has found the picture still not orderly after one hundred years of analysis. Although modern research has mostly laid to rest the idea that the Populists were simply hicks and hayseeds with an unsophisticated view of economics, the movement does not fit neatly into a standard ideological category. Miller concluded, "It was a thoroughly American, nonsocialist, anticapitalist movement that called for enough change in the institutions of land, transportation, and money to be considered moderately radical."[138]

But what happened locally? At the simplest, the People's Party in the year of its organization in Kansas, 1890, carried 96 of 125 seats in the lower house of the Kansas legislature and won 5 of Kansas's 7 U.S. congressional races. It then shook up the country with measures it at least proposed to carry out, and sometimes did.[139]

Most American history textbooks cover the Populist basics. The party advocated free coinage of silver, nationalization of transportation and communication, a secret ballot, direct election of U.S. senators, petition rights for direct influence of legislation, and a subtreasury plan to subsidize farm prices. It is the details in actual practice that confound. "Populism," wrote a Kansas City reporter in 1910, "was a great impressionist picture, full of violent daubs and colors, framed in depression, gloom, financial distress, hot winds, droughts, hard times, grasshoppers and tragedy."[140]

Typical of the literature that warmed things up in the boardrooms and legislative chambers of the rest of the country was a local piece published in Wichita in 1891, *Extortionate Taxation. Oppressive and Unjust Discrimination Against the Poor. Criminal Extravagance with Public Money. An Imperative Demand for Change.* The taxpayers were being stepped on, the pamphlet claimed, and would "growl." If Nature "had shut off her bounties and hard times were a providential necessity, no one could complain. But such is not the case. The masses are tired of fine oratory and legal talent. It pays not their debts, nor yields them bread." The depression conditions left the working people only two choices—to become tramps or take up a legal fight for natural rights. Beer and liquor were not the problem, but usury, unjust taxation, and public extravagance were. Perhaps official salaries should be cut down to those of common labor. "Select a mayor from the blacksmith shops, a council from the carpenter shops and street scrapers. . . . Let the working bees organize and with the ballot box rob them of their unworthy grip."[141]

The party was most successful politically in Kansas, where it grew from the activities of the Vincent brothers in Winfield and their newspaper, *Amer-*

ican Nonconformist and Kansas Industrial Liberator. But it had some impact also in other farming states and in the mining districts of Colorado, where its appeal for the free coinage of silver as a way to inflate the currency and relieve the burden of debtors spoke to those with silver to sell.

The platform of the Kansas People's Party in 1890 summarized the thrust: "The earth is the common heritage of the people; every person born into the world, is entitled equally with all others to a place to live . . . and [to] earn a living, and any system of government that does not maintain and protect this inalienable right is wrong and should be changed and abolished."[142] The next year, with great participation from Kansans, the party became national and ran a presidential candidate, James Weaver, in 1892. Before fusing with the Democrats in 1896 to support William Jennings Bryan, who emphasized the money issue with his famous Cross of Gold speech at the Democratic convention, the Populists raised many issues with the American electorate. It also produced, from Kansas particularly, many political originals, including Mary Elizabeth Lease, Annie Diggs, "Sockless" Jerry Simpson, and William Peffer.

The most distinctive aspect was the idea that a peoples' government, created through reform of the political system, could improve society through active intervention. This perhaps seemed more of a departure to the rest of the nation than it did to Kansas, where reform of that type had become a tradition. And many of the seeming changes were more complex than simply class rebellion.

There was the downfall of John Ingalls, for instance. Peffer defeated Ingalls, a U.S. senator since 1873, in the election in the Kansas legislature in 1891. That was certainly a surprising turn of events to outsiders. Ingalls, however, had long been vulnerable politically in Kansas. He represented an extreme, not only of view but also of temperament and expression. Articulate almost beyond imagination, satirical to a fault, and a famously dapper dresser, he seemed more of a contrast to the rumpled, seemingly hayseed Populist candidates than he really was. Warm and generous with his family and close friends, he yet had long suffered from bouts of depression and had an abrasive and cold public persona. He was an insult to Republican reformers, like Kansas congressman John Anderson, who had been at the forefront of railroad reform since the early 1880s, and Marshall Murdock, leading the "Murdock Rebellion" from Wichita.

His outspoken articulateness backed him into a corner. "The purification

"Sockless" Jerry Simpson.
Courtesy of the Kansas State Historical Society.

of politics," Ingalls said in a famous speech, "is an iridescent dream. Government is force. Politics is a battle for supremacy. Parties are the army. The Decalogue and the golden rule have no place in a political campaign."[143] The government, he thought, should leave the people alone.[144] "I have no sympathy with the paternal idea," he said, "but believe . . . the best results are attained when the people are left to settle the great questions of society by individual effort. All that legislation can do is give men an equal chance in the race of life." To that, Percy Daniels, a Populist activist from Crawford County responded, "I cannot see that the distribution of wealth is very closely allied to our individual capacities. There are men in Kansas . . . barely making a living raising grain, who are as able and *unscrupulous* as any of the Wall Street financiers. . . . Opportunity is the larger factor in most of these transactions— lack of integrity taking the second place, and capacity third."[145]

Ingalls seemed to prove his "politics as force" theories in his own affairs. There was a major Senate investigation of him in 1879 on a charge of bribery. He survived but not without adding to his bitterness. And his vindication technically and legally did not mean he was left without taint. George Martin, a Democrat, the editor of the *Junction City Union,* and a close observer of the Ingalls situation, received a letter from one of his reporters in Washington noting that Governor George Anthony, testifying in the case, "made a strong impression in favor of the Lord—which is *us,* of course—& against the beanpole son-of-hell who holds a seat in the Senate."[146]

On returning to his home in Atchison to give a kind of victory address in March 1880, Ingalls lashed out at Albert Horton, his nemesis in the case and chief justice of the Kansas Supreme Court, in a way that shocked even his friends.[147] One man wrote to Horton that "the Ingalls blow was . . . a piece of childish folly," attended only by hirelings for his campaign. "Is he lunatic to think that he can make these outrageous assaults upon the private characters of men of prominence?"[148] Another said Ingalls's speech was "unworthy the utterance of the town street corner politicians."[149]

On the Populist uprising itself, Ingalls was direct. He wrote a friend in summer 1890 that "we are contending with an enemy whose strength is unknown, a secret organization based upon discontent, bound by oath, led by malevolent and vindictive conspirators, who have everything to gain and nothing to lose in the conflict. . . . It is not a campaign for fire-works, oratory, or brass bands. It should be a business from the start."[150] Kansas had mixed feelings about it but in 1890 had to say goodbye to Ingalls, "the lover of her youth."[151] Interestingly, as Populist issues became middle class in the twentieth century, Ingalls's son Sheffield became a prominent Roosevelt Progressive in Kansas.[152]

The Populists, too, and their actions have been distorted by time and by the surviving description. It was great fun to pillory them and to create caricatures.[153] But just as the Ingalls defeat was not solely due to a simple sea change, one should not judge the Populist movement by its more insane public statements or gaudy personnel. As with the reputation of James Lane, the long-lived eventual winners have tended to dominate the telling of the story with perfect hindsight. Mary Lease said a lot of things besides "raise less corn and more hell," if she ever even said that. There was more to William Peffer than a long beard and a farming background, textbook descriptions notwithstanding. The temptation by historians to quote clever descriptions of Populist oddities written by glib newspaper editors who often happened to be Republicans is as great as was the contemporary desire of a fearful, well-educated establishment to write and read them.

The critics were indeed many and delighted in outdoing each other in invective, directed not only at the Populists but sometimes also against the new Kansas. Who could forget White's 1896 editorial, "What's the Matter with Kansas?" "Go east and you hear them laugh at Kansas; go west and they sneer at her; go south and they 'cuss' her; go north and they have forgotten her. Go into any crowd of intelligent people gathered anywhere on the globe, and you will find the Kansas man on the defensive." According to White, Kansas in the 1890s was filled with fools. "We need several thousand gibbering idiots to scream about the 'Great Red Dragon' of Lombard Street. We don't need population, we don't need wealth . . . you bet we don't."[154] The Populist idea of government, said the Honorable James Pigott, Democrat of Connecticut, was "paternalism of the worst kind. Every public ill, real or imaginary, is to be cured by some patent legislation. Money is to be printed, not coined and distributed, not earned."[155] A typical panegyric, looking back, proclaimed:

> We see her downtrodden plough joggers rattling about in devil wagons and shooting the Money Devil. Before our musing eye the mighty ones of old pass by—Lorenzo Lewelling, Mary Elizabeth Lease, Annie Diggs . . . the Sockless Socrates of Medicine Lodge, all the heroes and heroines of the perpetual age. Choirs of girls drive about singing "No man that ain't a

Populist shall ever marry me." Agricultural subtreasuries look real. Inter-state and intercontinental railroads follow the lines of latitude and have sidings and terminal facilities in every backyard. For Kansas was, is, and ever shall be in highest C. She stands upon the misty mountain tops and yells. . . . She is inebriated with the exuberance of her own strenuosity. The sunbeams are as buttered rum to her. The air is hashish. The water is sake. The soil is pulque. She is keyed beyond all keys. . . . She is the commonwealth of hyperbole.[156]

Mary Lease was a favorite target, called everything from a "petticoated smut-mill" to a "lantern-jawed, goggleeye nightmare." White noted, fa-mously and irrelevantly, that "she had no sex appeal—none!"[157] The People's Party, wrote Charles Gleed, was "a large winding of respectable and decent though inarticulate and incoherent discontent on a small nucleus of political deviltry compounded of vicious stupidity and unscrupulous cunning."[158] It was the Puritan spirit that had brought prohibition and Populism, Gleed thought, the desire to make people "good by compulsion. . . . Outside of Kansas one finds no counterpart of this spirit. It seems to be peculiarly a product of the soil."[159]

Yet just as John Brown and Jim Lane had an ability to speak not only to the masses but also to power and influence, so did Jerry Simpson and William Peffer. Simpson never lived down a comment he made, which left him with his sobriquet, about not taking silk socks to Washington. However, he was a considerable classical scholar, an attorney (as was Lease), and a down-to-earth thinker. He was well received when he spoke in New Hamp-shire in April 1891, attacking both major parties equally. In Kansas, he said, we came to the conclusion that rich men in Congress would only help themselves and not poor farmers. Thus, "instead of electing monopolists to make our laws we went down among the common people and took men from the plow and the cattle pen, men whose hands were horny from honest toil, who had heard the wind rustle through the corn field and who knew from personal experience the privations and toil of a Kansas farmer's life. We didn't take any of those gentlemen farmers who farm by proxy, through the medium of a mortgage on our places, I mean, but we took the farmer himself." In the lower house were men, he continued—in the upper were "creatures." Kansas was not alone. Every state was cursed with politicians. "The great trouble with the common people is that they are not aware what a power they have in their own hands. They have had drilled into them so long the idea that they were incapable of governing themselves that they have really come to believe it." When was the Roman nation strong? When its wealth was in the hands of the common people.[160]

Peffer was also well received when he gave a speech in Annapolis, Maryland, in March 1891. Observers noticed his neat clothes and dignified manner and thought that his speech made sense. "Such a type of the perfect, unassuming farmers is the newly famous Westerner in appearance and manner that his presence was not noticed when he entered the crowded hall," wrote a reporter. He told the audience that "the time has come when it is necessary in our own defense that the working people of this country, the farmers, mechanics, day laborers and all men and women who earn their living by hands or brains, organize against usurpation. . . . This is not a movement against the merchant, the lawyer, the beggar or anyone else, but a great uprising of the people." They say we want to destroy capital, he continued. That was not so. "But we want to restore the supremacy of the people, and we propose to do it. . . . The interest-bearing function of money is the fang of that great, red dragon, the money power."[161]

Eastern papers observed that it had been some years since Peffer had been an actual farmer and that the Populists in Congress quickly adapted to city ways and lived in expensive Washington homes. Still, their sincerity and their ability were obvious.[162] "This movement," Peffer said, "is not one for destruction; it is one for creation. . . . Is it the work of men demented? If so, then indeed is half the world gone mad."[163]

The legislative achievement in Kansas in the first biennial legislature (1891) in which Populists were involved was good, though the volume of bills passed (approximately 250) was the smallest ever. Perhaps it was a little more boisterous than sometimes. Noble Prentis thought the snow that fell on March 7 was heaven's way of marking the time, turning the streets of Topeka into "snowy plains and steppes and wide white wilderness, in which the electric lamps made circles and narrow vistas of light." In the capitol was "a mass of sound and wind and hair and boots and popcorn and yelling chairman and whooping members, who faced now in one direction and now in another," finally getting around to consideration of a bill to allow Kansas to participate in the Chicago Columbia Exposition.[164] There was a bill regulating state banks. There was an irrigation bill, eighty-five pages long, to aid western Kansas in the drought. Another bill made Labor Day a legal holiday

William Peffer.
Courtesy of the Kansas State Historical Society.

and limited labor hours to eight a day for those employed by government. The legislature created a Board of Public Works to have charge of public buildings. It authorized a chinch bug study under KU chancellor Snow. More controversial, but hardly socialistic, was a primary election bill, in which "primary elections, which have heretofore been conducted only as the politicians might arrange, are now controlled by law." The session passed a Metropolitan Police bill to enforce prohibition in the sinful cities and an Alien Land bill, forbidding nonresident aliens from owning land. This last was directed primarily at Lord Scully's property in Marion, Morris, and Chase Counties and was opposed by western members, Populist or not, who thought it would drive away capital. Bills to elect the Board of Railroad Commissioners and for a secret ballot, equal suffrage, and to cut railroad rates failed.[165]

Until 1893, the state retained a Republican governor, Lyman Humphrey of Independence, and the Populists worked tolerably with the other parties in the legislature. Indeed, the Republican reform agenda was liberal enough that some students of Populism have doubted that the Populists accomplished much that the Republicans would not have in time. Humphrey's 1889 legislative message, given before there was a People's Party, called for "a judicious system of public regulation of the railroad, firmly, but discreetly administered," and antitrust legislation to regulate what he called "an excrescent growth of the age—an ill-begotten child of avarice and mendacity, exhibiting in its most obnoxious form that lust for gain, regardless of the rights and interests of the people." No Populist could have phrased it more strongly. Humphrey advocated rights for women, "to open the doors to wider fields of usefulness" for them. He spoke also of an alien ownership bill and of abolishing the death penalty.[166] Though most modern historians do not accept the Republican-as-radical thesis, certainly some of the issues the Populists pushed were in the Kansas atmosphere anyway. "We are a happy state," Humphrey said, "where laws restrain cupidity and greed; a civilization that breeds neither barons nor beggars . . . whose prime factors are the railroad, the school house, the church, and the press."[167]

However, any possibility that the Kansas Populists would be accepted in the national media as a respectable reform movement was quite damaged by the spectacle of the Legislative War of 1893. In November 1892, with the help of the Democrats, who supported the Populist candidates at the state level, Kansas elected a Populist governor, Lorenzo Lewelling, and sent Simpson to

Congress. There was a triumphal march in Topeka with Mary Lease dressed in a new silk dress and bonnet and Congressman Simpson guiding tours of the gaily decorated legislative hall for the public. "We have come today," said Simpson, "to remove the seat of government of Kansas from the Santa Fe offices, back to the State-house where it belongs."

On January 9 Governor Lewelling gave his inaugural address.[168] "The 'survival of the fittest' (or strongest)," Lewelling said, "is the government of brutes and reptiles, and such philosophy must give place to a government which recognizes human brotherhood."[169] He went on with passion, and to a "mighty ovation," to say, "It is the mission of Kansas to protect and advance the moral and material interests of all its citizens. . . . Government is not a failure, and the state has not been constructed in vain. This is the generation that has come to the rescue. Those in distress who cry from the darkness shall not be heard in vain. Conscience is in the saddle, we have leaped into the bloody chasm and entered a contest for the protection of home, humanity and the dignity of labor."[170]

But problems with the smooth working of brotherhood quickly arose. Kansas had an indisputably Populist-dominated state senate along with its new governor. But in the house there was a question about several election returns. Both the Republicans and the Populists, claiming to be in the majority, tried independently to organize the chamber. On January 10, there was a standoff, and all members, fearing to adjourn, spent the night in the legislative chamber, the two speakers sleeping with gavel in hand. The next day the governor recognized the Populist house. Neither side, however, would concede the ground, and both threatened the use of force. "We are here by the will of the people," the Populists wrote the governor, "and will disperse only at the point of the bayonet."

There followed for over a month one of the strangest on again–off again legislative sessions on record, the Republicans using the chamber in the morning and the Populists in the afternoon. There was a bare minimum of appointments made and little legislative progress. On February 14, the Populists stayed in the house chamber overnight, and when the Republicans arrived for their morning session, the Populists barred them from entering. The Republican contingent then marched en masse from an organizational meeting at the Copeland Hotel to the capitol, where they smashed down the door of the house chamber and entered it by force. The Populists threatened that they would regain the hall with the help of state militia called by

Lewelling. This time the Republicans held the hall overnight, going in and out for food. They were uncomfortable, given the heavy snow, because the Populist janitor had turned off the heat to the building. The governor and the militia, however, backed off on the countercharge, and the house factions agreed to meet separately until the court decided the matter. That decision, when it came on February 25 from the Kansas Supreme Court, was in favor of the Republicans, as might be expected from that party's two-to-one majority on the court. The lone Populist justice dissented vigorously.[171]

It was just a piece of political silliness, not much different from any Kansas had experienced before. The Republicans generated as much of it as did the Populists. It was disappointing that only eleven days had been devoted to official business during the whole session, and the Populists could not blame their lack of progress on a reform agenda on the obstructionism of Republicans. What made it more than a usual mistake, however, was that the Populists, the harbingers of change, were vulnerable, and the strange standoff was perfect for the new mass media. It generated ink all over the nation, most of it critical of the Populists and their Kansas agenda. Joseph Hudson of the *Topeka Capital* published a series of letters to Governor Lewelling, noting, "Defying the constitutional rights of members of the Legislature is a more serious matter than talking anarchist 'rot' at picnics."[172]

Every incident of the war was selected for and blown up to the maximum possible ludicrousness. Reporters in January spoke of "howling mobs" dueling in the chambers where solons were supposed to debate.[173] The American Press Association reported, "There is always fun in Kansas politics, as to what that state will do next, but one thing is certain, and that is that it will not do what eastern people naturally expect it to do."[174]

When the conflict escalated in mid-February, so did the commentary. "It appears to be the determination of the opposing factions in the Kansas House," the *Kansas City Star* commented, "to superadd to the stupidity of a senseless deadlock the crime of an open revolution."[175] The door-smashing episode provided lithographs for illustration. And then came the militia, stationed outside and presumably ready for attack. "In addition to Mrs. M. E. Lease, who is already established at the Kansas seat of war," wrote the *Star*, "Wichita also contributes a Gatling gun to the fray which is raging at Topeka."[176] Wrote another reporter, "The latest Kansas hemorrhage appears to be an effusion from the jugular. . . . When it comes to a genuine crisis,

Broken door at the statehouse during the legislative war, 1893.
Courtesy of the Kansas State Historical Society.

Kansas can give the European war cloud heavy odds and beat it all hollow."[177] People came from all over the state and region just to watch.

In the aftermath came laughter but also sadness. "Kansas's Silly War," read one headline. "Tragedy Was Promised, but Farce Is the Only Outcome."[178] The "jaw and sledge hammer war" seemed to accomplish little positive.[179] A St. Louis reporter thought, "Kansas is nothing if not mercurial and sensational. She delights to advertise herself by performances of a remarkable character, and to relieve the monotony of life on her broad and lonesome prairies by presenting new phases of political activity and contention. But she sometimes overdoes the matter."[180] The only physical wound of the legislative war was a bloody nose when a militiaman tried to stop "maddened men with lunch baskets," but the state's reputation plummeted.[181] As one poet wrote,

> Everything appears disjointed, up to date.
> With no fool killer appointed for the state.
> While the world, aghast with wonder,
> Faintly questions, 'Why in thunder
> Do the idiots all in Kansas
> Congregate?'[182]

Kansans waited for the storm to blow over and for another crisis somewhere to divert the attention of the national press. "Legislatures like raging fevers run their course shortly and then pass away," wrote a Leavenworth attorney, "and we enjoy ourselves all the better for a severe dose now and then."[183] Many Kansans tried to distance themselves from these activities. Complimenting Chief Justice Horton on his decision in the *Gunn vs. Kansas* case that settled the legislative war and on his careful reading of it in public, D. J. Brewer, a justice of the U.S. Supreme Court from Kansas, wrote that the decision would strengthen "the hands of law and order, as against the vagaries and violence of all the fools and fanatics in the State."[184] Wrote another supporter of Horton, "There is yet a God in Israel, and a Chief Justice in Kansas."[185] We are not ashamed of Kansas, wrote one newspaperman. "To condemn her for all time because of her present anarchistic fit, would be like pronouncing as consumption the slight colicky fit of the small boy in the early green apple time of summer. . . . We are sincerely sorry she is sick. Our duty is to nurse her again to life and health."[186]

The People's Party itself declined, first slowly and then rapidly, filled with splits in its ranks that eventually led to fusion with the Democrats and the phenomenon of Popocrats in 1896. Lewelling lost the governorship in 1894 to Edmund Morrill, a Republican. Although Governor John Leedy, who was elected in 1896 for one term, was ostensibly a Populist, his election was by a Populist/Democratic fusion party, and he had by no means the zeal of Lewelling for radical reform.[187] In 1904 the Populists polled just over six thousand votes for president of the United States in Kansas, while the Prohibition Party had over seven thousand and the Socialists fifteen thousand.[188] The head of the Democratic State Central Committee that year declared, "The Populist party has been wiped off the map," most members having become Socialists.[189]

The ideas that engendered the party however, were not gone. Laura Johns, president of the Kansas Equal Suffrage Association, and several companions were locked into the house chamber during the legislative war and spoke on their issues there.[190] They continued to speak from 1894 until 1912, when Kansas women gained full suffrage. A woman noted, "Who made the political pool one of filth and iniquity? Not women; for their hands would have long ago poured a disinfectant in its putrid waters." Annie Diggs of Lawrence, a Populist speaker, said in a speech in 1894, "The women of Kansas are not claiming the right of suffrage because we are better than the men but because we want to try to make this world a little better for our having lived in it. . . . We have had a government of the men, for the men and by the men. It has been splendidly fathered but it has not been properly mothered."[191]

But by the 1890s the traditional regional hope of betterment had fallen on hard times. So had the economy. Kansas gained barely 3 percent in population overall during the decade and was buffeted by hot winds and unfavorable press.[192] A correspondent in Chicago wrote Eugene Ware, saying he would "like to ask certain questions of some level headed man about Kansas, and the actual position of the thinking portion of the people there upon the questions about which by common fame they have all gone daft. Everything one hears in the way of an authorized public utterance make that impression worse."[193]

There were attempts to defuse Populism by trivializing it. Editor George Martin of Junction City blamed Populism on the economic boom of the 1880s and consequent sour grapes from the losers in the bust. "Because we have borrowed wisely or unwisely, lived extravagantly, or expended money

Clara Jones McNees and Joel McNees, a Canton, Kansas, couple, 1900.
Courtesy of the Kansas State Historical Society.

for those things we could have done without, or suffered reverses and afflic-
tions which are the common lot of mankind, a large proportion of our
people for some years have settled into a state of chronic whine, and this
condition of the individual liver has developed into a political party which
proposes to run the government on a perpetual ache."[194] Charles Gleed
thought the credit of the state was not entirely ruined and wrote in 1894:

> The general reputation of Kansas is very bad among superficial observers;
> fair among the middle class observers, and first-class among those who
> observe critically. The superficial observers are those who know nothing
> of Kansas except what they find in the crime and freak departments of the
> big papers. . . . Every managing editor has his mind made up to accept
> and print anything, no matter how extraordinary, if it only has a Kansas

date line.... The man who merely had a bad Kansas mortgage, or several of them, cannot necessarily assume to know Kansas.[195]

Most people could not make those subtle distinctions. Robert Bader, in his study of the twentieth-century image of Kansas, dates the precipitous and seemingly permanent decline in self-esteem and of respect by others for the state to the Dust Bowl years of the 1930s. But he admits that the 1890s in Kansas were "a public-image nightmare," which left the citizens of the state "alternating in mood between sputtering anger and sullen defensiveness on every subject from economics to literature." It was 1901 before hope was enough alive that a local man could publish a poem, "Sneakin' Back to Kansas."[196] In general, it was a disoriented and suffering set of Kansans, chastened especially by the contrast of current conditions to the prosperity that seemed to prevail in the 1880s, who looked forward to the arrival of the twentieth century.

5

THE BONE AND SINEW OF THE STATE

In a hay field along Berryton Road southeast of Topeka, on September 2, 1911, Albin Longren started the Hall-Scott V-8 engine on a delicate-looking pusher biplane, the *Topeka*, which he and two other local men had constructed. "There was a whir," the *Topeka Capital* reported, "a series of regular explosions from the motor and a strong current of wind swept back from the propeller. The whole machine quivered and pulled impatiently, promising every moment to break away from several men who were holding it." Then one of the three who had wheeled the big bird onto the field mounted the driver's seat, grasped the control lever and signaled, "Let her go." That was Longren. He flew the craft six miles in perfect control, the first flight in Kansas in a Kansas-built airplane.[1]

J. C. Mars had made a cross-country flight in a Curtiss from Topeka toward Kansas City in 1910, and the Curtiss team gave demonstrations at Walnut Grove in Wichita in 1911 before a crowd estimated at thirty thousand. But these were not Kansas airplanes. Longren's obscure but important achievement occurred slightly before Clyde Cessna's. Cessna, from Kingman County, was in 1911 flying a modified kit plane, which he wrecked and repaired often enough that it soon became his own design.

All the craft of 1911 were far in advance of Roy Knabensue's airship, which had flown only a few hundred yards at Wichita's Peerless Prophet's street fair in 1908 before the Kansas wind tore the gasbag to ribbons and plummeted pilot and craft to earth. Henry Call's "woodpecker-headed creation," built in Girard that same year to carry people to the Socialist Party convention in Chicago, was a Kansas-built plane, to be sure, but not a practical one. It only taxied. Reported the local press: "It hasn't yet become addicted to the rising habit." William Purvis and Charles Wilson's helicopter, built in 1909 in Goodland, in far western Kansas, never got off the ground either, and had, one observer said, "all the grace of a crippled praying mantis." The same was true of A. E. Hunt's rotary flying machine, built by a blacksmith in Jetmore. They were no more promising than Dr. Foote's 1885 machine had been. The *Wichita Eagle* ran an aviation number in 1911, stating, "Contemporary progress is as unreal to us as foreign lands, as unreal as things of the historic past, unless we see them with our own eyes."[2] Seeing, however, was not believing. That took people like Longren and Cessna, who made aviation in Kansas into a business.

Longren built a plane for Phillip Billard, the son of the mayor of Topeka, and Billard flew it over the capital city on November 17, 1912. He reached a height of twenty-five hundred feet and a speed of seventy-five miles per hour as he buzzed over the Santa Fe railway shops, north to the Kansas River, and back over the statehouse and the business district. On Christmas Day he flew forty minutes at five thousand feet, to the wonder of gawking spectators.[3]

The Kansas that Phil Billard looked down upon on those flights and later ones over western Kansas was a state much changed from its Populist 1890s struggles. The native enterprise there, combined with a relative lack of regulation and the small capital needed to turn invention into industry, meant that aircraft manufacture was not the only industry beginning to compete with agriculture in Kansas.

The state took to the automobile as enthusiastically as it did to the airplane and was an "early adapter," too, of the gasoline tractor on farms. In 1916 at the old Burton Car Works factory in Wichita, a remnant of the 1880s boom, Cessna built aircraft for demonstration and sale. In the same space John Jones constructed the Jones Six automobile.[4] Other Kansas towns boasted auto plants. The Hagstrom brothers in Lindsborg had one.[5] Topeka had the Smith Automobile Company, employing fifty people to produce the "Great Smith" car.[6] There was the Cloughley, built in Parsons, the Sellers in Hutchinson, the Adams in Hiawatha, and the Gleason in Kansas City.[7] F. W. (Woody) Hockaday, proprietor of the Hockaday Auto Supply Company in Wichita, promoted automobiles with clever advertising stunts from 1905 on, and in 1915 he attracted national attention by issuing maps and automobile guides and marking highways in Kansas.[8] The first to have cars were the wealthy. Dr. John Northington of Emporia had probably the first car in Kansas, a blue single-cylinder Winton, bought secondhand in Chicago. It

Clyde Cessna in one of his early monoplanes.
Courtesy of the Kansas State Historical Society.

attracted so many onlookers that the doctor had "no real peace."[9] C. Q. Chandler, president of the First National Bank, was one of the early owners in Wichita, as was Arthur Capper, the newspaper publisher, in Topeka.[10]

"When the motor car first found its way to the Kansas farm," a Kansas City paper commented in 1909, "it appeared a luxury. Soon it became a not uncommon pleasure and then a necessity.... Many farmers have them and a majority of those who are not so fortunate have the motor car fever in a most virulent form."[11] A reporter in 1911 stated that the country town livery stable was a thing of the past.[12] In eighteen months in 1913 and 1914, owners registered over ninety thousand cars in Kansas.[13] In 1916 there was a car for every 22.5 people in the state and one for every 9.0 in Pawnee County in the west. Kansans had spent $37 million for automobiles in the last two years, and "the wheat counties have shown the most startling changes."[14] Nor was

Automobiling, 1908.
Courtesy of the Kansas State Historical Society.

the automobile the only high-technology item. In 1913, there were over two hundred fifty thousand telephones in Kansas, and radio was soon to come.[15]

But that prosperous, confident, and diversified world below Billard's wings did not spring up sudden and mature. It was a slow pull out of a pit and no more automatic than any other reinvention of the state. Senator Preston Plumb wrote Eugene Ware in 1891, encouraging Ware to stay in Kansas. "We sometimes get off our feet in various ways, but things will settle down."[16] Two years later, however, Ware still could write, "The bottom seems to have dropped out of things."[17]

The old leaders had had their day. Preston Plumb died in December 1891.[18] In 1894, it was Charles Robinson's turn to go.[19] In 1900, Ingalls died in Arizona, where he had gone for his health. His copper-lined cedar coffin was taken back to Atchison, where friends said goodbye to the strains of Chopin in the Episcopal Church.[20] "One by one," a friend wrote Sara Robinson, "are the old pioneers, like Autumn leaves, dropping all around us."[21]

It seemed that the glory of Kansas might pass with them. Carrie Nation raided the Carey House bar in Wichita in 1900, sweeping the glassware off the bar, throwing rocks at John Noble's painting of a nude Cleopatra, and creating a storm of publicity about Kansas as a crazy place.[22] "Mrs. Nation's use of the hatchet," wrote President Nathan Morrison of Wichita's Fairmount College, "in breaking into buildings, destroying furniture and disturbing the peace . . . should be treated by the courts precisely as the law requires them to treat other burglars. . . . Kansas is just now suffering deeply in the estimation of all substantial men in the East whom I meet. Remarks I am obliged to hear about the 'instability of society there,' 'lawlessness of professed good men,' 'low grade of civilization,' etc. are not easy to bear and are hard to refute."[23] Shortly, the headlines were about the battleship *Kansas* that had to be christened with pure water at the insistence of a Kansas governor who also tried to reform the drinking habits of the seamen, offering clean-living Kansans for the crew if necessary.[24] L. Frank Baum wrote a novel in 1900 about a little girl blown away by a cyclone to the Land of Oz from a very gray state of Kansas that had ruined her Uncle Henry and Aunt Em. Most people reading the novel at the turn of the century, or later, seeing the 1939 film, remembered the original dismal look of Kansas in Dorothy's eyes and not the moral of *The Wizard of Oz*: the wonderful qualities of our ordinary homes, those civilized countries where there are no witches and wizards at all.[25]

It seemed the only positive publicity Kansas was getting around the turn of the century concerned Frederick Funston, the Iola native who was a hero in the Spanish American War. Funston, the son of a Kansas congressman, made a reputation as an Arctic explorer in the early 1890s, partly through his own vivid writing for newspapers and magazines and partly through that by his friend, William Allen White. He volunteered to help the Cuban rebels before the United States was officially involved in the conflict and later captured the Philippine insurrectionist Emilio Aguinaldo, to great acclaim. One journalist wrote, "If in ages to come the mythology of Kansas should be written, Funston would figure as the unconquerable warrior who bore a charmed life."[26] Funston's book, *Memories of Two Wars* (1912), sold well. The *Louisville Star* hoped that he represented a new direction for Kansas, more pragmatic and scientific. "There was a time when [Kansas] . . . was straining at the leash and gritting her teeth in her frantic efforts to get at midnight conspirators, octopuses and things that chew them up raw; while the rest of the county laughed and poked jibing paragraphs at her." Perhaps Funston's calm heroics—in his exploration, in his war record, and in the efficient way he handled disaster relief after the San Francisco earthquake in 1906— heralded a welcome change.[27]

Frederick Funston.
Courtesy of the Kansas State Historical Society.

Kansas always had a solid strain of realism. The Atchison editor Ed Howe had garnered compliments for his portrayal of the dark side of rural life in his 1881 novel, *The Story of a Country Town*, from the scion of the literary realist movement, William Dean Howells.[28] Eugene Ware, the "short haired" poet with the pen name "Ironquill," demonstrated the same honest common sense. The realist poet, Ware wrote, "has no muse nor chief; / He sings of corn; he eulogizes beef; / And in the springtime his aesthetic soul / Bursts forth in vernal eulogies of coal."[29]

Ware had something to sing about in his state, even in the otherwise grim decade of national depression. Coal, salt, oil, and natural gas became commercial industries as agricultural prospects plummeted. So did new manufacturing and distribution enterprises, such as milling, broom-corn jobbing, and airplane building. William Coleman's gasoline lamp business thrived in Wichita, as did Albert Hyde's sales of Mentholatum, the "Little Nurse for Little Ills." Coleman quietly established his manufacturing operation in Wichita in 1900, just as the headlines were talking about Nation's saloon raid.[30]

Farmers were not stereotyped as innovators. But in Kansas, farmers welcomed the automobile, the tractor, and the Coleman lamp, and the people marketing these products were ingenious at making them acceptable to that class of customer. Just as Richard Sears had attracted the farmer to mail order with an iron-clad money-back guarantee, and Jerome Case had burned and replaced a farmer's reaper that he could not repair, Coleman kicked a lighted lamp down hardware store aisles to demonstrate safety. Coleman representatives visited Kansas towns not only to sell new products but to repair old ones. They claimed that a Coleman product was not to wear out or go out of fashion, any more than was Henry Ford's Model-T car.[31]

Thinking seriously about causes and solutions suddenly seemed a more fit task for regional college students than declension of Latin nouns. To the passion for growth and for change, it was thought, must be added a science of how to go about it and wisdom concerning appropriate and achievable goals for Kansas. Robinson gave one hundred thousand dollars, nearly his whole estate, to the University of Kansas, with the thought that education was the best guarantee of implementation of his reform agenda.[32]

This cast to matters did not spring up suddenly with the new century. Populist thinking went well beyond arguments for free silver and debt relief.

A little of everything in a small-town Kansas store in August 1911.
Courtesy of the Kansas State Historical Society.

Ignatius Donnelly and Henry Demarest Lloyd in the political realm and Ida Tarbell, Frank Norris, and Lincoln Steffens in the economic area built a case for a reasoned approach to issues that placed government planning at the forefront.[33] In Kansas there was practical thinking along with the eccentric or general statements so often quoted. Sam Wood did not just criticize the legislature of 1891; he analyzed it, bill by bill, employing statistics rather than rhetoric.[34] C. Wood Davis wrote pragmatic articles. In "The Farmer, the Investor, and the Railway," he blamed the troubles of the farmer not on political conspiracy but on the "difficulty experienced in forming combinations with his fellows for concentrated action."[35]

The new regulatory agencies were similarly down to earth. In the 1890 report of the Kansas Board of Railroad Commissioners was a section, "A Suggestive Review." The board thought that "circumstances and conditions" required a study of the relationship of the state to railroads, with a view toward answering "questions of statesmanship most difficult to master with wisdom and justice to the public and the companies." With a "foundation of public knowledge," there could be accurate public judgment and "the occupation of the demagogue will be gone."[36] By 1895 the board had decided over one thousand cases and had collected such information from hundreds of advocates for many positions.[37]

Charles Gleed and his brother Willis were partners in a Topeka law firm, along with Eugene Ware. Charles was an ATSF director and a regent of the University of Kansas; Willis was a regent and a professor of law and Greek at the university.[38] Both were active public speakers and managed to bridge the seeming gap between the academic world and that of business. "Knowledge is no longer to be monopolized," Charles Gleed wrote, "by those who chance first to get it; . . . it is no more to be kept covered in the cell of the monk or in the book-lined alcoves of the student's retreat; . . . its possessor is in every way morally obligated to impart what he has to his fellows in as direct and certain a way as possible."[39]

A means to this end was the building of public libraries. By 1891 the Kansas State Historical Library contained over sixty thousand volumes, the Kansas State Library about thirty thousand, the Topeka Public Library twelve thousand, Bethany College three thousand, Washburn six thousand, and the library of the Kansas Academy of Science five thousand.[40] Wichita, which had been laughed at during the 1880s for its failure to support school bond and library issues, and for its boast that its people were too busy selling real estate to read, changed its tune in the 1890s. Nathan Morrison, a scholarly Congregationalist originally from New England, pushed primarily at Wichita's Fairmount College (1895) for the creation of a library. When his eastern friends complained about the wild economic views of the Populists in Kansas, Morrison calmly listened. People, he observed, "think Kansas is plagued with populism, crankism, Leaseism, repudiation & free silver to an extent compared to which the plagues of Egypt are not a circumstance." When they finished, he asked their help to educate Kansans. By 1905, Fairmount Library had twenty-six thousand volumes.[41]

Charles Gleed thought that William Spooner's gift of one hundred thousand dollars to KU for a library, which came in 1891, was significant. Kansas had to diversify, to stop being exploited as a colony by the East, to replace the one hundred eastern insurance companies operating there with some of its own, to publish more books, and to manufacture more products. "Regions which produce only corn, or cotton, or timber, or silver, or coal, or fish, usually wear the same badge—the badge of poverty." Studying in a library was the way to learn how to do things. The Populists were right that something was wrong in the West, but they were wrong in their analysis and deficient in their expertise. There was, he wrote, "scarcely agricultural talent enough in all the [Populist] party's . . . office-holders combined to know the difference between cucumbers and cockle-burrs. . . . Like the one-drug doctors, they prescribe for all miseries their sole remedy."[42]

Willis Gleed recalled that when his class of 1879 graduated, there were only ten on the faculty at the University of Kansas and one building. In 1895 there were seven buildings and one hundred professors. That was helpful. But the greatest resource was students with varied backgrounds and a practical outlook. The average businessperson thought a liberal arts education was expensive (two hundred dollars a year per student in 1895) and failed to teach how to copy a letter in a letterbook without blurring it. But according to Gleed, it provided qualities both vital and ultimately practical—keener sensibilities, higher aspirations, and warmer affections—keeping alive "the power of emotion, the power to feel," which was basic to preserving good government on earth.[43] "Yes I have come all the way from Kansas," he told an Ohio audience in 1899, "just to say 'Be good'—be a good man and a good citizen—not negatively good—not conventionally good—but actively, aggressively good. . . . That is real life at the foundation."[44] That program required more than piety.

Many people felt a key was to educate more people more thoroughly. Kansas established an open admissions policy in 1915. All students who had completed a four-year course accredited by the Board of Education were entitled to enter the freshman class of the state universities.[45] Governor Capper emphasized in 1913 that the state appropriated $2 million a year for its colleges, but only seventeen of one thousand Kansans went to college, and only fifty-three of that number entered a high school. "I want every boy and girl in Kansas," Capper said, "no matter how humble his home, to have a fair chance at the door of opportunity. If we are going to do that, we must have education that fits NOT alone the few for the life they are to live, but an education that will fit the many, the great body of the common people, the bone and sinew of the state, for what they will undertake, an education that will make bread-winners rather than dreamers of the children of Kansas."[46]

There was another side to public demands on higher education: people who wanted quality as well as democracy. C. W. Smith of Stockton in 1902 suggested that the University of Kansas, where he intended to send his six children, "has fallen behind all the State Universities in the West during the past ten years," and the legislature should support its recovery from Populist restrictions on funding.[47]

Sound and universal education took money. Contemporary with the push for open admissions came a movement to charge tuition, based on public suggestions from Carl Swensson, president of the private Bethany College.[48] In 1904 the legislature directed the University of Kansas, an institution that had been free to state residents, to charge a "matriculation fee" of five dollars for Kansans and ten dollars for non-Kansans.[49] There were issues, too, of overlap of the missions among the state schools. KU, thought one critic, should be "more exclusively a graduate school and not a common college with a big name attached to it," Kansas State should be more narrowly an agricultural school, and the Normal at Emporia was "too much of a High School."[50] George Martin wrote in 1903, "Kansas is too rural to comprehend the enormous salaries with which the University must compete to keep the best talent." He recommended a special tax so that the regents could pay the salaries demanded by circumstances and so that the chancellor and faculty could be "relieved of the humiliating duty of whining about each session of the legislature for the means of business." He noted also that from 1899 to 1902, wealthy donors gave $242 million to colleges, libraries, and charities but none to Kansas institutions. During the forty years of Kansas's history less than $1 million had come to it from these sources. "Kansas, with all her prominence or notoriety, is still far from being an integral part of the globe," Martin concluded. "Our freaks and fads do not attract."[51]

To change that image abroad as well as the self-image at home was worth real effort. And much of that effort came from a new generation of Kansas newspaper editors. William Allen White of the *Emporia Gazette* was the most prominent of these, but there were many others of a sterling class. Charles Scott became associated with the *Iola Register* in 1897 and gave that paper tremendous character.[52] The same was the case with Frederick Brinkerhoff's longtime editorships in southeast Kansas (beginning in 1909), A. Q. Miller Sr.'s operation of the *Belleview Telescope* (beginning in 1904), or Rolla Clymer's of the *El Dorado Times* (beginning in 1918).[53] Henry Allen of the *Wichita Beacon,* Victor Murdock of the *Wichita Eagle,* and Arthur Capper were more famous than Scott, Brinkerhoff, Miller, Clymer, and their colleagues because they combined political careers with journalism. But the small-town editors with the large vocabularies and the big hearts stayed put into the 1960s and 1970s, keeping Kansas's Progressive Era conscience alive.

They pioneered in seeing global significance in the local, in collecting statistics, in doing what might now be called "investigative reporting," and in crusading for effective change across the street as well as in Topeka and Washington.[54]

Arthur Capper was not one of the great writers among newspapermen, but he was the master organizer of chains of Kansas newspapers, and he revolutionized both the technology and the organization of the regional newspaper business early in the twentieth century. He learned along the way that in Kansas, reform sold newspapers and that it even made up for loss of revenue suffered from turning down ads for liquor and cigarettes.[55] "A newspaper," wrote the Topeka minister Charles Sheldon to Capper in 1909, "should be the people's historian of world events, related with strict truthfulness, and in the right proportion as to quantity and emphasis. . . . One of the greatest weaknesses of many papers to my mind is the abnormal quantity of space given to abnormal human conduct."[56] Capper, Sheldon thought, should see his paper as not just his own property "but a great instrument for the tremendous cause of righteousness in general."[57] The *Capital* was not always edited as Sheldon himself edited it in 1900, when he was allowed to run it as he thought Jesus would have done. But some form of applied religion continued as part of the educational message of Kansas newspapers.

Rolla Clymer remembered working on the *Quenemo Republican* on the Marais des Cygnes River at the turn of the century at age thirteen, setting the body of the paper by hand in eight-point type and editor John Ellis's editorials in ten-point. "These deathless articles," he remembered, "written with a heavy lead pencil on large sheets, dealt mostly with political subjects of the day—all in one sentence. As my first chore at editing, I managed to drop in a few commas and semi-colons—no periods—as I went along." His hands at the end of the day were covered with blisters from the lye used in washing the forms, but he had run six hundred copies of the sheet that helped define the community for its citizens and their proper role in it.[58] He found newspaper work a wonderful combination of thought and craft, translating words into metal, into ink on paper, and then, just maybe, into prosperity and change.

Clymer worked at the *Emporia Gazette* with White, beginning in 1907. White, Clymer remembered, "burst in every morning with suggestions for timely news stories, which usually meant that the town's Sacred Cows were marked for another distressing series of shocks and outrages. He interpolated straightway news copy here and there with some twist of his own that raised ordinary reporting to a high level. . . . When something hot was coming off the griddle of his nimble mind, his flying fingers beat a tattoo on his old . . . typewriter that was nothing short of sheer assault."[59] Clymer said the town editor in the White mold brought "pride in community progress, firm faith in community stability and an immortal community destiny."[60] Clymer, like so many small-town Kansas editors, was a master of the personal obituary, knowing, as he did, the people of his town intimately. Those biographies became in turn part of a well-understood community legacy and provided a challenge to the next generation.[61]

With the infrastructure of everything from newspapers to airplane and auto plants, and with a more humble and grounded turn of mind, Kansas in the twentieth century resumed where it had left off politically. There was a rush of legislation and experiments on many fronts. The historian Robert LaForte, whose *Leaders of Reform* is one of the most careful studies of the regional politics of the era, called the Kansas Progressives "conservative radicals who were interested in practical solutions to practical problems." They were "naturally fair minded," said one of them, and would not endanger property rights. But they were not, LaForte argued, conservative in the same sense as Gabriel Kolko used that term in describing the national movement. Kolko in *The Triumph of Conservatism* made the point that Progressivism nationally actually helped establish the hegemony of big businesses in the era of mergers by rationalizing markets and creating competitive predictability. Kansas, in contrast, by no means approved of the established economic relationships and so was more liberal than the U.S. Congress in trying to change the balance. Kansas Progressives took over some Populist issues, but they were much more scientific in their approach and less passionate, hardly, as William Allen White once claimed, just Populists who had put on a clean shirt and moved to town.[62] The legislators even looked different. "The whisker . . . is in the minority," commented a Topeka paper at the 1915 session, "and the barber shops will not be kept from their rightful share of the legislative trade."[63]

There was a flurry of legislation on a wide range of subjects. Among the more innovative topics were bills on primary elections, football regulation, the public utilities commission, city commissions and city managers, consolidating state agencies, the state board of administration, anticigarette moves, initiative/referendum/recall, the civil service merit system, insurance

Rolla Clymer.
Courtesy of the Kansas State Historical Society.

regulation, workmen's compensation, blue-sky securities regulation, woman suffrage, the state art board, capital punishment, the pure shoe law, child hygiene, interracial marriages, displaying radical flags, mine and factory inspection, the juvenile court, eugenic matrimony, the bank guaranty law, the public defender, movie censorship, the eight-hour day, and the state printing plant.[64] Most of these were not private bills, or what were sometimes called "hobby bills," on trivial subjects, as had plagued the legislature for years, though there was one much-publicized proposal in 1915 forbidding women under forty-five from using face powder, rouge, hair dye, bleaching powder, and tooth powder or from wearing earrings.

The volume of bills introduced and passed increased rapidly.[65] No wonder order in the legislative chamber sometimes broke down, as in 1903 when at the end of the session there was a half-hour "wastebasket fight," with paper thrown by tired state legislators cleaning out their desks.[66] It was regularly suggested in these years that the fifty-day Kansas biennial meeting of the legislature was an "oxcart" system that hardly allowed for the careful consideration of the concerns referred to the legislature.[67] Yet no change came until 1966, when voters accepted an annual session as a constitutional amendment.[68] There was still a restriction that the sessions in the even-numbered calendar years should be limited to sixty days, changed to ninety days in 1974. Pay changes were slow in coming, also. From 1861 to 1949, Kansas legislators received a compensation of three dollars a day, as originally provided in the constitution, and a travel allowance for only one trip from home.

Those long-standing restrictions mirrored the view of some early-twentieth-century critics that all this legislating and regulating could go too far. The state budget in 1915 was already $10 million (40 percent for education).[69] In 1917, the statehouse was full of lobbyists—the Kansas Better Government League, the Kansas Good Roads Association, the Kansas League of Municipalities, the Four-in-One Organization of State Officers, the Farmers' Co-operative Grain Men's Association, the Kansas WCTU, the Council of Women, the Kansas Star Grange—seeking everything from a closed season on quail, to regulating cigarette ads in newspapers, to changing the tax exemption for college fraternity houses.[70] One reporter in 1915 was disturbed by a bill recommended by a lobbyist to regulate the Kansas farmer by requiring safety and sanitation devices.[71]

To avoid mental indigestion from the complexities of the Progressive Era in Kansas, certain evocative issues may serve as lenses on the style in which matters came to be approached and resolved in the state in the pre–World War I period. These issues, approximately in the order of their chronological appearance, were school textbooks, the flood of 1903 and conservation, the Standard Oil fight of 1905, railroad and anti-trust regulation, capital punishment, women's rights, public health, city reform and structural change, T. R. and the Bull Moose rebellion, and isolationism.

In the atmosphere of scientific management and the "gospel of efficiency" emerging in the early twentieth century, the cost advantages in either centralized purchase of schoolbooks or the publication of them directly by a state agency gained wide attention in Kansas. There were educational disadvantages, including the inability of teachers to choose their own textbooks and lack of competition. But with the new confidence in experts, there was little doubt that a board could wisely choose the right texts and that the uniformity would provide a standardized educational experience that suited both statisticians and advocates of fairness. The School Textbook Commission, created in 1897, was a late Populist measure. It was replaced in 1913 by the Schoolbook Commission, which weathered an investigation in 1931 and 1932, and lasted until 1937. The superintendent of public instruction was a member throughout.[72]

The original idea was that the state should use its mass purchasing power to reduce prices and perhaps to specify content from commercial publishers. This worked well to lower costs but became controversial because of opportunities for payoffs from publishers to members of the commission, the question of the competence of the political appointees on the commission, and questions about whether the system was flexible enough to support good teaching. George Crane of the Topeka publishing house of Crane and Company complained in 1905 that one man had been on the commission since 1897, had no children in school, and had managed, while spending most of his time as a volunteer member of the School Textbook Commission, to build one of the finest homes in Topeka. Crane thought this was due to kickbacks from the publisher Webb McNall and that it was no accident that his own firm, Crane, was never successful in its bids for Kansas schoolbook business. "The only way to avoid the widespread scandals of the past in regard to the Text Book Commission," Crane advised, "is to appoint fair and proper men."[73]

However, the experts who were supposed to be forthcoming, at little or no pay, to serve the state were not much in evidence.[74] "It is a notorious fact," wrote Professor W. H. Carruth from KU, that the books adopted by the state were out of date "and long given up in progressive communities, and also that these unfit books are nearly all published by one company." He suggested as appointees to the board the heads of the three state universities, three secondary school men and three "educated business men."[75] Another analyst suggested to Governor Edward Hoch that women be appointed. "The majority of school teachers are women, now do you not think it fair and just that they should have some representation on the board. . . . You surely have some pleasant recollections of women teachers when you were a boy, possibly some of them had much patience with you."[76] Many observers seemed to agree, whoever were the appointees, that the "school book octopus" was worse than what it was designed to cure.

Having the state print its own books at the Kansas State Printing Plant (established in 1904), either by contracting for reprinting of titles from other publishers or commissioning its own authors to write textbooks, seemed a way to control corruption while further reducing costs. But it established a major state business, which not only required sophisticated management but also led to criticism that it was a socialistic interference with free enterprise.[77] A businessman argued there were severe distortions in the state's estimate of savings from the printing of its own textbooks. The critic claimed that school readers in Kansas from commercial publishers were in 1913 selling for less in Kansas than they were in California from a state printing plant. If Kansas were clever, it could get its schoolbooks free from Sears Roebuck, as did Ontario, Canada, in return for allowing advertising in them.[78] Be that as it may, the campaign with the public for state printing of schoolbooks was irresistible.

The 1915 report of the reorganized and redirected Kansas Schoolbook Commission detailed the beginnings of a large state-run business. There was $150,000 for the purchase of grounds to expand the State Printing Plant, the erection of a building, and the purchase of printing and binding machinery; $50,000 for payment of authors, artists, and compilers and purchase of copyrights and plates; a salary of $2,000 a year for the secretary of the School Book Commission; and a $25,000 revolving fund for purchase of paper and printers and binders material and to pay labor. That year the state commissioned Anna Arnold to write a history of Kansas for a fixed fee of $3,500. Quickly produced, the Arnold history remained in print for its captive audience until the 1930s. It sold 34,951 copies in 1915 at 22¢ a copy and put over $7,500 back into the revolving fund. A primer was even more of a project, selling over 50,000 copies in 1915 at 12¢. The state also reprinted titles from commercial publishers at a deep discount. Ford and Ammerman's *Plane and Solid Geometry*, for instance, was sold from the State Printing Plant to schools for 70¢, including a 28¢ per book royalty to the Macmillan Company. The best price Macmillan had formerly offered the state to buy the book from it was $1.05 a copy.[79] In 1916 the board approved for school use *Bow-Wow and Mew-Mew, Nixie Bunny in Manner's Land,* Ware's *Selections from Ironquill,* and William Connelley's *John Brown,* among others. The last two volumes were publications of Crane and Company, Topeka.[80] By 1918 the state appropriation for the School Book Commission was only $7,500. It had generated a revolving fund from sales of $45,000 and was printing 200 to 300 titles. It had by then printed over 2.2 million books and sold 1.6 million, with revenue of over $330,000. State printer W. R. Smith boasted that the plant had 55,460 square feet of space and that "every art and device known to the modern successful printer," including six linotype machines, eight cylinder presses, and two quadruple folding machines, "each doing the work of twenty-seven girls," were present.[81] "The schools of Kansas," an official claimed, "as a whole are supplied with the best text books they have ever had and at prices much lower than the same books could be purchased in the open market."[82]

Not everyone agreed, especially when it came to the quality of the books. Henry Allen of the *Wichita Beacon* wrote an editorial in 1915 making fun of the poor grammar in the *Little Kansas Primer* and the sad halftones in the Kansas history. On more than 70 of the 143 pages of the *Kansas Primer,* Allen said, were found "by casual observation, errors in grammar, punctuation, rhetoric and quotation which would be inexcusable in any book of reasonably correct English, to say nothing of a textbook." There were "manifestly garbled" quotations, including fractured passages from the Bible.[83] The *Beacon* was in favor of free textbooks and of the state's printing them, the editor and future governor wrote, "but it does object to the state's printing any more books like the Kansas history and this new primer."[84] The reaction to that in Topeka was defensive, one legislator, during the twenty-minute discussion of the editorial, calling it a "libel on the state."[85] But criticism persisted.

A 1932 investigation led in 1937 to elimination of the commission and assigning its duties to the State Board of Education. The state printer, thereafter, could competitively bid on schoolbooks, but they were no longer required to be printed by the state.[86] The investigating committee concluded that the State School Book Commission had not functioned efficiently, that its members, serving as volunteers, did not give their duties the time required to do the job properly, and that pressure from private book publishers led to moving away from the ideal of uniformity and state printing. The investigators did conclude that the state had saved a good deal of money through the experiment.[87]

There was more hesitation about other species of public works. A case in point was flood control. The devastation of the flood of 1903 has been mentioned. What was different about it from earlier floods was the newfound feeling that there should be public action concerning natural disasters. Armourdale, the meatpacking district in Kansas City, which had a population of sixteen thousand, was deserted after the flood, and nearly ten thousand people were out of work in Kansas City.[88] "No private purse is large enough to provide for the sufferers," the mayor thought.[89] There was shock also at the looting and the raising of prices by merchants and calls for government intervention in that area.[90] Some people suggested that the federal government should help prevent floods through its powers under the Rivers and Harbors bill.[91] The relief commission set up by the Commercial Club in Topeka collected only about five thousand dollars in private money, and there were nine hundred applications filed for that aid.[92] In July, the state made an appropriation of seventy-two hundred dollars divided among four counties.[93] There were strong suggestions that it should have been $1 million.[94]

Some people, especially in Wichita where floods were not a problem until the next year, complained that government control would create fraud.[95] The *Topeka Journal*, however, argued that even if there were fraud, the emergency must be met. State relief was the right approach, but the current appropriation was far from enough. The state was spending two hundred thousand dollars at the St. Louis Lewis and Clark Exposition to show its wealth and resources. "I would hang my head in shame," wrote a Topeka reporter, "to enter that Kansas building at the St. Louis Exposition or point it out and say that Kansas is too beggarly, too penurious, to take care of her own distressed ones, or that the party that controls Kansas politics is so afraid of establishing a precedent."[96]

The *New York Times* agreed. In the editorial "A Willing Dependent," the newspaper wrote that it was thought in the East the Kansas legislature would appropriate $3 million for flood relief. "Kansas," the *Times* concluded, "is and always was a freak state. It claims to raise more cranks and impossible people generally to the acre than any other state of the Union, and the claim is not to be disputed. . . . When flood, or drought, or grasshoppers, make it again necessary to pass the hat, it is to be hoped that the satisfaction its legislators now derive from the economy of willing dependence upon the outside help in case of need will not be remembered to the disadvantage of the people."[97]

Kansas City focused on aid from the federal government to create public works. Its mayor went on a speaking tour to organize a lobby to convince the federal government to improve the Kansas River.[98] Kansas City leaders proposed a federal reservoir system costing $3.8 million.[99] Senator J. R. Burton of Kansas moved crowds by saying, "I would have tens of thousands of reservoirs, beginning at the headwaters of the stream and coming right to the rain belt. . . . The American engineer will solve the problem."[100]

It would take another flood in 1951 for the federal engineers to start moving earth in Kansas. But the idea that water control in the name both of property protection and conservation was a government function was gaining strength. At the time of the 1903 flood, Kansas and Colorado were embroiled in a lawsuit, pushed by Kansas, concerning the proper use of the Arkansas River and whether the taking of valuable water upstream by Coloradans for irrigation ought to be regulated or Kansas compensated for economic damage or both. Pump irrigation was already an important factor in western Kansas agriculture, evening the cycles at the expense of the aquifers.

In 1907 the *Kansas vs. Colorado* case decided by the U.S. Supreme Court established a concept of "equity" that has been used since, but water issues between the two states were still a bone of contention late in the twentieth century.[101] Even such a seemingly small issue as the proper treatment of the Cheyenne Bottoms wetlands area near Great Bend turned out to be complex. Proposals ran the gamut from draining, to use for farm irrigation, to creating a hunting reserve, to maintaining a wildlife habitat for migrating birds. The definition of "natural" became problematical as such wetlands areas became scarce and as the rights of local owners came into conflict with the public interest.[102] Senator Frederick Newlands of Nevada, active in promoting conservation, visited Kansas in 1915, and Governor Capper was named a member of the national Flood Prevention Congress that year.[103] A Western Kansas Water Conservation Association formed in 1927 and a volunteer State Commission on Flood Control and Water Conservation in 1928.[104]

The conservation issue, though by no means as significant in Kansas as it was in the great national debates of the Theodore Roosevelt era over wilderness and national forests, did crop up in ways other than the water question. Oil and gas conservation legislation began in 1889 with a petroleum inspection statute. In 1891 the state required casing of all oil and gas wells and specified a means of plugging abandoned wells to minimize environmental damage. Acts of 1901 and 1905 regulated the waste of natural gas, which previously had been vented in "fire fountains" for lack of a ready market. In 1905 oil and gas pipelines became common carriers, and in 1907 came a series of safety regulations on vendors of gasoline. In 1917 the state regulated the movement of housing, derricks, and other oil field equipment along public roads, as the highways near the El Dorado oil strike had become almost impassable.[105]

Fish and game issues were prominent, and the state fish hatchery at Pratt developed during the era into one of the premier facilities in the nation. Pratt's was so big, with one hundred fishponds in 1915, that citizens complained about the six men hired in winter to feed the fish and the thirty-five-hundred-dollar engineer's house—"a wicked waste," a detractor thought.[106]

Pond building by farmers became almost a fad, to the delight of J. C. Hopper of Ness City, who had been advocating a "dam the draws" solution to drought and flood since the 1880s. "I am for Ponds, Silos, and Good Roads," wrote a sloganeer to Governor George Hodges in 1913.[107] Pond Day joined Arbor Day, Fire Prevention Days, and other government-promoted educational days. Governor Capper, however, drew the line at the suggestion of a Gold Fish Day.[108] Stocking ponds was "artificial" surely, but there was the recognition, paralleled in the increased attention to urban and state parks in Kansas, that there was more to life than business and that the state was responsible for preserving and creating opportunities for outdoor recreation.

There were the early stirrings of a state role in historic preservation. The buildings at Shawnee Mission were some of the earliest structures in Kansas and had played a significant role in the territorial period and earlier. But in the twentieth century, they had deteriorated. In 1909, the mission was for sale for fifteen thousand dollars, having originally cost the government

Shawnee Mission in poor repair.
Courtesy of the Kansas State Historical Society.

seventy-five thousand dollars to build. Citizens thought that the Daughters of the American Revolution or some similar organization "ought to purchase this ground so replete with traditions and historic interest" before it was snapped up for a sanitarium.[109] Women's groups were active in historic preservation generally, and in 1910 Mrs. Homer Reed suggested turning Shawnee Mission into an inn.[110]

There was a drive in 1907 to restore and preserve the first state capital in Pawnee. The cost to restore it was estimated at fifteen hundred dollars, and though state ownership was not considered, promoters asked the legislature for restoration funds to be administered by the Kansas State Historical Society.[111] The funds were appropriated.[112]

Such public/private cooperation was the approach also with Pawnee Rock, a landmark on the Santa Fe Trail that had suffered from quarrying off its top. Mrs. J. S. Simmons, president of the Kansas Day Club, helped by Mrs. W. Y. Morgan of Hutchinson, in 1907 took charge of the effort to purchase and preserve Pawnee Rock. The townspeople of Pawnee raised $820, but the landowner wanted $1,500. The state legislature passed a resolution supporting the women, but provided no funds.[113] The women were able to buy the property in 1908 and then deed it to the state. The owner's conditions of sale required the state to expend $4,000 for improvements and for a driveway on the site and to maintain it as a public park.[114]

The awareness created by the private efforts of women in historic preservation did eventually create interest in more direct state action. One state senator in 1925 pushed legislation to preserve Shawnee Mission, the Kaw Mission, the Potawatomie Mission, Ft. Harker, Ft. Hays, and other sites. "If Kansas is to preserve her history and traditional landmarks," he said, "she must begin to act promptly. We can't wait much longer, for these old landmarks are rapidly disappearing."[115]

Of potentially more direct economic import than any of these issues was the Standard Oil fight of 1905. Perhaps success operating the state-run printing plant, as well as a twine and mining industry at the state prison, encouraged the solution proposed by Kansas in 1905 to declining wholesale prices offered by the Standard Oil refinery in Neodesha. The suggestion was to establish and operate a state-owned and operated refinery. It was to be run by prisoners to avoid the prohibition on state-owned internal improvements in the Kansas Constitution. Appropriations were made, but the refinery was never built, since its constitutionality was upset by a court test. However, the debate over it, pitting reforming Kansas against one of the most powerful corporations in the United States, created much journalistic ink with mixed results for the reputation of the Sunflower State.

Commercial oil was a relatively new industry in Kansas, though the original discoveries dated to G. W. Brown's activities in the 1860s. The T. J. Norman Number One well in Neodesha produced twelve barrels a day in 1892 and pumped profitably until 1917. Its success led to the construction of a refinery in Neodesha by Standard Oil and to a boom in the region. The Chanute field, developed in 1899 by I. N. Knapp, resulted in the city of Chanute by 1903 controlling twenty-one gas wells with a capacity of 41 million cubic feet a day. It was said that "it is . . . cheaper to keep warm in Chanute than it is to freeze to death" and that "matches are used in Neodesha only to light cigars." Chanute's population went from 4,200 in 1900 to 7,115 in 1903. There were one hundred oil and gas companies in Kansas in 1903, one-third headquartered in Chanute. Oil companies there had a monthly payroll of one hundred forty-five thousand dollars. New magazines appeared, the *Chanute Oil and Gas Review* and the *Kansas Derrick* (Iola). In

1904 Kansas ranked seventh in the nation in oil production, pumping over 4 million barrels that year.[116]

William Connelley could not resist during these years putting his writing and promotional talents to work for the Keystone Oil and Gas Company in the Chanute field. "If I were as big a liar as W. E. Stanley [recent governor of Kansas]," Connelley wrote Eugene Ware in fall 1903, "I think I might be able to get up to a truthful account of what is going on here. Men are making millions so quickly and easily that the world hears little of it. This is really the most wonderful field ever discovered."[117] Oil was $.96 a barrel at tanks in the field when Connelley arrived: a few months later it was $1.14, and the *Wall Street Journal* was predicting a rise to $2.50.[118] Connelley's only complaint was lack of intellect in the oil fields. "There is plenty of oil here but there are few people who care whether cabbage is spelled with a little *k* or a capital Q."[119]

There was the downturn in 1905, when the Kansas fields produced faster than Standard could refine.[120] Heavy oil then sold for $.17 a barrel in Kansas and water for $.42. Ida Tarbell visited the Kansas fields to gather material from disgruntled operators there for her muckraking *History of Standard Oil*.[121] The issue warmed up Kansas politics. A ditty on John Rockefeller in the *Topeka Capital* appeared:

I sing the multi-millionaire
Whose pate is destitute of hair,
Perhaps it's hardly right to hate him
And not just civil to berate him
But surely we can legislate him.[122]

Legislate it did. On February 10, 1905, as a state refinery bill made its way through the legislature, Standard Oil announced it would buy no more Kansas oil and shut down its refinery. On February 15, the bill for running a four-hundred-thousand-dollar state refinery using inmates was signed by Governor Hoch. On March 6 Standard ceased all operations in Kansas, and many people questioned whether the state had cut off its nose to spite its face.[123] Governor Hoch had some doubts about the cost of the proposed refinery but said that though "its garb is Socialist . . . its real purpose is competitive." The Kansas solution, he added, "may or may not be a wise one, but it is at least an honest and courageous one."[124]

Reactions from elsewhere were of two kinds. Some people praised the state for standing up to the corporate monster. A Kansas City attorney thought that a state refinery was needed as a comparative model to show that unreasonable profits were being made by Standard.[125] Hoch, wrote another man, would have the chance of "being placed in the same class of reformers as President Roosevelt . . . and Governor [Robert] Lafollette," if he succeeded in the plan.[126] "Don't let Kansas be bluffed or cheated out of her purpose," wrote a third correspondent. "Don't let Kansas surrender to these pirates."[127] The alternate view was that, however popular the move might be, it did not make economic sense. Standard's $3.5 million refinery in Neodesha was a small one. What could a four hundred thousand dollar state refinery do?[128] James Humphrey, an attorney in Junction City, wrote the governor that he was against the state's running a business enterprises on principle. Some people said loyalty would cause Kansans to buy exclusively from the state, even at a higher price. That, said Humphrey, was nonsense. "There is as much public spirit in Kansas as anywhere else, but in a case of this sort you probably could not find a hundred men in the state, including the oil men, whose patriotism would rise to the level of a nickel a gallon." The state would be in the business of guaranteeing oilmen's profits and "every succeeding legislature will be besieged, bullied and bribed to tax the people to maintain or increase profits of the oil field. Then will come a carnival of corruption such as no American state has ever beheld before." Did people like Hoch not once laugh at the Populists and their schemes to guarantee profit to farmers? Was this Republican measure for the oilmen any different?[129]

Many Kansans, though, liked the spirit of the attack on Standard. They were proud, too, of the pipeline law, the antidiscrimination law, and the maximum freight law passed in the same legislative session. "What an illuminating spectacle," wrote a Kansas oilman, "that a raw Kansan should drive the cormorants into the bathrooms of the Waldorf. . . . The Kansas idea is becoming the American idea."[130]

Despite numerous warnings that the oil industry would disappear in the state because of this radical atmosphere, it did not. The state refinery scheme failed at the level of the courts. There was a dip in Kansas oil production between 1905 and 1910, then a steady increase, which became spectacular with the drilling of Stapleton Number One, the discovery well of the world-class oil field in El Dorado in 1915. In 1918, with war prices of over three dollars a barrel for crude, the El Dorado field alone produced 29 million barrels of oil, over nine times the total output for all of Kansas in 1915, and

An oil field in the El Dorado district.
Courtesy of the Kansas State Historical Society.

was the leading oil field in the United States.[131] And that was only 64 percent of Kansas production that year.[132] In 1923 Carrie Oswald Number One, "the western wonder," opened western Kansas production, which thrived in the 1930s and beyond.[133] At the peak production of the industry in 1956, Kansas produced nearly 124.5 million barrels of oil from forty-three thousand wells in 1,669 oil fields located in 78 of its 104 counties.[134]

A similar story could be told for other extractive industries. Coal, lead, and zinc mining were features of southeast Kansas. Natural gas was a boon to industry, being cheap and clean, especially in light of the freight-rate problems connected with shipping in coal and the unsatisfactory burning qualities of local coal. When Wichita was able in 1906 to eliminate its inefficient coal gassification plant and connect homes, industries, and even its electric plant to natural gas brought in by pipeline, it was a major step, often underemphasized, in the whirl of political news.[135] Salt was first produced in Kansas in the 1860s in wells through the evaporation of brine. But in 1887 rock salt was discovered by oil companies drilling near Hutchinson, and since that time Kansas has been a major producer of salt, and ancillary to that, in recent times, a provider of document storage in the even environment of the played-out salt caverns seven hundred feet below ground. From 1888 through 1974 Kansas produced nearly 59 million tons of salt valued at about $455 million. It gave Hutchinson the moniker Salt City.[136]

These industries, combined with a nascent manufacturing establishment in the larger cities and an upturn in agricultural productivity and price in the period before and during World War I that has ever since been called by historians the "golden age of American agriculture," gave Kansas renewed confidence and wealth. The state had a population of over 1.7 million in 1917, up from 1.4 million in 1900.[137] A Tennessee editor, writing in 1915, commented that "the Kansas mind seems to turn to practical things. . . . The people are riding around in their 65,000 automobiles . . . attending state and county fairs, where they have exhibits, etc. and studying ways to improve farming. . . . It would seem that this unusual commonwealth, whose picturesque course has aroused prejudice, has succeeded better than some others, because, among other reasons, first, it early recognized the need for practical training for its youth of both sexes; and, second, because it was progressive in its legislation along similar practical lines and led the way in instituting reforms."[138]

Railroad regulation and trust busting were the bywords of the times after Theodore Roosevelt came to the White House. Sometimes the actions of Kansas in this field seemed trivial compared to the national movement. Moving against the local cream trust, for example, specifying proper content for shoes sold in the state, or outlawing oleomargarine in the interest of dairy farmers was not on a level with the Northern Securities case. However, these activities were similar in kind, if not in scale. And in the case of railroad regulation, Kansas was a national leader, as it had been earlier in the construction of railroad mileage.

Kansans had long thought about the railroad issue and had mixed feelings. Eugene Ware wrote in 1911, "I consider the Santa Fe Railroad as one of the great achievements of man. I do not think the pyramid of Cheops is to be compared either mechanically, intellectually or beneficially with the Santa Fe Railroad."[139] But criticism was endemic. Victor Murdock, the Kansas congressman from Wichita, wrote in the 1920s that "for twenty-five years or so the town had, upon occasions, two grand passions, the first to get more railroad corporations attached to it and the second to grow inflamed over the attitude of the railroad corporations after the town got them. . . . After a season of indignation the town would gird up its loins and go out to get another railroad."[140]

Industrial threshing, July 18, 1912.
Courtesy of the Kansas State Historical Society.

The Walter Stubbs administration (1909–1913) fell in one of those "seasons of indignation." Not only did Kansas want to become more involved in rate making, but it also wanted to approach that task, as well as that of proper taxation of railroads, scientifically, using physical valuation as a basis.[141] Stubbs gained national publicity when he began releasing to the press correspondence between himself and Edward Ripley, president of the ATSF. Ripley thought that a fair valuation of railroad property by the state would be impossible, and he was concerned that in limiting railroad profits to some percentage of a valuation, the risks of future downturns and the costs and benefits to Kansas society of the original development of the line would not be sufficiently recognized.[142] State officials were concerned that if a valuation expert were appointed whose "education has been on the railroad side," the move to substitute science for emotion might backfire.[143] But Stubbs was determined to try it.

The political support was there. Many people in Kansas were frustrated that the state was discriminated against in rates. Charles Gleed in an 1893 article, "Railroad Rights and Duties," had written, "The attrition of transportation frequently cuts the life out of the commodities transported. It often reduces a steer to its horns and a bushel of grain to the bag it started in.

Railroad in the open: Dorrance, looking east, 1910.
Courtesy of the Kansas State Historical Society.

The Kansas farmer who hauls his produce to New York and exchanges what he has left on his arrival for cloth or hardware, and hauls that back to Kansas, is likely to find that he has got little for his pains—but his pains."[144]

Wichita brought several cases before the Board of Railroad Commissioners in the late 1880s, arguing successfully that it was disadvantaged in rates relative to Kansas City, especially on livestock, packinghouse products, coal, flour, and lumber. It was important, the Wichita attorneys said, to diffuse the markets for raw products, thus diminishing the danger of "unjust combinations." This required "practical equality" in rates with other industries in the same territory. Freight rates on livestock to Wichita within a distance of 110 miles were over 16 percent higher on average than the same for corresponding distances to the stockyards in Kansas City. Representatives of Wichita's Dold Packing Plant and Burton Car Works testified to the effect on their industries.[145] It was a festering issue, and Stubbs thought it was time to face it in a general, rather than in a case-by-case, way. "We are going into this agitation," wrote the mayor of Waterville, "with grim determination born of a long time imposition, and we intend to bring things to pass. We hold that the laws of the state are made in the interest of the people, and that the standards of railroad service which our state demands are intended to be lived up to."[146] The railroads had argued that the Board of Railroad Commissioners Law of 1883 would bankrupt them, but they seemed quite prosperous in 1909.[147]

Ripley tired of such agitation. He wrote Stubbs in 1910 from his private rail car that he had read one of the governor's speeches, and "I am pleased to know that 'you would like to have the east and the eastern newspapers understand that you do not want to tear up the tracks of the railroad companies.' Assurances of this kind from the Governor of the State naturally will make those who have investments in the railways feel more secure." Would Stubbs allow the railroad investor the same rate of return he [Stubbs] got on his holdings in the Lawrence National Bank?[148]

Santa Fe director Charles Gleed questioned also the state's ability to regulate railroad return so closely, emphasizing that "the vicissitudes of the railroad business" were "enormous."[149] What made the general public such experts on everything? "Patent methods for eliminating human traits from human beings," Gleed thought, were doomed to failure. "We have in Kansas, I am sorry to say, many people who bear the same relation to politics that they do to astronomy and chemistry. They know nothing about astronomy and chemistry and they let them alone. They know nothing about lawmaking but they work at it."[150]

Stubbs, however, felt fair regulation was possible. He called a conference of "conservative, representative, sober-minded business men" representing eight states to study the question in Topeka. If neither valuation nor capitalization had anything to do with fixing rates, what was the basis for it? Was it arbitrary? A mystery?[151] Ripley said that it was certainly a mystery to any regulatory board and that rates were the result of competition with other modes or transportation, "a growth—a result of experience; of contact with shippers; of conference and compromise—and in many cases a concession to public opinion even when we believed that public opinion was mistaken." Capitalism was a wonder that ran partly of itself and ran well if regulating bodies did not "cast stones into the meshes of the machinery."[152] The direction, however, was clear. "For many, many seasons and sessions," wrote a Topeka newspaperman in 1915, "the paramount thought with every legislature was: 'Gig the railroads.' It isn't done now, you know. . . . The railroads have been gigged to a frazzle."[153]

Railroads were not any longer the only big businesses with which the state had to deal. Electric utilities, for example, had reinvented themselves in the early twentieth century. Regional companies, like Kansas Gas and Electric (1910) and Kansas Power and Light (1924), replaced the decentralized local concerns. They used Samuel Insull's system of large-scale power plants and depended on time and seasonal variations in peak demand, new equipment, the corporate form, and substantial capital coming from eastern banks to reduce electric costs for the consumer. This approach, however, increased the need for government to regulate these "natural monopolies."[154] The Public Utilities Commission, established in 1911, became increasingly busy with nonrailroad items.

Antitrust and antimonopoly sentiment was in the air. A Topeka real estate man wrote to Governor Hoch in 1907 that the pioneers "could not foresee that little by little . . . corporations would be enthroned, monopolies and syndicates placed in power, and a system of tribute be established . . . which would create an unrighteous combination of greed that would, in turn, fix the price of daily life, control the ebb and flow of business, rob the *farmer,* the *producer* of his produce, and debauch the voter at the polls. But such is the case today in this mammon-worshipping, dollar-crazed, trust-ridden Government of ours." The Republican Party of Kansas, he said, had better change this or "make the necessary arrangements with the undertaker."[155]

Railroad and antitrust regulation involved economic nitty-gritty. But issues like capital punishment touched directly the moral sphere in which Kansans seemed to specialize. Kansas had an unusual history regarding capital punishment. There were some state-ordered executions in the first years of state government, the last in 1869; but in 1872 the legislature passed a law specifying that the governor alone had the power to order executions, and that could happen only after the condemned criminal had been in prison for at least a year. Since then, no Kansas governor had ordered one.[156]

When a minister wrote Governor Hoch in 1906 asking that he hang together the fifty murderers then under sentence of death in Kansas, the governor blanched at the idea of such a spectacle.[157] Modern times had no room, he wrote a student in Michigan, for the "hanging exhibitions" that used to draw great crowds. These hangings brutalized spectators and "contributed to the crimes they were intended to prevent and punish." The electric chair, hidden out of the way, was really no different. Hoch thought that civilization, accepting the advice of penologists, should "relegate this final method of taking life to the ash heap where it belongs."[158]

The Kansas legislature agreed and abolished capital punishment early in 1907.[159] Even federal executions on Kansas soil were controversial. When in 1916 Robert Stroud, who had been convicted of murdering a prison guard at Leavenworth Penitentiary, was sentenced to be hanged, the Kansas press reported that it "naturally shocks the sensibilities of a people who believed Kansas soil was safe from such a contingency." No federal prisoner had been hanged in Kansas since 1889.[160] There was relief when four years later President Woodrow Wilson commuted Stroud's sentence to life in prison. He was transferred to Alcatraz, pursued his study of ornithology, and became the "Bird Man of Alcatraz" of book and movie fame.[161] Capital punishment was not reinstituted in Kansas until 1935, and no executions were carried out until 1944.[162] And as the later history of the issue in Kansas shows, that was not the end of debate on the matter.

Women's rights was another issue with strong moral overtones and one of long standing. There were plenty of issues connected with the Kansas women's movement other than suffrage, but the culmination of that stage came in 1912 with the granting of full suffrage and political rights to Kansas women. The legislature passed the bill to amend the state constitution to that effect, and it prevailed in an election held in 1912. The first jury containing women entered the courtroom in El Dorado that December. The women bowed their heads in silent prayer, listened to the instructions, and returned a verdict in three hours.[163]

It did not happen without struggle. Bills to grant women presidential suffrage only, which the legislature could do without a vote of the people, came close to passage in 1902 and 1905 but ran into stout opposition. J. W. Adams, a representative from Sedgwick County, noted that only a few states had gone further with woman suffrage than Kansas already had. "We do not doubt the integrity of women," he said. "We don't doubt their ability; we don't doubt their valor. But I do not believe we should divert the minds of women with politics." Bill Hackney of Atchison added that he would pay no attention to the "army of cacklers" that had been besieging the Kansas

House, pushing for suffrage.[164] In 1911 Governor Stubbs received a letter from a real estate man in Larned, saying that "the Great Creator, knowing the end from the beginning, and seeing the delusion of Satan, under which mankind would become dissatisfied with the natural order of things . . . wisely settled this question of man's domination by Divine decree."[165] Women felt otherwise. "Wouldn't it be fine to have Kansas numbered with the *true* Commonwealths?" Lucy Johnson, president of the Kansas Equal Suffrage Association, wrote Stubbs in 1908. "*Women are people.*"[166]

Women, as their male counterparts in reform had done so successfully, used organization and statistics to press their case. The Kansas State Teachers' Association, the State and District Federation of Woman's Clubs, the State and District WCTU, the State Sunday School Association, and others passed resolutions favoring the 1912 suffrage amendment. "The number of educated, refined Kansas women who have thus expressed themselves as desiring the ballot reaches up to twenty or twenty-five thousand," wrote one woman activist. "In the face of all these facts and because just a few Kansas women, wrapped in their robes of indifference or selfish ease say 'I don't care to vote,' will any honest voter cast his ballot against the amendment. . . . What! Continue the entire feminine constituency in bonds because a tiny portion of it are satisfied with their chains?"[167] Jane Addams of Hull House fame spoke for suffrage in Wichita to two packed houses at the new Forum Auditorium in 1912.[168] Kansas at the time of the election was flooded with antisuffrage literature, but a majority of its men agreed with those working for women's rights and voted that way.[169]

As with municipal suffrage, the new dispensation worked well. "Kansas is again up to its old tricks," a Kansas City man wrote in 1914, "upsetting precedents." There were then twenty-three women in appointive official positions in Kansas, more than in any other state.[170] The next year, a reporter concluded that "women who feel that they are tied by conventionalities or by law should move to Kansas. . . . The women boss in Kansas. Fact is, they do just about as they please."[171] To prove the point, the state reported nineteen woman lawyers in 1916—modest, but a definite start.[172]

Women's influence was important in advancing public health consciousness and practice in Kansas, as were the findings of the new science and the training of medical specialists. Dr. Samuel Crumbine of Kansas was probably the best-known advocate of public health in the nation in the early twentieth century. Crumbine, who first located in Spearville, near Dodge

City, in 1872, became a member of the State Board of Health in 1898, and in 1904 he moved to Topeka as its executive officer, a post he held for nineteen years. Crumbine was a crusader and an excellent writer. His campaign against the common drinking cup, as well as his "Swat the Fly," "Bat the Rat," and "Don't Spit on the Sidewalk" publicity campaigns for public hygiene, drew wide attention. Political opposition to him by certain food and drug interests headquartered outside the state only made the whole issue more interesting to Kansans. Crumbine was active in achieving a pure food act after an outbreak of food poisoning from a shipment of poorly refrigerated oysters. He investigated municipal water supplies, questioning those who argued that river water "purified itself." And he supported women in their crusade for pure milk and for employees of the State Board of Health to visit new mothers, particularly poor ones, and educate them in ways to reduce the startling infant mortality that had prevailed in the late nineteenth century. In 1907 he convinced the state legislature to appropriate one thousand dollars for a traveling tuberculosis exhibit. In 1909 he persuaded the State Board of Health to specify paper drinking cups in public places. He sought and received cooperation from the state universities on research in health. In 1911 he pushed a vital statistics law through the Kansas legislature, requiring that all births and deaths in the state be recorded. He promoted sex education. He investigated diseases caused by conditions in the lead and zinc mining areas of southeast Kansas and pushed for a full-time health service in Cherokee County. In 1915 his influence caused the creation of a Division of Child Hygiene in Kansas. "We suffer from disease through ignorance," Crumbine put on posters; "we may escape through knowledge."[173]

Crumbine was not the only crusader for public health in Kansas. Dr. E. C. McAdams, who served on the city council of Wichita in the 1880s, was interested in testing river water used for drinking, in the regulation of privies, in the purity of milk, and in the collection of mortality statistics.[174] The medical specialists arriving in Kansas in the early twentieth century supported the public efforts of Crumbine. Dr. Howard Norton, Wichita's first pediatrician, sponsored baby contests beginning in 1916. The contests were not for beauty but to judge the health of local infants and to promote good care. The "pest house," where victims of epidemic disease were quarantined, was thoroughly reformed. Wichita had a public health nurse in 1918, thanks to the support of the Wichita Equal Suffrage Association, and a city bacteriologist soon after. In 1919 came the establishment of the "Fresh Air

Baby Camp," to focus on the survival of low birth-weight infants. In the 1920s "Mother" Elizabeth Hughes and her corps of Sunday School helpers established hospital maternity care, and the Wichita Junior League single-handedly supported outpatient clinics in poor neighborhoods. Upper-class women used their automobiles to drive poor women and their children to medical care. "Wichita is through with civic indecency," wrote a reporter in 1921, "and has put the past behind here."[175]

Crumbine formed "Little Mother's Leagues" throughout the state and appointed juvenile health officers in many schools. The traveling Pullman health-exhibit car "Warren" devoted much of its time to child hygiene, and well-baby clinics were conducted there. In 1918 the Board of Health made house-to-house visitations in the state to promote infant health and the care of crippled children. The campaign had as a goal a 50 percent reduction of infant mortality.[176]

Crumbine could organize private resources. In 1915 a mother and her thirteen-year-old mentally retarded son appeared before the Kansas legislature in support of the bill creating the Division of Child Hygiene. He was a normal infant, but the mother had not known the signs and waited too long to take him to a doctor for what would have been a curable ailment. "The state of Kansas, gentlemen," she said, "has been very kind to my children. For three of them the state has built universities and colleges. . . . But for this baby, he will never be anything more, for this baby the state has built an asylum at Winfield. Some time he will have to go there."[177] Crumbine, standing before a delegation of women visiting the statehouse, added, "Give us the cost of killing one soldier in the European war to save the lives of a thousand babies in Kansas." In four months after establishing the visiting nurse's association in Topeka, he said, the death rate among infants decreased 36 percent.[178] A few legislators thought that it was unnecessary "to create a new bureau just for the purpose of sending circulars about raising babies to the mothers of the state."[179] But the emotional appeals, the phalanx of women, the statistics, and the science to take measures to improve life with public funding was a hard combination to resist.

The public initiative on health helped encourage private organizations like the Society for Crippled Children, headed for years by the Wichita banker C. Q. Chandler and administered almost entirely on volunteer executive time.[180] Of the greatest significance for the future was the founding in 1919 of the Menninger Clinic in Topeka by Dr. Charles Menninger and his son Karl, recently graduated from Harvard Medical School. Charles and his wife Flora had been active earlier in private social services, taking in and boarding many of the homeless after the flood of 1903, but the new enterprise specialized in mental health. It was a unique family enterprise, later involving several generations of Menningers and based on a strong conviction that a homelike, residential atmosphere was important to mental balance in severely disturbed persons. The clinic became world famous and so did Karl Menninger's many books, beginning with *The Human Mind* (1930) and followed by such classics as *Man Against Himself* (1938), *Love Against Hate* (1942), and *The Vital Balance* (1963). The Menninger Clinic attracted specialists from all over the world and gave Topeka an international flavor that was an adjustment to both the visitors and the townspeople. Karl himself often made the connection between the development of the clinic and the Kansas reform era, emphasizing the support that he had in his home state for a rather radical experiment.[181]

These efforts added up to a great change. Governor Capper advertised in 1915 that Kansas was leading the way in a national movement to organize against dirt and disease. And here, again, government must be active. "It is the part of the good citizen not only to protect his own health, but to do everything possible to protect the health of his community. And it is the business of the state to see that the individual does this. . . . It is the idea of society protecting itself against the ignorance, the carelessness, the indifference of the individual."[182]

As was typical of the Progressive Era nationally, most issues in Kansas could be categorized as "social reform." They were moral debates about what goals were desirable for the future of Kansas society, and the struggle was to consolidate public opinion and to pass legislation. But there was a minority of issues that fit what historians have called "structural reform." These addressed not any special social or moral change but the inefficiencies and injustices in the organization of the political machinery itself. The civil service law and the primary election law were examples. Perhaps the most prominent changes of this type, however, were the creation of city commissioners and managers in Kansas cities and of the Board of Administration at the state level.

The idea of the commission came from a successful experiment with a voluntary commission of business people in Galveston, Texas, in 1900 after the disastrous tidal wave there. The city's affairs were divided into categories with a commissioner in charge of each. The Kansas state statute authorizing city commissions passed in 1907, and Wichita created one in 1909. These commissioners, instead of being elected by wards, as was the case with the earlier city council system, were elected at large and served at token pay, lest anyone make a career of local government. In 1917 came the additional innovation of the city manager system, Wichita again pioneering that. The city manager operated like the CEO of a corporation, and, while serving at the behest of the elected city commission, made all daily administrative and hire-and-fire decisions on his own, removing this practice from the direct realm of politics. The city commission then became the equivalent of a board of directors. The model for the manager system was that of Dayton, Ohio, instituted in 1913.[183]

These structural changes were elaborations on basic civil service rules that had been applied in Kansas since 1908. The change was also a response to the muckraking national literature exposing what Lincoln Steffens called "the shame of the cities." Wrote Victor Murdock, the editor of the *Wichita Eagle*, in 1908, "The way policemen are knocked about in the shuttle of city politics is a shame and a disgrace to enlightened municipal government. Every little two-by-four ward 'heeler' takes a crack at them and the councilman or alderman who does not respond to the 'pull' or the 'push' is marked for slaughter at the next coming election."[184] The Wichita commission had several notable immediate successes, the most significant being convincing the local railroads to build a union station and elevated tracks, largely at the expense of the railroad. And the reform atmosphere was evident when the city held a recall election in 1911 over supposed scandals in the police and water departments and removed the mayor and two commissioners. The push to add a manager in 1917 was organized by W. M. G. Howse, president of the Greater Wichita Civic League. It was actively backed also by Henry Allen, the editor of the *Wichita Beacon,* and by the local Rotary Club. Howse stated, "Not a city in the United States has such a clean citizenship as Wichita, and such a dirty government."[185]

Cities in Kansas were ever more important, and therefore their problems were more evident. Between 1900 and 1910 the population of the state defined by the census as urban increased 49 percent, from 330,000 to 492,000. By 1920, it increased by another 125,000, or 25 percent. And the investment in infrastructure, particularly paving and sewers, was enormous.

The League of Kansas Municipalities, formed in 1909 under the direction of Richard Price, was based at the University of Kansas and studied the regional urban scene from an academic perspective with a view of implementation. Abilene experimented unofficially with an officer called a city manager as early as 1913, when Kenyon Riddle, its city engineer, took over public works projects and personnel. Riddle toured the state advocating the system and attended national meetings of the City Manager's Association. The city commission system, said Clarence Dykstra, a political science professor at the University of Kansas, had worked well, but "it is one thing to represent public opinion. It is quite another to carry out public demands wisely, economically and continuously." For that a trained professional was needed at the helm. It caught on. By the mid-1980s, fifty-two Kansas cities, comprising 42 percent of the state's urban population, had a city manager form of government, and thirty-three more had city administrators.[186]

The urban element of Progressive reform in Kansas was significant beyond these structural changes. The Metropolitan Police bill of the 1890s had attempted to impose state control on local police departments with the view of enforcing official morality. The same goal was evident in the investigation of Wichita vice enforcement by State Attorney General C. W. Trickett in November 1911. The new Wichita mayor, the dentist W. W. Minick, sat embarrassed at hearings in which Trickett questioned Wichita police officers about their lack of enforcement of ordinances against prostitution and drug use. What about photograph parlors all over the city where pictures of nude girls were taken and sold? What about innumerable houses that were obviously places of prostitution? When police said they could not make arrests just because people were dressed in a certain way or because there was certain paraphernalia lying about, the state officials averred that anyone "who is not able to discover that a place is a bawdy house or not hasn't the ability for a detective. . . . When you go into one of those houses and you see a woman in there with short skirts and short sleeves and a cigarette in her mouth and a poodle dog on her lap, or probably sitting on some fellow's lap . . . what would you suppose the place was?"[187] Kansas might be becoming more urban, but the state was concerned that cities should not mean it would become a moral cesspool. "We are at last beginning to understand," said Capper in a 1914 speech, "that as much expert knowledge is required for cleansing the morals of a city as for cleaning of its streets or disposing of its sewage. . . . Zeal is necessary but it is valueless, and indeed often harmful, without knowledge to guide it."[188]

City leaders seemed to agree with that sentiment. C. L. Davidson, mayor of Wichita, speaking at the University of Kansas in 1911, asserted, "There is nothing so vital to the nation's welfare as correct solutions to the problems of municipal government. If the city is a breeding place of idlers, poverty and crime; if it is the refuge of criminals and its life is polluted with suffering and broken hearts, murder and suicide; if the lure of the lights and the unlimited possibilities of its business life are drawing the boys and girls to our larger cities in greater numbers, then surely the municipal problem is the problem of problems." Davidson could point to the White Way lighting system in Wichita, which both promoted business and reduced crime. He argued that the root cause of these urban problems, poverty, must be attacked by the city and the state through the regulation of tenements, of sanitation and of wages, and particularly of the low wages of women working as clerks. "We must tear away the old customs, but when this is done, we must be able to substitute something better and more useful in their place."[189] The city, he said in another address the same year, was like a beautiful painting and was at a disadvantage at close inspection. Time would tell. "Only the lapse of time weeds out the insignificant and trivial things, and preserves for all time those that are of lasting benefit." He hoped the reforms would be so lasting.[190]

Citizens expected the same kinds of improvements from the structural reforms of establishing a primary law in Kansas, done at a special session of the legislature in 1906, and from the 1915 establishment of a modest Civil Service Commission, with a budget of only one thousand dollars but including over one thousand employees.[191] For years, some counties in Kansas had had a primary election system, and, said J. N. Dolley, speaker of the Kansas House in 1909, "while it was far from perfect and was only regulated by public opinion and by the moral sense of the proprieties of political ethics, yet it was preferred to the convention system, for the convention system was also wholly unregulated by law." There would be no more manipulations by corporations and party bosses, he thought, and this would result in "an entirely new type of politician."[192] The Civil Service office barred questions about political or religious affiliation in state hiring, and it outlined grounds for dismissal, including habitual use of intoxicating beverages or cigarettes or "notorious, disgraceful or infamous conduct." There were competitive exams in penmanship, spelling, and letter writing.[193]

The Board of Administration, created in 1913, had the primary object of coordinating the financing and operation of state colleges and universities. In 1917, charitable and correctional institutions were added to its responsibilities. In 1925, the new Board of Regents took over the colleges and universities, and the Board of Administration broadened its scope in other areas.[194]

The Board of Administration was a logical outgrowth of an emphasis on economy and efficiency. Governor Capper declared in 1916, "There will be strong opposition to the concentration of responsibility in either state or county government, but we must come to it, and the sooner the better."[195] He noted in 1917 that the Board of Administration was structured much as the commission-manager plan, which had "worked . . . admirably in every city that has adopted it." If taxes were "to cease growing by leaps and bounds, red tape and waste must be cut out. . . . The tendency toward multitudinous and overlapping commissions and boards is one of the weaknesses of modern governmental machinery. . . . There is not a great business in the state that would give a moment's consideration to a proposition to abandon existing business methods and systems of management and adopt the political system that prevails in Kansas." He thought the Board of Administration would save two hundred thousand dollars a year in salaries and operating expenses and "absolutely cut out politics in the management of state institutions."[196]

Beyond all these specific issues—maybe it would be better to say behind them—was not only an attitude and a philosophy but also certain powerful and influential people in Kansas who considered themselves Republican insurgents, and who, after the Roosevelt Bull Moose bolt from the national Republican Party in 1912, moved Kansas politics, Republican though it remained, in a more liberal direction generally.[197] Chief among these was a man who held no elective political office—William Allen White, the Sage of Emporia. Although he was awkward at speechmaking, White was not only creative and determined but also articulate in print. He wrote nationally known books, and the *Emporia Gazette*, though far from the largest newspaper in the state, was doubtless the most influential. White influenced public opinion and corresponded voluminously with a wide range of Kansas leaders, both advising them and reacting to their ideas. Reading his correspondence leads one to the conclusion that individuals as well as ideas and trends shape policy.[198] "Be of good cheer about Kansas," White wrote Victor Murdock in 1910. "She never was so much Kansas as she is today. It's grand."[199]

Perhaps in retrospect White has been made into too much of a saint in

Kansas, but for better or worse, he was a heavy hitter there for most of the first half of the twentieth century. He had the organizational skill to manage the program that the Populists only imagined. A friend wrote to White, "I could entertain a very much higher opinion of men like Lewelling and Leedy . . . when I saw them afar than when I came to know them intimately. But, however weak and selfish and ignorant they were, they had certainly some vision of a new earth wherein dwelt righteousness, and I have no doubt that, as you say, the modicum of truth they preached had something to do with forming the spreading public opinion that now demands the removal of the burdens the strong are ever placing upon the weak."[200] T. A. McNeal, editor, state printer, and sometime Kansas historian, thought White was one of the smartest men he had ever known, "and I think that you are honest and helping to fight the battle of the ages . . . and today I regard you as the strongest single force in the state of Kansas."[201]

White was a bridge between Washington and Topeka, supporting in 1908 both Congressman Joseph Bristow and his relatively radical program in Washington and Governor Wilbur Stubbs and his relatively radical program in Kansas, though Bristow and Stubbs did not personally agree on much.[202] Bristow was not sure about Stubbs's ability. He "seems to be making a good impression by his speeches," he said, "but he has not the slightest conception of perfecting an organization. He simply goes into a county, disturbs the atmosphere, creates a good impression, and goes away and permits things to aimlessly drift away or evaporate."[203] Could White do something about that? Stubbs defended himself to White. "The talk that reform in Kansas," he wrote, "is an expensive luxury is so ridiculous that it is hardly worthy an-swering." He could find fifty thousand dollars a year in savings in the state printing law and twenty-five thousand dollars more in the interest the banks paid on public funds. He thought railroad reform saved $3 million a year and that the "political parasites" were the only ones complaining.[204]

White coordinated education and politics. "The University above every-thing just now needs to appeal to that quickened conscience of the people that is manifest in all our activities of life," KU regent White wrote to the chancellor in 1910.[205] But he was no strict ideologue. "It does not interest me whether the planks of the Kansas platform are modifications of the Socialist party, or the Populist party, or the Prohibition party, or the Democratic party. I do not care who has written them, but I am interested in knowing whether or not they expound the truth."[206] He was for practical changes to

William Allen White.
Courtesy of the Kansas State Historical Society.

improve people's lives, "for no man can give a government an intelligent vote whose life and environment is cramped."[207] But even he knew that efficiency could go too far. When the state commission on efficiency proposed in 1911 to put every employee of state universities on an exact hour-of-service basis, White rebelled. The commission should know, he wrote, "that a college professor cannot be hired and paid with a time clock key."[208]

White recognized privately that not everyone was with him, and despite his public scorn of "standpatters," he accepted that as healthy. He knew that his most powerful and persuasive nemesis among conservatives was Charles Gleed of the *Kansas City Journal.* "It takes all kinds of people to make a world," he wrote Gleed in 1912, "and I am willing to admit that the conservative brake on the progressive wheel is a good thing. . . . One thing is certain, the thing that seems so revolutionary to you is just beginning."[209] Sometimes White became discouraged, as he could not see the implications of his own decisions in the future. He wrote Charles Scott in Iola in 1919, "I note that you ask is the country going to hell. Before you read any further, close the door and let me tell you something in dead confidence, and for Heaven's sake don't let it get out that I said so; but I really don't know! Tuesdays, Thursdays, and Saturdays, I think it is. Mondays, Wednesdays, and Fridays, I am more hopeful."[210]

Gleed supported much of the Kansas Progressives' program, but he had a stomach full of what he considered the pious and impractical rhetoric of people like White and Roosevelt, who would throw out the good with the bad of a long tradition of becoming civilized. He said of Capper in 1911: "Of course Arthur is rather queer in some of his republicanism, but under the idiotic political methods which we have borrowed from Oregon or elsewhere, there seems to be no possibility of a better selection."[211] The same year he complimented White on a sensible suggestion: "When I read the average stuff that is running on this subject . . . I grow so furious I cannot eat my next meal. I have almost trained myself to forget the whole subject and let the great, lazy leviathan public crawl round to the right position when it gets ready."[212] As for T.R., Gleed called him "Boss" Roosevelt and suggested his type would replace one tyranny with another.[213]

But there was cooperation on means amid disagreement on ends. Capper often asked Gleed's advice as businessman to businessman, stating that "administratively, the state of Kansas is, of course, nothing more or less than a big business corporation." He invited Gleed to a "Conference on Modernized and Simplified State and County Government," which was to hear the report of the Economy and Efficiency Commission.[214] Gleed was concerned wholly with implementation. It would not be enough, he said, "to paste the word 'city manager' over the old word 'mayor' in somebody's title."[215]

Tensions had always been a part of Kansas history. White was a contrast to

Republican boss Cy Leland, Senator Joseph Bristow to Senator Chester Long and Senator Charles Curtis, Governor Arthur Capper to Governor Henry Allen. Yet they were all popular and electable in Kansas. And together, from their more conservative and more radical perspectives, they made a change that lasted.

As it happened, however, the new world toward which these ideas were tending was not so wholly bright as they imagined. Nor was it one that could be formed and controlled wholly in the cities and wheat fields and public buildings of the State of Kansas. In 1914, while Kansas was legislating away on social and economic problems, Europe went to war—the most terrible war yet, as the new technology turned to the grinding up of people.

War to the Kansas Progressives was another example of inefficiency and waste. It was particularly repugnant to Governor Capper, who was a Quaker. In 1914 he told the Wichita YMCA, "Civilization is a moving tide. It is a joyous journey if we undertake it in the spirit of 'glorious company' of those who have made the world what it is today. To be *afraid* of the present or the future is cowardice." Kansas was now, he said, "on the threshold of a grander era."[216] Shortly after, however, looking at the carnage in Europe, he was not so sure. "All Europe," he wrote, "has been plunged into a senseless butchery, millions of brave men mobilized for murder, by greedy, quarrelsome, ambition-crazed monarchs gratifying a wicked lust for power and further-ing their own wretched plots."[217] He opposed "preparedness" as a "specious name and false pretense."[218] Joseph Bristow felt the same. "You may think it patriotic," he wrote a U.S. congressman, "to draw the youth of this land to die in the trenches of Europe and to permit the bloated munitions maker to escape proper taxation and keep his blood-stained gold—*but we do not.*"[219] In 1916, at the state meeting of the Kansas Peace and Equity League in Topeka, the unquestioned leadership elite of the state poured out antiwar invective in what a writer in hindsight called "the lowest ebb to which red-blooded American patriotism ever receded in our commonwealth."

But the war fever escalated, and in 1917 the nation and Kansas entered the conflict in spirit and in fact. Kansans quickly enough became ashamed of ever having felt doubtful. It seemed, said one citizen, that "Teuton pro-pagandists had our schools, press, public men and churches completely under their direction," causing the "ridiculous and un-Kansan" position of isolationism. The writer admitted, however, that perhaps isolationism was

Camp Funston, 1918.
Courtesy of the Kansas State Historical Society.

not missing from the Kansas historical tradition. A Kansas Populist congressman had once asked why the United States needed battleships, since they could not plow corn.[220]

Phillip Billard was one of the volunteers in the new flying service. He had flown a Curtiss plane, as well as his Longren, quite a bit in 1916 and felt well prepared.[221] True, his girlfriend Dorothy Berry from California was worried about his flying. "I would be the *happiest* person in the world if you wouldn't fly anymore," she wrote him. "This is an awful lonesome old world if you're not with some one you care about."[222] But the military aircraft seemed good, and Billard was a great pilot. He covered sixty-eight miles from Topeka to Kansas City in forty minutes in November 1916. He circled over the playing field in Lawrence during a football game between the University of Missouri and the University of Kansas and managed to land in a pasture with no problem.[223] In August 1917, he did thirteen consecutive loop the loops at two thousand feet over Topeka to demonstrate his skill to Major Alvarado Fuller, the examining officer for pilots for the U.S. Signal Corps and chief of the Aviation Corps. He passed all tests and was declared scientifically fit for

Phil Billard beside his Topeka-built Longren airplane.
Courtesy of the Kansas State Historical Society.

anything the war could dish out.[224] "Don't you dare let some Egyptian Sphinx steal you entirely away," Dorothy wrote that winter, "for you know you've promised to come back to *me* some day when this war is over."[225]

Phil wrote his brother Bob from France in March 1918 that he was a "tired human," having been in the air that day over six hours and reaching sixteen thousand feet wearing five sweaters and a helmet. Still, he was "growing more and more enthused over these machines every time I go up in one."[226] In April he wrote, "Hate to plan anything in the future, that I'm not sure will materialize."[227] In May a friend from the *Topeka Capital* wrote, "Do be careful! You are fearless and cool headed, but don't be *risky needlessly.*"[228]

The Longren plane Billard flew over the Topeka statehouse those reform-filled winter days in 1912 hangs still in the Kansas State Historical Society Museum. But Phil himself never came back from Europe alive. He died late in July 1918 in a testing accident in an American-made plane with a 450-hp Liberty engine.[229] The Kansas that reared Billard and where his first machine was created never returned, either, to quite the state of optimism about bringing heaven to earth with which it had been so long associated.

CHASTENED AND CHANGED

On the evening of April 17, 1918, a mob of fifteen hundred people attacked David Schwarztman, a popcorn merchant with a street stand at Lawrence Street and Douglas Avenue in Wichita on the grounds that he was not displaying the American flag and had refused to buy Liberty Bonds. Schwartzman, a Polish Jew who had been in the United States eleven years, tried to explain that he had displayed the flag but that some boys had torn it down. His son Heine and his daughter Lena stood with him, petrified with fear. They were forced to kiss the flag, and the girl to salute it. The local paper reported, "Schwartzman was so terror-stricken that he could not drive a nail through the staff of the little flag thrust into his hands. . . . His legs trembled, his hands shook and his lips quivered so that he could not speak." There were shouts of "string him up," and it might have happened had not the police spirited him away. The crowd dragged the stand over a block to South Topeka Street and burned it. While the flames rose, Frank Westfall drove up in "a machine" and began making patriotic speeches from the seat. The crowd then marched from place to place, visiting another popcorn stand, whose proprietor had a flag and promised to buy bonds from the Liberty League in the morning. They proceeded to Gus Sauer's drugstore at 624 East Douglas. There were no flags, but the proprietor showed a bond. A cafe and a chili stand were next, and then the crowd began to look for Schwartzman's house. They surged about the house of a suspected pro-German along the way, but Will Jochems, a local attorney, came out from across the street and protested. Some people said he had a revolver. About midnight the crowd dispersed but not before emphasizing that they would like to "hang the brutes and burn the devils. . . . The sanctity of home, the honor of women is endangered so long as a pro-German is allowed to poison the air of Wichita with his vile breath."[1]

The next day Wichita's new city manager, L. R. Ash, said that he would add more police to prevent further incidents of this sort. Mayor L. W. Clapp said, "Every considerate, fair and loyal citizen of Wichita must regret the street turmoil and occurrences of Wednesday night." He emphasized that at least there was little property damage (one man's popcorn stand notwithstanding). A police investigation revealed that one ringleader of the supposedly patriotic mob action, O. B. Bozarth, was a parolee convicted of beating his wife; the other, R. B. Poage, had been arrested for running a house of prostitution.[2]

The incident in Wichita was in extreme contrast to Governor Arthur Capper's idealistic antiwar and antiviolence statements of a year earlier. So was an occurrence there a few days earlier when eighty-five employees of the Domestic Laundry on East Douglas, mostly women, averring they would "not stand for a slacker in their crew," threatened to ride three fellow employees on a rail from the laundry to Main Street if they refused to kiss Old Glory.[3] There were rumors of a Negro uprising in Kansas, encouraged by the Germans. There were attacks throughout that year on Mennonites in central Kansas, who were visited by nightriders. They were tarred and feathered, had their heads shaved, their buggies burned, and were otherwise humiliated for their religious conviction against supporting that war or any war. The main building at the Mennonite-backed Tabor College in Hillsboro burned to the ground in a suspected case of arson.[4]

The Mennonites argued that they had left Germany centuries ago and had no more interest in the kaiser than other Americans.[5] "The war?" wrote one in 1913. "God pity all who must fight. . . . May God forgive all who are responsible for this war. . . . But we are not for Germany or Russia, either one."[6] The Mennonites emphasized that they were not against this war because it was waged on Germany but were against all wars and had been for centuries. "When our people came to this country, we were often contemptuously called 'Russians,' but now we have suddenly become 'Germans' in the eyes of those who have nothing but contempt for our non-resistant principles."[7] But a district court reversed the decision of a Marion County draft board that had given exemptions to seven Mennonites, saying that religious views were not a valid excuse for exemption from the draft.[8] Governor Henry Allen told a man from Tabor College that there was nothing that the governor could do about prejudice against conscientious objectors or Mennonites or both groups. "The attitude of the public which has been engaged in the war . . . is a perfectly natural attitude, and it cannot be changed by argument."[9]

It was clear that there had been some malevolent turn in Kansas progressivism, some dark spirit that arose as efficiency and unanimity were turned to the service of jingoism and hate. Randolph Bourne thought that World War I was a tragedy, not only because young people died but also because their idealism, that most precious resource for the future, died with them.[10] The assault on slackers, on conscientious objectors, on suspected pro-Germans, on supposed radicals of any kind, and, by implication, on diversity itself in Kansas during World War I and immediately after was hardly limited to a few mob incidents. When threatened, Kansas optimism became intolerance, Kansas uniqueness became parochialism, Kansas morality became peevishness and stubborn pride. The historian Henry May called the war "the end of American innocence."[11] It was clearly a reminder in Kansas that "the American mixture of democratic freedom and democratic tyranny is complex indeed."[12]

The Kansas State Council of Defense, established in April 1917 and based on the city manager plan, was, unlike the "listless and inept" councils in other states, an efficient organization. "It mapped the strategy," wrote the historian Patrick O'Brien, "kept everyone on the same page, and led cheers." That last included operating the Americanization program, part of the effort to make "the war everyone's business." Included were eliminating the "baneful influences of German psychology and unsound philosophy" from the University of Kansas. German language newspapers all but disappeared, and many German Americans in Kansas filed in court to anglicize their names.[13]

Kansas patriotism and moral certainty showed up in other ways. During the war, the Kansas YWCA organized young women to go to Europe to establish "hostess houses" and to protect soldiers from the "harpies of the French streets." "The YWCA," wrote a Kansas paper, "is one great organization of women to which has been given the responsibility of working for social morality in war times." Four hundred Kansas women listened to Mrs. Sherwood Eddy speak in Topeka in 1917 about the "loneliness, the temptations, and the moral triumphs and falls" she had seen on a visit to France.[14]

Liberty Bond sales not only were vital but were also a loyalty test. Kansas was proud that it was among the top states in those sales, but some of the sales methods were heavy-handed. Governor Capper himself in 1918 wrote to a prosperous farmer in Enterprise, Kansas, that the man's neighbors had informed the governor that the farmer had refused to invest in the Fourth Liberty Loan. "It surely cannot be that your sympathies are not with your Government in our great fight for humanity. It surely cannot be that you are disloyal to the Government, which has done so much for you. It surely cannot be that you are a slacker who is willing to let others bear the entire burden of this fight. . . . Surely your sympathies are not with the autocratic tyrants of Prussia. Surely you are not indifferent to the fate of the hundreds of thousands of American boys who are going to the trenches in France and Belgium."[15]

There were many such letters, a most extraordinary introduction for German Americans and others to the official arm of their state government. There was a consistent program also in Kansas to suppress the German language, during the war and after. Governor Allen instituted a Speech Week in 1919, on the grounds that "every true citizen . . . should use his American Language."[16] In doing so, he was responding to local opinions such as that of a Cheney man, who pleaded for the continuance of wartime restrictions on the speaking of German and the use of German in church, or even socially. "Why let them teach foreign in church or Sunday School or over telephone. The sooner these people are made to respect America the sooner everything will be settled. . . . I am raising three sons and want them to be true Americans."[17]

There was much resentment in Kansas over the exemption of aliens from the draft by local boards and against conscientious objectors.[18] Prejudice against things German extended so far that the Kansas Senate narrowly defeated authorization in 1919 of an Americanization Board, to be a part of the Committee on Public Relations of the Kansas State Council of Defense. One man wrote the governor's office, "In the light of recent events in our country, I believe most of us are convinced by this time, that our labor problem is interwoven with the problem of the foreign speaking population. To solve one, we must solve both."[19] Another bill nearly passed forbidding public meetings to be held in any foreign language, much to the chagrin of the Hispanic population.[20] In Wichita the chief of police complained that Mexicans were storing up arms for an insurrection. There was criticism of African Americans on the grounds that they were avoiding the draft.

Labor organizations could conveniently be attacked for disloyalty, especially the Non-Partisan League, which was active in Kansas in advocating state-owned grain elevators and packinghouses, state hail insurance, and rural credit banks. William Allen White at the *Emporia Gazette* called it the "Hun-Partisan League" and said it disguised "pro-German pacifism" with an economic program. Many members of the Industrial Workers of the World (IWW) were ushered out of communities under vagrancy laws, which allowed such action against people who refused to work for "fair wages." Some people complained that they were even threatened by the Red Cross for not coming up with a large enough donation. When a McPherson schoolboy did not salute the flag, other youths, with the sanction of the school board, soaked him with "American water" from a hose. An Italian-American coal miner in Pittsburg was dumped in grease and hanged for a short moment for refusing to buy a war bond. A boy was expelled from the teachers' college at Hays for saying he was only pretending to support the war. Locals refused permission to Congressman Joseph Bristow to speak in several towns in Kansas because of his criticism of the war.[21] At one point a bill appeared in the Kansas legislature forbidding any noncitizen to possess a gun or bowie knife. The headline on that one ran, "Aliens in Kansas Must Now Hunt with Clubs."[22] It was probably no accident that the Bone Dry law, amending the Kansas prohibition rules to close all loopholes on dispensing liquor even for medicinal purposes, rode on a wave of revulsion for German brewers.[23]

Among the controversial violations of civil rights by federal action during World War I was a denial, by terms of the Espionage Act, of second-class mailing rights for the newspaper *Appeal to Reason*, published in Girard, Kansas, from 1897 to 1922. Julius Wayland founded the *Appeal* in 1895, and it was the most widely circulated socialist newspaper in the United States in the decade prior to World War I. It reached a regular circulation of over .5 million, sometimes as much as 4 million on special issues. Its stated purpose was to "war against oppression and vast wrongs, dispelling the tears, the blood, the woe of capitalism," and to imbue Americans with egalitarian, nonexploitative values. All the major socialists, including labor organizer and sometime presidential candidate Eugene Debs, were closely associated with it. It serialized important works, the best-known being *The Jungle* by Upton Sinclair.[24]

In the hands of Emanuel Haldeman-Julius in the 1920s and 1930s—a man with an eighth-grade education who was called the "Henry Ford of publishing"—the old *Appeal* printing plant at Girard, though less radical, still shook the nation through the publication of the Little Blue Books. There were 6,000 titles printed and over 500 million copies.[25] These were full of stimulating ideas on topics from censorship to companionate marriage, capital punishment, prohibition, immigration, behaviorism, evolution, the Ku Klux Klan, sex, the open shop, and even Emily Brontë and Henry James. Haldeman-Julius published the Blue Books in large quantities on cheap paper, and they retailed always for less than a quarter and for a time at under a nickel.[26] "The great virtue of the Little Blue Books," the author of one of them said, "is that they make knowledge a living and human thing—place it among the realities of life." That much was pure Kansas.[27] Blue Book number 1512, published in 1930, was entitled, "Is This Century the Most Admirable in History?" The answer was yes . . . but.[28] Kansas, Haldeman-Julius wrote, was more forgiving about dress and etiquette than the East but less so when it came to opinions.[29]

The Kansas "Balkans," where Girard was located, had been radical since the Cherokee Neutral Lands War of the late 1860s. The development of mining and the immigration of miners from Europe reinforced that reputation. Sometimes townspeople made fun of their local socialists. When the Call airship prepared to fly to Chicago in 1908, a Kansas City wag said the awkward airship was not the only thing in Girard "that was supposed to appeal to reason, but doesn't."[30] But by 1912, few people could fail to recognize the *Appeal* as a force, enough so that the federal government was proceeding against it with every sort of legal action, including charges of obscenity. Wayland, a John Ingalls look-alike who had once traveled Kansas leaving pamphlets at the doors of farmhouses, committed suicide late in 1912, "hounded to his death," the paper said, "by the relentless dogs of capitalism." The paper, without his leadership, suffered.[31] But in the meantime, it created a scare in Kansas and the nation.[32]

Charles Gleed, who was not too sure about Roosevelt Progressivism, was appalled by the *Appeal to Reason* and in his newspaper questioned its honesty and credibility. The word regionally was that Wayland was an expert capitalist. Local proceedings against the company in 1912 charged that "under pretense of espousing Socialism, teaching economics, and variously furthering the interest of the working man, the *Appeal to Reason* has operated to but one end, and that the amassing of wealth for the owner and his confederates." The *Appeal* subsidiaries included the Girard Cereal Company, the

Girard Manufacturing Company, the Girard Novelty Company, and the Appeal to Reason School of Law, all using the newspaper's mailing list to sell products.[33] Wayland was aware that his ownership of the newspaper conflicted with socialist principles, but like William Morris in England, he was too good a businessperson and too strong an ideologue to put up with the compromises that collective ownership brought.[34]

The *Los Angeles Times* ran an investigation, which revealed that some of the key witnesses in the lawsuit were disgruntled former employees of these *Appeal* enterprises, who themselves wanted to publish a muckraking book on it. The evidence of any fraud was not very sound. A reporter paid by Gleed on behalf of Harrison Gray Otis of the *Los Angeles Times* did find that the *Appeal* itself in 1912 was a big business. It operated five linotype machines. Wayland earned forty thousand dollars a year, lived in a twelve-thousand-dollar home, and was said to be worth over $1 million. There were suspicious practices, playing on the gullible, such as a contest to be won by the person who sent in five subscriptions a week for the longest continuous period of time, those failing to do so in any one week being dropped. The prize was supposed to be a farm in Tennessee, whose value had been misrepresented. The farm would be awarded, it was promised, if and when the contest ever ended. There was nothing strictly illegal about it.[35] It was, however, an enterprise that did not seem to fit in World War I–era Kansas.

The Russian Revolution in 1917 and the addition of the word "Bolshevik" to the language, however vaguely it was understood, added another rhetorical weapon to the arsenal of the superpatriots. Kansas had its own version of the Red Scare, an era when strikes all over the country were widely interpreted as being a part of the Bolshevik Trotskyite plan to spread the revolution to the industrialized nations. Although the *Appeal* rejected the official socialist antiwar plank and supported Wilson's idealistic fourteen points for the remaking of the world after the storm, it printed plenty of material on the horrors of the war and was tarred with the same brush in Kansas as the rest of the "disloyal" radicals.[36]

One of the best known of many IWW trials occurred in Wichita, when, as the union was organizing oil field workers in Butler County, it ran into the wartime hysteria. A federal raid on an IWW local resulted in 1917 in an indictment in Wichita, the defendants charged with conspiracy to impede the war effort. For two years, while awaiting trial, they were held in a jail so inhumane and unsanitary that their case resulted in the reform of county jails as well as in questions about civil rights.

The Wichita case was the only successful federal prosecution directed specifically against the IWW's concept of industrial unionism. One piece of evidence was a letter written to the chamber of commerce in Augusta (Butler County), Kansas:

> Your damned speaker from Missouri in a speech to you and your members advised you to take steps to unlawfully suppress the W.C.U. [Working Class Union] and all organized workers, who are against your blood sucking, cowardly conscription. We warn you that the first dirty move you make against the workers, whether they be organized or unorganized, we will reply with a handful of matches, and numerous sticks of dynamite and nitro.

Police arrested three hundred to four hundred people in Butler County that summer on vagrancy charges. Deputy U.S. Marshal Sam Hill reported that there were fifteen federal and state officers in the Butler County oil fields rounding up IWW members and that the jail and improvised stockades in Augusta and El Dorado were filled with the prisoners. There were two thousand IWW members in the Kansas and Oklahoma oil fields at the time. There was a dynamiting in Tulsa, Oklahoma, and another one was feared in Kansas. People charged that the union organized the field purposely to deprive the United States of petroleum products in the war effort.

The decision on the Wichita detainees came in December 1919, and the accused went to the Leavenworth Federal Penitentiary. In 1920, Butler County's district attorney obtained an injunction against the IWW's oil field subsidiaries operating in Kansas, a decision eventually reversed on appeal to the Kansas Supreme Court.[37] Kansans had no doubt about the meaning of the trial. The *El Dorado Times* headline on the verdict was "Victory for Americanism."[38] The Wichita newspapers, criticized for a jail filled with rats and bedbugs, which one observer said "combines the efficiency of modern invention with the insensibility of the thirteenth century," defended the city's reputation for progressivism and argued that the IWW people hated work worse than "cooties."

The defendants were presumed guilty and therefore thought to deserve what they suffered.[39] The *Kansas City Times* reported that the Wichita trial of thirty-two IWW members was "as far reaching in its interest and sensational in its developments" as any ever held on the question of radicalism. "It is the purpose of the government to lift the cover from the organization known as the Industrial Workers of the World and let the country take a look at the inside works."[40] The jail, said a report from Wichita, "is not a dungeon," though it was "out of date." It was not dark all the time, and the IWW indictment was "one of the most serious ever brought up against anyone in the federal court, involving the question of the very existence of the government, its war against Germany and rights of life and property and the peace and dignity of the nation."[41]

The wheat fields were an organizing area for the IWW also, as evidenced by the case of *Fiske v. Kansas* concerning the unionization attempts there.[42] There were rumors that the IWW planned to poison cattle with a mixture of lye, muriatic and nitric acid, and roach powder as an antiwar plot.[43] In 1919, a volunteer police force of "young farmers with shot guns" formed in Kansas to guard against IWW "locusts" who might sabotage the harvest.[44]

Governor Henry Allen of Wichita wrote that year that the IWW and the Non-Partisan League were dangerous to Kansas agriculture. He became well acquainted with the league in North Dakota, its state of origin, when investigating it for his newspaper, the *Wichita Beacon*. "It is not only a class minded organization," he wrote, "which seeks to exist by arraying members of one occupation against another, but it is my belief that some of its leaders are not loyal Americans and are seeking to do with the agricultural population of this state, just exactly what the IWW and other members of the red organization are doing with the industrial proposition. . . . There is not a thing that a Kansas farmer today desires in the way of legislation which he cannot get by methods which do not organize him as a class."[45]

Organizers, however, were effective. A Non-Partisan League man said at Great Bend that those who put on the Liberty Loan and Red Cross drives were "spit-straws for Wall Street" and offered ten dollars to anyone who would debate him on the subject. "They are inflaming our farmers and laborers," wrote Phillip Zimmerman, who ran the Kansas Anti-Bolshevik Campaign office headquartered in Wichita, "and hell is bound to break loose very soon unless a way is found to muzzle them."[46]

Among the ways for muzzling was an American Day, promoted by the governor's office, sponsored by the National Security League, and celebrated in Kansas on the international radical holiday of May Day, beginning in

1920. "The movement is typical of the state," wrote a newspaper in Ohio. "It studies tradition and history merely that it may learn how to move and occupy new ground."[47]

American Day was abstract education. More concrete was the state's use of the fire marshal to investigate radicals on the grounds of protecting wheat fields from "fire bugs."[48] More direct still was action taken by local American Legion groups against IWW and Non-Partisan League speakers. When the Non-Partisan League scheduled a picnic and speech at Ellinwood, Kansas, in spring 1919, some of the local youths surrounded the speaker's car and told him it would not be advisable for him to appear. They then escorted him to Great Bend and marched him around the square before fifteen hundred people, where locals pelted him with eggs.[49] Why should a state park, wrote the Hays sheriff, be "desecrated by its use as a camping ground for a band of Bolshevik outlaws?"[50] Zimmerman thought it was "plainly evident that Kansas has more than her share of these disciples of despair, sowing discord among our farmers and laborers."[51] Another man reported that there was a lot of IWW literature abroad in Kansas and that "if the Bolsheviks get too raw, the returning soldiers will handle them in the good old fashioned way."[52]

The governor's files in 1919, the peak year of the Red Scare nationally, were filled with broadsides from radical organizations. "The war is over," proclaimed one:

> Your exploiters have quickly placed their profits in safety. You, the working slaves, will soon find yourselves on the streets, facing a hard winter, looking for work . . . BECAUSE YOU LACK THE COURAGE TO USE OTHER METHODS! You have tolerated all the moral and physical slaveries during the war. . . . What were your profits out of this war? You lost all the little liberty you had, and you gave your sons, brothers and fathers away to be shot down like dogs to rot in the fields of France. For what? For the glory of the American flag! So that your masters may have bigger markets to sell merchandise and exploit other people like you.[53]

Kate Richards O'Hare, a socialist and feminist from Kansas and the first woman to run for the U.S. Senate, wrote for the *Appeal to Reason* and served a jail term under the Espionage Act. She composed a tribute to a dead colleague: "We shed no tears of grief; grief is for the naked lives of those who have made the world no better. . . . Sleep on, our comrade. . . . We bring no ostentatious tributes of our love, we spend not gold for flowers for your tomb, but with hearts that rejoice at our deliverance offer a comrade's tribute to lie above your breast—the red flag of human brotherhood."[54]

There was enough truth and power there to attract. After all, the socialist idea of a better future and an improved human race was hardly alien to Kansas. The Kansas government itself had often been accused of socialistic practices. The broadsides, crudely printed on newsprint, as well as newspapers like the *Appeal to Reason,* with their striking cartoons, popular education programs, attention to problems of women and racial minorities, and bold editorials, worried state officials. "You have got to line up with Uncle Sam," said Governor Capper in 1918, "or leave Kansas. We now have nearly one hundred state guard units who will see that disloyalty does not get a foothold in Kansas."[55]

The coal strike of 1919, organized in southeast Kansas by Alexander Howat, president of District Fourteen of the United Mine Workers, increased the stakes. Howat made radical statements beyond the official positions of the national union. Personally, he behaved aggressively. And the coal strike, coming as it did at the beginning of winter 1919–1920, fundamentally affected the rights of what the new governor, Henry Allen, called "the party of the third part," the public. "It is the duty of government," Allen said in November 1919, "and it has the inherent power, to protect the people whose welfare is dependent upon it. . . . If government is to mean anything, then its obligation is to prevent innocent people from becoming the victims of a fuel famine, which, in the course of events, is both unnatural and unnecessary." Allen asked for and got volunteers to run the strip mines until the strike was settled. He then made for himself a national reputation by creating the Kansas Court of Industrial Relations, the express purpose of which was to prevent such situations from again arising from the "ruthless quarrels" between management and labor.[56]

Kansas had in some ways pioneered in rights for labor, building on its relatively liberal reaction to the 1885 rail strike. Miss Linna Bresette, a state factory inspector and secretary of the welfare commission, investigated conditions among employed women in Kansas in 1916 with a view toward regulating working conditions, hygiene, and salaries required to "maintain a self supporting woman in frugal, but respectable condition" in twenty Kansas communities.[57] Kansas was a national leader in regulating safety.[58] It passed an eight-hour law for work on public contracts in Topeka in 1890 and in the state in 1893.[59] It specified in 1916 that laundries in the state had to provide women employees with seats to use when not at a machine requiring standing. It also had to provide them drinking fountains or individual drinking cups, adequate supplies of soap and towels, separate toilets, good ventilation, clean and sanitary plants, separate dressing rooms, and proper lighting.[60] There was even a suggestion of ten-hour workdays for Kansas farmers. "The joys of plowing from daylight to dark or working in the harvest fields 18 hours with a half hour off for meals," said farm organizer Henry Richardson of Ft. Scott in 1915, "will not be tolerated by the Independent and Respected Order of Farm Employees."[61]

William Kerle of Topeka, a union carpenter who had lobbied for much of the regulatory legislation of the 1890s, said that he became a union member because of the long hours his wife had to work. She awakened at five in the morning to prepare breakfast and did not finish the supper dishes until nine at night. "No self-respecting man wants his wife to work that way." But he thought conditions so much better in 1916, and the press so much more sympathetic than before, that "many of the present day union men do not realize what we older ones have gone through to get what we have for unionism today."[62] Governor Capper, an honorary member of the Topeka Typographical Union, paid tribute to what he called the "real labor leaders who have fought the battles of the working men, insisting upon justice and fairness between employer and employee."[63] Howat, however, did not qualify as one of those "real labor leaders," and the 1919 mine strike pushed beyond the limits of state tolerance.

There had been strikes before in the Kansas coal district. In 1910 Governor Walter Stubbs had refused to call out the militia to deal with a strike of thirty-five thousand coal miners against the Central Coal and Coke Company.[64] One of the issues then was the impact of thirty-seven steam shovels that had been operating in the district in the three years previous, displacing miners.[65] In 1917 the mine operators in Pittsburg and Howat were at odds again and eighteen mines closed, idling about twenty-five hundred workers. The operators said that Howat was trying to take advantage of war demand to squeeze concessions from them. Howat said the operators were using the war to discredit the union and that new electrical devices used to set off blasts were dangerous to the workers who used them.[66]

In 1919 the state militia supplied young volunteers to operate the mines in Crawford and Cherokee Counties.[67] Allen justified his actions by saying that strikes were getting out of hand. Over 364 mine strikes had occurred in Kansas between April 1916 and December 1918, "most of them called upon the most trivial ground." He said that miners were making no progress through this strike technique and that the mine unions, "the aristocracy of organized labor," had "instituted the present insane notion that an organized minority is greater than government itself." In thinking this approach would work in Kansas, Allen said, they "underestimate the Kansas spirit."[68]

Intervening in an individual strike, however, was one thing; creating permanent machinery for compulsory arbitration of strikes in Kansas was another. The debate over the so-called Freeman bill, which created the Kansas Court of Industrial Relations in 1920, was therefore both fierce and national. "Labor does not relish a strike," said a union leader from Wichita, "any more than the South used to enjoy yellow fever. No legislation was ever attempted in an effort to brand a yellow fever patient a criminal but every means was employed to discover and remove the cause of the trouble."[69] Another man wrote, "The Child brought forth by the legislature, it would seem, is sired by the Kansas City Star and out of William Allen White, and is not a legitimate son at all of Kansas. Dr. Allen should let this child die."[70] Clarence Darrow, the nationally known criminal lawyer, said in Topeka on Labor Day 1920 that "Kansas farmers had better burn their corn than pass such ignominious legislation."[71] The Brotherhood of Railway Clerks wrote that if the bill passed in Kansas, it would deny them the rights for which their forefathers fought and died at Bunker Hill and Gettysburg.[72] The League of Kansas Municipalities, however, came out for the bill, as did the mine owners and the Association of Railway Executives.[73] "The remedy for bolshevism, anarchy and IWW," wrote the president of the American Sash and Door Company in Kansas City, "is clearly within our own hands. . . . Our people read and do their own thinking, it remains only to stop the stream of poison that flows out and through certain newspapers and publications printed chiefly in foreign languages."[74] Wrote a Ft. Scott attorney, "The time has passed in Kansas (the most forward State in matters of the improvement of conditions of society) when the necessities of the people of this good State, are to be either forgotten, or used as chess men, to play out a waiting game or a game of 'strong arm' between two powerful and rich organizations for the purpose of determining who is to win in a big contest of freeze out, with the public's necessities as the goal."[75] And an insurance man in Salina wrote to Governor Allen, "I feel just like hugging you."[76]

Eleven cases were filed in February 1920, the first month of the existence of the Court of Industrial Relations, and people of all perspectives closely watched the result of this new "industrial umpire" idea.[77] Allen, his presidential ambitions aroused, gave matters no time to cool down but delivered a speech on Lincoln's birthday in Chicago justifying the court. He said that there was a new demand for the "consecrated service of every citizen" to the "ideals of America" and to put that above selfish concerns. The coal strike did not fit. "With a callousness that is without parallel both operators and miners settled down in the dead of winter to hold a deliberate wage controversy, while the mines were idle and the public freezing." The state did not have the power to force them back to work but did have the power to take over the two hundred mines with the help of the Supreme Court and ten thousand volunteers. Their work, often in subzero temperatures, was an inspiration, Allen said, and taught everyone that government could protect citizens against industrial strife just as it had always protected them against criminals. He said the Kansas court was no irresponsible experiment and could be applied nationally.[78] In his files was a letter quoting Plutarch, the ancient Greek philosopher and biographer, to the effect that public conflagrations did not always begin in public buildings and that it was the duty of the state "to heal . . . private animosities, and to prevent them from growing into public divisions."[79]

Allen promulgated his views of the labor problem and the court widely. He debated Samuel Gompers of the American Federation of Labor (AFL) at Carnegie Hall in New York City in May 1920 to wide national publicity, and he published *The Party of the Third Part* in 1921.[80] "Gompers and his crowd," Allen said, "realize that they must fight the Kansas court which stands for justice, because if the court continues there will no longer be any market for the tin gods they have been selling to labor for the last forty years." Moreover, these "hard-faced, soft-headed radical leaders" had "cost the farmers of this country more than all the natural pests."[81]

There were plenty of incidents to heat up opinion. The state prosecuted Howat and four other members of the United Mine Workers local for refusing to appear before the Court of Industrial Relations in its mining investigation. Howat said, "We officials of the United Mine Workers of District 14 do not recognize this industrial court. Let its members go down into the mines and dig coal and learn the business the same as we did. If they do not know the coal mining business they are unfitted for the position and are wholly incompetent."[82] He served some time in a Kansas jail.[83] The next year Howat called a strike in protest, although he denied it was specifically aimed at Allen and his "joke" court.[84]

Late in 1921 the women's march, the wives and relatives of the striking miners, took place in Cherokee County. It was headed "by the girl's band of Arma, playing martial music. 'General' Annie Stovich, the Joan of Arc of the 'Amazon army' led her invading hosts . . . into the enemy country." Word that troops were coming "only increased the pent-up fury of the women," and local officials were frightened, for "it was believed that even bayonets will not deter the strong, highly temperamental foreign women who compose the bulk of the marching hosts."[85] When the state did send troops, local labor leaders complained about using such force against women, especially in the era of the industrial court and so-called peaceful processes.[86] More threatening than the march were the actions of George W. Reid, the African-American leader of a 1922 packing plant strike in Kansas City. Reid stopped a streetcar on a viaduct, drew two revolvers, and began firing shots through the windows, yelling that he was going to "dump all the scabs in the river."

The same year William Allen White, who was more dangerous with a pen than Reid was with a revolver, hung a poster in the window of the *Gazette* office supporting the union in a current railway shopmen's strike as long as it avoided violence. White saw putting up the poster as a freedom of speech issue. Allen felt otherwise and had a warrant served on the editor. White insisted on going to trial to massive publicity. A judge, in dismissing the case, said it had been brought "maliciously or recklessly" by a state that was getting too enthusiastic about its new labor policies to the detriment of fundamental rights.[87]

White's defection was serious, as he had been one of the strongest supporters of the Industrial Commission bill and had testified for it in the legislature. He thought Bolshevism should be fought "not with guns, but with steady employment" and felt that, in that regard, the interests of management and labor could be reconciled.[88] The court, he said, "was the furthest step toward the socialization of industry ever taken in America, and perhaps in the world."[89] That, to him, was preferable to strikes. He commented that Howat was "an energetic man, one rather more intelligent than the usual labor leader, but ill-tempered and pig-headed, and I am almost persuaded selfish, although he has a lot of martyr blood in him." As for the women's march, he noted that women were not afraid of infantry but would scatter before cavalry.[90] But White's being indicted on a charge of conspiracy to stop Santa Fe trains for putting up a poster in 1922 convinced him the state was going too far. "We are coming into serious times," he wrote. "The industrial question—the difference between the man who owns the machines and the man who runs them—must be settled by reason; not by force. And if it is settled by reason, we must guarantee to every man, free utterance of what he finds best suited to his place in the world." Justice, he said, was the only means that would bring peace.[91]

Allen responded that the controversy must go to his impartial tribunal. President Warren Harding "has suggested a Christian Science treatment when what was needed was an operation."[92] Allen dispatched troops to strike centers in 1922 against the advice of White and pleaded with White "to get hard-headed."[93] That attitude, White thought, was fatal to the court. He wrote in 1923 that the Court of Industrial Relations, created not as a true court but as an arbitrative body with representatives from labor as well as management and the public, had "got itself into being called a labor hater." It was, therefore, doomed in the court of public opinion, whatever the ultimate decision on its constitutionality.[94]

The operations of the court itself were of more modest significance than all the rhetoric might suggest. It took up 166 cases and eight investigations during its five-year life. But it never faced a situation parallel to the coal strike of 1919. It solved few disputes, and there is no evidence that strikes were reduced in Kansas compared to surrounding states. Some of its teeth were drawn in 1923 when the U.S. Supreme Court reversed a Kansas court and ruled that the act creating the Court of Industrial Relations curtailed the rights of both employer and employee to contract about their own affairs, thus violating the due process clauses of the Fourteenth Amendment. "To say that a business is clothed with the public interest," wrote a Wichita attorney, "is not to import that the public may take over its entire management and run it at the expense of the owner."[95] The demise of the Court of Industrial Relations came in 1925 after U.S. Supreme Court decisions denied the right of states to regulate wages.[96]

The 1919 coal strike was national, a part of a flurry of strikes, including the well-known general strike in Seattle, which led to the federal investigating agency that became the FBI.[97] Although there was plenty of talk about the relationship between Bolshevism and labor around the country that year, the Court of Industrial Relations was a pragmatic response particularly

Kansan. There was a mix of cynicism in it, to be sure, but also a typical optimism that reason could and would prevail had it only a structure in which to work.

As the incident with Allen illustrates, White was as opposed to right-wing as to left-wing abuses of rational procedure. Thus came his nationally known campaign for governor of Kansas in 1924 on a platform including strong and straightforward opposition to the Ku Klux Klan. The renewed Klan, organized in 1915 by William Simmons, incorporated the race prejudice of the nineteenth-century group along with its sheeted rituals and penchant for direct action, but it was also a money-making organization, sweeping in many other prejudices, including those against "modernism," "urbanism," and German Americans, Jews, and Catholics.[98] In Kansas the Klan was strong. It had about forty thousand members there in 1922, perhaps six thousand of them in Wichita.[99] It made inroads at the level of local government, so precious to White. This tarnished the image of small-town America that his moving 1921 essay on the death of his daughter Mary had cast so powerfully across the country. That the Klan should be winning city elections in Emporia was too much for him, and so he ran, without much hope of winning, against a state establishment that he thought had become complacent.

The Klan, White wrote, "is an organization of cowards." He wanted "to offer Kansans afraid of the Klan and ashamed of that disgrace, a candidate who shares their fear and shame." The Klan attacked groups that made up one-quarter of the Kansas population, and it preached and practiced "terror and force."[100] White thought the Klan was an example "of the tyrannies of men in masses." Imagine, he wrote, "Christ chasing the Pharisees out of the temple behind a mask, and Lincoln riding around in his shirttail before signing the Emancipation Proclamation."[101] It was "based upon such deep foolishness that it is bound to be a menace of good government in my community. Any man fool enough to be Imperial Wizard would have power without responsibility and both without any sense. That is social dynamite." He called the group a "self-constituted body of moral idiots."[102]

White's strong showing in the election did bolster courage. Imperial Wizard Simmons ran into trouble with his followers about his own lack of moral probity in regard to his secretary, damaging the national organization, and in 1925 the Klan was ousted from Kansas through the device of refusing it a charter.[103] To White, it was another example of what the Free

Kansas Ku Klux Klan rally, 1920s.
Courtesy of the Kansas State Historical Society.

State people had proved against such great odds in the 1850s: that when "decent elements exhibit courage and hard work," no matter how entrenched may seem the forces of evil or however long standing an abuse, the future can be changed.[104] It was another pivotal moment testing the regional culture to make its choices and define itself.

The Klan issue involved the broader issue of race, one with which the state continued to struggle. Gordon Parks, the well-known photographer of the late twentieth century, published *The Learning Tree* in 1963, a fictionalized account of his own growing up black in Ft. Scott, Kansas, in the 1920s.[105] It was a far from idyllic experience, and, like the experience of many farmers suffering a depression beginning in 1923 or of Howat's coal miners, the lives of most black families were a long way from the general economic boom and a jazz-age social life that Kansas and the nation experienced in that decade.

Kansas had an ambiguous record on race. There was sympathy, with a long tradition behind it, for the situation of black people. Governor Allen noted in 1919 that the year before, sixty-eight men and women, mostly black, had been put to death by mobs in the United States, and that he was fully in sympathy with the desire of the National Association for the Advancement of Colored People (NAACP) to "suppress lawlessness and improve the condition of the colored people in this country."[106] The state received national publicity in 1920 when Governor Allen refused to extradite from Kansas to Arkansas a black man, Robert Hill, accused of instigating a deadly riot there. Allen said he refused extradition, not in fear that Hill might be lynched, "but through fear of that equally unfortunate thing that he might be tried by passion and racial bitterness."[107] For his trouble, Allen received a note addressed to "the Kansas Nigger Lover Gov. Harry [*sic*] J. Allen." The text read, "You Kansas Nigger Lover, It is too bad you were not at Elaine on October 1, 1919 and had your nasty 'white liver' shot out by some of your beloved brethren. From One who suffered."[108] That kind of mail from Arkansas, Allen said, was even more reason not to return Hill there.[109] The Kansas Negro Civil League expressed its appreciation to him.[110] Hill thanked him, too, claiming he was innocent, and that if convicted, "it would simply prove to me and thousands of my race—a race that have been handicapped throughout the south over three hundred years that the law is not the thing for us to call on."[111]

The handling of that incident seemed tolerant and liberal. On the other hand, school segregation by race and housing discrimination were definite realities in Kansas cities by the early twentieth century. An 1879 Kansas law authorized boards of education in cities of the first class (population over fifteen thousand) to provide separate educational facilities for black and white children in the primary grades.[112] Most cities moved to do so immediately. Blacks in Topeka complained, "We hear of no Irish or German school. All children are at liberty to attend the school closest to them, except the black child." They also protested that the school board did not hire blacks. Blacks in Topeka sued in 1890 on the grounds that one of the black schools was inferior, "a veritable cesspool," but the school board prevailed.

The broader question arose: "Why do we send our children to high schools . . . to earn $1.50/day cleaning the sewers?" The efforts of the Reverend Charles Sheldon, whose Central Congregational Church was adjacent to the Topeka African-American area of Tennesseetown, to establish a kindergarten, library, and training classes there did not much allay the basics of discrimination in housing, education, and jobs. "There is not a restaurant or lunch counter in this city," wrote the Reverend George Shaffer of St. John AME, "where a Negro can obtain a meal . . . or a cup of coffee." With the exception of Edwin McCabe of Nicodemus, who became state auditor in 1882, blacks were invisible in the state and largely so in the urban power structure. An 1899 survey in Tenneseetown revealed that men's wages averaged $1.43 a day; yet only 11 percent received any aid from the city or county.[113]

Segregation in Wichita was delayed by an 1889 action making that city an exception to the 1879 law. But in 1906, thinking that a 1905 state law had

Tennesseetown kindergarten, Topeka, 1899.
Courtesy of the Kansas State Historical Society.

eliminated that restriction, Wichita instituted a segregation rule. Although only 1 percent of blacks attended Wichita High School, mixing at the elementary school level was controversial, and the *Eagle* in 1905 said that separate schools would be best "for the colored race." Blacks took more interest in separate schools, the newspaper article said, because they felt these belonged to them. That year the Kansas state superintendent of public instruction justified segregation in public schools in his annual report, saying, "The conclusion is not based on prejudice, but on common sense and pedagogical principles. We need teachers of the same race as the pupils." Wichita officials said that separate schools "were more in keeping with the ideals and wishes of a majority of patrons."

National law in the wake of the Supreme Court decision in *Plessy v. Ferguson* (1896) justified the "separate but equal" legal doctrine upon which segregation was based. However, it did not sit well with many black parents, who appeared before the Wichita school board to protest, claiming to represent two-thirds of the black population, which was in turn about 5 percent of the population of Wichita. Wichita, they said, had as yet no "black belt or

Tennessee town" and did not need one, and there was no need to go to the expense of separate schools. The *Wichita Searchlight*, an African-American newspaper, advised, however, that blacks not make a scene when turned away from white schools or be "ungentlemanly or unladylike," as that would accomplish nothing.

The preferred strategy was legal action. A suit filed in Sedgwick County District Court by a black parent wishing her child to be admitted to a white school failed there, but the Kansas Supreme Court sustained the mother's position in 1907.[114] The high court rejected Wichita's argument that a 1905 state action reaffirming the general 1879 permission to segregate primary schools applied there.[115] This forced the Wichita school board to go to the state legislature for stronger authority to separate students. Achieving this in 1909 removed the last barrier in the state to segregating primary schools. In 1911 Wichita voters approved the Toussaint L'Overture School as strictly for blacks and authorized busing to it from those homes outside the "colored colony." Nineteen twelve was the first year for total separation of black and white students in Wichita, a situation that lasted until the Kansas *Brown v. Topeka Board of Education* case of 1954 and beyond.[116] The Wichita school board members reaffirmed in 1912 their opinion that "the lot of a Negro pupil in a white school would be as unpleasant for the Negro as obnoxious to the white children."[117]

There was demand that the segregation be extended to smaller cities and to high schools. But Kansas was not ready to go that far. A case brought concerning Galena in 1916 resulted in a court's deciding that cities of the second and third class could not under existing legislation segregate schools, even when the facilities were equal.[118] A 1919 legislative bill to segregate schools in second- and third-class cities failed.

The arguments against segregation at that time were familiar—that dual schools would increase cost and that they "breed racial antagonism; in the white children is bred a spirit of condescension, and the colored children have thrust upon them a feeling of inferiority." The common and integrated public school was just the answer, some people thought, to eliminate the prejudices Kansas was experiencing in the wake of the war.[119] A petition by Kansas blacks protested that the segregation bill was "a backward step and inconsistent with Kansas history." The American black was "being robbed of his self respect by a treatment in schools and public places which accentuates complexion differences and masses all into a single body without regard to personal worth or character." In most respects, Kansas was progressive, wrote a Topeka man, but "on the race question we are reactionary." No such suggestion as the segregation law could have been made in the Kansas of forty years earlier, he thought.[120]

The Supreme Court of Kansas passed down its last opinion upholding the segregation in Kansas schools in 1930.[121] It was some time, however, before the law or the situation there changed, and when it did it was in the dramatic matter of *Brown vs. Topeka Board of Education,* which changed policy much more broadly than in Kansas alone.

That school segregation paralleled increasing housing segregation, and that separate education did nothing to relieve poverty among blacks, was highlighted by the Wichita Squattertown issue of the mid-1920s. Motivated partly by the violent 1921 Tulsa race riot to look into the racial situation, the Wichita Council of Churches in 1924 published a study of the sixty-five hundred blacks residing in town and found that more than 20 percent lived "far below the level of decency and comfort." Many urban blacks worked as trash collectors and lived on land they did not own in the so-called Squatter-towns, developing at the margins of the city. The Wichita Council of Social Agencies concluded that the Squattertowns were "a condition of the City rather than a district of the City" and that city government should do something about it. An interracial conference took place in 1924 and ad-dressed the question of school segregation as well as discrimination in hiring in the city police and fire departments and in private industry. But nothing major changed. In 1927 a group of local attorneys submitted to the city commission a report charging that Wichita police regularly violated the civil rights of racial minorities and that the city manager's office ignored it. The city filed the report and advised that individual suits could be filed on individual grievances.[122]

One seeming high point for Kansas of the 1920s in race relations was the banning of the film *Birth of a Nation* in the state. That epic silent film, released in 1915, portrayed the Ku Klux Klan as a heroic and patriotic force designed to put aggressive blacks during Reconstruction in their place. Kansas blacks naturally objected. So did the Grand Army of the Republic organi-zation of Union veterans in Kansas, both on the grounds that the film was a serious distortion of history.[123] "We all agree that it is a powerful picture," wrote Governor Allen to the head of the Department of Visual Education at the Kansas State Normal School in Emporia in 1919, "but it undoubtedly has an unfortunate racial effect for the very reason that it is powerful." Allen saw the film in Los Angeles and concluded, "It was [built] around a theme the presentation of which has no constructive value whatever. Its only effect is to rearouse the memories of a period which it is best to forget." He could not allow it to be used for special educational purposes any more than to be shown generally.[124] One of the Kansas film censors defended in strong terms the board's actions. It was, he wrote in 1920, "a tissue of misrepresentations of the north, the Negro, and our country's history to the final culminating travesty which pictures peace on earth and good will to men as the outcome of passion, of hate and of murder." The film was "immoral," not because it was sexually suggestive "but in its whole revelation of race prejudice and sectional bitterness."[125] The Kansas City branch of the NAACP agreed, calling *Birth* vicious propaganda, "with the intention of arousing and keeping alive prejudice which an oppressed race has suffered long."[126]

By 1923 Kansas was the only state in the Union continuing the ban on *Birth of a Nation,* by then considered a sort of classic by most people. The next year, however, for commercial reasons, Kansas began showing it also. The U.S. Supreme Court had ruled that it was an accurate account of the Civil War and Reconstruction.[127] It was, wrote one man to Governor Jonathan Davis, a "morally clean" and "purely historical" picture, which was immensely popular across the country.[128]

The Wichita Ministerial League, representing ten thousand African-American communicants, still felt otherwise (as have professional historians always). The film "tended to excite the unthinking mind" in all the wrong directions, wrote the Ministerial League. "It barters the security and happiness of the citizens of a commonwealth on the counter of ordinary commercial endeavor; it gives an incentive for lynching, mob violence, and economic prejudice against a group of the citizens of the state in which it is placed on exhibition. . . . It is absolutely contrary to the high ideas and ideals of Kansas History."[129] Some cities, including Wichita, passed ordinances to continue to ban the film, but courts overturned these.[130] And it was clear there was pent-up demand. In Topeka in February 1924, *Birth* ran eleven days at the Grand Theater, a record for any picture there, and was seen by twenty thousand people.[131]

In considered hindsight, that particular movie ban was a moral victory for Kansas. But the agency out of which it grew, the Kansas State Board of Review, one of seven movie censorship boards that came to exist in the nation, was a controversial feature of the teens and twenties in Kansas. It lasted into midcentury, beyond the life of any other motion picture censorship board in the United States, and some people thought it was a source of ridicule for the state.[132]

When motion pictures first appeared in Kansas, the state superintendent of public instruction judged their suitability. After 1913, any films banned by that officer could appeal to a new board, the Moving Picture Censorship Appeal Commission. That consisted of the governor, the attorney general, and the secretary of state, who soon found they had things to do other than to decide film controversies. The State Board of Review therefore originated in 1917. Its three members, all women for a long while, viewed every film to be shown in Kansas and cut them if they felt it necessary.[133] The work was supported by a two-dollar-a-reel tax, instituted some years earlier.[134]

The board created a stir from the first. A Santa Fe railroad official wrote Arthur Capper in 1915 that he was shocked that the film *Carmen* could not be shown in Kansas. He and his wife had seen it in Houston and thought its ban meant that "hypocritism has certainly reached its limit in Kansas."[135] How could the state superintendent of instruction's office possibly deal fairly with the four hundred films a week presented for its inspection?[136]

But the new board did view them, and it published an annual list of changes it had made and the reasons. In July 1918 the women censored *A Tight Squeeze* by the Fox Film Corporation so as to "eliminate man finding himself in water and seeing cow, suggesting vulgar situation." The film *Bathing Beauties and Big Boobs,* whose title the slang of the time had not yet made offensive, was censored to eliminate a man having his trousers pulled off by fish. In *Brass Bullet No. 8,* the subtitle, "We're in a hell of a fix," was not seen in Kansas. In *The Death Dance,* reel five, the board cut the subtitle, "So your new lover keeps you in the same nest my husband built for his plaything." A scene showing a man and woman drinking from the same glass was eliminated. *The Golden Fleece* had to cut scenes showing "tough women smoking." In *The Great Love,* the subtitle "there are reasons why we must be married" was not allowed to engender speculation in the Sunflower State.[137]

Kansans debated films seriously and, as usual, were divided in their opinions. Clyde Reed, who was creating a political and journalistic career in Kansas, wrote that the Max Sennet comedy *Cupid's Day Off* was "the rottenest picture I have ever seen on the screen" and argued that if it could get the board's approval, which it did, there was no need for maintaining a censorship board at all.[138] "The movie screens," wrote a man from Wichita that year, "are the prime factor in demoralizing and destroying our homes. Every phase in the category of crime is minutely shown in detail upon the screen, where it is imprinted in the minds so indelibly, that they can never be obliterated. . . . Thousands of girls receive their first thrills of sex knowledge in the movies. Every step taken, showing the unfaithfulness of wives, is vividly portrayed and including forgiveness and reconciliation." It was, he thought, worse than strong drink. "Are we drifting into open 'Free Love?'"[139]

There was plenty of opinion, too, on the other side. N. W. Huston, the editor of the *Columbus Advocate*, wrote in 1920 that there were too many women on the film board and that they did not fairly represent views, even of Kansas women. The censors needed to be "broad-minded enough to look at pictures with their entertainment value in mind,—rather than their Biblical application." What a system! "Three women (God bless them!) sit up there in K.C., criticize the many wonderful pictures presented, quibble over whether comedies are decent,—butcher many splendid pictures, to such an extent that producers refuse to come into Kansas at all, rather than chop up their pictures." The women, he thought, carried "the Puritan view to an extreme. . . . They insist upon the wronged girls being all 'secretly married' in the first reel." Women might be "good cooks, but some of them are punk censors."[140]

The supporters of censorship prevailed. Why could there not be just a good story, wrote a Kansan in 1921, showing "life's joys and sorrows . . . the cause and remedy afforded. . . . But no, each door I walked up to had a picture out showing some desperado in the act of assassinating a human and stomping his 'innards' out."[141] Of course, it was convenient to ban such pieces as *The Marching Amazons of the Kansas Coal Fields*, which the board did in 1922.[142] Movie censorship in Kansas, however, survived because most people agreed with the editor of the *Oskaloosa Independent* that here also Kansas must be a leader in the "revolt against the crime and loose moral suggestiveness of the picture business as it exist[s] now," rather than sitting back and crying against the evils of society.[143] And so, with little support from the rest of the country, it continued to be.

Indeed, it was not the showing of films to which Kansans objected, or to modern technology in general. On the contrary, they were fascinated by it, as evidenced by their early adoption of the automobile and the airplane. In the

A muddy road.
Courtesy of the Kansas State Historical Society.

1920s these two devices thrived in the state. The airplane made its way into the open sky without much incident. The Kansas automobilist, however, long struggled with some of the worst and most unsystematically designed roads in the nation.

Floyd Hockenhull remembered a four-hundred-mile trip with his father from Natoma, Kansas, to Longmont, Colorado, in a new Model-T Ford in 1916. The experience was typical of the times. "Here were father and I," Floyd recalled, "both inexperienced with automobiles, about to take off blithely on a long trip through country unknown to us, without maps, charts or anything to guide us." There were five people in the car with all the supplies on their laps. The departure was fine. "We rolled down the street with an air of frivolity, all of us smiling . . . speeding at seven miles an hour where five was the limit." Since the Ford had over twenty horsepower, the family felt "we could pass and outrun almost anybody." They averaged sixteen miles per hour to Plainville, checking the gas at Palco with a ruler from the tank under the front seat. Checking the oil involved going under the car with pliers to open the top petcock on the crankcase—"if no oil flowed out, you needed oil." After Palco, the roads were unknown to them, and they had three flats in ten miles. The afternoon brought a storm, which involved putting up the side curtains on the car and placing raincoats over the suitcases. They became stuck in the mud up to the axles, and the radiator boiled over. They drove into Colby on the wheel rim that night, having traveled eighty-eight miles in twelve hours. The next morning, after taking off the front floorboards to tighten the transmission bands, they headed for Colorado.[144]

The Good Roads movement in Kansas was a powerful regional political lobby from the early years of the twentieth century. Farmers, with some reservations, were part of it. *Kansas Farmer* questioned central administration of a state highway system and the arrogance of urban expertise but not the usefulness of the car or decent roads in ending rural isolation. In 1914, Kansans owned 50,000 cars; 30,000 of the owners were farmers. The 1920 census showed that Kansas ranked third in the percentage of farmers who owned autos, with 62 percent, and was one of eleven states that had 10.7 or more cars for every 100 residents.[145] In 1921 it was said that Kansans were buying 300 autos a day.[146] A journalist noted as early as 1911 that "the country town livery stable is passing." The horse suddenly was a hobby rather than a necessity.[147]

Agitation for better roads began early. A 1905 bill made the township boards of Kansas the boards of commissioners of highways and gave them power to appoint overseers of highways at two dollars a day. That, to one member of the state Good Roads Association, was not satisfactory, as it perpetuated a system where control was local, improvements were not standard, and there was no coordination of through and way routes across the state, much less a rational system of marking.[148] The time was "ripe," wrote a manufacturer of bicycles and motor bikes to Governor Hoch in 1906, for the federal government to aid in connecting the larger cities by road and to use skilled supervision and regional legislative assistance to follow a plan.[149] There were suggestions at that time from the Kansas Motor League that there be a state highway commission, which would appoint county highway commissions to ensure that all road building was done by "competent road builders, separating road building from farming." The machinery should be owned by the state and include heavy road rollers. The state, the critic said, was spending over three hundred thousand dollars a year on roads through local taxing units, but about half of that was wasted due to poor technique.[150] It was an embarrassment that football fans had to be told by the newspapers in 1914, "How to Reach the Kansas-Missouri Football Game in Lawrence Next Sunday by Motor," including alternative routes under different weather conditions.[151]

The Good Roads movement was on the defensive often, and progress was slow, but its people were determined. John Wright of Junction City was the first president of the Good Roads Association, organized in 1900 with the slogan, "Keep Kansans Out of the Mud." He wrote that he was "confronted by some men who seem to think that this good road movement means higher taxes, and giving someone a lucrative position with little work. . . . What we want is good wholesome laws, by which the road taxes can be and will be collected and then expended in an economical judicious manner under competent supervision."[152] In 1909, one thousand people attended a convention of the National Good Roads Association in Topeka.[153] Organizations emerged within the state promoting individual routes, and local chambers of commerce, automobile clubs, and individual business people backed these.[154] By 1911, there was a Santa Fe Trail Highway Association for a road following the Arkansas River; a Meridian Road Association, contemplating "building of a good road along the Sixth Principal Meridian from the north to the south line of the state" (later state highway 81), with J. C. Nicholson of Newton as its spark plug; a Central Kansas Boulevard group that was improving roads from Great Bend through Ness City to the Colorado line (later state highway 96); the Sunflower Trail from the Santa Fe Route north; the Golden Belt Route from Kansas City to Denver (later Interstate 70); a group promoting a road following Coronado's track; and a lobby for the Salt Bed Route passing through the central Kansas salt area.[155] Men like Nicholson and A. Q. Miller of the *Belleville Telescope* (who for years promoted what became U.S. 36) were strong publicists for modern highways.[156] Everyone wanted to build more concrete roads, after the first one in the state opened in 1914.[157] "It seems to me," said a man attending the state Good Roads convention in Wichita in 1911, "that if there were a place in God's great outdoors where nature had lavishly prepared the plans and specifications for beautiful highways, it was in Kansas."[158]

By the time of World War I, the automobile habit was entrenched. The Kansas bank commissioner wrote in 1915 that it seemed to him that "the craze is getting to the point where men are buying cars and going without overcoats."[159] Arthur Capper used his speechmaking ability in the cause. "Kansas wants good roads," he said, "and Kansas will have them." The problem, he said, was that farmers had regarded the Good Roads movement "as a scheme of the pleasure-seeking automobilist to construct smooth highways upon which reckless drivers might risk their own foolish necks." That, he said, was not true, and much of the cost would come from licenses and gasoline, instead of from general property tax. The car was no longer a toy.

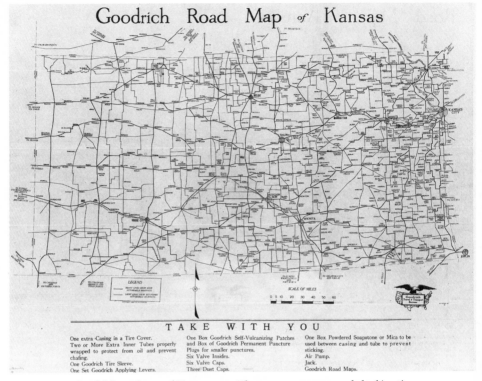

Goodrich road map of Kansas, 1920. The company recommended taking tire
sleeves, levers, patches, and valve caps along, just in case.
Courtesy of the Kansas State Historical Society.

"Kansas will have good roads, if not for the mere comfort and pleasure
which come from a highway in perfect condition twelve months in the year,
than from a deeper economic cause; the added value which a good road
gives to every acre tributary to it; the decrease in the cost of marketing farm
products; the increased earnings which come to the farmer who is able to
hold his grain until the market is right, no matter what the weather; the
bringing of the farm nearer the market place; the improvement in social
conditions and the added cultural influences which good roads bring."[160]
Good roads would come, wrote *Poultry Farming and Rural Life*, "and bless us
like sunshine, wind and rain, without expense, but will require system,
money and labor to build them. . . . A good road is a universal public
benefaction."[161]

After World War I, increased federal aid to the states for highways put

Kansas in the awkward position of having to request special federal legislation each year because its constitutional prohibition against investing in internal improvements meant that it was unable to generate the state match required by the federal funding. By the mid-1920s, this situation was endangering that federal funding, which amounted to more than $2 million a year for Kansas. A three-person state commission to coordinate federal funds, created in 1917, was insufficient as a permanent solution. Consequently, a campaign began in earnest to modify the constitution and to create a state highway system.[162] It came none too soon. In 1922 Kansas was twenty-second among the states in hard-surfaced road mileage, or 611 miles of a total road mileage of over 112,000, much of which did not connect logically.[163]

The stopgap measure in the early 1920s was a gas tax to fund the highway commission and to preserve federal funds. There were plans for a coordinated state system of main and secondary roads, using standard culverts and bridges, to connect all trade centers. Brochures noted that Kansans in 1923 owned 349,038 automobiles and 26,446 trucks, using 158,327,000 gallons of gasoline a year. A three-cents-a-gallon gas tax would raise nearly $5 million a year, with license fees bringing in another $3.5 million—enough to make steady progress in construction. Such a system would allow repeal of the county road levies. "In other words we take the tax from the home that does not earn, from the farm that is not paying, from the stock of goods that is not selling, and from the bank that is not paying dividends and place that tax on the fellow who is using the roads." That included the nonresident tourist and salesman, so the proposal appealed to farmers, who were in the midst of a depression. Advocates also argued that paved roads saved tires and gas. Tires lasted nearly twenty thousand miles on paved roads as opposed to eleven thousand on dirt.[164] Rolla Clymer, editing a newspaper in a mostly rural community, came out for a state system in 1925. "I am no nut on the matter," he wrote Governor Ben Paulen, "but I try to keep informed, and I certainly hope our state will not make the mistake of trying to build roads in a hodge-podge fashion."[165] Many people decried the "legislative lethargy" as a position as damaging as neglecting railroads would have been a few years earlier.[166] "Bad roads are keeping Kansas farmers poor," wrote the Salina Chamber of Commerce. "The heaviest tax they pay is the mud tax."[167] Nicholson argued for the issuance of bonds, to be paid off by a gasoline tax. "You have to pay anyway," he said, "why not get good roads, NOW?"[168]

But opposition was strong, particularly in the western sections. The publisher of the Hill City newspaper, Charles Emmons, wrote the governor in 1926 that "any attempt to concentrate matters in the hands of the State Highway Commission . . . will upset political matters here in the west. . . . Any road bond scheme would be like shaking a red rag in the face of an angry bull." The county commissioners objected to being deprived of their present advantages in distributing funds.[169] "Think of the farmers of Western Kansas," wrote a state representative from there, "being asked to pay four cents per gallon tax, and their money put into a free fund to be spent in Eastern Kansas."[170] Most Kansans were for good roads, said another correspondent, "but they are not all insane on the subject." He advised Governor Paulen not to give in to the "Gypsies" and "road fiends."[171]

In 1928, as it appeared federal highway aid would surely be lost, a special session of the legislature recommended, and Kansans passed, a constitutional amendment allowing a state highway system. The next February the legislature passed the first state road bill and appropriated $15 million to advance the highway system.[172] A second constitutional question for the voters gave the state the power to levy special taxes on motor vehicles and on fuel for state highway purposes.[173]

In the local logic of Kansas history, 1928, with its roads amendment, was a landmark date. It was one of the first regional pivotal moments in which the resolution of a regional question was influenced strongly by federal pressure, and it would be far from the last. But whether pressured on not, Kansans seemed glad they had done the deed. The era was over, crowed the *Wichita Eagle* at the opening of Highway 81 in 1930, when Kansas roads were "two ruts between market centers" and intrepid motorists carried Blue Books to find their way.[174]

There were no such ambiguities about aviation. Everyone thought it a wonderful development, with the exception of a few Wichita merchants who asked for ordinances banning low-flying planes to abate noise. Wichita created a sustainable aviation industry, beginning with the establishment of the E. M. Laird Airplane Company in spring 1920.[175]

Jake Moellendick of Wichita, who had made his money in the El Dorado oil fields, was a believer in the usefulness of the airplane, not only for his business but also for air freighting the products of the Coleman Company around the country, and he was willing to invest his fortune in it. He and others attracted Emil "Matty" Laird from Chicago, and shortly the Laird Swallow was in regular air mail service. Laird left Wichita in 1923, but his company remained, and its alumni founded other corporations. Walter Beech, a Laird test pilot, joined Clyde Cessna to form Travel Air in 1925. Lloyd Stearman, another Laird graduate, formed Stearman in 1926 to build his own biplane. He went to California temporarily, but Wichita merchants lured him back. Cessna formed his own firm, Cessna Aircraft Company, in 1927, partly because he preferred monoplanes and because Beech did not want to build them at Travel Air. The city hosted the National Air Congress in 1924, where local planes bested military fighters in performance. Attention from all over the country was at that time focused on the "California section," a piece of virgin prairie that soon became Wichita's airport. By 1927, when Charles Lindbergh's flight across the Atlantic drew the attention of the nation to aviation; when the *Wollaroc*, a Travel Air, won the Dole prize for the first nonstop flight from California to Hawaii; and when Transcontinental Air Transport was stopping in Wichita on a New York to California route for the rich and famous, Wichita advertised itself as the Air Capital. The city had in 1929 sixteen aircraft-related factories, its own airline, thirteen flying schools, sixteen hundred acres of flying fields, and six aircraft-engine plants. That year it manufactured one thousand airplanes, or 26 percent of the total U.S. production of commercial aircraft.

The rest of Kansas caught the spirit and shared some of the business. Kansas City and Wichita built major airports, and the network expanded by the construction of airfields in Topeka, Lawrence, Coffeyville, and Garden City in 1928. "In the nocturnal hours," wrote a WPA author of the Wichita airport,

the airport becomes an abode of romance superseding the public parks. . . . They loiter, they linger . . . their serenade to be broken presently by the roar of a pair of twin-motors as a giant air-liner swoops down and pulls up within the glare of floodlights to empty its human cargo. The intent crowd in the gallery lining the enclosure murmur with a ripple of excitement as a fluttering figure steps out to promenade—a Hollywood star bound either east or west. . . . She treads upon native prairie terrain where gophers were burrowing only a few years before. . . . Suave and glamorous under the flame of lights, she flickers like that butterfly that she is on the silver-sheet, re-enters the cabin, and flies away to light again either at Kansas City or Albuquerque, depending upon which way the winds of fortune blow her.

It was proposed that Kansas should eventually have airports every thirty miles. "The air route of today," noted a speaker to a crowd of four thousand at the Topeka airport, "will be the trade route of tomorrow."

Kansas flyers became famous. The Atchison native Amelia Earhart in June 1928 became the first woman to fly the Atlantic. Female Kansas flyers— Betty Browning, Ruth Haviland, Louise Thaden, Mary Haizlip—attracted considerable publicity by their success in the air races of the 1920s and 1930s. Ben Howard's custom-built DGA racers were constructed at Fairfax Field in Kansas City. Dwane Wallace won numerous prizes in the 1930s with his Cessnas, and the Beech Mystery ships were world-renowned racers.

Participation by Kansas airplanes in the Ford Reliability Tour to demonstrate the practicability of flying led to initiation of the All-Kansas Air Tour. For years the regional chambers of commerce had sponsored a Booster Train. This changed to automobiles in 1924 and to airplanes in 1928. During the first week of April, a promotional party, including Governor Paulen, toured the state in a fleet of twenty-five airplanes "to spread the air gospel." Marcellus Murdock of Wichita, president of the National Aeronautic Association, spoke at each stop on the advantages of flying, and the tour drew large crowds. Thirty-five thousand saw it the first day. Eight thousand greeted the tour at Newton, seven thousand at Hutchinson, and ten thousand at McPherson. Aviation, wrote Murdock, was the best lens to "give the searcher a peep into the marvels of tomorrow."

The industry was a marvel. Beech and Cessna, both men listed in the Wichita telephone book, became familiar corporate names all over the world. It was a high-tech image, inconsistent with the agricultural rube stereotype so often associated with the state. Aircraft manufacture was no flash in the pan, either. By 1993, over two hundred sixty-six thousand airplanes had been manufactured in Kansas by at least eighty-six companies. One of these, the Longren Aircraft Corporation, which opened a factory in Topeka in 1921, had modest production but represented the continued contribution of the man who had first flown a Kansas-built plane in 1911.[176]

Industry in the 1920s burgeoned in many other ways. The oil and gas business, which boomed mightily with $3.50 oil prices during the war, combined with the development of the vast El Dorado, Augusta, and Towanda fields, thrived in the decade. It was handicapped in the 1930s, not in its pace of discovery but only by low prices.[177] Kansas oil production during the 1920s was 30 to 40 million barrels a year, with about one thousand oil wells drilled annually. Of national significance was the discovery of enormous natural gas reserves in Barber County and in the Hugoton field in Stevens County in far southwest Kansas. The latter was one of the major reserves in the nation, with gas piped directly from there to Detroit and Chicago markets, and it was responsible for Kansas gas production reaching over 45 trillion cubic feet a year by 1928. Prices were strong in the 1920s: as much as $2.26 a barrel for oil and nearly $.08 per 1,000 cubic feet at the wellhead for gas. Oil prices had traditionally paralleled wheat prices—a barrel going for about the same as a bushel. That would happen again in the 1930s, when both were around $.25. But in the 1920s oil was twice the price of wheat and definitely the more desirable product.[178] High crude prices, however, did not slow driving, since gasoline in Kansas was $.16 a gallon in 1923.[179]

The El Dorado field remained a big producer. But the major new player in the 1920s was in the "Golden Lanes" of Marion and Greenwood County's Flint Hills grassland and in the far west, where the surprising discovery of the Carrie Oswald well and the Fairport field near Russell opened the whole region to exploration in 1923. There were many one-thousand-barrels-a-day wells also in the Peabody area in Marion County, and one well there produced thirty-five hundred barrels a day for a time.

Doomsayers then as always talked about the oil and gas supply of Kansas being nearly exhausted. But the cable-tool wildcatters, working for $4.20 a day and living in shotgun houses in the new fields, did not think so. The Great Southern, Phillips Petroleum, Mid-Kansas Oil, and Kansas City Refining were organized and active concerns. For a time the population of Greenwood County, in the center of the Flint Hills grazing region, where populations are generally the lowest per acre in Kansas, reached twenty thousand, the highest ever, before or since. Refineries across the state, like the Skelly facility in El Dorado, were no longer the little glorified stills they had been in the early twentieth century but substantial and scientific industries on their own. "I have reported oil on the Wichita Daily Eagle for the past ten years," wrote Kent Eubank in 1928. "I have seen the gushers and the dry holes, the joys and the sorrows, the hilarious mirth and the weaker member of the fraternity sent to the asylum when he held four acres and fate held the gun in the game of oil. . . . When I see the thousands of lights shining from the derricks of an oil field, I think of the python with button eyes gleaming yellow, charming the dove."

The industrial look extended beyond the extractive companies. A combine was used at a harvest in Great Bend in 1901, and these factories on wheels became popular in the 1920s. A major company manufacturing combines, Baldwin, which made the Gleaner, originated in Nickerson, Kansas. Kansans purchased 1,500 combines in 1919 and 1920, and by 1926 there were 8,274 combines in use in the state, harvesting over 30 percent of the wheat there. That reduced the time required to harvest an acre of wheat from 2.8 man-hours to .75 and hastened the urbanization as well as the mechanization of Kansas. In 1930, there were 75,000 combines in the United States and 27,000 in Kansas. By 1938 nine-tenths of the acreage in Kansas was harvested by combine. By the 1940s the Sunflower State was not only one of the heaviest users of combines itself but the major center for custom-cutting crews traveling each year all over the Great Plains.[180]

Wichita, the second largest city in the state with a population in 1924 of 90,465 to Kansas City, Kansas's, 118,780, had an industrial look independent of its aircraft plants. It instituted zoning and planning in 1921 and 1922, after significant controversy, and published a 174-page city plan, crafted by Harland Bartholemew of St. Louis, in 1923.[181] Bartholomew wrote that cities required "intelligent direction," and the *Wichita Beacon* added, "Plans must be made for a unified city just like a skyscraper or a factory or bridge."[182] The city created industrial districts and separated railroad grades from auto traffic.[183] In 1923 there was one car or truck for every five residents and the highest motor vehicle ownership in the nation.[184] In 1927 the Santa Fe railroad alone ran thirty-two passenger and fourteen freight trains a day into Wichita and had thirty-six miles of yards to serve its industry.[185] Production of fast foods, later a Wichita specialty, was already under way, with the Dye Chili Company distributing full bore and Walter Anderson, Wichita's "hamburger king," operating twenty-two of his White Castle fast-food outlets.[186] Glen Rose founded the Rose Neon Company in Wichita in 1928, gained a national reputation in the field of Art-Deco signage, and made Wichita in the next decade one of the most "artistically" advertised cities in the country.[187]

The Coleman Company of Wichita was by the 1920s truly a global concern. In 1920 it shipped 462,600 lamps and reported sales of $4 million. It used fifty-nine different kinds of material gathered from all parts of the United States and the world, making its factory "a veritable world's fair of the industrial arts." Knitting machines there created fifty thousand mantles a day, and Coleman's "Sunshine of the Night" ads were seen in magazines nationwide. In the 1920s it established branches in Canada, Australia, and

The Coleman Company, Wichita.
Courtesy of the Kansas State Historical Society.

New Zealand and had marketing outlets in China, Malaysia, Central and South America, the Pacific Islands, and Africa.[188] In 1921 the Coleman factory in Wichita covered one hundred thirteen thousand square feet and used 471 machines, leading a newspaper reporter to comment, "After touring the factory any visitor . . . will attach new meaning to such words as the Genius of Invention, the Forward Strides of Science, a Busy Hive of Industry."[189]

Kansas City, Missouri, was also greatly changed, in attitude and in appearance. J. C. Nichols in 1923 developed the Country Club Plaza, a residential and shopping complex planned like no other before it. Restrictive covenants on housing and carefully laid out parking and services created a kind of utopian community with none of the accidental, overlaid growth typical of areas influenced by the uncoordinated decisions of thousands of individuals. It was scientific management and the progressive dream of betterment through environmental control and planned influences at its most sophisticated. "Boys and girls reared in a place of flowers, lawns and shrubbery, of clean air and sunshine," claimed the advertising, "have an unquestioned advantage over the children from closely-built houses, apartments and dusty traffic streets." The Country Club District was the prototype of the "shopping center." It was also, according to critics, elitist, racist, and sterile.[190]

Technology touched everything. Rolla Clymer in El Dorado purchased in 1929 a new press for his newspaper. It was a "12 page tubular (duplex) press," costing over thirteen thousand dollars and capable of printing his five-thousand-copy edition in about twenty minutes. The newspaper corporation built a whole building around it, and local people came for tours. "People who rather are inclined to believe the town is going to the dogs," Clymer wrote, "are bucked up by the fact that we have invested $25,000 in new and modern equipment looking forward to an increased business."[191] El Dorado was not a big city, but if one wanted to publish a newspaper anywhere in the 1920s, it required large investments in technology.

William Allen White installed a similar modern press at the *Gazette* in Emporia and said that the Emporia of the 1920s was a place where "the character of every street is changing."[192] He refused an offer of four hundred thousand dollars for his printing plant in 1929 and wondered whether the business office aspect and the advertising agencies were permanently changing the role of the local editor.[193] In his ongoing correspondence with Sinclair Lewis over whether Kansas small towns were really as awful as the Gopher Prairie portrayed in Lewis's *Main Street,* White claimed that 1920s Emporia was modern and generally better for it. "Kansas towns are, for the most part, coming into the County Club stage."[194]

The impact of urbanization was not all business. In 1926, Fairmount College, a liberal arts institution founded by the Congregational Church in 1895, became the University of Wichita, only the ninth municipal university in the United States. The ideas were two: the city itself would serve as a laboratory for realistic and practical learning, and the graduates as well as students would provide expert employees for the city's industries. There were pioneering interchanges between town and gown in city government, in police science, and in laboratory work for industrial research.[195]

Leisure itself became a business, including, prominently, sports. Dr. James Naismith, who had invented the game of basketball, came to the University of Kansas in 1898 and started the team there in 1899. Forrest "Phog" Allen continued from 1909 until 1956. Between 1900 and 1930, KU won 377 of 549 basketball games played and got the attention of fans across the state.[196] Regular accounts of the overwhelming importance of football in Wichita illustrated that the college athletics mania was not limited to Lawrence. The University of Wichita lost its accreditation for a time in 1933 due to a perceived overemphasis on sports.[197]

Kansans doted on their native sons in national sports, probably the most famous of whom in the 1920s was Walter "Big Train" Johnson of Coffeyville, a star pitcher with the Washington *Senators*. His shutting out the New York Giants for four innings in relief to win the World Series in October 1924 was doubtless bigger news for most Kansans than the constitutional troubles of the Court of Industrial Relations or the founding of Travel Air. Other Kansas athletes, from heavyweight champion Jess Willard forward, garnered an attention that presaged the mass identification of place with athletic prowess and the perception that if these individual sports figures or Kansas teams had achieved fame, "we" must have done it also.[198]

The same logic applied to movie stars, if the 1920s notoriety of Wichitan Louise Brooks, the bobbed-haired, tough-talking, Jazz Baby "It" girl and liberated "Kansas Cleopatra" is any indication. When Brooks said that "love is a publicity stunt, and making love . . . is only another . . . way to pass the time," it was clear that she was not in Kansas anymore but unclear whether Kansas was still Kansas.[199]

There was a general air of advertising and of publicity stunts in Kansas in the 1920s, brought on partly by the radio, partly by the national brands and advertising in the newspapers, partly by its own native exuberance. Woody Hockaday called on the office of the Kansas Daily Newspaper Advertising Agency in Hutchinson in 1924 to tell about his appearance in Atlantic City at a national convention of bakers on behalf of Kansas, Incorporated, and its slogan, "Kansas Grows the Best Wheat in the World." His next idea was to select the most beautiful farm girl in Kansas and send her to Washington with a sack of wheat to present to President Coolidge. That should be front-page news, Hockaday thought.[200] Vada Watson, who was selected, did go on Kansas Day 1929 and had her picture taken with the president and Senator Capper.[201] An El Dorado man criticized papers that had "cheapened themselves and given to the minds of many readers a colored glass through which to think" but had to admit that it was common. "Every move," he wrote in 1925, "is interpreted in terms of sex or of graft."[202]

To the further shock of such people, Kansas in 1927 passed a law legalizing the sale of cigarettes, after fifteen years of banning them. One woman complained that it was a victory for the big tobacco interests and did not represent Kansas. "If there is any earthly use for tobacco, it is only as an insecticide, a wash for sores on sick quadrepeds [*sic*]. And yet, sad to relate, the biped man, eats it—smokes it, and uses it as an all around flimsy prop." Legalizing it, she thought, would only create "more subnormal, narcotic, alcoholic protoplasms to clutter the earth."[203] Wrote a minister, "Kansas has backed up. The sovereignty of the state has been assailed, and the enemy has won."[204] Editor Clymer felt, by contrast, that more availability of cigarettes was a good thing for Kansas, and so did the American Legion, which supported repeal of the ban. The new cigarette law had restrictive amendments, but Clymer thought those would disappear in time and that Kansas "thus has taken a step out of the freak state class."[205] Now if it could only repeal prohibition!

Kansas history was one means to mollify these "acids of modernity." It became, like so many subjects, more and more the purview of professionals. James Malin, teaching history at the University of Kansas, started two Ph.D. students in the late 1920s on Kansas history dissertations.[206] He held a seminar in 1930 on Kansas history and was pleased to report in 1932 that the new head of the state historical society "knows nothing of history and has sense enough to know it."[207]

There was no avoiding the conclusion that the old Kansas was threatened, partly by national influence, partly by the changes in the makeup and views of the local population, and partly by its own excesses. Some people hoped to stop or reverse the process. A minister from Ellis, writing Governor Paulen in 1925 in opposition to changes in the cigarette law, summed up his feelings: "Unless we are very careful at these points we shall throw to the winds the results of consecrated efforts of men and women who all through the years have fought the battles of the boys and girls and men and women of our fine state. . . . I can have no word of commendation for the man who turns his face from a better day and retraces steps which have been bought at so great a price."[208]

But change, accelerated by crisis, was sweeping over Kansas like the "electric wind" of the dry, roiling storms of the Dust Bowl—dark and forbidding, stirring its native soil in unaccustomed ways and bearing unavoidable loads of material from somewhere else.

7
DUST AND DEMOCRATS

Nineteen thirty-five was a bad year for Ray Hugh Garvey's farming operations in western Kansas. He had dismantled his farming corporation after Kansas outlawed these in 1931, and he had taken on a satisfactory local manager and profit-sharing partner, John Kriss, in 1933. However, neither the size nor the efficiency of his operation freed him from the troubles that weather and low prices were causing all Kansas farmers in those seasons of doom.

"Personally I am not in favor of spending much money farming until it rains," Garvey wrote the banker W. D. Ferguson in Colby in January 1935.[1] By late March, it had not rained appreciably in Thomas County for nearly twenty months. Ferguson wrote concerning some land in Logan County that "the whole field looks like a rock pile. . . . It is as hard as bricks. . . . It is going to have to break loose in good order right soon or the spring crop work will be a joke out here."[2]

It was a nightmare. In 1932 the wheat price in Colby sank to twenty-five cents a bushel, and in September it was over 100 degrees ten days straight, reaching 108 in Colby and 111 in Hays on September 5. There was an "electric wind" that lit up the tops of windmills with static electricity. "With the temperature up to 105 degrees," a local man wrote the next year, "and the horizon lined with roiling clouds that seems to promise ten inches of rain but delivered three feet of dirt, the plains took on a phantasmagorical dreadfulness." The University of Wichita's Department of Geology estimated that 5 million tons of dust hung one mile thick over that city of one hundred thousand. The wheat crop was nearly a total loss.[3] "Down in the dust," wrote a Kansas poet, "We could not bear it except we must, / For all our values are

Approaching dust storm, 1935.
Courtesy of the Kansas State Historical Society.

shaken. What is earth? Is there / anything solid and sure? And what is air? / Is there sun anywhere?"[4] Garvey, like most entrepreneurs, was an optimist. He wrote Ferguson that he need not worry too much about Rex Tugwell's statement that he would like to see 7 million acres of Dust Bowl farmland turned back to sod. Garvey concluded, "This is an interesting period to live through, if one lives through it."[5]

After some delay and argument, Garvey participated in the Agricultural Adjustment Administration program, which provided price subsidies to farmers in exchange for production limits. However, he did not think much of governmental solutions: "I presume there will be a liberal sprinkling of exhibits at your Fair, consisting of allotment checks, WPA checks, and relief checks. They seem to be the leading producing items during this Administration in Thomas County."[6]

The weather was awful. A Garden City woman wrote, "All we could do about it was just sit in our dusty chairs, gaze at each other through the fog that filled the room and watch that fog settle slowly and silently, covering everything—including ourselves—in a thick, brownish gray blanket. When we opened the door swirling whirlwinds of soil beat against us unmercifully. . . . Our faces were as dirty as if we had rolled in the dirt; our hair was gray and stiff and we ground dirt between our teeth."[7] Dust covered the fields

Boy on sand dune, which is threatening his home, March 1936.
Courtesy of the Kansas State Historical Society.

in dunes; children struggled to school with damp towels over their faces, risking getting lost in the gloom on the way home. The air filters on cars had to be changed many times as often as standard; a car's or truck's ignition system could malfunction due to the static electricity in the air and leave the driver stranded; and the vehicles themselves did not last very long, as sifting dust ruined the crankshaft and connecting rods.[8] Kriss reported that a young man trapped beside his tractor by a sudden dust storm was in danger of his life. Grasshoppers swarmed in the summer to eat any crops remaining, as they had in the dark days of the 1870s, and jackrabbits gathered by the thousands around any growing stalk, plagues it seemed on sinners.[9] "The thing that impressed me the most," wrote a resident, "was probably not the dust storms but the devastation on the land. . . . There would just not be any vegetation at all on the land for maybe a half a mile in any direction. . . . I don't know how anyone survived."[10]

It came amid searing dry heat and strong winds. Garvey reported in August 1936 that there had been .28 inches of rain in relatively moist Wichita since June 1, and August 23 was the seventeenth successive day there where temperatures exceeded 100 degrees.[11] His Wichita neighbor Charles Good-rum wrote of that time, "Kansas has a heat that has to be felt to be believed, and having experienced it few people can bring themselves to talk much about it afterwards. . . . By midsummer the heat is shimmering off the pavement, and the sky has turned to a brilliant yellow whiteness that pulses at your eyeballs. . . . Caveth Wells, the explorer, once said that the only place he knew as bitterly hot as Wichita was Cairo, Egypt, and in Cairo they dressed for it."[12] Garvey thought, "We may expect some fairly good crops if any are being planted along about 1945 or 1950."[13] He wrote to Ferguson in Colby in spring 1935, "I guess you folks have almost been impounded with millions of pounds of dust in the past ten days. . . . I doubt if sales will be very good until rain and Republicans replace dust and Democrats."[14]

The crisis in the weather and in the financial markets was fully reflected in Kansas in the gubernatorial elections of 1930 and 1932, some of the closest in count and unusual in issues ever in a state that had seen its share of contro-versy. Governor Clyde Reed, elected in 1928, was a brusque man. He also had overwhelming challenges to face. The taxpayers' league in Kansas was active as early as summer 1929. It wanted prisoners to work on the roads. It wanted a tax on lawsuits. It wanted national banks to pay more taxes. It wanted expenditures for sports in schools cut, and in the classroom "less hibrow stuff. Less so called Kulture. A cariculum [sic] that prepares our children for every day life of home instead of this pilgrimage of the over educated into the cities." Politically, the league thought it was best to discard those officials "nominated at the behest of Washington or Topeka. Also those whose in-spiration comes from New York and Wichita."[15]

By 1930 the anti–chain store movement and the anti–corporate farming movements were fully under way in the state. The small farmer, it was said, was being crowded out "by these land hogs," who could farm cheaper be-cause they could afford big acreages and large machines. The Wheat Farm-ing Company, organized in 1927 and headquartered in Hays, farmed over sixty thousand acres in 1930 and at harvest operated thirty combines, rolling through fields "like a fleet of ships at sea." It owned four grain elevators and farmed in shifts day and night.[16] Garvey's Mutual Farming Company, head-quartered in Colby, operated on a smaller scale (about fifteen thousand acres), as did the Sledd Farming Corporation out of Lyons, but to the same end.[17] "Chain merchandising is bankrupting the towns of Kansas by daily draining the communities of their profits," wrote a Coffeyville attorney, who soon became a Kansas congressman, to Reed, and chain banking and chain farming were just as bad. The fifteen thousand acres a chain farm handled represented potentially forty-seven family farmers tilling a half-section each. Chain farming would depopulate the wheat belt. "We needed corporations to build railroads," the attorney wrote, "because no individual could build a railroad." They were not needed to farm.[18]

The sort of state action directed against corporations, however, did not solve basic problems, like the drought. Reed could only say to one farmer, "Your situation is similar to that in which thousands of Kansas farmers find themselves. It is to help such cases that we have been struggling to find a way to take care of them. Up to date we have not been successful as the state has absolutely no power."[19]

Instead, state government seemed to respond more to local fears. It returned to one of the questionable legacies of Populism in emphasizing in the crisis homogeneity of population. Many Kansans believed that railroads should use white laborers instead of the Mexican that had been the rule previously. This was partly at the behest of the President's Employment Commission, but it partly came from Kansas itself, advanced by regional labor unions.[20] The governor wrote all the railroads asking for reports of the number of Mexicans employed.[21] The track work, which, one man wrote, "American citizens do not seem to care for," had become desirable to whites for lack of alternatives.[22]

On broader matters, it was the trend to look for federal help. Yet there was embarrassment about that and nostalgia for the tradition of regional regulation and self-help. One woman was ashamed "that Kansas would be made an object of public charity."[23] An El Dorado man noted that with $.5 billion at their disposal, the Department of Agriculture in Washington "have made the great discovery that if the farmers grow less wheat the price of wheat may rise! Great discovery! Say, I could have saved the government a lot of money. Had they simply written me or my sixteen-year-old son either and enclosed a stamp for answer we could have told them that and saved all the expense of a special session of congress and the thousands of barrels of perfectly good ink used in editorials and the millions of feet of high pressure gas consumed in and out of congress in talking and arguing about this matter."[24] Nevertheless, sufferers thought they deserved and understood they needed aid from afar, however much they suspected it might interfere with future state independence. "If our government could loan and cancel many millions to our old enemies for war purposes," one Kansan wrote, "they could and should help the farmers that were ruined when they lost their crops."[25]

Not surprisingly, in this charged atmosphere, the election of 1930 was unusual, even for Kansas. The Kansas pundit R. G. Clugston wrote in his 1940 panegyric *Rascals in Democracy* that the gubernatorial race that year was "one of the most spontaneously concerted peaceable uprisings of enfranchised citizens history has ever recorded."[26]

The first shock was that Reed lost the Republican primary to a "model young farm boy," Frank Haucke. The second was the entry into the race as an independent of Dr. John R. Brinkley, the "goat gland doctor" from Milford, Kansas. Despite snickering among the intelligentsia about the billy goat implant operations designed to revive sexual vitality and cure prostate problems, and real outrage from the medical profession and the Federal Radio Commission about Brinkley's advertising over his powerful radio station KFKB, the doctor enjoyed great popularity. Part of his appeal stemmed from his role as the outsider, the friend of the poor and of those whom William Allen White called "ignorant." And he promised much, including better roads, a system of farm ponds, free schoolbooks, and a free state medical clinic while at the same time pledging to lower taxes. The religious commentary at his rallies, the country music, and the spectacle of his landing in his Ford Tri-motor or driving up in his fancy car pulled in the crowds.

Strict rules about how Brinkley supporters were to write his name probably cost him the election, but it was close. Harry Woodring, the Democrat, won with 217,171 votes; Haucke was second with 216,920; and Brinkley third with 183,278. The 1932 election was equally close. A Republican, Alf Landon, won with 278,581 votes. But Woodring polled 272,944 and Brinkley 244,607. Brinkley carried forty-seven counties.[27]

The local Republican establishment was appalled. The AMA *Journal* spoke of Brinkley as a "blatant quack . . . whose professional record reeks with charlatanism of the crudest type."[28] The *Leavenworth Times* editorialized that Brinkley's large vote was humiliating and showed that "any mountebank who has an unctuous manner and makes loud professions of piety can put forth any sort of fraud and get away with it." To William Allen White, it was Kansas gullibility, but Brinkley's showing should be a warning to the "smug, well-fed" group that things must get better or else.[29]

That Brinkley was almost exclusively the story of these elections nationally was partly due to the "freak state" pattern of reporting about Kansas.

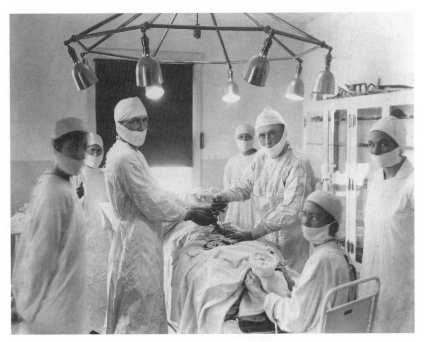

Dr. John Brinkley operating.
Courtesy of the Kansas State Historical Society.

White wondered whether the doctor was "a conscious knave or just a poor bedeviled and bewildered fool!" and claimed that he would be remembered by future historians "only as a sign that the people of Kansas in the collapse of the big stock boom of the 20s were amazed, confused, confounded and desperate; disgusted with themselves and their leaders."[30] The Brinkley vote, White wrote in 1930, was a sure demonstration that literacy was not wisdom. "We have paid taxes for the last forty years to teach them how to mark the ballot without giving them the brains to know what ballots to mark."[31]

But whatever White thought of Brinkley's character, the Emporia editor was surely wrong when he wrote at Brinkley's death in 1942 as a bankrupt who had lost his yacht and fine homes that "he made no lasting mark on Kansas."[32] Nearly twenty years after his death, Gerald Carson, in his biography *The Roguish World of Doctor Brinkley,* testified to the continued interest in him as a person who stood "head and shoulders above his fellows," both in "the crowded world of pseudo-medicine" and in the rarefied world of political demagoguery. As a pioneer in political advertising in the media, medical advertising, and in the uses of pseudoscience, sexual fears, and innuendoes of conspiracy, this "sunflower state Galen" was a figure of the future. And he had for a time a nearly forty-thousand-dollar-a-month income to prove his appeal.[33]

Both his appeal and his threat were evident in Kansas at the time. Mrs. C. C. McClure wrote Governor Reed that she was "satisfied that Dr. Brinkley is no worse than many surgeons we have in the State and is far better than most of them and was doing a wonderful work for many people that have utterly failed to receive help from other physicians. . . . The doctors are just jealous of him because he has success."[34] Ray Garvey in Wichita, no moron but certainly a Brinkley supporter, noted late in October 1930 that Haucke and Capper drew eleven hundred at the Wichita forum while Brinkley outdid that by far and ten thousand were turned away. "Saul has slain his thousands," Garvey proclaimed, "but David his tens of thousands."[35] He thought the vote in the state for Brinkley was "part of it enthusiasm for Brinkley, part of it a protest against general conditions, and a very large part of it an expression of the poor opinion in which both the other candidates and both the old parties are held."[36]

Rolla Clymer, the El Dorado editor, plugged away at Brinkley but admitted that he was a formidable vote getter and that his Citizens' Clubs were powerful in Butler County. "My reason tells me that Brinkley is a fearsome factor," he wrote in 1932; "my instinct leads me to believe that he cannot be again as serious a factor as he was, that surely the star of such a charlatan must be on the wane."[37] But that was a hope, not a conclusion, as long as the Dust Bowl raged. A correspondent wrote Clymer, "Many look upon Brinkley as a sort of Savior."[38] Clymer himself, after the 1932 election, predicted that Brinkley would be back. The doctor was, he concluded, "no small fry grafter; he is a colossal charlatan and must be given credit for extraordinary gifts along the line of deceiving the public. I think the Republican party in Kansas should take its licking in the same fashion that an ailing man takes castor oil. . . . We need to be more humble, to get closer to the people and to begin to build our party from the bottom."[39]

Kansas moved away a little from its traditional self politically, even leaving the Brinkley phenomenon aside. It elected two Democratic governors in the decade of the 1930s—Harry Woodring in 1930 and Walter Huxman in 1936. Legislative majorities, however, did not follow, and the general Kansas attitude and political stance hardly made it the special darling of the New Dealers when they came into their kingdom. Republicans of any kind hardly stood a chance in Washington. Clifford Hope, elected to Congress from Kansas in 1926, wrote to a constituent in the mid-1930s: "We might as well abolish Congress, . . . as long as the present situation continues. I mean there is no particular use in having a Congress which finally follows whatever suggestions that come from the White House."[40]

The Woodring administration took some seemingly radical actions for its time and place. But they were more neo-Populist than they were New Deal, and they were advanced amid an atmosphere of budget cutting, limited government, and corporate regulation that was traditional Kansan. Woodring pushed for equalization of the tax burden and got an intangibles tax, an increase in the gasoline tax, and a bank tax law. The legislature placed holding companies under the supervision of the Public Service Commission, instituted a prorationing plan to regulate oil production and subsidize price, gave county commissions the power to levy a poor tax, outlawed corporate farming, and prohibited utilities from engaging in merchandising. Woodring's warm personality was refreshing after Reed. The governor's public struggle with Henry L. Doherty, president of the Cities Service Company over the lowering of gas rates, was as popular as had been Walter Stubbs's 1905 attack on Standard Oil. Behind all this was a budget-cutting stance. The state budget declined nearly $1 million in Woodring's first year of office. He reduced his own salary by $5,000, and cut $2 million from the budget in his second year. Faculty salaries at the state universities declined more than 10 percent, and building programs diminished. "It is not my intention," Woodring said, "to be swept off my feet by an instant demand to meet certain conditions that I consider are only passing. I shall stand firm for a safe, sound, business administration."[41]

The ideology that Kansas should and could recover on its own, that it had its economic strengths, and that wealth was not everything remained strong. In a speech in fall 1931, Woodring noted that Kansas was the largest producer of winter wheat in the United States or any similar area in the world, was second in meatpacking and third in oil—achievements that might entitle "the Sunflower state to one niche in the hall of fame—in the eyes of the materialistically inclined." Yet these were "the things that make Kansas rich, but are not the items that make Kansas great." Where else in the last thirty years had a state picked a printer's devil, a railroad laborer, a popcorn boy, and a farmer to be governor? "Kansas has always been a firebrand of politics. It is to be sincerely hoped that the state will not let the modern ideas and business change her ways of thinking." The state was born in a trying time, and Woodring hoped it would continue to think for itself. Kansans, he said, "kick over the traces when things are not to their liking. They snort and sniff, fuss and fume at conditions and situations. Instead of just adopting resolutions that something ought to be done about it they go out and do it. . . . None ever accused the Sunflower State of not trying." Kansas had been among the first states to attempt to "solve economic ills by political action" and so should be able to deal with the present crisis on its own. It had one hundred sixty-six thousand farms, one hundred twenty-six thousand of them with radios. There were enough cars to take every Kansan on a ride at the same time. But the most important asset was "the spirit, the exuberance, the hopefulness, the aggressiveness, the determination of the people who inhabit the state."[42]

John Bird, president of the Wheat Farming Company, was not so sure how far spirit would go when finances were short. He tried to advance a philosophy of change and adaptation through modern business methods. He held that his corporation was formed to help save the region and consisted of Kansas investors. "We felt sure . . . that a large well-organized farm unit, carefully managed and adequately financed, can do more to give permanent assistance to agriculture in the Plains Region than almost any other agency. The greatest opportunity in agriculture today is in decreased costs and in better yields through better practices."[43] The Wheat Farming Company published a pamphlet in 1930, "An Independent Kansas Agriculture Through Self-Help."[44] The company seemed to do well. In 1931, it had assets of $3,635,820.62, still claiming that "the general effect of this kind of agriculture should prove good for all producers. The demonstration of lower production costs should be of great value to farmers both large and small."[45]

Bird lobbied Woodring aggressively for his new vision of agriculture. Four million people had quit farming between 1919 and 1927, and Bird thought that was fine: the family farm was a thing of the past. In a pamphlet, "The Path of Progress," he likened large corporate farming to other technological and business innovations. "The great forward development of farming will be along this line. There always has been, and there always will be those who bitterly oppose any new development; some because of mental inertia, some from honest convictions, others from ulterior and selfish motives. We are now witnessing a progress-parade which involves a conflict between economics and politics."[46] C. L. Clayton of Wellington wrote the governor that the farm corporations were only operating in sections of the state that were already mostly depopulated and were succeeding where the small farmer could not. The jealousy, he wrote, came "from the envy of people who have not succeeded themselves, and who do not want to see anyone else succeed."[47]

Garvey felt the same way. He argued that the farming corporations were only doing what the state was doing in its own administration, cutting costs. Looking back to previous periods of deflation in American history, he observed that only those who were able to cut costs parallel to price deflation— those who "tightened up their belts, faced facts and plugged away"—survived. He thought in 1930 that even with wheat at sixty cents a bushel, he could average two dollars an acre net profit through the corporation and large-scale farming under a single manager, rather than with scattered tenants. "There is no use in leaving machines idle," he wrote. Nor was the government plan of production control sound. "Cutting down acreage in Thomas County is bunk. It is a race to see who must quit, and I believe we are in an airplane and can beat the horse and buggy farmer on grain production. The whole world is in this competition."[48]

But the current of opinion on this issue in Kansas flowed strongly in another direction. An editor in Burlington wrote that cheery statements about the future of farming must "be viewing farm assets with a telescope and farm liabilities with the machine reversed." Deflation and the crash in commodities prices had come "like a cyclone from a clear sky, unknown, unseen, unexpected." The editor used the example of an old farm couple who, "as they stand homeless and helpless facing life's setting sun, are not sore because they gave their boys in the name of democracy, but they are bitter because autocracy in the form of profiteers has robbed them of the dearest spot on earth—Home."[49] Nine chain farming companies were operating in Kansas, wrote another, and used over one hundred fifty thousand acres. Bird boasted in *Business Week* that he was paying over 12 percent dividends. Yet jobs were lost in the wheat belt and traditional communities weakened.[50] Chester Sanders of Yates Center, a stockholder in the Wheat Farming Company, sent the governor a corporate pamphlet with the comment, "I think the sooner this corporation farming is nipped in the bud the better for young future American farmers and American homes." He would "rather see my stock in this company dwindle to nothing than to see one American farm home ruined. . . . I love these great Kansas plains and prairies, as I know you do. And I am sure sorry to know that my native state is falling into the hands of large corporations."[51] No strictly economic argument could address the outrage of Kansans at the passing of a way of life.

In January 1931 Kansas legislated against corporate farming of certain crops, including wheat, on the grounds that "it is contrary to public policy to permit a corporation to acquire large blocks of land." A series of ouster suits rid the state of such farming corporations as existed.[52] Efficiency was not the only consideration politically, and there was widespread discontent about the big operators. However, to keep the small farmers, with their relatively high costs, on the land, Kansas was ultimately left little choice but to turn to federal aid and accompanying federal control and initiative. In doing so it perhaps traded one master for another.

Not that positive local initiatives of the promotional type were lacking. There were campaigns from Kansas to promote the eating of cracked or ground wheat as a breakfast cereal, to issue scrip in exchange for stored wheat, to use wheat as fuel, to have the governor buy the entire wheat crop and hold the surplus until a lean year came along, to form a wheat growers union, to establish a moratorium on wheat buying at Kansas elevators for thirty days, to feed wheat to animals instead of selling it into the market, to build a cooperative mill owned by farmers, to shut down elevators for six weeks, and to have the state build mills and buy the supply.[53] But these measures were hardly adequate to deal with the situation. "We who live out here in the wheat belt," wrote a farmer, "and see the actual conditions every day, can I am sure be pardoned for getting somewhat hysterical about the situation."[54]

Woodring found the wheat problem a difficult one for a state. Controlling wheat, he wrote, was not like controlling oil, where the supply could be easily cut off at the source with the cooperation of a few companies.[55] He was not sure that anyone could help the wheat price, not even the governor of a state that produced 25 percent of the wheat in the nation. "It is a matter with which the Federal Government has more to do than the state," he wrote.[56] "It is easy to say," he stated on another occasion, "that the Governor should padlock the mills if they do not pay a higher price for wheat, or that he should order all the wheat shipments to stop until the market reaches a point that makes it profitable to the wheat grower, but there are many things which the Chief Executive of the State cannot do."[57]

State action was more definite on nonagricultural fronts. Woodring

noted that he could not promote one Kansas product over others and therefore could not force the public schools to use coal, as many people suggested.
But he could and did send out a circular letter advising industries using coal
to use Kansas coal in preference to that from other states.[58] K. A. Spencer,
president of the Pittsburg and Midway Coal Mining Company, headed a
committee charged with promoting the use of Kansas coal, and its campaign
managed to create an increase of 3 percent in domestic coal consumption in
1932, contrasted to a decline of 19 percent in the consumption of Kansas coal
elsewhere in the same period.[59]

In the long-range thinking, there was considerable discussion of the need
to create an industrial base for Kansas in order to diversify its economy and
make it less dependent on prices for a single commodity. Woodring, one
man advised, would face mobs if he did not do something "to head the
people out of Egypt" by rewarding latent talents for inventions and discoveries.[60] Kansas had 1,767 manufacturing establishments in 1931, employing
over forty-five thousand people, but that was only a start on the potential.
There needed to be a change of habit.[61] The models were Kansas City and
Wichita. To replicate them Kansas would have to accept urbanization and let
the image of the yeoman family farmer go.

But it was not until the Payne Ratner administration of 1939 that there
was serious organization by the state for industrial development. More typical earlier were the older style anti–big business moves against wheat corporations and preventing utilities from merchandising electrical appliances.
Woodring's speeches deplored the "panic of plenty" and blamed it on centralization in government and in business. Profits had gone to the manufacturer and distributor, he said, leading to lack of income by consumers and
consequently underconsumption. An Akron, Ohio, newspaper thought
Woodring was a reincarnation of Sockless Jerry Simpson when he said at
Hays: "It would seem that the goal of the pioneers has been attained, but
millions of men walk our streets and highways looking for work. . . . If these
pioneers whom we commemorate are looking down on us today, they must
feel that their sacrifices were in vain. For what purpose did they break the
sod of the Kansas prairies and suffer the hardships of the pioneer if the grain
from their fields cannot satisfy the hunger of the world, but must be stored
while men, women and children starve around the world?"[62] Why should a
quart of oil cost as much as two barrels of crude, he asked. "Four more years
of Hoover and we will have a nation of peasants and serfs to the overlords of

monopoly."[63] It was a conspiracy theory, and it calls to mind Richard Hofstadter's criticism of the Populists as idealists who did not understand or would not understand the farmers' place in a capitalistic economy.

Some people thought that government had to be larger. J. W. Cummins, editor of the *Wheat Grower's Journal*, published by the Kansas Cooperative Wheat Marketing Association in Kansas City, thought government must intervene strongly. If business did not want more government, it had better provide prosperity. "What is the function of government anyway? Is it to stand idly by while the strong ride down the weak?"[64]

But the old laissez-faire stance was strongly established in 1932 in the person and philosophy of the new governor, Alf Landon. Landon was from a no-nonsense business background. He thought it was time to go back to old values, and no time for the Kansas government to increase its role. The Republicans chose Landon as a presidential candidate in 1936 exactly because of his record in Kansas of working for limited government living within its means and opposing the deficit-spending trends that were prominent nationally. "Of course," Landon told Roy Bailey, the editor of the *Salina Journal*, in 1932, "I'll admit that I am very pessimistic as to the future. I think we are in the midst of a revolution, the far-reaching effects of which we have not yet felt and cannot yet see to the end. Every program that is being offered as at least a partial panacea for our ills is fundamentally based on prosperity by Government aid. . . . But in my judgment the only safe and sure footing is that we must save our way out."[65] Some Kansans went further than Landon about retrenchment. Garvey noted that commodity prices were down about 70 percent and real wages around 50 percent, making even the 20 percent cuts being made by state government inadequate.[66]

There was a widespread feeling that government programs, if necessary, were an unsatisfactory substitute for private initiative. "I seem to be doing most of my business with bureaucrats," Garvey wrote in 1934, "and the more business I attempt to do with them the less I like bureaucrats, charming fellows though they may be."[67] Jess Denious, a newspaper editor in Dodge City and a state legislator, felt the same way. "An independent investigation that I have made," he wrote a friend, "has convinced me that the wild animal to which you referred in your letter, is not the Washington County panther, instead I am inclined to believe that the tracks along the river were made by one of those slinking bureaucrats making a survey to determine whether the taxpayer had any money left."[68] An Ashland attorney, writing to Denious, expressed a common opinion: "This 'gimme' business is next to a public scandal and is destroying pride and initiative in many people who could otherwise get along fairly well. For great political parties to compete for this shifting vote by the use of the tax payers' money is the mounting disgrace of the age."[69] Laconic, mildly intellectual, pragmatic, caustic—those were the traditional Kansas traits.

Landon studied the messages of every president in time of depression from 1837 and found that all of them, including Hoover's, emphasized economy.[70] The 1933 state legislature appropriated $4,580,127 less than the 1931 legislature.[71] Legislators still earned just three dollars a day. Kansas's retrenching government spending, moving against corporate farming, stopping utility merchandising, opposing school consolidation, and sticking with strict prohibition fitted a back-to-basics, highly moral, antibigness model. Landon's estimate of the circumstances gave his plan and the Kansas image its color and effect, but much of the rest of the country was gazing through different colored glasses.[72]

Outsiders saw the situation clearly. A man from Minneapolis, Minnesota, wrote the southeast Kansas editor Frederick Brinkerhoff concerning Brinkerhoff's radio interview with Landon in summer 1936: "Governor Landon's distinctive merit, so his eulogists have declared, is his innocence of anything extraordinary. He is an average man, an 'everyday man.'" However, economy carried to an extreme, the *Parsons Sun* editorialized, was a vice. "Economy at the expense of humanity does not appeal to this newspaper," Brinkerhoff wrote. "This condition is becoming notorious in Kansas." The Minnesota correspondent quoted a union leader: "God help the American people if they must depend upon this little man out in Topeka, Kans., who has no more conception of what ails America or what to do about it than a goat herder in the hills of Bulgaria."[73]

Symbolically, perhaps, following the hottest and most threatening summer ever in Kansas, 1936, came the national presidential election pitting Landon against the popular Franklin Roosevelt. Rolla Clymer worked hard for Landon. He said that it was the "highest peak of his life" when he watched a Kansas man being nominated by acclamation at the Republican convention in Cleveland. He thought, "The strongest appeal that can be made in behalf of the Governor is that he is a fellow Kansan, a Kansas product, whose outstanding record was made in this state. . . . The Kansas character is being reflected over the nation by his personality. The prestige of

Kansas is at stake in the coming election."[74] Landon wore a sunflower in his lapel, his campaign train was called the "Sunflower Special," and Republican publicity played hard on his Kansas character as representing what the American people wanted. He was even coached to keep his speech delivery amateurish, to match what was expected from Kansas and to make Roosevelt appear flippant by contrast.[75] The *Hutchinson Herald* made a point of Landon's origin. "Landon is a Kansan," it editorialized. "We are Kansans. When he goes to the White House he is going to show the rest of the people what Kansas brains and Kansas honesty can do. He is going to give them a sample of Kansas culture."[76] William Allen White suggested the campaign say that a president who had lived among the people of the plains could deal better with the suffering than someone from another place. He would "see that no man wanted for food and clothes and shelter in these terrible times."[77] Landon, a campaign piece went, "found in Kansas . . . the human laboratory in which he might work out his destiny. He is a plain man of a plains people. He lives in a world of reality. . . . He does not distort true aspects by looking at them through the prism of emotionalism. . . . Here in the heart of the United States is the cradle of American liberties. Here in the heart of America comes the type of man who best reflects the true American spirit. It is something that we 'have loved long since, but lost awhile.' "[78]

Landon's defeat in 1936 was monumental. He lost 16,674,665 to 27,478,945; he failed even to carry his home state of Kansas.[79] In considering the defeat that November, Clymer looked to more than errors in campaign strategy. He saw the loss, instead, as a sign of a fundamental shift in the attitude of Americans and therefore in the reputation of Kansas. He wrote to a friend that "some of us . . . are clearly out of step in this country. The big majority expects the government to take care of it in numerous ways and is going to vote for the man who will promise most."[80] The election, he said, was "a real sweep—and left us gasping for breath." In Clymer's Butler County, the Republicans lost the entire legislative delegation, the whole board of county commissioners, and eight of nine contested offices on the county ticket.[81] "I have not taken down the banner," Clymer wrote, "but it will be necessary for me to step softly for awhile."[82]

Surely the Landon defeat represents some kind of watershed in Kansas history, although big changes can never be dated precisely or perfectly identified with a certain event. The first result was to give Kansas a heightened version of its old inferiority complex, and the second, which took a period to

Alf Landon's presidential campaign, Canton, Ohio, August 1936.
Courtesy of the Kansas State Historical Society.

develop, was to convince it that it needed to "play the game" and be, as David's Israel was in its time of temporal power, more "like the nations."

But there were signs, even before the Dust Bowl publicity, that the rest of the country found Kansas and Kansans more humorous than profound and increasingly beside the point. Kansas congressman Hope found people in Congress from eastern states referring to Kansas when they meant Nebraska and to Nebraska when they meant Kansas. When confronted with the error, they said, "Oh well, what's the difference anyway? Who cares what goes on in either state?"[83] In 1928 the *Chicago Tribune* called White "an old lady" and the "chief duenna of the Kansas matriarchy, where the hem-stitching championship is a masculine honor." The state was "monotonous," the Chicago writer said, "buried in snow in the winter and baked in heat in the summer." Its electorate was "composed of nice, amiable people too listless to be disorderly . . . only the grasshoppers are active."[84] By 1933, with the Brinkley furor dying down, White almost wished for something at least to illustrate again the old Kansas energy. He himself was too fat, he admitted, and with "the cosmos riding astraddle my neck; so many people out of jobs, so many people needing help, so many people wanting advice these days and so much misery and so little to check it with," he felt tired. He wrote a friend, "Did you ever dream of anything like the docility of the American people under the crushing burden of these times? Why don't they smash windows? . . . The slow crushing of this thing, the inexorable grinding down of social and economic status is something I have never seen in all my life."[85]

Historians have noticed this seeming malaise. Robert Bader, whose book on the 1933 bond scandal involving the Emporia scion Ronald Finney highlighted a particularly seamy aspect of the times, argued in *Hayseeds, Moralizers, and Methodists* that modern Kansas as an "eclipsed civilization" could be traced to the Dust Bowl.[86] He defined the "modern era" in Kansas as beginning in the 1930s, when a "permissive, urbanizing, and industrialized nation marched off to its own drummer, leaving the traditional, puritanical, rural and agricultural province in its wake." Kansas, he wrote, has since been involved in "a persisting and futile struggle to improve the negative image— to catch up with the ever-accelerating national parade." This "me-tooism" involved "a concurrent reduction in state salience and purpose as a sociocultural entity." A commentator in 1951 argued that Kansas had become "staid and prosperous . . . increasingly barren of the ferment that produces challenge and conflict of ideas." Kansas history, Milton Eisenhower said about that time, was "five decades of epic poetry . . . followed by three decades of pedestrian prose."[87]

That judgment was harsh, but Bader was not alone. Donald Worster takes the line of the 1930s film *The Plow That Broke the Plains* in regarding the agricultural revolution in Kansas, touted since the removal of the bison and the Native American, as an enormous miscalculation. In other words, "progressive" Kansas farmers over the years were not just hicks but malevolent, and the Dust Bowl proved it. Far from being an accidental event that should generate sympathy for Kansans, the coming of the dust, in Worster's view, was inevitable, given the history of Kansans' relation to their environment— a just punishment for their ecological sins. "Farms have come to be considered too much as business ventures," wrote the *Sublette Monitor* editor in 1933, "yielding good and easy returns. . . . Profits will be welcome, of course, but this is not the day to put profits ahead of home."[88]

Other scholarly studies take a milder view. Pamela Riney-Kehrberg and Paul Bonnifield, for example, notice the majority of farmers that stuck and survived—though it might be a stretch to call them successful—to benefit

Hired man, Sheridan County, August 1939.
Courtesy of the Kansas State Historical Society.

from the turn of the cycle in the 1940s when the rains returned.[89] Douglas Hurt, though expressing admiration for the New Deal's land purchase program in Morton County, shows that it distorts the seeming "failure" rate of farmers in that area. There were complaints at the time that federal officials were "spotting and purchasing the better farms with good improvements, driving many owners and tenants out of the country or onto the W.P.A. rolls."[90] In many ways the 1930s were not so different from the 1890s in Kansas. There was the same drought, the same talk of mass exodus, the same low commodity prices and high mortgage payments, and the same self-doubt. Probably the region and its people again would recover well enough.

Still, many popular accounts followed the "black legend" of the Dust Bowl in Kansas, originated by journalists and government reports at the time. A classic in the doomsday style was Lawrence Svobida's *An Empire of Dust,* the bitter recollections of one who, after seven crop failures in eight years and suffering from "dust pneumonia," moved away from the state. Meade County, where Svobida resided, has never been regarded as a prime wheat area, and Hurt has noted that Svobida was neither typical of farmers of the region nor was he particularly objective.[91] But the stories of suffering were touching and, unquestionably, real. Those who experienced them or studied them often wrote movingly. As Svobida wrote, "With youth and ambition ground into the very dust itself, I can only drift with the tide."[92]

Traditional Kansas reforms, like prohibition, seemed by this time to some people in the state as signs of backwardness. Clymer was himself enough of a drinker that he lost his driver's license over it, and for a time he had to commit himself to a sanitarium to cure his habit. He corresponded regularly in the mid-1930s with his advertising agent in the East about the attitude of Kansans toward drink. The agent pushed for the right to run liquor ads legally in Kansas on the grounds that the nondrinker "has just as much right not to want a drink as I have to want it. I should respect his attitude and he mine. . . . I know a great many more people who suffer from ills induced by over-eating than I do drunkards; yet nobody wants to cut off their supply of food or deny them their cornbeef and cabbage if that's what they get full of."[93] Clymer responded that the letter was logical, but that the change was not going to happen in Kansas. "The actual majorities in both houses for the dries are brutal. We have been able to keep beer on the bars by fast foot-work. . . . Hard liquor is wholly taboo. . . . I don't know much but I know Kansas. It is dry and is going to stay that way for some time."[94] Other

Kansans agreed, but like Clymer, felt ambiguity about it. An attorney in Dodge City wrote the *Dodge City Globe* editor Jess Denious in 1937 that if the legislature would pass a 3.2 percent beer law and tax beer at five cents a pint, it would raise several million for farmers. "If this country again becomes a part of the Great American Desert it makes little difference whether we vote it wet or dry. Camels will take the place of tractors and some provision will have to be made to get them something to drink."[95]

The depression naturally brought forth two types regionally: the lunatics with schemes for curing the world's ills, and the entrepreneurs, who found opportunity in every situation. Both seemed particularly active in Wichita, where Gerald K. Winrod advanced his Christian anticommunist movement and where a seemingly moribund aircraft industry found survival and better in the 1930s in the hands of enterprising people.

Bad times always brought forth the radicals in Kansas. Winrod was a kind of latter-day Brinkley, in scope of appeal. Perhaps he had a larger national following. Senator Arthur Capper was careful to defend Winrod's right to speak, through Winrod's own widely circulated *Defender* magazine and on Capper's radio stations or newspapers. Capper was not frightened by Winrod's run for the U.S. Senate in 1938.[96] Certainly Winrod was anti–New Deal and opposed the court-packing scheme in 1937. Certainly he opposed U.S. intervention in Europe before Pearl Harbor. But so did many other Kansans.[97] Capper rejected the idea that Winrod was a tool of the German fascists and wrote him in 1942: "I have never had any doubt as to your desire to be a useful and loyal citizen of Kansas."[98] His brand of protest, just as much as that of Waldo McNutt, who advanced procommunist views in the state through the American Youth convention, was in the Kansas strain. Kansas in ensuing years became a rallying point for the German-American Bund, an organizing center for the John Birch Society, and the home of Earl Browder, head of the American Communist Party. "I shall count it a joy to thus serve Christ in adversity," Winrod wrote. "Christian stock of the twentieth century comes from a long line of martyrs who, by enduring great suffering, have demonstrated their right to existence."[99]

But it was the entrepreneurs who promised Kansas a positive image. An agricultural state with prominently agricultural values and no balance of industry and urban culture would be a backwater someday, with or without Kansas history and a new line of eccentrics behind it. In the wake of the Landon defeat, attitudes in Kansas slowly changed, and so did the circum-

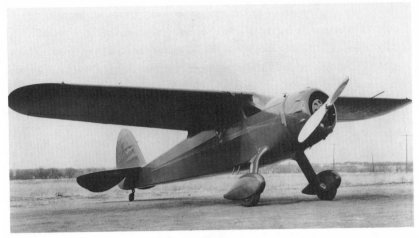

The Cessna Airmaster.
Courtesy of the Kansas State Historical Society.

stances of the economy. There was change enough at least that in the late 1930s, with the war approaching in Europe and federal spending and initiative increasing further to create a United States Rampant, Kansas had both the desire and the wherewithal to join the national parade rather than to sting at its tendencies from its unique moral height.

Two components of the new industrial Kansas were aviation and oil. At first Wichita's situation in the depression seemed disastrous. In 1929 the "Air Capital's" companies manufactured one thousand airplanes. City economists predicted it would manufacture two thousand planes in 1930, and the governor of Kansas believed that thirty thousand planes a year would be made there by 1933.[100] The truth was that in 1938 only three hundred planes were manufactured in the city. From the heady days of 1929, when Curtiss-Wright bought out Wichita's Travel Air and United Technologies (capitalization $80 million) purchased Stearman, the early 1930s saw nothing but bankruptcies. Cessna closed its doors in 1931; Travel Air in 1932, as Curtiss-Wright went broke; and Stearman barely limped on with military contracts in the face of United Technologies' bankruptcy.[101]

Who would have guessed then that a young Dwane Wallace, right out of college at the University of Wichita with a degree from its tiny aeronautical engineering program, would successfully market the C-34, later called the Airmaster, one of the classic private aircraft of the 1930s? Or that Walter Beech would return to Travel Air, rename it Beech Aircraft Company, and

The Beech plant, Wichita, c. 1946, with the first twelve Model D18S executive planes.
Courtesy of the Kansas State Historical Society.

succeed with the D-17 Staggerwing, an expensive executive craft of prodigious performance and appetite for fuel? Or that Stearman would attach
itself to another subsidiary of the failed United Technologies, the Boeing
Company of Seattle, to succeed with the Model 75 Kaydet in the 1930s and to
extend its military contracting by World War II to include being the center of
manufacture for the secret B-29 bomber? But it happened. By the end of the
decade Beechcraft was producing the Model-18 Twin and Cessna the T-50
Twin, both of which became heavily produced bomber-training craft in
World War II. At the air racing events of the 1930s, Wichita planes were as
dominant as they had been in the 1920s.[102] No doubt the big conglomerates
could not have done it, but the local men, with their low costs and disciplined local workforce, could.

The regional oil business thrived also. There was tremendous exploration
activity, particularly in the western part of the state, and improved technology. Seismic techniques made location more sure, the rotary rig replaced
cable tools to put wells down faster, and acidizing and fracturing techniques
created significant secondary recovery in wells that once would have been
abandoned. In 1934, twenty-six new oil fields opened in Kansas, more than

in any other state but Texas. Fifty fields were connected to pipelines in 1935, fifty-four in 1936, and fifty in 1937. By 1938, sixty of the one hundred five Kansas counties had oil production, and six western Kansas counties combined had the capacity to produce enough oil to meet the requirements of the entire nation. By 1944 there were seven hundred fifty oil fields in Kansas and a $30 million investment in the industry.[103]

But oil at fifty cents a barrel was as damaging to the petroleum business as wheat at twenty-five cents a bushel was to agriculture. In both cases there was government intervention, providing a direct or indirect subsidy to maintain these businesses at some level. In the case of agriculture, it was the federal Agricultural Adjustment Act (AAA), passed in 1933, that subsidized price through a government loan program in return for cuts in acreage, much in the manner of the subtreasury idea proposed by the Kansas Populists in the 1890s. With the oil business, it was a prorationing program (passed in Kansas in 1931 and one of the earliest in the country), administered at the state level by the Kansas Corporation Commission and advertised as a conservation measure, not a price-enhancing one. This state control of production happened despite Governor Landon's campaign against the Prairie Oil and Gas Company's private attempt to shut off the supply from small "stripper" wells in eastern Kansas. Setting "allowables" for new wells limited supply and increased market price. In the case of both oil and agriculture, however, it was no secret to the beneficiaries that they, as private business people, were not calling the shots anymore.[104]

Governor Huxman, a Democrat, motivated by the deepening depression, made a move to the left in government action and in cooperation with national trends. Then Governor Ratner, a Republican, motivated by the opportunities and dangers of the coming war, completed this roll left and, in a sense, made it politically native.

There were continued suggestions to Huxman that Kansas needed industry and could build on Wichita's aircraft manufacturing establishment. Wichitan Fred Bailey had several patents on aircraft and airship improvements, and it seemed logical for the government to build its airship plants in Kansas rather than to ship the helium they were using for lift from Kansas, where it was almost exclusively produced, to Dayton and Akron, where the Goodyear facilities were. Bailey had perfected a process for making lumber from asphalt, straw, and other materials, and there could be a straw-board manufacturing plant in south-central Kansas, which had both oil development and straw production.[105]

Kansas was now more willing to appeal to Washington without stint or hesitation. In April 1937 a Dust Bowl committee, with H. A. Kinney of the Liberal, Kansas, Chamber of Commerce as its secretary, sent a telegram to FDR:

> Drought conditions of the dust bowl have reached an emergency stage requiring desperate action. Stop. We appeal to the federal government for the preservation of life and property in the dust bowl area. Stop. Present program inadequate under individual operation to cover the area in time to accomplish necessary results. Stop. Work must be done under federal supervision working the soil with an army of tractors and listers planting seed with the first operation and covering the area systematically under orders beginning at the south and west sides of the dust bowl leaving no cultivated land untouched until the entire area is covered. Stop. Imperative that the federal government declare an existing emergency and place martial law in effect throughout the dust bowl requiring immediate listing and planting. Stop. Blowing and shifting of the soil daily moving eastward at alarming rate. Stop. Concentrated and maximum effort vitally necessary to prevent utter destruction of the soil.[106]

Kinney thought that the "chiseler who farms primarily for the benefit checks and who farms every available acre with little attempt to prevent blowing" was creating an environmental disaster. Adding to it were those who were "financially unable to properly farm their land even with the assistance of the benefit payments and others . . . too stubborn or indifferent to realize the seriousness of the situation but depend entirely on some act of God, nature, or time to correct all troubles." The Dust Bowl was too large for that, and dealing with it required coordinated and forced action.[107]

Kansas joined the New Deal. A high percentage of farmers there enrolled for AAA aid (9,100 farmers in the state were paid $1.3 million in 1933), and by 1938 Kansas was second in its district in number of applications filed for Public Works Administration (PWA) federal projects. Between 1933 and 1938, there were 291 PWA projects in Kansas, costing over $28 million.[108] Similarly the Works Progress Administration, which began operating in Kansas in 1935, funded a large number of public buildings and runways as well as employing artists and writers in making surveys of urban services and in writing *Kansas: A Guide to the Sunflower State* (1939) as part of the state guide series. The WPA distributed $56 million in Kansas. William Allen White thought the WPA as "demoralizing as the dole," but the Wichita-based labor paper the *Plaindealer* commented that "if this is boondoggling, let the good work continue."[109]

As though to recognize locally the increased role of government in some areas, Kansas went along with twenty-one other states in requiring a driver's license and driver's license examination, beginning in 1937.[110] To recognize the modern trend of the government's decreased role in other matters, such as the regulation of morals, the state authorized the sale of 3.2 beer the same year.[111] Beer was served in the Kansas State Senate for the first time in fifty years.[112] There were protestations that Kansas and its legislature "wasn't a carbon copy of congress" or a "rubber stamp," but the need to protest indicated the opinion of many people that it was.[113]

By the time the *Guide* was published, it could be said that Kansas was thoroughly federalized. This condition extended even to the federal owner-ship of land, a category in which Kansas was far behind most of the western states. The Land Utilization Commission had purchased over one hundred thousand acres of submarginal Kansas land in 1939 on which to carry out experiments in terracing, contour tillage, and listing.[114] Much of this land, first under the control of the Soil Conservation Service and then the Forest Service, became eventually the Cimarron National Grassland in Morton County.[115] William Allen White wrote the introduction to the *Guide*, but it was a brief characterization of the differences between western and eastern Kansas rather than White's usual paean to the Kansas character. Charles Edson, who worked on the *Guide* project, wrote in 1937 that "White's stuff has reached the point where the poor deluded people of Kansas can no longer stomach him; they vomit his stuff up."[116] Edson thought that was fine, as it was time Kansas stopped being "in the nuttiest section of a nutty old-stock Nordic nation."[117]

Edson thought that Payne Ratner made a mistake by going on a Carib-bean cruise in a private yacht after his 1938 election ("he takes a cruise in the ever-sunny seas while winter cracks down on Kansas and poor folks have no shoes") and worried that the new governor's Jewish ethnic ancestry (though Ratner himself was a Christian) would not fit with some of the anti-Semitic Kansas complaints about the Roosevelt administration.[118] But Edson was a

WPA recreation for blacks, about 1939, Junction City.
Courtesy of the Kansas State Historical Society.

Republican-hater generally. Many people believed that Ratner had a strong start, combining traditional Kansas Republicanism with modern directions, both in government and industry.

Ratner's two early prime concerns were the reorganization of state government, with special attention to civil service reform, and taking active steps to advance Kansas industry. But his agenda for government activity was broad. "Kansas," he said in his first message to the legislature, "is confronted today with a peculiar combination of old and new difficulties." He listed among government priorities care of the needy, education, law enforcement, "maladjustment in the development of our oil resources," and more equitable tax distribution. "We all realize the grave problems which confront Kansas at this time. We all realize that they are serious, and that we must work together if we would solve them. . . . Diversity of interests and differences of opinion make it difficult sometimes to take action that will please all of us. But our legislative halls are ideal places in which to work out a solution to our common problems."[119]

He advocated "an honest, intelligent and good faith merit system."[120] Each new administration began with an unseemly rooting for patronage.

"The governor and other appointing authorities," noted a contemporary report, "are besieged, not only at their offices but even at their homes, by office seekers clamoring for jobs."[121] Kansas had passed a civil service law in 1915, but it became inoperative in 1921 due both to failure to appropriate money to administer it and through weaknesses in the law itself. Ratner supplemented it in 1941 with legislation that had teeth, providing for competent employees and taking the administration of state charitable and penal institutions out of politics.[122] "The spoils system has had its day," he said, "and in the light of modern demands it must be displaced by an intelligent and thoroughgoing system of government based on merit and service."[123]

In instituting this brand of reform, Ratner was able to utilize an unusual institution in Kansas government, the research department of the Kansas Legislative Council. It created a report with a catchy title, "Personnel Administration: Analysis of Modern Employment Procedures, Present Personnel Practices in Kansas, and Merit Systems of Other States," to guide the Ratner merit initiative.[124] The Legislative Council had originated in 1933 to apply scientific management principles to the operation of state government and to provide a research service to back proposed legislation with careful study. The council consisted of ten state senators and fifteen representatives who met quarterly, even when the legislature was not in session.[125] The research department's initial funding was a fifteen-thousand-dollar grant from the Rockefeller Foundation.

A reporter for the *Topeka Journal,* who had reported on every state legislature since 1909, wrote in 1937 that the council had been successful in developing the "framework and general outline" for many proposals. It reduced the number of bills by about half—from nearly two thousand to about one thousand a session, and they were better bills. "Ten or a dozen years ago a situation such as faces the legislature at this time would have developed the greatest confusion and produced a multiplicity of proposals based on untested theories and vapory ideas of individual solons. Instead of that situation the general legislature is meeting the issues with cool deliberation and their action will be as sane and sound as that of any state in the nation."[126] Kansas was the pioneer in establishing a legislative council, a month before Michigan did it, and the device became more popular as lawyers and political scientists praised it. The legislature could discuss "questions of policy and the broad principles applying to the proposed legislation while the council worked out the details."[127] That was in great contrast to the earlier situation. A reporter had commented on the 1933 legislature: "It hasn't enough leadership and organization to guide a wheelbarrow."[128]

A central element of Ratner's 1939 address to the state legislature was an aggressive program of industrialization, beginning with more state support of the aviation industry.[129] But the *Kansas City Star* emphasized, as war developed in Europe, that there needed to be action with the words. "With the best strategic location in the United States for the safe production of war planes and the instruments and accessories that mean so much to their successful employment the 'movement' (if it can be called that) to bring more aviation industries to this part of the country has bogged down entirely."[130]

There were immediate moves to change that. The Wichita attorney Edward Arn, who would later be governor himself, met with the Wichita Chamber of Commerce in summer 1939 with the view of stemming the animosities that existed between Wichita's National Aeronautics Association and "the boys who really do things in aviation in the State."[131] Earl Shaefer, president of Boeing-Wichita, started his own lobbying program in Washington. He wrote Kansas senator and former governor Clyde Reed, emphasizing that the coasts could be attacked and saying that his interest in having aircraft defense plants in the center of the country was pure patriotism, not just self-interest.[132]

The aviation initiative was vital to the future of Kansas. But Ratner's industrial program went beyond that. One of his first acts as governor was to establish the Kansas Industrial Development Commission (KIDC). This institution, consisting of nine members serving without pay, not only created one of the pioneering permanent state lobby offices in Washington—an office instrumental in gaining for Kansas more than $2 billion in defense spending during World War II—but also employed traveling representatives (one was named, appropriately, R. H. "Dusty" Rhoads) to collect data from Kansas towns and industries and help them write proposals for all sorts of defense plants. The commission researched Kansas resources and prospects and, in addition, had as a major purpose the improvement of the Kansas image through publicity of its own and through responding to publicity from elsewhere that it considered off base. It was a blue-ribbon commission of outstanding Kansans, including journalists Rolla Clymer and Oscar Stauffer; businessman George Gano, the elevator builder; J. C. Nichols, the Kansas City developer; and, perhaps most important, Richard Robbins, whose background as president of TWA in the 1930s qualified him uniquely to contact fellow CEOs in the aviation field and elsewhere about the industrial future of Kansas.[133]

The charge to the KIDC stated that Kansas was too much an agricultural state and did not have a tax and corporate law structure suited to an industrial economy. But it did have cheap gas and an abundance of oil and coal. State colleges and independent research think tanks, if supported by state government, could learn a great deal about new methods for using traditional grain crops to manufacture goods made from these raw materials.[134]

Former governor Woodring did not mind that it was a Republican's idea; he liked the KIDC very much.[135] So did the citizens of Horton, Kansas, who were losing the Rock Island railroad shops there and were aided by the commission in finding new occupants for the buildings and new jobs for the former railroad employees.[136] The KIDC published a booklet in 1939, "Kansas Facts Pertinent to New Industries in Kansas," which was much more focused on specific results than the older sort of state puff/promotional piece.[137]

The concentration on image was central, especially an attempt to counter the newsmaking machines on the coasts with more authentic information from the heartland. The KIDC offered a fifty-dollar prize for the best photography of Kansas and attracted nearly seven hundred entries.[138] It made a promotional film, "Kansas: Modern Queen of the Prairie," in color, though without sound and a little heavy on hogs and chickens.[139] It put the editors Rolla Clymer and A. Q. Miller to work on the state's image. "It would be a good thing," Clymer wrote, "for the people of Kansas to forget their warts, dust storms, chinch bugs, tornadoes and the like and flaunt their graces and blessings a bit."[140] He responded to articles in the national media and consulted with Kansans who were writing them.[141] And he went for the implicit as well as obvious jibes. Late in 1939, Clymer wrote to the King Features Syndicate about the content of one of their "Bringing up Father" cartoon strips. Jiggs and Maggie were driving along Kansas highways lined with billboards and hot dog stands so that the "beautiful fields of corn and grass" they were seeking were obliterated. That, Clymer wrote, was far from the real situation. Kansas had one hundred thirty-two thousand miles of maintained highways, the second largest system in the country, and these were "remarkably free from the annoyance of billboard canyons which cut off the scenery of the 'sweet countryside.'" It was time to stop kidding Kansas. "Kansas

Richard Robbins, of the Kansas Industrial Development Commission.
Courtesy of the Kansas State Historical Society.

admits to harboring a deep green pain over being freely termed by outlanders a place only of dust bowls and 'cyclones' and horned toads. . . . It
frankly feels it has been slandered by other sections long enough." Why not
give the cartoon characters a return visit to the Sunflower State, where they
would be shown "tooling along dustless roads and drinking in great gulps of
tree-fringed meadows . . . of smoky, mystic hills—unmarred by ten feet of
lumber in a league?"[142]

The KIDC studied many industries with a view to building either on raw
materials or modest industrial starts. There was a soap plant in Hays, run by
Ray Kippes, which made washing compounds from local deposits of vol-
canic ash and rendered its own fats and oils from Kansas rabbits. It then sold
the rabbit hides.[143] Leavenworth had a battery company. The C. W. Parker
Amusement Company, which originated in Abilene, had been doing a business in manufacturing carousels for many years.[144] Galesburg, in Neosho
County, built garden tractors.[145] Frank Webb had developed a successful
calcium carbide plant in Arkansas City in 1934 and sold his product in over
fourteen states. The KIDC gathered information about cyanide fertilizer
plants, which used calcium carbide. The calcium carbide in turn was the
base for a host of other chemical compositions: lacquers, rayon, paint, synthetic resins, molded products. Kansas could make acetylene gas, explosives,
dope for airplanes, films, and safety glass as easily as any place in the East.
Was it not ridiculous that Kansas, with its great salt production, was buying
$2.5 million a year's worth of sodium chlorate to eradicate bindweed, all of it
manufactured at Niagara Falls? There was good Kansas coal, but not a coke
oven in the state. Why not have an aircraft plant in Dodge City? There was
talk of a dinnerware factory in western Kansas, of advancing flax production
in the eastern section, of establishing a plastics plant to produce auto tags,
and of getting the Exline Diesel Engine Works in Salina a navy contract. How
about soybean oil?[146]

There were some major achievements in industrial fields outside aviation. The Hercules Powder Company established the Sunflower Ordnance
Works near Lawrence in 1942 and used the University of Kansas for employee training in chemistry.[147] The Jayhawk Ordnance Works at Baxter
Springs was a $20-million ammonium nitrate plant employing three hun-
dred people, which was converted after the war into a fertilizer plant run by
Spencer Chemical Company.[148] By 1943 the plant was using 14 million cubic
feet of natural gas a day. "The visitor blinks his eyes," wrote a reporter then,

"when a pretty girl in a tailored suit is seen standing on top of a tank car, sampling ammonia. He blinks again when he learns that some of the men in overalls have Ph.D degrees, and when he finds women and men working side by side in a chemical laboratory requiring high professional skills. . . . This is a 'guinea pig' among Kansas war industries . . . a 'guinea pig' capable of prolific production challenging past laurels of the entire field of chemistry."[149] Kenneth Spencer commented in 1946 that the war demand for the four hundred thousand tons of high explosives the plant produced had created the investment that made the postwar fertilizer plant possible: "No private concern would have gambled thirty million dollars to build a chemical plant so far from industry."[150]

Clymer suggested a slogan for the KIDC: "Kansas: Where East Meets West and Farm Meets Factory."[151] The group made plans to copy the Mellon Institute for Industrial Research at the University of Pittsburgh.[152] William Jardine, former secretary of agriculture in the Coolidge administration, established a similar organization at the University of Wichita. It was called the Foundation for Industrial Research, was funded by Wichita companies, and lasted until 1955, collecting over seven hundred fifty thousand dollars in fees for research in wheat flour, vegetable conditioning, cement block fabrication, chrome plating, and record player design, among other things.[153]

The great opportunity, of course, came with the war and massive federal defense contracting. Not that Kansans were willing to go into the war for the potential profit alone. As in World War I, there was a strong strain of isolationism in the state as Hitler and Mussolini did their work across Europe. Arthur Capper, the Quaker governor who had opposed American entry into World War I so vigorously, did the same as a senior U.S. senator from Kansas in the late 1930s. He noted then that World War I took 10 million lives and "crippled or broke or crazed 20 million more." It wasted wealth to no purpose, and it was questionable whether civilization could survive another such conflict. "Kansas people do not believe in mud, blood and rotting corpses as a means of settling international questions," he wrote. "They have ceased to believe that it is necessary to plunge the world into a state of poverty to decide comparatively trivial international disputes."[154] Jess Denious wrote in 1940, "Whatever happens in Europe, I can see nothing but ruin for us if we too enter into the war. Then there would be no democracy left upon the earth, and all our ideas of freedom and progress and peace would have to be abandoned. . . . The worst has already happened in many countries, and it is feared everywhere else."[155] The Kansas delegation in Congress even went so far as to oppose the Burke-Wadsworth bill for Selective Service in 1940, speaking against the principle of peacetime conscription and minimizing the Nazi triumphs in Europe. Even with amendments to weaken it, only one person in the Kansas delegation voted for it.[156]

Ray Garvey supported Lindbergh and the America First Committee while fuming that Roosevelt was stirring up war hysteria to excuse his do-nothing domestic policy. "He knows how to squander and quarrel and meddle and gabble but that is not getting our defenses in any better shape."[157] Yet he admitted that "it is hard to buck a war trend when they are beating the war drums. . . . There will be a hell of a reaction against the war mongers later, but that might not prevent an expeditionary force every twenty-five years."[158] Garvey favored keeping America First together after Pearl Harbor to work for administrative efficiency in government but was not surprised when on December 18, 1941, he received notice it was disbanding.[159] His comment, looking at how few airplanes the country had was, "They'd better nail down the Capitol Dome."[160]

Garvey corresponded with William Allen White about isolationism. Finally, however, White gave up trying to change Garvey's mind and broke off the correspondence. White did accept, however, that the extreme isolationist opinion Garvey represented was a typical Kansas and even midwestern one. White's more extensive correspondence with Verne Marshall, the Pulitzer Prize–winning editor of the Cedar Rapids, Iowa, *Gazette,* was enough to illustrate that. Marshall, like Garvey, was anti–Eastern Seaboard, suspicious of Wall Street's influence, and against the New Deal and "Dictator Roosevelt." The war seemed to him just one more New Deal program. "The crazy foreign policy at Washington," he wrote, "is going to become crazier still." All of it, Marshall thought, was "poisonous to the American way of life."[161]

White did not think that "Hitler will come sailing into New York harbor," but he had read *Mein Kampf* and thought that totalitarian ideas were on the march.[162] His personal compromise was to head the Committee to Defend America by Aiding the Allies, thus hoping to aid Britain without involving the United States directly.[163] He found, however, that even this was unpopular in Kansas. In June 1940, after a committee ad stated that anyone "who believes the Germans will wait is either an imbecile or a traitor," White's mail ran five to one against aiding the Allies. Some of it was openly anti-Semitic.[164] But he had to recognize reality. He could not, for example, oppose isolationists running for political office, as many supporters of his committee wished, or he would have had to fight all the Kansas Republican incumbents and support their Democratic opponents. This would have jeopardized not only the tenure of Ratner as governor but also the pending constitutional amendment instituting the state merit system so dear to Ratner and the old Bull Mooser White. White's Kansasness in this case split his loyalties and gave him pause.[165] And Kansas was hardly alone. "What is true of Kansas," he concluded, "is true everywhere."[166]

White's position made this near Kansas saint somewhat unpopular in his own state.[167] Ray Yarnell of *Capper's Farmer* wrote him that he had made "shameful use of this great talent of yours in increasing the war hysteria that is gripping this country. . . . I am ashamed of you."[168] White understood that he could not explain to many people, as he did to his friends, that "the only reason in God's world I am in this organization is to keep this country out of war."[169] Confessing that "I am a liability to my friends," he resigned from the Committee to Defend America early in 1941 and awaited developments.[170]

By then developments were irreversibly under way, and Kansas decided to adapt. In 1940 Wichita aircraft leaders were called to Washington and briefed just before Roosevelt made his public address calling for the rapid manufacture of fifty thousand aircraft to buttress U.S. readiness. The entire U.S. aircraft industry had built fewer than forty-five thousand planes in the history of powered flight. The war was obviously going to be a great task and a potentially great opportunity for Wichita's plants.[171] Kansas established an office in Washington that year to meet with the Kansas senators and representatives and to camp at the doors of the right offices.[172] At the same time it established the infrastructure in Kansas, such as vocational training programs for aircraft workers in Wichita, that would be needed to take advantage of such contracts as might come.[173] It learned diplomacy: Clymer should stop beating U.S. senators at golf.[174] And the state backed the initiatives, increasing the appropriation for the KIDC from sixty thousand to one hundred thousand dollars per year for the biennium ending June 30, 1943. Clymer thought defense industry would, or at least should, be decentralized and located partly in the central part of the nation. Kansas stood a good chance to get some of it.[175] The KIDC organized regular trips for Governor Ratner to Washington, with a specific industrial agenda each time.[176] Ratner also pushed the idea of decentralization, which certainly came in for a follow-up from Kansas after the Pearl Harbor attack demonstrated the vulnerability of the coasts.[177]

"The work of keeping our contacts here in representing Kansas," Clymer wrote from Washington in summer 1940, "goes on continually." We will get nothing "on a platter," Clymer wrote, "but . . . consideration in any degree will come only after ceaseless and aggressive efforts on the part of every agency and interest."[178] J. C. Nichols wrote late in 1941, "Believe me, Payne, I am keeping up the fight, working two extra stenographers all the time; telephoning and telegraphing, and doing everything in my power to get a more fair distribution of defense plants and defense orders in our area. You can depend that I will not quit."[179] That summer a Kansas War Industries Board was formed as a single incorporated unit to join Kansas cities together in a more effective lobby.[180] That took not just reams of statistics but also "personal contacts and unremitting salesmanship."[181] It was exciting to those involved. Wrote Oscar Stauffer, "Of all the ages in which men have lived, how could any have been more interesting than the one we share now?"[182]

An example of how effective the KIDC could be in helping local industries with war contracts was the case of the Coleman Company of Wichita. A successful manufacturer of gasoline lamps and outdoor equipment since 1900, Coleman found itself in 1941 handicapped by materials shortages and changes in national priorities. Nearly one-third of its workforce was laid off in 1941. However, Sheldon Coleman, the son of founder William Coffin Coleman, used personal initiative and the help of the KIDC people in Washington to make the right contacts for the company with the contract distribution division of the Office of Production Management. Coleman burst into a private compartment on a train to talk to the proper military officer about a contract for manufacturing .50mm ammunition chests, but his assertiveness might have been in vain without the right information from the people who had surveyed the Washington scene already. "It is an excellent type of work," Coleman wrote Ratner, "and you are to be congratulated . . . on the foresight that you have shown in setting up an organization of this kind to help the industries of our state." The farmers might complain about the tax money spent on the commission, but they did not understand the importance of its work to the future of Kansas.[183]

The first major coup was the location of the North American aviation plant for building B-25s in Kansas City, Kansas, in 1941. The KIDC credited Kansas City editors Roy Roberts and Lacey Haynes with cleaning out the Pendergast urban machine and promoting new industry through lobbying in Washington. Richard Robbins was key also.[184] Eventually that plant, built

B-29s in front of the assembly plant at night in Wichita.
Courtesy of the Kansas State Historical Society.

adjacent to Fairfax Airport and designed to use automotive assembly techniques, produced thirteen bombers a day—a total of over six thousand or 67
percent of all the B-25s produced during World War II.[185]

That achievement paled in comparison with landing a production contract for the B-29 bomber for Wichita. Boeing-Wichita produced over sixteen hundred of these craft during the war, about 44 percent of total B-29
production. The statistics were remarkable, even in wartime. Boeing-Wichita had 766 workers in July 1940 and close to 30,000 by the end of the war.
Wichita as a whole employed 60,000 people working in aircraft alone during
the war period, housed in three federally constructed communities (Planeview, Hilltop Manor, and Beechwood), and its population nearly doubled.
The federal government built forty five hundred of the six thousand new
homes provided for air workers in Wichita. Boeing's Plant II, built by the
War Department, cost $27 million, and nearly seventy thousand phone calls
a day came through the Wichita company's switchboards.[186]

Every Wichita aircraft plant grew accordingly. Beech built the AT-10 and
AT-11 bomber trainers and Cessna a version of its T-50 Bobcat twin in
numbers beyond all dreams of the earlier decade. Wichita alone produced

Overview of Boeing, Wichita, with Planeview in the background.
Courtesy of the Kansas State Historical Society.

twenty-six thousand three hundred military aircraft during World War II,
and production in the rest of Kansas made the state's total thirty-four thousand five hundred aircraft. It was a massive change from Wichita's production record of three hundred planes in 1938.[187]

There was much to recommend Kansas for defense work, including its
rural tradition. George Trombold, the personnel director at Boeing-Wichita,
stated that persons from modern farm backgrounds did especially well in
aircraft manufacturing jobs. "Most persons from rural areas have been indus-
trious all their lives and are used to hard work. Nearly all Kansas farms are
highly mechanized and Kansas farmers have learned the use of power machinery as well as hand tools." About 50 percent of workers at Boeing-Wichita
in 1942 had farm backgrounds, and they were encouraged to continue farming while employed there as long as it did not interfere with war production.
Wichita workers reduced the time necessary to build a B-29 from one hundred fifty-seven thousand worker hours for the first one hundred units to
fifty-seven thousand worker hours for the third one hundred.[188]

The urban atmosphere in Wichita in the 1940s quickly disabused any
visitor of bucolic images of a quiet life. The city's population was 114,634 in

1940, up only a little from the 111,110 it had in 1930. But in 1942 the population in the metropolitan area was 133,011 (164,994 in the metropolitan area where the commuting suburbs boomed); in 1943, 184,515 (218,619); and in 1944, 176,316 (226,724). That growth and the boom of the Korean conflict in the 1950s outdistanced the Kansas end of Kansas City and made Wichita the largest city in Kansas. By 1953, when it was building the B-52 jet bomber, Wichita proper had a population of 238,302. The busiest intersection in Kansas in February 1941 was Central and Broadway in Wichita, where north-south Highway 81 met east-west thoroughfare Highway 54. Fifty-five thousand cars a day passed that way. Wichita had to hire a traffic consultant from Yale to advise its new traffic commission, put in parking meters, and ban angle parking. The city ran twenty-four hours, with all-night groceries and child care, emergency bus service to the plants, and all the other changes that had to be made with a workforce that included women. Wrote the local author Kunirade Duncan for the *New York Herald Tribune:*

> When a community expands so suddenly, living conditions are upset. There are too many people in stores, on buses, at the bank, gas, water and electricity pay windows. It takes forever to get nothing done. There are too many traffic tangles and accidents, too few lodgings for airplane workers, too few seats in school rooms. . . . It is a headache to try to telephone. . . . Motor drone is an all-day and most of the night noise. . . . Traffic signal change has been increased to thirty-two seconds to get the sidewalk crowds across safely, and around every filling station is a ring of trailers in which new arrivals await a demountable house, fabricated to the stage where you can put tired little children to bed. . . . How many inhabitants has Wichita today? No one knows. Old-timers look on dazed at buses unloading commuters from towns seventy miles away.

A reporter from *Colliers* that year visiting all the small machine shops in Wichita turning out war materials thought he was seeing a revolution.[189]

Certainly, what was sometimes called the Battle of Kansas, organizing and implementing rapid aircraft production, was a remarkable achievement. The number on industrial payrolls in Kansas rose from 137,811 in the first quarter of 1940 to a peak of 284,262 in the third quarter of 1943, mostly in the manufacturing sector. Aircraft plants and the two ordnance plants in Kansas (the Kansas Ordnance Works near Parsons and Sunflower Ordnance near Lawrence) accounted for 80 percent of that total. But smaller concerns, like the Manville shell-loading plant near Parsons and the ammonia nitrate plant at Baxter Springs had an impact on Kansas communities. Employment figures in aircraft plants alone by the war's end were higher than those in all Kansas manufacturing in 1940.

The distribution was anything but random. Wichita and Kansas City accounted for 92 percent of the state's total industrial employment. Wichita was a "classic boom town," having the highest per capita war-contract volume of any American city, and, along with San Diego, was most noted in the nation for its industrial growth.[190] And clearly, the balance of the economies within these cities changed during the war and forever thereafter. Only 3 percent of Wichitans depended for their livelihood on aviation in 1939; in 1943, it was 50 percent.[191]

The federal influence was obvious, not only in investment in physical plants and housing but also in promoting social changes. Wichita at first wanted only skilled male workers, many of whom had to be imported from outside the city, rejecting the option of training local women, African Americans, or both. Doing so required the construction of nearly twelve thousand housing units in that city by the federal government. But by 1943 that same government pushed companies for the employment of more women and blacks, and it happened. African Americans, who had been used only in janitorial positions by Wichita aircraft plants early in the war, were working on the assembly lines by the end of it, partly at the strong urging of Senator Capper. Women, at first recruited only to fit into tight places in the B-29 assembly process, were by the end of the war placed in all sorts of industrial jobs.[192] Half of Boeing's employees in Wichita in 1945 were women.[193]

Social change was deep and permanent. The war started with horse-mounted cavalry still stationed at Ft. Riley and ended with the B-29. High wages and strong crop prices changed consumption patterns, and war threats increased community organization and unity. Child rearing and the travel scope of custom combiners changed dramatically. Yet Patrick O'Brien, writing about the home front in Kansas, emphasized, "Kansans believed strongly in the values inherited from the past; to preserve those values in a society transformed by war would be their next challenge."[194] In Wichita's Planeview, dubbed the Miracle City, grew the elements that allowed that city to "shake off the doldrums of the Great Depression to become one of the nation's busiest military production centers." The planned housing communities, drab as they were, were prototypes for the Levittown cul-de-sac suburbs of the postwar period. A regimented system of community leadership there, as well as rigid planning for upkeep and activity, had a large impact on resident's attitudes. The Planeview federal housing district became, by the end of the war, the seventh largest city in Kansas. Its high school had fourteen hundred students. Although much of the war housing physically disappeared after the war, the social, political, and demographic changes it brought and allowed did not.[195]

Large amounts of money were involved. Kansas by 1942 was tenth overall in the nation in volume of defense spending and third in aircraft expenditures. Most of the money went to Wichita—a remarkable $2,002,187,000. Other figures for Kansas were ships, $5,992,000; industrial facilities, $240,923,000; nonindustrial facilities, $105,446,000; and all others, $86,235,000. The total federal investment in the state's economy was nearly $2.5 billion.[196] Wichita employed sixty thousand people at its aircraft plants by 1943 and had a payroll of $9 million a month. There were major army airfields in Coffeyville, Dodge City, Kansas City, Topeka, Garden City, Great Bend, Herington, Independence, Liberal, Wichita, Pratt, Salina, Winfield/Arkansas City, and Ellis County. There were naval air stations in Hutchinson and Olathe. Scattered all over the plains were runways for bomber training, and the little towns of Kansas absorbed thousands of pilots while gaining vast and expensive facilities for postwar uses. Walker Air Field in Ellis County, western Kansas, had ten-thousand-foot runways for B-29 testing and was home in 1944 to six thousand people.[197] Kansas farmers benefited, also. The $595 million cash income they had in 1942 was more than double the average for the years 1936 to 1940.[198]

The *Christian Science Monitor* was only one of many publications that covered the look of it. On April 2, 1945, its reporter observed of Boeing-Wichita:

The vast building is as clean and light and convenient as a modern university. It turns out one of the mightiest, most intricate, and most beautiful machines ever produced—the B-29 Superfortress. Perfect engineering, flawless construction, unerring precision are required. Never have bulk and minutiae been more intimately combined. Inspecting it, one wonders if the production of any other single machine anywhere at any time has called upon so many men and women so completely to adapt themselves to teamwork and so unreservedly to follow directions.

The work ethic, the democracy ("the big chief's old Chevrolet parked right with the workers' cars") seemed traditional Kansas, but going out into the countryside, the *Monitor* reporter found a thoroughly modern state. He found no "comic provincialism"; rather, "they are . . . as familiar with fast automobiles, splendid roads, crack trains, and silver planes as any community on earth. . . . One may say that America has made the dreams of the ages come true."[199]

As with World War I, however, there were some drawbacks for the state to the great "arsenal for democracy" bounty. One had to do with racial and ethnic homogeneity, one of the arguments advanced by Kansas in attracting defense industry, and clearly, along with its central location and trained workforce, a deciding factor. Wichita had one of the lowest alien population percentages among cities its size in the United States. In the 1940 census, out of a population of 114,966, only 910 aliens were listed, a much lower percentage than, for example, Topeka. It had only 317 Germans in 1940 and almost no Asians. Knowing the security advantages in that, Wichita throughout the war resisted relocation of Japanese Americans from the coast to the heartland. The city manager, Russell McClure, wrote the Society of Friends in 1943: "On the basis of a few previous experiences we have had, we know that our regular citizens here will not accept these Japanese and trouble would result." During the war's last days, cars sprouted bumper stickers showing B-29s dropping bombs with the legend: "From Wichita to Japan. Excuse Please."[200] President Harold Focht of the University of Wichita, who had written books on Japan and actively recruited Japanese students to his school, had been surprised one morning in the early 1930s to find scrawled on the sidewalk in front of his home, "America for Americans."[201] Ten years later, he might have expected it.

Others in Kansas felt the same drive toward Americanism in everything. The Kansas Industrial Development Commission flirted with the idea of working with the War Relocation Authority in Washington to relocate Japanese from internment camps to Kansas, where they could be employed. An experiment with German prisoners at "Stalag Sunflower" worked well during the war in relieving some of the shortage of agricultural workers. Germans were located near fourteen Kansas towns, and there is evidence that the experience with these individual Germans softened the attitude of Kansans toward the German nation as a whole.[202] But the same was not true for the Japanese. Richard Robbins inquired in 1943 what the sentiment might be in Kansas toward employing some of about one hundred thousand Japanese located in ten camps, mostly American citizens and mostly under twenty-five.[203] He quickly found out. It was necessary to establish that those to be moved would be welcomed in their new home, circumstances that could not be demonstrated in Kansas. Ratner made a public statement indicating that Kansas wanted none of this type of labor. When representatives of the KIDC met with the new governor Andrew Schoeppel to encourage him to make a statement saying that Japanese-born Americans were entitled to some rights, his staff determined that, given the negative feeling in the state, it would be unwise for Schoeppel to "stick his neck out." There was agreement that "this problem is with us and will have to be met after the war is over," but wartime did not seem a good time to start the regional diversity educational process.[204] The KIDC did get permission for Henry Hosuke Ikeda, who had been employed for years by the Fred Harvey organization in Dodge City, to acquire a permit to teach Japanese in a navy school, but that was as far as the race initiative went in Kansas.[205]

Perhaps the war fever was partly responsible for the first executions taking place in Kansas in the twentieth century. A death penalty law, after vetoes of earlier bills by Governor Woodring, finally passed in 1935, amid protest, but was not implemented. At the time, the protesters argued that Kansas had become too civilized for executions.[206] Still, when Governor Huxman commuted a death sentence to life in prison, it probably contributed to his defeat for reelection.[207] Governor Schoeppel in 1944 refused to commute several death sentences on the grounds that the governor should not interfere with the will of the people as expressed in legislation.[208] On March 10, 1944, Ernest L. Hoefgen, convicted of killing a Kansas State College student in a cornfield near Peabody, was hanged in the old warehouse of the state penitentiary in Lansing.[209] A little over a month later Fred Brady and Clark Knox met their ends with the hangman.[210]

One Kansan wrote that it was a terrible turn. "I never dreamed but what you would carry out our Kansas traditions," he wrote the governor, "and save us from the shame and disgrace that will come to our state if these hangings are permitted. . . . I cannot believe that the people of the state of Kansas will relish the spectacle of a scaffold built on Kansas soil."[211] But other people disagreed. "Pay no attention to the 'sob sisters' governor," wrote one man. "They elected you and thus hired you to protect 'sleeping Kansas,' and if, in the line of your duty, you make it dangerous to wantonly kill in Kansas, you are simply handling your job of making Kansas safe for Kansans."[212]

Also odd for Kansas, and perhaps attributable to the war, was that women, though active in industry, were nearly invisible in regional politics. In the legislature meeting in 1931, among 163 men there were only 2 women, Mrs. T. T. Solander of Osawatomie, the first woman senator in Kansas, and Miss Kathryn O'Loughlin of Hays. O'Loughlin was the daughter of a state representative from Ellis County: "Tall, slender, a thick crop of bobbed hair confined beneath a close-fitting hat, she is a conventional picture of an efficient young professional woman as she enters the big doors of the state-house for the daily legislative session." A reporter noted that Solander wore "chic dresses . . . cleverly tailored and usually softened with a bit of lace at throat or wrists. There is something feminine about the Kansas senator, even while she discusses labor or railroad legislation." She was careful to say to the press that she was there due to the "generosity and indulgence" and "sense of humor" of her husband, a locomotive engineer, and would never think of serving had she had children.[213] Solander presided over the state senate and brought cheers when she said, "Gentlemen of the senate, I call you to witness that contrary to all the traditions concerning women, I have remained silent and allowed you to do all the talking."[214] O'Loughlin assured the public that she was not out to seduce the governor: "Miss Lida Woodring is a most capable, charming and gracious hostess; an ideal first lady of the state and I have no designs on the governor and no intention to supplant Miss Lida."[215] This is not the kind of coverage one would have expected of Clarina Nichols in 1867, or of Laura Johns in 1887, or of Annie Diggs and Mary Lease in 1892.

Although there was some ambiguity among Kansans about the meaning of World War II, the feeling was strong that it had prevented "our area from dying on the vine" in the wake of the Dust Bowl.[216] The legislature, adopting the 1873 Kansas-composed "Home on the Range" as the state song in 1947, did object that deer and antelope were not the current type of stock but accepted that "knocking out 'buffalo' and putting in 'Jersey milk cow' would naturally play hob with the meter of the thing."[217] The Coronado "Cuarto-Centennial" of 1941 was maybe more hype than history, but it matched the new tourism program.[218] There was an effort to change the "freak legislation" for which Kansas had long been famous. There were bills in 1941 to repeal the thirty-year Kansas law against eating snakes in public. That would relieve Kansans, said a reporter, "who for more than a third of a century may have felt an undue restraint on their desire to eat snakes and other reptiles in public places. . . . There was no penalty against eating snakes in private."[219] Wichita was not certain it liked the tacky war housing that changed its cityscape, or the dependence it felt on federal dollars to maintain its enlarged population and to provide water, sewers, and highways. Had the federal government been a Santa Claus to Wichita, one local man asked, or had Wichita "been Santa Claus to the whole United States?"[220]

Rolla Clymer thought that the wartime bargain, though it might seem to have been with the devil, at least paid the state well. It had industries now, even a nascent tourist business, and it had a grudging respect. "Various officials could not 'see' Kansas as an industrial state," Clymer told a group of Kiwanis, "but patience and a high type of salesmanship finally broke down this view." That there was a TNT plant in Eudora or that land-locked Kansas City furnished not only gun turrets and armor plate but also boats for the navy seemed to revive the old Kansas confidence that its people could build ex nihilo through pure verve and reinvent the state at every crisis.[221] How much of this development had been its own doing and how much outside circumstance Kansans were no more willing than ever to evaluate impartially. The KIDC in 1943 published one of its colorful pamphlets, printed by the state printing office. It was called "On the Road to Fulfillment."

CONCRETE STEPS

One political pundit called Kansas governor Fred Hall "a vigorous young man, a little on the noisy side." Hall, elected in 1954, was, according to a reporter, "for all his charm with the voters . . . quite uncharming with the legislators."[1] His attacks on "rascals" in state government resulted in a stand-off during his administration. His enemies called him a "spendthrift," partly because of his upgrading of the governor's mansion, and he referred regularly to the "overdraft" legislature. There were charges that Hall's union support came as much from payoffs as from the governor's opposition to Right-to-Work bills outlawing the closed shop. A "truth squad" toured Kansas campaigning against Hall in 1956, noting that the governor had spent $1,100 on pictures of himself and had run up a $106 hotel bill one night in Wichita. Hall lost the Republican primary, and Democrat George Docking won the gubernatorial election handily in a strongly Republican state in a year when Eisenhower swept the presidential election and Kansas Republican senator Frank Carlson won easily.

That seemed to be the end of it. But at 9:00 A.M. on January 3, 1957, Hall held a press conference. He entered the room followed by two justices of the Kansas Supreme Court and announced the retirement of Chief Justice William Smith, due to failing health. That was the first and least surprising step of what became known as the "triple play." The second announcement woke up every reporter. Hall, just days from the end of his term, announced his own resignation as governor of Kansas. That made Lieutenant Governor John McCuish the governor for about ten days. The third element of the triple play was the most surprising. New Governor McCuish, sworn in then and there, appointed former governor Hall to the Kansas Supreme Court to fill the vacancy created just minutes earlier. Hall looked up after taking the oath and simply said, "The ceremony's over," after which Battery C, 154th Field Artillery Battalion of the Kansas National Guard, fired a nineteen-gun salute for McCuish. The triple play, an observer remembered, "took its place as one of the most bizarre political events in Kansas history."[2]

Though it had some competition in Kansas history for the title of most bizarre, the Hall administration and its unusual ending showed that Kansas had not quite allowed itself to be fitted into the straitjacket of federal policy and modern bureaucracy. Hall argued that the way to maintain state sovereignty against federal power was to meet modern needs by increased state action. He pushed a minimum wage law, a bill regulating interest, increases in workmen's compensation, a direct primary law, and the vote for eighteen-year-olds.[3] Still, his program matched national trends. One Kansas paper said it was "a virtual echo of what the New Deal Democrats have been saying."[4] Nevertheless, when there was talk in 1955 of Hall as a Republican presidential candidate, the *Kansas City Star* editorialized that "what almost surely would kill off any chance he might otherwise have had would be the fact of his being from Kansas, and its governor. The Kansas tradition in that respect is hardly conducive to presidential prospects."[5]

Allan Nevins delivered an address at the Kansas Territorial Centennial Conference in 1954, "Kansas and the Stream of American Destiny." Not since Carl Becker wrote his famous essay "Kansas" in 1910 after a sojourn in the state had such a respected academic reflected in a general way upon the place of Kansas in the nation. In his talk, Nevins highlighted the dilemma of Kansas, as a state with a tradition of innovation, trying to maintain its character in an age of bureaucracy and centralization.

Nevins was well aware that Kansas puritanism and moral certainty had had its dark side historically. "In cold fact," he wrote, "liberalism in its classic sense—the maintenance of individual freedom of thought, of speech, of conscience, of economic and social action within legitimate bounds—has sometimes fared ill within Kansas." The state now faced a "terrible and inescapable dilemma," however, of how to protect the positive aspects of its individual character while "pursuing a path of consolidation and centralization fixed by economic and social circumstance." Liberals defended the growth of federal power as a means of countervailing the power of corporations, but there was a "constant threat of regimentation."

The solution Nevins suggested was easier stated than accomplished. He

Governor Fred Hall's inauguration, 1951.
Courtesy of the Kansas State Historical Society.

recommended that Kansas continue to be an "inspiring rebel" but that it should become more "mature" and "intelligent" in its protest. The "great central cable in Kansas history," agrarianism, had weakened and so should "the force of the Kansas divergence." It was time for Kansas to grow up, take advantage of its basic honesty and courage, and thus to realize its "self-contained possibilities" without rocking the ship of state so hard. The United States needed "variegation" among its states, Nevins thought, a melding of distinct traditions. However, his closing statement—he hoped "that after the soft prairie zephyr has blown mildly away, the rousing Kansas cyclone will return"—was inconsistent with the tone of the rest of his speech and with the reality he was describing.[6] There was no room for any but a rhetorical cyclone. "Honestly the federal welfare outfit doesn't want any common sense used," wrote a Kansan in 1950. "They held up all federal welfare funds for Kansas 17 days in January, because we 'were not in conformity' to the federal plan. . . . How long it will be before they put us over a barrel again I do not know."[7]

As the centennial of the creation of Kansas Territory (1954) and of statehood (1961) came around, there were plenty of analysts trying to link the

The Kansas state legislature in session, 1950s.
Courtesy of the Kansas State Historical Society.

Kansas past and future. But observers spotted disorientation and hesitation where there had been little before. Politicians could generalize in platitudes. Governor Edward Arn in his inaugural address in 1953 said, "Our course in Kansas is charted for us with remarkable clarity of outline. It is our bounden duty to maintain our house in order to husband our resources, and to labor in full harmony with the national purpose."[8] But how would that be done with actual cranky Kansans? A Kansan could be guided, wrote one of its newspapers in the 1950s, "but try to tell him he has to do something and he promptly hits the ceiling. . . . It's a state for progress, but slow progress that doesn't cost too much."[9]

Carl Bridenbaugh has suggested that sometime around World War II a fundamental link had been broken, demographically, politically, economically, and spiritually, with the American past that Kansas had always represented. An "artificial" environment was substituted for a natural one, and the personal connection with sky, animals, and land that had characterized human civilization for thousands of years disappeared. There was a city presence in the country that brought "the Huntley-Brinkley news and the Madison Avenue claptrap to the summit of Moosilauke and the High Sierras." A bland toleration, what historians of the era in applying it backward in time called "consensus," made the great religious and political battles of the past seem irrelevant. Teachers and students of history, Bridenbaugh wrote, had lost "the priceless asset of a shared culture." Without the connection to the past there could be no confident movement into the future, the "cult of the contemporary" notwithstanding. "Mankind," Bridenbaugh concluded, "is faced with nothing short of the loss of its memory."[10]

Perhaps it was this historical amnesia, combined with enormous external pressures and a changing populace, that led to the end of constitutional prohibition of liquor in Kansas in 1948. Statistics about alcohol's continuing cost and its damage to health and the economy could no longer overcome an embarrassment about image, and there was an unwillingness to stand on such different ground. A Wichita group, spearheaded by an Episcopal priest and a Catholic bishop, pushed for repeal. The 1948 vote showed that wets were strongest among veterans, urban residents, Democrats, and young people.

There was heavy pressure to be "modern" and to live down the legacy of Kansas's provincialism and hypocrisy.[11] But there was stress in it. "Kansans are babes in arms regarding the liquor business," a reporter commented in 1949. "Now Kansans find themselves bewildered and wandering in a strange land. They are going to sea without a compass or a ticket."[12] Still, they were swept inevitably away from the shore. Kansans as late as 1983 still consumed only 73 percent as much alcohol as the national average (up from 14 percent in 1916), but the trend was obvious. "Kansas was once known around the world for high moral principles," wrote a member of the WCTU, "but not now."[13]

Kansas had a national leader hailing from the state in the 1950s, as it had had in the 1930s, but Eisenhower Republicanism implied something much different from the Landon Republicanism of that earlier era. Payne Ratner had said in his inaugural address in 1939, "Kansas has in her blood and history, the vision, the capacity for solving her own problems, for living her own life, for overcoming her own difficulties."[14] But that was before World War II. Rolla Clymer rode in the *Life* car at the media event that surrounded Eisenhower's visit to his boyhood home in Abilene in 1952 and thought he had met the future there. "The most amazing fact about the whole affair," he wrote his fellow editor Frederick Brinkerhoff, "was not Ike, or the home-coming events or anything else but the communications coverage by news-papers, wire groups, magazines, radio and television—especially the last. We don't know much about TV out here, but political managers are keenly aware of it and are playing it for all it is worth, which is a lot." Clymer used to tell his reporters in El Dorado, "if the Good Lord had intended us to run the *Kansas City Star*, he would have set us down in Kansas City." But now the world and its technology were coming to Abilene and El Dorado, and people like Clymer became dinosaurs.[15]

Clymer's friend Richard Robbins wrote that he visualized Clymer not being "overwhelmed by all the 'Whoopla' for the 'Man from Abilene,' par-ticularly in our own fair state. I am still suffering from the dose of this kind of dope which the patent medicine vendors slipped down my craw in 1940. Therefore, I am taking a second look before I let myself come under the magic spell of the snake charmers of the Vintage of 1952."[16] But there was no avoiding it. "This is once again the District of Confusion," wrote a Kansas visitor to the nation's capital. "The Bureaucrats are again extremely happy in the prospect of running the national economy with their cute little mimeo-graphs and directives."[17] Whitley Austin of the *Salina Journal* added, "I can't help feeling Topeka is a little Washington."[18]

Although Dwight Eisenhower's ballyhooed roots were in Abilene, his military and administrative career in centralized and standardized com-mand hardly reflected the independent, offbeat reputation of historical Kan-sas. Kenneth Davis credits Kansans' identification with Ike, which corre-sponded with the enormous new industrial prosperity brought by federal spending in World War II and the Cold War, in initiating a "phase-change" in the nature of the state. "A *Kansan* had become the supreme soldier of the greatest war in history! The subsequent crushing of Hitler was rendered, thereby, a peculiarly Kansan triumph!" But Eisenhower of Abilene was a different man from that city's hitherto most famous resident, Wild Bill Hickok. Davis described Eisenhower as a person who promoted a psychol-ogy of "middleness" and worked against "unequivocal either–or choices and *for* coalitions, amalgamations, homogenizations on the basis of perceived common denominators among diverse people and things and forces." His approaches "were essentially conservative attributes of a successful 'chair-man of the board.' " As Milton Eisenhower, speaking to the Native Sons and Daughters of Kansas in Topeka in 1949, pointed out, "The State's remarkable energies have been spent too often upon issues which are no longer of crucial importance in a world struggling to organize itself for the atomic age. It is as though a huge tractor, badly needed for plowing acres of wheatland, were being used to plow and replow a kitchen garden." When Dwight Eisenhower in 1945 could speak of a "kinship" between London and Abilene, it meant that things had changed in Abilene.[19]

One sure local sign of the change in the 1950s was the struggle over the building of the Tuttle Creek dam near Manhattan. As early as 1933 there had been a proposal for Kiro dam and reservoir west of Topeka, and there were federal studies in 1938 of the possibility of placing a dam along the Big Blue River, where it flowed into the Kansas River through limestone hills. Tuttle Creek, for which the eventual dam was named, was a tributary of the Blue, but controlling the Blue was the main event. A dam at such a strategic site, the Corps of Army Engineers argued, would provide recreational opportunities in the large lake behind it and, more to the point, control the flooding that had done so much damage to Manhattan, Topeka, and Kansas City in 1903.

From the beginning, however, there was determined and organized opposition in the Blue Valley, where rich farms and towns and a scenic landscape would be destroyed. The residents thought the dam would be an environmental disaster and that flood control would be better handled through "stopping the water where it falls" by means of small ponds and watershed management. The latter could be accomplished partly by contouring and terracing on farms. In 1944 the opposition published a booklet, "Flood Control in Reverse," showing people and animals fleeing to the hills to escape the rising waters and painting a picture of "social destruction" through federal engineering and financing. They found hope in the 1944 Flood Control Act that provided for review by the affected states of proposed projects. Until 1951, at least, the critics seemed in a strong position to stop this particular project.

In that year, however, came the floods, panic, and, on the part of the Corps of Engineers, hubris. The head of the corps said that had the Tuttle Creek dam existed, the damage of the 1951 flood (estimated at nearly $1 billion and affecting 183 towns) could have been prevented. "Those who saw the Kaw basin in July 1951," said a Corps of Engineers representative, "with flood waters extending from bluff to bluff, must sense that nothing short of great works is needed to control the torrents that will otherwise flood the

lowlands of our rivers and their tributaries." For a time there were thirty–
four federal dams proposed for Kansas, to cost over $700 million.[20] "Sitting
here and watching the by-play by the papers," wrote Rolla Clymer in 1952, "I
have come to the conclusion that Kansas can hardly escape having three–
four big dams. I don't know what else will satisfy some of these red-hots or
how they can be prevented from having what they lust for."[21]

Brinkerhoff wrote that the flood controversy "baffles description" and
that in it was "the making of a fine quarrel coming up in Kansas unless
everybody gets what everybody wants." He added that the Corps of Engineers proposals were

> a farce of the first degree. I have been disgusted no end with the pell mell
> rush on the part of some politicians and some would be leaders to pre-
> vent future floods. It has been my contention for some time that the
> crackpot outfit in Washington is trying to build dams everywhere for the
> purpose of making power and for recreation purposes, instead of provid-
> ing for flood control. "Flood control" is largely a disguise for the idea of
> creating boating and fishing and picnicking along with power. The power
> is to be used for destroying private industry. The recreation is to be
> provided for those in the future who work one day a week and play the
> other six.[22]

The outspoken editor wondered if he might have lived too long.

The Blue Valley Association, through its spokesman Glen Stockwell,
fought on. Rural farmwives visited the new presidential nominee, Eisenhower, in Denver to present their case. Congressman Albert Cole, who, after
the flood, had thrown his support to the dam builders, was defeated in the
Republican landslide year of 1952 by a seventy-three-year-old Democrat,
Howard Miller, on that single issue. For a time, there seemed to be agreement that Tuttle Creek would be a "dry" dam, where farming would be
possible except in times when it was needed for flood control. Ultimately,
however, the project went up as originally planned. Construction on the
Tuttle Creek dam, towering 135 feet over the valley and backing up a lake fifty
miles long, was completed in 1962.[23]

Kansas's minority reaction to this modern solution, though ultimately
futile, is instructive about the cultural as well as the economic stakes. "They
will pay us for our land," wrote a woman to Governor Frank Carlson in 1948,
"but what about all the beautiful old memories we will be leaving behind?"[24]

Construction of the Tuttle Creek dam, 1958.
Courtesy of the Kansas State Historical Society.

Wrote another opponent, "What right have we to destroy farm homes and thousands of acres of valuable land to build frog ponds, there is no more logic to this than Hitler's scheme to drive the Jews out of Germany."[25] The regional propaganda spoke of "Dam Foolishness."

Stockwell worked hard and long, with some help from the Isaac Walton League and other nascent national environmental organizations, as well as the National Farmers' Union, to make a case more general than one of bitterness harbored by a few farmers at having to sacrifice for the greater good.[26] He wrote Governor Arn in 1951 that his association wanted "an honest evaluation of all known means of water control, knowing that it would take more than a silly row of dams above a valley full of local water." He wanted a "western program for western men." Meanwhile, farmers refused entrance to their land to dam planners and warned, "we would not like to have any violence in our peaceful valley."[27] The Blue Valley organization wrote the Kansas senators that the flood had created a "panic psychology" and that reaction should not be allowed to cause the nation "to plunge blindly into a career of reckless, wasteful and destructive river basin spending."[28] Stockwell collected his own statistics on the prediction that the dam could have stopped the 1951 flood. It would not have stopped it, he said, particularly if it were not a dry dam and already backing up a lake nearly full for recreational purposes. Was there not a simple solution? "I maintain that it is both moral and criminal negligence to allow people to rebuild in the flooded area without adequate warning of the danger."[29] It was, he said, "almost a personal feud" from the point of view of the army engineers. "They have long resented the fact that a group of residents of the Blue Valley have stymied them. They have laid low for years waiting until a big flood. The trouble now is that the flood was too big."[30]

Stockwell thought their side had a chance. "We are just a small group of farmers and small town people," he wrote, "without political support, no slush fund, or lobby but we have the right side of the argument and a spirit to fight for it."[31] That might have been enough at one time in Kansas, or had the debate been limited to Kansas (an independent Kansas study recommended against the dam), it might have been enough, even in 1951.[32]

The arguments were strong, and Stockwell's allies many. Arthur Carhart, who wrote an article in *Atlantic Monthly* on the issue and then a book, *Water—or Your Life,* agreed with Stockwell that the corps schemes were "screw-ball, unsound, fantastic, in many instances."[33] Walter Kollmorgen from the Department of Geography at the University of Kansas pointed out in an article that "floodplains sometimes flood" and suggested adapting to the environment rather than modifying it. "It seems somewhat unkind . . . to picture a flooding river as a vicious beast that has escaped its cage." The federal Tennessee Valley Authority (TVA) "in fact liberated the Tennessee Valley from flood hazards by the simple expedient of flooding the entire valley. . . . This is a cure with a vengeance."[34] Stockwell said, "Civilized man has shed his ancient mores like a coat. He draws his water from a faucet and dumps his sewage into the streams and is so far removed from his environmental landscape that he locates indiscriminately in the flood plains."[35] A Kansas farmer could advise him better, if anyone would listen. Elmer Peterson, once private secretary to Kansas governor Henry Allen, told the Kansas Watershed Association in Topeka that it was "gallant" of Kansans to oppose "the most powerful lobby ever seen" and that such opposition was right. The dam projects were "scientifically as obsolete as the horse and buggy." Floods dumped topsoil not only on front porches but also on land, and that process was the "elixir of life." One hundred years hence, he said, "historians will say that one of the most stupid political policies of the year 1951 was to try to control plowland area floods by imprisoning huge bodies of muddy water—behind high midstream dams. Of course it is spectacular, and how unthinking people love it!"[36]

However, the U.S. environmentalist movement was young, and as so many people were learning around the country, the postwar federal government was both powerful and patient.[37] The Flood Control Act of 1936 had put the federal government in control of national water resources.[38] This dam was a $90 million project, and those who believed in it in Washington and in Kansas were not ready to abandon it. Stockwell called it an "orgiastic fantasy," going well beyond the dictates of reason.[39] "They are diabolically clever," Elmer Peterson wrote. "All they have to do is to sit around in swivel-chairs in Washington and think up new devilment."[40] The Blue Valley Association's propaganda film never showed the faces of the army engineers—just their boots tramping through Kansas.[41] "The Corps of Engineers," countered a corps representative to a Kansas audience, "builds dams that do not fail."[42]

Congressmen Clifford Hope, relying on his long experience with Kansas and with Congress, at first held out some prospect to Stockwell that the dam, which Hope personally opposed, might be stopped. But, he said, it would be due to a technical accident, not a groundswell of popular opinion. It might get lost among so many hundreds of projects. But should it come up, it would pass. "I doubt if anyone in the Kansas delegation would want to take the responsibility of trying to eliminate the item in the bill which provides for starting work on Tuttle Creek. I further doubt that it could be done if there was anyone who would wish to undertake that step."[43]

There continued to be questions. Perhaps the watershed management would work, some observers said, but implementing it required nine hundred small dams, which might take twenty years to complete, and the downstream cities wanted immediate relief. A second alternative, recommended by the 1953 governor's independent survey board report provided by the Kansas Industrial Development Commission, suggested development of flow ways and local protection, such as was done by Wichita's Big Ditch, combined with flood zone planning. The report called the big dam system "obsolete." But the fact that Tuttle Creek "never had any official sanction" from the State of Kansas did not really matter.[44]

Kenneth Davis, who grew up in Manhattan and was once an employee of the Soil Conservation Service, added a Personal Conclusion to his 1976 history of the state, in which he commented on the changes Tuttle Creek brought in a manner reflecting the view of those people who were adapting to modern trends.[45] The sixteen-thousand-acre lake was a surprising sight, he thought, but, he said, "The completed project . . . with its picnic and camping areas, marinas, and swimming beaches, does definitely enhance the quality of life in my old hometown." There were twenty flood control and recreation reservoirs across the state by the time Davis wrote, and it was, he said, a boon to "a state whose natives used to drive for hours to recreate themselves in or beside a muddy five-acre pond." He thought there was grandeur in historic Kansas streams (the Wakarusa, Walnut, Marais des Cygnes, Neosho, Republican, Solomon, Smoky Hill) "caught and held by twentieth-century engineering, in quiet and deep repose." The lakes they formed (Clinton, Melvern, Perry, Waconda, John Redmond, Milford, Glen Elder, Webster, Fall River, Toronto, Pomona, Webster, Kirwin, Cheney, Wilson, Wolf Creek, El Dorado, Cedar Bluff, Kanopolis) "startle the vision when first encountered," he wrote. "One sees them initially as contradictions of the drouthy treeless plain. . . . They jar and grate upon the sensibilities as contradictions and artificialities commonly do." Soon, however, "the vision becomes accustomed; whereupon each lake acquires a beauty at once strange and natural."[46]

Not only were there reservoirs that impounded floodwaters, but also there were those whose primary purpose was to provide drinking water for growing cities. Such a project was Cheney reservoir, west of Wichita, completed in 1965.[47] But a reservoir was only part of what Wichita needed to supply its water.

The city's population doubled in the decade of the 1940s; and its infrastructure, including the supply and delivery system for water, based on the unreliable Arkansas River, was inadequate. Compounding the problem was the drought of the 1950s, in which day after day the state's climate was compared unfavorably with that of the Sahara Desert, and people had only their green Wichita-built Vornado fans and air conditioners to comfort them. There was increased demand for irrigation water by regional farmers and increased use of pesticides and commercial fertilizers by the same farmers, which polluted runoff into reservoirs. To bypass these problems, Wichita built a large pipeline to the Halstead area in the 1950s to use water from wells in the so-called Equus Beds there, an underground aquifer that was said to contain enough water to supply Wichita for one hundred years. In doing so, the city created conflicts not only with farmers but also with sportsmen who hunted ducks in the wetlands of that area.[48]

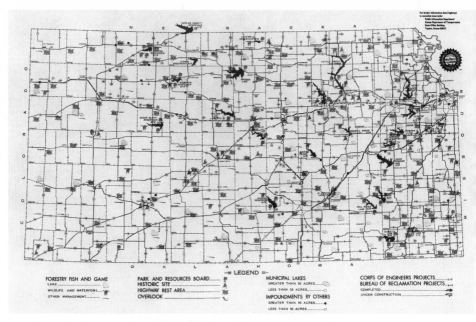

Map of Kansas recreation areas, 1983.
Courtesy of the Kansas State Historical Society.

A. E. Howse led the move for Wichita's tapping the Equus Beds, named for the Latin word for horse because fossils of prehistoric horses were found in these Tertiary period sands.[49] He emphasized that the beds extended over one thousand square miles and that the water there was five-and-one-half-times greater than all the surface water in Kansas. It was "underutilized," he averred, and could supply Wichita without hurting others. Besides, it was a modern, high technology method for solving a modern problem. Howse responded to members of the Central Kansas Water Conservation Association, who sued Wichita, that he had "made clear in the most friendly possible way, that we must have additional water, and we intend to get it in an orderly, decent, neighborly fashion if possible. Failing that, we would be derelict in our duty to the citizens of Wichita if we did not pursue every remedy the law permits."[50] Industry, growth, urban modernism, and the environment were coming into conflict—a contest that was to be typical of Kansas in the late twentieth century.

Studies of the Equus Beds began in the 1930s, and Wichita had pumped some water from them since 1940, but serious moves to develop them began in 1952 when Wichita voters approved the development of twenty wells and a pipeline.[51] It cost the city over $11 million, which was supplemented by a federal grant of over $1 million on the grounds that there was a water emergency at the defense plants in Wichita that were building planes for the Korean War and at nearby McConnell Air Force Base, training fighter pilots for the same conflict.[52] Farmers felt blindsided. Charles Wilson of Burrton, speaking for the conservation association, paraphrased William Jennings Bryan's 1896 protest in saying, "They come with this $11 million cross of gold after our water, and they offer us a cross of thorns." There were threats by farmers to interrupt the laying of the pipeline, and the conservation association raised $25,000 to fight it through legal action.[53] The water would not last Wichita or anyone else for a hundred years, the protestors said, but the aquifer would be quickly drawn down and an irreplaceable resource would be lost.[54] By 1954 there were eleven lawsuits pending against the Equus project.[55] The good old days around Halstead began to be designated as "B.W."—i.e., Before Wichita.[56]

Everyone seemed to have a solution, especially the "tablecloth engineers" in the small towns, who thought that Wichita should dam the Ninnescah River as a cheaper solution to its water problem. Wichita said it was not cheaper and that the water was not as good.[57] However, in 1955 the Wichita City Commission voted to build a $30 million reservoir on the Ninnescah, in case the Equus Bed use was slowed by the lawsuits.[58] That never happened, but Cheney reservoir transpired to supplement the well supplies. The Kansas Supreme Court upheld the constitutionality of the 1945 Kansas Water Rights law providing for permits to the Equus Beds.[59] The U.S. Supreme Court upheld Wichita's right to condemn land for its pipeline to the Equus Beds, and the opposition slowly used up its cards.[60] A small flow of 4 million gallons daily began through the sixty-six-inch pipeline to the Equus Beds in June 1956. The *Wichita Eagle* wrote that it represented "a victory by the city over some of the most determined opposition ever faced in Kansas over a water pipeline."[61] Heavy rains in 1958 recharged the Equus Beds and further weakened the farmers' environmental arguments.[62] Cheney water began to be used in 1965, relieving some pressure on the wells.[63]

The forces of evil in Wichita could then turn their attention to fluoridating the water that was coming from the Equus Beds in order to promote dental health. This piece of modernism, however, they were never able to sell to local people, losing a local vote on the subject in 1964.[64] Supporters of fluoridation, which included most of the medical profession, were charged with being procommunists who were trying to promote "mass medication for a non-communicable disease" in a violation by government of individual rights. Kansas was still Kansas in the sense that moral idealism continued to enter heavily into everyday pragmatic decisions. But modernism and science, and doing things as others did them, was a much stronger force than heretofore.

The passion to be modern in Kansas could be seen, not only in the snaking through the state of the federally funded and mandated Interstate Highway system but also in the organization and construction of the Kansas Turnpike. At its completion in 1956, befinned cars could roar through the Flint Hills at a posted speed limit of eighty miles per hour, a national record. The Maine Turnpike, which opened in 1947, demonstrated that turnpikes worked and that four-lane, limited-access roads were safer than older roads.[65] In 1953 there were over eight hundred fifty thousand cars licensed in Kansas.[66] That year Governor Arn named a Kansas Turnpike Authority, whose expenses were funded not from the general fund but from the income of the state highway commission. The power of eminent domain was extended to this authority, and it had the right to issue bonds.

The route was never much in doubt. It was to connect the two urban population centers of the state, Kansas City and Wichita, by way of Topeka and Lawrence. True, for a time it ended in a field at the border of Kansas south of Wichita, but shortly the interstate system took care of connections.[67] The idea, the promoters said, was "to build ultra-modern express highways with private money, pay them out and maintain them through tolls . . . and ultimately turn the paid-out investment into the state road system."[68] Except for the last promise that the turnpike would eventually become a free state highway, it all came to pass.

The turnpike was a vast undertaking. Its $160 million bond issue was the largest ever to that time in Kansas.[69] Its 236-mile ribbon shortened the former route by two-lane road by thirty-six miles. Originally it had nine interchanges, 227 grade separations, and several service plazas.[70] At the groundbreaking ceremony at the frozen Kansas River in Lawrence, Governor Arn, who operated a power shovel himself to turn the first earth, said the toll highway "begins a great new era of progress for Kansas."[71] Wrote the first general manager, Gale Moss, borrowed from the highway department and paid the then-surprising salary of twenty-five thousand dollars a year: "I live the business of building roads."[72]

Kansas turnpike in the Flint Hills, 1960.
Courtesy of the Kansas State Historical Society.

The English poet laureate John Masefield wrote a paean to the turnpike ("Our White Road Westward"), read at its opening in 1956. To be kind, it was perhaps not his best effort. "May this Road's Angels blessedly fulfill / The inmost Hope of travelers of goodwill / May those who seek Love, find; those Knowledge, learn. / To all gay, going-forth and glad return."[73] Perhaps on a more appropriate level of culture, Gene Autry and his horse Champion pushed through a large paper map of the highway in Kansas City to open it figuratively.[74]

But whether turnpike travelers found love or knowledge at the end of the trip, they certainly got to a business meeting in Wichita or a football game in Lawrence much faster than before. At its opening, the turnpike boasted six swank restaurants at the service areas, which included futuristic water towers that looked like golf balls on tees to many observers. Estimates were that 7 million trips would be made on the turnpike the first year and nearly 10 million by 1961.[75] People were impressed, particularly in the early months

Highway 10 east of Lawrence, 1950.
Courtesy of the Kansas State Historical Society.

when there was no speed limit at all. The road made high speed seem easy and secure. The sharpest curve was three degrees and the steepest hill has a 3 percent rise. Porcelainized green aluminum signs with raised reflective lettering, developed exclusively for the Kansas Turnpike and later used almost universally on interstates, made navigation at speed easy. Reflectors at the roadside kept hurtling drivers on track at night almost in the manner of runway landing lights at an airport.[76]

Financial success, however, was not immediate. Governor Hall intervened to lessen the help the Turnpike Authority was getting from the state highway department, insisting it sink or swim as a purely private venture. No one liked to contemplate what would happen to hundreds of miles of concrete diagonally crossing Kansas if it were simply to be abandoned.[77] However, not only were projections of traffic and revenue not met in the early years, but there were also concerns about safety and about the impact on the environment.[78] One farmer said, "As far as we're concerned, it's the same as if they'd routed the Kaw River up through these hills."[79] Some people thought the speed limit was outrageous and were surprised that one could get a ticket on the turnpike for going too slowly. The Wild West had returned, an editor commented: "The Sunflower state must be switching to lilies of the valley."[80] The road's fatality rate, although lower than standard roads per passenger miles traveled, was in 1963 the worst among eighteen toll roads in the nation.[81] It took five years for the turnpike to turn a profit, compared with the predicted three, and the high maintenance costs made it unlikely that it would ever become a free road.[82] Wrote one editor, "Even Rome, we imagine, looked a little ragged around the edges the first year of its existence."[83]

There was competition in the 1970s and 1980s from interstates, particularly from a piece of I-35, which many people took from Emporia to Kansas City as a free alternative to the turnpike. However, other turnpike proposals for Kansas, prominently one from Kansas City to Galena along the eastern border of the state and another connecting southeast Kansas and Wichita, did not come to fruition.[84] The turnpike's use was increasingly heavy. By 1976 nearly 8 billion miles had been traveled on it since the opening, and one observer called the "new super cow trail" the "best and longest road of its type west of the Mississippi River."[85]

There was a "predictable plasticity" about turnpike and interstate culture. The franchised Howard Johnson's along the turnpike were not like the little home-cooking restaurant at Alma in the Flint Hills where people used to stop, but it was fast, and one could get gas and maybe read a historical marker. The new roads went through dull and flat sections of Kansas and whisked people "right past most of the byways where America's distinctiveness dwells." But a three-hundred-mile trip, once a day's work, was nothing, and people thought of one-thousand-mile days with the wife and kids and the boat behind. The sacred Waconda Springs was deep beneath the reservoir where the motorboat pulled the skiers. A virtual sea behind Tuttle Creek buried the Blue Valley. But fewer people remembered those former local landscapes anyway. The roads had "extended the practical horizons of the everyday citizen by leagues, and become the ultimate agent of his liberation from the bonds of geography." Kansas was proud that an eight-mile segment of what became I-70 was the first in the country to be completed with funds provided by the Federal Aid Highway Act of 1956 that brought interstates into being by paying 90 percent of their cost. That system cost $62 billion by 1976.[86] It was frustrating to drive the fast roads during the fifty-five-mile-

Flint Hills, Waubaunsee County.
Courtesy of the Kansas State Historical Society.

speed-limit days of Jimmy Carter, but over 11 million vehicles used the turnpike in 1978, despite tolls that had gone to $5.75 from the $3.80 it originally had cost to make the trip.[87] Governor Robert Bennett's "potty patrol" had made sure the rest rooms were clean. In the mid-1980s the toll was $7.00, but people still loved to tear through the Flint Hills on their way somewhere in a hurry, connected with the world.[88]

Kansas continued to be a seedbed for entrepreneurial development. Hill's dog food facility in Topeka created an employee program that was the subject of business case studies, and Frank and Dan Carney in 1958 started a small pizza restaurant in Wichita called Pizza Hut, which shortly revolutionized both the fast food and franchising business far more than had its Kansas fast food predecessors, White Castle hamburgers and Kings-X. Sam Marcus developed MBPXL into a national force in meatpacking from his Kansas base. And perhaps most striking, though less well known internationally, were the varied activities of Ray Hugh Garvey. In the 1950s Garvey's major focus was the building of grain elevators.

The Garvey family ran its business in the 1950s as individual proprietorships. Ray Garvey had bought and constructed some small elevators in western Kansas and Colorado in the 1930s and 1940s to serve his wheat farming operation. That farming empire expanded to one hundred thousand acres in the early 1940s on his hunch that returning rain would allow

R. H. Garvey's Wichita elevator.
Courtesy of the Kansas State Historical Society.

wheat to be grown in the deserts of eastern Colorado. High storage prices, short supply of warehousing, and a federal program to offer tax benefits through rapid cost amortization for people willing to build large terminal elevators pushed or tempted the Garveys into the terminal storage business. By the time of Ray Garvey's death in an auto accident in 1959, the Garvey elevators incorporated about 200 million bushels of capacity, most of it in Kansas, and had shifted the former regional concentration of storage and milling in the Kansas City area to various points in the region. Garvey had major terminal elevators in Topeka, Salina, Atchison, and Wichita as well as in Lincoln, Nebraska, and Ft. Worth, Texas.[89]

The banks with which the family dealt in New York City and Chicago at first thought that elevators were devices used to reach the upper stories of tall buildings. Therefore it was difficult getting financing, even in the 1950–1955 period when rapid amortization for tax purposes and federal guarantees of storage in the new elevators seemed to make loan repayment nearly a sure thing. The Garveys convinced financial institutions and continued elevator building long after the special government incentives ceased. Over half the eventual capacity was constructed after 1955. Garvey "paid tuition," as he put it, and learned the business so well that he and his construction partners, Chalmers and Borton of Hutchinson, became well known in the trade as some of the most efficient builders and operators of large elevators in the nation. Garvey would send out postcards showing his latest structures with the simple message, "Aren't Elevators Beautiful!"[90]

He was criticized often, almost as virulently as when he had tried a farming corporation in Kansas in the 1930s. A *Chicago News* article in 1954 took the standard line that "big Kansas wheat growers had a front seat on the gravy train carrying federal 90 per cent parity price support loans on the 1952 crop." Garvey's name showed up as one of the biggest recipients of farm subsidies in the nation, not to mention the tax incentives for the elevator building. The Garvey family's annual storage rent from the federal government was about $20 million in 1959. Therefore, to the critics, it appeared that despite Garvey's free enterprise and antigovernment talk, he was, as were so many new-style Kansans, in the position of being a kind of federal dependent.[91] Garvey's response was always that he did not make the rules, he only played by them, that "we pay considerably more taxes than we get, as do most people," and that to be without subsidies in a subsidized industry was to court disaster. His son James was more caustic about it. He noted that the *News* was sent out through subsidized bulk mail prices.[92] "The Congress and bureaucrats offered the programs," James wrote; "we participated, complied, and are criticized."[93] The *Hutchinson News* editorialized, "This fretting about Garvey merely points up the curious nature of America's half-breed economy which, with the abandon of a roving pack of canines, has become part socialism, part free enterprise."[94]

There was the matter, too, of simple challenge. In 1892 Topeka had been the second largest milling center in the United States, next only to Minneapolis, and Garvey thought it was time for Kansas to be big again in storage and milling. Salina had 6.5 million bushels of storage in 1953 when Garvey started operations there; in 1958, it had 40 million. Topeka went from 2.5 million to 30 million from 1950 to 1958.[95] In 1958 Garvey's Wichita elevator, at 23 million bushels capacity, was the largest in the world and expanding as fast as tanks could be added. "It gives a utilitarian beauty to the landscape southwest of Wichita," the local newspaper commented.[96] "We are probably a bit silly to extend ourselves to build this," Garvey wrote in 1954. "We are in a position, however, to build these, we believe, as few others are, and feel that those who can should. We have an interest in this entirely separate from the financial incentive. While not easy, it is a lot of fun to build elevators."[97]

Politics was not dismissed in such an age of business, although business issues did loom large at the statehouse. The Eisenhower era in the Kansas legislature was characterized by regular debates about two issues—a severance tax on oil and gas and a Right-to-Work law. The severance tax was the more surprising of the two to some people who hardly thought of Kansas as having an environmental agenda, but it reflected national trends toward regarding oil and gas as not only the property of landowners but also as an irreplaceable resource of the state. For conservatives, such a tax had the virtue of promising a reduction in property taxes. A severance tax passed in 1957 but was declared unconstitutional, and the issue hung fire into the 1980s when a severance tax law was eventually passed. Not so with the Right-to-Work law, which became an amendment to the Kansas Constitution in 1958 after vigorous debate.

Right to Work was as unpopular with unions as had been the Court of Industrial Relations in the 1920s, and they regarded it as directed toward the same end, union busting. The labor movement in Kansas was hardly radical. Former governor Payne Ratner and the Catholic Church were among those opposing Right to Work. Wichita's union publication, the *Plaindealer*, represented a continued strong Kansas tradition of union sympathy and liberal thought but was hardly akin to the old *Appeal to Reason*. It often contained conservative Christian editorials along the lines of "Jesus the Worker." The paper editorialized in 1953, "Kansas has reason to be very proud of its sound labor legislation and of the splendid record of labor and management reflected in steady production." But it warned that a Right-to-Work proposition, essentially outlawing the union shop, represented a dangerous trend.[98] That year's bill, called the "Right to Scab" or "Right to Jerk" bill by the labor press, failed, thanks to a massive lobby. "The legislation is particularly shocking," wrote one labor leader, "because it deals with imaginary evils that have never existed in the state of Kansas."[99]

Employer groups, however, continued to promote Right-to-Work legislation of a type that existed in about seventeen other states, mostly in the South.[100] Kansans for the Right to Work, headed by Reed Larson, who went on to head the national Right to Work Office, and by Louis Weiss of Augusta, was a well-organized, well-funded organization and effective in advancing its argument. The name of the movement itself was a masterpiece and evinced the strong political appeal of the argument against the closed shop.

The organization's 1955 film *The American Way* was well made, according even to labor groups, and Larson and Reed dared to present it to labor groups at the Electrical Workers Hall on South Broadway in 1956. They argued that the law was not directed against unions but that it was "against moral and democratic rights" to force a person to join a union. The union men there confessed that speaking to unions and answering questions was a good gesture, but one commented, "You can't change a good union man's mind in 15 minutes, in 15 years, or ever, on this question of 'right-to-work.'"[101] Labor made a film, *The Strongest Link,* to counter it.[102] The union people quoted Finley Peter Dunne, the mock Irish humorist of the early twentieth century, who had defined the open shop as "where they kape the door open to accommodate the min comin in to take jobs cheaper than the min that has the jobs."[103]

Governor Hall vetoed a bill that passed the legislature in 1955, with five Democrats and sixty-one Republicans supporting it in the House.[104] That action made Hall, already controversial, considerably more so. "No public reaction to an executive move in the last third of a century," wrote the Kansas political observer A. L. Schultz, "has equaled the protests following veto of the labor bill. Thousands of letters, telegrams, phone calls and personal interviews swamped Governor Hall and his secretarial staff."[105] Hall spoke at the national Young Republican convention against the GOP old guard, saying that the progressive Republican tradition that William Allen White and the Bull Moosers had once represented in Kansas was still alive and well and represented the future of the party. The delegates and the eastern press were impressed, and a Topeka paper noted, "Kansas is no longer scorned by the politically wise among the national news writers."[106] Hall debated with the Democratic governor of Georgia (which had a compulsory open shop bill) on Right to Work in fall 1955 to national publicity. The Kansas governor said that Right-to-Work bills were designed "to put an instrument in the hands of the unscrupulous employer to do away with the principle of collective bargaining." Weiss, of the Kansas Right to Work movement, responded that Hall's talk was an "insult to the Kansas legislature" and came from Hall's "apparent obligation to the union czars." His "distortion of the facts," Weiss said, "is aimed at smoke-screening the real issue and justifying his denial of a fundamental American right."[107] The lines were drawn.

The major issue in the party platforms in Kansas in the 1956 elections was the Right-to-Work question. Democrats argued that the right to contract included the right to organize unions and make them exclusive, and they advanced the union argument that it was an unjustified "free ride" for employees to benefit from union gains without supporting the organization that made them. Republicans emphasized that Kansas had had a law for over fifty years guaranteeing a worker's right to join a union but that a worker should have the right also to refuse to join a union.[108] George Docking, a banker and a Democrat who "combined conservatism on fiscal policy with social liberalism," became governor in 1956, beginning the most successful Democratic dynasty in Kansas history. But even that did not mean the end of Right to Work.[109] The legislature was still Republican, and Kansans were still split on the issue. A Right-to-Work joint resolution passed in spring 1957, easily in the state senate but barely in the house. It went to the voters at large in 1958 as a constitutional amendment, and the voters approved it.[110]

Labor mounted a strong defense against the amendment, touring the rural districts of the state on Labor Day 1958 to make the argument to farmers that they should be sympathetic to the problems of their urban working brethren.[111] George Meany of the AFL–CIO called Right-to-Work laws a "high-powered, brazen lie," and William Smith, S.J., characterized them as "an appeal to exaggerated individualism."[112] After the vote, the unions concluded that they were poorly funded amateurs compared to the Right to Work movement in Kansas.[113] In 1958 Right-to-Work laws failed in five of the six states where they were proposed, Kansas being the only exception.[114] "The films they had on television," wrote the editor of the *Plaindealer,* "even though they were pure fiction, certainly had their effect, especially on women voters."[115] The proponents used modern political techniques well to push an issue with some national momentum to passage in Kansas. The opponents could answer only that the states that had Right to Work were not growing as fast as others and that Kansas union members would work for repeal.

Another controversial area where Kansas history provided an ambiguous legacy was that of race. The institution of partial school segregation, beginning in 1879, belied the liberal attitudes of the majority of Kansans during the territorial struggles. Familiarity with the segregation system in the twentieth century seemed to serve mostly to solidify an "out of sight, out of mind" set of racial attitudes in Kansas, the battle over *Birth of a Nation* notwithstanding. Segregation was a question on which Kansas showed little originality until forced to change by the federal courts.

Certainly there had always been doubts among Kansans as to the justice of the issue. The Kansas Supreme Court, in *Board of Education of Ottawa, Kansas v. Leslie Timmon* (1881), upheld on the narrowest possible technical grounds the right of local school boards to institute segregation while ques-

tioning in the written opinion the general premises upon which state authorization for such separation was based. Justice Daniel Valentine wrote, "Is it
not better for the grand aggregate of human society, as well as for individuals, that all children should mingle together and learn to know each other?"
Why should two children, "equally intelligent and equally advanced in their
studies," be separated in school because of their color? One historian, com-
paring the segregation situation in Louisiana and Kansas, noted that unlike
the stark contrasts between pro- and anti-integration forces in Louisiana,
"in Kansas, divisions were blurred, struggles often inconclusive, and legal
questions narrow." There were at least fourteen cases on school integration
in Kansas between 1880 and 1910, though the basics did not change. Often
blacks, represented by black attorneys, won these cases, and integration was
ordered in those many school districts and situations where segregation was
illegal in Kansas. The court even sometimes declared that integration "was a
fitting remedy for extreme inequalities even in first-class cities," where it was
technically legal but not required that elementary schools be segregated.
However, in 1900, when the Kansas Supreme Court squarely faced the issue
of whether any segregation was constitutional, it decided that it was.[116]

And so the issue rested until 1950, when Linda Brown, an eight-year-old
black girl, was denied permission to enroll in Sumner Elementary School in
Topeka. Her father took her there, concerned about the danger of her walking to and from Monroe Elementary School, which she had attended for
some time. The fact that both these Kansas schools became national historic
landmarks resulted from the train of legal events that that rather mundane
and not unexpected experience set off. A challenge to the tenuous segregation laws of Kansas led on appeal to the overthrow nationally of the separate
but equal doctrine promulgated by the U.S. Supreme Court in the case of
Plessy v. Feguson (1896). And it changed American society in a fundamental manner.[117]

Of course, in many ways it was incidental that the test case that finally led
to the change came from Kansas. Few Kansans, a participant in the case
remembers, "were conscious of the significance of the case," even when it
was being adjudicated before the U.S. Supreme Court, "nor could they
foresee its impact on history." However, the National Association for the
Advancement of Colored People had been pursuing legal remedies actively
for nearly two decades, and the Brown family was far from alone or unsup-
ported in its case. Moreover, according to Paul Wilson, a Kansas attorney on

the *Brown* case, the NAACP concentrated on Kansas especially because of its unusual history and the role of race in that history. It was also true that segregation was less firmly entrenched there, practically and philosophically, than in many of the twenty-two other states that allowed it in schools. At any rate, it was *Brown v. Board of Education of Topeka*, commenced in February 1951 in the U.S. District Court for the District of Kansas, that became the test case ending segregation as an option in schools nationwide.[118]

The *Brown* case marked not only the end of segregation in schools but also the beginning of a new day in social relationships beyond the school, in Kansas and in the nation. Topeka had been known as a Jim Crow town, despite there being no separate waiting rooms or facilities on buses. According to the historian Richard Kluger, it was in the 1950s a town that "viewed with alarm almost anything that smacked of liberalism or foreign infiltration of the Topekean psyche." There were few black members of unions and "a black clerk at a retail shop or a black stenographer at an insurance company was almost unknown." The main black businesses were beauty and barbershops, barbecue restaurants, and after-hours bars and brothels. Charles Scott, a black attorney, remembered that "you'd look up and down Kansas Avenue early in the morning, and all you could see were blacks washing windows."[119]

The situation was the same elsewhere in Kansas. The *Plaindealer*, a black-owned newspaper in Kansas City edited by James A. Hamlett, kept up a regular barrage of criticism during World War II and immediately after about color-conscious employment at aircraft plants. The president of North American Aviation reportedly announced that blacks would not be hired above the level of janitor in the new Kansas City defense plant. The Kansas legislature responded to that quickly by sending a resolution of protest to the federal government against discrimination in defense industries. This was a factor leading to the issuance of Executive Order 8802, ensuring fair employment in these industries. Yet in 1948 Hamlett reported that white and black students eating lunch together in Lawrence were evicted by the police.[120]

Through the 1960s, however, Lawrence, the home of the University of Kansas and by reputation one of the most liberal of Kansas communities, experienced not only ongoing racial tensions but also considerable open organizing and protests from blacks and whites designed to upset the status quo. Sit-ins and rallies for civil rights mixed with Vietnam War protests to give life, on the cusp of change, a special flavor. In 1970 there were violent riots in Lawrence organized by the Black Student Union in response to the killing of a young black man by a member of the Lawrence Police Department. On the other extreme, a Lawrence group called Loyal American Whites demanded a payment of $500 billion from the "Negro race" to pay for the "expense of educating them from slavery into the American mainstream." In the moderate center, the Lawrence League for the Practice of Democracy aided the Lawrence–Douglas County chapter of the NAACP in passing local antidiscrimination laws.

Issue by issue, in the wake of the *Brown* decision, there was success on the peaceful front. A grassroots campaign to integrate the swimming pools of Lawrence worked, as did one to remove landlords who discriminated against university-approved housing, and one forcing campus organizations to affirm that race was not a consideration for membership. Wilt "the Stilt" Chamberlain of the University of Kansas basketball team claimed that in the 1950s his fame, combined with KU Chancellor Franklin Murphy's threat to open barber shops and cafes on campus to compete with Lawrence's segregated establishments, allowed the seven-foot athlete to integrate establishments for miles around.[121]

Wichita, too, experienced considerable civil rights activity. Ronald Walters and a dozen other members of the Wichita NAACP Youth Council, ranging in age from fifteen to twenty-two, and advised by local attorney Chester Lewis, staged an organized sit-in in 1958 at the Dockum Drug Store downtown. They sat quietly at the counter as though expecting service. The resulting disruption of business forced the entire Rexall chain, of which the Dockum outlet was a part, to begin serving blacks at the counter rather than at a take-out position in the rear as before. This predated the famous sit-in in Greensboro, North Carolina, in February 1960, which is immortalized by the preservation of the counter at the Smithsonian Institution. Lewis led also the successful Wichita campaign in the 1960s for a fair housing ordinance. "There are 25,000 Negroes in Wichita," Lewis said in 1967, "with about 18,000 of them stakeless, powerless and hopeless."[122] There were street riots in protest of what was called the "chittlin' curtain," and a message came from the black community that the election of Wichita's first African-American mayor, Price Woodward, in 1967, and the presence of a few outstanding black businessmen and athletes, was not enough.[123] At the University of Wichita, the president avowed that none of the local fraternities and sororities would be allowed to affiliate with national organizations until those national fraternities and sororities had removed race discrimination clauses from their constitutions.[124] Clearly, it seemed that some of the ideals first advanced during Reconstruction were implemented in the grassroots prairie in the center of America. Kansas in the next decades learned to adjust to a much greater range of diversity. But with African Americans, who had been there and been an object of controversy from the very beginning of Kansas Territory exactly one hundred years before the *Brown* decision, the Sunflower State came to a more definite understanding, overcoming the ambiguous legacy of local option and benign neglect that had so long prevailed.

The division between the unions and the Right-to-Work advocates, as well as the concentration of civil rights direct action in the larger cities of Kansas, reflected the increasing division of interests between rural and urban Kansans. That division, plus the unusual historical situation that had resulted in most of the state's political and educational institutions being located in its northeast corner and the shift in the population centers toward the west, accounted for the special political heat that surrounded a proposal, advanced seriously for the first time in 1955, to admit the Municipal University of Wichita into the state's Board of Regents system.[125]

Harry Corbin, one of the youngest presidents of a major university when he took over the University of Wichita in 1948, envisioned that the school, in addition to its late role as a trainer for Wichita industry and government, would excel in research and graduate programs. He hoped it would increase the quality of its faculty to the point where the term "urban university" would suggest Socrates teaching in the marketplace in Athens more than a smorgasbord of service and technical courses that led to notions of a "trade school" or "Hillside High." Joseph Hudnot of Harvard, speaking in Wichita, noted that the urban university in the future would provide the beauty that the palace gave to the city of the Renaissance and the life that the cathedral gave to the medieval city. More strictly to the point in lobbying with the legislature was that Wichita was the largest city in Kansas and that the local mill levy, which had supported the school since the Congregationalist Fairmount College had become the University of Wichita in 1926, was insufficient to take it where Corbin and some other city leaders wanted it to go. The university had plans to build a new education center designed by Frank Lloyd Wright, and it was in no mood to play educational second fiddle to any state university because of structural bonds.

The battle, however, was fierce and reflected the momentum of a history where colleges were not in large cities and where large cities were not such a factor in the makeup of Kansas. The 1955 joint application of Washburn University and the University of Wichita to be admitted to the state system failed, and WU then went it alone. Wichita, wrote the advocates, was an urban learning laboratory unique in the state. To say that having a state institution there was a duplication of effort was the equivalent of saying that "one marriage partner [could] breathe for both since *both* breathing would be a duplication of effort. . . . No institution is simply one thing or service. . . . The children of the agricultural workers in this country need not all become farmers. The children of the great portion of city dwellers, together with those who migrate to the city from small communities, cannot be confined to a narrow range of educational possibilities." Whitley Austin of the *Salina Journal* felt distinctly otherwise. He wrote, "The basic and ancient difficulty is that each community is concerned only with its own welfare and that each faculty is concerned only with its own dreams of empire." Clyde Reed of the *Parsons Sun* agreed. "Kansas," he wrote, "has no conceivable or plausible need for another state university. . . . This is not a chamber of commerce project."

The state commissioned a series of reports by consultants, beginning with one authored in 1960 by Dr. Robert Keller of the University of Minnesota. This report recommended that WU become part of the state system, accepting Wichita's arguments that state colleges had been established much earlier (in Hays in 1901 and in Pittsburg in 1903) to recognize demographic changes, and now it was time for Wichita. A second report, authored by Alvin Eurich of the Ford Foundation and submitted late in 1962, pleased Wichitans much less. Wichitans were not invited to the press conference in Topeka announcing the results, which were that Eurich recommended that WU be admitted not as a self-standing university but as an "attendance center," to be called the State Universities Center at Wichita. A joint committee from KU and KSU would govern it, and professors would commute from those places on the turnpike. Wichita would provide students and buildings, but all decisions would be made in Lawrence and Manhattan. An editor in Manhattan thought that was just fine: "Kansas . . . shouldn't further dilute the standards of the schools it already has, and it doesn't owe a darn thing to an ambitious Wichita U."

There were protests in Wichita. Corbin said that a complete "severance" from the past of the Wichita school would be unwise. "A basic need of any institution is to be strong enough to elicit pride and loyalty, strong enough to attract excellent teachers and students, strong enough to participate in some meaningful way in the definition of its own purposes in a manner comparable to other institutions with which it shares in fulfilling the State's educational responsibilities and obligations. You cannot provide adequately for the educational needs of the young people in southern Kansas merely by providing a series of classes in which they may enroll."

The Board of Regents, though favoring taking the University of Wichita into the state system, was "unalterably opposed" to a third state university operating independently of the others. The bill making its way through the senate, said Austin, "implies that Wichita would be a full size university granting doctors' degrees." Joe Jagger, a member of the board of directors of the Kansas Farm Bureau, said, "Putting it bluntly, it has been a real strain on our state to keep even with our neighbors. . . . To take on a third costly university can very well be the millstone that could impair forever the quality of the university program in Kansas."[126] Wrote another, "It looks like a pure Chamber of Commerce booster plan to build up a university in Wichita . . . which at first will duplicate present facilities and eventually may try to dominate all other institutions."[127]

At last, and after a series of proposals were tested, Wichita State University entered the state system in 1964. Corbin concluded accurately, "It was more than an education fight. It was a political and economic struggle as well. There will be some resentment of our gains for many years, particularly in some rural areas."[128] His claim that the final bill did open the way for a full third state university offended many legislators, who threatened to withdraw the approval. "Dr. Corbin's statements, I feel," said one, "are an insult to the Legislature and are unique in that he kicks us in the teeth before we even get home. This is not done in the better circles—integrity or no integrity."[129]

The bill was a compromise. The university was required to maintain some of its mill levy to make up for limited private endowment; it was forced for a time into an associate status, with a lot of input from the other state universities in its management; it was de facto prevented from competing in expanding its graduate programs in competition with Manhattan and Lawrence. However, the bill allowed it to retain the title "University" and its own faculty. Corbin resigned as a sacrifice to his enemies, and WSU quickly grew from about six thousand to around fifteen thousand students. Doctoral programs eventually appeared in certain areas consistent with the "urban mission" developed for WSU, but this did not happen until the 1980s.

Ironically, perhaps, but tellingly, there were some observers who believed that a key factor in swinging votes in the state legislature for accepting the Wichita school into the system was legislators' attendance at a basketball game at the new University of Wichita Roundhouse. Dave "the Rave" Stallworth was an all-American, the WU team was nationally rated, and the local fans packed the hall with vociferous enthusiasm. There were some people who thought that the national prominence of Wilt "the Stilt" Chamberlain, the great KU player, was a boon for Kansas, the equivalent to Walter "Big Train" Johnson all over again. And it appeared that legislators who had some doubt about the quality of and the need for WU's academic programs were convinced that night in the Roundhouse that it must be a real university to have such a powerhouse sports program.

The drama of the creation of WSU was played out in the later twentieth century, an era more characterized than ever by publicity and by public relations. The university had a public relations adviser on its lobbying team and understood well that without the image, the reality of a bigger or better university would never advance. Its advisers also understood that Wichita, from which the heroes of Bleeding Kansas did not hail, would have a long road to parity. However, in 1964, the pain was absorbed and the process begun.

Indeed, if everything was up to date in Kansas City, the same was true of Wichita. William Lear arrived there in 1962 from Switzerland, where he had been developing a business jet of revolutionary performance. Wichita attracted him with the issuance of over $1 million in industrial revenue bonds and the provision of land for a plant near the Municipal Airport. In October 1963 a test pilot flew the first Lear Jet from that airport, and it looked and performed wonderfully. By spring 1966, Lear's company had delivered more than one hundred of these craft, representing sales of more than $38 million and adding Lear to the aviation names familiar worldwide that related to Kansas. Frank Sinatra and other famous people visited Wichita so often to check on their Lear Jets that it began to be called Hollywood East.[130]

About the same time occurred another more obscure but equally surprising event, with symbolic and dreary significance for the new age in Kansas. On April 14, 1965, Richard Hickock and Perry Smith were hanged at the state prison for the murder of four members of the Herbert Clutter family near the small western town of Holcomb in November 1959. It was a grisly crime committed by strangers in a heartland farm village where farmers did not even lock their doors and where the motive was jailhouse rumors of money, which Mr. Clutter did not in fact have in the house. Such was the intrusion of modern crime on the supposed idyllic landscape and of sudden death on the Norman Rockwell–type lives of the Clutters that it would have been a kind of regional icon of change in any case. It became more so because the novelist Truman Capote, a flamboyant New Yorker whose society novel *Breakfast at Tiffany's* had been a best-seller, noticed a clipping about the event in the *New York Times* and traveled to Kansas. There he undertook the historical documentary for which his writing talent and near photographic memory for interviews uniquely suited him. Capote in Garden City, the nearest fair-sized town to Holcomb, was a phenomenon. But he gained the confidence of the townspeople, the police, the Kansas Bureau of Investigation officers, and eventually of Hickock and Smith themselves after their arrest and during their long incarceration. He was present that day in 1965 at the hanging, and shortly after, his *New Yorker* articles on the case were incorporated into surely a classic and perhaps unique book of its type: *In Cold Blood.*

Until one morning in November 1959, Capote wrote, few Americans, or Kansans, had heard of Holcomb. "Like the waters of the river, like the motorists on the highway, and like the yellow trains streaking down the Santa Fe tracks, drama, in the shape of exceptional happenings, had never stopped there." But after those shotgun blasts and the discovery of Mr. Clutter with his throat cut, sixteen-year-old Nancy Clutter became the most publicly grieved dead young Kansas woman since Mary White in the 1920s. Moreover, "many old neighbors viewed each other strangely, and as strangers."[131] The riveting detail of Capote's documentary added to the drama through his depiction of the crime and the hanging, written from the point of view of the criminals as well as the victims, the law enforcement people, and members of the community. "The crime was a psychological accident," Capote wrote, "virtually an impersonal act; the victims might as well have been killed by lightning. Except for one thing: they had experienced prolonged terror, they had suffered." The Kansas Death Row, and the hangman in his stained cowboy hat, had its own form of terror. "I believe in hanging," Hickock told Capote, "just so long as I'm not the one being hanged." The four Clutter graves in Garden City's Valley View Cemetery had to be balanced against the "childish feet" of Perry Smith, a man with "the aura of an exiled animal" dangling in the air from a rope.[132]

On capital punishment, federal initiative again ruled. A 1972 U.S. Supreme Court decision, *Furman v. Georgia,* invalidated all existing American death penalty laws, leading to a hiatus in all executions until Gary Gilmore died in Utah in 1977. Kansas struggled especially with the issue, as it always had. Before a new restrictive death penalty law passed in Kansas in 1994, nearly fifty bills were considered in eighteen legislative sessions.

"Kansas' tradition," wrote one student of modern capital punishment, "resembles an abolitionist state more than a death penalty retensionist state, in that it infrequently used the death penalty even when available." The Kansas legislative debate on capital punishment between 1973 and 1994 "reflected a normative ambivalence toward the death penalty that is part of the state's cultural tradition." But the Clutters were remembered. Wrote one journalist in 1994, "Almost 35 years after the Clutter family homestead became a slaughterhouse, Kansas legislators debating the death penalty still speak movingly, almost intimately, of Herb, Bonnie, Nancy, and Kenyon, the four victims no one can forget."[133] It was a shock of shocks to the "it can't happen here" school of regional analysis.

LIKE THE NATIONS

The new year of 1979 in Kansas began with record low temperatures —twenty below zero in some areas on the first several days of January. Not by accident, this was the time chosen for the delivery of the 380-ton, $50 million Westinghouse nuclear reactor that was to be the core of the first nuclear generating plant in Kansas, the Wolf Creek plant near Burlington. The plant was to create the steam to drive the turbines that would provide electricity for Kansas City and Wichita in the late twentieth century. The reactor vessel was forty feet long and twenty feet in diameter, made of carbon steel with a covering of stainless steel, and with space for over fifty thousand uranium fuel rods. It had come by barge from Chattanooga, Tennessee, and made its final journey into Kansas on a two-hundred-foot, twenty-two-axle rail car, attached to a train that the local protestors dubbed the Wolf Creek Express. The train entered Kansas on Thursday evening, January 11. One small boy commented about the reactor vessel: "I thought it was going to be a bomb." And it did look like one, but it had a banner on its side: "Wolf Creek Plant: Saves Oil . . . Makes Jobs . . . Saves Money."

Scattered along the back roads in Coffey County, where the plant was under construction, were members of the Kansas Natural Guard, camped in tents and teepees. They flew an early U.S. flag with thirteen stars to mark what they thought was a new revolution against the tyranny of centralization and a kind of high-tech mercantilism. They planned to stop the train by lying on the tracks, thus expressing their strong opposition to a nuclear future. Tony Blaufuss, a Roman Catholic priest with the protestors, said, "We decided to participate only after a lengthy study of the problems and prayerful consideration of the effects of our action. It seemed to us that we needed to exercise our responsibility to alert people to the danger. . . . There are situations when we disregard laws for a more important reason. . . . We believe our action is in the Christian tradition."

On January 12 around 2:00 P.M. the Missouri Pacific train carrying the reactor and the small group of protesters met on the Kansas prairie northwest of Aliceville. The group joined hands and marched to the railroad tracks, shouting "take that damn thing back to Chattanooga, Tennessee." Police arrested thirty-six people. Seven went to jail, and the rest paid fines of forty dollars. The train stopped for only thirty minutes. When the reactor—a thing "of technical beauty" according to the Kansas Gas and Electric engineers who welcomed it—arrived at the construction site, Superintendent Jesse Auterburn walked over to it and said, "Welcome Home, Baby." To others, however, nothing seemed less at home than a nuclear reactor in Kansas.[1]

But it was a time of surprises and of anomalies, when the Puritan and Hebraic images of Kansas seemed no longer appropriate. Some people were enthusiastic about the coming of the new age, others accepted it philosophically, and some chafed bitterly at this different kind of future as an imposed abomination. Kansas had always had a range of opinion with equal and earnest factions polarized. It had been so with the slavery issue in Bleeding Kansas; it had been true in the era of the People's Party; it had been there in the struggles over prohibition or the Ku Klux Klan; and it made for tight elections when the dust blew in the 1930s. There had been entrepreneurs and socialists in Kansas in strength, politicians and poets. In the 1970s, with record high interest rates, an energy crisis, and a growing environmentalist movement nationally, new parameters accompanied the traditional passionate tensions. The 1980s and 1990s only increased the pressures of change. Agricultural Kansas and small-town, family-farm Kansas were seriously threatened, as were some of the last pristine prairies in the United States. The definition of Christian morality, once so unequivocal to Kansas, was in flux. Some of the premier battles of the late twentieth century over the abortion issue in the United States took place in the legislature and courts of Kansas as well as on the streets of Wichita. Demographics, changed already by World War II, changed more. Asians became a significant presence after the Vietnam War and with the development of beefpacking jobs in western Kansas. Who would have imagined ever seeing a sign on a motel in Dodge City advertising that it was "American-owned"? And the coming of computer

Wolf Creek Nuclear Power Plant.
Courtesy Wolf Creek Nuclear Operating Corporation.

processing, the dot-com virtual reality, and remote consumer communication made the old threat of the chain store seem tame.

There were political groundswells of an unfamiliar type. Who would have imagined in the old days that a Democratic governor could serve four terms in Kansas, as Robert Docking did between 1966 and 1972? Television coverage caused issues and candidate image to rival party identification in influencing voting behavior. Moreover, Docking managed to distance himself from the liberalism of the national party. But whatever the changes, it remained true that social issues came to the fore in idealistic regional politics much in the manner of days past, though without the same result.[2] Culture adjusted, but culture never moves as quickly as the future shock that was typical of the end of the century. And as was always true in Kansas, minority views were advanced with vigor by advocates who became ever more sure of their ground as it seemed to be cut out from under them.

Some people found in the shopping malls and the franchise restaurants of the era a new kind of home, a portable environment, which was comfortable because it was the same everywhere. But there were those in Kansas who were restive at the bland future represented by absorption into the global economy. When Wendell Berry spoke in a barn at the annual prairie festivals at the Land Institute in Salina, Kansas, he passed on a strong message of localism and regional community. Former Harvard professor Wes Jackson founded the Land Institute in 1976 to experiment with prairie perennials and sustainable agriculture. Eventually he moved to projects having to do with restoring the viability of small communities, particularly the near ghost town of Matfield Green in Chase County. Jackson had deep Kansas roots. His great-grandfather rode with John Brown, and Jackson was a first cousin once removed to Dwight Eisenhower. But he definitely was more Brown than Eisenhower in personality, not only making an articulate protester against Wolf Creek but also working a quiet revolution in demonstrating an alternative future on his own prairie acreage. He was one of the most aggressive regionalists in the Kansas of the late twentieth century and as such a prominent anomaly in that era. "To consult the genius of the place in all," and to resist centralization, standardization, and bureaucratization, was a near mantra of the sustainable agriculture movement, and to Jackson it was as natural as being a lifelong Kansan born in the environmentally reverse years of the Dust Bowl.[3] He asked in one of the early issues of his journal, the *Land Report*, "What, after all would Black Elk think of these alternatives for the twenty-first century? Or for that matter, Lao Tzu? Or Don Juan, or even Aristotle?"[4] The "vagrant sovereign" of the modern world, Berry said, had lost his limits and therefore his moorings in a plethora of standardized things. His geography was artificial. "He could be anywhere, and he usually is."[5]

That aggressively surviving local spirit was also evident in William Least Heat-Moon, an English professor from Missouri whose best-seller *Blue Highways* found an audience among those who had forgotten the delights of following routes marked in blue on maps as secondary roads. In the late 1980s Heat-Moon moved to Kansas for a time and immersed himself in the history and culture of a single county—Chase—in the Flint Hills. The result was *PrairyErth*, a book that was somewhat controversial among the folk it portrayed but that is surely a masterpiece of its type. History, interviews, and observation—passions, hedges, limestone, archives, biographies, mental and physical maps—are mixed in this big book in a way Heat-Moon calls "deep landscape." It calls to mind Andrew Wyeth's lifetime of painting the Pennsylvania country where he was born. "You can't civilize men," said Senator George McDuffie in 1843, "if they have an indefinite extent of territory over which to spread."[6] In each may be all. In the late twentieth century, so many things so long taken for granted disappeared—replaced surely, and in abundance, with the new, but to ends that were neither certain nor local. The

Wes Jackson.
Courtesy of the Land Institute.

countercurrent was relatively weak, but it was certainly there and perhaps grew by what it fed on.

Biblical intonations about "the nations" seemed to resonate in these Kansas times, if not of physical exile, then at least of a kind of cultural exile from regional roots. "The nations roar like the roaring of many waters," Isaiah wrote.[7] In the twentieth century, as in the time of the ancient prophet, the siren song for any people that might want to consider itself a light to the gentiles was sweet as well as strong. According to Ezekiel, the Israelites had the temerity to question Yahweh, saying, "Let us be like the nations, like the tribes of the countries, and worship wood and stone."[8]

At first the new directions seemed relatively uncomplicated. Kansas Gas and Electric could publicize in 1957 a design for a breeder-type nuclear reactor, which produced plutonium as its own fuel. But given Kansas's supply of cheap natural gas, which fueled regional power plants, it was thought that it would be many years before the nuclear option would ever be implemented in the state.[9] Proposals for a prairie park to preserve areas of tallgrass in Pottawatomie County near the Tuttle Creek reserve met firm opposition when introduced in 1959 and seemed a distant and unlikely scenario. Kansas had little federally owned land, and the Flint Hills had long prospered from raising cattle rather than antelope and prairie chickens.[10] But in the next thirty years there was a radical transformation in the status of these two initiatives. Kansas ended up with both a nuclear plant and a park, but they came from a cauldron of struggle that illustrated both how strong was the suspicion of modern technology and its social concomitants in the state and how weak was support for fundamental alternatives to its imperatives.

The nuclear plant was a child of the energy crisis.[11] Kansas Gas and Electric (KG&E) and Kansas City Power and Light (KCP&L) joined in advancing the project of building a nuclear plant along Wolf Creek in Coffey County after natural gas suppliers informed them in 1967 that there could be no steady supply of natural gas guaranteed in the future at any price. The necessity became even clearer after the federal government passed the Fuel Use Act of 1978, promising prison terms for utility executives who did not seek alternatives to natural gas for firing boilers. But the great difficulties, technical, economic, and political, which Wolf Creek came to face in Kansas were the result of a long construction lead time combined with rapidly changing rules, interest rates, and attitudes on the part of the public and the Kansas Corporation Commission. What began as a protest by a few farmers and ranchers against the exercise of eminent domain powers in taking their land for the plant spread to individuals concerned about the implications in time of drought of the plant's water rights to the John Redmond reservoir and the Neosho River. Then antinuclear activists and the Nuclear Regulatory Commission itself joined in, in the wake of the Three Mile Island plant accident of 1979 in Pennsylvania. Finally, a broad spectrum of Kansans balked at a final cost for Wolf Creek of over $3 billion, triple the original estimates. Construction Work in Progress (CWIP) was not allowed by the Kansas Corporation Commission (KCC), since charging ratepayers for the plant in advance of its providing them with power was politically suicidal. Yet with interest rates at an all-time high in the 1970s and with KG&E, the contracting utility, suffering from a reduced credit rating, the borrowing alone added over $1 billion to the cost. Wilson Cadman, chief executive of KG&E in Wichita, made many speeches and issued many press releases arguing that the utility had invested in both coal and nuclear plants to hedge its bets in the face of a seeming crisis in the supply and escalation in the cost of natural gas and oil. Still, he received death threats on his home phone and saw people dressed in grim reaper costumes marching in front of his office building. The Wichita utility, recently popular because of its low rates and community philanthropy, suddenly responded to taunts that its cute little symbolic lightning man, Reddy Kilowatt, should now be called "Reddy Kill-a-Lot." Wrote one Kansan, "Nuclear power is a religion to its supporters, and a fanatical obsession to its opponents."[12]

Wolf Creek was completed, one of the last of its kind actually to go into operation. It came on line in 1985 and produced power efficiently into the twenty-first century. But the enormous debate that took place before the KCC in the rate hearings, the reams of consulting reports and press clippings, and the voluminous testimony of expert witnesses from all viewpoints showed that power plant authorization was no longer the same inbred bureaucratic process in the state that it had once been. "This hungry Wolf," noted a press report in 1983, "has been on the loose for a decade. . . . There seems no end to the waste, the billions upon billions we will be forced to cough over for a project that should have been shut down in the name of common sense years ago. . . . Reading through the flack and between the lines, the utilities have lost their collective shirt, pants and shoes on this boondoggle and they want us to pay for their folly."[13]

The legal requirement for asking the ratepayers to bear the cost was that the decisions made by the utilities in initiating and completing the project be "prudent." Utility attorneys emphasized that this did not mean "perfection" and that they could not have foreseen the changes in energy supply, interest rates, and nuclear reputation that unfolded during the long construction period for Wolf Creek. They had joined with other utilities around the country to build a standardized plant. This had increased the cost (to protect against earthquakes in some places and tornadoes in others) but had improved the safety and reliability. To punish the companies now would be to change the rules by which "regulated monopolies" were encouraged to build facilities in the public interest and in turn were promised limited, but secure, profits on their investments.

Opponents strongly objected to that scenario, arguing that the utilities were private companies that had made egregious errors, for which their stockholders should largely pay. There was an overcapacity that was beyond the usual, and in hindsight it appeared that there was no need to abandon natural gas in the first place. There were elements of the old Populist anticorporate fire in the rhetoric of the interveners, but there was also an element of suspicion that the helmet of modernity that was being clapped down on Kansas did not entirely fit. "There is plenty of blame to go around on Wolf

Creek," wrote R. H. Garvey's son Willard. "But isn't the root cause that politicians and political monopolies have little incentive to control or reduce cost to the citizens?" What next? "Will KG&E," wrote one man, "ask that we give our first born, our blood, or the gold from our teeth?"[14] The battleground was not the technical factors on which the legal battles rested but a questioning of the whole process by which utilities had traditionally been approved. "The real issue," wrote state representative Robert Miller in 1977, "was whether the utilities could continue to successfully sidestep the Legislature and the people of Kansas in setting nuclear policy. . . . The real issue in nuclear power in Kansas is who's going to set policy for the state."[15]

Utility witnesses saved the plant itself, but the rate increases that the utilities asked and thought they had been virtually guaranteed when they gained permission to start building were not granted. KG&E had to scramble to survive, taking out insurance policies on its executives to meet its obligations in lieu of expected rate income. It ended up being taken over in a merger with Kansas Power and Light after narrowly fending off an unfriendly takeover attempt by KCPL. Its public relations director at one conference had to end with the statement, "We are not a monster."

In the year 2000 there was still vague concern about how and at what cost the Wolf Creek plant would be decommissioned at the end of its useful life. Mayor Bob Knight of Wichita was active on behalf of that city in complaining about the continued electric rate differential to the detriment of the Peerless Princess. But absorption of all the participating companies and the plant itself into Western Resources, Incorporated, combined with lowering of interest rates, a good long-term deal on uranium fuel, and the rapid growth of the Kansas City–Johnson County area, softened the predicted negative impact of Wolf Creek's expense on the state considerably.

Wilson Cadman, speaking in 1989, said that even the critics gave the plant as it actually had operated a grudging respect and that its temporary excess capacity was a "golden commodity" for a future that would need nonpolluting nuclear capacity but that could not afford to go through the pain of building a new one. "They're going out of their way now," said Cadman, "to reanalyze this thing and say 'Hey, maybe this thing wasn't all bad.' If it were anything other than a nuclear power plant, people would say: 'Holy Christ! In Kansas, you've done this?'"[16] Interveners and attorneys on both sides of the battle came to regret that the adversarial process had polarized positions to the point of suppressing creative thinking that might have led to better solutions. Passion and self-consciousness and a play to the media in a way highly conditioned by national events and current national priorities and trends made Wolf Creek almost an icon rather than a power plant—something that could hardly be examined purely on its merits for the region by anyone. In the planning for Wolf Creek, space and water were set aside for a second nuclear plant on the site. But it was doubtful that one would ever be constructed there.

But as one KG&E director put it, nothing has ever been perfectly predictable or perfectly safe, and decisions for the future must be made with information available in the present, with the result sometimes that "you have to sit on your own blisters."[17] Had there been levels of regulation, public access, and media coverage of the sort in the ninth century that existed in the 1980s, doubtless someone would have told the Vikings that their wooden ships with the dragon prows were dangerous and they would have been forced to stay home and jog. The complications of late-twentieth-century technology made adequate and appropriate public discussion of consequences more difficult, but to allow the entire direction to rest in the hands of distant experts was a danger perhaps greater than any hazard likely from a nuclear accident. As with the coming of the railroads in the mid-nineteenth century, the arrival of nuclear power in the mid-twentieth was an ambiguous presentation, full of promise and of threat. Whether regions can respond in a way that reflects and preserves their special character as regions is the question indeed.

The Prairie Park issue seemed, by contrast, simple. But here the new environmentalist, preservationist, and tourism consciousness in Kansas was pitted against the near sacred image of the family farm and ranch and the decentralized small-community-based economy. Again the juggernaut of the federal government, with its vast financial and persuasive powers, was key. The locals, who had lost the battle over Tuttle Creek dam, had some influence in changing the direction in the Wolf Creek controversy and perhaps a little more in the case of the Prairie Park. Perhaps what seemed the inevitable shape of the future in Kansas at the end of World War II will become a more variegated scenario in the twenty-first century, as Kansans recover their feet, reexamine themselves, and learn the ropes. But it will not be like the old days.

The Flint Hills, running diagonally through eastern Kansas, were in the 1960s a resource long taken for granted as one of the nation's premier places for fattening cattle as well as a well-kept secret among Kansans for its subtle but compelling scenery. The one did not seem to interfere much with the other, as cattle ranchers burned the ranges regularly to suppress any trees and simply replaced the bison with Herefords and Angus. Long ago experience had taught that the Flint Hills, where horses' hooves could raise sparks, were not a good place for small family farms, and it had seemed, therefore, that the preservation of the basic landscape, so compatible with its economic employment as cattle ranches, was not a problem.[18]

However, old certainties no longer applied, and familiar factions had metamorphosed. Even the environmentalists were divided into preservationist and conservationist wings, and this time the Kansas urbanites constituted the core of those arguing for wilderness while the rural folks were arrayed on the front of development. The development faction was in turn divided. Economic use through cattle grazing was one thing. Development through suburban vacation properties, or ownership by outside corporations, or tourism development through the national park system raised other issues. The permutations were many, but the complexity did not sooth the passions.

The tall prairie was once a major presence in the Midwest. By the 1960s it had largely disappeared in places like Illinois, where it once had dominated. It was one major ecosystem that was not represented in the national park system and that, though nominally accessible to any citizen by public roads, was, as private property, not subject to the sort of structured experience the park service provided at other sites. The realm of the Big Bluestem, the area that was, in the phrase of John Madson, "beyond the wooden country . . . where the sky began," was a dramatic landscape to the eye, and the mature climax prairie, often centuries in developing, contained an enormous variety of plants. These had for millennia been used by natives and could be of use to modern medicine, also.[19] There had been some thought of a prairie preserve in Kansas as early as 1914 and some serious study of one in 1925.[20]

With these considerations, the National Park Service contracted with professors at Ft. Hays State College in 1954 and 1956 to study potential areas in Kansas that might preserve a tallgrass environment. In 1956 an advisory board on national parks passed a resolution favoring a prairie project. Locating it in Kansas was backed by the Manhattan Area Park Development Association, with the editor of the *Manhattan Mercury* as its vice president. The park service studied three Kansas sites during summer 1958 in Pottawatomie, Wabaunsee, and Chase Counties. Bills appeared in Congress in 1959, and there was talk of a park as large as sixty thousand acres. "The area," wrote a journalist commenting on the bill for a park northeast of Manhattan, "combines tall grass prairie with wooded, spring-fed streams areas. If the park is authorized, the park service plans to re-establish native game such as buffalo, antelope, and deer. It is also planned as a natural propagation ground for game birds such as quail and prairie chicken." It was the old multiuse technique, which had been so effective in garnering support for the Corps of Engineers dam projects.

The Prairie Park Natural History Association, which originated among professors at KU and KSU, began organized lobbying for a park. Dr. Raymond Hall, professor of biology and director of the Dyche Museum of Natural History at the University of Kansas, said in 1960 that "time is running out" on preserving the "vastness" that was a primary characteristic of prairie. The turnpike had ruined several prime sites.[21] Although the prairie was tough and had a "remarkably stable ecology," prolonged overgrazing of the type that Hall believed was occurring destroyed it.[22] Therefore, even should other types of development not intrude, a grazed Flint Hills was not the kind of "original" landscape, subject only to occasional heavy grazing by roaming herds, that park proponents wished to reestablish. And there was prestige to be considered. Floyd Amsden of Wichita, vice president of the new association, expressed the belief that if Kansas were to acquire a national park, it "would greatly help the national image of our state in the eyes of the nation."[23] Opposition, however, appeared—from county commissions, from ranchers, from people worried about loss of tax base, and from those suspicious of government projects in general.[24]

Although the Kansas City press predicted as early as 1961 that a Prairie Park, if established in 1965, could have more than 1 million visitors a year by 1970 who would spend $6 million a year in the area, most people doubted that a park was practical.[25] "A prairie national park?" an editor wrote in 1960. "Who in the world would be interested in a park out on the lonely prairie of Kansas? . . . Many Kansans are so close to the prairies they don't see anything unusual about them."[26]

But in 1961 Secretary of the Interior Stuart Udall landed in a government helicopter at a point in the Flint Hills called Twin Mound to examine the site for a potential federal prairie park. There he was met by rancher Carl Bellinger with a shotgun and sent swiftly away.[27] In January 1962, the Pottawatomie County Planning Commission approved plats for an airport, country club, and housing development in part of the area studies had designated as prime for the Prairie Park.[28] In 1963 a U.S. Senate subcommittee held hearings in Kansas lasting more than four hours and drawing over three hundred people.[29] Suddenly a park seemed possible.

Ben Hibbs of the *Saturday Evening Post* talked about his nostalgia for the prairie of his native state. "For a long time," he wrote, "some of us who grew up on these prairies and learned to love them, as other men love the mountains and the forests and the sea, have yearned for the day when some remnant of this immense grasslands of the West would be set aside as a national park, so that this generation and the generations to come could see what they once were. . . . The synthetic cowboys on television are not enough."[30] *Time* magazine quoted Secretary Udall as saying that "it's too bad when a member of the President's Cabinet tries to take a walk on a hill, he is told to get off. But the National Park will remedy that."[31] Udall said he recognized that "some of the sturdy owners would not like to give up their property" but added that "if we're going to save a few pieces for future generations, someone has to give."[32]

Local ranchers did not take kindly to that kind of talk. Bellinger became a rallying point for those who organized the Twin Mound Ranchers' Association, soon joined in opposition by the Farm Bureau and the Farmers' Union.[33] People began putting up hand-lettered signs, still to be seen in the hills in the year 2000, with slogans such as "Private Lands in Private Hands."[34]

As with any measure during that period, the Prairie Park issue was fought in the media and in forums, and it was fought more by organizations than by individuals. At first the organizations were small, if vocal. But in the 1970s, as the prospect for a park in Kansas seemed to grow closer, the organizational net was thrown wider on both sides. The early efforts of the Prairie Park Natural History Association were supplemented in the 1970s on the promotional side by larger and more diverse coalitions, Save the Tallgrass Prairie, Incorporated (STP), the Sierra Club, and the Nature Conservancy. The last provided a private alternative to federal ownership and offered preservation without massive tourism. The STP, founded in 1973, and with photographer Patricia Duncan spearheading a strong verbal and visual campaign, was the most sophisticated of the organizations surrounding the Prairie Park debate. The opposition formed the Kansas Grassroots Association, again a broad coalition that used publicity and petition drives effectively. There appeared in the 1970s middle-of-the-roaders also, who proposed a prairie parkway, a kind of "ribbon park" that would allow tourists to see the area better without any change in ownership of the land.[35]

Generally, the preservation movement was initially an urban phenomenon. Wichita's local historic preservation ordinance, designed to protect buildings, was the first such law in the state and became a model for others. Its Historic Preservation Board members were regularly called socialists or communists by a general citizenry that was not well attuned to the idea that local government might regulate property rights in the interest of history. However, grassroots groups like Wichita's Midtown Citizens' Association called themselves "urban pioneers" in opposing the federally mandated Urban Renewal mindset of the 1960s, which wiped out older neighborhoods with zoning and financing policies that supposedly were instituted in the name of progress. And just as the STP in the Prairie Park matter or Kansas City's Mid-America Coalition for Energy Alternatives in the Wolf Creek plant fight had done, they drew help and inspiration from similar citizens' organizations around the country.[36]

Clearly grassroots movements, when well organized and financed, could do more than delay in the manner of the Blue Valley Association in the 1950s. They could serve as a medium for discontent and with the right arguments could attract unlikely allies from the seeming mainstream establishment. After all, at the turn of the twenty-first century, both Wichita and Kansas City have thriving Old Town districts and multimillion-dollar restoration projects for major historic downtown buildings. These projects have not only the support of local business and government but also, in a total reversal of the Urban Renewal mindset about what modern cities should be like, the active financial help of the federal government. Books like Jane Jacobs's *Death of the American City* may have helped raise consciousness, and organizers elsewhere may have provided models, but it was Kansans in the local trenches who changed slum and blight to valuable homes and derelict commercial property to some of the hottest real estate in town. The STP was a parallel kind of organization, but its idea of preservation was a little less subject to "adaptive use" than that of the building preservationists and so was in sharper counterdistinction to the agriculturalists and the real estate promoters.

The propaganda coalesced into certain key points on both sides. Primary for those favoring a park was the idea that the prairie was a rare spiritual resource for a hurried age. There was little population in the area, and although some families were admittedly old, increasing numbers were rent-ers.[37] A prairie preserve would be a haven for a stressed urban Kansas and nation, more important to their psychological health than the beef the land would raise would be to their physical well-being.[38] A tallgrass preserve would provide a habitat for 850 native flowering plants, which, with grazing pressure lessened, would grow to "their natural proportions" and in their natural profusion.[39] Absentee owners, including major American corpora-tions, were buying Flint Hills land, perhaps initially as a hedge against in-flation or as a tax shelter, but who knew for what purpose in the long run. In 1973 Mercedes Benz bought six thousand acres near Eureka. And who was to say that ranching was the only use? Harvey Feldman of Topeka, head of the Kansas Motel and Hotel Association, which supported the park, drew some shudders even from his erstwhile allies when in 1973 he said that he believed the new park should include a "Disneyland-like amusement center."[40]

There was species preservation to consider, also. There were more prairie chickens in the Flint Hills than in the rest of the world combined, an Au-dubon Society representative noted.[41] It would be a fine thing, some people thought, to bring back the primeval hills. "The present grassland," wrote a proponent, "no matter how well managed for perpetual productivity, is grassland for cattle and is not the complete prairie that first greeted white settlers. The full diversity of grasses and forbs and the original variety of wildlife, including large herbivores, are no longer present."

At most, it was only 2 percent of the hills that could be preserved without power lines, military bases, power plants, and reservoirs. Could one depend on the owners to resist development, especially if future owners were Chase-Manhattan Bank clients? "Will not the beauty of these hills invite their subdivision by second-home speculators and developers who sell beauty to the first 5% of their buyers, but suburban sprawl to the last 5%?"[42] *Audubon* magazine in 1975 noted, "No living man will see again the long-grass prairie, where a sea of prairie flowers lapped at the stirrups of the pioneer," but there could be a facsimile of sorts.[43] "The national rape of our resources," wrote a Salina editor, "placed a premium on our virgins."[44]

The beauty of the hills in all seasons was of course the coup de grace for those promoting a park. Here perhaps the most quoted person was Rolla Clymer, "The Sage of the Bluestem," who, over the years, had written so many editorial essays in the *El Dorado Times* on the subject of the land-scape's look. Reprints of these were distributed to turnpike travelers at the service centers. Clymer was eighty-five years old in 1973 but had lost none of his style or political savvy. He had always been drawn to the idea of a park. "Frankly," he wrote in 1964, "I doted on the idea of the park. It pleased all my feelings of fitness." But he had to respect the ideas of his neighbors. "They seemed to abhor the idea of a park, with their exaggerated fears of tourism and commercialism, and never took down their flag. So I felt I could not put mine up against them."[45] Charles Stough of the STP wrote Clymer in 1974, "It disturbs me that any one who writes so eloquently of the Flint Hills would object to the preservation of an area of sufficient size to give assurance that a small part of this beautiful land would be left unimpaired for the enjoyment of future generations."[46]

One of Clymer's 1973 editorials, "The Hills Change Not," indicated that the way he reconciled the matter personally was by emphasizing that there would be continuity, no matter what.[47] In his printed collection of editorials, "Glory of the Hills," he wrote, "Today more wayfarers are passing through the Hills than ever before—since these mounds pushed up from the basin of an ancient sea. The questing race of man has carved a giant slash through the Hills—a mighty roadway wriggling with sinuous curves upon whose surface swiftly passes the traffic burden of the outside world." More often than not the auto drivers did not "lift up their eyes unto the hills" but raced on to another objective. But, wrote the hills poet, "The Hills look upon this display of animation tolerantly. They are changeless. They have vast patience—and they can wait."[48] Clymer had to come out against "nationalization" of the hills. "The Flint Hills will retain their natural birthright," he wrote in 1973, shortly before his death, "as God made them, without the help of the Tall-grass parkers."[49]

With Clymer's death in 1977, opposition to the park lost one of its most powerful voices—powerful because eloquent and because the voice belonged to a man who certainly belonged to the region and had deep empathy with some of the values the proponents were trying to advance. "It's hard to understand why there could be a Watergate," wrote Nyle Miller of the Kansas State Historical Society to Clymer in 1973, "when there's such a world as you describe."[50]

As a counterpoise to Clymer, the pro groups brought in some big guns of the environmental movement with their own brand of eloquence. Their meeting in 1973 in Emporia hosted David Brower, founder and president of Friends of the Earth, as the major speaker.[51] Dr. Karl Menninger and Thomas Hart Benton were appointed to the honorary Board of Trustees of the STP.[52] Even the opponents had to give the propark lobby credit for determination as true believers. "Burn them at the stake," wrote one critic, "draw and quarter them, bury them under the sod, they will keep right on pushing for a prairie park. . . . To them the prairie is its own reason for being and anyone who can't see the beauty and importance of the tallgrass is a little off balance."[53]

The opposition, however, was also not without resources, financial, technical, and rhetorical. Probably the principal argument in its quiver was Clymer's: that there was no need to protect the Flint Hills, as cattlemen had and always would leave the land pretty much as it was while at the same time providing protein to the world and income to their communities. Access was by public road, and after all, what more did one need to experience the simple vastness and beauty of the place?[54] A park, according to the opponents, would ruin the place it was designed to protect by bringing in too many people with their accompanying inappropriate behavior. Proponents were not seeing the real future, they said, "but are furthering the scheme with appealing, romantic and enchanting presentations and with half truths or untruths, generated by ignorance of design." Opponents argued that they were not, as portrayed, "ignorant, selfish, and totally lacking in esthetic and artistic appreciation." Indeed, esthetics was part of their concern. The park would become, they thought, an "oversize zoo," where wild animals would spread disease to neighboring cattle herds and maybe even chase the tourists.[55] The tourists, said one newspaper, would "run all over it and have beer cans all over and set fire to it."[56] Government ownership itself, the critics thought, was a scary prospect, as the federal government already owned over four hundred thousand acres in Kansas. Much of this was underwater in reservoirs, and it was much less than in many western states. But it was too much for many Kansans. The park proponents, they said, were not the true ecologists; the ranchers were. Those pushing government ownership were "people from Lake Quivira, Mt. Oread, our representatives in Washington, and the women of the little green thumb garden clubs" in Kansas City and Wichita. The tallgrass left ungrazed would be a fire hazard, which, if not tended with controlled fire and sprays would soon be overrun by intruder plants and "a bunch of 'green horns' turned loose in it to study the birds, bees, bugs and ecology of the bluestem wilderness." The federal lands around reservoirs, critics said, were a "disgrace." Wrote rancher Jack Ferrel, "Next we'll want a Smoky Hills nationalization, then a Gyp Hills nationalization . . . or maybe a National Monument of tired, beat up, arthritic, weathered, drought fighting, blizzard battling cow nut admirers of the Hills who use them as they think the Creator meant them to be used—to feed his children."[57]

The park proposal, the crusty opponents said, was a trendy initiative pushed by well-meaning but ignorant and impractical people. Editor Bill Krause in the *Douglas Tribune* wrote that it was a "crummy idea, with prac- tically no merit, no purpose, and ought to be buried right along with Polack jokes and cucumber salads." The urban types that promoted it were not true Kansans but "a few idealistic souls with a reading knowledge of grass culture and a smattering of historical aroma."[58] The opponents thought that Pat Duncan of the STP, who appeared on the *Today* show and quoted Chief Seattle's fabricated speech that "whatever befalls the earth befalls the sons of the earth," was a kind of hippie without practical experience.[59]

Congressman Joe Skubitz, though favoring a limited park, shared much of that anti-intellectual rhetoric and prided himself on practicality. He reg- ularly thwarted the efforts of Congressman Larry Winn, representing a dis- trict including suburban Kansas City, to introduce bills establishing a sizable park.[60] "I pointed out a long time ago," Skubitz wrote, "that mighty few tourists were going to spend much time in 100 degree plus heat in Kansas wandering through chigger-infested prairie grass with very few trees."[61] A biology professor at the Kansas State College in Pittsburg agreed: "Tourists just don't flock in droves to scenes of unbridled monotony." Letting the tallgrass grow "would serve to ruin your vacation by reminding you of your unattended back yard at home."[62]

Although the struggle escalated to a moral issue as much as a practical one, fought out by equally matched groups, as was usual in Kansas, the proponents did gain strength in changing times. In 1963 the *Chicago Tribune,* writing about the Prairie Park issue, had asked whether "displacing about 100 ranchers and their cattle and installing highways, camping grounds, trails, and toilets to attract thousands of tourists who otherwise would give the area a wide berth is not actually defeating the purposes of conserva- tion."[63] But by the mid-1970s there were people in positions of power in Washington and in Kansas with considerably different attitudes. The *Wall Street Journal* noted in 1975 that people were starting to value the prairie, perhaps as a "reflection of a deep-felt national anxiety about the dizzy pace of social change." The environmental movement had begun to "appreciate unspectacular landscapes, as well as spectacular ones," as important and threatened and as good for reasons other than "for plowing up or mowing down."[64]

The Kansas political establishment was accordingly changed also. Nancy Landon Kassebaum, the daughter of former Kansas governor Alf Landon, became the first female U.S. senator from Kansas in 1978 and the first woman in the United States elected to the Senate on her own, without first following her husband.[65] The other Republican senator from Kansas, Bob Dole, was a far more complicated character than had once been associated with Kansas. Gerald Ford, with Dole as his running mate, promised in 1976 to spend over $1 billion expanding the national park system, a promise that resonated well with the Prairie Park supporters in Kansas.[66]

Kassebaum, who had grown up around prairie, took the Prairie Park specifically as a special project and in the 1980s used her considerable influence, ability to get along with diverse groups, and unquestionable Kansas credentials to bring about some compromise to preserve tallgrass in some formal way. Dan Glickman, a Democrat from Wichita serving in the U.S. House, also took up the cause, partly on the grounds that a park would be good for the Kansas image and made economic sense. Glickman, who became secretary of agriculture in the Clinton administration, illustrated not only that the Prairie Park had urban support but also that preservation had come to have broad-based regional support.

Be that as it may, the Prairie Park proposals suffered hard times around 1980. The *Eureka Herald* in 1977 suggested that Congressman Winn's National Prairie Park be located in Overland Park, Kansas, where the city folk could see it, and that the industry from that area should be moved to Greenwood County in the Flint Hills to help in the economic development of rural America.[67] Winn's 1979 proposal for a three-hundred-thousand-acre park covering parts of three counties toward the west end of the Flint Hills seemed to overwhelm even the supporters.[68] Winn announced before his reelection in November 1980 that he would not press a tallgrass bill again. Farmers and ranchers gained new encouragement from the so-called "Sagebrush Revolution" in the far West against federal land management. Secretary of the Interior James Watt, a pariah to conservationists, told Kansas congressman Bob Whittaker in 1981 that "as long as this [Reagan] admin-

Nancy Kassebaum.
Courtesy of the Kansas State Historical Society.

istration is in place there will be no prairie park." Winn estimated that it looked as though it would take a century for the park proponents to achieve their goal.[69] State action certainly indicated that. In 1980 Governor John Carlin signed a bill passed by the Kansas legislature that would restrict federal acquisition of land in Kansas to eighty acres or less. Attorney General Robert Stephan doubted whether that would stop the federal government from establishing a Prairie Park if it really wanted one but declared that he would fight any proposals on the ground that they did not serve a public purpose.[70]

Several events happened to change that mood, though certainly not to revive any quarter-million-acre dreams. For one, it became clear that there were private organizations and individuals who were willing to purchase Flint Hills land for the purpose of prairie preservation or study rather than for cattle ranching. That was hard for free enterprise proponents effectively to oppose. The Nature Conservancy, beginning in the 1970s and extending right through the turn of the twenty-first century, was an active buyer of extensive ranch properties in Kansas, initially in the Flint Hills and later in western Kansas. In 1971 it purchased 916 acres near Manhattan.[71] In 1973 it purchased 1,500 acres of Flint Hills grass around Cassoday from the Matador Cattle Company of Wichita for two hundred fifty thousand dollars.[72] Later additions meant that this Cassoday tract, called the Flint Hills Prairie and used by Emporia State University for research, amounted by 1979 to about 2,100 acres.[73] To those early purchases the conservancy had added by 1977 land in Douglas, Linn, Butler, Greenwood, Harvey, and Clark Counties. It continued, while restoring prairie, to pay local property tax. In 1977, with the financial help of Katherine Ordway, a New York philanthropist who asked only that the new preserve be given an Indian name, the conservancy purchased the 7,200-acre Dewey Ranch south of Manhattan, joined it to its former 916-acre purchase in the area, and leased the eleven-square-mile plot to Kansas State University as a research area called the Konza Prairie. By that date the conservancy owned about 40,000 acres in Kansas and over 1 million acres in the United States.[74]

A second approach that resulted in de facto prairie preservation, though not perhaps in the form some people desired, was to compromise on the national park issue by reducing both the area requested and the ambitions for its use, improvements, and tourist numbers. This endeavor included the possibility of keeping a traditional ranch, marked for prairie preservation, in operation as a working cattle ranch without elk or wolves and with the modest goal of preventing irreversible alternative uses.[75]

The focus here was the Z-Bar Ranch near Strong City. Although encompassing only about ten thousand acres, the ranch included a historic 1880s ranch home, a large stone barn, and a picturesque schoolhouse. It was relatively accessible from the turnpike, the farmhouse was on the National Register of Historic Places, and in the mid-1980s the whole property was offered for sale. In 1989 the Audubon Society bought an option on it. It at first proposed to sell $400 one-acre shares to conservationists to finance the purchase of the $4.5 million ranch but soon began working to transfer the place to the National Park Service.[76]

Again the opposition arose, but this time, given the modest proposal, there was a core of local people as well as outsiders who favored the change. Some in jest called the Kansas Grassroots Association the KGB. One rancher asked, "If you KGA boys are so opposed to federal this and that, why do you accept agricultural subsidies?"[77] "We agree," said one STP member, "with KGA in wanting to preserve a century-old way of life, but we also want to preserve one that's twenty million years old." The mistake had been "barging in here as 'experts,' tramping around and mapping people's land, and not making them part of things right at the beginning. . . . The perception of us here was as city people from Johnson County, the place known across the state as the home of spoiled brats of all ages."[78]

In 1989 there was a switch in emphasis from national park to possible national monument. The *Wichita Eagle* pushed hard for this, quoting Laura Ingalls Wilder, Bishop William Quayle, John Ingalls, Aldo Leopold, and William Least Heat-Moon on the "pull of the prairie."[79] The *New York Times* in 1991, speaking of proposals for a tallgrass park in Kansas or Oklahoma, called the area "the essence of America" and supported some such move.[80] "Look across the stark and rolling vastness of the Flint Hills in Chase County," an *Eagle* writer urged. "You can see the past. You don't even have to use your imagination."[81]

The National Park Service did a feasibility study but concluded in 1991 that the Z-Bar Ranch, at 10,849 acres, was too small for a national monument that would include the introduction of bison. Congressman Glickman, who had pushed legislation, was upset and accused the Park Service of changing its bureaucratic mind.[82] However, former Kansas governor Mike Hayden, who was an Interior Department official, supported the Park Service decision. Senator Dole commented that there were and had been a number of park proposals in Kansas and this one was "not a big deal."[83]

A bill for a national monument did make its way through the U.S. House. Hearings were held at Emporia State University late in August 1991, with a panel of proponents and opponents there as well as Glickman and members of the House committee handling the park issue.[84] It was a lively session, as was any invitation to debate the matter in those times, but ultimately the monument bill failed. It seemed that again all proposals were tabled.

Kassebaum, however, emerged with a compromise initiative, which could create one of those newly fashionable "public-private partnerships," with the Park Service operating the ranch and a private trust as the chief owner. The *Eagle* called Kassebaum's move "sad, bad," though the senator was from Wichita and wildly popular there.[85] But the paper admitted that "some Kansas ranchers and farmers, the saying goes, would rather invite the ghost of Karl Marx to dinner than see even a single acre of private land go to the federal government."[86] Kassebaum called a meeting in December 1991 at Wichita State University to discuss ways and means of taking some action on prairie preservation.[87] The result was the creation of a commission, headed by Ross Beach of Hays, which met for over a year without much visible result. Glickman commented, "We'll be like 'Waiting for Godot' to get anything to happen with it. The only way people will be really interested in moving this along is if you have a legislative threat."[88]

Nevertheless, by January 1993 the commission was ready to make an offer for the Z-Bar Ranch.[89] The atmosphere in Washington for some cooperation from the Park Service had improved, too, with the arrival of the Clinton administration and the activist interior secretary Bruce Babbitt.[90] There was worry that the credit for the tallgrass park would go to Oklahoma, where the Nature Conservancy had bought about thirty thousand acres of the Osage Hills, an extension of the Kansas Flint Hills, in 1989 and introduced a herd of three hundred bison.[91] Negotiations with Boatman's Bank in Kansas City went on seemingly interminably, but in spring 1993 the National Prairie Trust, which despite its government-sounding name was a private organization, purchased the entire Z-Bar Ranch except for one hundred eighty acres around the farmhouse, barn, and school.[92] This last piece was to be owned by the National Park Service, with the restriction that it was to interpret not only the primeval prairie but also the history of cattle ranching.[93] The negotiations there took until fall 1996, when at last a bill for the National Park Service to operate the ranch (called the Tallgrass Prairie National Preserve) and to own its small piece passed in the final days of Kassebaum's tenure in the Senate. It was seen widely as a tribute to her on her retirement.[94]

One of the first actions of the Park Service was to create a questionnaire asking supporters whether the Z-Bar should or should not continue being a cattle ranch.[95] Edward Bass, a Texas multimillionaire, then leased the Z-Bar from the Trust for thirty-five years for cattle grazing.[96] The public could visit the farmhouse, have a tour with uniformed guides, and walk a nature trail between the house and the schoolhouse. The schoolhouse in 1998 received a gift from the estate of pop artist Andy Warhol for its preservation.[97] Several Kansas politicians, including Kassebaum and Glickman, received awards in 1997 from the National Parks and Conservation Association for their work on behalf of the Tallgrass Preserve.[98] Things had come to quite a different pass from what anyone in 1965 would have expected.

The Prairie Park was an interesting case, ranging rural against urban interests, tradition against a new kind of Kansas consciousness, and local against federal initiative. The result was mixed but surely could be seen as a victory of sorts for a local economic interest, whatever the implications for the future of ecology tourism in the state. The *Eagle* and Wichita and Kansas City backers ultimately failed to shape up the opposition to persuade them to "give up their paranoia of the federal government and their rigid self-interest." The Z-Bar Ranch, though attractive, was not exactly the "proper monument to the vanishing tallgrass prairie" so many people had desired.[99]

Certainly, however, setback on broad environmental goals did not mean surrender. The people of rural Kansas, the staff ecologist of the Kansas Advisory Council on Ecology had written in 1972, "need to be made aware that the ecological crisis has long since reached Kansas and does indeed affect them." He thought it was scandalous that newspapers in the state did not print the annual report of the council and that few environmental bills introduced in the Kansas legislature seemed to pass.[100] "We can sympathize with their wiry heritage," wrote the *Kansas City Star* about the ranchers' opposition, "fight off the sheepmen, stomp the coyotes, poison the prairie dogs, keep the fences tight," but really there was no room in the modern world for people who "still think the .30–.30 caliber rifle is the solution to their problems."[101] Did not Kansas have an obligation to share its treasure? Travel and tourism were by 1987, some observers claimed, the second leading industry in the state, yet Kansas, laughing at itself for attractions like the World's Largest Prairie Dog and the Second Largest Ball of Twine, ranked thirty-fourth among the states in the mid-1980s in money spent to promote tourism.[102] "No city child," said the Wichita paper, "should be deprived of the chance to hear the dickcissel's incessant call . . . or to view a prairie wildflower display."[103] Congress should listen, the newspaper said, "not to angry landowners who would fight to keep any land out of the U.S. Park Service's hands, but to the countless voices of conservation who would do what's right for all of the people of Kansas and the nation."[104] It seemed that in the long run Emporia State Associate Professor Jim Mayo was right in calling the Flint Hills farmers and ranchers the endangered species here—the "designated victims"—eventually, if not now. "Can I tell you [an expanded park] won't ever happen 50, 100, 150 years from now?" Glickman asked. "No I can't."[105] For all the fits and starts and the epicycles of progress and regression that would do credit to the Ptolemaic scheme of the universe, federal initiative and the national media still seemed to call the tune and to have endless power and patience, as the pockets of resistance aged and faded.

This truth was demonstrated vividly in the fate of the long-standing severance tax struggle and in massive changes in some of the vice issues, over which the state had become famous for more than a century for its alternative resolutions. In many ways, in the mid-1980s Kansas joined "the nations," these issues being merely the most prominent, particularly in contrast to the regional political and moral tradition. Governor John Carlin and a state delegation visited China in 1979, and by 1985 Kansas had a sister state in the Peoples' Republic, Henan Province.[106] Carlin regularly preached that it was time to "liberate our image."[107]

The year 1985, close as it was to George Orwell's dystopian year *1984,* was an unusual time in Kansas history. The nuclear plant came on line; a severance tax on oil and gas was in place; liquor by the drink and parimutuel betting bills cleared the legislature; L. Ron Hubbard, the founder of the Church of Scientology, was declared an honorary Kansas citizen; the attorney general was charged in a sexual harassment suit; serial killers were tried for a murder rampage in western Kansas; and the governor was divorced for the second time during his term, with pundits doubting that it would affect his political career. No wonder a state legislator, desperate to preserve something of the state's traditional image, introduced a bill to make "wholesome" milk the official Kansas state drink.[108]

The severance tax competed with liquor reform as the change longest in arriving. The Kansas Independent Oil and Gas Association (KIOGA), formed in 1937, spent years struggling against the severance tax on the grounds that the oil and gas industry was already taxed sufficiently and that the extra burden would severely damage one of the state's leading industries. In 1955, when the Kansas oil and gas industry earned $7 billion, it paid out more than half of that in taxes. Further political intervention and taxation were, according to some critics, the kind of economic suicide that Kansas had nearly committed in the Populist era and with the attack on Standard

Oil in 1905. Innis Harris, an attorney for the Kansas Corporation Commission, said in 1938 that "we should not be surprised at a time when the politically ambitious seek to use the problems of the oil industry for personal advancement even at the expense of truth." But he added, "The problem cannot be solved politically. There is no Democratic or Republican way of building a bridge or constructing a building. These are matters of sound engineering."

There had been talk of a Kansas severance tax since 1915. It was a major item of discussion in the legislature through the 1950s. The political attraction was clear. Who could object to more money for education, particularly when it came from wealthy oilmen? But the opposition was strong, also. A 1 percent severance tax to aid state high schools failed in 1955, and a 3 percent tax that passed in 1957 was invalidated by the state supreme court on a technicality. But it arose again. "Every regular session of the Kansas legislature since the mind of man runneth not to the contrary," observed a journalist in 1965, "has seen the tribe of severance taxers, marching in solid phalanx, seeking desperately to inflict a tax on oil and gas." The price increases during the energy crises of the 1970s only stepped up pressure. But a serious attempt to pass a 2 percent tax failed in 1978.[109]

The rhetoric in the long debate was quite elevated. In more than a three-hour discussion of the tax in spring 1947, county commissioners, oil people, and school officials appeared. William Ainsworth, a Wichita oil executive, said, "When you apply a gross income tax to your net profit you've got something pretty vicious." School people, however, saw an untapped source of revenue. Representative John McCormally of Chapman, an author of the bill, was sarcastic about the oil industry lobby. "I must agree with Lincoln that God must have loved the poor because he made so many of them. This has turned into a recital of the poverty of oil companies." Another representative said that "while we're shedding crocodile tears for the oil men," who were carrying 25 percent of the tax burden of Kansas, "let's shed a few for the widow who will lose her home if you raise her property tax. This will step on fewer toes than would an increase in sales tax or property taxes."[110] In 1949 one severance tax headline read "Figures Fly, Fists Pound." A representative of the Kansas Council of Women and its two hundred thousand members said at that time, "The women know what this tax means—and we will continue to work for our objective if it takes a hundred years." Looking around him at a crowd of eight hundred in Topeka, Judge W. D. Jochems of

John Carlin.
Courtesy of the Kansas State Historical Society.

Wichita, representing KIOGA, said, "I have seen here tonight the best demonstration of pressure groups ever put before any legislative body in any
state. . . . When you practically threaten the Legislature by saying 'we have so
many votes to cast against you,' that's not Americanism." The lobbyists for
the Kansas Congress of Parents and Teachers felt otherwise. They characterized the KIOGA presence as representing a "special interest" while they
represented "the people."[111]

Carlin, a former dairy farmer from the tiny town of Smolan, thirty-two
years old when elected in 1979, found the issue congenial and pressed for a
severance tax through the early 1980s when a downturn in oil prices made
the industry less able to afford it than in the previous decade. He argued that
proceeds would benefit schools, bring about highway improvements, provide a tax credit for utility bills, and compensate counties for reducing the
valuation of farm machinery.[112] The issue was regarded as a test "of just how
effective the governor is in rallying Kansans around him. He eagerly sought
out arenas where he could publicly wrestle with members of the oil and gas
industry, and was quietly disappointed when his jaunts around the state
failed to yield the forum for him to play David against the oil and gas
industry's Goliath."[113]

Despite the nearly equal strength of the factions, which had so long
delayed a severance tax, Carlin eventually made progress. A severance bill
failed in what he called "a collective disaster known ceremoniously as the
1981 legislative session."[114] KIOGA claimed that the industry was not as
strong as proponents said and that the "tax simply would squeeze blood
from a dwindling resource when America is trying to restore energy independence." The revenue wasn't needed, the association said, "because government will always squander whatever you give it." Carlin painted the GOP
as obstructionists who protected rich and powerful industry instead of
doing what most urban voters thought should be done, taxing the oil and
gas industry rather than letting property taxes continue to rise.[115] In May
1983, after Carlin's reelection in a campaign in which the severance tax was a
major issue, the long battle ended with the passage of a law. At the last
minute, Republicans had gathered to write their own version of the bill, but
it was too late. That attempt, Carlin had said, was "like having King George
III writing the Declaration of Independence."[116] Kansas joined other states in
having such a tax, the argument finally prevailing that the industry was so

diversified that only about 5 percent of the payers of the severance tax would be Kansans. Nothing was purely state-based anymore, it seemed.

But it was only the beginning of Carlin's declaration of independence. He argued that gambling should be allowed in Kansas and that allowing liquor by the drink "was vital to improving the state's image and aiding economic development."[117] Traditionalists of the era, it seemed, were reduced to arguing about the appropriateness of putting a statue of a pagan goddess, Ceres, atop the statehouse dome or debating the question of whether Kansas needed a state reptile.[118]

The vice issues were particularly evocative. The United Dry Forces organization had soldiered on after the repeal of the prohibition amendment in 1948, taking on lotteries, slots, and dog racing as well as trying to hold the line on liquor through strict regulation. "Surely Kansas will not join the nations that forget God," one woman said. But the historian of Kansas prohibition, Robert Bader, noted, "Like a politician or a criminal with a record, the dries had to explain and defend the past. And since the mid-1940s, even they had to admit that the past left much to be desired." Prohibition, far from being regarded in the late twentieth century as something about which Kansans should be proud, was regarded by pundits and historians as a "beclouding" issue that had been used to distract people of the Sunflower State from its need for modernization in general.[119]

It was as though the long tradition of fighting vice in Kansas reversed itself. In 1890, a Kansas newspaper could say that "the moral sense of the country" was "startled" by the political corruption connected with the Louisiana lottery. That concern, the newspaper said, was using "its millions of net revenue from its demoralizing and corrupting business" to be certain that it was legal to sell lottery tickets in Kansas. A correspondent was clear on his position: "There is perhaps nothing more foolish than an investment in a lottery by an individual, unless it be for a state to allow this business within its borders."[120] In 1894 the State of Kansas prosecuted lottery salesmen as vagrants.[121] Seven councilmen in Kansas City, Kansas, who voted in 1906 to uphold an ordinance licensing poolrooms for racehorse gambling were all in immediate danger of losing their positions, even though most agreed that Kansas City was not really a full part of Kansas.[122] "Gambling has been illegal so long in Kansas," wrote a reporter in 1961, "that the ban's origins are lost to most citizens, except for a vague notion that it has something to do with the first settlers coming from Puritanistic New England."[123]

The slot machine issue was always in the news. Kansas law from the 1920s forward prevented "setting up and keeping slots" but did not outlaw owning one. Many clubs in Kansas paid federal tax on machines they claimed were simply collectors' items. "There is one unfailing yardstick for measuring moods of Kansas voters in meeting moral trends," the *Topeka Journal* commented in 1951. "That's the course and reaction of the vote hunting politician, with both ears glued to the grass roots and his tootsies well inside the cook stove door on frosty mornings. Back in the good old days when Kansas pursued every form of suspected vice with dogs, the slot machines and its numerous cousins wouldn't have had a chance." But times had changed since "the passing of cold-nosed, tight-laced, pioneer state builders." Cigarette sales were bringing $5 million a year into the state treasury by then, and pinball machines by 1963 produced $400 a week profit on single machines, which cost less than that to buy.[124] "The pounding of horses' hooves on racetrack turf," a lobbyist told a Kansas House committee in 1965, "would sound like the ringing of a cash register to Kansas."[125] And why should Kansas law enforcement worry itself about charity bingo games?[126] Why worry about slots? "Kansas may find the one-arm bandits no greater threat to her moral fibre than an afternoon ladies' bridge game. Folks who want to gamble do so."[127]

Kansas vice raids still made national news through the 1970s, especially because of the activities of Vern Miller, sheriff of Sedgwick County, who once leaped out of the trunk of a police car to apprehend offenders in person. In Wichita, people sharing a view represented by James Lawing of the ACLU debated those siding with Ron Adrian, pastor of the Glenville Bible Baptist Church, about everything from gay rights, to fluoridation of the water supply, to nude dancing, to performances of *Hair* and *O Calcutta* at public facilities, to the salacious lyrics of rock concerts, to the film openings of the Erotic Arts Society at Wichita State University.[128]

The legalization of liquor by the drink, the last major vestige of Kansas's restraints on alcohol, was pushed hard by the legislature from 1969 forward.[129] In 1978 state lawmakers "surprised even themselves" by approving a bill to circumvent the prohibition against the open saloon by deciding that private clubs should be allowed to sell liquor by the drink if county voters approved.[130] The house passed the bill sixty-three to sixty-one and the senate twenty-five to twelve.[131] Governor Robert Bennett, who favored liquor by the drink, thought the compromise was flawed. He did not sign the bill but

THE KANSAS ISSUE

| Volume 37 | January - February - March 1988 | Number 1 |

Please picture me talking to you, face to face.

I have talked with many of you face to face, stayed in your home, spoken in your church, eaten with you in a restaurant.

If today I could speak to you face to face, what would I say? I'd thank you for prayers, for your generous support, for your contacts with Representatives and Senators in Topeka.

Then I would ask you to continue praying, to send a gift for this year, to write <u>many</u> letters to your lawmakers, send petitions, phone them, speak with them when they are home on weekends, attend their Saturday restaurant meetings.

If you have followed multi-state lotto gambling in the news media, you know how busy have been since January 14 trying to defeat this measure now signed into law.

The poor in Kansas are victimized enough with lottery ticket sales and Kansas lotto (computer gambling). Should we hurt them <u>more</u> with a joint state Lotto America?

Kansas does not have enough people to supply the large number of losers needed to pay all the dollars required for the unbelievable large lotto jackpots that attract the po Lotto America provides this large population base for multi-million dollar jackpots with odds that are astronomical. But poor people see only the prize as they lose $10 and $20 and more each week. They do not understand that millions and millions of people must lose everything to pay for the multi-million dollar jackpot.

One year ago an opinion was issued saying Kansas could join a multi-state lottery. Based on that opinion, the Kansas legislature approved Lotto America. Because the Revisor of Statutes and many lawmakers believe the multi-state lottery law is unconstitutional, we hope to challenge it in court. <u>We need a lawyer and we need money.</u>

An opinion issued by the Attorney General stands until overturned by a court. We have never fought for less suffering through the courts. <u>This would be a first.</u> Attorney General Robert Stephan has issued many opinions helping those who deal in our most abused drug and those who promote gambling. Concerned citizens who love their neighbor would like to overturn this opinion. Will you help?

The Reverend Richard Taylor, who was in charge of the United Dry Forces.
Courtesy of the Kansas State Historical Society.

did not veto it either, allowing it to pass without his signature.[132] But Bennett favored loosening restrictions. "To impose the requirement of abstinence on all," he wrote in 1973 while president pro-tem of the Kansas Senate, "because of the vicissitudes of a few is, in my view, neither appropriate nor necessary."[133]

The 1978 bill was based on the theory that, although the open saloon remained unconstitutional in Kansas (the general prohibition repeal amendment of 1948 had specifically stated that), the legislature had the authority to define what an open saloon was and was not. The 1978 legislation stated that a restaurant that served liquor was not a saloon and therefore alcohol could be allowed. That theory, however, did not sit well with many people in the state, and there was a considerable struggle. In 1970 voters had narrowly rejected a constitutional amendment that would have allowed liquor by the drink without restriction.[134] Some thought that should have been the end of the debate for a good long time. The Reverend Richard Taylor, a Methodist minister who took over the lobby effort of the United Dry Forces (which shortly after became Kansans for Life at Its Best) in 1971, well represented that strain of opinion. The United Dry Forces had had a newsletter, the *Issue*, since 1948. Taylor made it a depository for his research and opinion and mailed it to seventy-five thousand Kansas homes.[135]

Taylor admitted that it was too late for total prohibition but urged Kansans to be "realistic and honest by acknowledging that alcohol is available enough now. Let us not increase our problems and our taxes by pushing for increased consumption of our most abused drug." Consumption in Iowa increased 51 percent in the decade after liquor by the drink went into effect in 1963, and the national average consumption increased 38 percent in the same period. The Kansas increase was only 17 percent.[136] Taylor, when asked to give a prayer in 1975 before the state legislature, said, "Help us, Father, to understand just what are the foundation stones which make for a great state. May we be wise enough to build on those principles that support true greatness. We do not want to wake up some morning and wonder why Kansas is crumbling."[137]

Bennett's mail in the 1970s, both as a senator and governor, was so overwhelmingly critical of liquor by the drink that he regularly advised supporters that he did not think any bill loosening liquor restrictions could pass. Many people were upset about the time spent on the issue. "We want our legislators to spend their time solving problems," wrote one man, "not creating them."[138] Maxine Oliver of Paola wrote "Ode to the Kansas Legislature" in 1985:

It really made us stop and think,
You spend all those hours arguing "liquor by the drink"
(which was voted down—but what do voters know?)
And discussing whether we could play—bingo!
Then, when the session was almost past
You got down to "trivial" things at last,
Bills on health care—and education—
New highways—and less taxation.[139]

Supporters could point to ironies, too. Why should people in country clubs "have the pleasure of a relaxing cocktail before dinner," as they had had since a private club act passed in 1965, when the rest of the people could not? "My relatives and friends from Chicago call you archaic. They DO NOT enjoy going to dinner in Wichita."[140] In 1973 several people sent Bennett a copy of a *Wall Street Journal* article, "If You Own a Whistle, Don't Try to Wet It in the State of Kansas." The article said that Taylor "has parlayed old-time religion and modern media techniques into persuasive political action" designed to keep "spirits down in these parts." Asked whether he had ever tasted liquor, Taylor said he had a sip of beer once but that "it tasted just like what it looked like." The irony in the text was not lost on Kansas supporters of liquor by the drink. "I hope you agree," wrote one, "that publicity of this type does untold harm to the economy of Kansas and builds up the very bad image our state already has."[141]

The urban chambers of commerce were for liquor by the drink, as were the hotel and motel people looking for convention business. A potential convention provider wrote in 1977, "Until the liquor law of Kansas joins the Union we can't bring large meetings to the state. . . . People everywhere travel too much anymore to be satisfied by the throw it on the table—Greasy Spoon concept."[142] To get a drink at a restaurant, one either had to join a private club, pay a fee and wait fifteen days, or be satisfied with beer.[143] The club license was "the most unwieldy system you can imagine. . . . It only makes it expensive and annoying to do business."[144] A Wichita-based group, Kansans for Moderate Alcoholic Beverage Control, tried to match Kansas for Life at Its Best in organization and publicity.[145] Bennett defended bills allowing drinking in the governor's mansion, Cedar Crest, and for selling beer on college campuses; and he pushed for open liquor by the drink everywhere. The moderate use of alcohol, he said, "is a part of our general public ethic," and, he thought, "we must deal with that ethic as it exists, rather than turn our backs on it and in the process force it underground."[146]

Taylor's hope to have the 1978 law declared unconstitutional was disappointed. Attorneys established that the definition of a saloon was not limited to an Old West bar with swinging doors and full-length mirrors. The legislature was within its rights under the 1948 constitution to allow liquor to be served in public restaurants where food was 50 percent of the business.[147]

There continued to be support for a constitutional amendment to legalize liquor by the drink in public anywhere. Kansas was a fine state, Governor Carlin wrote, with clean air and water, good soil, and good education.

> There is no doubt but that we can compete with other states and that we are a forward-looking, growth-oriented state. However, we do not always communicate that message to outsiders. . . . Let me state clearly, that liquor by the drink will not guarantee immediate and large scale business investments in the state. Nor is it the only thing standing between us and progress. But it is a powerful symbol that contributes to a stereotype of our state that is not accurate. . . . We are now in a cycle of exporting our best talent to other parts of the country and world because that's where the opportunities are. . . . We have learned from past experience that prohibition will not stop consumption. We must accept that people will drink.[148]

The impression that Kansas was not modern had implications far beyond its moral status. There were two pictures of Kansas, Carlin thought. One was "painted without vision. It is a picture of a state with inadequate educational programs, of highways in disrepair, of businesses leaving the state, of depleted water supplies, of an ever-aging population, of young people leaving for better opportunities." The other was a picture of "continuous progress."[149] Many people felt that the way to progress was through less government regulation, particularly of personal behavior. Motorcycle riders flocked to the statehouse to protest against laws requiring helmets for adult riders. One legislator was quoted in 1979, when there were bills banning bottle rockets and requiring color pictures on Kansas drivers' licenses and when there were debates about ratification of the Equal Rights Amendment to the federal Constitution, that the legislature had taken away his cherry bombs and three-inch firecrackers already: what was the world coming to now?[150]

Taylor was not distressed about the coming of the modern age or about restrictions in general. But he said the legislature had no backbone on the vice issues. It was, he said, "a sieve, not a funnel for such issues."[151] He objected to the whole idea of talking about "sin" in this context. He argued that alcohol was a health issue, a highway safety issue, a child abuse issue, and a mental health issue more than it was a moral question.[152] "Like a teenager in school," a reporter who was an opponent of freer liquor laws wrote, "the government is succumbing to peer pressure." Was Kansas so backward in its concern with health and highway safety? "Governor John Carlin is a noted Democratic progressive and would be shocked to be branded as a tool of big business profiteers. But that's what he looks like as he starts carrying water for the booze business." He was no blue nose, the reporter said. "I just hate to see my old home state become like every place else."[153]

Taylor made a strong and reasoned argument that the revenues from vice were not worth the cost to society and that Kansas should have learned that in the cattle-town era. He wrote that "gambling destroys the best of the human fabric and pollutes the human spirit."[154] Paul Harvey took up the theme. "Kansas must have something," the conservative radio commentator broadcast in 1986. It had the highest per capita income on the Great Plains. It was near the bottom in the United States in per capita crime, highway deaths, and job absenteeism and near the top in productivity and mental health. Per capita liquor consumption was only half the national average, and there were billboards in the state saying, "Buy Beef; Boycott Booze!"[155]

However, fewer and fewer people seemed to be convinced. Robert Bader said that although his research convinced him to support continued restrictions, quite in contrast to his original view, most liberals did not feel that way. "Sane and sensible liquor control is opposed and alcohol abuse ignored," Bader wrote, "because these sane citizens believe, incorrectly, that this is the domain of the irrational, blue-nosed puritanical crank."[156]

Liquor by the drink as a constitutional amendment passed in November 1986 along with the other "sin amendments": the authorization of a state lottery and parimutuel wagering. The winning margins were all high, the lottery passing by 64 to 36 percent.[157] The proceeds, it was said, would help fund roads and schools.[158] Supposedly, there were limits. Liquor by the drink was instituted initially only in thirty-six counties, leaving private club laws in force in the others. "Neither the Kansas Legislature nor the Kansas public is going to let liquor drinking get out of hand," said a press report.[159] The legislature claimed that it would apply restrictions to be sure "that racetrack gambling in the state is scrupulously clean."[160]

But unquestionably the 1986 constitutional questions brought about a change in the order that the 1928 amendments creating the state highway system had wrought. The state itself was now in the gambling business, and Indian tribal casinos, pushed by federal initiative, were not far behind. Kansas also in the 1986 flock of constitutional amendments exempted business inventories from property tax (one of the last seven states to do so) and allowed the state to invest in business projects when they were "for the purpose of stimulating economic development and private sector job creation." Out of that last permission came the Kansas Partnership Fund, operated through the Kansas Department of Commerce, to provide money to cities and counties for economic development. There was an industrial training program, a series of small business centers, the Kansas Development Finance Authority, the Business Enterprise Loan Fund, Kansas Venture Capital, Incorporated, and the Ad Astra Venture Capital Fund, mostly financed through lottery earnings. At first about 60 percent of lottery revenues went to economic development, 30 percent to a county reappraisal fund, and 10 percent to a correctional institutions building fund. But in 1991 the formula was changed to provide 90 percent of lottery revenues to economic development.[161] No wonder that the term "public/private partnership" became ubiquitous in the 1990s. There was no question that the state had passed to the other side of a great divide.

Perhaps it was not surprising. Taylor had an operation for throat cancer in 1974, which reduced his rich baritone voice to a whisper. The 1986 amendment cut the circulation of his magazine by half as he fought on against what was left of gambling and liquor restrictions. Governor Joan Finney met with him in 1991 but was firm in her belief that Taylor was an impressive throwback to a time that was gone.[162] In 1983 the legislature discussed Pac-Man bills to tax video games.[163] By 1987 state university faculties were unionizing, and there was a bill requiring premarital AIDS testing.[164] In 1988 Kansas even authorized microbreweries.[165] The first number of the *Kansas Issue* in 1948, advising against voting for the constitutional amendment that year repealing total state prohibition, had defined the "issue" as "the question of whether Kansas shall give up her climb 'ad astra per aspera' and turn downward along the slippery path of booze to the bottom of the moral hill."[166] By the 1990s most Kansans did not frame the question that way at all.

Governor Finney herself symbolized the changes. She was a woman, a Roman Catholic, and a Democrat, all three features unusual historically in the governor's chair. That she was considered and considered herself a Populist was not unique, harking back as it did to state politics of exactly one hundred years earlier, but it had been a long time since anyone in Kansas had talked about the People's Party except as an unfortunate diversion from the mainstream of more conservative reform. The 1990 census showed an increasingly urban state, and it was perhaps no surprise that to represent these people was a different proposition than to represent the people of the 1890s.

Finney took several controversial stands. In 1991 she negotiated compacts with Indian tribes to open casinos in the wake of the federal Indian Gaming Act of 1988 but was sued by the attorney general and criticized by the U.S. secretary of the interior for moving beyond her authorization in this area. It was 1994 before the state legislature officially declared that she had a right to establish such agreements. Finney thought it was hypocrisy to declare "the Year of the American Indian," as President George H. W. Bush did in 1992, and then to block the gaming compacts. She saw herself as defending "the rights to self-determination and economic opportunity of all Indian Nations and their people," emphasizing that it was "the result of land gifts of Native Americans" that Kansas was first established in 1854. Like Carlin before her, Finney saw economic development and diversity as more important than any antique ideas about gambling. "Gaming," she said, "is a far better choice than illiteracy, unemployment, [and] poverty."[167]

She also was a strong supporter of an Initiative and Referendum for Kansas, a view consistent with the direct democracy ideas of the earlier Populists. She was not successful in her term in having such legislation passed but spoke a great deal about it. "For almost a century and a half," she said in 1991, "the citizens of Kansas have been denied direct participation in state government." Kansans had been forced to live with the mistakes made by elected officials. "The people," said Finney, "should be allowed to make their own mistakes."[168]

The legislative changes indeed seemed mostly to reflect changes in the makeup of the state's population and the mix of its industries, though the switch was neither so rapid nor so unequivocal as to happen without debate and resistance. The abortion issue, for instance, was hotly debated in Kansas.

That struggle was typical throughout the country, but there was a reason why Randall Terry and his radical Operation Rescue organization picked Wichita for a 1991 Summer of Mercy campaign to close abortion clinics. Dr. George Tiller of Wichita was one of the relatively few physicians in the nation performing late-term abortions, operating under some surprisingly liberal Kansas laws on the topic.[169] "It's funny," a newspaper wrote in 1972, "that in Kansas you cannot buy a drink but you can have an abortion, and in Chicago you can buy a drink, but not have abortions."[170] Wichita was also a place where street and court confrontation could develop full-blown for the media. The Pro-Choice people were as strong at least in Kansas as the Pro-Lifers. Both groups saw their issue as a practical as well as an ideological matter and were highly disciplined in advancing it. Terry's group practiced civil disobedience, chaining themselves to fences. Many were arrested, and the ensuing court action gained national publicity. Protestors held vigils outside Tiller's home, singing "Jesus Loves the Little Children," the Wichita police budgeted thirty thousand dollars extra for overtime and expenses, Terry tried to have a fetus in formaldehyde shown on local TV, and crowds on both sides confronted one another in rallies.[171] Pro-Choice forces concluded, "I think the patience of the people in this community is being pushed to the limit. This is a much larger issue now than an abortion issue. This is a city under siege. This is anarchy."[172] The publicity over Operation Rescue accomplished one goal. It demonstrated that people from all over the nation were converging on Kansas for a certain type of medical procedure. Ironically, puritanical, Republican Kansas in the 1990s was "the abortion capital of the nation."[173]

An equally surprising new reality was the influx of an Asian population, combined with the agricultural industrialization of western Kansas through the development of feedlots and packing plants to serve a more decentralized national economy. Arthur Capper in 1916 had claimed that "Kansas is a product of the melting pot and proud of it," but certainly the state had a mixed record in the treatment of immigrants and ethnic minorities.[174] The persecution of the Mennonites and the ethnic Germans in the World War I era is a case in point. Hispanics, though valuable to the railroad and the salt mines, were confined largely to Little Mexicos on the outskirts of Kansas towns.[175] Labor unions in the 1970s were particularly concerned about illegal aliens among Mexicans. Nearly one thousand were discovered in Kansas in 1976 with forged green cards.[176] There had been severe anti-Chinese riots in Kansas in the 1880s, backed by labor unions, despite the relatively few Chinese living there.[177] And clearly, there was strong anti-Japanese sentiment in the Kansas defense plant areas during World War II.

Garden City had considerable experience with a Mexican community following the promotion of immigration there in about 1907 to construct a sugar beet processing factory. There were 131 Mexicans in Finney County by 1915, and more came after the Mexican revolution in 1919, when a Mexican mission was established in the western Kansas town. However, the 1930s depression led to heavy pressure from labor unions and local governments to hire American labor only. There also began to be a combination of harsher discrimination in the town and more resistance to such treatment by the Mexican-American residents. Returning veterans, accustomed to equal treatment in the military, found the racial situation in Kansas particularly hard to bear. Yet inroads were made, and Mexicans began to be employed in western Kansas towns in many occupations other than in traditional field labor.[178]

Asians were few in evidence in the early years. The first Chinese national from Kansas to be admitted to U.S. citizenship was Frank Yobe Yokoyama of Wichita, naturalized in 1953.[179] However, in 1983 there was enough of an Asian population that the Kansas Governor's Cabinet Subcommittee on Migrant Concerns studied the immigrant situation in Garden City, where about fifteen hundred Asians, mostly Vietnamese, Laotian, and Cambodian, worked for IBP packing company (opened in 1981) and lived in what the committee found to be substandard housing. "You wouldn't want a dog in some of these places," said a witness. The influx also created problems with school capacity and health care.[180] There were five thousand Asians in Sedgwick County at the 1980 census, but that number was thought to have dropped 50 percent by mid-decade as these people took jobs in the western Kansas packing plants.[181] In 1988 Southeast Asians made up 8 percent of the population of Garden City. The community college was by then offering English language courses at the mobile home parks, and the school district provided bilingual education and tours of the IBP plant to all new teachers so that they could see where their students' parents worked.[182] There was a Southeast Asian Mutual Assistance Association, offering translation help with rules and documents, assistance with employment, and legal, health, and family advice. One of the major mental health problems was the depression the immigrants experienced, both over leaving family and homeland and in trying to adjust to such a different physical and cultural landscape.[183]

The industry that employed the Asian and Hispanic population in western Kansas was itself controversial, though economically useful. Feedlots, which finished cattle for the packing plants, were efficient in putting weight on cattle but controversial because of the smell and potential water pollution that such concentrated biological units generated. More tense yet was the specter of corporate hog farming, a potential economic bonanza but an environmental disaster. The general anticorporate farming law passed in

Kansas in 1931 was repealed in 1970, but there remained restrictions on corporations owning land in Kansas for farming purposes.[184] Such innovations as hog farms required special legislative consent. In the mid-1980s farming was in a considerable slump, and western Kansas towns and counties were desperate enough for new hope. In 1984 there were seventy-four thousand farms in Kansas, four thousand fewer than in 1974. The average size was 749 acres, 43 acres more than a decade before. And in a survey, only 8 percent of Kansas farmers said they wanted the government to keep out of farming; they needed the support to get by, ideology aside.[185]

Corporate hog farms were clearly a mixed blessing. A bill to allow them in the state passed the senate in 1984 but died in the house. Kansas hog producers feared that large-scale corporate operations would have an unfair competitive advantage and might not attract hog packers to the state as promised. Some hog raisers did not want to "see the Kansas hog industry go the way of the beef industry, where corporate and investor ownership has helped develop huge cattle feedlots." Still, they had to admit that the number of cattle fed in Kansas was growing dramatically while hog production had declined from 2.1 million in 1980 to 1.5 million in 1985. Production of hogs was only about half of what it had been in the 1950s. Kansas producers also got less for their hogs because they had to ship them to out-of-state packing plants.[186] There were studies indicating that the western Kansas population was aging and declining. Still, small hog farmers and their organizations worried that the state would officially sanction the corporate farms and that communities would issue industrial revenue bonds and offer property tax write-offs to them in the name of economic development.[187] The same fears were raised about proposed poultry operations.

Quality of life issues are complex. Economic development might involve compromise, but what quality of life was there if life in general could not be supported by the jobs the new kinds of agricultural industry provided? Representative Bruce Larkin expressed the view of the opposition on this matter in 1987: "The real issue is, what type of economy and society do we want? Do we want a corporate farm economy, where tax-subsidized investors feed hogs in lots employing Kansans at little more than a minimum wage with the profits drained out of state? Or do we want an efficient family farm economy where the people who do the work also enjoy the benefits of ownership and support their communities?"[188] But it was hardly that simple. A study in 1987 predicted that Kansas, then the nation's ninth-largest pork-producing state, could have virtually no commercial swine production by the twenty-first century unless the situation changed.[189] Consequently, in 1988 the Kansas Pork Producer's Council reversed its position and decided not to oppose changes in the state law that would allow corporate hog farms. There were two conditions: the legislature should prohibit tax breaks to corporate farms, and it should finance research for technology to keep hog producers competitive.[190]

The process did seem amazing. DeKalb Swine Breeders produced one hundred eighty thousand animals a year for breeding stock near the southwest Kansas town of Plains, employing 175 people and spending $14 million a year in the area. "Each animal's life is tracked by computer," said a spokesperson, "its vital statistics, weight, feed consumption and health recorded at regular intervals. Littermates are kept together, since research has shown that family harmony results in improved growth rates."[191] A representative from DeKalb Swine Breeders told the legislature that the company was going to build more hog farms whether Kansas changed its law or not, and it would like to do so in southwest Kansas, where it had a start. Said DeKalb's president Roy Poage, "Corporate hog raising is essential if Kansas is to become a dominant swine-producing state. Kansas has prospered in the past partly because it was willing to adapt to new methods of food production. Corporate hog farming is part of the future of American agriculture. If Kansas is to participate fully in the new farm economy, it must allow corporate hog farming."[192]

To some people, however, these words sounded as if they had come from George Orwell's *Animal Farm*—a frightening prospect. And the opponents had influence. DeKalb failed to get permission to expand its operation; the legislature would not modify the corporate farming law to fit the company plans. A Wichita headline read, "Hogs Head South: Economic Suicide in Kansas." DeKalb then announced plans for a $3.6 million large-scale hog farm near Turpin, Oklahoma, only about ten miles south of Liberal, Kansas. The farmers, the *Wichita Eagle* editorialized, "have left Kansas a reputation as hostile to business." And that was a pointless action, the newspaper thought. "Kansas can resist modern agribusiness and, most likely, wind up a financial victim, or it can work with corporations to keep the state's rural economy viable." As it was, the economic future of Kansas was "cloudy," with the modernists and traditionalists locked in an ancient battle.[193] Corporate hog farming remained a debate right into the twenty-first century, symbolizing a much wider set of issues about the regional future.

So divided indeed were interests within the state in the late twentieth century, and so much did these divisions turn on the geographical lines that split industrial and urban Kansas from the rural, small agricultural traditionalists, that there was at least a half-serious attempt in the 1990s to have western Kansas secede from the state. Reapportionment, school finance, and mineral taxation issues left the west feeling more isolated from the Topeka establishment than it ever had.

Secession attempts were not new. The Wichita editor Marshall Murdock had promoted it in the 1880s. In the 1950s a Lamar, Colorado, editor proposed that western Kansas, eastern Colorado, and the Texas panhandle break away from their dissimilar governmental partners and form a new state. Don Concanan, a Hugoton attorney and former Republican state chairman, revived such talk in 1992 when Governor Finney proposed a uniform state levy for school taxes, which would remove local school boards' authority to set property tax levies. That was the drop of the other shoe after the school consolidation that many western Kansas counties had opposed years earlier. It also smacked of the centralization of the state highway system, which those same counties had opposed in the 1920s. It was centralization and standardization, telling the districts how much money to spend on each pupil and redistributing the tax revenue (which in the form of the severance tax was quite substantial in Stevens County around Hugoton) to poorer school districts elsewhere in the state. It might seem modern and efficient and the way the nations did things, but to a minority, those were fighting words.[194]

A sign in front of a motel on U.S. 50 near Lakin read, "To heck with Topeka—let's secede." The owner stated, "What triggers me is the whole attitude of eastern Kansas legislators toward us out here in Western Kansas." It seemed the west paid and the east benefited, being in relation to eastern Kansas much the same as Kansas had once been in relation to the eastern United States—an oppressed colony in a mercantilist system. Governor Finney's press secretary responded, "I think the governor feels that despite differences that regions of the state might have, we are . . . when it comes right down to it, all Kansans."[195] But that attitude was far from universal. An editorial writer in Wichita was half serious in saying that maybe Wichita should secede. But that would not get rid of "Wichita-bashing" in Topeka.

"Secession, if anything, would intensify that problem because it would give folks in the rest of Kansas what they lack now—a valid reason to hate us."[196]

Legally, secession clearly was impossible. Attorney General Bob Stephan said that there was no way any Kansas county would be allowed to secede. "You could petition the good Lord himself to secede," he wrote, "but it would be an exercise in futility." Concannon, however, claimed that if the residents were allowed to vote, secession would win.[197] Disgruntled leaders of twenty-four western counties met in Garden City in March 1992 to discuss secession and to complain about Sedgwick, Johnson, and Shawnee Counties, largely urbanized, exempting more than $1 billion in property from the tax rolls to promote their economic development at the expense of the rest of the state. Maybe the western counties would boycott and not send their severance tax to Topeka. A Morton County commissioner asked, "Are you going to lock up the whole southwest corner of Kansas and put us in jail?"[198]

There was an unofficial vote on secession, which carried with a margin as high as 95 percent in some areas, but naturally it was mostly the enthusiasts who voted. The overall vote was 5,402 to 966.[199] Their point was heard. "Kansas is a big, diverse state that's hard to govern in the best of times," declared an editorial. "But as long as urban forces to whom power now is shifting understand the futility and stupidity of allowing rural Kansas to languish, Kansas will be a prosperous—if not completely happy place."[200]

The issue did not go away, nor was it only about the school finance package and the severance tax of recent years. The real problem, Concannon said, was "an insensitive, unresponsive state government willing to usurp authority that rightly belongs at local levels."[201] California had a secession movement also, but the *Eagle* reminded readers that "California is one of the wackiest states in the Union, while Kansas tends to be one of the more practical ones. . . . California dreaming about forming a new state won't work there or in Kansas." It was time, the paper said, to "get on with some practical Kansas-like solutions."[202]

There was humor in the whole matter. Some suggested that the new state joining parts of Kansas, Oklahoma, and Texas might be called Kotex. The danger was in those who did not see humor in it and who took the constitutional convention held in the west that fall seriously. Southwest Kansas did have a great sense of place, and that sense was of a different Kansas. "There's something called 'the plains eye,'" wrote a Garden City resident, "that enables people to see life differently—to have a deep feeling for community, to appreciate the subtle beauty of the land, to respect nature, to develop self-reliance and isolation." The Denver-based Center for the New West in a 1992 study rated that part of Kansas as particularly high in the traditional pan-Kansas values of entrepreneurial spirit, quality of life, and community. The key to preserving it, the study said, was local leadership.[203]

The secession talk and threats of civil war faded soon enough, but there were lessons for those with ears to hear. If the key to preserving values worth having in the future for western Kansas was local hegemony, the same might be said for Kansas as a whole vis-à-vis the nation. As was western Kansas to Topeka in the late twentieth century, so was Topeka to Washington. But there was no talk of revolution anymore at the capital.

Instead, the publicity from Kansas picked up by the wire services and the national magazines in the late 1990s was, as it had been in the 1890s and earlier, that the state was a weird place where the politics and the culture were out of line and not in a productive but in a freakish way. The tinder was there, waiting only for the right spark, which in time seemed always to come. Just at the end of the century, it came when the Kansas State Board of Education voted six to four in August 1999 to leave Darwin's theory of evolution out of its detailed science standards for Kansas students. It was up to local school boards whether or not to include Darwin in the curriculum.

The decision was hailed by individuals on and off the board who said that the Bible was the sole authority on creation, that evolution could not be proved (in fact, one board member went so far as to say there was "no evidence for it" and that the board dealt only with facts), and that teaching it undermined students' moral values. Opponents said that the new science standards would make Kansas a laughingstock and allow creationism back into the public schools. Kansas governor Bill Graves issued a one sentence statement: "This is a terrible, tragic, embarrassing solution to a problem that did not exist." He soon talked of eliminating the board or stripping it of authority. The cochair of a panel of science experts who had been commissioned to produce science standards asked that their names be removed from the final standards adopted by the Board of Education.[204]

Although it was clear that the decision did not represent the majority of Kansans (57 percent opposed it in a November poll and 15 percent were neutral), and even though it was changed when a new board took office in 2001, reaction nationally was not kind.[205] Reform and the efforts of Kansans to resist national patterns and to find their own cultural direction became

linked to reaction, and individuality was smeared with the brush of backwardness, even foolishness. At least one high-tech company, Broadcast Soft-
ware International of Eugene, Oregon, which was considering a move to
Kansas, called off its studies in the wake of the evolution decision. The
cultural shock to people moving from liberal, environmentalist Oregon to
Kansas, full of "monkey business" as it now appeared, would be too great.[206]
The publishers of a new school history of Kansas decided to remove parts of
the chapter on geology and paleontology. A part of the minority on the state
Board of Education reacted to that by saying, "The next thing you know, we
will be removing the Holocaust from history textbooks because it is objec-
tionable to some people."[207] Richard Crawson, the *Wichita Eagle* cartoonist,
drew a panel showing a family visiting Mt. Rushmore with paper bags over
their heads, the father saying, "You know . . . being a Kansan on vacation was
a lot more fun before the State Board of Education's evolution vote."[208]

"Forget tornadoes, abortion protests and [antigay activist] Fred Phelps,"
advised a local editorial. "Like it or not and deservedly or not, Kansas may
have a new claim to national infamy these days, thanks to the conservative
majority on the State Board of Education. . . . Will possible job recruits for
Kansas' high-tech industries, many of them with school-age children, really
rush to relocate to a state that, on the brink of the 21st century, still can't find
consensus on a debate dating from the 19th century?" Stories about the vote
ran immediately on TV on *News Hour with Jim Lehrer* and *Politically Incor-
rect with Bill Maher*. It was on the front pages of the *New York Times* and the
Washington Post and soon made all the national news magazines. The *Post*
described Kansas as "a state where fights over evolution are as common as
cornfields," and the headline in the *Los Angeles Times* was "New Creationism
Debate Is a Twister in Kansas."[209] Maybe, wrote a Boulder, Colorado, man,
"the next thing would be to require teaching that the stork delivers babies,
that the Earth is really flat, and that the moon landings were faked in a giant
soundstage in New Mexico. It is a sad day indeed for Kansas." A former
Kansan writing from Albany, New York, was typical of outlanders in asking,
"How did the bigoted and ignorant gain control of the State Board of
Education?"[210]

Attacks mounted. The *New York Times* ran the headline, "Willful Ignorance on Evolution." It averred that "deep sadness" was the most sensible
response to the Kansas decision "to downgrade the teaching of evolution" in
the state's public schools. "If local school boards follow the state board's lead,

bright students who might be inclined to pursue scientific careers may now reach college age with little or no exposure to the fundamental organizing principle of modern biology, and all students will be the poorer for lacking scientific literacy."[211] The *Washington Post* was no kinder with its headline: "And God Said, Let There Be Light in Kansas." Staff writer Gene Weingarten sent a memo to the members of the state board signed God. "Thank you for your support, much obliged." But God then went on to admit he was not perfect. He had made errors: "Armpit hair—what was I thinking?" But surely Kansans did not "seriously believe that I dropped half-a-billion-year-old trilobite skeletons all over my great green Earth by mistake?" People were supposed to find them and then draw appropriate conclusions. "That's what I made you for. To think."[212] The headline from *Time* was "Darkness in Kansas." Stephen Jay Gould had commented negatively on the decision, and so had other readers. One man suggested that Kansas backwardness might have changed Dorothy's itinerary in *The Wizard of Oz*. "Seems as though Dorothy could have saved herself the trip [to a fantasy world] by just attending the Kansas school board meeting. . . . Fortunately neither ruby slippers nor creationist rhetoric can repeal reality."[213]

The Thomas Fordham Foundation report, "The State of State Standards, 2000," gave Kansas a C+ grade, up from D− in 1998, but it condemned roundly the evolution decision and the removal of references to evolution in the working draft of "Kansas Science Education Standards." It went beyond biology proper. "By means of these cuts, the Kansas State Board of Education has reduced biology to natural history, geology to rock collection, and astronomy to stargazing." The standards, the foundation said, were "a disservice and an insult to the young people of Kansas. Dorothy went from Kansas to Oz seeking wonders and there found empty pseudoscience. She had the good sense to return to Kansas. Sadly, the State Board of Education seems to wish to issue a one-way ticket to all the state's children."[214]

There had been no such ruffle over evolution since the Scopes trial of 1925, and then it was the Round Lick Primitive Baptists of Tennessee in the catbird's seat. Now Kansas, for all its efforts since Payne Ratner took office in 1938 to modernize and industrialize and shed its Dust Bowl image, was, to the nation, in that same Old South backward category.

It was a truism that change was inevitable, desirable, and irresistible. But it was part of sententious wisdom, too, that unexamined movement was merely isometric exercise. The people who were not just drinking and shooting off fireworks on New Year's Eve 1999 were thinking about the future and its possibilities. And some of them in Kansas must have had the thought that a future separated from the past, or a future that was a copy of someone else's dream, might be powerful in its way but not at home with them and with their country.

So many businesses, founded and pursued in Kansas by Kansans, were by 2000 operated from headquarters elsewhere. Wichita's Beechcraft, whose founder Walter Beech had always had his name in the local telephone book, was now a branch of Raytheon. Pizza Hut's absorption into the Pepsi Company was only the beginning of its loss of local identity. The franchise businesses, which Kansas had helped spawn, now did away with individuality in people's daily lives. The MacDonald's on the corner might as well have been in Omaha. The same was true for banks all over the state, as changes in banking laws and megamergers blotted out the family enterprises once so typical. Even the iconographic prairie sky, with its 180-degree horizon and bright Milky Way looming over the marvelous quiet of swishing grasses, and the sense of awesome distances, had given way to Mercury-vapor lamps, highway noise, and the instant gratification of the World Wide Web. Kansans were glad they no longer had to live in dugouts and sod houses, but their residences, along cul-de-sacs, in houses whose plans came from pattern books, located in suburbs with British and Italian names, muted the sense of place mightily. They narrowed the possibilities of the future while seeming to free it of parochialism.

Two thousand one was not the year the movie with the Richard Strauss fanfare had predicted. The Kansas Cosmosphere in Hutchinson was indeed in place as the "Smithsonian of the West" and a major repository for antique NASA hardware. It was the top tourist attraction in the state in 2001. And Joe Engle, Ron Evans, and Steve Hawley, astronauts, were from Kansas.[215] However, people in the state were still rooted to old mother earth and to time and place. And Kansas itself had much more in common with the times and places of its past—of the New England Emigrant Aid Company people trying to build up Lawrence near the Delaware reserve in 1854, or of towns on the western steppes competing for railroads and industries in the 1870s and 1880s, or of the reformers of 1910 Kansas trying to make their ideology practical by training a generation of disciplined people, or of those laborers grinding the grit in their teeth in the Dust Bowl, or of the promoters working for industry and government contracts adapted to the strengths of their region amid a great international war crisis—than most Kansans, ignorant of their past and relatively morose about their present and future in any but a shallow promotional way, seemed to understand and appreciate.

There was an "eclipse" indeed, not in basic promise but in far vision—that long look that Rolla Clymer had talked about as being necessary to take from some high hill in communion with oneself in one's home place, before marching forward in what would otherwise be blind fury. Ideas and knowledge—scholarly, religious, historical, grounded in place—Wes Jackson has said, are as much a part of any future plan for a better world as hedge posts. Perhaps that local knowledge lay hidden for a time. Maybe the dazzle of the digital age and the power of widespreading institutions distracted people from remembering the ground on which they stood and had their being, causing them to think they could fly and never land. But the ideas were there, waiting to be shaped in the new mix the future would give them. "We must," Jackson claimed, "build cultural fortresses to protect our emerging nativeness."[216]

Aeneas had to leave familiar Troy in flames and seek a new country. He faced forward without tears. But he carried his aged father on his back and his household gods in his hand, never forgetting whence he sprang.

CONCLUSION: HORIZONS

"Love a place like Kansas," wrote former Wichitan Earl Thompson in 1970, "and you can be content in a garden of raked sand." It was the flattest, he thought, and its economy, culture, and history were a mishmash. "Big sky, wheat sea, William Inge, bottle clubs, road houses —Falstaff and High Life, chili and big juke road houses—John Brown, Wild Bill Hickcok, Carry A. Nation, cockeyed Wyatt Earp, Pretty Boy Floyd, and shades of all those unspoken Indians." But there was something compelling still to the novelist in the ungrasped relationships implicit in the passage of time in the place. "Out there on the flat, in the wheat sea, on the spooky buffalo grasses where the ICBMs go down into the shale and salt of the prehistoric sea wherein the mighty monosaurs once roamed and the skies were not cloudy all day," remarkable things had happened.[1] The Wichita of Thompson's youth in the 1930s and 1940s had been, from the perspective of his mobile home, gritty and tough, but it engaged his imagination still. The checkered past of experiment in Kansas gave it dignity, made it a genuine, exceptional home. Richard Hinton remarked once that although the English historian Thomas Macaulay once wrote that democracy carried no romance about it, "we point to the story of free Kansas as an all-sufficient reply."[2]

The New Western History has made a point of reemphasizing place and continuity, as contrasted to Frederick Jackson Turner's focus on a frontier "process." Historians of this school have reintroduced complexity and diversity into the western "myth" and have questioned that the "development" of the West was seamless "progress" carried out by independent and self-reliant people, or that it represented "redemption" rather than conquest and exploitation of wild land and wilder people by capitalism and Christianity.[3] They have pointed out, too, that human culture is as important as geography and climate in defining the West. Richard White in his new history of the American West wrote that "geography did not determine the boundaries of the West; rather history created them. . . . The environment . . . limits as well as creates human possibilities, but it simultaneously reflects the actions of human beings upon it." Choices were made, he says, at every turn—the kind of choices that have been isolated in the "pivotal moment" structure of this history. The choosers were, according to White, "trying to shape the way that people would use . . . information and the kind of society—however hazily envisioned—that these people would create." History, that is, was creating and importing culture, as well as destroying it, as it plodded along, seemingly benignly and pragmatically, month by month.[4] The New Social History chimes in with emphasis on the inarticulate ordinary folk, whose unsung annals do not appear in traditional historical sources. Business historians have pointed out a relative neglect in documenting the entrepreneurial achievements through which the United States has spoken most loudly.

This state history addresses the selection and interpretive shortcomings these critics locate, and there is certainly material in the real history of Kansas to support some of their insights. But the writing of history moved beyond the strictly political long ago. Some of the shortcomings in practice of historical writing are more matters of the nature of survival in archives than of practitioners' ideology. Historiographers debate the question of "exceptionalism" and the whole matter of whether the United States was a "New Eden" or just more of the same ancient wheel-spinning with a new gloss. At least one theorist wonders whether in the late twentieth century, with its global technology, seeming universal decline of dictatorships, and the rise of matters of personal self-esteem, we may not indeed have come to the "end of history," in the sense of factions and nations struggling over the shape of the future. Are there any longer real choices anywhere for anyone?[5]

Still, with all the emphasis on upsetting Turner's theories about the fading frontier, its nature, and its influence on the American character, there has been relatively little attention paid to Turner's second major focus: the impact of region and section in American history. Turner was influenced by Josiah Royce, who wrote that there was a need for "vigorous development of a highly organized provincial life to offset dead national conformity that tends to crush the individuals." Unless such regional entities emerged, Royce feared that the nation "was in danger of becoming an incomprehensible monster, in whose presence the individual loses his right, his self-consciousness, and his dignity." A "sense of place, in geographical environs," was vital to a sense of community.

In "The Significance of the Section in American History" (1925), Turner developed the idea that the cultural dimension was a dominant factor in the development of landscapes.[6] He found that in moving to local and regional history from his broader sweeps through American history, the picture nearer the ground, so to speak, became more complex. Turner's broadly interdisciplinary study and extensive note taking on all aspects of the slices of time and space he chose to interpret consumed so much time and energy that he managed to publish very little. As his biographer Ray Billington put it, Turner discovered that "sections must be defined in geographic, economic, political, cultural, and psychological terms."[7] The unique characteristics of a region manifested themselves not only in political and economic behavior, but also in literature, the arts, and in every facet of social life. That scholarship has had many heirs. Region, defined as "an *ensemble de rapports* between man and the natural milieu," has been a laboratory for testing the exceptionalism theories as well as for applying some of the insight and direction of the New Historians.[8]

The best-known Kansas proponent of regionalism was William Allen White. His theme, pursued in novels as much as in editorial writing, was the quest for morality in an immoral world. "What better force than the ethos of the small town to cleanse an amoral world?" The Kansas village could be the city on the hill, the place where, as utopian reformers in the nineteenth century had thought, the practical consequences of reform could be played out. In *The Revolt from the Village, 1915–1930,* Anthony Channell Hilfer explains not only that such a place did not really exist in Kansas or anywhere else at any time, but also how powerful was the myth of it in the minds of many Americans. It was neither farm nor city, but somehow combined the best of both. "It is not really of arms and the man that this story is written," White wrote in 1917 of his trip to Europe with Henry Allen, "but it is the eternal Wichita and Emporia in the American heart that we shall celebrate." Their mistake no doubt was in thinking that World War I was a "colossal annex to their progressivism" and in White's belief that he had "at last carried Kansas to the planet."[9]

Another problem with regionalism is that the longtime awareness among historians of region (the South, the West, the Northwest) has had a sweep that is perhaps too wide to reveal important but more subtle distinctions. Not only do states have regional cultures based on their unique political and social history, as well as climate and geography, but they also often consist of several substate cultures. If Minnesota were a milking stool, it has been observed, it "would have one leg in the northern pine forests, one leg in the corn belt and one in the Great Plains."[10] St. Paul is not Brainerd anymore than Topeka is Hays.

True, the forces of homogenization have been at work. I have a 78-rpm recording of myself at four years reading "The Night Before Christmas" for my dad. The little boy reading the poem has a heavy southern accent in comparison to the college professor by the same name listening to it over fifty years later. Certainly, some southern expressions, even family speech peculiarities, are still found in his lectures, to the surprise of students, but what happened to the definite regional accent of 1948? Is it TV, politico-speak, or what else? Indeed, the local DeCoursey and Steffens Dairies no longer compete for the home milk-delivery business, and even the neighbor-hood Dillon's grocery has grown into a regional giant. But just what is left of region, and how important is it to the future?

Granted, there is virtue in toning down parochial passions insofar as they are violent and intolerant, as those of Kansas sometimes were. But is it desirable to dispense with regional cultures, or simply to allow them to disappear along with Indian languages, accidentally and unmissed? And what of local history? Is it of use only as a case study of national trends? From some dissertation titles and editorial comments, one might think so. Is its purpose primarily pride, even if that is based on mythology? Is it enough to skim the simple surface and pull out the people and events that happen to be remembered or that a given establishment or counterculture thinks are appropriate to remember, no matter how untypical, stereotyped, or ex-treme? And is the weight of historical accounts to be measured by their chronological or geographical scope or by the extent to which they general-ize without local detail? Are things really so much the same everywhere, or should they be? Should local and regional history be left in the hands of antiquarians and genealogists, thus deteriorating into a useful but clearly subsidiary subcategory of the real thing? And why should the local history of an English shire or a New England colonial town be academically respect-able, capable of revealing universal truths, but a study of a Kansas town is perceived as narrow to insignificance?

There is a bromide that all history is local, and that, as Oliver Wendell Holmes Sr. once observed, what we had for breakfast, or the traffic on our commuting street, may have more actual effect on our lives than our philo-sophic, political, or religious opinions. Yet writing about the everyday, close up, is difficult—perhaps more so than the broader study. What seems orderly from a distance looks chaotic from the center. William James talked about the necessity for habit in action and for simplification, even stereotype, in analysis to deal with "the buzzing, blooming confusion of the actual world." Walter Lippmann added, "It is beyond the power of any mind—to deal continually and effectively with the data of experience in all their raw, hetero-geneous fullness."[11] Henry Adams, one of the pioneers in writing detailed social history, wrote in the midst of his late-life depression that "historians undertake to arrange sequences—called stories, or histories—assuming in silence a relation of cause and effect. These assumptions hidden in the depths of dusty libraries, have been astounding, but commonly unconscious and childlike; so much so, that if any captious critic were to drag them to light, historians would probably reply, with one voice, that they had never sup-posed themselves required to know what they were talking about."[12]

Still, the enterprise of history does go on, and even though historians may never reach the ideal of telling it as it actually happened, modern source accessibility and techniques allow regional historians to approach more closely in their writing the purpose of catharsis that the realist novelists of the nineteenth century set as their purpose.[13] That is, the story should be realistic enough that readers can identify with the characters and their situa-tion and learn vicariously, to the end of avoiding some painful experience and building upon what people have already sustained and suffered.

One would not imagine that the *Kansas Statistical Abstract* would make especially fascinating reading. However, its data, running through June 1999, reveal some trends that are surprising and thought provoking. It illustrates the distance traversed since the Emigrant Aid Company people set up their tents in Lawrence nearly 150 years ago.

The population of Kansas in 1998 was 2,629,067, or 0.97 percent of the population of the United States. In 1890 the state had only 1,428,108 people, but that was 2.27 percent of the U.S. population, the highest ever for Kan-sas. Though it is obvious that Kansas was never a big population center for the nation, it has not been such a demographic nonentity as it is now since the 1870s.

Rates of growth over time are also revealing. Once Kansas was one of the fastest-growing places in the nation, not only when and because it was new, but in the 1880s at least, because it was genuinely booming economically. Compared to an overall growth rate per decade for the nineteenth-century United States of about 25 percent, Kansas grew over 200 percent in the 1870s and over 40 percent in the 1880s. Then came the disastrous 1890s, when the population growth rate was still positive but reduced to 3 percent. The Progressive Era was another peak, right in the midst of all the controversial Kansas reform. The state grew 15 percent between 1900 and 1910 but then settled down to a 4 to 6 percent growth rate, with the exception of the 1950s, when it reached nearly 15 percent again.

Population growth by region within Kansas in the 1990s shows the south-western part of the state, where the new feedlot and packing plant industry is, up by nearly 7 percent while the rest of the west was down by about 5 percent. Certain very rural counties were down significantly more: Comanche by 13 percent, Ness and Trego by about 10 percent. The big growth areas were the urban areas. The east-central area, including Lawrence, Topeka, Kansas City, and Manhattan, grew by 12.24 percent in the 1990s, and the south-central area, including Wichita, was up 8.21 percent. Individual urban counties or counties, like Butler, adjacent to a major city, skyrocketed. Butler County, admittedly the largest in area in the state, gained over 20 percent in population in the 1990s, and Johnson County, where the Kansas City suburbs are, was not far behind. Density for Johnson County was over 900 per square mile; Chase County in the Flint Hills had a population density of 3.8, and Wallace in the far west 2.0. Hardly anything in the west had a population density over about 13 people per square mile, which may help explain the secession sentiment there. Urban counties were becoming more urban, though it was clear this was a trend dating at least from the 1920s. Sedgwick was 78.3 percent urban in 1920 and 82.4 percent urban in 1990. Wyandotte went from 89.1 to 99.1. There were a few small towns, like Holton, showing dramatic recent increases, but that is explained by the development of tribal casinos.

The Kansas population was aging and becoming more diverse. The median age in 1990 was 32.9; in 1998, 35.2. Five percent of the state's population was over 75 in 1970; the figure was 6.4 percent in 1990. Hispanic population increased over 40 percent in the 1990s and Asian by 35 percent.

Kansas, long thought of as the quintessentially rural state, not only was losing rural population in the late twentieth century as fewer people ran larger farms, but the contribution of agricultural products to the total state economy also was declining precipitously. The amount of Kansas land in farms has remained fairly steady since 1920. But in 1920 there were 167,000 farms in Kansas; in 1996 only 64,000. The average Kansas farm size in 1920 was 272 acres; in 1996, 747 acres. The value per acre was $62 as opposed to $575, and the value per farm was $16,900 as against $429,453. In calculating the gross state product of a bit over $71 billion, farms in 1997 contributed $2.554 billion. The farm contribution to the state economy had actually increased over 40 percent between 1965 and 1980, but between 1980 and 1999 it dropped over 30 percent in absolute dollars, not adjusted for inflation. One would have to call that a free fall.

Meanwhile, other sectors grew rapidly to change the balance. The Kansas economy as a whole grew in constant dollars from $12.259 billion in 1965 to $71.737 billion in 1999, or about 500 percent. Retail and wholesale trade, however, was $12.861 billion of that total, up 1,200 percent since 1965. Manufacturing increased 400 percent, to an output of $12.784 billion. Services contributed similarly in 1999—$12.298 billion, up a whopping 1,700 percent since 1965. The figure for government was $9.759 billion in 1999, up 700 percent since 1965. The top Kansas industries by employment in 1999 were government (about 20 percent of the workforce in 1990) and services (about 20 percent also). In the latter category, health services and eating and drinking led the way. Agriculture, by contrast, in 1990 employed fewer than 6 percent of Kansans.[14]

The pace of change is even more extreme than prophets predicted in past years, although in the same direction. The *Kansas 2000* report (1975) underestimated population growth slightly by the turn of the millennium by about 300,000. The suggestion there that Kansans might decide to "people the countryside, towns and small cities of the state" in the next quarter-century was a possibility in which doubtless even the planners did not believe. The report was more in error still on the changes in the balance of the economy. It estimated manufacturing in 2000 would be about double what it was in 1965; that was half too low. Service was projected at a 150 percent increase— far below the actual. By contrast, the projection was that agriculture would increase in contribution to gross product by about 40 percent after 1980, rather than declining by 40 percent as it actually did.[15] In short, the state is considerably wealthier in 2000 than the 1960s and 1970s planners imagined it would be, but its demographic makeup and economic balance are changing more rapidly than they predicted. Does this imply the "end of history" as we have known it? Does it imply that the regional culture developed over 150 years of experiment and challenge is as endangered, maybe as irrelevant, as the family farm?

Kansas is not alone in these threats to regional identity. The "acids of modernity" are working everywhere to erode emotional and physical connections to community and state. A revealing case in point is Minnesota, whose combination of icons and personalities is as diverse, contradictory, and in danger of eclipse as that in the Sunflower State. Though Minnesota is a prosperous state and, most people think, "a decent place to live," the industrial revolution, the central state, global markets, and nationalism have left less room than before for variation and peculiarities in local landscapes and minds. The new century is one in which "distinct places and unique localities matter less and less in shaping human experience, sensibility and memory."[16] Recently, the journal *Daedalus* devoted an entire issue to trying to understand Minnesota, and in so doing, contributed significantly to organizing serious consideration of the issue of regionalism everywhere.

The editors conceived their idea in conversations with colleagues in Europe, aware of the distinct regions and subcultures in their countries, who questioned whether the United States still had true regions. European travelers flew coast to coast over the middle of the United States and got most of their news from the media centers on those coasts. When news came from the midlands, it was something startling, like the Oklahoma City bombing, or some weird AP wire copy from Kansas. The study of Minnesota showed that it was changing rapidly in the late twentieth century; that a cerebral image of it at least remained, and was perhaps strengthening, as its former physical status as a real place declined; and that, for all the changes, it was "certainly not becoming Illinois or Iowa, New Jersey or Oregon."[17]

Minnesota's tradition and present problems, according to the authors, contain much that is reminiscent and reflective of Kansas. True, its status as a "pure" land of ice and snow, as a recreational haven, or as the Star of the North has no parallels in Kansas. But like Kansas, it has historical heroes far more varied and broadening than the easily named ones, like Charles Lindbergh or Hubert Humphrey. It had, like Kansas, a history of confidence and of moral hegemony, followed by self-doubt and criticism. Its past was one of "complex and contradictory truths," and it was "a hard someplace to be sometimes."[18] The literary image of its small towns, from Sinclair Lewis's Gopher Prairie to Garrison Keillor's Lake Woebegone, was hardly unmixed boosterism. And its rural heritage has been subsumed by access into it and out from it so pervasive that the very meaning of place has changed. "Nothing restrains the forces of the outside world. . . . The agents of change enter . . . without knocking, and, trafficking in the contraband of wishes and daydreams, they steal minds and hearts."[19]

Yet something remains of the iconographic Minnesota—something important in allowing people in a world beyond their comprehension to "take measure of who they are and what they value."[20] Part of it is mysterious. Minnesotan Robert Zimmerman (aka Bob Dylan) gave his own musical interpretation in "Girl from the North Country" and sometimes came forth with a prosier version of the prominence of place. He claimed in a *Playboy* interview in 1977 that the ore country of Minnesota formed his music. The stillness of the winter was part of it. "You can have some amazing hallucinogenic experiences doing nothing but looking out the window. . . . The air is very metallic. There is a lot of Indian spirit. The earth is unusual, filled with ore. . . . There is a great spiritual quality throughout the Midwest. Very subtle, very strong, and that is where I grew up. New York was a dream."[21]

The question is whether even this artificial, maybe nostalgic, local iconography will last very long in the world of virtual reality. The *Daedalus* authors seem to think that in the case of Minnesota it will, if only because nationality, "the quintessential identity of modern times, drowns in complexity, divisions and corruption. It pales in the limelight in which it stands."[22]

Even Carl Becker, that great early interpreter of the Kansas spirit, seemed to the historian Dudley Cornish, speaker at the state historical society meeting in 1974, to have oversimplified considerably and based his 1910 essay on narrow research and limited observation. It would surely be inadequate in 1975, and Cornish apologized a little—"I task the ghost of Becker for what he did not know, what he could not know"—but stuck to his guns that "memorable phrases" are not enough in interpreting the state.[23]

Perhaps the "Kansas spirit," however described, will strengthen the more it is threatened. Keillor talks about the "dark Lutherans" of Minnesota worrying about whether they will be embarrassed by not being able to start their cars some cold morning or for forgetting whether Galatians or Ephesians comes first—a people afraid to be happy, else they would have moved out of that climate to California long ago. But Keillor in the year 2001 was living in New York talking about Minnesota. By contrast Bill Holm moved back to his hometown in Minneota, Minnesota, where there was precious little opportunity to teach in his field of English literature but a great chance to reconnect with place, to rediscover what Ole Rolvaag was talking about. Holm, in his delightful *The Heart Can Be Filled Anywhere on Earth*, quotes Flannery

O'Conner on fashionable novelists: "You know what's the matter with them? They're not from anywhere."[24] Being connected, even if it sometimes seems like failure, is to Holm the best kind of spiritual success. That he was a fat man of Icelandic background from latter-day Minnesota homesteader stock seemed to him something he had better face sooner than later. It was a part of mental health.

Kansas has experienced dramatic economic changes before. The railroad and aviation industries are two examples. But through the changes, it has maintained and developed, mostly to its clear advantage, its recognizable regional character and approach. It has also valued its history, however much debate there was on the heroes and villains of the piece.

Central to that character has been an abiding faith, tempered in the fires of the territorial struggle and developed in a hopeful people in a sometimes harsh environment, that storms were inevitable, maybe even exciting, and that after them came the sun, a gentle breeze, and a particularly peaceful day. Kansans have traditionally faced the day, like their state flower, and survived in their rough cheeriness as it does in the heat of late summer when seemingly all else fades. They have done so largely because they have believed consistently in the knowability and applicability of morality and have pursued their belief in the improvability, if not the perfectibility, of the human species and its society, even at the risk of great ridicule by the cynics. "Kansas was, is and ever shall be in highest C," wrote an 1890s journalist of the Sunflower State. "She stands upon the misty mountain tops and yells. . . . She is keyed beyond all keys. She is the Commonwealth of Hyperbole."

Taking such delight in the seeming ordinary, and thus transforming it by a mental and psychological alchemy into something valuable, was the high art long practiced on the prairie. Charles Driscoll of Wichita wrote that when his father had arrived in that town in the 1870s, he took one look at the environs of the hot and dreary station and asked when the next train out was. "Ain't none from here," said a man on the platform. "End of the line. But this is Wichita, the Peerless Princess of the Plains. Stay here and you will be rich in no time." Driscoll was so struck by that he walked on into town and his family stayed there for generations, embarrassed perhaps to admit that the "Nile of America" was not all it was cracked up to be. Yes, there was an inferiority complex at times—what Kenneth Davis called a cycle of "self-assertion and self-abnegation"—but there was always a determination that no circumstance, personal or environmental, was forever. Kansans' hope was written on their hearts and seen in their deeds. There were no lucky breaks in Kansas. It was all, as the *Wichita Eagle* editor Marshall Murdock put it, "spell-created." The meek may inherit the earth, went a joke in the Kansas oil patch, but they will never get the mineral rights. G. K. Chesterton once wrote, "Gullibility is the key to all adventures. The greenhorn is the ultimate victor in everything; it is he that gets the most out of life." There is a fine line between healthy gullibility and hayseedism, but the cynic never created anything. What kept Kansas going, asked a Boston reporter visiting the state during the great 1880s boom. The answer was, "Confidence, Confidence."[25]

Surely it was not an in-your-face sort of confidence, or arrogance, that was the Kansas tradition. However offensive the smugness might be at times, the general impression was more often a kind of laughable innocence, or naiveté. It seemed Kansans were innocent as doves but had missed the part about being wise as serpents, concerning the real ways of the world.

They seemed often to be promoting a utopia, though in many ways one much closer to home than those from Plato to More to Bacon to Bellamy and Morris—something seemingly just around the corner, almost real. Still, it was some sort of City of God on earth, repugnant to the simply hard-headed, and therefore it had qualities in common with the naive yet insightful characters of the utopian romances so popular in the United States around the turn of the twentieth century among those cultivating a mild sense of guilt in their parlors.

In William Dean Howell's *Traveler from Altruria,* a strange man, from an unknown but Christian country, with an unidentifiable accent, and socialist, feminist, and labor reform views, shakes up guests at a New England resort with his innocent comments on the damaging customs that are assumed by the rest of them to be unimpeachable and unalterable. When told that personal virtue is not legislated in America, the man from Altruria asks if there are not marriage laws. "You have laws, I believe, against theft and murder and slander and incest and perjury and drunkenness?" There were laws against cruelty to animals. Why stop there? "We have everything on a large scale here," commented a diner, flicking an ash from his cigar, "and we rather pride ourselves on the size of our inconsistencies even." But Mr. Homos from Altruria was not easily dismissed. "I imagine," he said, "that the difference between your civilization and ours is only one of degree, after all, and that America and Altruria are really one at heart."[26] That oneness was close to what the rest of the country thought and feared for a century about its heartland of Kansas.

Surely all that has changed. The business statistics of Kansas in the year 2000 are not the only facts that would make it unrecognizable to a Kansan of 1861 or 1891 or 1911 or 1931. But as every conservative thinker (Edmund Burke may be primary among them) has noted, change, to be solid, must have continuity with what has gone before in that place. The sculptor Leonard Baskin, in complaining about the extremes of modern art, has written that it is tragic that the tradition of the representation of the human figure has been abandoned, rather than just advanced, by abstract expressionists. "The fig-ure and meaning of man," Baskin wrote, "is a vast terrain, crusted and reticulated with his passage from time to time and place to place. Here is he pitched and in this lambent configuration is his future and his hope."[27] That study is never over, always new. And if we are to look for guidance in the past, it helps to look at things happening where we are now. "It is human nature," a *Wichita Eagle* editorial pointed out in 1911, "that contemporary progress is as unreal to us as foreign lands, as unreal as things of the historic past, unless we see them with our own eyes." The piece then put the new airplane not only into local context but also into historical context, compar-ing it with the arrival of the freight wagon, the locomotive, the bicycle, and the automobile on these same plains. That connecting in time and place was a part of a culture's understanding of what was happening to it. "The aero-plane is unreal to Wichita until we see it soar over our own local habitat. Then . . . the aeroplane is ours, and we are of the aeroplane age."[28]

Certainly, too, there is the historical and contemporary planning issue of leadership. The physical and cultural environment has shaped Kansans to a degree, but doubtless individual Kansans have shaped it more. Perhaps they have been self-selected and then winnowed by the challenges of the state— certainly there was a selective process going on in the 1850s "cockpit of the nation" era. But the figures of earth that emerged were both towering and unusual. What a crew were Senators Pomeroy, Lane, Ingalls, Peffer, Capper, Kassebaum, Dole, for example; or journalists Brown, Clymer, Howe, Miller, Wilder, Ware, Prentis, White; or feminists Nichols, Johns, Lease, Diggs; or entrepreneurs Holliday, Chanute, Hyde, Menninger, Anderson, Koch, Yost, Harvey, Hall, Gott, Grant, Dillon, Warkentin, McCoy, Longren, Coleman, Beech, Garvey, Carney, Wallace. Is William Allen White's Kansas gone be-cause conditions have so changed as to make a White impossible, or because there is no White to create the circumstances that he in turn interpreted and under which he thrived? Is Kansas an "eclipsed civilization" or an extinguished one?

Without venturing far into Carlyle's "hero in history" mode, it is clear that biography has mattered to Kansas and that the cliché that its greatest resource is its people is more than a little true. At present, there are indeed studies being conducted in Kansas of those circumstances that may encourage entrepreneurship and entrepreneurs, in which the state, especially in the twentieth century, has been so strong. And the consultants on such studies are considering local history as part of the data. But the question is broader than the sources of business acumen and verve. It must have been something other than accident (since accident is such a negligible factor in Kansas history) that drew or made such giants. There was a combination of challenge and opportunity—a hope of achievement just difficult enough, but just possible to realize—to stimulate a certain kind of person to action. That type tended to be articulate, but not purely literary, and to put words and reason to work in newspapers, in politics, and in business rather than in poetry or plays. Kansas was perceived for a long time as a relatively new country, a frontier, where young people could make a difference, and definitely as an economy that was growing and as a society that was improving. The thought was obviously in the atmosphere too that control was largely local and that Kansans could reap what they sowed. There has been some future shock indeed, but there is reason to believe something like that combination could recur should the level of leadership that created and sustained it in the first place, and the supporting cast in Kansas communities and their media, return. Shedding an inferiority complex involves more than social psychoanalysis. It requires finding or creating something unique and regional in which to take pride. A motivational speaker in Wichita in 1908, when there was discouragement about the long economic downturn and the loss of many of the boom businesses of the 1880s, addressed a crowd of sixteen hundred amid the carnival atmosphere of the Wonderland Amusement Park. He dared again to pick up Reverend Sheldon's theme that business should take Jesus as a partner and watch profits rise. He suggested a return to the Kansas tradition, fostered locally despite the new twentieth-century emphasis on centralized and merged corporate power and on big and federally mandated government programs; and he proposed the slogan, "Find Good and Advertise It." Shortly, the autumn street fairs in that city under the electric "Watch Wichita Win" sign included the first demonstrations of the airplane. Not coincidentally, and not incompatibly, in the same years Wichita established a local historical society.

"What is your community?" editor Murdock asked. "It is your family. To whom do you look in sorrow? To whom do you turn in trouble? To whom do you first go for approbation when successful? It is not to the indefinite nation . . . but to that community where you have settled down to pass your life, to achieve your fortune, to rear your children, to build your home. . . . The community's joys are your joys. The community's sorrows are your sorrows. The community's success is your success. Pull the community down to a small town and you pull yourself down to small opportunities. Enlarge it by your help and you enlarge your field and yourself."[29] The whole White school would have said, "Amen."

The novelist Reynolds Price has gone so far as to suggest, almost in the manner of Einstein, that space is, in a way, time and that our geographical nomadism, our fear of home, represents a fundamental fear of the process of the passage of time itself. "If we stay at home," he wrote, "we acknowledge as past which, as one of its functions, has given birth to us (contingency then, no spontaneous generation); and worse, we see that past die before us—our parents age, sicken, dissolve in pain; we tend them as they go and learn our mortality. But flight—ah flight! To leave all is to cancel its claims. In a strange far place we are free to be ourselves . . . and the chance of evading decay and companions—the touch of others' bodies. That touch is the friction which begins to wear us; and time finds us anywhere, the ultimate police." No wonder that in an age of divorce, mobility, and supposed cosmopolitanism there are few sacred places, those places defined by Roman law as one a person makes by carrying the dead into them and being willing to live with and for those tombs. Moving does not satisfy. "They change their skies, but not their souls, who run across the sea," Horace wrote. A safe and rewarding home, according to Price, may be built only around a nucleus of sound and realistic people who have a keen sense of their own possibilities, "as these possibilities are foretold and restricted by visible successes and failures of . . . ancestors." Wisdom comes from prolonged observation in place. The constant movers "crippled themselves—the breadth of vision, depth of feeling— by abandoning the only places and people they stood some chance of comprehending."[30] Similarly handicapped are those who remain but do not reflect adequately on the history of where they are rooted. "No man," wrote

C. S. Lewis, "would find an abiding strangeness in the moon unless he were the sort of man who could find it in his own backyard."[31]

Local history both stimulates and limits, just as a horizon does. Limits are in fact endemic to the environment. Elliott West makes this clear in discussing the centrality of Liebig's Law to the Plains—that maxim that one must calculate survival in the worst times and cycles there rather than the average or the best.[32] "Dakota," Kathleen Norris wrote, "is a painful reminder of human limits, just as cities and shopping malls are attempts to deny them." And amid those limits, she notes, one must dig in to live. "The Plains are not forgiving. Anything that is shallow—the easy optimism of a homesteader; the false hope that denies geography, climate, history; the tree whose roots don't reach ground water—will dry up and blow away."[33]

Rootedness involves truth telling and coming to terms with the local past, not as isolated mythology but as present direction. Joseph Levenson noted in an essay once that when the Chinese communists wished to destroy Confucianism as a current influence, they did so by honoring it, mythologizing it, and thus confining it to museums.[34] That way of proceeding is a flaw in the modern emphasis on cosmopolitanism, as equated with sophistication. The etymology of the word suggests both urban concentration and Faustian yearning. It is contrasted to the maligned parochialism or provincialism of people who do not regard or treat the whole world as their habitat. Yet like tasteless computer-generated typography, cosmopolitan behavior is not desirable because it is suddenly possible. Local history, continuity, is as much a part of the enabling and humbling atmosphere of place as is climate or landscape. "Dakota can be terrifying enough," Norris observes, "without the loss of one's cultural context."[35]

Webster defines "horizon" as the circle that bounds that part of the earth's surface visible from a given point, the seeming junction of earth and sky called the apparent, local, or visible horizon. Figuratively, it is the limit or range of perception or experience. Anthropologically or geologically, it can be a particular historical period or a deposit from a particular time. In painting, a "horizon" is the imaginary line on which is projected the point of sight or station point of the spectator, especially in landscapes where this horizon replaces the natural horizon. The Oxford English Dictionary adds that "horizon" can be an embryological stage of development, or "a boundary, the frontier or dividing line between two regions of being." According to a quotation from 1551, "The horizonte is a cyrcle whiche parteth that parte of the worlde that we see, from that which we see not." From 1812 comes, "Stars rose and set, and new horizons glowed." That is, metaphorically expressed, as it must ultimately be, very much the way it is with the relation of local history in Kansas to the future of the state and its people.

Regions can lose their way, loose their historical moorings, just as people in them can. Samuel Johnson wrote to James Boswell in 1775 concerning a trip Johnson had made to the middle counties of England: "Having seen nothing I had not seen before, I have nothing to relate. Time has left that part of the island few antiquities; and commerce has left the people no singularities." He confessed to a perhaps related weariness of being at home and being abroad, which modern ideals of mobility as sophistication and the modern fact of frequent and easy divorce from spouse as well as from home only tend to strengthen. However, Johnson noted that reading, especially of history, sometimes helped relieve the seeming pallidness of the sensed immediate environment. As for the world weariness, "all the wise and all the good say, that we may cure it."[36]

Local knowledge, which comes through study as well as observation and experience, clearly does have the power to transform the atmosphere in which people's lives are lived. William Phillips of Salina, reflecting on Kansas history in 1890, noted, "History is the crystallization of thought into institutions." Those institutions in turn had their influence on thinking among local residents of the future. Phillips remembered when he first came to Kansas Territory, meeting with White Antelope and Roman Nose and Black Kettle. "The wife of each soldier," he wrote of the tribes, "when the sun rose, erected in front of their tent, on a spear and club, her husband's shield and his arms across it all burnished. Little did the people dream how soon all these forms and customs should be swept away. . . . Long years have passed since I saw an elk. . . . The animated life of the Kansas of a quarter of a century ago is now completely blotted out as if it had never been."[37] But another atmosphere was made in its place from thought, and there is still a need to mark our tents somehow with emblems of ourselves.

"I was the world in which I walked," wrote Wallace Stevens, "and what I saw / or heard or felt came not from myself / And there I found myself more truly and more strange."[38] Virgil wrote that before plowing an unfamiliar patch of ground, "it is well to be informed about the winds / About the variations in the sky / The native traits and habits of the place / What each locale permits, and what denies."[39] Eugene Ware, the Kansas poet, expressed similar feelings about possibilities and limits inherited from place and fore-bears:

> States are not great
> Except as men may make them.
> Men are not great except they do and dare.
> But states, like men
> Have destinies that take them—
> That bear them on, not knowing why or where.[40]

NOTES

PREFACE

1. James Malin, *In Commemoration of the Centennial Anniversary of the Admission of Kansas into the Union 1861: An Essay to Accompany an Exhibition of the Kansas Statehood Centennial* (Lawrence: University of Kansas Library, 1961).
2. James Malin to Eugene Davidson, editor, Yale University Press, June 2, 1951, James Malin Papers, box 3, Kansas State Historical Society (KSHS).
3. Roy Nichols, "Kansas Historiography: The Technique of Cultural Analysis," *American Quarterly* 9 (spring 1957): 91.
4. A careful account of published Kansas histories with idiosyncratic commentary is James Malin, "Notes on the Writing of General Histories of Kansas," published in five parts in the *Kansas Historical Quarterly*, autumn 1954 through winter 1955.
5. Malin, "Notes," part 2 (winter 1954): 282, 286; part 4 (summer 1955): 407. The historical society had a complex earlier history under various names dating to the late 1850s.
6. Barbara Brackman, comp., *Kansas Trivia* (Nashville: Rutledge Hill Press, 1997), 133.
7. Bessie Wilder, *Bibliography of the Official Publications of Kansas, 1854–1958* (Lawrence: Governmental Research Center, University of Kansas, 1965), unpaged preface, and Bessie Wilder, *Governmental Agencies of the State of Kansas, 1861–1956* (Lawrence: Governmental Research Series, University of Kansas, 1957), unpaged preface.
8. Homer Socolofsky and Virgil Dean, comps., *Kansas History: An Annotated Bibliography* (New York: Greenwood Press, 1992).
9. William Connelley, *A Standard History of Kansas and Kansans*, 5 vols. (Chicago and New York: Lewis, 1918), 1: v.
10. Tacitus, *De Vita et Moribus Iulii Agricolae Liber* (Boston: Merrymount Press, 1904), 1 (my translation).
11. Isaiah Berlin, *The Crooked Timber of Humanity* (Princeton: Princeton University Press, 1991), 62.

INTRODUCTION: THE FAR LOOK

1. *Speech of William H. Seward, for the Immediate Admission of Kansas into the Union. Senate of the United States, April 9, 1856* (Washington, D.C.: Buell and Blanchard, 1856), Kansas Collected Speeches and Pamphlets, vol. 1, KSHS.
2. Fred Trigg, quoted in Leo Oliva, "Kansas: A Hard Land in the Heartland," in *Heartland: Comparative Histories of the Midwestern States*, ed. James H. Madison (Bloomington: Indiana University Press, 1990), 250.

3. The "electric light" phrase is from *Topeka Daily Capital*, March 1, 1885, Mounted Clippings, Charles Gleed Papers, box 48, KSHS.

4. John Ingalls, "Kansas," May 10, 1896, in *A Collection of the Writings of John James Ingalls: Essays, Addresses, and Orations* (Kansas City, Mo.: Hudson-Kimberly, 1902), 483.

5. *Salina Herald*, February 17, 1893, Essays Clippings, vol. 1, KSHS.

6. John Ingalls, "Kansas, 1541–1891," in *Collection of the Writings of John Ingalls*, 465.

7. *Topeka Journal*, July 8, 1931, Kansas Description Clippings, vol. 2, KSHS.

8. William Simpson, "The Kansas Idea," *Our State* 1 (October 1889).

9. Edwin Manning, "Kansas in History," *Collections of the Kansas State Historical Society* 12 (Topeka: State Printing Office, 1912): 10.

10. Simpson, "The Kansas Idea."

11. Speech by Arthur Capper before the Kansas Society of Washington, 1927, Arthur Capper Papers, box 13, KSHS.

12. Ibid., typescript of speech to real estate men, 1911, box 46.

13. Ibid., radio address by Capper, WINX, July 3, 1941, box 13.

14. Lawrence: University Press of Kansas, 1988.

15. Karl A. Menninger, "Bleeding Kansas," *Kansas Magazine* (1939), quoted in *Kansas Revisited: Historical Images and Perspectives*, ed. Paul Stuewe, 2d ed. (Lawrence: University of Kansas Division of Continuing Education, 1998), 38.

16. Charles Edson to Reed Harris, August 30, 1937, Charles Edson Papers, microfilm MS-811, KSHS.

17. Paul Jones, "Kansas the Beautiful: Answering Heywood Broun," unidentified clipping [1931], Kansas Description Clippings, vol. 2, KSHS.

18. Nelson Antrim Crawford, "The State of Kansas," *American Mercury* (April 1950), clipping in Capper Papers, vol. 13, KSHS.

19. Fred Brinkerhoff to Rolla Clymer, January 28, 1964, Frederick Brinkerhoff Papers, box 8, KSHS.

20. In *Esquire* (November 1969), Kansas Description Clippings, vol. 4, KSHS.

21. Frank Popper and Deborah Popper, "The Great Plains: From Dust to Dust, a Daring Proposal for Dealing with an Inevitable Disaster," *Planning* 53 (December 1978): 12.

22. Among many other places, the story is told by Cecil Howes in a typescript from the 1940s, "Grand Duke Alexis," in the collection "Jayhawk Sketches," in Cecil Howes Papers, box 1, KSHS. For Kansas humor generally, see Robert Haywood, *Tough Daisies: Kansas Humor from "The Lane County Bachelor" to Bob Dole* (Lawrence: University Press of Kansas, 1995).

23. Charles Gleed, "As Others See Us," in *Hiawatha World*, n.d. [1894], Mounted Clippings, Gleed Papers, box 49, KSHS.

24. *Oxford English Dictionary*, 2d ed., 20 vols. (Oxford: Clarendon Press, 1998), 4: 497.

25. William Allen White, *The Autobiography of William Allen White* (New York: Macmillan, 1946), 281.

26. Charles Gleed, "As Others See Us."

27. Noble Prentis, "Is Kansas Corrupt?" *Topeka Mail*, March 3, 1891, in Essays Clippings, vol. 1, KSHS.

28. John Ingalls, "Kansas: 1541–1891," 456.

29. J. W. Gleed, *Sectionalism. An Address Delivered Before the Quill Club, New York City, February 15, 1898* (n.p., n.d.), 7, 17–18, Kansas Collected Speeches and Pamphlets, vol. 24, KSHS.

30. Governor Lyman Humphrey, *Inaugural Address*, January 14, 1889, 5–7, 10, in Lyman Humphrey Clippings, Kansas Collection, Spencer Research Library, University of Kansas (KU).

31. Gleed, "As Others See Us."

32. Charles Sheldon, "Why I Prefer to Live in Kansas," *Topeka Capital*, March 15, 1931, Kansas Description Clippings, vol. 2, KSHS.

33. Leverett Spring, *Kansas: The Prelude to the War for the Union* (Boston: Houghton Mifflin, 1885).

34. James Malin, *John Brown and the Legend of Fifty-six* (Philadelphia: American Philosophical Society, 1942), 436.

35. "The Preacher's Book," *Topeka Commonwealth*, October 10, 1885.

36. *Hiawatha World*, undated clipping [1885], Mounted Clippings, Gleed Papers, box 51, KSHS.

37. Ibid., F. B. Sanborn, in *Springfield Republican*, n.d.; Sanborn's piece was reprinted in *Topeka Commonwealth*, December 16, 1885.

38. Spring, *Kansas*, 145–46, 303–5.

39. See Malin, *Brown*, 359–439, for the definitive account of these arguments generally.

40. "One Who Knew Brown," in *Christian Register*, Sara Robinson Scrapbooks, vol. 4, KU.

41. Ibid., *Weekly Inter-Ocean* (Chicago), January 25, 1883.

42. Ibid., Ingalls in clipping, n.d. [*North American Review*, February, 1884].

43. *Union* (Junction City), May 2, 1885, Kansas State Historical Society Clippings, vol. 7, KSHS.

44. Malin, *Brown*, 409.

45. *Christian Register*, July 26, 1883, Sara Robinson Scrapbooks, vol. 4, KU.

46. G. W. Brown to editor, n.d. [1884], clipping in ibid. For G. W. Brown's fullest statement, see George W. Brown, *False Claims of Kansas Historians Truthfully Corrected* (Rockford, Ill.: author, 1902).

47. *Daily Press*, December 13, 1879, Kansas History Clippings, vol. 4, KSHS.

48. Malin, *Brown*, 437.

49. Charles Gleed, in *Topeka Daily Capital*, October 18, 1885, Mounted Clippings, Gleed Papers, box 48, KSHS.

50. Noble Prentis, in *Olathe Mirror*, June 7, 1888, clipping in James Lane Papers, KU.

51. Charles Gleed, in *Topeka Daily Capital*, October 18, 1885, Mounted Clippings, Gleed Papers, box 48, KSHS.

52. Don Wilson, *Governor Charles Robinson of Kansas* (Lawrence: University Press of Kansas, 1975), 161–62.

53. Malin, *Brown*, 355.

54. Charles Robinson to Madam [Miss Emmee Willard], March 30, 1860, Charles and Sara Robinson Papers, reel 1 (MS 640), 00510–12, KSHS.

55. Charles Robinson, *The Kansas Conflict* (New York: Harper and Brothers, 1892), v.

56. E. F. Ware to Mrs. Ingalls, December 7, 1901, Eugene Ware Papers, KU.

57. William Connelley, *John Brown* (Topeka: Crane, 1900), 170.

58. E. F. Ware to William Connelley, March 17, 1903, Ware Papers, KU.

59. *Kansas City Star,* October 14, 1928, Reminiscences Clippings, vol. 4, KSHS.

60. William Leuchtenberg, *Theodore Roosevelt: The New Nationalism* (Englewood Cliffs, N.J.: Prentice-Hall, 1961), 10.

61. William Allen White to Theodore Roosevelt, August 4, 1910, microfilm selection by Walter Johnson from William Allen White Collection, Library of Congress, 9 reels, MS-0045, reel 3, no. 473, KSHS.

62. Walter Johnson, ed., *Selected Letters of William Allen White, 1899–1943* (New York: Henry Holt, 1947), 113.

63. Robert LaForte, "Theodore Roosevelt's Osawatomie Speech," *Kansas Historical Quarterly* 32 (summer 1966): 192.

64. Oswald Villard, *John Brown, 1800–1859: A Biography Fifty Years After* (Boston and New York: Riverside Press, 1910), viii.

65. *Lawrence Journal–World,* May 13, 1914, Kansas History Clippings, vol. 4, KSHS.

66. James Malin to Professor T. L. Harris, November 26, 1926, Malin Papers, box 1, KSHS.

67. *University Daily Kansan,* January 6, 1929.

68. James Malin, in *University Daily Kansan,* January 10, 1929.

69. James Malin to Nyle Miller, May 26, 1953, Malin Papers, box 3, KSHS.

70. Nichols, "Kansas Historiography," 86.

71. M. Sue Kendall, *Rethinking Regionalism: John Steuart Curry and the Kansas Mural Controversy* (Washington, D.C.: Smithsonian Institution Press, 1986), 43.

72. Bret Waller, "Curry and the Critics," *Kansas Quarterly* 2 (fall 1970): 47.

73. Calder Pickett, "John Steuart Curry and the Topeka Murals Controversy," *Kansas Quarterly* 2 (fall 1970): 30, 37–40.

74. Henry Allen to Payne Ratner, March 8, 1941, Ratner Papers, Governors' Papers, 27-11-05-08, KSHS.

75. Ibid., Mrs. H. T. Bishop to Payne Ratner, August 13, 1943.

76. Ibid., *El Dorado Times,* reprinted article by Richard Lloyd Jones from *Tulsa Tribune,* enclosed in secretary to Payne Ratner, August 15, 1942.

77. William Zornow, *Kansas: A History of the Jayhawk State* (Norman: University of Oklahoma Press, 1957).

78. Charles Edson to Governor Huxman, November 17, 1938, Edson Papers, KSHS.

79. Ibid., Charles Edson, preface to unpublished novel, "Booms and Ballies," 1, 2, 10. This preface is what remains of the suppressed text Edson wrote for the WPA *Guide to Kansas.*

80. James Malin to Robert Henry, April 1945, Malin Papers, box 2, KSHS.

81. Nichols, "Kansas Historiography," 85.

82. Rolla Clymer, speech at dedication of Olathe Methodist Church, 1917, Rolla Clymer Papers, box 50, KSHS.

83. *Wichita Eagle,* September 6, 1999.

84. Quoted in Craig Miner, *West of Wichita: Settling the High Plains of Kansas, 1865–1890* (Lawrence: University Press of Kansas, 1986), 119.

85. Clipping, February 21, 1917, no newspaper identified, Frederick Funston Papers, box 3, KSHS.

86. The phrase is from Arthur Capper, "A Tribute to Kansas," speech given March 8, 1945, excerpt from *Congressional Record,* in Capper Papers, box 13, KSHS.

87. Crawford, "The State of Kansas," in ibid.

88. R. H. Garvey to W. D. Ferguson, March 26, 1935, R. H. Garvey Papers, box 7, KSHS.

89. *Rolla Weekly Herald,* May 31, 1888.

90. Edith Coe to Rolla Clymer, January 8, 1975, Clymer Papers, box 48, KSHS.

91. *Chanute Tribune,* January 30, 1932, Kansas Description Clippings, vol. 2, KSHS.

92. A. R. Greene to Charles Gleed, December 5, 1915, Gleed Papers, box 15, KSHS.

93. See James Nottage and Floyd Thomas, " 'There's No Place Like Home': Symbols and Images of Kansas," *Kansas History* 8 (autumn 1985).

94. Haywood, *Tough Daisies,* 53.

95. Joseph Collins, ed., *Natural Kansas* (Lawrence: University Press of Kansas, 1985), 98, and Nottage and Thomas, " 'There's No Place,' " 141.

96. *Harper's Weekly,* November 11, 1899, clipping in Funston Papers, box 3, KSHS.

97. Nottage and Thomas, " 'There's No Place,' " 142.

98. Quoted in *Mail and Breeze,* February 12, 1900, Poetry Clippings, vol. 4, KSHS.

99. Collins, *Natural Kansas,* 98.

100. *Kansas City Star,* October 23, 1930, Sunflower Clippings, vol. 1, KSHS.

101. Thomas Wolfe, "The Four Lost Men," in *From Death to Morning* (New York: Grosset and Dunlap, 1935), 118.

102. Typescript, n.d. [1915], Capper Papers, box 13, KSHS.

103. Victor Murdock, in *Kansas City Star,* January 22, 1928, Kansas Description Clippings, vol. 1, KSHS.

104. Introduction of Dr. Cherrington of the League of Industrial Democracy, Topeka, October 23, 1934, Capper Papers, box 13, KSHS.

105. Allen, in *Kansas City Star,* January 22, 1928, Kansas Description Clippings, vol. 1, KSHS.

106. The phrase is from Olin Templin in *Graduate Magazine* (February 1934), Capper Papers, vol. 13, KSHS.

107. Ibid., speech before Kansas Society of Washington, 1927.

108. Quoted in Noble Prentis, *Kansas Miscellanies,* 2d ed. (Topeka: Kansas Publishing House, 1889), 185.

109. *Topeka Journal,* July 18, 1931, Kansas Description Clippings, vol. 2, KSHS.

110. Speech at Pittsburg Normal Banquet, May 5, 1915, in Capper Papers, box 47, KSHS.

111. *Kansas City Star,* January 29, 1936, Kansas Description Clippings, vol. 2, KSHS.

112. Olin Templin, in *Graduate Magazine* (February 1934), in Capper Papers, box 13, KSHS.

I. CHILD OF THE GRASSY PLAIN

1. *Address Delivered at the Quarter-Centennial Celebration of the Admission of Kansas as a State by Gov. John A. Martin. Topeka, Kansas, January 29, 1886* (Topeka: Kansas Publishing House, 1886), Kansas Collected Speeches and Pamphlets, Miscellaneous, vol. 23, KSHS.

2. Raymond Wood, ed., *Archaeology on the Great Plains* (Lawrence: University Press of Kansas, 1998), 5.

3. Paul Carson, *The Plains Indians* (College Station: Texas A&M University Press, 1998), 29, 35.

4. Elliott West, *The Contested Plains: Indians, Goldseekers, and the Rush to Colorado* (Lawrence: University Press of Kansas, 1998), 18, 33.

5. Ibid., 57.

6. James Mead, "Wichita's Industrial History—In the Beginning," in *History of Wichita and Sedgwick County, Kansas,* ed. O. H. Bentley, 2 vols. (Chicago: C. F. Cooper, 1910), 1: 115–16.

7. Elliott West, "A Story of Three Families," *Kansas History* 19 (summer 1996): 112–13.

8. Charles Sternberg, *Life of a Fossil Hunter* (New York: Henry Holt, 1909), 16.

9. Bill Sharp and Peggy Sullivan, *The Dashing Kansan: The Amazing Adventures of a Nineteenth-Century Naturalist and Explorer* (Kansas City, Mo.: Harrow Books, 1990), 72–75.

10. Most of Dyche's 1893 World's Fair exhibits are still in place at the University of Kansas, as are the early fossil discoveries. The other great repository is the Sternberg Museum in Hays.

11. Sternberg, *Fossil*, 104. An excellent overview is John Peterson, "Science in Kansas: The Early Years, 1804–1875," *Kansas History* 10 (1987): 201–40.

12. John Rydjord, *Kansas Place-Names* (Norman: University of Oklahoma Press, 1972), 288.

13. John McPhee, *Annals of the Former World* (New York: Farrar, Straus, and Giroux, 1998), 214.

14. Huber Self, *Environment and Man in Kansas: A Geographical Analysis* (Lawrence: Regents Press of Kansas, 1978), 36, 38, 40–49. Graphic representation of much that is basic about Kansas may be found in Homer Socolofsky and Huber Self, *Historical Atlas of Kansas* (Norman: University of Oklahoma Press, 1972).

15. William Allen White, "The Story of Agua Pura," from White, *The Real Issue: A Book of Kansas Stories* (Chicago: Way and Williams, 1897), 23.

16. *Encyclopedia Britannica,* 11th ed., 29 vols. (New York: Encyclopedia Britannica, 1911), 11: 654–55.

17. Self, *Environment,* 52.

18. William Least Heat-Moon, *PrairyErth* (Boston: Houghton Mifflin, 1991), 43.

19. Self, *Environment,* 55.

20. "Kansas Weather," *Topeka Commonwealth,* January 7, 1874, Weather Clippings, vol. 1, KSHS.

21. Ibid., *Topeka State Journal,* August 30, 1913, vol. 2. Flora wrote a book, *Tornadoes of*

the United States (Norman: University of Oklahoma Press, 1953), which details the most severe Kansas storms.

22. "Western Kansas, Its Climate," *Kansas City Journal,* November 30, 1879, Weather Clippings, vol. 1, KSHS. See also Miner, *West of Wichita,* 46–51.

23. *Topeka Capital,* July 14, 1911, Weather Clippings, vol. 2, KSHS.

24. Ibid., *Republic County Journal,* June 21, 1879, Storms and Cyclones Clippings, vol. 1, and *Wichita Eagle,* March 15, 1953, vol. 5, KSHS.

25. Ibid., *Seneca Tribune,* June 17, 1881, vol. 2.

26. Ibid., *Wichita Star,* vol. 3.

27. See Thomas Averill, "Oz and Kansas Culture," *Kansas History* 12 (spring 1989): 2–12.

28. *Atchison Champion,* May 30, 1879, Storms and Cyclones Clippings, vol. 1, and *Topeka Daily Capital,* June 2, 1879, vol. 1, KSHS.

29. Ibid., "The Kansas Tornado," *Harper's Weekly,* June 18, 1882, vol. 4.

30. Ibid., *Topeka Daily Capital,* March 17, 1956, vol. 5.

31. Ibid., February 3, 1956.

32. Ibid., *Wichita Eagle,* May 26, 1955, and *Topeka Capital,* May 27, 1955.

33. Quoted in Wilson, *Robinson,* 75.

34. *Wichita Eagle,* April 15, 1880.

35. *Kansas City Star,* August 17, 1913, Weather Clippings, vol. 2, KSHS.

36. Joseph Gambone, "Economic Relief in Kansas, 1860–1861," *Kansas Historical Quarterly* 36 (summer 1970): 149–74.

37. John Ingalls to Father, May 16, 1862, John Ingalls Papers, box 1, KSHS.

38. Elizabeth Custer, *Tenting on the Plains or General Custer in Kansas and Texas* (New York: Charles L. Webster, 1887), 614, 636, 640, 644, 646, 651–52.

39. Alden Stevens to All at Home, May 30, 1859, Robert Stevens Papers, box 1, KSHS.

40. Ibid., Robert Stevens to Levi Parsons, June 20, 1873, box 3.

41. *Kansas City Star,* June 3, 1902, Floods Clippings, vol. 1, KSHS.

42. Ibid., *Topeka Herald,* May 29, 1903.

43. Ibid., *Kansas City Star,* May 30, 1903.

44. Ibid., *Topeka Capital,* May 31, 1903.

45. Ibid., *Kansas City Journal,* May 31, 1903.

46. Ibid., June 1, 1903.

47. Ibid., P. J. Ryder in *Topeka Herald,* June 2, 1903, vol. 2.

48. *Topeka Journal,* June 8, 1908, vol. 6; *Kansas City Journal,* September 9, 1914, vol. 7; *Kansas City Times,* September 13, 1926, vol. 7; and *Topeka Journal,* June 4, 1935, vol. 8, all in ibid.

49. Ibid., *Kansas City Star,* May 17, 1951, vol. 9.

50. Ibid., *Topeka Journal,* May 25, 1951.

51. Ibid., June 29, 1951.

52. Ibid., *Topeka Capital,* July 12, 15, 1951, vol. 10, and *Kansas City Kansan,* July 11, 1971, vol. 15.

53. Ibid., *Lawrence Journal–World,* July 16, 1951, vol. 11.

54. Quoted in Craig Miner, *Uncloistered Halls: The Centennial History of Wichita State University* (Wichita, Kans.: Wichita State University Endowment Association, 1995), 5.

55. *Wichita Eagle*, August 3, 1941, Weather Clippings, vol. 2, KSHS.

56. John Ingalls to Father [Elias Ingalls], October 24, 1858, Ingalls Papers, box 1, KSHS.

57. Ibid., January 8, 1863.

58. *Wellington Press*, December 4, 1880, Weather Clippings, vol. 1, KSHS.

59. Sara Robinson, *Kansas: Its Interior and Exterior Life* (Boston: Crosby, Nichols, 1856), 179.

60. John Ingalls to Father, January 19, 1861, Ingalls Papers, box 1, KSHS.

61. William Roe to William Howard, February 2, 1879, William C. Howard Papers, box 3, KU.

62. The source here is the author's twenty-five years of experience as an amateur astronomer and his reading of experiences of others in Kansas.

63. E. H. Taylor, Swarthmore, Pa., to Rolla Clymer, March 5, 1961, Clymer Papers, box 35, KSHS.

64. "Western Kansas: Its Climate," from *Kansas City Review* in *Kansas City Journal*, November 30, 1879, Weather Clippings, vol. 1, KSHS.

65. Oliver Bidwell and William Roth, "The Land and the Soil," in *The Rise of the Wheat State: A History of Kansas Agriculture, 1861–1986*, ed. George Ham and Robin Higham (Manhattan, Kans.: Sunflower University Press, 1987), 3.

66. Dennis Farney, in *Wall Street Journal*, quoted in *Wichita Eagle and Beacon*, June 14, 1975, Save the Tallgrass Prairie Collection, box 2, KU.

67. Willa Cather, "On the Divide" (1896), quoted in Diane Quantic, *The Nature of the Place: A Study of Great Plains Fiction* (Lincoln: University of Nebraska Press, 1995), 23.

68. Dennis Farney, in *Wall Street Journal*, quoted in *Wichita Eagle and Beacon*, June 14, 1975, Save the Tallgrass Prairie Collection, box 2, KU.

69. Heat-Moon, *PrairyErth*, 158.

70. John Stilgoe, *Metropolitan Corridor: Railroads and the American Scene* (New Haven: Yale University Press, 1983).

71. Michael Steiner, "Robert Hine, Sense of Place, and the Terrain of Western History," *Pacific Historical Review* 70 (August 2001): 461–62.

72. John Madson, *Where the Sky Began: Land of the Tallgrass Prairie*, 2d ed. (Ames: Iowa State University Press, 1995), 294.

73. Oliver Bidwell and William Roth, "The Land and the Soil," in Ham and Higham, eds., *The Rise of the Wheat State*, 3.

74. E. G. Heyne, "The Development of Wheat in Kansas," in ibid., 43, 51; Self, *Environment*, 98, 108.

75. Heat-Moon, *PrairyErth*, 156–57; Miner, *Discovery*, 1–2; Daniel Merriam, *The Geologic History of Kansas* (Lawrence: University of Kansas, 1963), 182; see also Rex Buchanan, ed., *Kansas Geology: An Introduction to Landscapes, Rocks, Minerals and Fossils* (Lawrence: University Press of Kansas, 1984).

76. James Sherow, *Watering the Valley: Development Along the High Plains Arkansas River, 1870–1950* (Lawrence: University Press of Kansas, 1990), 83.

77. Self, *Environment and Man*, 104, 206.

78. Ibid., 159, 160; see also Miner, *Discovery*, 179–80.

79. Since there can be no such thing as an undifferentiated encylopedic account, contained in one volume, of everything that might have gone on in the Kansas region, there are at times in this study narrative bridges of no special originality, which, in the interest of space, are not cited in the notes. The information contained in them may be found in numerous, easily available sources, one of a medium level of detail being William Zornow's, *Kansas*. Also useful for straight chronology are the Kansas annals. See Daniel Wilder, ed., *The Annals of Kansas, 1541–1885*, 2d ed. (Topeka: Kansas Publishing House, 1886); Kirke Mechem, ed., *The Annals of Kansas, 1886–1925*, 2 vols. (Topeka: Kansas State Historical Society, 1954–1956); and Louise Barry, ed., *The Beginning of the West: Annals of the Kansas Gateway to the American West, 1540–1854* (Topeka: Kansas State Historical Society, 1972).

80. See William Unrau, *The Emigrant Indians of Kansas: A Critical Bibliography* (Bloomington: Indiana University Press, 1979), for a good summary essay and guide to study.

81. A good source for these early fundamentals is Barry, ed., *The Beginning of the West*.

82. Theodore Parker, *Some Thoughts on the New Assault upon Freedom in America and the General State of the Country* (Boston: Benjamin B. Mussey, 1854), 56, in Kansas Collected Speeches and Pamphlets, Miscellaneous, vol. 3, KSHS.

83. *Speech of Hon. Sam Houston, of Texas . . . in Favor of Maintaining the Public Faith with the Indian Tribes* (Washington, D.C.: Congressional Globe Office, 1854), February 14, 1854, in ibid., vol. 1.

84. *Nebraska and Kansas. Speech of William H. Seward Against the Abrogation of the Missouri Compromise* (Washington, D.C.: Buell and Blanchard, 1854), in ibid., vol. 14.

85. Craig Miner and William Unrau, *The End of Indian Kansas: A Study of Cultural Revolution, 1854–1871* (Lawrence: Regents Press of Kansas, 1978), 4.

86. Ibid., 7–13.

87. Henry Beecher, *Defense of Kansas* (Washington, D.C.: Buell and Blanchard, 1856), 5, in Kansas Collected Speeches and Pamphlets, Miscellaneous, vol. 19, KSHS.

88. Robinson, *Kansas Conflict*, 97.

89. James Malin, *The Nebraska Question, 1852–1854* (Lawrence: author, 1953), 15.

90. John N. Holloway, *History of Kansas from the First Exploration of the Mississippi Valley to Its Admission to the Union* (Lafayette, Ind.: James, Emmons, 1868), 115.

91. James Shortridge, *Peopling the Plains: Who Settled Where in Frontier Kansas* (Lawrence: University Press of Kansas, 1995), 10–11.

92. Brown, *False Claims*, 10–11.

93. Charles Robinson to Dr. Thomas Webb, July 24, 1855, New England Emigrant Aid Company Papers, reel 1 (MS 619), 00240-43, KSHS.

94. The poem was printed in the *Herald of Freedom* (Lawrence), October 21, 1854, and

was for years inscribed behind the desk of the Kansas governor. The complete words are in Wilder, ed., *Annals*, 51.

95. Speech of Eli Thayer, March 25, 1858, reported in *Washington Intelligencer*, October 26, 1858, Speeches Clippings, vol. 1, KSHS.

96. Undated, unidentified clipping, Kansas Territorial Clippings, vol. 3, KSHS.

97. The Amana Historical Society at Middle Amana, Iowa, has the German diary of the expedition and a short typewritten summary by Cliff Toumpold, "The Kansas Odyssey."

98. Connelley, *Kansas and Kansans*, 1: 341–48.

99. Samuel Johnson, *The Battle Cry of Freedom: The New England Emigrant Aid Company in the Kansas Crusade* (Lawrence: University Press of Kansas, 1954), 48, 269, 295.

100. Ibid., 62.

101. Phillips, Sampson & Co. to E. E. Hale, July 12, 1854, reel 1 (MS 619), 00048-50, and August 4, 1854, 00085-86, both in New England Emigrant Aid Company Papers, KSHS.

102. Ibid., M. D. Phillips to Hale, August 21, 1855, 00310-12.

103. Edward Hale, *Kanzas and Nebraska* (Boston: Phillips, Sampson, 1854), 226, 240, 243.

104. Webb to Eli Thayer, May 26, 1854, New England Emigrant Aid Company Papers, reel 1 (MS 619), 00038-41, KSHS.

105. Ibid., Greeley to E. E. Hale, 00080-82.

106. Ibid., Wm. Haley to E. E. Hale, March 9, 1855, 00166-70.

107. Charles Robinson, handwritten remarks at Old Settlers' Meeting in Emporia, September 25, 1889, Charles Robinson Papers, box 1, KU.

108. Eli Thayer, *A History of the Kansas Crusade: Its Friends and Its Foes* (New York: Harper and Brothers, 1889), 187.

109. "Council City. American Settlement Company. The Great Kanzas Enterprize, Composed of the Bone and Sinew of the New England, Northern, Middle and Western States," Isaac Goodnow Papers, box 1, KSHS.

110. Ibid., Isaac Goodnow to Stephen French, December 16, 1854.

111. Ibid., Isaac Goodnow diary, February 20, 1855, box 7.

112. Ibid., Minutes, January 31, 1855, Isaac Goodnow to William Goodnow, April 9, 1855; Ellen Goodnow to Isaac Goodnow, April 12, 1855; and Goodnow diary, March 10, 1855, box 7.

113. Ibid., Goodnow diary, March 21, 1855, box 7.

114. Ibid., March 25, 1855.

115. Ibid., March 27, 1855.

116. Ibid., March 30, 1855.

117. Ibid., Ellen Goodnow to Isaac Goodnow, April 24, 1855.

118. Ibid., William Holt, Lake Shore and Michigan Southern Railroad, to Mrs. I. T. Goodnow, May 26, 1855; Sam Tappan to Mrs. Goodnow, June 29, 1855.

119. Ibid., H. Goodnow to William Goodnow, May 27, 1855.

120. Ibid., Harriet Goodnow to Husband, June 24, 1855.

121. Nicole Etcheson, "Laboring for the Freedom of This Territory," *Kansas History* 21 (summer 1998): 68, 71–72, 76, 87.

122. A biographical sketch of Miller is in the Kansas State Historical Society, *History of Kansas Newspapers* (Topeka: Kansas State Printing Plant, 1916), 27–28.

123. Josiah Miller to Mother and Father, June 4, 1855, Josiah Miller Papers, box 1, KU.

124. Ibid., August 29, 1855.

125. Thomas Webb to Charles Sumner, April 12, 1856, New England Emigrant Aid Company Papers, reel 2 (MS 620), 01159-50, KSHS.

126. Ibid., Thomas Webb to Charles Robinson, October 9, 1854, 00762-65.

127. Ibid., Thomas Webb to Charles Robinson, October 16, 1854, 00772-74.

128. Ibid., [Thomas Webb] to S. C. Pomeroy, November 6, 1854, 00791-98.

129. Ibid., Thomas Webb to Nicholas Brown, February 5, 1856, 00998-1000.

130. Ellen Goodnow mss on early history of Manhattan, Goodnow Papers, box 14, KSHS.

131. Ibid., William Goodnow to Wife, June 17, 1855, box 1.

132. Letter from Kansas, August 1, 1855, no newspaper identified, Legislative Clippings, vol. 1, KSHS.

133. Spring, *Kansas,* 53.

134. Mrs. Reeta Hadden to Representative-elect Miss Kathryn O'Loughlin, in *Hays Daily News,* November 14, 1932, Legislative Clippings, vol. 1, KSHS.

135. Wilder, ed., *Annals,* 66.

136. Sam Tappan to Mrs. Goodnow, June 29, 1855, Isaac Goonow Papers, box 1, KSHS.

137. Ibid., William Goodnow to Wife, June 17, 1855.

138. Clarina Nichols, in *Evening Telegraph* (Boston), January 9, 1855, Kansas Territorial Clippings, vol. 1, KSHS. Richard Cordley, *A History of Lawrence, Kansas, from the First Settlement to the Close of the Rebellion* (Lawrence, Kans.: Lawrence Journal Press, 1895), 13, has a good description of the earliest vernacular architecture there.

139. Charles Robinson to "Sir," August 27, 1855, Robinson Papers, reel 1 (MS 640), 00037-39, KSHS.

140. Typescript of speech, July 4, 1855, Robinson Papers, box 1, KU; Goodnow diary, July 4, 1855, Goodnow Papers, vol. 7, KSHS; Sara Robinson, *Kansas,* 69–70.

141. *Independent Democrat,* April 19, 1855, Kansas Territorial Clippings, vol. 1, KSHS.

142. Robinson, *Kansas Conflict,* 103; Wilder, ed., *Annals,* 49.

143. Spring, *Kansas,* 63.

144. The state of Kansas towns in fall 1854 was described in T. B. Mason and Charles Boynton, *A Journey Through Kansas; with Sketches of Nebraska: Describing the Country, Climate, Soil, Mineral, Manufacturing and Other Resources. The Results of a Tour Made in the Autumn of 1854* (Cincinnati: Moore, Wilstach, Keys, 1855). A guide to town founding in general is Robert Baughman, *Kansas Post Offices, May 29, 1828–August 3, 1961* (Topeka: Kansas State Historical Society, 1961). He records that sixty-two post offices were established in Kansas in 1855 and only eight discontinued (240). The year before, only one post office was established, indicating the

lack of services to towns that definitely existed. C. K. Holliday, one of the founders of Topeka, gave a delightful talk on early towns to the State Historical Society in 1886 (see *Kansas Historical Collections* 3 [1886]: 396–401).

145. Wilder, ed., *Annals*, 55.

146. Malin, *Nebraska Question.*

2. TRAMPLING OUT THE VINTAGE

1. Robert Stevens to Folks at Home, August 23, 1863, Stevens Papers, box 2, KSHS. The detail about the railroad meeting came from William Connelley, *Quantrill and the Border Wars* (Cedar Rapids, Iowa: Torch Press, 1910), 341.

2. "Personal Recollections of Mrs. Sara T. D. Robinson of the Quantrill Raid of August 21, 1863," Robinson Papers, reel 12 (MS 651), 00672-00688, KSHS.

3. Robert Stevens to Folks at Home, August 23, 1863, Stevens Papers, box 2, KSHS.

4. "Personal Recollections of Mrs. Sara T. D. Robinson of the Quantrill Raid of August 21, 1863," Robinson Papers, reel 12 (MS 651), 00672-00688, KSHS.

5. Robert Stevens to Folks at Home, August 23, 1863, Stevens Papers, box 2, KSHS.

6. Cordley, *A History of Lawrence,* 223.

7. H. M. Simpson to Hiram Hill, September 7, 1863, Hiram Hill Papers, box 1, KSHS.

8. [Richard Cordley, D.D.], *The Lawrence Massacre by a Band of Missouri Ruffians Under Quantrell, August 21, 1863* (n.p., n.d.), 53, in Special Collections, no. 161, Ablah Library, Wichita State University. Cordley's account was first published in Boughton and McAllister's Lawrence City Directory for 1866. A later version is in Cordley, *History of Lawrence,* 239.

9. Robert Stevens to Folks at Home, August 23, 1863, Stevens Papers, box 2, KSHS.

10. John Ingalls to Father, September 5, 1863, Ingalls Papers, box 1, KSHS.

11. H. M. Simpson to Hiram Hill, September 7, 1863, Hill Papers, box 1, KSHS.

12. Thomas Carney to Maj. Gen. J. M. Schofield, August 24, 1863, Thomas Carney Papers, KU.

13. Ibid., Thomas Carney to E. M. Stanton, August 24, 1863.

14. John Ingalls to Father, September 5, 1863, Ingalls Papers, box 1, KSHS.

15. Albert Castel, *Civil War Kansas: Reaping the Whirlwind,* 2d ed. (Lawrence: University Press of Kansas, 1997), 132. Castel's book was originally published in 1958 as *A Frontier State at War.* Recent accounts of the raid itself include Thomas Goodrich, *Bloody Dawn: The Story of the Lawrence Massacre* (Kent, Ohio: Kent State University Press, 1991), and Edward Leslie, *The Devil Knows How to Ride: The True Story of William Clarke Quantrill and His Confederate Raiders* (1996; reprint, New York: Da Capo Press, 1998). An older standard is Connelley, *Quantrill and the Border Wars.* As with the vast literature on the Custer battle, historians have left hardly any detail of that day in Lawrence undocumented.

16. H. M. Simpson to Hiram Hill, September 7, 1863, Hill Papers, box 1, KSHS.

17. Robert Stevens to James Denver, April 25, 1858, James Denver Papers, KSHS.

18. John Martin, *Address Delivered at the Quarter-Centennial Celebration of the Admission of Kansas as a State by Gov. John A. Martin. Topeka, Kansas, January 29, 1886*

(Topeka: Kansas Publishing House, 1886), Kansas Collected Speeches and Pamphlets, vol. 23, KSHS.

19. Thayer, *The Kansas Crusade*, 1.

20. Lyman Humphrey, *Inaugural Address of Governor Lyman U. Humphrey of Kansas. Delivered in the Hall of the House of Representatives, January 14, 1889* (Topeka: Kansas Publishing House, 1889), in Humphrey Clippings, KU.

21. Douglas Brewerton, *The War in Kansas: A Rough Trip to the Border Among New Homes and a Strange New People* (New York: Derby and Jackson, 1856), 289.

22. Johnston Lykins to James Denver, December 18, 1857, Denver Papers, KSHS.

23. Robert Richmond, *Kansas: A Land of Contrasts*, 4th ed. (Wheeling, Ill.: Harlan Davidson, 1999), 68.

24. Mary Denver to James Denver, January 9, 1858, Denver Papers, box 1, KU.

25. Charles Robinson to Allen, Blood, Hutchinson, and others, August 16, 1856, Charles and Sara Robinson Papers, reel 1 (MS 640), 00136-37, KSHS.

26. Paul Gates, *Fifty Million Acres: Conflicts over Kansas Land Policy, 1854–1890* (Ithaca, N.Y.: Cornell University Press, 1954), 1, 19.

27. Dale Watts, "How Bloody Was Bleeding Kansas? Political Killings in Kansas Territory, 1854–1861," *Kansas History* 18 (summer 1995): 123–24.

28. William Phillips, *The Conquest of Kansas by Missouri and Her Allies* (Boston: Phillips, Sampson, 1856), 377.

29. Thomas Goodrich, *War to the Knife: Bleeding Kansas, 1854–1861* (Mechanicsburg, Pa.: Stackpole Books, 1998), 91–92, 185.

30. The "cockpit" phrase comes from undated, unidentified clipping, Lane Papers, folder 7, KU.

31. Quoted in William Treadway, *Cyrus K. Holliday: A Documentary Biography* (Topeka: Kansas State Historical Society, 1979), 171.

32. James Sands to Hiram Hill, December 21, 1878, Hill Papers, box 2, KSHS.

33. Goodnow, introduction to Robinson, *Kansas Conflict*, xiii.

34. Ibid., 365, 377, 429.

35. [Hannah Ropes], *Six Months in Kansas by a Lady* (Boston: John P. Jewett, 1856), 144–45.

36. Charles Robinson, "Speech to Commander and Members of the Loyal Legion," January 3, 1889, Robinson Papers, box 1, KU.

37. The six volumes of the Sara Robinson Scrapbooks at the University of Kansas are loaded with newspaper documentation of the war of words between the two.

38. Sara Robinson commissioned Professor Frank Blackmar of the University of Kansas to write a biography of her husband; the book, *The Life of Charles Robinson: The First State Governor of Kansas*, was published in 1902.

39. Brewerton, *The War in Kansas*, 258.

40. George Brown, *Reminiscences of Gov. R. J. Walker; with the True Story of the Rescue of Kansas from Slavery* (Rockford, Ill.: author, 1902), 136.

41. Brewerton, *The War in Kansas*, 258, 284.

42. John Ingalls to Father, February 23, 1862, Ingalls Papers, box 1, KSHS.

43. *New York Daily Times,* January 10, 1855, Territorial Clippings, vol. 1, KSHS.

44. Ibid., *Independent Democrat,* no date [1855].

45. Ibid., unidentified clipping, summer 1856.

46. Goodrich, *War to the Knife,* 155.

47. Zornow, *Kansas,* outlines most of it clearly at a medium level of detail (67–75). A more detailed account is Connelley, *Kansas and Kansans,* 1: 298–594, and 2: 595–797. A popular account is Alice Nichols, *Bleeding Kansas* (New York: Oxford University Press, 1954). The musical chairs of changing governors can be followed in outline in Homer Socolofsky, *Kansas Governors* (Lawrence: University Press of Kansas, 1990). For economy, basic facts covered in such works as these are not cited in the notes.

48. The comment is from John Gihon, M.D., *Geary and Kansas* (Philadelphia: Charles C. Rhodes, 1857), 40–41.

49. Charles Robinson, "Topeka and Her Constitution," speech given before the Kansas State Historical Society, 1877, 7, Robinson Papers, box 1, KU.

50. Gihon, *Geary,* 47.

51. Frémont to Robinson, March 17, 1856, Robinson Papers, reel 1 (MS 640), 0068-70, KSHS.

52. Ibid., Sara Robinson to Celia Sherman, May 10, 1856, 00077-79. The details on the house come from Sara Robinson, *Kansas,* 192.

53. C. [Robinson] to S. [Robinson], January 15, 1857, Robinson Papers, reel 1 (MS 640), 00186-87, KSHS.

54. Charles Robinson, "Topeka and Her Constitution," speech before the State Historical Society, winter 1877–1878, 12–14, Robinson Papers, box 1, KU.

55. Amos Lawrence to Charles Robinson, June 31, 1856, Robinson Papers, reel 1, 00045, KSHS.

56. Henry Ward Beecher, *Defense of Kansas,* 1, Kansas Collected Speeches and Pamphlets, vol. 19, KSHS.

57. E. J. Nute Jr. to E. E. Hale, October 3, 1855, New England Emigrant Aid Company Papers, reel 1 (MS 619), 00450-57, KSHS.

58. Proceedings of National Kansas Convention, June 26, 1856, Thaddeus Hyatt Papers, reel 1 (MS 0086), KSHS.

59. Ibid., A. L. Searl to Thaddeus Hyatt, August 21, 1856.

60. Ibid., Thaddeus Hyatt to New York Tabernacle Committee, August 16, 1856.

61. Ibid., C. I. H. Nichols to Thaddeus Hyatt, October 4, 1856.

62. For example, Helen Burnham to Thaddeus Hyatt, October 8, 1856, in ibid.

63. E. Nute to E. E. Hale, August 24, 1856, New England Emigrant Aid Company Papers, reel 1 (MS 619), 00664-67, KSHS.

64. Ibid., 00702-09.

65. I. G. to ?, undated, Goodnow Papers, box 1, KSHS.

66. Ibid., Wm. Goodnow to Wife, May 16, 1856.

67. G. W. Brown to Friends, August 16 or 17, 1856, William Hutchinson Papers, KSHS.

68. Sara Robinson, *Kansas,* 3, 6, 117, 148, 215, 249, 337, 348.

69. Phillips, *Conquest of Kansas,* 114, 332, 410.

70. A guide to the bibliography of nineteenth-century publications on Kansas is David Dary, *Kanzana, 1854–1900* (Lawrence, Kans.: Allen Books, 1986).

71. Ropes, *Six Months in Kansas*, 133.

72. Thomas Gladstone, *An Englishman in Kansas; or Squatter Life and Border Warfare* (New York: Miller, 1857), 23, 74, 328. The book was originally published as *Kansas; or Squatter Life and Border Warfare in the Far West*, by G. Routledge, London, but the American edition contains some additional comments.

73. *Report of the Special Committee Appointed to Investigate the Troubles in Kansas* (Washington, D.C.: Cornelius Wendell, 1856).

74. Undated clipping, Lane Papers, KU.

75. Quoted in Villard, *Brown*, 225–26.

76. The "strip tease" comment is from W. G. Clugston, *Rascals in Democracy* (New York: Richard R. Smith, 1940), 67.

77. *Kansas City Times*, October 19, 1938, Lane Papers, KU.

78. This summary account follows Zornow, *Kansas*, with some supplementation from other general texts.

79. [Isaac Goodnow] to Friend Sherman, April 1, 1858, Goodnow Papers, box 2, KSHS.

80. Ibid., Ellen Goodnow to Husband, June 27, August 3, 1858.

81. Ibid., Thomas Webb to Goodnow, July 21, 1858.

82. Ibid., Resolution, September 13, 1858. The cornerstone for the college building was laid May 11, 1859. See Julius Willard, *History of the Kansas State College of Agriculture and Applied Science* (Manhattan: Kansas State College Press, 1940).

83. Isaac Goodnow, "Personal Reminiscences and Kansas Emigration, 1855," *Collections of the Kansas State Historical Society* (Topeka: Kansas Publishing House, 1890), 4: 251, 253.

84. Ibid., *Message of the President of the United States, Communicating a Constitution for Kansas as a State, and Presenting His Views in Relation to Affairs of That Territory*, S. ex. Doc. 21, 35th Cong., 1st sess., vol. 6.

85. Ibid., S. Rept. 82, 35th Cong., 1st sess., vol. 19.

86. For background, see George Barns, *Denver, the Man: The Life, Letters and Public Papers of the Lawyer, Soldier and Statesman* (Wilmington, Ohio: [author], 1949). For the gold rush, see West, *Contested Plains*.

87. Summary texts can be well supplemented here by Goodrich, *War to the Knife*, and Stephen Starr, *Jennison's Jayhawkers: A Civil War Cavalry Regiment and Its Commander* (Baton Rouge: Louisiana State University Press, 1973). A contemporary account, highly favorable to Montgomery, is William Tomlinson, *Kansas in 1858: A History of Recent Troubles in the Territory* (New York: H. Dayton, 1859). On the Jayhawk, see Kirke Mechem, *The Mythical Jayhawk* (Topeka: Kansas State Historical Society, 1967).

88. Barns, *Denver*, 148–49.

89. J. Thompson to James Denver, January 28, 1858, Denver Papers, box 1, KU.

90. Barns, *Denver*, 155, 159, 164, 166.

91. J. Thompson to Denver, February 28, 1858, Denver Papers, box 1, KU.

92. Barns, *Denver*, 209.
93. Thomas Hendrick to J. W. Denver, April 3, 1858, Denver Papers, box 1, KU.
94. Ibid., Mike to James Denver, April 14, 1858.
95. J. W. Williams to Denver, May 16, 1858, Denver Papers, KSHS; Tomlinson, *Kansas in 1858*, 181.
96. George Clark to Samuel Jones, June 2, 1858, Denver Papers, KSHS.
97. Tomlinson, *Kansas in 1858*, 195, 215, 218.
98. Goodrich, *War to the Knife*, 219; Tomlinson, *Kansas in 1858*, 231, 259.
99. J. Thompson to Denver, June 21, 1858, Denver Papers, box 1, KU.
100. Hugh Walsh to Lewis Cass, November 19, 1858, Denver Papers, KSHS.
101. Samuel Medary to Denver, January 12, 1859, Denver Papers, box 1, KU.
102. Samuel Medary to Denver, January 13, 1859, Denver Papers, KSHS, and S. C. Smith to Charles Robinson, January 6, 1859, Robinson Papers, box 1, KU.
103. Good discussions of all the constitutions are Robert Stone, "Kansas Laws and Their Origin," in Connelley, *Kansas and Kansans*, 2: 935–52, and Rosa Perdue, "The Sources of the Constitution of Kansas," *Collections of the Kansas State Historical Society* 7 (1901–1902): 130–51. The Wyandotte Constitution is printed in *Kansas Constitutional Convention. A Reprint of the Proceedings and Debates of the Convention Which Framed the Constitution of Kansas at Wyandotte in July, 1859* (Topeka: Kansas State Printing Plant, 1920), 574–92. That book also contains the debates on the constitution. A careful discussion of the proceedings is G. Raymond Gaeddert, *The Birth of Kansas* (Lawrence: University of Kansas, 1940), 28–60; the quotations in this paragraph came from this source.
104. Mary Gray, reminiscences, c. 1903, Biographical Scrapbook, G, 5, KSHS.
105. Connelley, *Kansas and Kansans*, 1: 301–4.
106. Abelard Guthrie diary, July 4, 1859, Abelard Guthrie Papers, KSHS.
107. Ibid., July 7 and October 4, 1859.
108. A. Lincoln to M. W. Delahay, May 14, 1859, Mark Delahay Papers, KSHS.
109. Ibid., M. W. Delahay to A. Lincoln, November 14, 1859.
110. *Wichita Eagle Magazine*, February 8, 1959, Lincoln, in Kansas Clippings, vol. 2, KSHS. For an account by a later journalist, see Fred Brinkerhoff, "The Kansas Tour of Lincoln the Candidate," *Kansas Historical Quarterly* 13 (February 1945): 204–307.
111. "Lincoln in Kansas," *Collections of the Kansas State Historical Society* 7 (1901–1902): 538.
112. *Kansas City Star*, February 8, 1960, Lincoln, in Kansas Clippings, vol. 2, KSHS. Lincoln's Leavenworth speech was a version of the talk he was to give at the Cooper Institute in New York City early the next year.
113. J. J. I. to Father, October 24, 1858, Ingalls Papers, box 1, KSHS.
114. *Topeka Capital*, June 4, 1905, Lincoln, in Kansas Clippings, vol. 1, KSHS.
115. Gambone, "Economic Relief," 150.
116. Nathan Starks to Hiram Hill, June 27, 1860, Hill Papers, box 1, KSHS.
117. Ibid., July 1, 1860.
118. J. J. I. to Father, August 21, 1861, Ingalls Papers, box 1, KSHS.

119. C. to S., October 20, 1860, Robinson Papers, reel 1 (MS 640), 00575-77, KSHS.

120. Gambone, "Economic Relief," 152.

121. Appeal for aid signed by Hyatt, September 25, 1860, Hyatt Papers, reel 1 (MS 0086), KSHS.

122. Ibid., S. C. Pomeroy to Thaddeus Hyatt, October 9, 1860.

123. Ibid., Thaddeus Hyatt broadside, August 24, 1860.

124. *Emporia News,* January 19, 1861.

125. *Leavenworth Conservative,* January 31, 1861.

126. Mary Holliday to "H," February 18, 1861, Holliday Papers (MS 146), KSHS.

127. Thaddeus Hyatt to Lilly, September 25, 1860, Hyatt Papers, reel 1 (MS 0086), KSHS.

128. Burton Williams, *Senator John James Ingalls: Kansas' Iridescent Republican* (Lawrence: University Press of Kansas, 1972), 32.

129. *New York Times,* January 6, 1861.

130. *Emporia News,* February 2, 1861. *Leavenworth Conservative,* January 30, 31, 1861. See "When Kansas Became a State," *Kansas Historical Quarterly* 27 (spring 1961): 1–21.

131. J. J. I. to Father, January 19, 1861, Ingalls Papers, box 1, KSHS.

132. *Emporia News,* January 26, 1861.

133. "Osage," in *Lawrence Republican,* September 24, 1860, Legislative Clippings, box 1, KSHS.

134. Ibid., *Topeka Daily Capital,* September 18, 1886.

135. Castel, *Civil War Kansas,* 26, 28.

136. Lyman Trumbull to M. W. Delahay, February 16, 1861, Delahay Papers, KSHS.

137. J. J. I. to Father, March 21, 1861, Ingalls Papers, box 1, KSHS.

138. Castel, *Civil War Kansas.*

139. J. J. I. to Father, May 15, 1861, Ingalls Papers, box 1, KSHS.

140. Ibid., February 23, 1862.

141. Charles Robinson, "Address Written for Reunion at Leavenworth," Robinson Papers, box 1, KU; Connelley, *Kansas and Kansans,* 2: 712–13.

142. Charles Robinson, Message to Legislature, 1861, Robinson Papers, box 1, KU.

143. See Castel, *Civil War Kansas,* chap. 11, "The Great Raid," 184–202, and Samuel Crawford, *Kansas in the Sixties* (Chicago: A. G. McClurg, 1911), 139–63.

144. Richmond, *Kansas,* 93.

145. C. to S., January 11, 1860, Robinson Papers, reel 1 (MS 640), 00596-97, KSHS.

146. Ibid., February 5, 1861, 00605-06.

147. Ibid., February 11, 1861, 00610.

148. Castel, *Civil War Kansas,* 24, 28, 30–31.

149. Lane to Dr. Delahay, December 18, 1860, Delahay Papers, KSHS.

150. Quoted in Gaeddert, *Birth of Kansas,* 103.

151. Joseph Gambone, in his study of Pomeroy's role in relief, concluded that he had been treated unfairly by previous historians, in that context at least ("Economic Relief," passim).

152. Castel, *Civil War Kansas,* 32, 33.

153. Ibid., 34–35.

154. Undated clipping [1894], probably Sol Miller in *Troy Kansas Chief*, Sara Robinson Scrapbooks, vol. 5, KU.

155. Ibid., *Express* (Buffalo), May 15, 1892, vol. 6.

156. Ibid., Review of Robinson's *Kansas Conflict*, in *New York Mail and Express*, n.d. [1892], vol. 6.

157. Testimony of James H. Lane, *Proceedings in the Case of the Impeachment of Charles Robinson, Governor* (Lawrence: Kansas State Journal Steam Press, 1862), 23–25.

158. The summary is from Castel, *Civil War Kansas*, 39, 71–77.

159. Wilson Shannon to Robert Stevens, April 24, 1860, Stevens Papers, box 1, KSHS.

160. C. to S., April 17, 1862, Robinson Papers, reel 1 (MS 640), 00730-31, KSHS.

161. Ibid., C. to S., May 4, 8, 1862.

162. For the Republican Party's origin, see Gaeddert, *The Birth of Kansas*, 13–15.

163. Castel, *Civil War Kansas*, 53–54.

164. Robinson to Frémont, September 1, 1861, *The War of the Rebellion: A Compilation of the Official Records of the Union and Confederate Armies*, series 1 (Washington, D.C.: Government Printing Office, 1881), 3: 468–69.

165. Ibid., Lane to Frémont, August 16, 1861, 446.

166. Ibid., Lane to Frémont, September 24, 1861, 505–6.

167. Transcript of Lane speech in Springfield, November 8, 1861, in *Speeches of Gen. J. H. Lane, of Kansas* (Washington, D.C.: McGill and Witherow, Steam Printers, n.d.), Kansas Collected Speeches and Pamphlets, Miscellaneous, vol. 9, KSHS.

168. George Martin to D. R. Anthony Jr., March 22, 1910, and Adjutant General of the U.S. to D. R. Anthony Jr., March 26, 1910, James Lane Papers, KSHS.

169. Castel, *Civil War Kansas*, 132.

170. Charles Robinson, in *Christian Record*, April 15, 1893, Sara Robinson Scrapbooks, vol. 5, 146–47, KU.

171. Thomas Carney to Abraham Lincoln, June 25, 1863, Carney Papers, KU.

172. Ibid., Thomas Carney to Maj. Gen. J. M. Schofield, September 11, 1863.

173. Dudley Cornish, *The Sable Arm: Black Troops in the Union Army, 1861–1865* (1956; reprint, Lawrence: University Press of Kansas, 1987), 63, 70–78; see also Gaeddert, *Birth of Kansas*, 158–59.

174. *Vindication of the Policy of the Administration. Speech of Hon. J. H. Lane of Kansas, in the Senate of the United States* (Washington, D.C.: Gibson Brothers, Printers, 1864), Kansas Collected Speeches and Pamphlets, Miscellaneous, vol. 9, KSHS.

175. Castel, *Civil War Kansas*, 77–80.

176. Samuel Smith, "Kansas Troops in the Civil War," handwritten manuscript, April 17, 1897, in Robinson Papers, reel 12 (MS 651), 00690-00711, KSHS.

177. Abelard Guthrie diary, January 18, 1862, Guthrie Papers, KSHS.

178. Ibid., February 27, 1862.

179. Castel, *Civil War Kansas*, 118–19, 166–76, 202; S. D. B. to editor of *Boston Journal*, January 12, 1865, Legislative Clippings, vol. 1, KSHS.

180. *Speeches of Hon. James H. Lane in the Cooper Institute, New York, and of General Neal Dow in the New City Hall, Portland* (Washington, D.C.: William H. Moore,

Printer, 1864), Kansas Collected Speeches and Pamphlets, Miscellaneous, vol. 14, KSHS.

181. Ibid., *Vindication of the Policy of the Administration,* vol. 9.

182. W. O. Stoddard, "The Story of a Nomination," *North American Review* 138 (March 1884): 271.

183. "Kansans Who Played a Part in the Career of Abraham Lincoln," *Kansas City Star,* February 7, 1909, Lane Papers, box 1, KU.

184. Ibid., James Lane to Henry Wilson, May 30, 1866.

185. *Boston Commonwealth,* June 23, 1866, Sara Robinson Scrapbooks, vol. 1, KU; John Speer, *Life of Gen. James H. Lane,* 2d ed. (Garden City, Kans.: John Speer, 1897), 313–14, 340–42.

186. Castel, *Civil War Kansas,* 231–32.

187. Clipping account of Lane's suicide by W. H. Morris, n.d., Lane Papers, box 1, KU.

188. Ibid., J. H. Lane to John Speer, April 11, 1866.

189. Speer, *Life of Lane,* 315–16.

190. Clipping account of Lane's suicide by W. H. Morris, n.d., Lane Papers, box 1, KU.

191. C. to S., Robinson Papers, April 3, 1865, reel 1 (MS 640), KSHS.

3. "HOW THE IRON MUST BURN"

1. Miner, *Wichita,* 20–23.

2. W. Stitt Robinson, "The Role of the Military in Territorial Kansas," in *Territorial Kansas: Studies Commemorating the Centennial* (Lawrence: University of Kansas Publications, 1954), 81.

3. Robert Wright, "Frontier Life in Southwest Kansas," *Collections of the Kansas State Historical Society* 7 (1901–1902): 69.

4. Miner and Unrau, *End of Indian Kansas,* 139.

5. Quoted in Miner, *Wichita: The Early Years,* 30.

6. Gates, *Fifty Million Acres,* xi, 3.

7. G. W. Brown to Secretary of Historical Society, October 7, 1887, G. W. Brown Papers, box 1, KSHS.

8. Ibid., G. W. Brown to Gentlemen, July 21, 1885.

9. Ibid., G. W. Brown to [M. L. Field], August 17, 1903.

10. Craig Miner, *The Fire in the Rock: A History of the Oil and Gas Industry in Kansas, 1855–1976* (Wichita: Kansas Independent Oil and Gas Association, 1976), 16.

11. Francis Schruben, *Wea Creek to El Dorado: Oil in Kansas, 1860–1920* (Columbia: University of Missouri Press, 1972), 1; Miner, *Fire in the Rock,* 13.

12. G. W. Brown to [M. L. Field], August 17, 1903, Brown Papers, box 1, KSHS; Miner, *Fire in the Rock,* 15.

13. Erasmus Haworth, "Historic Sketch of the Gypsum, Cement and Plaster Industry in Kansas," 85, and Irene Stone, "The Lead and Zinc Fields of Kansas," 243–60, both in *Collections of the Kansas State Historical Society* 7 (1901–1902).

14. Richmond, *Kansas,* 104; Charles Glaab, *Kansas City and the Railroads: Community Policy in the Growth of a Regional Metropolis* (1962; reprint, Lawrence: University

Press of Kansas, 1993), 2. A good summary of early rail development in Kansas is A. Bower Sageser, "The Rails Go Westward," in *Kansas: The First Century*, ed. John Bright, 5 vols. (New York: Lewis Historical Publishing Company, 1956), 1: 221–54.

15. Charles Gleed, "The First Kansas Railway," *Collections of the Kansas State Historical Society* 6 (1897–1900): 358.

16. Craig Miner, "Stereotyping and the Pacific Railway Issue, 1845–1865," *Canadian Review of American Studies* 6 (spring 1975): 59–73; Frank Hodder, "The Railroad Background of the Kansas-Nebraska Bill," *Mississippi Valley Historical Review* 12 (June 1925): 3–22.

17. William Gilpin, *The Central Gold Regions* (Philadelphia: Sower, Barnes, 1860), 20–21.

18. James Rawley, *Race and Politics: Bleeding Kansas and the Coming of the Civil War* (Philadelphia: J. B. Lippincott, 1969), 58–59.

19. *Sixth Annual Report of the Board of Railroad Commissioners for the Year Ending December 1, 1888. State of Kansas* (Topeka: Kansas Publishing House, Clifford C. Baker, state printer, 1888), 4.

20. Glaab, *Kansas City and the Railroads*, 33.

21. Junius to *Missouri Democrat*, May 28, 1857, Sara Robinson Scrapbooks, vol. 4, KU.

22. John M. Giffen to Robert Stevens, January 13, 1860, Stevens Papers, box 1, KSHS.

23. Charles Chadwick to Herman Hill, June 23, 1860, Hill Papers, box 1, KSHS.

24. Ibid., December 2, 1867.

25. Glaab, *Kansas City and the Railroads*, 14.

26. Treadway, *Holliday*, 111–12, 115.

27. Jeff Thompson to C. K. Holliday, March 5, 1858, Holliday Papers (MS 146), KSHS.

28. Samuel Pomeroy to Thaddeus, August 6, 1857, and March 6, 1859, Samuel Pomeroy Papers, box 1, KSHS.

29. Railroad speech in Lawrence, December 23, 1858, Hutchinson Papers, KSHS.

30. I. E. Quastler, *Railroads of Lawrence, Kansas* (Lawrence, Kans.: Coronado Press, 1979), 21.

31. Ibid., in *Western Argus*, February 13, 1860, 3.

32. Sageser, "The Rails Go Westward," 226–27.

33. C. to S., January 6, 1859, Robinson Papers, reel 1 (MS 640), 00396-97, KSHS.

34. Ibid., S. C. S. [Samuel C. Smith] to Charles Robinson, 00379-81.

35. Quastler, *Railroads of Lawrence*, 41–42.

36. Alan Farley, "Samuel Hallett and the Union Pacific Railway Company in Kansas," *Kansas Historical Quarterly* 25 (spring 1959): 5, 7.

37. Quoted in Joseph Snell and Robert Richmond, "When the Union and Kansas Pacific Built Through Kansas," *Kansas Historical Quarterly* 32 (summer 1966): 167.

38. Sageser, "The Rails Go Westward," 228–47. For color on the construction phase, see O. P. Byers, "When Railroading Outdid the Wild West Stories," *Collections of the Kansas State Historical Society* 17 (1926–1928): 339–51. Byers started with the Kansas Pacific in 1878.

39. C. K. Holliday to Messrs. Alfred and Edgard Huidekoper, Meadville, Pa., September 28, 1858, Holliday Papers (MS 146), KSHS.

40. Holliday address, January 29, 1886, in Treadway, *Holliday,* 125.

41. G. W. Brown to Miss Gracie, November 14, 1895, Brown Papers, box 1, KSHS.

42. Ibid., G. W. Brown to Editors, *Republican,* November 18, 1882.

43. William Phillips to Samuel Wood, January 29, 1860, Samuel Wood Papers, box 1, KSHS.

44. Ibid., M. Corn to Samuel Wood, January 19, 1864, box 2.

45. Ibid., Wm. Wood to Samuel Wood, February 15, 1872, box 4; Miner, *West of Wichita,* 224–25.

46. Quoted in Gates, *Fifty Million Acres,* 102.

47. Miner and Unrau, *End of Indian Kansas,* 28–37.

48. Diary of Abelard Guthrie, April 22, 1858, Guthrie Papers, KSHS.

49. Ibid., December 16, 1858.

50. Ibid., September 15, 1862.

51. P. C. Ferguson to Lyman Trumbull, March 22, 1862, Stevens Papers, box 2, KSHS; Miner and Unrau, *End of Indian Kansas,* 40.

52. Diary of Abelard Guthrie, January 27, 1863, Guthrie Papers, KSHS.

53. I. C. to *Lawrence Republican,* July 1, 1857, Stevens Papers, box 1, KSHS.

54. Ibid., flyer, June 2, 1868, box 2.

55. On the Kansa, this has been done particularly by William Unrau in *The Kansa Indians: A History of the Wind People* (Norman: University of Oklahoma Press, 1971), and his *Mixed-Bloods and Tribal Dissolution: Charles Curtis and the Quest for Indian Identity* (Lawrence: University Press of Kansas, 1989).

56. For a detailed account, see William Unrau and Craig Miner, *Tribal Dispossession and the Ottawa Indian University Fraud* (Norman: University of Oklahoma Press, 1985).

57. Gates, *Fifty Million Acres,* 154.

58. Craig Miner, "Border Frontier: The Missouri River, Fort Scott & Gulf Railroad in the Cherokee Neutral Lands, 1868–1879," *Kansas Historical Quarterly* 35 (summer 1969): 105–29. For a personal reminiscence, see Eugene Ware, "The Neutral Lands," *Collections of the Kansas State Historical Society* 6 (1897–1900): 147–69.

59. Gates, *Fifty Million Acres,* 139, 143–45, 151, 181, 195.

60. Ibid., 194–200.

61. T. F. Rager, *History of Neosho and Wilson Counties, Kansas* (Ft. Scott, Kans.: Monitor Printing Company, 1902), 82, 86.

62. Thomas Osborn to President of the U.S., September 2, 1873, Thomas Osborn Papers, Governors' Papers, 27-02-08-04, KSHS.

63. Peter McVicar to Isaac Goodnow, July 6, 1868, Goodnow Papers, box 3, KSHS.

64. Treadway, *Holliday,* 198.

65. Gates, *Fifty Million Acres,* 221–22; see also Miner and Unrau, *End of Indian Kansas,* 121–32.

66. Miner, *Wichita: The Early Years,* 30.

67. The work of Elliott West is filled with such environmental insights, from which I am borrowing generally here.

68. Miner, *West of Wichita*, 15.

69. Socolofsky and Self, *Historical Atlas of Kansas*, map 20. An excellent series of short histories of Kansas forts, several by Leo Oliva, has been published by the Kansas State Historical Society.

70. Leo Oliva, *Fort Larned: Guardian of the Santa Fe Trail*, rev. ed. (Topeka: Kansas State Historical Society, 1997), 26.

71. F. B. Smith to Samuel Wood, May 15, 1864, Wood Papers, box 2, KSHS.

72. Ibid., Gen. S. R. Curtis, in Alexander Banks, to Samuel Wood, September 17, 1864, box 3.

73. Zornow, *Kansas*, 160.

74. Miner, *West of Wichita*, 14–25, 109–18.

75. Quoted in ibid., 16.

76. David Jordan, *Winfield Scott Hancock: A Soldier's Life* (Bloomington: Indiana University Press, 1988), 187.

77. Ibid., 191.

78. Joseph Rosa, *Wild Bill Hickok: The Man and His Myth* (Lawrence: University Press of Kansas, 1996), 85.

79. Crawford, *Kansas in the Sixties*, 49, 231, 248–49, 253–60, 277–78.

80. Miner, *Wichita: The Early Years*, 34–35.

81. James Mead, "The Little Arkansas," in Bentley, ed., *History of Wichita and Sedgwick County*, 1: 130.

82. James Mead, *Hunting and Trading on the Great Plains* (Norman: University of Oklahoma Press, 1986), 11, 254–57.

83. James Sherow and William Reeder, "A Richly Textured Community: Fort Riley, Kansas, and American Indians, 1853–1911, *Kansas History* 21 (spring 1998): 9.

84. James Harvey to Gen. John Pope, May 2, 1870, John Harvey Papers, Governors' Papers, 27-02-08-04, KSHS.

85. Ibid., May 25, 1870.

86. Ibid., July 14, 1870.

87. Ibid., James Harvey to President of U.S., April 4, 1871.

88. Wright, "Frontier Life in Southwest Kansas," 74, 78.

89. Snell and Richmond, "Union and Kansas Pacific," 346.

90. "Touring Kansas and Colorado in 1871: The Journal of George C. Anderson," *Kansas Historical Quarterly* 22 (autumn 1956): 210–11.

91. W. E. Webb, *Buffalo Land* (Cincinnati and Chicago: E. Hanford, 1872), 161–62, 281.

92. Thomas Osborn to William Street, Central City, Decatur County, April 30, 1873, Osborn Papers, Governors' Papers, 27-02-08-04, KSHS.

93. Charles Robinson, "The Indian War Exposed," *Lawrence Standard*, April 1875, Sara Robinson Scrapbooks, vol. 6, KU. Extensive testimony may also be found in File no. 16, Special Files, Indian Division, Record Group (RG) 48, National Archives (NA), Washington, D.C.

94. Report of Commissioners, Lawrence, September 28, 1874, File no. 16, Special Files, Indian Division, RG 48, NA.

95. James Christiansen, "The Kansas–Osage Border War of 1874: Fact or Wishful Thinking?" *Chronicles of Oklahoma* 63 (fall 1985): 292–311.

96. *Kansas City Times,* February 19, 1875, in File no. 16, RG 48, NA.

97. Ibid., Thomas Osborn to Columbus Delano, January 16, 1875.

98. Ibid., ? Smith, Commissioner to Secretary of Interior, January 5, 1875.

99. Thomas Osborn to President, September 5, 1874, Osborn Papers, Governors' Papers, 27-02-08-04, KSHS.

100. Charles Robinson, "The Indian War Exposed," *Lawrence Standard,* April 1875, Sara Robinson Scrapbooks, 6: 50–51, KU.

101. Miner, *West of Wichita,* 109–10.

102. Charlie [Sternberg] to Friend Hattie, July 18, 1869, Goodnow Papers, box 3, KSHS.

103. Clifford Griffin, *The University of Kansas: A History* (Lawrence: University Press of Kansas, 1974), 1, 16, 18, 24, 25–26; Willard, *History of the Kansas State College,* 11. The public schools' origin is covered in C. O. Wright, *One Hundred Years in Kansas Education* (Topeka: Kansas State Teachers Association, 1963).

104. Amos Lawrence to Charles Robinson, February 11, April 29, 1857, Robinson Papers, box 1, KU.

105. C. to S., January 19, 1864, Robinson Papers, reel 1 (MS 640), 00875-77, KSHS.

106. Ibid., January 21, 1864.

107. C. Robinson to Frank Snow, January 3, 1866, Robinson Papers, box 1, KU; Griffin, *The University of Kansas,* 33, 35.

108. Frank Snow to Robinson, December 2, 1865, Robinson Papers, reel 1 (MS 640), 01011-13, KSHS.

109. James Marvin to Robinson, February 18, 1876, Robinson Papers, box 1, KU.

110. J. A. Lippincott to Robinson, June 2, 1887, Robinson Papers, reel 4 (MS 643), 00025-26, KSHS.

111. Griffin, *University of Kansas,* 17, 300–301, 309.

112. Thomas Webb resolution, September 13, 1858, Goodnow Papers, box 2, KSHS.

113. Ibid, July 21, 1858.

114. Ibid., Ellen Goodnow to husband, June 27, 1858.

115. Ibid., August 16, 1859, and diary, July 25, 1861, box 7.

116. Ibid., Isaac Goodnow to C. E. Blood, May 5, 1859, box 2.

117. Ibid., J. W. Robinson to Goodnow, June 13, 1861; Willard, *History of the Kansas State College,* 13.

118. Isaac to Ellen Goodnow, January 16, 1862, Goodnow Papers, box 2, KSHS.

119. Ibid., February 19, 1862.

120. Ibid., March 2, 1862.

121. Ibid., February 15, 1863.

122. Ibid., Isaac Goodnow to Brother [Joseph] Denison, February 26, 1864.

123. Ibid., Isaac Goodnow to Ellen Goodnow, February 15, 1866.

124. Ibid., Joseph Denison to Goodnow, July 26, 1871, box 3.

125. Ibid., Isaac Gooodnow to A. R. Taylor, February 22, 1889, box 5.

126. See Robert Richmond, "Kansas Builds a Capitol," *Kansas Historical Quarterly* 38 (autumn 1974): 249–67.

127. Joseph Gambone, "The Forgotten Feminist of Kansas: The Papers of Clarina I. H. Nichols, 1854–1885," *Kansas Historical Quarterly* 39 (spring 1973): 22, 24; G. W. Brown to Miss Cowgill, April 8, 1903, Brown Papers, box 1, KSHS.

128. Michael Goldberg, *An Army of Women: Gender and Politics in Gilded Age Kansas* (Baltimore: Johns Hopkins University Press, 1997), 14; Gambone, "Nichols," 13.

129. Gambone, "Nichols," 25–27.

130. Goldberg, *Army,* 14–15.

131. Richard Sheridan, "Charles Henry Langston and the African American Struggle in Kansas," *Kansas History* 22 (winter 1999–2000): 273, 275, 277.

132. Sister Jeanne McKenna, " 'With the Help of God and Lucy Stone,' " *Kansas Historical Quarterly* 36 (spring 1970): 15, 18.

133. Gambone, "Nichols," 32–33, 240, 417, 518.

134. H. B. B., in *Woman's Journal,* Boston, August 25, 1894, Sara Robinson Scrapbooks, 5: 34, KU.

135. C. to S., January 13, 1869, Robinson Papers, reel 2, 00217-18, KSHS.

136. Gambone, "Nichols," 526, 528.

137. Sidney Clarke to S. N. Wood, July 5, 1867, Wood Papers, box 3, KSHS.

138. Ibid., Attorney General to J. M. Harvey, April 29, 1871, box 3; A. L. Williams to S. N. Wood, July 3, 1872, and H. S. McCarthy to S. N. Wood, July 15, 1872, box 4.

139. Lucy Stone to Sol Miller, February 7, 1887, Sol Miller Papers, vol. 1, KSHS.

140. Susan B. Anthony to John St. John, August 21, 1881, John St. John Papers, Governors' Papers, 27-03-08-07, KSHS.

141. Gambone, "Nichols," 522.

142. Peter Beckman, *Kansas Monks: A History of St. Benedict's Abbey* (Atchison, Kans.: Abbey Student Press, 1957); C. L. Edson to Reed Harris, August 30, 1937, Edson Papers, MS-811, KSHS.

143. Charles Edson to Reed Harris, August 30, 1937, Edson Papers, MS-811, KSHS. For a general church history, see Blanche Taylor, *Plenteous Harvest: The Episcopal Church in Kansas, 1837–1972* (Topeka: Episcopal Diocese of Kansas, 1973).

144. These summaries come from Emory Lindquist, "The Protestant and Jewish Religions in Kansas," in Bright, ed., *Kansas,* 2: 351–71. Lindquist's *Smoky Valley People: A History of Lindsborg, Kansas* (Lindsborg, Kans.: Bethany College, 1953) is a classic Kansas local history, focusing on the Swedish Lutherans; for the Olsson quotations, see 15–16.

145. Miner, *Wichita: The Early Years,* 158.

146. For the Volga German social impact, see Miner, *West of Wichita,* 81–92.

147. Prentis, "The Mennonites at Home," in *Kansas Miscellanies,* 162–70.

148. Norman Saul, "Myth and History: Turkey Red Wheat and the 'Kansas Miracle,' " *Heritage of the Great Plains* 22 (summer 1989): 1–13.

149. *The Railroad Policy of Kansas. Speech of Hon. Sidney Clarke, Delivered at Paola,*

Kansas, September 8, 1865 (Lawrence, Kans.: Daily Tribune Book and Job Office, 1865), Kansas Collected Speeches and Pamphlets, Miscellaneous, vol. 14, KSHS.

150. Miner, *West of Wichita*, 27–30. The most complete history of the UPED/KP is William Petrowski, *The Kansas Pacific: A Study in Railroad Promotion* (New York: Arno Press, 1981), first done as a dissertation in 1966. See also Snell and Richmond, "Union and Kansas Pacific," 161–86, 334–52. There is an anomaly in the construction of the UPED, which stalled it at the terminus town of Sheridan in Logan County in far western Kansas from July 3, 1868 until early in 1870, when construction was resumed to complete the few remaining Kansas miles and to reach Colorado.

151. Wilder, ed., *Annals*, 486, 519.

152. *Topeka Commonwealth*, January 11, 1884, and *Topeka Record*, November 24, 1860, ATSF Clippings, vol. 1, KSHS.

153. Ibid., *Topeka Commonwealth*, March 20, 1881.

154. Joseph Snell and Don Wilson, *The Birth of the Atchison, Topeka and Santa Fe Railroad* (Topeka: Kansas State Historical Society, 1968), 4, 59.

155. C. B. Schmidt in *Topeka Commonwealth*, July 23, 1881, ATSF clippings, vol. 1, KSHS.

156. *Topeka Capital*, March 13, 1882, and *Topeka Commonwealth*, March 20, 1881, August 5, 1883, ATSF Clippings, vol. 1, KSHS. Standard ATSF histories are L. L. Waters, *Steel Trails to Santa Fe* (Lawrence: University of Kansas Press, 1950), and Keith Bryant, *History of the Atchison, Topeka and Santa Fe Railway* (New York: Macmillan, 1974).

157. Charles Gleed, "The Great Railway Systems of the United States—The Atchison, Topeka & Santa Fe," *Cosmopolitan* (February 1893), in Gleed Papers, box 44, KSHS.

158. Bryant, *History of the Atchison, Topeka and Santa Fe*, 12–13.

159. "To the Voters of Shawnee County," n.d. [1865], Holliday Papers (MS 146), KSHS.

160. V. V. Masterson, *The Katy Railroad and the Last Frontier* (Norman: University of Oklahoma Press, 1952), 30, 46–71, 184–85. A convenient map of railroads in Kansas in 1878 is found in Socolofsky and Self, *Historical Atlas of Kansas*, 30.

161. The local strategy is well covered in Quastler, *Railroads of Lawrence*.

162. Levi Parsons to Robert Stevens, December 13, 1870, telegram, Stevens Papers, box 2, KSHS.

163. Ibid, December 20, 1870.

164. Ibid., Robert [Stevens] to Mary [Stevens], July 19, 1870.

165. Ibid., Robert Stevens to Mary Stevens, June 5, 1870.

166. Leslie Decker, *Railroads, Lands, and Politics: The Taxation of the Railroad Land Grants, 1864–1897* (Providence, R.I.: Brown University Press, 1964), 28. Decker's detailed economic study moves far beyond the scope of a survey of state history but contains much Kansas information.

167. Robert Stevens to George Denison, May 27, 1873, Stevens Papers, box 3, KSHS.

168. Ibid., July 30, 1873.

169. Ibid., June 18, 1873.

170. Ibid., Robert Stevens to William Bond, January 9, 1874.

171. Ibid., Robert Stevens to Levi Parsons, November 4, 1872, box 2.

172. Sageser, "The Rails Go Westward," in Bright, ed., *Kansas,* 1: 247–48.

173. The basics here are well known; so, as with certain earlier sections, detailed citations in the notes will be omitted. Good sources for an overview of the social and
economic impact of the cattle trade are Robert Dykstra, *The Cattle Towns* (1968;
reprint, Lincoln: University of Nebraska Press, 1983); Miner, *Wichita: The Early
Years;* and "North to Abilene," in *Settling the West* (New York: Time-Life Books,
1996).

174. Webb, *Buffalo Land,* 103.

175. Wichita quotations are from Miner, *Wichita: The Early Years,* 110.

176. Basic secondary sources on Scully and Case are Homer Socolofsky, "The Scully
Land System in Marion County," *Kansas Historical Quarterly* 18 (November 1950):
337–75, and Sondra Van Meter, *Marion County, Kansas, Past and Present* (Hillsboro,
Kans.: M. B. Publishing House, 1972).

177. Alexander Case to Messrs. Cochran and Brown, September 6, 1871, Alexander Case
Papers, box 46, KU.

178. Ibid., Alexander Case to A. R. Bardick, March 15, 1876.

179. Ibid., A. Backus to Hiram Hill, March 25, 1870, box 2.

180. Ibid., December 22, 1873.

181. Ibid., October 22, 1874.

182. Daniel Warden to Cecil Howes, August 24, 1874, Howes Papers, box 1, KSHS.

183. Ibid., Daniel Warden to Uncle, February 15, 1875.

184. Miner, *West of Wichita,* 142, 146. A delightful memoir of farming in the 1870s in
Kansas in Anne Bingham, "Sixteen Years on a Kansas Farm," *Collections of the
Kansas State Historical Society* 15 (1919–1922): 501–23.

185. Broadside on stationery, June 11 1874, Wood Papers, box 6, KSHS.

186. James Sands to Hiram Hill, October 27, 1873, Hill Papers, box 2, KSHS.

187. Ibid., December 26, 1873.

188. Ibid., June 29, 1875.

189. Ibid., March 8, 1877.

190. Ibid., February 27, 1878.

191. Ibid., December 5, 1883.

192. Leslie Fitz, "The Development of the Milling Industry in Kansas," *Collections of the
Kansas State Historical Society* 12 (1911–1912): 58.

193. Angelo Scott, "How Natural Gas Came to Kansas," *Kansas Historical Quarterly* 21
(winter 1954): 234.

194. Frank Vincent, "History of Salt Discovery and Production in Kansas, 1887–1915,"
Collections of the Kansas State Historical Society 14 (1915–1918): 358–59.

195. Fred Howell, "Some Phases of the Industrial History of Pittsburg, Kansas," *Kansas
Historical Quarterly* 1 (May 1932): 274, 276.

196. Stone, "Lead and Zinc Fields of Kansas," 254–55.

197. Rob to Eugene Ware, January 20, 1874, Eugene Ware Papers (Nies acquisition), box
3, KSHS.

198. H. T. to Charles Martin, September 20, 1874, and Thomas Osborn to Messrs.

Donnell, Lawson & Co., September 3, 1874, both in Osborn Papers, Governors' Papers, 27-02-08-04, KSHS.

199. D. W. Wilder to Eugene Ware, June 13, 1875, Ware Papers (Nies acquisition), box 3, KSHS.

200. Ibid., ? Rossington to Eugene Ware, November 5, 1880, box 4.

201. A. M. Holmes to W. C. Howard, June 1, 1878, Howard Papers, box 2, KU.

202. Ibid., Wm. Roe to W. C. Howard, February 2, 1879, box 3.

203. Quastler, *Railroads of Lawrence,* 243–44.

204. County Clerk, Douglas County [B. F. Diggs] to Hon. George Nettleton, July 19, 1879, Robinson Papers, reel 3 (MS 642), 00147-55, KSHS. Former Governor Robinson represented Douglas County with the Boston bondholders.

4. TOWARD A BRIGHTER DAY

1. H. M. Hoxie to John Martin, March 9, 1885, Martin Papers, Governors' Papers, 27-05-01-06, KSHS; *Third Annual Report of the Board of Railroad Commissioners for the Year Ending December 31, 1885. State of Kansas* (Topeka: Kansas Publishing House, T. D. Thacher, state printer, 1885), 23.

2. John Martin to H. M. Hoxie, March 9, 1885, Martin Papers, Governors' Papers, 27-05-01-06, KSHS.

3. James Brucker, "Workers, Townsmen and the Governor: The Santa Fe Enginemen's Strike, 1878," *Kansas History* 5 (spring 1982): 23–32.

4. John Martin to Thomas Carroll, March 19, 1885, Martin Papers, Governors' Papers, 27-05-01-07, KSHS.

5. Edith Walker, "Labor Problems During the First Year of Governor Martin's Administration," *Kansas Historical Quarterly* 5 (February 1936): 33–34.

6. John Martin to A. B. Campbell, March 14, 1886, Martin Papers, Governors' Papers, 27-05-01-06, KSHS.

7. Ibid., John Martin and John Marmaduke to H. M. Hoxie and attachments, March 21, 1886; Thomas Carroll to John Martin, April 4, 1886.

8. Ibid., John Martin to H. M. Hoxie, March 12, 1885.

9. Ibid., Hugh Camerson to John Martin, June 1, 1885, 27-04-05-06.

10. Ibid., John Martin to Prof. James Canfield, March 24, 1885; Griffin, *University of Kansas,* 93–94.

11. John Martin to Samuel Hamilton, April 24, 1885, and Martin to Emily Newcomb, May 1, 1885, Martin Papers, Governors' Papers, 27-04-05-06, KSHS.

12. Walker, "Labor Problems," 52–53.

13. *St. Joseph Herald,* July 24, 1877, Sara Robinson Scrapbooks, vol. 6, KU.

14. *Topeka Commonwealth,* March 8, 1885, Strikes Clippings, vol. 1, KSHS.

15. Ibid., *Tribune* (Lawrence), August 15, 1886, reprinted from *Kansas Farmer,* April 21, 1886.

16. Henry Armstrong to John Martin, March 26, 1886, Martin Papers, Governors' Papers, 27-04-05-06, KSHS.

17. Ibid., David Kelso to John Martin, March 30, 1886.

18. Ibid., John Martin to Sheriff Frank Shaw, March 30, 1886, and A. B. Campbell to John Martin, March 31, 1886.

19. Ibid., C. H. Kimball to John Martin, April 6, 1886.

20. *Third Annual Report of the Board of Railroad Commissioners,* 26–28.

21. P. B. Plumb to John Martin, April 17, 1886, Martin Papers, Governors' Papers, 27-05-01-06, KSHS.

22. Shortridge, *Peopling the Plains,* 46; *Fifth Biennial Report of the Kansas State Board of Agriculture, 1885–1886* (Topeka: Kansas Publishing House, 1887), 14.

23. *Sixth Biennial Report of the Kansas State Board of Agriculture, 1887–1888* (Topeka: Kansas Publishing House, 1889), 6.

24. Mechem, ed., *Annals of Kansas,* 1: 414.

25. Craig Miner, *Wichita: The Magic City* (Wichita: Wichita–Sedgwick County Historical Museum Association, 1988), 56–57. A careful study of the impact of the boom on one Kansas town is James Malin's "The Kinsley Boom of the Late Eighties," *Kansas Historical Quarterly* 4 (February, May 1935): 23–49, 164–187.

26. C. Borin, "Kansas: Her History, Her History-Makers, and Her Historical Society," *Collections of the Kansas State Historical Society* 4 (1886–1888): 270.

27. Sageser, "The Rails Go Westward," 249, 251.

28. *Fifth Annual Report of the Board of Railroad Commissioners for the Year Ending December 1, 1887. State of Kansas* (Topeka: Kansas Publishing House, Clifford C. Baker, state printer, 1887), 1–7; *Sixth Annual Report of the Board of Railroad Commissioners for the Year Ending December 1, 1888. State of Kansas* (Topeka: Kansas Publishing House, Clifford C. Baker, state printer, 1888), 4–6.

29. *Fifth Annual Report of the Board of Railroad Commissioners,* 7.

30. James Malin, *Power and Change in Society: With Special Reference to Kansas, 1880–1890* (Lawrence, Kans.: Coronado Press, 1981), 424.

31. Kos Harris, "Chronicles," in Bentley, ed., *History of Wichita and Sedgwick County,* 1: 207, 219.

32. *Sixth Annual Report of the Board of Railroad Commissioners,* 4.

33. *Eighth Annual Report of the Board of Railroad Commissioners for the Year Ending December 1, 1890. State of Kansas* (Topeka: Kansas Publishing House, Clifford C. Baker, state printer, 1890), iv.

34. *Tenth Annual Report of the Board of Railroad Commissioners for the Year Ending December 1, 1892. State of Kansas* (Topeka: Press of the Hamilton Printing Company, 1892), iii.

35. Ibid., viii–ix.

36. Miner, *Magic City,* 34, 91.

37. See the *Sixth Biennial Report* and *Eighth Biennial Report of the State Board of Agriculture, 1891–1892* (Topeka: Kansas Publishing House, 1893), part 2, 5. These biennial reports of the State Board of Agriculture are in general a good source for Kansas population statistics between the dates of the state and federal census collection.

38. Miner, *Magic City,* 86; *Eighth Biennial Report of the State Board of Agriculture,* part 2, 5. Wichita's population in 1892 was 20,938.

39. Quoted in Miner, *Magic City,* 71.

40. John St. John to W. H. Slavens, January 20, 1880, St. John Papers, Governors' Papers, 27-03-01-06, KSHS.

41. Ibid., John St. John to George Calderwood, February 9, 1880.

42. Ibid., John St. John to John Knowlton, March 1, 1880.

43. Ibid., John St. John to L. A. Currotte, March 2, 1880.

44. The principal secondary sources are Robert Athearn, *In Search of Canaan: Black Migration to Kansas, 1879–80* (Lawrence: Regents Press of Kansas, 1978), and Nell Painter, *Exodusters: Black Migration to Kansas After Reconstruction* (New York: Knopf, 1977). Unless otherwise noted, my introductory overview is based on these.

45. F. W. Giles, *Thirty Years in Topeka: A Historical Sketch* (Topeka: Kansas Publishing House, 1886), 367–71.

46. Painter, *Exodusters,* 187.

47. *Kansas Pioneer* (Wyandotte), April 12, 1879, Negroes Clippings, KSHS.

48. Giles, *Thirty Years in Topeka,* 368.

49. *Daily Times* (Leavenworth), March 7, 1879, Negroes Clippings, KSHS.

50. Glen Schwendemann, "Wyandotte and the First 'Exodusters' of 1879," *Kansas Historical Quarterly* 26 (autumn 1960): 233, 240.

51. Glen Schwendemann, "The 'Exodusters' on the Missouri," *Kansas Historical Quarterly* 29 (spring 1963): 25–40.

52. Miner, *Wichita: The Early Years,* 164–65.

53. *Wichita Eagle,* August 14, 1879, Negroes Clippings, KSHS.

54. Giles, *Thirty Years in Topeka,* 368.

55. Athearn, *In Search of Canaan,* 62.

56. John St. John to Rev. R. Haney, January 2, 1880, St. John Papers, Governors' Papers, 27-03-01-06, KSHS.

57. Ibid., John St. John to J. R. Jackson, January 2, 1880.

58. Ibid., John St. John to Mrs. Henry Cheever, January 16, 1880.

59. Ibid., John St. John to Horatio Rust.

60. Ibid., John St. John to J. M. Cavanass, March 23, 1880.

61. *Colored Citizen,* April 19, 1879, Negroes Clippings, KSHS.

62. Ibid., May 3, 1879.

63. Ibid., Laura Haviland, printed appeal from Kansas Freedmen's Relief Association Employment Bureau, 1879.

64. Athearn, *In Search of Canaan,* 155.

65. Giles, *Thirty Years in Topeka,* 369–70.

66. *Topeka Commonwealth,* April 23, 1880, Negroes Clippings, KSHS.

67. John St. John to Jay Gould, December 29, 1879, and John St. John to A. J. R. Smith, January 28, 1880, both in St. John Papers, Governors' Papers, 27-03-01-06, KSHS.

68. Ibid., John St. John to H. P. Stultz, January 26, 1880.

69. Ibid., John St. John to A. J. R. Smith, January 28, 1880.

70. The source for the summary information on prohibition is Robert Bader, *Prohibition in Kansas* (Lawrence: University Press of Kansas, 1986).

71. Final quote is from Bader, *Prohibition, 256.*

72. "The Prairie Was in Labor," mss in Charles Driscoll Papers, KU.

73. Quoted in Miner, *Magic City,* 113.

74. Robinson, in *Atchison Champion,* May 9, 1880, Sara Robinson Scrapbooks, vol. 6, KU.

75. Ibid., C. Robinson in *Gazette* (n.p.), August 23, 1890, vol. 5.

76. Ibid., *Standard,* June 1, 1880, vol. 6.

77. A fine account of St. John's specific prohibition activities is Edna Frederickson's "John P. St. John: The Father of Constitutional Prohibition" (Ph.D. diss., University of Kansas, 1931).

78. John St. John to George Martin, March 18, 1880, St. John Papers, Governors' Papers, 27-03-01-06, KSHS.

79. Ibid., John St. John to J. B. Brodnix, January 26, 1880.

80. Ibid., John St. John to George Martin, March 18, 1880.

81. Ibid., John St. John to R. E. O. Byone, March 19, 1880.

82. Ibid., John St. John to J. W. Ady, December 17, 1880, 27-03-02-03.

83. Ibid., John St. John to H. W. Brady, April 30, 1881.

84. Mechem, ed., *Annals of Kansas,* 1: 32.

85. Frederickson, "John P. St. John," 6–7.

86. Wilder, ed., *Annals,* 986–87, 998.

87. Bessie Wilder's pamphlet, *Governmental Agencies in the State of Kansas, 1861–1956,* is vital here, as it often is, to sorting out these patterns.

88. Malin, *Power and Change,* 402–4.

89. *Topeka Commonwealth,* September 17, 1883, Gleed Mounted Clippings, Gleed Papers, box 50, KSHS.

90. Ibid., *Kansas City Journal,* October 3, 1883.

91. Ibid., *Topeka Capital,* November 25, 1883.

92. Malin, *Power and Change,* 376, 402–4, 419.

93. Albert R. Greene, "The Kansas Railroad Commission," *Cosmopolitan* (January 1892), Kansas Board of R.R. Commissioners, Miscellaneous Pamphlets, vol. 2, KSHS.

94. R. W. P. Muse to Glick, February 4, 1883, George Glick Papers, Governors' Papers, 27-04-05-05, KSHS. The history of the bills for railroad regulation in this legislature is covered in detail in Malin, *Power and Change,* 235–39, 247-300.

95. Thomas Kimball, E. P. Vining, C. S. Stebbins, *The Railroad Problem: Memorial to the Legislature of the State of Kansas* (Topeka: Crane, 1883), in Kansas Board of R.R. Commissioners, Miscellaneous Pamphlets, vol. 1, KSHS.

96. Ibid., Norris Gage, *The Relations of Kansas Railroads to the State of Kansas* (Topeka: Kansas Publishing House, 1884), vol. 2, KSHS.

97. Democratic State Committee to G. W. Glick, November 26, 1882, Ware Papers (Nies acquisition), box 4, KSHS.

98. Ibid., Iowa Office of Railroad Commissioners to E. Ware, December 5, 1882, and Massachusetts Board of Railroad Commissioners to Ware, December 6, 1882.

99. E. F. Ware, *A Proposed Railroad Commissioner Law for the State of Kansas* (Ft. Scott, Kans.: Monitor, 1882), Kansas Board of R.R. Commissioners, Miscellaneous Pamphlets, vol. 2, KSHS.

100. Gleed speech at Valley Falls, July 4, 1886, Gleed Papers, box 44, KSHS.

101. Malin, *Power and Change*, 304–6.

102. James Drury, *The Government of Kansas*, 3d ed. (Lawrence: Regents Press of Kansas, 1980), 75.

103. *Topeka Commonwealth*, January 13, 1874, Legislative Clippings, vol. 1, KSHS.

104. Drawn from Wilder, *Governmental Agencies*. Wilder's *Bibliography of the Official Publications of Kansas, 1854–1958* (Lawrence: Governmental Research Center, KU), provides a reading list of what these agencies were doing.

105. F. P. Harkness, T. B. Murdock, C. H. Kimball, M. C. Kelley, and Joel Moody to Governor L. Humphreys in *Topeka Daily Capital*, December 28, 1890, Legislative Clippings, vol. 2, KSHS.

106. Wright, *One Hundred Years in Kansas Education*, 65–79.

107. *Wichita Eagle*, March 18, 1887.

108. Ingalls quoted in *Daily Gazette* (Abilene), May 21, 1887, Kansas Biography Scrapbook, vol. 2, KSHS.

109. *Wichita Eagle*, May 27, 1887.

110. Ellen DuBois, *Feminism and Suffrage: The Emergence of an Independent Women's Movement in America, 1848–1869* (Ithaca, N.Y.: Cornell University Press, 1999), 19, 79–80, 84.

111. Quoted in *Topeka Daily Capital*, October 29, 1880, Woman Suffrage Clippings, vols. 2–3, KSHS.

112. Susan Anthony to John St. John, August 21, 1881, St. John Papers Governors' Papers, 27-03-08-07, KSHS.

113. *Topeka Daily Capital*, October 27, 1886, Woman Suffrage Clippings, vols. 2–3, KSHS.

114. Ibid., October 29, 1886.

115. Ann Birney and Joyce Thierer, "Shoulder to Shoulder: Kansas Women Win the Vote," *Kansas Heritage* 3 (winter 1995): 67.

116. Eliza Homans to John Martin, n.d., Martin Papers, Governors' Papers, 27-05-01-07, KSHS.

117. Ibid., Nannie Stephens, M.D., to John Martin, n.d. [February 1887].

118. Ibid., Eva Stevens to John Martin, February 7, 1887.

119. Ibid., Edith Grains and Belle McCoy to John Martin, February 7, 1887.

120. Ibid., Mary Bowman, Abilene, to John Martin.

121. Ibid., Sarah Hall to John Martin, February 8, 1887.

122. Ibid., D. C. Milner to John Martin, February 15, 1887.

123. Mechem, ed., *Annals of Kansas*, 1: 35.

124. Richmond, *Kansas*, 193.

125. Birney and Thierer, "Shoulder to Shoulder," 68.

126. *Topeka Daily Capital*, April 30, 1887, Woman Suffrage Clippings, vols. 2–3, KSHS.

127. S. S. N. Foote to John Martin, September 27, 1885, Martin Papers, Governors' Papers, 27-04-07-03, KSHS.

128. Ibid., November 12, 1885.

129. Ibid., June 11, 1886, and May 11, November 21, 1887.

130. Hal Sears, *The Sex Radicals: Free Love in High Victorian America* (Lawrence: Regents Press of Kansas, 1977), 55, 63–64, 81, 87, 120.

131. *Kansas City Journal,* May 15, 1883, and *Topeka Commonwealth,* June 5, 1883, clippings in George Glick Papers, Governors' Papers, 27-04-05-02, KSHS. The entire matter of the Dodge City war is detailed in the Glick correspondence in the Governors' Papers.

132. Miner, *West of Wichita,* 214, 224–26.

133. Thomas Beer, *The Mauve Decade: American Life at the End of the Nineteenth Century* (1926; reprint, New York: Vintage Books, 1961), 42.

134. Miner, *West of Wichita,* 166–67, 215.

135. Gene Clanton, *Populism: The Humane Preference in America, 1890–1900* (Boston: Twayne, 1991), xiv, xvi, 8.

136. Richard Hofstadter, *The Age of Reform* (New York: Knopf, 1955), 94–95.

137. Elizabeth Barr, "The Populist Uprising," in Connelley, *Kansas and Kansans,* 2: 1115–16.

138. Worth Robert Miller, "A Centennial Historiography of American Populism," *Kansas History* 16 (spring 1993): 54–69.

139. Ibid., 54. For the historiography of Populism, see also C. Vann Woodward, "The Populist Heritage and the Intellectual," *American Scholar* 29 (winter 1959–1960): 55–72.

140. *Kansas City Journal,* October 30, 1910, Populist Party Clippings, vol. 2, KSHS.

141. *Extortionate Taxation. Oppressive and Unjust Discrimination Against the Poor. Criminal Extravagance with Public Money. An imperative demand for Change* (Wichita, 1891), in Special Collections, Ablah Library, Wichita State University.

142. Clanton, *Populism,* 1, 25.

143. Ibid., 24, 31.

144. John Ingalls to Rev. W. C. Wheeler, July 7, 1895, Ingalls Papers, box 2, KSHS.

145. Clanton, *Populism,* 30.

146. W. C. Webb to George Martin, January 17, 1880, Martin Papers, box 4, KSHS.

147. Williams, *Ingalls,* 94–95.

148. C. W. Johnson to Judge [Horton], March 3, 1880, Albert Horton Papers, box 2, KSHS.

149. Ibid., C. W. Pierce to A. H. Horton.

150. John Ingalls to P. I. Bonebrake, August 18, 1890, Ingalls Papers, box 2, KSHS.

151. Ibid., in *Atchison Weekly Globe,* August 28, 1900, Banks Scrapbook, box 5.

152. Box 3 of the Ingalls Papers (KSHS) is filled with the affairs of Sheffield Ingalls.

153. *Sectionalism. An Address Delivered Before the Quill Club, New York City, February 15, 1898, by J. W. Gleed* (n.p., n.d.), Kansas Collected Speeches and Pamphlets, Miscellaneous, vol. 24, KSHS.

154. Quoted in White, *Autobiography*, 281–83.

155. *The Leaders Who Have Inaugurated the So-Called Populist Party Purpose*, August 13, 1894, Kansas Collected Speeches and Pamphlets, vol. 19, KSHS.

156. Quoted in Miner, *Fire in the Rock*, 50.

157. Clanton, *Populism*, 43.

158. Charles Gleed, *A Bird's-Eye View of the Political Situation in Kansas, with Especial Reference to the People's Party* (Topeka: Republican State Headquarters, 1893), 5.

159. *New York Times*, July 23, 1889, Gleed Mounted Clippings, Gleed Papers, box 50, KSHS.

160. *Mirror and Farmer* (Manchester, N.H.), April 2, 1891, Populist Party Clippings, vol. 1, KSHS.

161. *Baltimore Sun*, March 11, 1891, in Richard Ely Papers, KU.

162. Ibid., *Chicago Evening Journal*, February 27, 1892.

163. Connelley, *Kansas and Kansans*, 2: 1160.

164. *Brown County World*, April 3, 1891, Essays Clippings, vol. 1, KSHS.

165. *Topeka Daily Capital*, March 14, 1891, Legislative Clippings, vol. 2, KSHS.

166. *Biennial Message of Lyman U. Humphrey, Governor, to the Legislature of Kansas* (Topeka: Kansas Publishing House, 1889), Humphrey Clippings, KU.

167. Ibid., Governor Lyman Humphrey, "Inaugural Address," January 14, 1889.

168. Connelley, *Kansas and Kansans*, 2: 1122, 1168–69. Mechem, ed., *Annals of Kansas*, 139.

169. Clanton, *Populism*, 106.

170. *Leavenworth Times*, January 10, 1893, Populist Party Clippings, vol. 1, KSHS.

171. Zornow, *Kansas*, 201–2; Connelley, *Kansas and Kansans*, 2: 1175; William Parrish, "The Great Kansas Legislative Imbroglio of 1893," *Journal of the West* 7 (October 1968): 471–90; J. Ware Butterfield, "The Legislative War of 1893: Inside, Outside and Back Again," *Collections of the Kansas State Historical Society* 6 (1897–1900): 453–58; and W. P. Harrington, "The Populist Party in Kansas," *Collections of the Kansas State Historical Society* 16 (1923–1925): 403–50. For a Populist partisan interpretation, see *The Legislative Conspiracy* (Topeka: Aurora Library, 1893). For a Republican partisan view, see Joseph Hudson, *Letters to Governor Lewelling* (Topeka: Topeka Capital, 1893).

172. Hudson, *Letters*, 5.

173. *Topeka State Journal*, January 10, 1893, Legislative Clippings, vol. 3, KSHS.

174. Ibid., American Press Association in *Kansas State Journal*, January 11, 1893.

175. Ibid., *Kansas City Star*, February 15, 1893.

176. Ibid., February 16, 1893.

177. Ibid., *Kansas City Journal*, February 16, 1893.

178. Ibid., *World*, February 17, 1893, vol. 4.

179. Ibid., *Western Spirit* (Paola).

180. Ibid., *St. Louis Globe Democrat*, vol. 5.

181. Ibid., *St. Paul Dispatch*, February 18, 1893.

182. Ibid., *Minneapolis Tribune*, February 20, 1893, vol. 6.

183. J. H. Gillpatrick to A. H. Horton, March 17, 1893, Horton Papers, box 2, KSHS.

184. Ibid., D. J. Brewer to A. H. Horton, March 26, 1893.

185. Ibid., James Humphrey to A. H. Horton, February 28, 1893.

186. *Kansas City Gazette,* February 16, 1893, Populist Party Clippings, vol. 1, KSHS.

187. Socolofsky, *Kansas Governors,* 123, 126.

188. *Kansas City Times,* November 27, 1904, Populist Party Clippings, vol. 2, KSHS.

189. Ibid., December 12, 1904. For an interesting insight into Lease's bolt, see O. Gene Clanton, "Intolerant Populist? The Disaffection of Mary Elizabeth Lease," *Kansas Historical Quarterly* 34 (summer 1968): 189–200.

190. Connelley, *Kansas and Kansans,* 2: 1185.

191. *The Kansas Democrat* (Hiawatha), May 17, 1894, Woman Suffrage Clippings, vols. 2–3, KSHS.

192. Robert LaForte, *Leaders of Reform: Progressive Republicans in Kansas, 1900–1916* (Lawrence: University Press of Kansas, 1974), 11.

193. James Steele to Eugene Ware, October 12, 1893, Ware Papers (Nies acquisition), box 8, KSHS.

194. Talk by George W. Martin, 1894, Martin Papers, box 3, KSHS.

195. *The Advocate,* May 9, 1894, Gleed Mounted Clippings, Gleed Papers, box 49, KSHS.

196. Robert Bader, *Hayseeds, Moralizers, and Methodists* (Lawrence: University Press of Kansas, 1988), 11–14.

5. THE BONE AND SINEW OF THE STATE

1. *Topeka Capital,* September 6, 1911, quoted in Richard Taylor, *Henry Ford of the Air* (Topeka: privately printed, 1996), 3–4.

2. Frank Rowe and Craig Miner, *Borne on the South Wind: A Century of Kansas Aviation* (Wichita, Kans.: Wichita Eagle and Beacon, 1994), 18–22, 26–29, 38–41.

3. Ibid., 35.

4. Ibid., 41.

5. *Topeka Capital,* March 13, 1910, Automobiles Clippings, vol. 1, KSHS.

6. Ibid., *Topeka Capital,* August 13, 1950.

7. Ibid., *Wichita Eagle,* June 15, 1954, and *Kansas City Star,* November 19, 1961, vol. 2.

8. Miner, *Magic City,* 111–12.

9. *Kansas City Star,* August 23, 1914, Automobiles Clippings, vol. 1, KSHS.

10. Ibid., *Wichita Eagle,* October 2, 1949, and *Topeka Capital,* August 13, 1950.

11. Ibid., *Kansas City Star,* February 12, 1909.

12. Ibid., September 17, 1911.

13. Ibid., *Topeka Journal,* January 23, 1915.

14. Ibid., *Topeka Capital,* February 8, 1916.

15. Charles Gleed, "The Kansas of 1912," speech, January 29, 1913, Gleed Papers, box 44, KSHS.

16. Preston Plumb to Eugene Ware, February 21, 1891, Ware Papers (Nies acquisition), box 6, KSHS.

17. Ibid., Eugene Ware to H. B. Humes, January 19, 1893, box 28.

18. William Connelley, *The Life of Preston B. Plumb* (Chicago: Browne and Howell, 1913), 431.

19. *Topeka Commonwealth*, August 24, 1894, Sara Robinson Scrapbooks, vol. 5, KU.

20. Williams, *Ingalls*, 144, 149.

21. Sarah Coates to Sara Robinson, August 27, 1894, Robinson Papers, box 2, KU.

22. Bader, *Prohibition in Kansas*, 150–55; Miner, *Magic City*, 113–14.

23. Quoted in Miner, *Uncloistered Halls*, 43.

24. E. W. Hoch to editor, *Kansas City Journal*, May 2, 1907, in Edward Hoch Papers, Governors' Papers, 27-06-03-08, KSHS.

25. The University Press of Kansas in 1999 published the "Kansas Centennial Edition" of L. Frank Baum's *Wonderful Wizard of Oz*, with a foreword by Ray Bradbury.

26. *Topeka Capital*, April 2, 1899, Funston Papers, box 3, KSHS.

27. Ibid., *Louisville Courier*, March 20, 1901, and *Chicago Daily Chronicle*, April 27, 1906.

28. Calder Picket, *Ed Howe: Country Town Philosopher* (Lawrence: University Press of Kansas, 1968), 73–74.

29. Eugene Ware, *Some of the Rhymes of Ironquill*, 5th ed. (Topeka: Crane, 1896), 250.

30. Miner, *Magic City*, 129–30. On Mentholatum, see John Hyde, "A Balm in Gilead," *Kansas History* 9 (winter 1986–1987): 150–63.

31. There is no published history of the Coleman Company, but the company historian, Herbert Ebendorf, has composed an excellent typescript history, "The Coleman Story," from which this information is drawn.

32. *Topeka Commonwealth*, August 24, 1894, Sara Robinson Scrapbooks, vol. 5, KU.

33. For recent views on Kansas Populist ideology, see Scott McNall, *The Road to Rebellion: Class Formation and Kansas Populism, 1865–1900* (Chicago: University of Chicago Press, 1988), and Gene Clanton, *Congressional Populism and the Crisis of the 1890s* (Lawrence: University Press of Kansas, 1998).

34. S. N. Wood, "Wood's Manifesto: An Address to the People of Kansas. Delivered at Herington, Kansas, April 29, 1891," 6–7, in Margaret Wood, *Memorial of Samuel N. Wood by Margaret L. Wood* (Kansas City, Mo.: Hudson-Kimberly, 1892).

35. C. Wood Davis, "The Farmer, the Investor, and the Railway," *Arena* 3 (February 1891): 291.

36. *Eighth Annual Report of the Board of Railroad Commissioners*, vi–viii.

37. *Thirteenth Annual Report of the Board of Railroad Commissioners for the Year Ending November 30, 1895. State of Kansas* (Topeka: Kansas State Printing Company, J. K. Hudson, state printer, 1896), 13.

38. For the Gleeds, see Terry Harmon, "Charles Sumner Gleed: A Western Business Leader, 1856–1920" (Ph.D. diss., University of Kansas, 1973).

39. C. S. G. in *Topeka Capital*, September 6, 1891, Gleed Mounted Clippings, Gleed Papers, box 49, KSHS.

40. Ibid., unidentified clipping, October 31, 1891; *Eighth Biennial Report of the Kansas State Board of Agriculture, 1887–1888* (Topeka: Kansas Publishing House, 1889), 5.

41. Miner, *Uncloistered Halls*, 42, 47, 56.

42. Charles Gleed, "The Wealth and Business Relations of the West," and "What the

Farmers Have Netted," in *Forum* (January, April 1893), Gleed Mounted Clippings, Gleed Papers, box 49, KSHS; Griffin, *University of Kansas,* 105–6.

43. *Kansas City Journal,* October 5, 1895, Gleed Mounted Clippings, Gleed Papers, box 50, KSHS.

44. *Kansas City Journal,* June 25, 1899, Speeches Clippings, box 2, KSHS.

45. Griffin, *University of Kansas,* 309.

46. Arthur Capper, Speech at Wakeeney, Kansas, 1913, Capper Papers, box 46, KSHS.

47. C. W. Smith to Willis Bailey, December 25, 1902, Willis Bailey Papers, Governors' Papers, 27-06-02-03, KSHS.

48. Ibid., Carl Swensson to Willis Bailey, January 30, 1903, and ? to Bailey, n.d. [1903].

49. Griffin, *University of Kansas,* 233.

50. ? to Bailey, n.d. [1903], Bailey Papers, Governors' Papers, 27-06-02-03, KSHS.

51. George Martin to Graduate Magazine (Lawrence), January 12, 1903, Martin Papers, box 4, KSHS.

52. *Iola Register,* October 6, 1932, Journalism Clippings, vol. 2, KSHS.

53. Of these there is a book about Miller; see James Callahan, *Jayhawk Editor* (Los Angeles: Sterling Press, 1955), but the legacy of the others is mostly in their newspapers themselves and in the extensive personal papers they left to the state historical society.

54. For White's famous statement of purpose, see Sally Griffith, *Home Town News: William Allen White and the Emporia Gazette* (Baltimore: Johns Hopkins University Press, 1989), 32; for White's view, see his *Autobiography.*

55. Homer Socolofsky, *Arthur Capper: Publisher, Politician, Philanthropist* (Lawrence: University of Kansas Press, 1962), 53–62.

56. Charles Sheldon to Arthur Capper, January 14, 1909, Capper Papers, box 31, KSHS.

57. Ibid., February 8, 1911.

58. Clymer Address at Kansas Editors' Day, "Newspapers' Sons of the Morning," September 23, 1961, Clymer Papers, box 50, KSHS.

59. Ibid., Rolla Clymer, speech on W. A. White, 1968.

60. Rolla Clymer, "Civic Ideals of the Kansas Press," address, Salina, January 22, 1926, published in *Jayhawker Press* 3 (April 1926).

61. These obituaries have been collected in R. A. Clymer, *Farewells,* ed. William Galvani (El Dorado, Kans.: Butler County Historical Society, 1986).

62. LaForte, *Leaders of Reform,* 6–8.

63. *Topeka State Journal,* January 12, 1915, Legislative Clippings, vol. 12, KSHS.

64. This list was compiled from volumes 3–17 of the Kansas Legislature Clippings file at the Kansas State Historical Society. For a published summary of the early movement, see Charles Hill, "Progressive Legislation in Kansas," *Collections of the Kansas State Historical Society* 12 (1911–1912): 69–77. Instructive studies of elements of Kansas Progressivism are Nina Swanson, "The Development of Public Protection of Children in Kansas," *Collections of the Kansas State Historical Society* 15 (1919–1922): 231–78; Edith Hess, "State Regulation of Woman and Child Labor in Kansas," *Collections of the Kansas State Historical Society* 15 (1919–1922): 279–333; Domenico Gagli-

ardo, "A History of Kansas Child-Labor Legislation," *Kansas Historical Quarterly* 1 (August 1932): 379–411; Domenico Gagliardo, "Some Wage Legislation in Kansas," *Kansas Historical Quarterly* 8 (November 1939): 384–98; Domenico Gagliardo, "The First Kansas Workmen's Compensation Law," *Kansas Historical Quarterly* 9 (November 1940): 384–97; Domenico Gagliardo, "Development of Common and Employers' Liability Law in Kansas," *Kansas Historical Quarterly* 10 (May 1941): 155–74.

65. *Topeka Capital,* February 12, 1915, Legislative Clippings, vol. 13, KSHS.

66. Ibid., *Topeka Journal,* March 10, 1903, vol. 7.

67. Ibid., *Kansas City Star,* March 13, 1917, vol. 14.

68. Ibid., *Topeka Journal,* October 25, 1966, vol. 35.

69. Ibid., *Topeka Capital,* March 22, 1915, vol. 14.

70. Ibid., *Topeka Capital,* January 8, 1917.

71. Ibid., *Topeka State Journal,* vol. 13.

72. Wilder, *Governmental Agencies,* 119.

73. George Crane to Edward Hoch, March 7, 1905, Hoch Papers, Governors' Papers, 27-06-05-05, KSHS.

74. For an overview of these ideas nationally, see John Sproat, *"The Best Men": Liberal Reformers in the Gilded Age* (New York: Oxford University Press, 1968).

75. W. H. Carruth to Edward Hoch, January 7, 1905, Hoch Papers, Governors' Papers, 27-06-05-05, KSHS.

76. Ibid., Bertha Marlatt to Edward Hoch, February 6, 1907.

77. W. R. Smith, "The Kansas State Printing Plant," *Collections of the Kansas State Historical Society* 14 (1915–1918): 354–55.

78. John Alford and H. L. Shirer, Kansas Book Company, typed statement, February 5, 1913, Gleed Papers, box 13, KSHS.

79. A. M. Thorman, Secretary of Kansas School Book Commission, to Arthur Capper, September 1, 1915, Arthur Capper Papers, Governors' Papers, 28-03-07-02, KSHS, and *A Price List of School Books Published by the State and the Books Adopted and Approved by the State School Book Commission of Kansas. August, 1915* (Topeka: Kansas State Printing Plant, 1915).

80. Ibid., A. M. Thorman to Arthur Capper, September 1, 1916.

81. Smith, "The Kansas State Printing Plant," 356–57.

82. A. M. Thorman to Arthur Capper, September 1, 1918, Capper Papers, Governors' Papers, 28-03-07-02, KSHS.

83. *Wichita Beacon,* January 23, 1915.

84. Ibid., January 27, 1915.

85. *Topeka Capital,* January 26, 1915, vol. 12, and *Topeka State Journal,* February 3, 1915, vol. 13, Legislative Clippings, KSHS.

86. Ibid., *Topeka Capital,* March 26, 1937, vol. 17.

87. Kansas Legislature, *Report of the Committee for Investigation of the School Textbook Question* (Topeka: n.p., 1932), 4, 17–20.

88. *Kansas City Star,* May 30, 1903, Floods Clippings, vol. 1, KSHS.

89. Ibid., *Kansas City Times,* May 31, 1903.

90. Ibid., *Topeka Capital,* June 3, 1903, vol. 2.

91. Ibid., *Kansas City Star,* June 9, 1903.

92. Ibid., July 2, 1903, vol. 4.

93. Ibid., *Topeka Capital,* July 10, 1903.

94. Ibid., June 23, 1903.

95. Ibid., *Wichita Eagle,* July 21, 1903.

96. Ibid., *Topeka Journal,* June 26, 1903, vol. 4.

97. Quoted in *Topeka State Journal,* enclosed in Frank MacLellan to Eugene Ware, July 11, 1903, Ware Papers (Nies acquisition), box 18, KSHS.

98. *Kansas City Star,* September 22, 1903, Floods Clippings, vol. 4, KSHS.

99. Ibid., *Kansas City Times,* October 5, 1903.

100. Ibid., J. R. Burton, "Twin Ideas," from *North American Review,* in *Kansas City Times,* October 9, 1903.

101. See Sherow, *Watering the Valley.*

102. For Cheyenne Bottoms, see Douglas Harvey, " 'Drought Relief Efforts Delayed by Rain': The History of Cheyenne Bottoms Wildlife Area" (master's thesis, Wichita State University, 2000). A part of this thesis was published as "Creating a 'Sea of Galilee': The Rescue of Cheyenne Bottoms Wildlife Area, 1927–1930," *Kansas History* 24 (spring 2001): 2–17.

103. *Topeka Capital,* August 18, 1915, Floods Clippings, vol. 7, KSHS.

104. Ibid., April 21, 1927, and February 9, 1928.

105. Miner, *Fire in the Rock,* 84–85.

106. "Pratt Fish Hatchery," n.d., Capper Papers, Governors' Papers, 27-08-06-04, KSHS.

107. J. F. Elliott to George Hodges, August 20, 1913, and J. C. Hopper to George Hodges, August 18, 1913, 27-07-04-01; J. C. Hopper to George Hodges, December 13, 1915, 27-08-06-04, all in George Hodges Papers, Governors' Papers, KSHS.

108. Arthur Capper to W. C. Tegmeier, November 8, 1915, Capper Papers, Governors' Papers, 27-08-06-04, KSHS.

109. Clarence Spellman to W. R. Stubbs, June 16, 1909, Walter Stubbs Papers, Governors' Papers, 27-06-08-04, KSHS.

110. *Kansas City Star,* February 19, 1910, Kansas History Clippings, vol. 4, KSHS.

111. Ibid., *Topeka Journal,* December 1907.

112. Ibid., *Junction City Sentinel,* April 24, 1908.

113. Mrs. J. S. Simmons to Edward Hoch, February 13, 1908, Hoch Papers, Governors' Papers, 27-06-04-04, KSHS.

114. Ibid., undated clipping from *Hutchinson Daily News,* [April 1908].

115. *Topeka Capital,* March 22, 1925, Kansas History Clippings, vol. 6, KSHS.

116. Miner, *Discovery,* 32–42, 79, 83–85, 89. The cigar quote is from *Topeka Capital,* April 10, 1897, Oil and Gas Clippings, vol. 1, KSHS.

117. William Connelley to Eugene Ware, September 4, 1903, Ware Papers (Nies acquisition), box 18, KSHS.

118. Ibid., November 12, 1903.

119. Ibid., June 11, 1904, box 19.

120. Schruben, *Wea Creek,* 71.

121. William Connelley to Eugene Ware, March 30, 1905, Ware Papers (Nies acquisition), box 21, KSHS.

122. *Topeka Capital,* February 15, 1905, Oil and Gas Clippings, vol. 1, KSHS.

123. Mechem, ed., *Annals of Kansas,* 1: 416–17; Schruben, *Wea Creek,* 77–78.

124. Edward Hoch, Message to Legislature, February 16, 1905, Hoch Papers, Governors' Papers, 27-06-04-04, KSHS.

125. Schruben, *Wea Creek,* 80.

126. J. G. Maxwell to Edward Hoch, February 4, 1905, Hoch Papers, Governors' Papers, 27-06-04-04, KSHS.

127. Ibid., Thomas Sawyer to Edward Hoch, February 4, 1905.

128. Schruben, *Wea Creek,* 82.

129. James Humphrey to Edward Hoch, February 6, 1905, Hoch Papers, Governors' Papers, 27-06-04-04, KSHS.

130. Ibid., A. F. Robertson to Edward Hoch, January 15, 1906.

131. Miner, *Discovery,* 124–29.

132. Schruben, *Wea Creek,* 156.

133. Miner, *Discovery,* 169.

134. Self, *Environment and Man,* 154–55.

135. Craig Miner, "Report on Executive Manor Case," for Blackwell, Sanders, Matheny, Weary and Lombardy, October 1991, paper detailing the history of energy in Wichita in the early twentieth century.

136. Self, *Environment and Man,* 142.

137. Population statistics can be conveniently traced in Mechem, ed., *Annals of Kansas.*

138. *Chattanooga News,* quoted in *Topeka Capital,* October 30, 1915, Kansas Description Clippings, vol. 1, KSHS.

139. Eugene Ware to ? Robinson, January 11, 1911, Ware Papers, KU.

140. Quoted in *Wichita Eagle,* February 9, 1964.

141. F. Dumont Smith to Walter Stubbs, December 18, 1908, Stubbs Papers, Governors' Papers, 27-06-08-02, KSHS.

142. Ibid., E. P. Ripley to Walter Stubbs, May 15, 1909.

143. Ibid., J. S. George to Walter Stubbs, May 25, 1909.

144. From *Kansas City Star,* n.d. [1893], Gleed Mounted Clippings, Gleed Papers, box 49, KSHS.

145. *Decisions of the Board of Railroad Commissioners. State of Kansas. The City of Wichita, by the Mayor, Complainant versus The AT&SFRR Co, The Mo. Pac. Ry. Co.* (Topeka: Kansas Publishing House, Clifford C. Barker, state printer, 1889), Kansas Board of Railroad Commissioners, Miscellaneous Pamphlets, vol. 1; *Seventh Annual Report of the Board of Railroad Commissioners for the Year Ending December 1, 1889. State of Kansas* (Topeka: Kansas State Printing House, Clifford C. Baker, state printer, 1889).

146. Franklin Adams to Board of Railroad Commissioners, November 19, 1909, Stubbs Papers, Governors' Papers, 27-06-08-02, KSHS.

147. Ibid., O. P. Byers, mss for article, "Intra-State Freight Rates," in J. S. George to Walter Stubbs, October 1, 1909.

148. Ibid., E. P. Ripley to Walter Stubbs, October 1, 1910.

149. Charles Gleed, "Facts and Comment on Railroad Agitation in Kansas," for *Sun* (Chanute, Kans.), September 18, 1906, Gleed Papers, box 44, KSHS.

150. Ibid., Gleed speech, "The Kansas of 1912," January 29, 1913.

151. Walter Stubbs to E. P. Ripley, October 19, 1910, Stubbs Papers, Governors' Papers, 27-06-08-02, KSHS.

152. Ibid., E. P. Ripley to Walter Stubbs, October 25, 1910.

153. *Topeka State Journal*, February 13, 1915, Legislative Clippings, vol. 13, KSHS.

154. Miner, "Report on Executive Manor Case"; Edward Nelson, *KPL in Kansas: A History of the Kansas Power and Light Company* (Lawrence, Kans.: Center for Research in Business, 1964); Craig Miner, *Wolf Creek Station: Kansas Gas and Electric Company in the Nuclear Era* (Columbus: Ohio State University Press, 1993), 10–11.

155. W. R. Kuykendall to Edward Hoch, February 6, 1907, Hoch Papers, Governors' Papers, 27-06-04-06, KSHS.

156. Ibid., E. W. Hoch to Mrs. Anna Williams, February 4, 1907, 27-06-03-08; *Kansas City Star*, February 13, 1944, Capital Punishment Clippings, vol. 1, KSHS.

157. E. W. Hoch to Thomas Marshall, June 26, 1906, Hoch Papers, Governors' Papers, 27-06-04-08, KSHS.

158. Ibid., E. W. Hoch to Robinette Scheier, March 23, 1907.

159. Ibid., E. W. Hoch to Mrs. Anna Williams, February 4, 1907; James Galliher and John Galliher, " 'Deja Vu All Over Again': The Recurring Life and Death of Capital Punishment Legislation in Kansas," *Social Problems* 44 (August 1997): 373.

160. *Kansas City Star*, July 6, 1916, Capital Punishment Clippings, vol. 1, KSHS.

161. Ibid., *Topeka Journal*, November 24, 1919, with handwritten reference to Wilson pardon.

162. Ibid., *Wichita Eagle*, April 9, 1937, and *Topeka Capital*, March 10, 1944.

163. Mechem, ed., *Annals of Kansas*, 2: 3, 52. See Lorraine Gehring, "Women Officeholders in Kansas, 1872–1912," *Kansas History* 9 (summer 1986): 48–57.

164. *Topeka Journal*, February 10, 1905, Legislative Clippings, vol. 8, KSHS.

165. W. R. Adams to Walter Stubbs, April 27, 1911, Stubbs Papers, Governors' Papers, 27-06-08-04, KSHS.

166. Ibid., Lucy Johnson to Walter Stubbs, July 7, 1908.

167. E. S. A. Peulosa in *News*, October 10, 1912, Woman Suffrage Clippings, vol. 6, KSHS.

168. Ibid., *Emporia Gazette*, October 23, 1912.

169. Ibid., *Ness City News*, October 26, 1912.

170. *Kansas City Times*, September 27, 1914, Women Clippings, vol. 1, KSHS.

171. Ibid., *Topeka Capital*, August 24, 1915.

172. Ibid., February 4, 1916.

173. Samuel Crumbine, *Frontier Doctor* (Philadelphia: Dorrance, 1948), 23, 110–12, 114, 116, 121, 132, 143, 146–47, 156, 165, 169, 198–99, 211; *Wichita Eagle*, September 8, 1918.

174. Miner, *Magic City*, 40.

175. See Craig Miner, "History of Pediatric Medicine in Wichita," paper, and Melissa Grubb, "Mother Hughes and Female Guardians: Progressive-Era Women Promoting Infant and Maternity Health Care Reform in America" (master's thesis, Wichita State University, 1999). See also *Wichita Eagle*, March 11, May 1–3, 6, August 22, 1918; July 22, 1923; June 5, 1936, and *Wichita Beacon*, March 18, 1928.

176. Crumbine, *Frontier Doctors*, 212.

177. *Topeka Capital*, February 11, 1915, Kansas Legislature Clippings, vol. 13, KSHS.

178. Ibid., January 22, 1915, vol. 12.

179. Ibid., *Kansas City Times*, January 22, 1915.

180. Billy Jones, *The Chandlers of Kansas: A Banking Family* (Wichita, Kans.: Center for Entrepreneurship, 1983), 51–54.

181. Lawrence Friedman, *Menninger: The Family and the Clinic* (New York: Knopf, 1990), 4, 8, 24, 33.

182. Capper speech at Sanitation Day, Fredonia, October 3, 1915, Capper Papers, box 47, KSHS.

183. Miner, *Magic City*, 139–41; H. Edward Flentje, "The Political Roots of City Managers in Kansas," *Kansas History* 7 (summer 1984): 139–40, 148.

184. Miner, *Magic City*, 140.

185. Ibid., 136–37, 143, 146; Flentje, "Political Roots," 144.

186. Flentje, "Political Roots," 141–42, 158.

187. An extensive verbatim transcript is in Stubbs Papers, Governors' Papers, 27-06-08-02, KSHS.

188. Capper speech at National Purity Conference, November 8, 1914, Capper Papers, box 46, KSHS.

189. C. L. Davidson speech, April 21, 1911, Gleed Papers, box 4, KSHS.

190. Miner, *Magic City*, 141.

191. Wilder, *Governmental Agencies*, 34; speech of Arthur Capper before Womens' Federated Clubs, April 11, 1916, Capper Papers, box 48, KSHS.

192. J. N. Dolley to Arthur Luddington, February 6, 1909, Stubbs Papers, Governors' Papers, 27-06-07-03, KSHS.

193. Ibid., Set of Rules for Civil Service, 1915, 27-08-06-04.

194. Wilder, *Governmental Agencies*, 8–9.

195. Arthur Capper to E. T. Hackney, March 25, 1916, Capper Papers, Governors' Papers, 27-08-06-04, KSHS.

196. Ibid., Arthur Capper to State Senate, February 21, 1917.

197. The definitive account of state political alignments in this era is LaForte, *Leaders of Reform*.

198. In addition to the biased, maybe even partly fictional *Autobiography*, a good combination of primary and secondary sources for the study of White is found in Walter Johnson, *William Allen White's America* (New York: Henry Holt, 1947), and Johnson, ed., *Selected Letters*.

199. William Allen White to Victor Murdock, White Papers, reel 3, no. 420, KSHS. The

main White manuscript collection is in the Library of Congress. A substantial selection, far beyond those published, filmed by Walter Johnson, is available at the Kansas State Historical Society, from which these citations come.

200. Ibid., H. W. Young to White, no. 1090.

201. Ibid., T. A. McNeal to White, November 13, 1909, no. 1085.

202. Ibid., Joseph Bristow to William White, February 22, 1908, no. 34.

203. Ibid., May 10, 1908, no. 37.

204. Ibid., W. R. Stubbs to White, October 5, 1909, no. 1080.

205. Ibid., William Allen White to Chancellor, June 27, 1910, no. 459.

206. Ibid., William Allen White to S. A. Smith, September 7, 1910, no. 490.

207. Ibid., William Allen White to H. Vincent, September 3, 1910, no. 487.

208. William Allen White to W. H. Carruth, April 18, 1911, in Johnson, ed., *Selected Letters,* 118–19.

209. William Allen White to Charles [Gleed], February 10, 1912, White Papers, reel 4, no. 629, KSHS.

210. Ibid., William Allen White to Charles Scott, October 27, 1919, reel 5, no. 196.

211. Charles Gleed to Albert Greene, November 24, 1911, Gleed Papers, box 15, KSHS.

212. Ibid., Charles Gleed to William Allen White, December 1, 1911, box 5.

213. Ibid., Charles Gleed to John Fletcher, October 15, 1912, box 2.

214. Ibid., Arthur Capper to Charles Gleed, February 11, 1916.

215. Ibid., Charles Gleed to Walker Hines, March 6, 1917, box 18.

216. Speech of Arthur Capper at Wichita YMCA, February 1, 1914, Capper Papers, box 46, KSHS.

217. Ibid., Arthur Capper speech, n.d. [1914], box 47.

218. Ibid., Arthur Capper, "The Military Policy as Viewed in the West," n.d., box 25.

219. Bower Sageser, *Joseph L. Bristow: Kansas Progressive* (Lawrence: University Press of Kansas, 1968), 163.

220. George Morehouse, "Kansas as a State of Extremes, and Its Attitude During the World War," *Collections of the Kansas State Historical Society* 15 (1919–1922): 20.

221. Billard's flight records are in Billard Family Papers, box 1, KSHS.

222. Ibid., Dorothy [Berry] to Phillip Billard, February 1913, box 2.

223. Ibid., Billard flight report, November 30, 1916.

224. Ibid., Report of Major Alvarado Fuller, August 5, 1917.

225. Ibid., Dorothy Berry to Phil Billard, November 8, 1917.

226. Ibid., Phillip Billard to Bob Billard, March 27, 1918.

227. Ibid., Phillip Billard to Bob Billard, April 4, 1918.

228. Ibid., Karolyn Whitterey to Phillip Billard, May 4, 1918.

229. Ibid., speech of Arthur Capper, July 24, 1938.

6. CHASTENED AND CHANGED

1. *Wichita Eagle,* April 18, 19, 1918.

2. Ibid., April 22, 1918.

3. Ibid., April 6, 1918.

4. Ibid., April 20, 24, 1918; James Juhnke, "Kansas Mennonites in World War I," paper delivered at World War I Conference, Newman College, November 6–7, 1998; James Juhnke, "Mob Violence and Kansas Mennonites in 1918," *Kansas Historical Quarterly* 43 (autumn 1977): 334–50.

5. *Topeka Journal,* September 12, 1917, Mennonite Clippings, KSHS.

6. Ibid., *Topeka Capital,* May 30, 1913.

7. Ibid., June 3, 1918.

8. Ibid., November 27, 1917.

9. Henry Allen to J. G. Evert, February 11, 1919, Allen Papers, Governors' Papers, 27-08-07-07, KSHS.

10. Randolph Bourne, *War and the Intellectuals: Essays by Randolph S. Bourne, 1915–1919* (New York: Harper Torchbooks, 1964).

11. Henry May, *The End of American Innocence: A Study of the First Years of Our Own Time, 1912–1917* (New York: Knopf, 1959).

12. Juhnke, "Mob Violence," 350.

13. Patrick O'Brien, " 'War Was Everyone's Business': The Kansas State Council of Defense," paper presented at World War I Conference, Newman College, November 7–8, 1998.

14. *Topeka Capital,* January 12, January 27, 1918, and *Topeka Journal,* October 27, 1917, YWCA, in World War I Clippings, KSHS.

15. Arthur Capper to J. F. Faigley, April 25, 1918, Capper Papers, Governors' Papers, 27-08-05-02, KSHS.

16. Ibid., Henry Allen to Prof. E. M. Hopkins, December 2, 1919, 27-08-07-07.

17. Ibid., Timothy Shea to Henry Allen, June 23, 1919.

18. Ibid., P. A. Patterson to Henry Allen, February 6, 1919, and J. G. Evert to Allen, February 5, 1919.

19. Ibid., Martin Greabner to Henry Allen, December 15, 1919.

20. Ibid., Henry Allen to Rev. Arthur Gowdy, March 22, 1919.

21. Herbert Pankratz, "The Suppression of Alleged Disloyalty in Kansas During World War I," *Kansas Historical Quarterly* 42 (autumn 1976): 277–307.

22. *Topeka Capital,* February 14, 1917, Kansas Legislative Clippings, vol. 14, KSHS.

23. Bader, *Prohibition,* 186–88.

24. David Sterling, "The Federal Government vs. the *Appeal to Reason,*" *Kansas History* 9 (spring 1986): 31, 42; John Graham, ed., *"Yours for the Revolution": The Appeal to Reason, 1895–1922* (Lincoln: University of Nebraska Press, 1990), x–xi, 10.

25. Mark Scott, "The Little Blue Books in the War on Bigotry and Bunk," *Kansas History* 1 (autumn 1978): 155, 158. Haldeman-Julius bought the *Appeal to Reason* in 1919.

26. Blue Books nos. 452, 652, 656, 861, 883, 884, 1250, 1348, 1423, 1424, 1425, and 1549, from the author's collection.

27. John Gunn, *E. Haldeman-Julius—the Man and His Work* (Girard, Kans.: Haldeman-Julius, 1924), 57; Blue Book no. 678.

28. E. Haldeman-Julius, *Is This Century the Most Admirable in History?* (Girard, Kans.: Haldeman-Julius, 1930); Blue Book no. 1512.

29. Scott, "Blue Books," 159; Graham, *"Yours For the Revolution,"* 26.

30. Rowe and Miner, *Borne on the South Wind,* 12.

31. Sterling, "Federal Government," 39.

32. For a content analysis of the *Appeal,* see David Nord, "The *Appeal to Reason* and American Socialism, 1901–1920," *Kansas History* 1 (summer 1978): 74–89.

33. A. M. Lovejoy and F. M. Eastwood to E. N. Martin, January 6, 1912, Gleed Papers, box 17, KSHS.

34. Graham, *"Yours for the Revolution,"* 7.

35. N. H. Martin to Gen. Harrison Gray Otis, January 11, 1912, Gleed papers, box 17, KSHS.

36. Graham, *'Yours for the Revolution,"* 250.

37. Earl White, *The United States v. C. W. Anderson et al.: The Wichita Case, 1917–1919,* in *At the Point of Production: The Local History of the I.W.W.,* ed. Joseph Conlin (Westport, Conn.: Greenwood Press, 1981), 143–44, 149, 151, 153, 155, 159–60; unidentified clipping, November 2, 1917, IWW–Non-Partisan League Clippings, KSHS.

38. Clayton Koppes, "The Kansas Trial of the IWW, 1917–1919," *Labor History* 16 (summer 1975): 355.

39. Clayton Koppes, "The Industrial Workers of the World and County-Jail Reform in Kansas, 1915–1920," *Kansas Historical Quarterly* 41 (spring 1975): 67, 72–73, 82–83.

40. *Kansas City Times,* March 12, 1919, IWW–Non-Partisan League Clippings, KSHS.

41. Unsigned report, n.d., Henry Allen Papers, Governors' Papers, 27-09-01-01, KSHS.

42. Richard Cortner, "The Wobblies and *Fiske v. Kansas*: Victory and Disintegration," *Kansas History* 4 (spring 1981): 30–38.

43. *Topeka Journal,* January 9, 1918, IWW–Non-Partisan League Clippings, KSHS.

44. Ibid., June 24, 1919.

45. Henry Allen to Byron Blair, November 10, 1919, Allen Papers, Governors' Papers, 27-09-01-01, KSHS.

46. Ibid., P. E. Zimmerman to Henry Allen, November 9, 1919.

47. Ibid., *Ohio State Journal,* in Clarence Richards to Henry Allen, April 26, 1928, 27-08-06-07.

48. Ibid., Henry Allen to P. E. Zimmerman, June 14, 1919, 27-08-07-07, KSHS.

49. Ibid., Testimony of Jeff Yancey, sheriff of Barton County, June 18, 1920, 27-08-06-07.

50. Ibid., Jack Downing to "D. O.," September 9, 1919.

51. Ibid., P. E. Zimmerman to Henry Allen, April 16, 1919.

52. Ibid., John Barrett to C. E. Perkins, March 23, 1919.

53. Broadside in ibid.

54. Graham, *"Yours for the Revolution,"* 39; Sally Miller, "Kate Richards O'Hare: Progression Toward Feminism," *Kansas History* 7 (winter 1984–1985): 263–79.

55. *Topeka Capital,* May 1, 1918, IWW–Non-Partisan League Clippings, KSHS.

56. *Topeka Capital,* November 28, 1919, Labor Clippings, vol. 1, KSHS.

57. Ibid., *Topeka Journal,* January 10, 1916.

58. Ibid., *Topeka Capital,* February 28, 1916.

59. Ibid., April 16, 1916.

60. Ibid., November 27, 1916.
61. Ibid., *Topeka Journal,* June 17, 1915.
62. Ibid., *Topeka Capital,* April 6, 1916.
63. Ibid., September 7, 1915.
64. *Kansas City Journal,* May 7, 1910, Strikes Clippings, vol. 1, KSHS.
65. Ibid., *Topeka Capital,* February 7, 1910.
66. Ibid., *Kansas City Star,* May 30, 1917.
67. Henry Allen to Gen. Charles Martin, November 27, 1919, Allen Papers, Governors' Papers, 27-08-07-05, KSHS.
68. Ibid., Report of Allen speech, n.d. [1919], 27-08-08-02.
69. Ibid., J. J. Bulger to O. W. Sparks, December 20, 1919.
70. Ibid., J. Chenault to Henry Allen, January 18, 1920.
71. Mechem, ed., *Annals of Kansas,* 2: 284.
72. Committee of Brotherhood of Railway Clerks to Henry Allen, January 4, 1930, Allen Papers, Governors' Papers, 27-08-08-02, KSHS.
73. Ibid., Ira Clemens to Henry Allen, December 31, 1919, and Association of Railway Executives to Henry Allen, February 18, 1920.
74. Ibid., F. J. Moss to Henry Allen, January 6, 1920.
75. Ibid., John Crain to Henry Allen, January 6, 1920.
76. Ibid., John Eberhardt to Henry Allen, January 8, 1920.
77. Ibid., Henry Allen to Walter Gardner, February 27, 1920, and E. H. Murdock to Allen, enclosing clip from the *Cincinnati Post,* December 27, 1919.
78. Ibid., Speech of Henry Allen, n.d. [February 1920], 27-08-08-03.
79. Ibid., Charles Fenn to Henry Allen, December 31, 1919, 27-08-08-02.
80. Henry Allen, *The Party of the Third Part* (New York: Harper and Brothers, 1921), 93–94.
81. Domenico Gagliardo, *The Kansas Industrial Court: An Experiment in Compulsory Arbitration* (Lawrence: University of Kansas Publications, 1941), 240.
82. *Topeka Capital,* April 7, 1920, Labor Clippings, vol. 1, KSHS.
83. Ibid., April 10, 1920.
84. Ibid., February 6, 8, 1921.
85. Ibid., *Topeka Journal,* December 14, 1921. A study of the march is Ann Schofield's "The Women's March: Miners, Family and Community in Pittsburg, Kansas, 1921–1922," *Kansas History* 7 (summer 1984): 159–68.
86. *Topeka Journal,* December 14, 1921, Labor Clippings, vol. 1, KSHS.
87. Gagliardo, *The Kansas Industrial Court,* 157–59, 168–72. White's account is in his *Autobiography,* 610–14.
88. William Allen White to Paul Kellogg, December 2, 1919, White Papers, reel 5, no. 201, KSHS, and in Johnson, ed., *Selected Letters,* 203.
89. William Allen White to Carl Wheat, September 7, 1920, White Papers, reel 5, no. 237, KSHS.
90. Ibid., William Allen White to Gerald Villard of *Nation,* June 11, 1922, no. 283.
91. Ibid., William Allen White to Bill [Borah], no. 294, and in Johnson, ed., *Selected Letters,* 227–28.

92. Henry Allen to William Allen White, August 17, 1922, White Papers, reel 5, no. 299, KSHS.

93. Ibid., Henry Allen to William Allen White, July 12, 1922.

94. Ibid., William Allen White to ? Peterson, July 20, 1923, no. 320.

95. James Bulger to Jonathan Davis, June 22, 1923, Jonathan Davis Papers, Governors' Papers, 27-09-04-04, KSHS.

96. Gagliardo, *The Kansas Industrial Court,* 56, 227, 232.

97. For the Red Scare nationally, see Robert Murray, *Red Scare: A Study in National Hysteria, 1919–1920* (Minneapolis: University of Minnesota Press, 1955).

98. For modern Klan history, see David Chalmers, *Hooded Americanism: The History of the Ku Klux Klan* (Durham, N.C.: Duke University Press, 1987).

99. Charles Sloan, "Kansas Battles the Invisible Empire: The Legal Ouster of the KKK from Kansas, 1922–1927," *Kansas Historical Quarterly* 40 (autumn 1974): 393.

100. White, *Autobiography,* 606, 625–32. See also the chapter "Tolerance and the Ku Klux Klan," in David Hinshaw, *A Man from Kansas: The Story of William Allen White* (New York: G. P. Putnam's Sons, 1945), 234–49.

101. Hinshaw, *A Man from Kansas,* 240–41.

102. William Allen White to *New York World,* September 17, 1921, White Papers, reel 5, no. 270, KSHS, and in Johnson, ed., *Selected Letters,* 220–21.

103. Sloan, "Invisible Empire," 400.

104. Hinshaw, *A Man from Kansas,* 249.

105. Gordon Parks, *The Learning Tree* (New York: Harper and Row, 1963).

106. Secretary of Henry Allen to W. M. Martin of AME Church, Winfield, October 10, 1919, Allen Papers, Governors' Papers, 27-08-06-07, KSHS.

107. Ibid., Henry Allen to Gov. Charles Brough, April 20, 1920, 27-08-08-02.

108. Ibid., unsigned, postmarked Helena, Ark., March 24, 1920.

109. Ibid., Henry Allen to Ben Freeman, April 1, 1920.

110. Ibid., I. H. Anthony to Henry Allen, March 24, 1920.

111. Ibid., Robert Hill to Henry Allen, April 19, 1920.

112. Robert Bunting, "School Segregation in Kansas: A Study in Constitutional and Political Development" (master's thesis, Wichita State University, 1971), 38.

113. Thomas Cox, *Blacks in Topeka, Kansas, 1865–1915: A Social History* (Baton Rouge: Louisiana State University Press, 1982), 112–14, 146–47, 150, 168, 191.

114. *Wichita Eagle,* October 12, 1912.

115. Bunting, "School Segregation," 39.

116. Sondra Van Meter, *Our Common School Heritage: A History of the Wichita Public Schools* (Wichita, Kans.: Board of Education, 1977), 111–16, 147–50.

117. *Wichita Eagle,* October 12, 1912.

118. Bunting, "School Segregation," 48.

119. John Shillady to Henry Allen, February 18, 1919, Allen Papers, Governors' Papers, 27-09-01-02, KSHS.

120. Ibid., W. Sawyer to Henry Allen, January 11, 1919.

121. Bunting, "School Segregation," 52.

122. Miner, *Magic City,* 169–71.

123. Gerald Butters, "*The Birth of a Nation* and the Kansas Board of Review of Motion Pictures: A Censorship Struggle," *Kansas History* 14 (spring 1991): 8, 13.

124. Henry Allen to M. L. Smith, June 7, 1919, Allen Papers, Governors' Papers, 27-08-08-06, KSHS.

125. Ibid., W. D. Ross to Henry Allen, February 19, 1920.

126. Ibid., C. S. Matthews to Henry Allen, February 23, 1920.

127. Butters, "*Birth,*" 13.

128. ? Stater to Jonathan Davis, July 27, 1923, and S. E. Schwahn to Jonathan Davis, October 31, 1923, Davis Papers, Governors' Papers, 27-09-04-01, KSHS.

129. Ibid., Rev. B. C. Rannovalona to Jonathan Davis, December 3, 1923.

130. Butters, "*Birth,*" 14.

131. Mechem, ed., *Annals of Kansas,* 2: 380.

132. Butters, "*Birth,*" 2.

133. Wilder, *Governmental Agencies,* 98, 116.

134. I. C. Rush to Grant Harrington, April 25, 1913, Hodges Papers, Governors' Papers, 27-07-04-01, KSHS.

135. Ibid., A. Malmstrom to Arthur Capper, October 26, 1915.

136. Ibid., I. C. Rush to George Hodges, April 4, 1915.

137. *Complete List of Motion Picture Films Presented to the Kansas State Board of Review for Action from July 1, 1918 to September 30, 1918* (Topeka: Kansas State Printing Plant, W. R. Smith, state printer, 1918), 3–5, 7, 8–9.

138. Clyde Reed to Mrs. J. M. Miller, February 17, 1919, Allen Papers, Governors' Papers, 27-08-08-06, KSHS.

139. Ibid., G. W. Butts to Henry Allen, July 10, 1919.

140. Ibid., N. W. Huston to Henry Allen, March 22, 1920.

141. Ibid., J. W. Dibrell to Henry Allen, April 14, 1921.

142. Ibid., Dwight Harris to Henry Allen, January 27, 1922.

143. Ibid., T. H. Roberts to Henry Allen, May 15, 1920.

144. *Kansas City Star,* Automobiles Clippings, KSHS.

145. Paul Sutter, " 'Paved with Good Intentions': Good Roads, the Automobile, and the Rhetoric of Rural Improvement in the *Kansas Farmer,* 1890–1914," *Kansas History* 18 (winter 1995–1996): 286, 288, 292, 295.

146. Mechem, ed., *Annals of Kansas,* 2: 295.

147. *Kansas City Star,* September 17, 1911, Automobiles Clippings, KSHS.

148. E. A. Gilbert to Edward Hoch, March 1, 1905, Hoch Papers, Governors' Papers, 27-06-04-06, KSHS.

149. Ibid., Albert Pope to Edward Hoch, June 21, 1906.

150. Ibid., ? to Edward Hoch, December 25, 1906.

151. *Kansas City Star,* November 15, 1914, Good Roads Clippings, vol. 1, KSHS.

152. Ibid., *Mail and Breeze,* 1900.

153. Ibid., *Topeka Capital,* December 14, 1909.

154. Ibid., *Kansas City Star,* January 22, 1910.

155. Ibid., November 21, 1911.

156. For Miller, see Callahan, *Jayhawk Editor,* 73–93.

157. *Topeka Journal,* November 23, 1914, Good Roads Clippings, vol. 1, KSHS.

158. Ibid., *Topeka Capital,* January 22, 1911.

159. *Newton Kansan,* December 4, 1915, quoted in Christy Davis, "John C. Nicholson: Highway Builder," paper, Wichita State University, 1997.

160. Arthur Capper speech, n.p., n.d., Good Roads Clippings, 1: 28–39, KSHS.

161. Ibid., *Poultry Farming and Rural Life,* January 1, 1913, vol. 1.

162. Mary Rowland, "Kansas and the Highways," *Kansas History* 5 (spring 1982): 35, 37–38; *Topeka Capital,* September 6, 1917, Good Roads Clippings, vol. 1, KSHS.

163. *Topeka Journal,* September 3, 1921, and August 25, 1922, Good Roads Clippings, vol. 1, KSHS.

164. "A State System of Highways," n.d. [1923], Ben Paulen Papers, Governors' Papers, 27-09-04-04, KSHS.

165. Ibid., Rolla Clymer to Ben Paulen, November 20, 1925, 27-09-06-01.

166. Ibid., John Irving to Ben Paulen, November 14, 1925, 27-09-04-04.

167. Ibid., E. A. McFarland to Ben Paulen, November 4, 1925.

168. Ibid., John Nicholson, pamphlet, in H. V. Buck to John Nicholson, October 21, 1925.

169. Ibid., Charles Emmons to Ben Paulen, August 10, 1926.

170. Ibid., W. R. Simpson to Ben Paulen, 27-09-06-05.

171. Ibid., R. W. McGrath to Ben Paulen, November 19, 1927.

172. Rowland, "Kansas and the Highways," 49–50.

173. *Topeka Capital,* July 22, 1928, Good Roads Clippings, vol. 2, KSHS.

174. Ibid., *Wichita Eagle,* June 19, 1930.

175. The aircraft summary comes from Rowe and Miner, *Borne on the South Wind,* 52–126.

176. Longren information from Taylor, "Henry Ford of the Air," unpaged typescript.

177. The oil summary is from Miner, *Discovery,* 149–86.

178. Mechem, ed., *Annals of Kansas,* 2: 394.

179. Ibid., 2: 363.

180. Thomas Isern, *Custom Combining on the Great Plains* (Norman: University of Oklahoma Press, 1981), 13–15, 19, 52–54.

181. Miner, *Magic City,* 172–74.

182. *Wichita Eagle,* November 28, 1923.

183. For an account of the history of grade separation, see Craig Miner, "A Narrative History . . . of Local Attitudes, Actions and Policy Concerning Railroads and Railroad Crossings in Wichita Kansas, 1872–1997," 1997, in Special Collections, Ablah Library, Wichita State University.

184. *Wichita Eagle,* July 29, November 15, 1923.

185. Longman, Greene and Company, "Industrial Survey of Wichita, Kansas," October 1927, 43, 106, 118, in Wichita State University Library.

186. Mechem, ed., *Annals of Kansas,* 2: 424.

187. *Wichita Eagle,* May 12, 1940.

188. Coleman information is from Ebendorf, "Manuscript History of the Coleman Company," Coleman Company Archives.

189. *Wichita Eagle,* October 9, 1921.

190. William Worley's *J. C. Nichols and the Shaping of Kansas City: Innovation in Planned Residential Communities* (Columbia: University of Missouri Press, 1990) is an outstanding study of this phenomenon; the quotation is on 116.

191. Rolla Clymer to C. H. Pattison, September 17, 1928, box 5, and Rolla Clymer to P. M. Hoisington, March 22, 1929, box 6, Clymer Papers, KSHS.

192. White, *Autobiography,* 625.

193. Johnson, *William Allen White's America,* 486, 490.

194. William Allen White to Sinclair Lewis, November 23, 1920, White Papers, reel 5, no. 249, KSHS, and in Johnson, ed., *Selected Letters,* 211–12.

195. Miner, *Uncloistered Halls,* 104–9.

196. Griffin, *University of Kansas,* 666–67.

197. Miner, *Uncloistered Halls,* 52–53, 128–29.

198. Mechem, ed., *Annals of Kansas,* 2: 390.

199. See Barry Paris, *Louise Brooks* (New York: Knopf, 1989).

200. Marco Morrow to Rolla Clymer, October 1, 1924, Clymer Papers, box 2, KSHS.

201. Ibid., October 14, 1924, box 2. There is a picture of the scene in Mechem, ed., *Annals of Kansas,* 2: 415.

202. F. L. Preston to Rolla Clymer, October 14, 1925, Clymer Papers, box 3, KSHS.

203. Caroline White to Ben Paulen, February 2, 1927, Paulen Papers, Governors' Papers, 27-09-06-05, KSHS.

204. Ibid., Rev. F. L. Courter to Ben Paulen, February 7, 1927.

205. Unsigned typescript, n.d. [August 1927], box 4, and Rolla Clymer to C. M. Mc-Caughan, January 17, 1927, box 4, Rolla Clymer Papers, KSHS; Paul Coleman to Ben Paulen, February 2, 1927, Paulen Papers, Governors' Papers, 27-09-06-05, KSHS.

206. James Malin to E. R. DeLay, March 18, 1929, Malin Papers, box 1, KSHS.

207. Ibid., James Malin to Kirke Mechem, November 24, 1930, and James Malin to Mrs. Henderson, January 22, 1932.

208. John Jones to Ben Paulen, March 7, 1925, Paulen Papers, Governors' Papers, 27-09-06-04, KSHS.

7. DUST AND DEMOCRATS

1. R. H. Garvey to W. D. Ferguson, January 22, 1935, box 7, Garvey Papers, KSHS.

2. Ibid., W. D. Ferguson to R. H. Garvey, February 11, March 25, 1935.

3. Craig Miner, *Harvesting the High Plains: John Kriss and the Business of Wheat Farming, 1920–1950* (Lawrence: University Press of Kansas, 1998), 66, 100.

4. Thomas Vaerill, "Of Drought and Dust: Expressions in Kansas Literature," *Kansas History* 20 (winter 1997–1998): 237.

5. R. H. Garvey to W. D. Ferguson, January 5, 1934, Garvey Papers, box 7, KSHS.

6. Ibid., August 24, 1936.

7. Quoted in Donald Worster, *Dust Bowl: The Southern Plains in the 1930s* (New York: Oxford University Press, 1979), 17.

8. Lawrence Svobida, *Farming the Dust Bowl: A First-Hand Account from Kansas* (Lawrence: University Press of Kansas, 1986), 126–32, also including recollections of the author's father of life in Ness City at the time.

9. Miner, *Harvesting the High Plains*, 112. Svobida, *Farming the Dust Bowl*, 142, records a similar tractor isolation story; the rabbit information is on 175.

10. Quoted in Pamela Riney-Kehrberg, *Rooted in Dust: Surviving Drought and Depression in Southwestern Kansas* (Lawrence: University Press of Kansas, 1994), 1.

11. R. H. Garvey to W. D. Ferguson, August 24, 1936, Garvey Papers, box 7, KSHS.

12. Charles Goodrum, *I'll Trade You an Elk* (New York: Funk and Wagnalls, 1967), 3–4.

13. R. H. Garvey to W. D. Ferguson, August 24, 1936, Garvey Papers, box 7, KSHS.

14. Ibid., March 26, 1935.

15. S. Murdock to Clyde Reed, August 22, 1929, Clyde Reed Papers, Governor's Papers, 27-10-02-07, KSHS.

16. Ibid., Elmer Stocking to Clyde Reed, July 7, 1930, 27-10-03-05.

17. Miner, *Harvesting the High Plains*, 75.

18. Harold McGugin to Clyde Reed, February 22, 1930, Reed Papers, Governors' Papers, 27-10-03-05, KSHS.

19. Ibid., Clyde Reed to George Capeheart, LaCygne, September 29, 1930.

20. Ibid., E. L. Jenkins, Topeka Federation of Labor, to Clyde Reed, November 30, 1930, 27-10-02-02.

21. Ibid., W. B. Strong to Clyde Reed, November 22, 1930.

22. Ibid., Fred Morris to Clyde Reed, November 24, 1930.

23. Ibid., Mary Boyd to Clyde Reed, August 2, 1930.

24. Ibid., Frank Caldwell to Clyde Reed, July 9, 1930, 27-10-03-05.

25. Ibid., Josef Knilig to Clyde Reed, September 16, 1930, 27-10-02-07.

26. Clugston, *Rascals in Democracy*, 143.

27. Francis Schruben, *Kansas in Turmoil, 1930–1936* (Columbia: University of Missouri Press, 1969), 25–38, 99, 110.

28. *Kansas City Times*, May 28, 1942, in Medicine Clippings, vol. 2, KSHS.

29. Schruben, *Kansas in Turmoil*, 43–44.

30. *Kansas City Times*, May 28, 1942, Medicine Clippings, vol. 2, KSHS.

31. William Allen White to George Hanna, November 7, 1930, White Papers, reel 6, KSHS.

32. *Kansas City Times*, May 28, 1942, in Medicine Clippings, vol. 2, KSHS; Gerald Carson, *The Roguish World of Doctor Brinkley* (New York: Rinehart, 1960), 175.

33. Carson, *Roguish World*, 3, 7, 82.

34. Mrs. C. C. McClure to Clyde Reed, July 3, 1930, Reed Papers, Governors' Papers, 27-10-04-01, KSHS.

35. R. H. Garvey to W. D. Ferguson, October 29, 1930, Garvey Papers, box 1, KSHS.

36. Ibid., November 8, 1930.

37. Rolla Clymer to Judge A. T. Ayres, July 14, 1932, Clymer Papers, box 9, KSHS.

38. Ibid., J. D. Joseph to Rolla Clymer, September 9, 1932.

39. Ibid., Rolla Clymer to M. T. Williams, November 16, 1932.

40. Cliff Hope Jr., *Quiet Courage: Kansas Congressman Clifford R. Hope* (Manhattan, Kans.: Sunflower University Press, 1997), 111.

41. Keith McFarland, *Harry F. Woodring: A Political Biography of FDR's Controversial Secretary of War* (Lawrence: University Press of Kansas, 1975), 37–55.

42. Harry Woodring, message, October 29, 1931, Woodring Papers, Governors' Papers, 27-11-01-06, KSHS.

43. J. H. Bird to Clyde Reed, July 18, 1930, Reed Papers, Governors' Papers, 27-10-03-05, KSHS.

44. Ibid., John Bird to Clyde Reed, October 15, 1930.

45. *Report of Annual Stockholders Meeting of the Wheat Farming Company, Inc. Hays, Kansas, January 12, 1931*, R. H. Garvey Papers, box 3, KSHS.

46. J. S. Bird to Harry Woodring, February 3, 1931, Woodring Papers, Governors' Papers, 27-11-01-05, KSHS.

47. Ibid., C. L. Clayton, Wellington, to Harry Woodring, February 6, 1931.

48. R. H. Garvey to W. D. Ferguson, July 8, 1930, Garvey Papers, box 1, KSHS.

49. J. A. Mahurin to Harry Woodring, March 18, 1931, Woodring Papers, Governors' Papers, 27-11-01-05, KSHS.

50. Ibid., Ballard Dunn to Harry Woodring, n.p., n.d. [1931].

51. Ibid., Chester Sanders to Harry Woodring, January 29, 1931.

52. R. H. Garvey to Stockholders and Directors, Mutual Farming Company, December 16, 1931, Garvey Papers, box 3, KSHS; Schruben, *Kansas in Turmoil*, 63; see also Emy Miller, "Corporation Farming in Kansas" (master's thesis, University of Wichita, 1933).

53. J. D. Evans to Harry Woodring, March 10, 1931; F. C. Larsen to President Hoover, July 21, 1931; W. E. Coniff to Harry Woodring, July 22, 1931; W. A. Doershlag to Harry Woodring, July 25, 1931; Harry Woodring to William Thummel, August 3, 1931; W. H. Kerr to Harry Woodring, n.d. [August, 1931]; Harry Woodring to W. W. Culver, August 11, 1931; Leslie Wallace to Harry Woodring, August 24, 1931; Harry Woodring to A. E. Barker, September 11, 1931; William Aaron to Harry Woodring, October 12, 1931, Woodring Papers, Governors' Papers, 27-11-01-05, KSHS.

54. Ibid., W. A. Doershlag to Harry Woodring, July 31, 1931.

55. Ibid., Harry Woodring to Fred Laucick, August 29, 1931.

56. Ibid., Harry Woodring to Harry Friend, August 3, 1931.

57. Ibid., Harry Woodring to R. E. Crandall, September 11, 1931.

58. Ibid., R. W. Hurt to Harry Woodring, April 23, 1931; Harry Woodring to Coal Merchants of Kansas, January 4, 1932, 27-11-01-04.

59. Ibid., K. A. Spencer to Harry Woodring, September 10, 1932.

60. Ibid., L. M. Basset to Harry Woodring, August 12, 1931.

61. Ibid., Ed Gill, Kansas City Chamber of Commerce, to Harry Woodring, August 7, 1931.

62. Ibid., Park Sumner to Harry Woodring, July 14, 1931.
63. Ibid., Harry Woodring to J. D. Shepherd, July 14, 1931.
64. Ibid., J. W. Cummins to Harry Woodring, May 16, 1931.
65. Alfred Landon to Roy Bailey, December 14, 1932, Alfred Landon Papers, Governors' Papers, 27-11-03-05, KSHS.
66. R. H. Garvey to W. A. Ayres, December 28, 1932, Garvey Papers, box 3, KSHS.
67. Ibid., R. H. Garvey to W. D. Ferguson, August 24, 1934, box 6.
68. Jess Denious to Thale Skovgard, December 20, 1937, Jess Denious Papers, box 4, KSHS.
69. Ibid., Francis Price to Jess Denious, February 2, 1939, box 4.
70. Alfred Landon to Roy Bailey, December 14, 1932, Landon Papers, Governors' Papers, 27-11-03-05, KSHS.
71. *Topeka Capital,* March 23, 1933, Legislative Clippings, vol. 16, KSHS.
72. Alfred Landon to Roy Bailey, December 14, 1932, and Alfred Landon to W. D. Jochems, February 10, 1933, Landon Papers, Governors' Papers, 27-11-03-05, KSHS. On the effects of the merchandising law, see E. A. Briles to Kansas legislature, January 2, 1933, Clymer Papers, box 9, KSHS.
73. R. L. Baird to Frederick Brinkerhoff, August 10, 1936, Brinkerhoff Papers, box 2, KSHS.
74. Rolla Clymer to George Brannon, June 25, 1936, box 12, and Clymer to Paul Jones, September 9, 1936, box 13, both in Clymer Papers, KSHS.
75. Donald McCoy, *Landon of Kansas* (Lincoln: University of Nebraska Press, 1966), 343.
76. *Hutchinson Herald,* August 30, 1936, in Denious Papers, box 2, KSHS.
77. Ibid., W. A. White to Will West, August 20, 1936.
78. Typescript campaign piece, 1936, Clymer Papers, box 13, KSHS.
79. McCoy, *Landon of Kansas,* 340.
80. Rolla Clymer to Robert Carr, November 5, 1936, Clymer Papers, box 13, KSHS.
81. Ibid., Rolla Clymer to E. Ross Bartley, December 24, 1936.
82. Ibid., Rolla Clymer to Harold McGugin, December 14, 1936.
83. Cliff Hope Jr., *Quiet Courage,* 81.
84. *Chicago Tribune,* April 4, 1928, White Papers, reel 6, KSHS.
85. Ibid., William Allen White to B. C. B., January 11, 1933.
86. Robert Bader, *The Great Kansas Bond Scandal* (Lawrence: University Press of Kansas, 1982).
87. Bader, *Hayseeds,* 93–95.
88. Worster, *Dust Bowl,* 153.
89. Riney-Kehrberg, *Rooted in Dust;* Paul Bonnifield, *The Dust Bowl: Men, Dirt, and Depression* (Albuquerque: University of New Mexico Press, 1979).
90. R. Douglas Hurt, "Gaining Control of the Environment: The Morton County Land Utilization Project in the Kansas Dust Bowl," *Kansas History* 19 (summer 1996): 146.
91. Svobida's account was originally published by Caxton Printers, 1940, and was republished by the University Press of Kansas in 1986 under the title *Farming the Dust*

Bowl: A First-Hand Account from Kansas; Hurt's comments are in the introduction to the Kansas edition, 26–27.

92. Svobida, *Farming the Dust Bowl,* 172, 175, 233.
93. E. Katz to Rolla Clymer, June 17, 1935, Clymer Papers, box 11, KSHS.
94. Ibid., Rolla Clymer to E. Katz, June 14, 1935.
95. Walter Bullock to Jess Denious, February 16, 1937, Denious Papers, box 3, KSHS.
96. Arthur Capper to Charles Perry, May 18, 1938, Capper Papers, box 28, KSHS.
97. Ibid., Gerald Winrod to Arthur Capper, October 24, 1938, and January 30, 1943.
98. Ibid., Arthur Capper to Gerald Winrod, June 17, 1942.
99. Ibid., Gerald Winrod to Vincent Miles, June 6, 1942.
100. Miner, *Magic City,* 165.
101. Ibid., 177–78.
102. Rowe and Miner, *Borne on the South Wind,* 97–126.
103. Miner, *Discovery,* 212–13.
104. Ibid., 187–209.
105. Helen Harrow to Walter Huxman, January 13, 1937, Walter Huxman Papers, Governors' Papers, 27-11-05-04, KSHS.
106. Ibid., Emergency Dust Bowl Committee to FDR, April 23, 1937.
107. Ibid., H. A. Kinney to Walter Huxman, April 29, 1937.
108. Ibid., speech of Royden Reed, July 29, 1938; Schruben, *Kansas in Turmoil,* 111.
109. Schruben, *Kansas in Turmoil,* 180–81.
110. *Topeka Capital,* February 2, 1937, Legislative Clippings, vol. 17, KSHS.
111. Ibid., *Topeka Journal,* March 25, 1937.
112. Ibid., March 31, 1937.
113. Ibid., February 9, 1938, vol. 18.
114. *The WPA Guide to 1930s Kansas* (Lawrence: University Press of Kansas, 1984), 18.
115. Riney-Kehrberg, *Rooted in Dust,* 126.
116. Charles Edson to Reed Harris, December 13, 1937, Edson Papers, MS-811, KSHS.
117. Ibid., Charles Edson to Henry Alsberg, July 20, 1938.
118. Ibid., November 21, 1938.
119. *Topeka Journal,* January 11, 1939, Legislative Clippings, vol. 19, KSHS.
120. Payne Ratner to W. A. White, March 10, 1941, Ratner Papers, Governors' Papers, 27-11-05-08, KSHS.
121. Ibid., Legislative Council Report, 1938.
122. *Kansas City Times,* April 10, 1941, Legislative Clippings, vol. 18, KSHS.
123. Ratner address, WIBW, March 3, 1940, Ratner Papers, Governors' Papers, 27-11-05-08, KSHS.
124. Ibid., Legislative Council Report, 1938.
125. *Topeka Capital,* November 10, 1934, Legislative Clippings, vol. 16, KSHS.
126. Ibid., *Topeka Journal,* February 4, 1937, vol. 17.
127. Ibid., Cecil Howes in *Kansas City Times,* August 30, 1938, vol. 18.
128. Ibid., *Topeka Journal,* March 16, 1933, vol. 16.

129. Ibid., January 11, 1939, vol. 19.

130. J. E. Schaefer to R. W. Reid, July 27, 1939, Ratner Papers, Governors' Papers, 27-11-05-07, KSHS.

131. Ibid., Edward Arn to Payne Ratner, July 24, 1939.

132. Ibid., J. E. Schaefer to Clyde Reed, May 30, 1939.

133. Ibid., Payne Ratner to A. B. Block, June 30, 1939, 27-11-06-04. As a young professor I interviewed Robbins at his home in Pratt in the early 1970s, realizing then that he was clearly a major neglected figure in the latter-day history of the state of Kansas.

134. Ibid., H. N. Carver to Oscar Stauffer, June 26, 1939.

135. Ibid., Harry Woodring to Payne Ratner, May 19, 1939.

136. Ibid., *Horton Headlight*, May 25, 1939; Charles Browne to Payne Ratner, October 29, 1939.

137. Ibid., John Chambers, "Kansas Facts Pertinent to New Industries for Kansas," [1939].

138. Ibid., Payne Ratner to J. W. McManigal, September 28, 1939.

139. Ibid., memo, April 19, 1940. The film is available still on video from the Kansas State Historical Society.

140. Rolla Clymer to W. L. White, July 18, 1939, Clymer Papers, box 16, KSHS; A. Q. Miller to Payne Ratner, January 23, 1940, Ratner Papers, Governors' Papers, 27-11-06-04, KSHS.

141. Rolla Clymer to Albert Severance, July 27, 1939, Clymer Papers, box 16, KSHS.

142. Ibid., Rolla Clymer to King Features, November 21, 1939.

143. Rolla Clymer to Payne Ratner, February 19, 1940, Ratner Papers, Governors' Papers, 27-11-06-04, KSHS.

144. Ibid., undated newspaper clipping, January 6, 1940.

145. Ibid., Payne Ratner to Rolla Clymer, March 25, 1940.

146. Ibid., Frank Webb to Payne Ratner, December 25, 1939; Solon Wiley to Ratner, January 24, 1941; Walter Ross to Ratner, November 26, 1941; William Exline to Ratner, November 12, 1941. See also Richard Robbins to Jess Denious, June 19, 1940, and C. W. Foreman to Robert Geoffroy, June 15, 1942, Denious Papers, box 6, KSHS.

147. Griffin, *University of Kansas*, 495–96. For locations, see chart 68, "World War II Installations," in Socolofsky and Self, *Historical Atlas of Kansas*.

148. *Kansas City Times*, July 11, 1941, Kansas Ordnance Plant Clippings, KSHS.

149. Ibid., *Topeka Capital*, May 28, 1943.

150. Ibid., August 6, 1946.

151. R. A. Clymer to Payne Ratner, April 1, 1940, Ratner Papers, Governors' Papers, 27-11-06-04, KSHS.

152. Ibid., E. R. Weidlein to Oscar Stauffer, March 20, 1940.

153. Miner, *Uncloistered Halls*, 166–67.

154. Speech, "War and Peace," July 24, 1938, Capper Papers, box 26, KSHS. For details on Capper's position, see John Partin, "The Dilemma of 'A Good, Very Good Man,'" *Kansas History* 2 (summer 1979): 86–95.

155. Jess Denious to Clarence [?], January 18, 1940, Denious Papers, box 5, KSHS.

156. Phillip Gant, "The Kansas Congressional Delegation and the Selective Service Act of 1940," *Kansas History* 2 (autumn 1979): 201–2, 204.

157. R. H. Garvey to Frank Knox, May 20, 1940, Garvey Papers, box 12, KSHS.

158. Ibid., R. H. Garvey to Frank Carlson, September 23, 1941, box 13.

159. Ibid., Robert Wood to R. H. Garvey, December 18, 1941.

160. Ibid., R. H. Garvey to Ken Crumly, December 29, 1941.

161. William Tuttle, ed., "William Allen White and Verne Marshall: Two Midwestern Editors Debate Aid to the Allies versus Isolationism," *Kansas Historical Quarterly* 32 (summer 1966): 203, 206.

162. W. A. White to Rev. Allen Keedy, January 3, 1940, White Papers, reel 3, KSHS.

163. Ibid., W. A. White to Clark Lawrence, June 1, 1940, reel 1.

164. Ibid., W. A. White to E. K. Bugbee, October 11, 1940.

165. Johnson, ed., *William Allen White's America*, 536.

166. W. A. White to Robert Sherwood, June 14, 1940, White Papers, reel 1, KSHS. White wrote a book at this time called *Defense for America*.

167. Hinshaw, *A Man from Kansas*, 282–83.

168. Ray Yarnell to W. A. White, June 13, 1940, White Papers, reel 1, KSHS.

169. W. A. White to Roy Howard, December 20, 1940, in Johnson, ed., *Selected Letters*, 416.

170. W. A. White to Mrs. Esther Brunauer, February 7, 1941, White Papers, reel 3, KSHS; W. A. White to Hugh Moore, January 6, 1941, in Johnson, ed., *Selected Letters*, 426.

171. Rowe and Miner, *Borne on the South Wind*, 129.

172. E. C. Mingenback to Oscar Stauffer, May 18, 1940; Arthur Capper to Payne Ratner, May 25, 1940, Ratner Papers, Governors' Papers, 27-11-06-04, KSHS.

173. Ibid., C. M. Miller to Payne Ratner, July 10, 1940.

174. Ibid., Payne Ratner to Rolla Clymer, August 24, 1940.

175. Ibid., R. A. Clymer to Floyd Shoaf, September 24, 1940, and Richard Robbins to Roy Roberts, February 28, 1941.

176. Ibid., C. Y. Thomas to Payne Ratner, April 26, 1941, and Richard Robbins to Payne Ratner, May 1, 1941.

177. Ibid., Payne Ratner to Floyd Oldum, September 29, 1941, and Payne Ratner to Kansas Industrial Development Commission, December 10, 1941.

178. Ibid., Rolla Clymer to Kansas Industrial Development Commission, August, 1940.

179. Ibid., J. C. Nichols to Payne Ratner, December 19, 1941.

180. Kansas War Industries Board Plan [December 1940], Clymer Papers, box 16, KSHS.

181. Ibid., Rolla Clymer to Ormund Hill, February 14, 1941, box 17.

182. Ibid., Oscar Stauffer to Rolla Clymer, December 29, 1941.

183. Sheldon Coleman to Payne Ratner, November 1, 18, 1941, Ratner Papers, Governors' Papers, 27-11-06-04, KSHS.

184. Ibid., Richard Robbins to J. H. Kindelberger, January 3, 1941.

185. Rowe and Miner, *Borne on the South Wind*, 140, 142.

186. Ibid., 131, 133, 151; Anthony Brusca, "A National Effort for Victory: The B-29 Development Program and the Battle of Kansas" (master's thesis, Wichita State University, 1999), 46.

187. Rowe and Miner, *Borne on the South Wind*, 151.

188. Brusca, "A National Effort," 20–21, 45.

189. Miner, "Railroads and Railroad Crossings," 68–69. The Duncan and *Colliers* articles are excerpted in Craig Miner, ed., *The Wichita Reader: A Collection of Writing About a Prairie City* (Wichita: Wichita Eagle and Beacon, 1992), 93–95, 130–31.

190. Peter Fearon, "Ploughshares into Airplanes: Manufacturing Industry and Workers in Kansas During World War II," *Kansas History* 22 (winter 1999–2000): 301; Patrick O'Brien, "Kansas at War: The Home Front, 1941–1945," *Kansas History* 17 (spring 1994): 9.

191. O'Brien, "Kansas at War," 20.

192. Fearon, "Ploughshares into Airplanes," 299–302, 307–9, 311.

193. O'Brien, "Kansas at War," 21.

194. Ibid., 6, 9, 14, 17.

195. Julie Courtwright, "Want to Build a Miracle City? War Housing in Wichita," *Kansas History* 23 (winter 2000–2001): 218, 224, 226, 228, 235.

196. James H. Price to Members of KIDC, October 29, 1942, Clymer Papers, box 18, KSHS.

197. Rowe and Miner, *Borne on the South Wind*, 141, 153; see also "U.S. Army and Air Force Wings over Kansas," *Kansas Historical Quarterly* 25 (summer and autumn 1959): 129–57, 334–60, and Brusca, "A National Effort for Victory."

198. O'Brien, "Kansas at War," 330.

199. *Christian Science Monitor*, April 2, 1945, clipping in Andrew Schoeppel Papers, Governors' Papers, 27-12-06-07, KSHS.

200. Miner, *Magic City*, 184–85, 187.

201. Miner, *Uncloistered Halls*, 133.

202. Patrick O'Brien, Thomas Isern, and Daniel Lumley, "Stalag Sunflower: German Prisoners of War in Kansas," *Kansas History* 7 (autumn 1984): 182–98.

203. Richard Robbins to E. E. Frizell, Larned, January 17, 1943, Denious Papers, box 7, KSHS.

204. Ibid., Claud Cave to Jess Denious, March 18, 1943, and Denious to Cave, March 22, 1943.

205. Ibid., Jess Denious to Lester Luther, June 7, 1945, box 10.

206. *Wichita Eagle*, June 28, 1931, and *Topeka Capital*, March 15, 1931, Capital Punishment Clippings, vol. 1, KSHS.

207. Ibid., *Kansas City Star*, May 21, 1939, and *Kansas City Star*, undated clipping, Schoeppel Papers, Governors' Papers, 27-12-06-07, KSHS.

208. *Kansas City Star*, undated clipping, Schoeppel Papers, Governors' Papers, 27-12-06-07, KSHS.

209. *Topeka Capital*, March 10, 1944, Capital Punishment Clippings, vol. 1, KSHS.

210. Ibid., April 15, 1944, and *Kansas City Times*, February 8, 1944.

211. C. W. Brewster to Andrew Schoeppel, February 10, 1944, clipping from *Kansas City Star,* n.d.; clipping from *Rush County News,* April 13, 1944, Schoeppel Papers, Governors' Papers, 27-12-06-07, KSHS.

212. Ibid., F. Theodore Dexter to Andrew Schoeppel, March 10, 1944.

213. *Kansas City Star,* January 18, 1931, Legislative Clippings, vol. 16, KSHS.

214. Ibid., February 6, 1931.

215. Ibid., *Topeka Capital,* February 26, 1931.

216. Richard Robbins to Jess Denious, March 6, 1942, Denious Papers, box 6, KSHS.

217. *Topeka Capital,* March 28, 1947, Legislative Clippings, vol. 23, KSHS.

218. Ibid., *Topeka Journal,* January 19, 1939, vol. 20.

219. Ibid., February 19, 1941.

220. Quoted in Miner, *Magic City,* 196.

221. Rolla Clymer, Kiwanis speech, n.d. [1942], typescript in Clymer Papers, box 18, KSHS.

8. CONCRETE STEPS

1. W. L. White to Fred Brinkerhoff, September 27, 1954, Brinkerhoff Papers, box 7, KSHS; Roger Wilson, "The Triple Play," typescript, 16 (on loan to author).

2. Wilson, "Triple Play," 19−20, 23, 26, 31−34, 37, 42, 45. See also Socolofsky, *Kansas Governors,* 200−203, and contemporary accounts in *Topeka Journal,* January 3, 10, 1957, and *Topeka Capital,* January 4, 1957, in Politics Clippings, vol. 6, KSHS.

3. John Bright, "Kansas at Mid-Twentieth Century," in Bright, ed., *Kansas: The First Century,* 2: 493−94.

4. *Wichita Eagle,* December 1, 1955, Politics Clippings, vol. 6, KSHS.

5. Ibid., *Kansas City Star,* November 25, 1955.

6. Allan Nevins, in Bright, ed., *Kansas: The First Century,* 2: 502−15.

7. E. A. Biles to Frederick Brinkerhoff, March 18, 1950, Brinkerhoff Papers, box 3, KSHS.

8. *Topeka Capital,* January 13, 1953, Legislative Clippings, vol. 26, KSHS.

9. *Kansas City Star,* August 12, 1956, Politics Clippings, vol. 6, KSHS.

10. Carl Bridenbaugh, "The Great Mutation," *American Historical Review* 48 (January 1963): 315−31.

11. Bader, *Prohibition in Kansas,* 244−250, 254, 261.

12. *Topeka Journal,* March 10, 1949, Legislative Clippings, vol. 24, KSHS.

13. Bader, *Prohibition in Kansas,* 257.

14. Payne Ratner, Inaugural Address, January 10, 1939, Payne Ratner Clippings, Kansas Collection, KU.

15. Rolla Clymer to Fred Brinkerhoff, June 6, 1952, Brinkerhoff Papers, box 4, KSHS.

16. Richard Robbins to Rolla Clymer, April 23, 1952, Clymer Papers, box 25, KSHS.

17. Ibid., Stanley Taylor to Rolla Clymer, n.d. [1951].

18. Whitley Austin to Brinkerhoff, August 27, 1952, Brinkerhoff Papers, box 3, KSHS.

19. Kenneth Davis, *Kansas: A Bicentennial History* (New York: W. W. Norton, 1976), 202, 204, 206, 214.

20. Phillip Meyer, "Tuttle Creek Dam: A Case Study in Local Opposition" (master's thesis, University of North Carolina, 1962), 3, 7, 15, 17, 24, 27–28, 32, 33.

21. Rolla Clymer to Dwight [Payton], March 7, 1952, Clymer Papers, box 25, KSHS.

22. Fred Brinkerhoff to A. L. Miller, July 19, 1951, Brinkerhoff Papers, box 5, KSHS.

23. Meyer, "Tuttle Creek Dam," 35, 53, 58. A second summary of the issue while it was still warm by a historian is Homer Socolofsky's "The Great Flood of 1951 and the Tuttle Creek Controversy," in Bright, ed., *Kansas: The First Century*, 2: 494–502.

24. Joan Roblyer to Frank Carlson, December 28, 1948, Frank Carlson Papers, Governors' Papers, 27-13-07-06, KSHS.

25. Ibid., William Bolan to Frank Carlson, January 10, 1949.

26. William Voigt to J. A. Hawkinson, March 11, 1949, and Benson Strong to Glen Stockwell, August 8, 1951, Glen Stockwell Papers, box 1, KSHS.

27. Ibid., Glen Stockwell to Edward Arn, August 28, 1951.

28. Ibid., William Voight to Sen. Andrew Shoeppel and Sen. Frank Carlson, August 28, 1951.

29. Ibid., Glen Stockwell to *Manhattan Tribune News*, September 3, 1951.

30. Ibid., Glen Stockwell to Mrs. Bliss Isley, September 24, 1951.

31. Ibid., Glen Stockwell to Arthur Carhart, October 9, 1951.

32. Ibid., Edward Arn, remarks before the Missouri Basin Inter-Agency Meeting, December 14, 1951, box 2.

33. Ibid., Arthur Carhart to Glen Stockwell, October 12, 1951, box 1.

34. Ibid., Walter Kollmorgen to James Reed, October 30, 1951.

35. Ibid., Stockwell statement, July 25, 1955, box 3.

36. Ibid., Elmer Peterson, "Muddy Water in Motion," December 6, 1951, box 2.

37. For a broader context on the rise of the critics, see Marc Reisner, *Cadillac Desert: The American West and Its Disappearing Water* (New York: Penguin Books, 1986), and Elmer Peterson, *Big Dam Foolishness: The Problem of Modern Flood Control and Water Storage* (New York: Devin-Adair, 1954).

38. Glen Stockwell to *Topeka Daily Capital*, March 31, 1952, Stockwell Papers, box 2, KSHS.

39. Ibid., Glen Stockwell to *St. Louis Post Dispatch*, May 18, 1953.

40. Ibid., Elmer Peterson to Glen Stockwell, March 14, 1952.

41. The film, "Tuttle Creek Story," was produced in 1955.

42. Col. L. J. Lincoln to Kansas Society of Professional Engineers, February 22, 1952, Stockwell Papers, box 1, KSHS.

43. Ibid., Clifford Hope to Glen Stockwell, August 16, 1951.

44. Socolofsky, "The Great Flood," 500–501.

45. For some background and some of Davis's philosophical approach to flood control and ecology, see Kenneth Davis, *River on the Rampage* (Garden City, N.Y.: Doubleday, 1953).

46. Davis, *Kansas*, 212–14.

47. *Wichita Eagle*, July 16, 1965, Wichita Water Supply Clippings, box 1, KSHS.

48. A summary of the issue may be found in Miner, *Magic City*, 180–81, 199–200.

49. *Kansas City Times,* November 5, 1954, Wichita Water Supply Clippings, box 1, KSHS.

50. Miner, *Magic City,* 199–200.

51. *Wichita Evening Eagle,* January 11, 1954, and *Kansas City Times,* November 8, 1954, Wichita Water Supply Clippings, box 1, KSHS.

52. Ibid., August 19, 1954.

53. Ibid., August 20, 1954.

54. Ibid., *Topeka Capital,* September 2, 1954.

55. Ibid., *Kansas City Times,* November 5, 1954.

56. Ibid., *Wichita Eagle,* September 3, 1954.

57. Ibid., November 9, 1954.

58. Ibid., May 5, 1955.

59. Ibid., February 11, 1956.

60. Ibid., November 8, 1955.

61. Ibid., June 27, 1956.

62. Ibid., May 3, 1958.

63. Ibid., July 16, 1965.

64. Ibid., *Wichita Beacon,* August 5, 1964.

65. *Topeka Capital,* July 27, 1952, Good Roads Clippings, vol. 3, KSHS.

66. Ibid., *Topeka Journal,* March 7, 1953.

67. *Topeka Journal,* May 20, 1953, Turnpike Authority Clippings, vol. 1, KSHS.

68. Ibid., May 22, 1953.

69. Ibid., March 30, September 22, 1954.

70. Ibid., March 15, 1954.

71. Ibid., *Lawrence Journal–World,* December 31, 1954.

72. Gale Moss to Fred Brinkerhoff, December 4, 1954, Brinkerhoff Papers, box 5, KSHS.

73. *Kansas City Star,* October 7, 1956, Kansas Turnpike Authority Clippings, vol. 1, KSHS.

74. Ibid., *Topeka Journal,* October 25, 1956.

75. Ibid., *Topeka Capital,* May 8, 1955.

76. Ibid., *Kansas City Star,* September 16, 1956, and *Kansas City Times,* November 20, 1956.

77. Ibid., *Topeka Capital,* February 7, 1955.

78. Ibid., *El Dorado Times,* October 28, 1957.

79. Ibid., *Lawrence Journal–World,* May 18, 1955.

80. Ibid., *Kansas City Star,* October 23, 1956.

81. Ibid., February 10, 1963.

82. Ibid., *Topeka Capital,* February 4, 1969.

83. Ibid., *El Dorado Times,* October 28, 1957.

84. Ibid., *Topeka Journal,* April 25, 1967, vol. 2.

85. Ibid., *Wichita Eagle Beacon,* October 24, 1976.

86. Ibid., *Kansas City Star,* November 14, 1976.

87. Ibid., *Wichita Eagle Beacon,* October 24, 1976.

88. Ibid, August 31, 1982.

89. An overview of Garvey's career is Olive White Garvey, with Virgil Quinlisk, *The Obstacle Race: The Story of Ray Hugh Garvey* (San Antonio, Tex.: Naylor Company, 1970). For the farming, see also Miner, *Harvesting the High Plains.*

90. Summary statements are drawn from the author's research in the R. H. Garvey Papers for an upcoming biography.

91. *Chicago Daily News,* February 11, 1954, clipping in box 27, and *Kansas City Star,* February 1, 1959, box 36, Garvey Papers, KSHS.

92. Ibid., James Garvey to R. H. Garvey, February 18, 1954, and R. H. Garvey to James Garvey, February 22, 1954, box 27.

93. Ibid., James Garvey to Cong. Wint Smith, March 21, 1957, box 32.

94. Ibid., *Hutchinson News,* June 7, 1959, box 36.

95. Ibid., R. H. Garvey to James Garvey, July 30, 1958, box 34.

96. Ibid., *Wichita Eagle,* September 14, 1948, box 33.

97. Ibid., R. H. Garvey to Marvin McClain, CCC, March 31, 1954, box 27.

98. *Plaindealer* (Wichita), January 30, 1953.

99. Ibid., March 27, 1953.

100. Ibid., January 29, September 10, 1954, and February 11, 1955.

101. Ibid., May 4, 1956.

102. Ibid.

103. Ibid., April 1, 1955.

104. Ibid., March 25, April 1, 1955.

105. *Topeka Journal,* April 14, 1955, Politics Clippings, vol. 6, KSHS.

106. Ibid., *Topeka Capital,* August 11, 1955.

107. Ibid., November 21, 1955.

108. Ibid., *Topeka Journal,* August 29, 1956.

109. Socolofsky, *Kansas Governors,* 206–7; the *Oswego Democrat,* October 12, November 16, 1956, has W. G. Clugston's comments.

110. *Topeka Capital,* April 4, 1957, vol. 29, and *Kansas City Times,* January 29, 1960, vol. 30, Legislative Clippings, KSHS; Drury, *The Government of Kansas,* 359.

111. *Plaindealer* (Wichita), September 19, 1958.

112. Ibid., February 28, April 25, 1958.

113. Ibid., November 7, 1958.

114. Ibid., November 14, 1958.

115. Ibid., November 7, 1958.

116. J. Morgan Kousser, "Before *Plessy,* Before *Brown*: The Development of the Law of Racial Integration in Louisiana and Kansas," in *Toward a Usable Past: Liberty Under State Constitutions,* ed. Paul Finkelman and Stephen Gottlieb (Athens: University of Georgia Press, 1991): 215–16, 233, 236–38.

117. Paul Wilson, *A Time to Lose: Representing Kansas in Brown v. Board of Education* (Lawrence: University Press of Kansas, 1995), 4, 9–10. For Linda Brown's story, see also Richard Kluger, *Simple Justice: The History of Brown v. Board of Education and Black America's Struggle for Equality* (New York: Knopf, 1976), 408–10.

118. Wilson, *A Time to Lose,* 10, 20, 25, 81, 154.

119. Kluger, *Simple Justice,* 374–76.

120. *Plaindealer* (Kansas City), April 18, March 28, May 16, June 20, 1941; September 6, 1946; April 30, 1948. My thanks to Virgil Dean, editor of *Kansas History,* for calling my attention to this material.

121. Rusty Monhollon, "Black Power, White Fear: The 'Negro Problem' in Lawrence, Kansas, 1960–1970," in *Race Consciousness: African-American Studies for the New Century,* ed. Judith Fosset and Jeffrey Tucker (New York: New York University Press, 1997), 248–52.

122. *Wichita Eagle,* November 11, 1990; February 25, 1993; May 14, 1994; and September 5, 1996. Gretchen Eick, *Dissent in Wichita: The Civil Rights Movement in the Midwest, 1954–1972* (Urbana and Chicago: University of Illinois Press, 2001), is a careful study of these events. The Dockum sit-in is covered on pages 1–10.

123. Miner, *Magic City,* 204–5.

124. Miner, *Uncloistered Halls,* 214–15.

125. Unless otherwise noted, the account of the WSU struggle comes from Miner, *Uncloistered Halls,* 235–49, which in turn is based on the Wichita State University archives, Special Collections Division, Ablah Library, Wichita State University.

126. *Topeka Capital,* February 20, 1963, Legislative Clippings, vol. 34, KSHS.

127. Ibid., February 22, 1963.

128. Ibid., *Wichita Eagle,* April 3, 1963.

129. Ibid., *Topeka Capital,* April 4, 1963.

130. Rowe and Miner, *Borne on the South Wind,* 202–6.

131. Truman Capote, *In Cold Blood: A True Account of a Multiple Murder and Its Consequences* (New York: Random House, 1965), 5.

132. Ibid., 245–46, 336, 341.

133. Galliher and Galliher, " 'Deja Vu All Over Again,' " 369, 377–80, 382.

9. LIKE THE NATIONS

1. Miner, *Wolf Creek Station,* 202–5.

2. Joel Paddock, "The Gubernatorial Campaigns of Robert Docking, 1966–1972," *Kansas History* 17 (summer 1994): 109, 119.

3. Heat-Moon, *PrairyErth,* 494–95.

4. The *Land Report: Twenty Years,* 55–56 (summer 1996), contains a series of essays on the history of the Land Institute, and the magazine in general documented it as it progressed. The excerpt from Jackson is on page four and is from an essay he wrote in issue number one of the magazine in December 1976.

5. Quoted in Miner, *West of Wichita,* 247.

6. Heat-Moon, *PrairyErth,* 246, 262.

7. Isaiah 17:13.

8. Ezekiel 20:32.

9. Miner, *Wolf Creek Station,* 32–33.

10. *Topeka Journal,* June 9, 1960, Parks Clippings, vol. 1, KSHS.

11. Unless otherwise cited, the account of Wolf Creek comes from Miner, *Wolf Creek Station.*

12. The quotation is from ibid., 228.

13. Quotation from ibid., 246.

14. Quotations from ibid., 258–59.

15. Miller quote from *Topeka Journal,* January 12, 1977, Legislative Clippings, vol. 37, KSHS.

16. Quotation in Miner, *Wolf Creek Station,* 314.

17. Quotation in ibid., 329.

18. For a summary of the history, see Joseph Hickey and Charles Webb, "The Transition from Farming to Ranching in the Kansas Flint Hills," *Great Plains Quarterly* 7 (fall 1987): 244–55, and Joseph Hickey, *Ghost Settlement on the Prairie: A Biography of Thurman, Kansas* (Lawrence: University Press of Kansas, 1995).

19. See Madson, *Where the Sky Began.*

20. *Topeka State Journal,* August 29, 1973, Save the Tallgrass Prairie Collection, box 1, KU.

21. *Kansas City Star,* June 19, 1960, Prairie Park Natural History Association Collection, box 1, KU.

22. Ibid., *Lawrence Journal–World,* February 13, 1962.

23. *Topeka Capital,* October 14, 1961, Parks Clippings, vol. 1, KSHS.

24. Ibid., *Topeka Capital–Journal,* February 19, 1961.

25. *Kansas City Times,* July 26, 1961, Prairie Park Natural History Association Collection, box 1, KU.

26. *Kansas City Star,* June 19, 1960, Parks Clippings, vol. 1, KSHS.

27. Gary Baldridge, "Pottawatomie County Says No to Prairie Preservation," *Kansas History* 16 (summer 1993): 96, 98, 100, 104–5.

28. *Topeka Capital,* January 27, 1962, Parks Clippings, vol. 1, KSHS.

29. Ibid., July 9, 1963.

30. Unidentified clipping, December 6, 1961, Prairie Park Natural History Association Collection, vol. 1, KU.

31. Ibid., undated clipping from *Time* [1961].

32. *Kansas City Star,* December 4, 1961, Parks Clippings, vol. 1, KSHS.

33. Ibid., *Topeka Journal,* April 16, 1963.

34. *Topeka Capital,* April 14, 1963, Prairie Park Natural History Association Collection, box 1, KU.

35. *Kansas City Times,* March 29, 1973, and *Emporia Gazette,* May 29, 1973, Save the Tallgrass Prairie Collection, box 1, KU.

36. The author was one of those called a communist while serving on Wichita's original Historic Preservation Board and is drawing here from personal experience.

37. *Kansas City Star,* January 17, 1962, Prairie Park Natural History Association Collection, box 1, KU.

38. *Ottawa Herald,* March 2, 1974, Save the Tallgrass Prairie Collection, box 2, KU.

39. *Kansas City Kansan,* July 12, 1963, Prairie Park Natural History Association Collection, box 1, KU.

40. *Kansas City Times,* August 31, 1973, Save the Tallgrass Prairie Collection, box 1, KU.

41. Ibid., *Wichita Eagle,* September 30, 1973.

42. Ibid., *Clearwater Times,* February 28, 1974, box 2.

43. Ibid., *Audubon,* January 1975.

44. Ibid., *Salina Journal,* March 14, 1975.

45. Rolla Clymer to Bill Colvin, April 6, 1964, Clymer Papers, box 38, KSHS.

46. Ibid., Charles Stough to Rolla Clymer, December 23, 1974, box 48.

47. Clipping in ibid., box 49.

48. Editorial, "The Indestructible Bluestem," in ibid.

49. *El Dorado Times,* July 14, 1973, Save the Tallgrass Prairie Collection, box 1, KU.

50. Nyle Miller to Rolla Clymer, December 22, 1973, Clymer Papers, box 48, KSHS.

51. *Lawrence Journal–World,* Save the Tallgrass Prairie Collection, box 1, KU.

52. *Kansas City Times,* November 23, 1974, Clymer Papers, box 48, KSHS.

53. *Kansas City Star,* April 15, 1973, Save the Tallgrass Prairie Collection, box 1, KU.

54. A good summary of this argument is Jack ? Beaumont to Rolla Clymer, July 11, 1975, Clymer Papers, box 48, KSHS.

55. Ibid., C. P. Doughlen to Rolla Clymer, n.d. [1973], box 47. Threats of wolves chasing tourists are detailed humorously in the *El Dorado Times,* March 29, 1975, Save the Tallgrass Prairie Collection, box 2, KU.

56. *Kansas City Times,* March 29, 1973, Save the Tallgrass Prairie Collection, box 1, KU.

57. Ibid., *El Dorado Times,* July 14, 1973.

58. Ibid., July 25, 1973.

59. Ibid., *Parsons Sun,* July 26, 1973; the hippie characterization is in ibid., in the *Topeka Daily Journal,* January 12, 1974.

60. Ibid., *Topeka Daily Capital,* May 29, 1975.

61. Ibid., *Topeka State Journal,* August 29, 1973.

62. Ibid., Kansas State College at Pittsburg, *Collegian,* December 7, 1973.

63. *Chicago Tribune,* February 5, 1963, Clymer Papers, box 37, KSHS.

64. *Wall Street Journal,* June 6, 1975, Parks Clippings, vol. 2, KSHS.

65. A convenient source of short biographies of famous Kansans is Dave Webb, *399 Kansas Characters,* rev. ed. (Dodge City: Kansas Heritage Center), 1994; for Kassebaum, see 57–58.

66. *Augusta Daily Gazette,* September 17, 1976, Save the Tallgrass Prairie Collection, box 3, KU.

67. Ibid., *Eureka Herald,* September 29, 1977.

68. Winn's proposal is summarized in *Hutchinson News,* October 17, 1979, Parks Clippings, vol. 2, KSHS.

69. Ibid., *Topeka Capital–Journal,* April 16, 1981.

70. Ibid., *Norton Daily Telgram,* April 17, 1980.

71. *Topeka Daily Capital,* January 22, 1977, Save the Tallgrass Prairie Collection, box 3, KU.

72. Ibid., *Topeka Capital*, March 14, 1973, box 1.
73. *Kansas City Star*, April 1, 1979, Parks Clippings, vol. 2, KSHS.
74. *Topeka Daily Capital*, January 22, 1977; *Manhattan Mercury*, January 23, 1977; and *Kansas Grass & Grain*, May 15, 1978, all in Save the Tallgrass Prairie Collection, box 3, KU.
75. *Topeka Capital*, November 21, 1979, Parks Clippings, vol. 2, KSHS.
76. *Wichita Eagle*, January 6, 1989.
77. There is a fine description of the Z-Bar and the issue surrounding it in Heat-Moon, *PrairyErth*, 162–66.
78. Ibid., 111.
79. *Wichita Eagle*, January 15, June 4, 1989; May 17, 1991.
80. Ibid., June 25, 1991.
81. Ibid., July 16, 1991.
82. Ibid., April 23, 1989; July 17, 1991.
83. Ibid., July 25, 1991.
84. Ibid., August 23, 1991. The author attended.
85. Ibid., November 14, 1991.
86. Ibid., September 29, 1991.
87. Ibid., November 23, 1991.
88. Ibid., December 1, 1992.
89. Ibid., April 14, 1993.
90. Ibid., April 9, 1993.
91. Ibid., June 18, 1989; October 24, 1992; October 19, November 15, 1993.
92. Ibid., March 7, June 4, July 24, August 7, 1994.
93. Ibid., May 17, 1998.
94. Ibid., April 7, 1995; October 4, 1996.
95. Ibid., April 7, 1998.
96. Ibid., March 9, 1995.
97. Ibid., December 29, 1998.
98. Ibid., April 10, 1997.
99. Ibid., December 8, 1991.
100. *Shawnee Sun*, Save the Tallgrass Prairie Collection, box 1, KU.
101. Ibid., *Kansas City Star*, April 15, 1973.
102. *Kansas City Star*, February 2, 1987, Legislative Clippings, vol. 43, KSHS.
103. *Wichita Eagle*, August 23, 1991.
104. Ibid., October 10, 1991.
105. Ibid., March 7, 1992.
106. "A Report on the Far East Trade Mission, July 20, 1984," John Carlin Papers, Governors' Papers, 58-10-02-12, KSHS.
107. Ibid., speech by John Carlin, June 19, 1985.
108. Ibid., *Manhattan Mercury*, March 15, 1985; *Kansas City Times*, June 21, 1985; clipping marked *UDK*, April 4, 1985; *Wichita Eagle*, July 25, 1985, 59-01-01-07.
109. Miner, *Discovery*, 206–7, 228–32.

110. *Topeka Capital,* March 13, 1947, Legislative Clippings, vol. 23, KSHS.

111. Ibid., March 9, 1949, vol. 24.

112. Ibid., *Topeka Capital–Journal,* February 6, 1981, vol. 39.

113. Ibid., April 30, 1981.

114. Ibid., May 6, 1981.

115. Ibid., February 15, 1982.

116. Ibid., *Wichita Eagle,* May 1, 1983, vol. 41.

117. Ibid., *Topeka Capital–Journal,* January 7, 1985, vol. 42.

118. Ibid., *Wichita Eagle,* February 27, 1980, vol. 38, on the Ceres debate.

119. Bader, *Prohibition in Kansas,* 237, 248–49, 245–56, 259, 267.

120. T. E. Bowman, in *Topeka Daily Capital,* February 23, 1890, Ethics of Amusement Clippings, KSHS.

121. Ibid., *Topeka Daily Capital,* April 14, 1894.

122. Ibid., *Topeka Journal,* January 6, 1906.

123. Ibid., September 26, 1961.

124. Ibid., *Topeka Capital,* February 28, 1963.

125. Ibid., March 18, 1965.

126. Ibid., *Wichita Beacon,* April 16, 1970.

127. Ibid., *Topeka Journal,* October 25, 1951.

128. Ibid., *Wichita Eagle,* August 4, 1977. For Wichita detail, see Miner, *Magic City,* and *Uncloistered Halls.*

129. *Wichita Eagle,* March 14, 1969, Legislative Clippings, vol. 36, KSHS.

130. Ibid., April 9, 1978, vol. 37.

131. Ibid., *Hutchinson News,* April 7, 1978.

132. Robert Bennett to Richard Taylor, April 17, 1978, Robert Bennett Papers, box 75, KU.

133. Ibid., Robert Bennett, position statement, n.d. [January 1973].

134. *Topeka State Journal,* February 25, 1972, in *Kansas Issue,* 21, 3, Rev. Richard Taylor Scrapbooks, KU. The Taylor collection at KU contains the complete *Issue* for the years of his fight against liquor by the drink. More extensive Taylor papers (over thirty boxes) are at KSHS.

135. Memo from Richard Taylor, fall 1993, *Wichita Beacon,* May 6, 1971 in the *Issue,* 20, 3, all in Taylor Scrapbooks, KU.

136. Ibid., *Topeka State Journal,* February 25, 1972.

137. Ibid., *Kansas Issue,* 24, 1; the prayer was February 14, 1972.

138. Clifford Eller to Robert Bennett, January 29, 1973, Bennett Papers, box 75, KU.

139. Ibid., a voter, Maxine Oliver to Robert Bennett, n.d. [January 1974].

140. Ibid., Eleanor Huddleston to Robert Bennett, February 4, 1973.

141. Ibid., Glen Dickinson to Robert Bennett, December 28, 1973, enclosing WSJ article.

142. Ibid., Edwin Wheeler, the Fertilizer Institute, March 4, 1977.

143. Ibid., Joy Stawderman to Robert Bennett, n.d. [April, 1977].

144. Ibid., H. C. Nanson to Bennett, August 30, 1977.

145. Ibid., *Pratt Tribune,* February 5, 1976, clipping.

146. Ibid., Robert Bennett to Ellsworth Dedrill, November 24, 1975.

147. See the amusing brief, "Wyatt Earp and the Winelist: Is a Restaurant an 'Open Saloon?' " in ibid.

148. John Carlin, "The Case for Changing Our Liquor Laws," December 4, 1984, Carlin Papers, Governors' Papers, 58-10-02-12, KSHS.

149. John Carlin, State of the State, January 14, 1986, in *Selected Papers of Governor John Carlin: An Index of Social and Political Change,* ed. Joe Pisciotte (Wichita, Kans.: Hugo Wall School of Urban and Public Affairs, Wichita State University, 1993), 119.

150. *Topeka Daily Capital,* March 23, 1979, Carlin Papers, Governors' Papers, 58-11-03-13, KSHS.

151. *Topeka Capital–Journal,* January 17, 1985, Legislative Clippings, vol. 42, KSHS.

152. *University Daily Kansan,* April 14, 1977, in Taylor Scrapbooks, KU.

153. Ibid., John McCormally, Harris News Service, October 1984. McCormally worked for the *Hutchinson News* for many years.

154. *Topeka Journal,* February 10, 1971, Legislative Clippings, vol. 36, KSHS.

155. Paul Harvey transcript, n.d., Taylor Scrapbooks, p. 48, KU.

156. Ibid., Bader, in *Topeka Capital–Journal,* October 28, 1986.

157. February 5, 1987, Legislative Clippings, box 43, KSHS.

158. Ibid., *Topeka Capital Journal,* November 5, 1986.

159. Ibid., February 19, 1987.

160. Ibid., February 26, 1987.

161. John Clements, *Kansas Facts* (Dallas: Clements Research II, 1990), 6, 12.

162. Taylor memo, December 27, 1991, Taylor Scrapbooks, pp. 35–36, KU.

163. Ibid., February 4, 1983.

164. Ibid., *Wichita Eagle,* March 14, 1987, and *Topeka Capital–Journal,* March 31, 1987.

165. Ibid., *Topeka Capital–Journal,* January 8, 1988.

166. Ibid., *Kansas Issue,* 1, 1.

167. Warren Armstrong and Dee Harris, eds., *Populism Revived: The Selected Records of Governor Joan Finney, 1991–1995* (Wichita, Kans.: Hugo Wall School of Urban and Public Affairs, Wichita State University, 1998), 38, 68, 122.

168. Ibid., 513, 518.

169. *Wichita Eagle,* April 25, 1969; May 30, July 14, 1991, Abortion Clippings, Local History Division, Wichita Public Library.

170. Ibid., September 21, 1972.

171. Ibid., July 14, 15, 19, 22, 1991.

172. Ibid., July 19, 1991.

173. Ibid., September 3, 1999.

174. *Kansas City Star,* July 20, 1916, Immigration Clippings, vol. 1, KSHS.

175. Ibid., *Topeka Capital,* January 5, 1939, and *Lyons Daily News,* June 26, 1972, vol. 2.

176. Ibid., *Wichita Eagle,* January 23, 1977.

177. Miner, *Magic City,* 47, 66, 97–99.

178. Henry Avila, "Immigration and Integration: The Mexican American Community in Garden City, Kansas, 1900–1950," *Kansas History* 20 (spring 1997): 23–37.

179. *Kansas City Times,* September 4, 1953, Immigration Clippings, vol. 2, KSHS.

180. Ibid., *Garden City Telegram*, December 1, 1983.

181. Ibid., *Wichita Eagle*, November 22, 1984.

182. Ibid., *Topeka Capital–Journal*, June 5, 1988.

183. Ibid., *Garden City Telegram*, August 5, 1988.

184. *Wichita Eagle*, May 15, 1988.

185. Ibid., February 25, 1985.

186. Ibid., December 14, 1986; February 3, 1987.

187. Ibid., January 20, 1987.

188. Ibid., February 4, 1987.

189. Ibid., December 10, 1987.

190. Ibid., January 12, 1988.

191. Ibid., March 13, 1988.

192. Ibid., February 18, 1988.

193. Ibid., November 12, 1988.

194. Ibid., February 4, 1992.

195. Ibid., February 16, 1992.

196. Ibid., February 21, 1992.

197. Ibid., March 13, 1992.

198. Ibid., March 18, 1992.

199. Ibid., April 8, 1992.

200. Ibid., April 12, 1992.

201. Ibid., May 24, 1992.

202. Ibid., June 2, 1992.

203. Ibid., June 28, September 12, 1992.

204. Ibid., August 12, 1999; *New York Times*, August 14, 1999.

205. *Wichita Eagle*, November 7, 1999.

206. Ibid., August 14, 15, 1999.

207. Ibid., August 21, 1999.

208. Ibid., August 15, 1999.

209. Ibid., August 13, 1999.

210. Ibid.

211. *New York Times*, August 13, 1999.

212. *Washington Post*, August 14, 1999.

213. *Time*, September 13, 1999.

214. Information taken from ⟨*www.edexcellence.net*⟩.

215. Webb, *399 Kansas Characters*, 18.

216. Wes Jackson, *Becoming Native to This Place* (Lexington: University Press of Kentucky, 1994), 97. See also *The Land Report: 20 Years* 55–56 (summer 1996).

CONCLUSION: HORIZONS

1. Quoted in Miner, ed., *Reader*, 25–27.

2. Richard Hinton, "The Nationalization of Freedom, and the Historical Place of Kansas Therein," *Collections of the Kansas State Historical Society* 6 (1897–1900): 185.

3. For this type of approach, see Patricia Limerick, *Legacy of Conquest: The Unbroken Past of the American West* (New York: W. W. Norton, 1988), and Richard White, *"It's Your Misfortune and None of My Own": A History of the American Frontier,* 5th ed. (Norman: University of Oklahoma Press, 1991). A convenient summary of various views is *Does the Frontier Experience Make America Exceptional?* ed. Richard Etulain (New York: St. Martin's Press, 1999).

4. White, *Misfortune,* 3, 135.

5. Francis Fukuyama, *The End of History and the Last Man* (New York: Free Press, 1992).

6. Gerald Nash, *Creating the West: Historical Interpretations, 1890–1990* (Albuquerque: University of New Mexico Press, 1991), 101, 104, 110, 114.

7. Ray Billington, *Frederick Jackson Turner: Historian, Scholar, Teacher* (New York: Oxford University Press, 1973), 214–15.

8. Merrill Jenson, ed., *Regionalism in America* (Madison: University of Wisconsin Press, 1951), 133.

9. Edward Agran, "William Allen White's Small-Town America: A Literary Prescription for Progressive Reform," *Kansas History* 17 (autumn 1994): 162, 168–69, 175–76.

10. Rhoda Gilman, "The History and Peopling of Minnesota: Its Culture," *Daedalus* 129 (summer 2000): 1.

11. Quoted in Walter Lippmann, "Government Philosophy in a Sick World," speech before New York Academy of Medicine, December 19, 1935, in *Bulletin of the Sedgwick County Medical Society* 6 (April 1936): 8.

12. Henry Adams, *The Education of Henry Adams* (Boston and New York: Houghton Mifflin, 1918), 382.

13. For a discussion, see William Dean Howells, *Criticism and Fiction* (New York: Harper and Brothers, 1892).

14. Statistical comparisons come from the University of Kansas, Institute for Public Policy Research, *Kansas Statistical Abstract 1998,* 33d ed. (Lawrence: University of Kansas, 1999), sections 2-2, 2-3, 2-4, 2-6, 2-9, 2-16, 2-53, 2-61, 2-64, 7-5, 7-43, 16-6; Division of State Planning and Research, *Kansas 2000* (Lawrence, Kans.: Institute for Social and Environmental Studies, 1974), 55; and Clements, *Kansas Facts,* 5, 23.

15. *Kansas 2000,* 13, 51, 55.

16. Joseph Amato and Anthony Amato, in "Minnesota: Real and Imagined: A View from the Countryside," *Daedalus* 129 (summer 2000): 55.

17. Ibid., Stephen Graubard, "Minnesota: A Different America," v–vi.

18. Ibid., Annette Atkins, "Facing Minnesota," 51.

19. Ibid., quotation from Joseph Amato and Anthony Amato, "Minnesota," 71.

20. Ibid., 74.

21. Ron Rosenbaum, "Playboy Interview: Bob Dylan," *Playboy* (March 1978), 62.

22. Amato, "Minnesota," 76.

23. Dudley Cornish, "Carl Becker's Kansas: The Power of Endurance," *Kansas Historical Quarterly* 41 (spring 1975): 12.

24. Bill Holm, *The Heart Can Be Filled Anywhere on Earth* (Minneapolis: Milkweed Editions, 1996), 20.

25. Craig Miner, "Civilizing Kansas," *Kansas History* 17 (winter 1994–1995): 254–61, passim.

26. William D. Howells, *A Traveler from Altruria* (New York: Harper, 1894), 30–31, 50.

27. *Leonard Baskin's Speech of Acceptance on Receiving the Medal of the American Institute of Graphic Arts, New York, April 28, 1965,* Typophiles Monograph no. 78 (Lynchburg, Vt.: Spiral Press, 1965).

28. Quoted in Miner, *Magic City,* 151.

29. Ibid., 93–94, 109, 118, 120, 131.

30. Reynolds Price, *A Common Room: Essays, 1954–1987* (New York: Atheneum, 1987), 231–32, 235.

31. Quoted in Douglas Gilbert and Clyde Kilby, *C. S. Lewis: Images of His World* (Grand Rapids, Mich.: William Erdmans, 1973), 137.

32. West, *The Contested Plains,* 91.

33. Kathleen Norris, *Dakota: A Spiritual Geography* (Boston: Houghton Mifflin, 1993), 2, 38.

34. Joseph Levenson, "The Genesis of Confucian China and Its Modern Fate," in *The Historian's Workshop: Original Essays by Sixteen Historians,* ed. L. P. Curtis (New York: Knopf, 1970), 288–89.

35. Norris, *Dakota,* 139.

36. *The Letters of Samuel Johnson,* ed. Bruce Redford, 5 vols. (Princeton: Princeton University Press, 1992), 2: 265.

37. William Phillips, "Kansas History," *Collections of the Kansas State Historical Society* 4 (1886–1890): 352–53.

38. Quoted in Miner, "Civilizing Kansas," 257.

39. Virgil, *Georgics,* trans. J. W. Mackail (Boston: Houghton Mifflin, 1904), 9.

40. Quoted in *Directory of the Kansas Historical Exhibit, Kansas State Building, World's Columbian Exposition, 1893* (Topeka: KSHS, 1893), 4.

BIBLIOGRAPHY

ARCHIVAL SOURCES

Manuscript Collections

Amana Historical Society, Amana, Iowa.
  Christian Mertz Kansas Expedition, handwritten account, 1854. Diary.
  Toumpold, Cliff. "The Kansas Odyssey." Typescript.

Coleman Company Archives, Wichita, Kansas.
  Ebendorf, Herbert. History of the Coleman Company.

Kansas State Historical Society, Manuscript Division.
  Billard Family. Papers.
  Brinkerhoff, Frederick. Papers.
  Brown, George W. Papers.
  Capper, Arthur. Papers.
  Clymer, Rolla. Papers.
  Delahay, Mark. Papers.
  Denious, Jess. Papers.
  Denver, James. Papers.
  Edson, Charles. Papers.
  Funston, Frederick. Papers.
  Garvey, R. H. Papers.
  Gleed, Charles. Papers.
  Goodnow, Isaac. Papers.
  Guthrie, Abelard. Papers.
  Hill, Hiram. Papers.
  Holliday, Cyrus. Papers.
  Horton, Albert. Papers.
  Howes, Cecil. Papers.
  Hutchinson, William. Papers.
  Hyatt, Thaddeus. Papers.
  Ingalls, John. Papers.
  Lane, James. Papers.
  Malin, James. Papers.
  Martin, G. W. Papers.
  Miller, Sol. Papers.

New England Emigrant Aid Company. Papers.
Pomeroy, Samuel. Papers.
Robinson, Charles and Sara. Papers.
Stevens, Robert. Papers.
Stockwell, Glen. Papers.
Ware, Eugene. Papers, including Nies acquisition.
White, William Allen. Papers.
Wood, Samuel. Papers.

State Archives, Governors' Papers.
Allen, Henry. Papers.
Arn, Edward. Papers.
Bailey, Willis. Papers.
Capper, Arthur. Papers.
Carlin, John. Papers.
Carlson, Frank. Papers.
Davis, Jonathan. Papers.
Glick, George. Papers.
Harvey, James. Papers.
Hoch, Edward. Papers.
Hodges, George. Papers.
Huxman, Walter. Papers.
Landon, Alf. Papers.
Martin, John. Papers.
Osborn, Thomas. Papers.
Paulen, Ben. Papers.
Ratner, Payne. Papers.
Reed, Clyde. Papers.
St. John, John. Papers.
Schoeppel, Andrew. Papers.
Stubbs, Walter. Papers.
Woodring, Harry F. Papers.

National Archives, Washington, D.C.
File no. 16, Special Files, Indian Division. Record Group 48.

University of Kansas, Lawrence, Spencer Research Library, Kansas Collection.
Bennett, Robert. Papers.
Carney, Thomas. Papers.
Case, Alexander. Papers.
Denver, James. Papers.
Driscoll, Charles. Papers.
Ely, Richard. Papers.
Howard, William. Papers.

Humphrey, Lyman. Papers.

Lane, James. Papers.

Miller, Josiah. Papers.

Prairie Park Natural History Association Collection.

Ratner, Payne. Clippings.

Robinson, Charles. Papers.

Robinson, Sara. Scrapbooks.

Save the Tallgrass Prairie Collection.

Taylor, Rev. Richard. Scrapbooks.

Ware, Eugene. Papers.

Printed and Typescript Material

Extortionate Taxation: Oppressive and Unjust Discrimination Against the Poor. Criminal Extravagance with Public Money. An Imperative Demand for Change. Wichita, 1891. Special Collections, Ablah Library, Wichita State University.

Kansas Board of Railroad Commissioners. Miscellaneous Pamphlets. Kansas State Historical Society.

Kansas Collected Speeches and Pamphlets. Kansas State Historical Society.

Longman, Green and Company. "Industrial Survey of Wichita, Kansas." October 1927. Wichita State University Library.

Miner, Craig. "A Narrative History . . . of Local Attitudes, Actions, and Policy Concerning Railroads and Railroad Crossings in Wichita, Kansas, 1872–1997." 1997. Special Collections, Ablah Library, Wichita State University.

Wilson, Roger. "The Triple Play." In Roger Wilson's possession.

ARTICLES

Agran, Edward. "William Allen White's Small-Town America: A Literary Prescription for Progressive Reform." *Kansas History* 17 (autumn 1994): 162–77.

Averill, Thomas. "Oz and Kansas Culture." *Kansas History* 12 (spring 1989): 2–12.

Avila, Henry. "Immigration and Integration: The Mexican American Community in Garden City, 1900–1950." *Kansas History* 20 (spring 1997): 23–37.

Baldridge, Gary. "Pottawatomie County Says No to Prairie Preservation." *Kansas History* 16 (summer 1993): 94–107.

Bedlow, James. "Depression and New Deal: Letters from the Plains." *Kansas Historical Quarterly* 43 (summer 1977): 140–53.

Bingham, Anne. "Sixteen Years on a Kansas Farm." *Collections of the Kansas State Historical Society* 15 (1919–1922): 501–23.

Birney, Ann, and Joyce Thierer. "Shoulder to Shoulder: Kansas Women Win the Vote." *Kansas Heritage* 3 (winter 1995): 64–68.

Borin, C. "Kansas: Her History, Her History-Makers, and Her Historical Society." *Collections of the Kansas State Historical Society* 4 (1886–1888): 269–71.

Bridenbaugh, Carl. "The Great Mutation." *American Historical Review* 48 (January 1963): 315–31.

Brinkerhoff, Fred. "The Kansas Tour of Lincoln the Candidate." *Kansas Historical Quarterly* 13 (February 1945): 204–307.

Brucker, James. "Workers, Townsmen and the Governor: The Santa Fe Enginemen's Strike, 1878." *Kansas History* 5 (spring 1982): 23–32.

Butterfield, J. Ware. "The Legislative War of 1893: Inside, Outside, and Back Again." *Collections of the Kansas State Historical Society* 6 (1897–1900): 453–58.

Butters, Gerald. "*The Birth of a Nation* and the Kansas Board of Review of Motion Pictures: A Censorship Struggle." *Kansas History* 14 (spring 1991): 2–14.

Byers, O. P. "When Railroading Outdid the Wild West Stories." *Collections of the Kansas State Historical Society* 17 (1926–1928): 339–51.

Christiansen, James. "The Kansas-Osage Border War of 1874: Fact or Wishful Thinking?" *Chronicles of Oklahoma* 63 (fall 1985): 292–311.

Clanton, Gene. "Intolerant Populist? The Disaffection of Mary Elizabeth Lease." *Kansas Historical Quarterly* 34 (summer 1968): 189–200.

Clymer, Rolla. "Civic Ideals of the Kansas Press." *Jayhawker Press* 3 (April 1926): 1–3, microfilm N581, KSHS.

Cornish, Dudley. "Carl Becker's Kansas: The Power of Endurance." *Kansas Historical Quarterly* 41 (spring 1975): 1–13.

Cortner, Richard. "The Wobblies and *Fiske* v. *Kansas*: Victory and Disintegration." *Kansas History* 4 (spring 1981): 30–38.

Courtwright, Julie. "Want to Build a Miracle City? War Housing in Wichita." *Kansas History* 23 (winter 2000–2001): 218–39.

Davis, C. Wood. "The Farmer, the Investor, and the Railway." *Arena* 3 (February 1891): 291–313.

Etcheson, Nicole. "Labouring for the Freedom of This Territory." *Kansas History* 21 (summer 1998): 68–87.

Farley, Alan. "Samuel Hallett and the Union Pacific Railway Company in Kansas." *Kansas Historical Quarterly* 25 (spring 1959): 1–16.

Fearon, Peter. "Ploughshares into Airplanes: Manufacturing Industry and Workers During World War II." *Kansas History* 22 (winter 1999–2000): 298–314.

Fitz, Leslie. "The Development of the Milling Industry in Kansas." *Collections of the Kansas State Historical Society* 12 (1911–1912): 53–59.

Flentje, Edward. "The Political Roots of City Managers in Kansas." *Kansas History* 7 (summer 1984): 139–58.

Gagliardo, Domenico. "Development of Common and Employers' Liability Law in Kansas." *Kansas Historical Quarterly* 10 (May 1941): 155–74.

——. "The First Kansas Workmen's Compensation Law." *Kansas Historical Quarterly* 9 (November 1939): 384–97.

——. "A History of Kansas Child-Labor Legislation." *Kansas Historical Quarterly* 1 (August 1932): 379–411.

——. "Some Wage Legislation in Kansas." *Kansas Historical Quarterly* 8 (November 1939): 384–98.

Galliher, James, and John Galliher. " 'Déjà vu All Over Again': The Recurring Life and Death of Capital Legislation in Kansas." *Social Problems* 44 (August 1997): 369–85.

Gambone, Joseph. "Economic Relief in Kansas, 1860–1861." *Kansas Historical Quarterly* 36 (summer 1970): 149–74.

——. "The Forgotten Feminist of Kansas: The Papers of Clarina I. H. Nichols, 1854–1885." *Kansas Historical Quarterly* 39 (spring 1973): 12–57.

Gant, Phillip. "The Kansas Congressional Delegation and the Selective Service Act of 1940." *Kansas History* 2 (autumn 1979): 196–205.

Gehring, Lorraine. "Women Officeholders in Kansas, 1872–1912." *Kansas History* 9 (summer 1986): 48–57.

Gleed, Charles. "The First Kansas Railway." *Collections of the Kansas State Historical Society* 6 (1897–1900): 357–59.

Goodnow, Isaac. "Personal Reminiscences and Kansas Emigration, 1855." *Collections of the Kansas State Historical Society* 4 (1886–1888): 244–53.

Harrington, W. P. "The Populist Party in Kansas." *Collections of the Kansas State Historical Society* 16 (1923–1925): 403–50.

Harvey, Douglas. "Creating a 'Sea of Galilee': The Rescue of Cheyenne Bottoms Wildlife Area, 1927–1930." *Kansas History* 24 (spring 2001): 2–17.

Haworth, Erasmus. "Historic Sketch of the Gypsum, Cement and Plaster Industry in Kansas." *Collections of the Kansas State Historical Society* 7 (1901–1902): 84–90.

Hess, Edith. "State Regulation of Woman and Child Labor in Kansas." *Collections of the Kansas State Historical Society* 15 (1919–1922): 279–33.

Hickey, Joseph, and Charles Webb. "The Transition from Farming to Ranching in the Kansas Flint Hills." *Great Plains Quarterly* 7 (fall 1987): 244–55.

Hill, Charles. "Progressive Legislation in Kansas." *Collections of the Kansas State Historical Society* 12 (1911–1912): 69–77.

Hinton, Richard. "The Nationalization of Freedom, and the Historical Place of Kansas Therein." *Collections of the Kansas State Historical Society* 6 (1897–1900): 175–86.

Hodder, Frank. "The Railroad Background of the Kansas-Nebraska Bill." *Mississippi Valley Historical Review* 12 (June 1925): 3–22.

Howell, Fred. "Some Phases of the Industrial History of Pittsburg, Kansas." *Kansas Historical Quarterly* 1 (May 1932): 273–94.

Hurt, Douglas. "Gaining Control of the Environment: The Morton County Land Utilization Project in the Kansas Dust Bowl. *Kansas History* 19 (summer 1996): 140–53.

Hyde, John. "A Balm in Gilead." *Kansas History* 9 (winter 1986–1987): 150–63.

Juhnke, James. "Mob Violence and Kansas Mennonites in 1918." *Kansas Historical Quarterly* 43 (autumn 1977): 334–50.

Koppes, Clayton. "The Industrial Workers of the World and County-Jail Reform in Kansas, 1915–1920." *Kansas Historical Quarterly* 41 (spring 1975): 63–86.

———. "The Kansas Trial of the IWW, 1917–1919." *Labor History* 16 (summer 1975): 338–58.

LaForte, Robert. "Theodore Roosevelt's Osawatomie Speech." *Kansas Historical Quarterly* 32 (summer 1966): 187–200.

The Land Report: Twenty Years. No. 55/56 (summer 1996).

"Lincoln in Kansas." *Collections of the Kansas State Historical Society* 7 (1901–1902): 536–62.

Lippmann, Walter. "Government Philosophy in a Sick World." Reprinted in *Bulletin of the Sedgwick County Medical Society* 6 (April 1936): 8–9, 17–19.

Malin, James. "The Kinsley Boom of the Late Eighties." *Kansas Historical Quarterly* 4 (February, May 1935): 23–49, 164–87.

———. "Notes on the Writing of General Histories of Kansas." *Kansas Historical Quarterly* 21 (autumn 1954): 184–223; (winter 1954): 264–87; (spring 1955): 331–87; (summer 1955): 407–44; (winter 1955): 598–643.

Manning, Edwin. "Kansas in History." *Collections of the Kansas State Historical Society* 12 (1912): 10–14.

McKenna, Sister Jeanne. "With the Help of God and Lucy Stone." *Kansas Historical Quarterly* 36 (spring 1970): 13–26.

Miller, Sally. "Kate Richard O'Hare: Progression Toward Feminism." *Kansas History* 7 (winter 1984–1985): 263–79.

Miller, Worth Robert. "A Centennial Historiography of American Populism." *Kansas History* 16 (spring 1993): 54–69.

Miner, Craig. "Border Frontier: The Missouri River, Fort Scott & Gulf Railroad in the Cherokee Neutral Lands, 1868–1879." *Kansas Historical Quarterly* 35 (summer 1969): 105–29.

———. "Civilizing Kansas." *Kansas History* 17 (winter 1994–1995): 254–61.

———. "Stereotyping and the Pacific Railway Issue, 1845–1865." *Canadian Review of American Studies* 6 (spring 1975): 59–73.

"Minnesota: A Different America?" Special issue, *Daedalus* 129 (summer 2000).

Morehouse, George. "Kansas as a State of Extremes, and Its Attitude During the World War." *Collections of the Kansas State Historical Society* 15 (1919–1923): 15–28.

Nichols, Roy. "Kansas Historiography: The Technique of Cultural Analysis." *American Quarterly* 9 (spring 1957): 85–91.

Nord, David. "The *Appeal to Reason* and American Socialism, 1901–1920." *Kansas History* 1 (summer 1978): 74–89.

Nottage, James, and Floyd Thomas. "There's No Place Like Home: Symbols and Images of Kansas." *Kansas History* 8 (autumn 1985): 138–61.

O'Brien, Patrick. "Kansas at War: The Home Front, 1941–1945." *Kansas History* 17 (spring 1994): 6–25.

O'Brien, Patrick, Thomas Isern, and Daniel Lumley. "Stalag Sunflower: German Prisoners of War in Kansas." *Kansas History* 7 (autumn 1984): 182–98.

Paddock, Joel. "The Gubernatorial Campaigns of Robert Docking, 1966–1972." *Kansas History* 17 (summer 1994): 108–23.

Pankratz, Herbert. "The Suppression of Alleged Disloyalty in Kansas During World War I." *Kansas Historical Quarterly* 42 (autumn 1976): 277–307.

Parrish, William. "The Great Kansas Legislative Imbroglio of 1893." *Journal of the West* 7 (October 1968): 471–91.

Partin, John. "The Dilemma of 'A Good, Very Good Man.' " *Kansas History* 2 (summer 1979): 86–95.

Perdue, Rosa. "The Sources of the Constitution of Kansas." *Collections of the Kansas State Historical Society* 7 (1901–1902): 130–51.

Peterson, John. "Science in Kansas: The Early Years, 1804–1875." *Kansas History* 10 (autumn 1987): 201–40.

Phillips, William. "Kansas History." *Collections of the Kansas State Historical Society* 4 (1886–1890): 351–59.

Pickett, Calder. "John Steuart Curry and the Topeka Murals Controversy." *Kansas Quarterly* 2 (fall 1970): 30–41.

Popper, Frank, and Deborah Popper. "The Great Plains: From Dust to Dust, a Daring Proposal for Dealing with an Inevitable Disaster." *Planning* 53 (December 1978): 12–18.

Richmond, Robert. "Kansas Builds a Capitol." *Kansas Historical Quarterly* 38 (autumn 1974): 249–67.

Rosenbaum, Ron. "Playboy Interview: Bob Dylan." *Playboy* (March 1978): 61–64, 69–74, 78–90.

Rowland, Mary. "Kansas and the Highways." *Kansas History* 5 (spring 1982): 33–51.

Saul, Norman. "Myth and History: Turkey Red Wheat and the 'Kansas Miracle.' " *Heritage of the Great Plains* 22 (summer 1989): 1–13.

Schofield, Ann. "The Women's March: Miners, Family and Community in Pittsburg, Kansas, 1921–22." *Kansas History* 7 (summer 1984): 159–68.

Schuyler, Michael. "Federal Drought Relief Activities in Kansas, 1934." *Kansas Historical Quarterly* 43 (summer 1977): 403–24.

Schwendemann, Glen. "The 'Exodusters' on the Missouri." *Kansas Historical Quarterly* 29 (spring 1963): 25–40.

——. "Wyandotte and the First 'Exodusters' of 1879." *Kansas Historical Quarterly* 26 (autumn 1960): 233–49.

Scott, Angelo. "How Natural Gas Came to Kansas." *Kansas Historical Quarterly* 21 (winter 1954): 233–46.

Scott, Mark. "The Little Blue Books in the War on Bigotry and Bunk." *Kansas History* 1 (autumn 1978): 75–89.

Sheridan, Richard. "Charles Henry Langston and the African American Struggle in Kansas." *Kansas History* 22 (winter 1999–2000): 268–83.

Sherow, James, and William Reeder. "A Richly Textured Community: Fort Riley, Kansas, and American Indians, 1853–1911." *Kansas History* 21 (spring 1998): 2–17.

Simpson, William. "The Kansas Idea." *Our State* (October 19, 1889): 2–3, microfilm T2725.

Sloan, Charles. "Kansas Battles the Invisible Empire: The Legal Ouster of the KKK from Kansas, 1922–1927." *Kansas Historical Quarterly* 40 (autumn 1974): 393–409.

Smith, W. R. "The Kansas State Printing Plant." *Collections of the Kansas State Historical Society* 14 (1915–1918): 354–57.

Snell, Joseph, and Robert Richmond. "When the Union and Kansas Pacific Built Through Kansas." *Kansas Historical Quarterly* 32 (summer 1966): 161–86.

Socolofsky, Homer. "The Scully Lane System in Marion County." *Kansas Historical Quarterly* 18 (November 1950): 337–75.

Steiner, Michael. "Robert Hine, Sense of Place, and the Terrain of Western History." *Pacific Historical Review* 70 (August 2001): 453–64.

Sterling, David. "The Federal Government vs. The *Appeal to Reason*." *Kansas History* 9 (spring 1986): 31–42.

Stoddard, W. O. "The Story of a Nomination." *North American Review* 138 (March 1884): 263–73.

Stone, Irene. "The Lead and Zinc Fields of Kansas." *Collections of the Kansas State Historical Society* 7 (1901–1902): 243–60.

Sutter, Paul. "Paved with Good Intentions: Good Roads, the Automobile, and the Rhetoric of Rural Improvement in the *Kansas Farmer*, 1890–1914." *Kansas History* 18 (winter 1995–1996): 284–99.

Swanson, Nina. "The Development of Public Protection of Children in Kansas." *Collections of the Kansas State Historical Society* 15 (1919–1922): 231–78.

"Touring Kansas and Colorado in 1871: The Journal of George C. Anderson." *Kansas Historical Quarterly* 22 (autumn 1956): 193–219.

Tuttle, William, ed. "William Allen White and Verne Marshall: Two Midwestern Editors Debate Aid to the Allies versus Isolationism." *Kansas Historical Quarterly* 32 (summer 1966): 201–9.

"U.S. Army and Air Force Wings over Kansas." *Kansas Historical Quarterly* 25 (summer and autumn 1959): 129–57, 334–60.

Vaerill, Thomas. "Of Drought and Dust: Expressions in Kansas Literature." *Kansas History* 20 (winter 1997–1998): 230–47.

Vincent, Frank. "History of Salt Discovery and Production in Kansas, 1887–1915." *Collections of the Kansas State Historical Society* 14 (1915–1918): 358–78.

Walker, Edith. "Labor Problems During the First Year of Governor Martin's Administration." *Kansas Historical Quarterly* 5 (February 1936): 33–53.

Waller, Bret. "Curry and the Critics." *Kansas Quarterly* 2 (fall 1970): 42–55.

Ware, Eugene. "The Neutral Lands." *Collections of the Kansas State Historical Society* 6 (1897–1900): 147–69.

——. "No Cranks in Kansas." *Our State* (October 12, 1889): 6, microfilm T2725.

Watts, Dale. "How Bloody Was Bleeding Kansas? Political Killings in Kansas Territory, 1854–1861." *Kansas History* 18 (summer 1995): 116–29.

West, Elliott. "A Story of Three Families." *Kansas History* 19 (summer 1996): 112–23.

"When Kansas Became a State." *Kansas Historical Quarterly* 27 (spring 1961): 1–21.

Woodward, C. Vann. "The Populist Heritage and the Intellectual." *American Scholar* 29 (winter 1959–1960): 55–72.

Wright, Robert. "Frontier Life in Southwest Kansas." *Collections of the Kansas State Historical Society* 7 (1901–1902): 47–83.

BOOKS

Adams, Henry. *The Education of Henry Adams.* Boston and New York: Houghton Mifflin, 1918.

Allen, Henry. *The Party of the Third Part.* New York: Harper, 1921.

Armstrong, Warren, and Dee Harris, eds. *Populism Revived: The Selected Records of Governor Joan Finney, 1991–1995.* Wichita, Kans.: Hugo Wall School of Urban and Public Affairs, Wichita State University, 1998.

Athearn, Robert. *In Search of Canaan: Black Migration to Kansas, 1879–80.* Lawrence: Regents Press of Kansas, 1978.

Bader, Robert. *The Great Kansas Bond Scandal.* Lawrence: University Press of Kansas, 1982.

——. *Hayseeds, Moralizers, and Methodists.* Lawrence: University Press of Kansas, 1988.

——. *Prohibition in Kansas.* Lawrence: University Press of Kansas, 1986.

Bare, Janet. *Wildflowers and Weeds of Kansas.* Lawrence: Regents Press of Kansas, 1979.

Barns, George. *Denver, the Man: The Life, Letters and Public Papers of the Lawyer, Soldier and Statesman.* Wilmington, Ohio: [author], 1949.

Barry, Louise, ed. *The Beginning of the West: Annals of the Kansas Gateway to the American West, 1540–1854.* Topeka: Kansas State Historical Society, 1972.

[Baskin, Leonard]. *Leonard Baskin's Speech of Acceptance on Receiving the Medal of the American Institute of Graphic Arts, New York, April 28, 1965.* Lynchburg, Vt.: Spiral Press, 1965.

Baughman, Robert. *Kansas Post Offices, May 29, 1828–August 3, 1961.* Topeka: Kansas State Historical Society, 1961.

Beckman, Peter. *Kansas Monks: A History of St. Benedict's Abbey.* Atchison, Kans.: Abbey Student Press, 1957.

Beer, Thomas. *The Mauve Decade: American Life at the End of the Nineteenth Century.* 1926. Reprint, New York: Vintage Books, 1961.

Bentley, O. H., ed. *History of Wichita and Sedgwick County, Kansas.* 2 vols. Chicago: C. F. Cooper, 1910.

Berlin, Isaiah. *The Crooked Timber of Humanity.* Princeton: Princeton University Press, 1991.

Billington, Ray. *Frederick Jackson Turner: Historian, Scholar, Teacher.* New York: Oxford University Press, 1973.

Bonnifield, Paul. *The Dust Bowl: Men, Dirt, and Depression.* Albuquerque: University of New Mexico Press, 1979.

Bourne, Randolph. *War and the Intellectuals: Essays by Randolph S. Bourne, 1915–1919.* New York: Harper Torchbooks, 1964.

Brackman, Barbara, comp. *Kansas Trivia.* Nashville: Rutledge Hill Press, 1997.

Brewerton, Douglas. *The War in Kansas: A Rough Trip to the Border Among New Homes and a Strange New People.* New York: Derby and Jackson, 1856.

Bright, John, ed. *Kansas: The First Century.* 5 vols. New York: Lewis Historical Publishing Company, 1956.

Brown, George W. *False Claims of Kansas Historians Truthfully Corrected.* Rockford, Ill.: Printed by the author, 1902.

——. *Reminiscences of Gov. R. J. Walker; with the True Story of the Rescue of Kansas from Slavery.* Rockford, Ill.: Printed by the author, 1902.

Bryant, Keith. *History of the Atchison, Topeka and Santa Fe Railway.* New York: Macmillan, 1974.

Buchanan, Rex, ed. *Kansas Geology: An Introduction to Landscapes, Rocks, Minerals, and Fossils.* Lawrence: University Press of Kansas, 1984.

Callahan, James. *Jayhawk Editor.* Los Angeles: Sterling Press, 1955.

Capote, Truman. *In Cold Blood: A True Account of a Multiple Murder and Its Consequences.* New York: Random House, 1965.

Carson, Gerald. *The Roguish World of Doctor Brinkley.* New York: Rinehart, 1960.

Carson, Paul. *The Plains Indians.* College Station: Texas A&M University Press, 1998.

Castel, Albert. *Civil War Kansas: Reaping the Whirlwind.* 2d ed. Lawrence: University Press of Kansas, 1997.

Chalmers, David. *Hooded Americanism: The History of the Ku Klux Klan.* Durham, N.C.: Duke University Press, 1987.

Clanton, Gene. *Congressional Populism and the Crisis of the 1890s.* Lawrence: University Press of Kansas, 1998.

——. *Populism: The Humane Preference in America, 1890–1900.* Boston: Twayne, 1991.

Clements, John. *Kansas Facts.* Dallas: Clements Research II, 1990.

Clugston, W. G. *Rascals in Democracy.* New York: Richard R. Smith, 1940.

Clymer, Rolla. *Farewells.* Ed. William Galvani. El Dorado, Kans.: Butler County Historical Society, 1986.

Collins, Joseph, ed. *Natural Kansas.* Lawrence: University Press of Kansas, 1985.

Complete List of Motion Picture Films Presented to the Kansas State Board of Review for Action from July 1, 1918 to September 30, 1918. Topeka: Kansas State Printing Plant, W. R. Smith, state printer, 1918.

Conlin, Joseph, ed. *At the Point of Production: The Local History of the I.W.W.* (Westport, Conn.: Greenwood Press, 1981.

Connelley, William. *John Brown.* Topeka: Crane, 1900.

——. *The Life of Preston B. Plumb.* Chicago: Browne and Howell, 1913.

——. *Quantrill and the Border Wars.* Cedar Rapids, Iowa: Torch Press, 1910.

——. *A Standard History of Kansas and Kansans.* 5 vols. Chicago and New York: Lewis, 1918.

Cordley, Richard. *A History of Lawrence, Kansas, from the First Settlement to the Close of the Rebellion.* Lawrence: Lawrence Journal Press, 1895.

——. *The Lawrence Massacre by a Band of Missouri Ruffians Under Quantrell, August 21, 1863.* N.p., n.d.

Cornish, Dudley. *The Sable Arm: Black Troops in the Union Army, 1861–1865.* 1956. Reprint, Lawrence: University Press of Kansas, 1987.

Cox, Thomas. *Blacks in Topeka, Kansas, 1865–1915: A Social History.* Baton Rouge: Louisiana State University Press, 1982.

Crawford, Samuel. *Kansas in the Sixties.* Chicago: A. G. McClurg, 1911.

Crumbine, Samuel. *Frontier Doctor.* Philadelphia: Dorrance, 1948.

Curtis, L. P., ed. *The Historian's Workshop: Original Essays by Sixteen Historians.* New York: Knopf, 1970.

Custer, Elizabeth. *Tenting on the Plain or General Custer in Kansas and Texas.* New York: Charles L. Webster, 1887.

Dary, David. *Kanzana, 1854–1900.* Lawrence, Kans.: Allen Books, 1986.

Davis, Kenneth. *Kansas: A Bicentennial History.* New York: W. W. Norton, 1976.

——. *River on the Rampage.* Garden City, N.Y.: Doubleday, 1953.

Decker, Leslie. *Railroads, Lands, and Politics: The Taxation of the Railroad Land Grants, 1864–1897.* Providence, R.I.: Brown University Press, 1964.

Directory of the Kansas Historical Exhibit, Kansas State Building, World's Columbian Exposition, 1893. Topeka: Kansas State Historical Society, 1893.

Division of State Planning and Research. *Kansas 2000.* Lawrence, Kans.: Institute for Social and Environmental Studies, 1974.

Drury, James. *The Government of Kansas.* 3d ed. Lawrence: Regents Press of Kansas, 1980.

Dubois, Ellen. *Feminism and Suffrage: The Emergence of an Independent Women's Movement in America, 1848–1869.* Ithaca, N.Y.: Cornell University Press, 1999.

Dykstra, Robert. *The Cattle Towns.* Lincoln: University of Nebraska Press, 1983.

Eick, Gretchen. *Dissent in Wichita: The Civil Rights Movement in the Midwest, 1954–1972.* Urbana and Chicago: University of Illinois Press, 2001.

Eighth Annual Report of the Board of Railroad Commissioners for the Year Ending December 1, 1890. State of Kansas. Topeka: Kansas Publishing House, Clifford C. Baker, state printer, 1890.

Eighth Annual Report of the Kansas State Board of Agriculture, 1891–1892. Topeka: Kansas Publishing House, 1893.

Eighth Biennial Report of the Kansas State Board of Agriculture, 1887–1888. Topeka: Kansas Publishing House, 1889.

Etulain, Richard, ed. *Does the Frontier Experience Make America Exceptional?* New York: St. Martin's Press, 1999.

Fifth Annual Report of the Board of Railroad Commissioners for the Year Ending

December 1, 1887. State of Kansas. Topeka: Kansas Publishing House, Clifford C. Baker, state printer, 1887.

Fifth Biennial Report of the Kansas State Board of Agriculture, 1885–1886. Topeka: Kansas Publishing House, 1887.

Finkelman, Paul, and Stephen Gottlieb, eds. *Toward a Usable Past: Liberty Under State Constitutions.* Athens: University of Georgia Press, 1991.

Flora, S. D. *Tornadoes of the United States.* Norman: University of Oklahoma Press, 1953.

Fosset, Judith, and Jeffrey Tucker, eds. *Race Consciousness: African-American Studies for the New Century.* New York: New York University Press, 1997.

Friedman, Lawrence. *Menninger: The Family and the Clinic.* New York: Knopf, 1990.

Fukuyama, Francis. *The End of History and the Last Man.* New York: Free Press, 1992.

Gaeddert, G. Raymond. *The Birth of Kansas.* Lawrence: University of Kansas, 1940.

Gagliardo, Domenico. *The Kansas Industrial Court: An Experiment in Compulsory Arbitration.* Lawrence: University of Kansas, 1941.

Garvey, Olive, with Virgil Quinlisk. *The Obstacle Race: The Story of Ray Hugh Garvey.* San Antonio, Tex.: Naylor, 1970.

Gates, Paul. *Fifty Million Acres: Conflicts over Kansas Land Policy, 1854–1890.* Ithaca, N.Y.: Cornell University Press, 1954.

Gihon, John. *Geary and Kansas.* Philadelphia: Charles C. Rhodes, 1857.

Gilbert, Douglas, and Clyde Kilby. *C. S. Lewis: Images of His World.* Grand Rapids, Mich.: William Erdmans, 1973.

Giles, F. W. *Thirty Years in Topeka: A Historical Sketch.* Topeka: Kansas Publishing House, 1886.

Gilpin, William. *The Central Gold Regions.* Philadelphia: Sower, Barnes, 1860.

Glabb, Charles. *Kansas City and the Railroads: Community Policy in the Growth of a Regional Metropolis.* 1962. Reprint, Lawrence: University Press of Kansas, 1993.

Gladstone, Thomas. *An Englishman in Kansas; or Squatter Life and Border Warfare.* New York: Miller, 1857.

Gleed, Charles. *A Bird's-Eye View of the Political Situation in Kansas, with Especial Reference to the People's Party.* Topeka: Republican State Headquarters, 1893.

Goldberg, Michael. *An Army of Women: Gender and Politics in Gilded Age Kansas.* Baltimore: Johns Hopkins University Press, 1997.

Goodrich, Thomas. *Bloody Dawn: The Story of the Lawrence Massacre.* Kent, Ohio: Kent State University Press, 1991.

———. *War to the Knife: Bleeding Kansas, 1854–1861.* Mechanicsburg, Pa.: Stackpole Books, 1998.

Goodrum, Charles. *I'll Trade You an Elk.* New York: Funk and Wagnalls, 1967.

Graham, John. *"Yours for the Revolution": The Appeal to Reason, 1895–1922.* Lincoln: University of Nebraska Press, 1990.

Griffin, Clifford. *The University of Kansas: A History.* Lawrence: University Press of Kansas, 1974.

Griffith, Sally. *Home Town News: William Allen White and the Emporia Gazette.* Baltimore: Johns Hopkins University Press, 1989.

Gunn, John. *E. Haldeman-Julius—The Man and His Work.* Girard, Kans.: Haldeman-Julius, 1924, Blue Book no. 678.

Haldeman-Julius, E. *Is This Century the Most Admirable in History?* Girard, Kans.: Haldeman-Julius, 1930, Blue Book no. 1512.

Hale, Edward. *Kanzas and Nebraska.* Boston: Phillips, Sampson, 1854.

Ham, George, and Robin Higham, eds. *The Rise of the Wheat State: A History of Kansas Agriculture, 1861–1986.* Manhattan, Kans.: Sunflower University Press, 1987.

Haywood, Robert. *Tough Daisies: Kansas Humor from "The Lane County Bachelor" to Bob Dole.* Lawrence: University Press of Kansas, 1995.

Heat-Moon, William Least. *PrairyErth.* Boston: Houghton, Mifflin, 1991.

Hickey, Joseph. *Ghost Settlement on the Prairie: A Biography of Thurman, Kansas.* Lawrence: University Press of Kansas, 1995.

Hinshaw, David. *A Man from Kansas: The Story of William Allen White.* New York: Putnam's, 1945.

Hofstadter, Richard. *The Age of Reform.* New York: Knopf, 1955.

Holloway, John. *History of Kansas from the First Explorations of the Mississippi Valley to Its Admission to the Union.* Lafayette, Ind.: James, Emmons, 1868.

Holm, Bill. *The Heart Can Be Filled Anywhere on Earth.* Minneapolis, Minn.: Milkweed Editions, 1996.

Hope, Cliff Jr. *Quiet Courage: Kansas Congressman Clifford R. Hope.* Manhattan, Kans.: Sunflower University Press, 1997.

Howells, William D. *Criticism and Fiction.* New York: Harper and Brothers, 1892.

——. *A Traveler from Altruria.* New York: Harper, 1894.

Hudson, Joseph. *Letters to Governor Lewelling.* Topeka: Topeka Capital, 1893.

Ingalls, John. *A Collection of the Writings of John James Ingalls: Essays, Addresses, and Orations.* Kansas City, Mo.: Hudson-Kimberly, 1902.

Isern, Thomas. *Custom Combining on the Great Plains.* Norman: University of Oklahoma Press, 1981.

Jackson, Wes. *Becoming Native to This Place.* Lexington: University Press of Kentucky, 1994.

Jenson, Merrill, ed. *Regionalism in America.* Madison: University of Wisconsin Press, 1951.

Johnson, Samuel. *The Battle Cry of Freedom: The New England Emigrant Aid Company in the Kansas Crusade.* Lawrence: University Press of Kansas, 1954.

Johnson, Walter. *William Allen White's America.* New York: Henry Holt, 1947.

——, ed. *Selected Letters of William Allen White, 1899–1943.* New York: Henry Holt, 1947.

Jones, Billy. *The Chandlers of Kansas: A Banking Family.* Wichita, Kans.: Center for Entrepreneurship, 1983.

Jordan, David. *Winfield Scott Hancock: A Soldier's Life.* Bloomington: Indiana University Press, 1988.

Kansas Constitutional Convention: A Reprint of the Proceedings and Debates of the Convention Which Framed the Constitution of Kansas at Wyandotte in July, 1859. Topeka: State Printing Plant, 1920.

Kansas Legislature. *Report of the Committee for Investigation of the School Textbook Question.* Topeka: State Printing Plant, 1932.

Kansas State Historical Society. *History of Kansas Newspapers.* Topeka: State Printing Plant, 1916.

Kendall, Sue. *Rethinking Regionalism: John Steuart Curry and the Kansas Mural Controversy.* Washington, D.C.: Smithsonian Institution Press, 1986.

Kluger, Richard. *Simple Justice: The History of Brown* v. *Board of Education and Black America.* New York: Knopf, 1976.

LaForte, Robert. *Leaders of Reform: Progressive Republicans in Kansas, 1900–1916.* Lawrence: University Press of Kansas, 1974.

The Legislative Conspiracy. Topeka: Aurora Library, 1893.

Leslie, Edward. *The Devil Knows How to Ride: The True Story of William Clarke Quantrill and His Confederate Raiders.* New York: Da Capo Press, 1998.

Leuchtenberg, William. *Theodore Roosevelt: The New Nationalism.* Englewood Cliffs, N.J.: Prentice-Hall, 1961.

Limerick, Patricia. *Legacy of Conquest: The Unbroken Past of the American West.* New York: W. W. Norton, 1988.

Lindquist, Emory. *Smoky Valley People: A History of Lindsborg, Kansas.* Lindsborg, Kans.: Bethany College, 1953.

Madison, James H., ed. *Heartland: Comparative Histories of the Midwestern States.* Bloomington: Indiana University Press, 1990.

Madson, John. *Where the Sky Began: Land of the Tallgrass Prairie.* 2d ed. Ames: Iowa State University Press, 1995.

Malin, James. *In Commemoration of the Centennial Anniversary of the Admission of Kansas into the Union 1861: An Essay to Accompany an Exhibition of the Kansas Statehood Centennial.* Lawrence: University of Kansas Library, 1961.

——. *John Brown and the Legend of Fifty-six.* Philadelphia: American Philosophical Society, 1942.

——. *The Nebraska Question, 1852–1854.* Lawrence, Kans.: By the author, 1953.

——. *Power and Change in Society: With Special Reference to Kansas, 1880–1890.* Lawrence, Kans.: Coronado Press, 1981.

Mason, T. B., and Charles Boynton. *A Journey Through Kansas; with Sketches of Nebraska; Describing the Country, Climate, Soil, Mineral, Manufacturing and Other Resources. The Results of a Tour Made in the Autumn of 1854.* Cincinnati: Moore, Wilstach, Keys, 1855.

Masterson, V. V. *The Katy Railroad and the Last Frontier.* Norman: University of Oklahoma Press, 1952.

May, Henry. *The End of American Innocence: A Study of the First Years of Our Own Time, 1912–1917.* New York: Knopf, 1959.

McCoy, Donald. *Landon of Kansas.* Lincoln: University of Nebraska Press, 1966.

McFarland, Keith. *Harry F. Woodring: A Political Biography of FDR's Controversial Secretary of War.* Lawrence: University Press of Kansas, 1975.

McNall, Scott. *The Road to Rebellion: Class Formation and Kansas Populism, 1865–1900.* Chicago: University of Chicago Press, 1988.

McPhee, John. *Annals of the Former World.* New York: Farrar, Straus, and Giroux, 1998.

Mead, James. *Hunting and Trading on the Great Plains.* Norman: University of Oklahoma Press, 1986.

Mechem, Kirke, ed. *Annals of Kansas, 1886–1925.* 2 vols. Topeka: Kansas State Historical Society, 1954–1956.

——. *The Mythical Jayhawk.* Topeka: Kansas State Historical Society, 1967.

Merriam, Daniel. *The Geologic History of Kansas.* Lawrence: University of Kansas Press, 1963.

Miner, Craig. *Discovery: Cycles of Change in the Kansas Oil and Gas Industry, 1860–1897.* Wichita: Kansas Independent Oil and Gas Association, 1987.

——. *The Fire in the Rock: A History of the Oil and Gas Industry in Kansas, 1855–1976.* Wichita: Kansas Independent Oil and Gas Association, 1976.

——. *Harvesting the High Plains: John Kriss and the Business of Wheat Farming, 1920–1950.* Lawrence: University Press of Kansas, 1998.

——. *Uncloistered Halls: The Centennial History of Wichita State University.* Wichita, Kans.: Wichita State University Endowment Association, 1995.

——. *West of Wichita: Settling the High Plains of Kansas, 1865–1890.* Lawrence: University Press of Kansas, 1986.

——. *Wichita: The Early Years, 1865–1880.* Lincoln: University of Nebraska Press, 1982.

——. *Wichita: The Magic City.* Wichita: Wichita–Sedgwick County Historical Museum Association. 1988.

——. *Wolf Creek Station: Kansas Gas and Electric Company in the Nuclear Era.* Columbus: Ohio State University Press, 1993.

——, ed. *The Wichita Reader: A Collection of Writing About a Prairie City.* Wichita: Wichita Eagle and Beacon, 1992.

Miner, Craig, and William Unrau. *The End of Indian Kansas: A Study of Cultural Revolution, 1854–1871.* Lawrence: Regents Press of Kansas, 1978.

Murray, Robert. *Red Scare: A Study in National Hysteria, 1919–1920.* Minneapolis: University of Minnesota Press, 1955.

Nash, Gerald. *Creating the West: Historical Interpretations, 1890–1990.* Albuquerque: University of New Mexico Press, 1991.

Nelson, Edward. *KPL in Kansas: A History of the Kansas Power and Light Company.* Lawrence, Kans.: Center for Research in Business, 1964.

Nichols, Alice. *Bleeding Kansas.* New York: Oxford University Press, 1954.

Norris, Kathleen. *Dakota: A Spiritual Geography.* Boston: Houghton Mifflin, 1993.

Oliva, Leo. *Fort Larned: Guardian of the Santa Fe Trail.* Rev. ed. Topeka: Kansas State Historical Society, 1997.

Painter, Nell. *Exodusters: Black Migration to Kansas After Reconstruction.* New York: Knopf, 1977.

Paris, Barry. *Louise Brooks.* New York: Knopf, 1989.

Parks, Gordon. *The Learning Tree.* New York: Harper and Row, 1963.

Peterson, Elmer. *Big Dam Foolishness: The Problem of Modern Flood Control and Water Storage.* New York: Devin-Adair, 1954.

Petrowski, William. *The Kansas Pacific: A Study in Railroad Promotion.* New York: Arno Press, 1981.

Phillips, William. *The Conquest of Kansas by Missouri and Her Allies.* Boston: Phillips, Sampson, 1856.

Pickett, Calder. *Ed Howe: Country Town Philosopher.* Lawrence: University Press of Kansas, 1968.

Pisciotte, Joe, ed. *Selected Papers of Governor John Carlin: An Index of Social and Political Change.* Wichita, Kans.: Hugo Wall School of Urban and Public Affairs, Wichita State University, 1993.

Prentis, Noble. *Kansas Miscellanies.* 2d ed. Topeka: Kansas Publishing House, 1889.

A Price List of School Books Published by the State and the Books Adopted and Approved by the State School Book Commission of Kansas. August 1915. Topeka: Kansas State Printing Plant, 1915.

Price, Reynolds. *A Common Room: Essays, 1954–1987.* New York: Atheneum, 1987.

Proceedings in the Case of the Impeachment of Charles Robinson, Governor. Lawrence: Kansas State Journal Steam Press, 1862.

Quantic, Diane. *The Nature of the Place: A Study of Great Plains Fiction.* Lincoln: University of Nebraska Press, 1995.

Quastler, I. E. *Railroads of Lawrence, Kansas.* Lawrence, Kans.: Coronado Press, 1979.

Rager, T. F. *History of Neosho and Wilson Counties, Kansas.* Ft. Scott, Kans.: Monitor Printing Company, 1902.

Rawley, James. *Race and Politics: Bleeding Kansas and the Coming of the Civil War.* Philadelphia: J. B. Lippincott, 1969.

Redford, Bruce, ed. *The Letters of Samuel Johnson.* 5 vols. Princeton: Princeton University Press, 1992.

Reisner, Marc. *Cadillac Desert: The American West and Its Disappearing Water.* New York: Penguin, 1986.

Report of the Special Committee Appointed to Investigate the Troubles in Kansas. Washington, D.C.: Cornelius Wendell, 1856.

Richmond, Robert. *Kansas: A Land of Contrasts.* 4th ed. Wheeling, Ill.: Harlan Davidson, 1999.

Riney-Kehrberg, Pamela. *Rooted in Dust: Surviving Drought and Depression in Southwestern Kansas.* Lawrence: University Press of Kansas, 1994.

Robinson, Charles. *The Kansas Conflict.* New York: Harper and Brothers, 1892.

Robinson, Sara. *Kansas: Its Interior and Exterior Life.* Boston: Crosby, Nichols, 1856.

[Ropes, Hannah]. *Six Months in Kansas by a Lady.* Boston: John P. Jewett, 1856.

Rosa, Joseph. *Wild Bill Hickok: The Man and His Myth.* Lawrence: University Press of Kansas, 1996.

Rowe, Frank, and Craig Miner. *Borne on the South Wind: A Century of Kansas Aviation.* Wichita, Kans.: Wichita Eagle and Beacon, 1994.

Rydjord, John. *Kansas Place-Names.* Norman: University of Oklahoma Press, 1972.

Sageser, Bower. *Joseph L. Bristow: Kansas Progressive.* Lawrence: University Press of Kansas, 1968.

Schruben, Francis. *From Wea Creek to El Dorado: Oil in Kansas, 1860–1920.* Columbia: University of Missouri Press, 1972.

——. *Kansas in Turmoil, 1930–1936.* Columbia: University of Missouri Press, 1969.

Sears, Hal. *The Sex Radicals: Free Love in High Victorian America.* Lawrence: Regents Press of Kansas, 1977.

Self, Huber. *Environment and Man in Kansas: A Geographical Analysis.* Lawrence: Regents Press of Kansas, 1978.

Settling the West. New York: Time-Life Books, 1996.

Seventh Annual Report of the Board of Railroad Commissioners for the Year Ending December 1, 1889. State of Kansas. Topeka: Kansas State Printing House, Clifford C. Baker, state printer, 1889.

Sharp, Bill, and Peggy Sullivan. *The Dashing Kansan: The Amazing Adventures of a Nineteenth-Century Naturalist and Explorer.* Kansas City, Mo.: Harrow Books, 1990.

Sherow, James. *Watering the Valley: Development Along the High Plains Arkansas River, 1870–1950.* Lawrence: University Press of Kansas, 1990.

Shortridge, James. *Peopling the Plains: Who Settled Where in Frontier Kansas.* Lawrence: University Press of Kansas, 1995.

Sixth Annual Report of the Board of Railroad Commissioners for the Year Ending December 1, 1888. State of Kansas. Topeka: Kansas Publishing House, Clifford C. Baker, state printer, 1888.

Sixth Biennial Report of the Kansas State Board of Agriculture, 1887–1888. Topeka: Kansas Publishing House, 1889.

Snell, Joseph, and Don Wilson. *The Birth of the Atchison, Topeka and Santa Fe Railroad.* Topeka: Kansas State Historical Society, 1968.

Socolofsky, Homer. *Arthur Capper: Publisher, Politician, Philanthropist.* Lawrence: University of Kansas Press, 1962.

——. *Kansas Governors.* Lawrence: University Press of Kansas, 1990.

Socolofsky, Homer, and Virgil Dean, comps. *Kansas History: An Annotated Bibliography.* New York: Greenwood Press, 1992.

Socolofsky, Homer, and Huber Self. *Historical Atlas of Kansas.* Norman: University of Oklahoma Press, 1972.

Speer, John. *The Life of Gen. James H. Lane.* Garden City, Kans.: John Speer, 1897.

Spring, Leverett. *Kansas: The Prelude to the War for the Union.* Boston: Houghton Mifflin, 1885.

Sproat, John. *"The Best Men": Liberal Reformers in the Gilded Age.* New York: Oxford University Press, 1968.

Starr, Stephen. *Jennison's Jayhawkers: A Civil War Regiment and Its Commander*. Baton Rouge: Louisiana State University Press, 1973.

Sternberg, Charles. *Life of a Fossil Hunter*. New York: Henry Holt, 1909.

Stuewe, Paul, ed. *Kansas Revisited: Historical Images and Perspectives*. 2d ed. Lawrence: University of Kansas Division of Continuing Education, 1998.

Stilgoe, John. *Metropolitan Corridor: Railroads and the American Scene*. New Haven: Yale University Press, 1983.

Svobida, Lawrence. *Farming the Dust Bowl: A First-Hand Account from Kansas*. Lawrence: University Press of Kansas, 1986.

Taylor, Blanche. *Plenteous Harvest: The Episcopal Church in Kansas, 1837–1972*. Topeka: Episcopal Diocese of Kansas, 1973.

Taylor, Richard. *Henry Ford of the Air*. Topeka: Privately printed, 1996.

Tenth Annual Report of the Board of Railroad Commissioners for the Year Ending December 1, 1892. State of Kansas. Topeka: Press of the Hamilton Printing Company, 1892.

Territorial Kansas: Studies Commemorating the Centennial. Lawrence: University of Kansas Publications, 1954.

Thayer, Eli. *A History of the Kansas Crusade: Its Friends and Its Foes*. New York: Harper and Brothers, 1889.

Third Annual Report of the Board of Railroad Commissioners for the Year Ending December 31, 1885. State of Kansas. Topeka: Kansas Publishing House, T. D. Thacher, state printer, 1885.

Thirteenth Annual Report of the Board of Railroad Commissioners for the Year Ending November 30, 1895. State of Kansas. Topeka: Kansas State Printing Company: J. K. Hudson, state printer, 1896.

Tomlinson, William. *Kansas in 1858: A History of the Recent Troubles in the Territory*. New York: H. Dayton, 1859.

Treadway, William. *Cyrus K. Holliday: A Documentary Biography*. Topeka: Kansas State Historical Society, 1979.

University of Kansas, Institute for Public Policy Research. *Kansas Statistical Abstract, 1998*. 33d ed. Lawrence: University of Kansas, 1999.

Unrau, William. *The Emigrant Indians of Kansas: A Critical Bibliography*. Bloomington: Indiana University Press, 1979.

——. *The Kansa Indians: A History of the Wind People*. Norman: University of Oklahoma Press, 1971.

——. *Mixed-Bloods and Tribal Dissolution: Charles Curtis and the Quest for Indian Identity*. Lawrence: University Press of Kansas, 1989.

Unrau, William, and Craig Miner. *Tribal Dispossession and the Ottawa Indian University Fraud*. Norman: University of Oklahoma Press, 1985.

Van Meter, Sondra. *Marion County, Kansas, Past and Present*. Hillsboro, Kans.: M. B. Publishing, 1972.

——. *Our Common School Heritage: A History of the Wichita Public Schools*. Wichita, Kans.: Board of Education, 1977.

Villard, Oswald. *John Brown, 1800–1859: A Biography Fifty Years After.* Boston: Riverside Press, 1910.

Virgil, *The Georgics of Virgil.* Trans. J. W. Mackail. Boston: Houghton Mifflin, 1904.

The War of the Rebellion: A Compilation of the Official Records of the Union and Confederate Armies. Series I. Washington, D.C.: Government Printing Office, 1881.

Ware, Eugene. *The Indian War of 1864: Being a Fragment of the Early History of Kansas, Nebraska, Colorado, and Wyoming.* Reprint. New York: St. Martin's Press, 1960.

——. *Some of the Rhymes of Ironquill.* 5th ed. Topeka: Crane, 1896.

Waters, L. L. *Steel Trails to Santa Fe.* Lawrence: University of Kansas Press, 1950.

Webb, Dave. *399 Kansas Characters.* Rev. ed. Dodge City: Kansas Heritage Center, 1994.

Webb, W. E. *Buffalo Land.* Cincinnati and Chicago: E. Hanford, 1872.

West, Elliott. *The Contested Plains: Indians, Goldseekers, and the Rush to Colorado.* Lawrence: University Press of Kansas, 1998.

White, Richard. *"Its Your Misfortune and None of My Own": A History of the American Frontier.* 5th ed. Norman: University of Oklahoma Press, 1991.

White, William Allen. *The Autobiography of William Allen White.* New York: Macmillan, 1946.

——. *The Real Issue: A Book of Kansas Stories.* Chicago: Way and Williams, 1897.

Wilder, Bessie. *Bibliography of the Official Publications of Kansas, 1854–1958.* Lawrence: Governmental Research Center, University of Kansas, 1965.

——. *Governmental Agencies of the State of Kansas, 1861–1956.* Lawrence: University of Kansas, 1957.

Wilder, Daniel, ed. *The Annals of Kansas, 1541–1885.* 2d ed. Topeka: Kansas Publishing House, T. Dwight Thacher, state printer, 1886.

Willard, Julius. *History of the Kansas State College of Agriculture and Applied Science.* Manhattan: Kansas State College Press, 1940.

Williams, Burton. *Senator John James Ingalls: Kansas' Iridescent Republican.* Lawrence: University Press of Kansas, 1972.

Wilson, Don. *Governor Charles Robinson of Kansas.* Lawrence: University Press of Kansas, 1975.

Wilson, Paul. *A Time to Lose: Representing Kansas in Brown v. Board of Education.* Lawrence: University Press of Kansas, 1995.

Wolfe, Thomas. *From Death to Morning.* New York: Grosset and Dunlap, 1935.

Wood, Margaret. *Memorial of Samuel N. Wood by Margaret L. Wood.* Kansas City, Mo.: Hudson-Kimberly, 1892.

Wood, Raymond, ed. *Archaeology on the Great Plains.* Lawrence: University Press of Kansas, 1998.

Worley, William. *J. C. Nichols and the Shaping of Kansas City: Innovation in Planned Residential Communities.* Columbia: University of Missouri Press, 1990.

Worster, Donald. *Dust Bowl: The Southern Plains in the 1930s.* New York: Oxford University Press, 1979.

The WPA Guide to 1930s Kansas. Reprint. Lawrence: University Press of Kansas, 1984.

Wright, C. O. *One Hundred Years in Kansas Education.* Topeka: Kansas State Teachers Association, 1963.

Zornow, William. *Kansas: A History of the Jayhawk State.* Norman: University of Oklahoma Press, 1957.

NEWSPAPERS

Abortion Clippings. Local History Division, Wichita Public Library.

Emporia News, 1861

Humphrey, Lyman. Clippings. Kansas Collection, Spencer Research Library, University of Kansas, Lawrence.

Kansas State Historical Society. Clippings books (multivolume by subject). The sets most used:

ATSF	Medicine
Automobiles	Mennonite
Capital Punishment	Negroes
Essays	Oil and Gas
Ethics of Amusement	Parks
Floods	Poetry
Good Roads	Politics
Immigration	Populist Party
IWW–Non-Partisan League	Prohibition
Kansas Biography	Strikes
Kansas Description	Territorial
Kansas History	Turnpike Authority
Kansas Reminiscences	Weather
Kansas State Historical Society	Woman Suffrage
Labor	Women
Legislative	

Leavenworth Conservative, 1861

New York Times, 1861, 1999

Plaindealer (Kansas City), 1941–1948

Plaindealer (Wichita), 1953–1955

Time, September 13, 1999

Topeka Commonwealth, 1885

University Daily Kansan, 1929

Washington Post, 1999

Wichita Beacon, 1915, 1928

Wichita Eagle, 1880, 1887, 1912, 1918, 1921, 1923, 1936, 1940, 1986–1994, 1996, 1998–1999

THESES AND DISSERTATIONS

Brusca, Anthony. "A National Effort for Victory: The B-29 Development Program and the Battle of Kansas." Master's thesis, Wichita State University, 1999.

Bunting, Robert. "School Segregation in Kansas: A Study in Constitutional and Political Development." Master's thesis, Wichita State University, 1971.

Frederickson, Edna. "John P. St. John: The Father of Constitutional Prohibition." Ph.D. diss., University of Kansas, 1931.

Grubb, Melissa. "Mother Hughes and Female Guardians: Progressive Era Women Promoting Infant and Maternity Health Care in America." Master's thesis, Wichita State University, 1999.

Harmon, Terry. "Charles Sumner Gleed: A Western Business Leader, 1856–1920." Ph.D. diss., University of Kansas, 1973.

Harvey, Douglas. " 'Drought Relief Efforts Delayed by Rain': The History of Cheyenne Bottoms Wildlife Area." Master's thesis, Wichita State University, 2000.

Meyer, Phillip. "Tuttle Creek Dam: A Case Study in Local Opposition." Master's thesis, University of North Carolina, 1962.

Miller, Emy. "Corporation Farming in Kansas." Master's thesis, University of Wichita, 1933.

INDEX

Abilene: cattle trade in, 136; city manager in, 227; Eisenhower and, 326; flooding in, 27; vice/violence in, 135

Abolitionists, 4, 48

Abortion issue, 56, 354, 388–89

Adams, Henry, 151, 404

Adams, J. W., 221

Ad Astra Venture Capital Fund, 387

Addams, Jane, 222

Adjutant General's Office, 163

Administrative state, emergence of, 162–63

Admiral (steamboat), 39

Adrian, Ron, 381

African Americans. *See* Blacks

Agencies, creation of, 163, 197–98

Agribusiness, 392

Agricultural Adjustment Act (AAA), 298, 299

Agricultural Adjustment Administration, 276

Agricultural Experiment Stations, 163

Agriculture, 130, 139, 191, 298, 354, 393; contribution of, 405; divergence and, 322; employment in, 406; industrialization of, 389; sustainable, 356. *See also* Corporate farming; Farming

Aguinaldo, Emilio, 194

Ainsworth, William, 377

Air Capital, 267

Aircraft: commercial, 267; early, 261; expenditures on, 315; photos of, 296, 311; private, 296; war, 303, 310, 311–12, 333. *See also* Aviation

Aircraft industry, 270, 295, 303, 306, 313; blacks and, 314; growth of, 266–67, 304, 314, 409; wartime, 303

Airfields/airports, 267–68, 315

Alcohol. *See* Liquor

Alexis, Grand Duke, 3

Alien Land bill, 182

Allen, Forrest "Phog," 272

Allen, Henry, 15, 16, 200, 233, 237–38, 246, 251, 257–58, 329, 402; coal strikes and, 248,

249, 250; Gompers and, 249; Hill and, 253–54; IWW and, 244; Speech Week and, 239; on textbooks, 207; White and, 252

All-Kansas Tour, 268

AMA *Journal,* on Brinkley, 280

America First Committee, 308

American Communist Party, 295

American Day, 244–45

American Federation of Labor (AFL), 249

American Legion, 245, 274

American Mercury, 3

American Nonconformist and Kansas Industrial Liberator, 174–75

American Populism: A Social History (McMath), 173

American Press Association, 184

American Sash and Door Company, 248

American Way, The (film), 341

Amsden, Floyd, 363

Anderson, George, 118

Anderson, John, 134, 175, 411

Anderson, Walter, 270

Animal Farm (Orwell), 392

Annals of Kansas (Wilder), xiii, 6, 141

Anthony, D. R., 80

Anthony, George, 143, 160, 177

Anthony, Susan B., 128, 165

Anticorporate farming law, 278, 390–91

Antidiscrimination law, 214, 346

Antinuclear activists, 358

Anti-Semitism, 12, 173, 300, 308

Anti-trust regulation, 205, 220

Apaches, 94

Appeal to Reason, 11, 241–42, 341; founding of, 240; O'Hare and, 245; state officials and, 246; women/minorities and, 246

Arapahoes, 54, 94, 113, 114, 115, 116

Arbor Day, 210

Argersinger, Peter, 173

Arkansas City, flooding in, 28

Arkansas River, 33, 94, 103, 117, 136, 157, 263, 331; flooding of, 28; irrigation from, 148; lawsuits over, 209; railroad for, 131